A County Community in Peace and War:
Sussex 1600-1660

A County Community in Peace and War: Sussex 1600–1660

Anthony Fletcher

LONGMAN London and New York

Longman Group Ltd.

Longman Group Limited
London and New York
Associated companies, branches and
representatives throughout the world
Published in the United States of America by
Longman Inc., New York

First published 1975

ISBN 0 582 50024 9

Set in Baskerville
and printed in Great Britain at
The Aberdeen University Press

For Tresna

Contents

Maps

Preface

The recent stress on county studies in seventeenth-century English history springs from an awareness of the need to test generalisations about the nature of the Great Rebellion by detailed local research. The diversity of the political and religious traditions of the counties and the individuality of their gentry communities is becoming increasingly evident as a result of these studies. My purpose in subjecting another county to close analysis is to illuminate the patterns of life and thought of a single corner of provincial England in the period of the civil war. A number of the aspects of Sussex's society, religious experience and modes of government which I discuss are certainly characteristic of other counties, but I would hesitate to claim that Sussex was a typical county in any particular respect. The arrangement of the book in four sections—society, religion, government and politics—provides a convenient means of organisation, but any such division is bound to be artificial. The notes contain numerous cross references. I am convinced that one of the most fruitful avenues towards fuller understanding of the Great Rebellion is through the study of local communities in all the aspects of their lives. So far as the sources permit, the scope of this book attempts to reflect that conviction.

One cannot work on the well-tilled ground of seventeenth-century England without being constantly aware of the debt owed to those historians who established the main lines of the political story in the last century and early in this century. Those who wrote of events at the national level are best remembered; others who worked on the records of the civil war period for their own county should not be forgotten. The frequent appearances of the *Sussex Archaeological Collections* (*SAC*) in the notes show how much easier their labours have made my task. Sir Charles Thomas-Stanford drew on a wide range of sources for his book *Sussex in the Great Civil War and Interregnum*, published in 1910. This book is not intended to supersede that pioneering study. It is written from a different viewpoint; it is bound to reflect present lines of interest towards civil war studies and present preconceptions. I have benefited greatly from the stimulus and encouragement of others working in the same field. Among those who have been generous in answering queries and providing information from their own research are Professor Gerald Aylmer, Miss Ruth Bird, Mr Graham Bungard, Mr James Casey, Mr Richard Gilbert, Dr Robin Jeffs, Mr Anthony Michell, Dr John Morrill, Professor Paul Pinckney, Professor Paul Seaver, Mr Keith Thomas, Dr Nicholas Tyacke and Professor Austin Woolrych.

I would like to express my gratitude to the staffs of the record offices where I have worked, and particularly those of the British Museum, the East Sussex Record Office, the Public Record Office and the West Sussex Record Office, for their helpfulness and courtesy. At Lewes Mrs Judith Brent has answered a stream of questions and provided me with many useful references; at Chichester Mr Timothy McCann has been equally generous of his time. Mr K. W. Dickins, the curator of deeds for the Sussex Archaeological Society and Miss G. M. A. Beck, the archivist-in-charge of the Guildford Muniment Room have taken much trouble in making available documents in which I was interested. I would like to thank Major James More-Molyneux for sending me a photostat copy of a letter relating to Sussex, from the bound volumes of his family's correspondence which are at Loseley House, and for allowing me to quote from the Loseley MSS.

Those who have read chapters of the book in draft have provided me with invaluable comments and suggestions: Colin Brent, Mark Greengrass, Kenneth Haley, Linda Kirk, Timothy McCann and Conrad Russell. So also has Ivan Roots, who has read the whole manuscript. Their kindness is much appreciated. The responsibility for the final form of the book is of course entirely my own. I am grateful to Miss Ruth Wells of Sheffield University Library for her patient pursuit of books about Sussex through interlibrary loan and to Mrs Patricia Holland, Mrs Shirley Hill, Mrs Mary Marsden, Miss Helen Pack and Mrs Doreen Spurr, who between them typed the book, for their cheerful persistence with my handwriting. A series of grants from the University of Sheffield research fund have been of great assistance towards the expenses of research for this book.

Finally I wish to record my gratitude to my family. My grandmother introduced me to Sussex and its history almost thirty years ago. Since then she has shared my explorations of the county on many occasions. While I have been working on this book from the distance of Sheffield, her hospitality has sustained me and her interest has encouraged me. My parents also have always encouraged me to write. My sons, both of whom were born during the genesis of this book, have been a constantly agreeable distraction from it. My wife, above all, has made its completion possible by her unfailing support and her insistence that it should be finished. Not least she has read the whole book in draft and made many suggestions.

Sheffield Anthony Fletcher
March 1974

NOTE ON TRANSCRIPTION

In quoting from seventeenth-century sources I have retained the original spelling but have modernised capitalisation, extended contemporary contractions and occasionally supplied punctuation necessary to the sense of the passage. Dates are given in Old Style, but with the year regarded as beginning on 1 January.

Part I

SOCIETY

I

Communications, towns, agriculture and industry

It lies all on the south side, upon the British Ocean, with a streight shore, as it were, more in length than breadth . . . The sea-coast of this country has very high green hills, call'd the Downs, which consisting of a fat chalky soil, are upon that account very fruitful. The middle part being chequer'd with meadows, pastures, cornfields, and groves, makes a very fine show. The hithermost northern-side, is shaded most pleasantly with woods, as anciently the whole countrey was, which made it unpassable.
William Camden[1]

To a messenger for carrying a letter to the looker of Pevensey Castle in the hard time of winter to give the runts meate there.
Accounts of Sir Thomas Pelham's steward 1658.[2]

The most striking contrast in Sussex's terrain is between the downland of the south and the Weald, or 'wild' as it was called in the seventeenth century, in the north. The South Downs form a belt of high and open chalk country, which runs from the Hampshire border to the sea at Beachy Head. The High Weald is now much less heavily wooded than it was three hundred years ago, but Ashdown Forest still preserves something of the old atmosphere of this heath and coppice country. On the coastal plain, in the Selsey peninsular and around Pevensey and Rye, there were saltmarshes in the seventeenth century. The rapes of Sussex, the administrative divisions created soon after the Norman Conquest, run from north to south, cutting across these geological strata. In the three western rapes of Chichester, Arundel and Bramber the clay vale behind the Downs is wide, stretching to the borders of Surrey. The High Weald is confined to the eastern rapes of Lewes, Pevensey and Hastings, and in the far east of the county, where the downland has petered out, wooded hillsides and valleys come right down to the flat marshland beside the sea. The Weald was much more heavily populated than the Downs in the seventeenth century. The iron industry attracted casual labour and the woodland of the inland parishes provided numerous opportunities for by-employments. Common grazings were extensive and there was virtually no restriction on immigration; settlement was dispersed. The small nucleated villages along the edge of the Downs and in the downland valleys contrasted sharply with typical

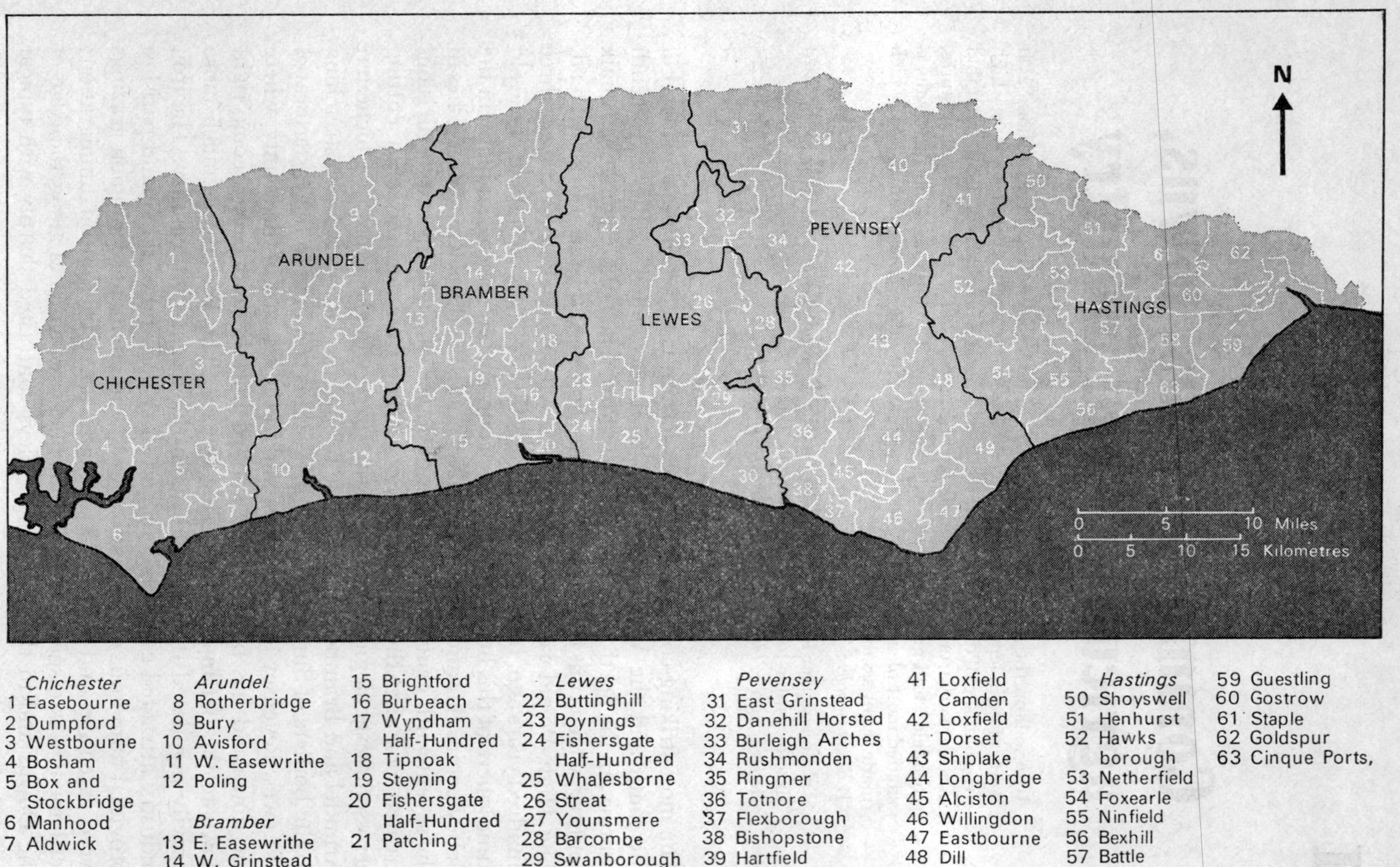
N
ARUNDEL
BRAMBER
LEWES
PEVENSEY
HASTINGS
CHICHESTER
0 5 10 Miles
0 5 10 15 Kilometres
Chichester
1 Easebourne
2 Dumpford
3 Westbourne
4 Bosham
5 Box and Stockbridge
6 Manhood
7 Aldwick
Arundel
8 Rotherbridge
9 Bury
10 Avisford
11 W. Easewrithe
12 Poling
Bramber
13 E. Easewrithe
14 W. Grinstead
15 Brightford
16 Burbeach
17 Wyndham Half-Hundred
18 Tipnoak
19 Steyning
20 Fishersgate Half-Hundred
21 Patching
Lewes
22 Buttinghill
23 Poynings
24 Fishersgate Half-Hundred
25 Whalesborne
26 Streat
27 Younsmere
28 Barcombe
29 Swanborough
30 Holmestrow
Pevensey
31 East Grinstead
32 Danehill Horsted
33 Burleigh Arches
34 Rushmonden
35 Ringmer
36 Totnore
37 Flexborough
38 Bishopstone
39 Hartfield
40 Rotherfield
41 Loxfield Camden
42 Loxfield Dorset
43 Shiplake
44 Longbridge
45 Alciston
46 Willingdon
47 Eastbourne
48 Dill
49 Pevensey
Hastings
50 Shoyswell
51 Henhurst
52 Hawks borough
53 Netherfield
54 Foxearle
55 Ninfield
56 Bexhill
57 Battle
58 Baldslow
59 Guestling
60 Gostrow
61 Staple
62 Goldspur
63 Cinque Ports,

wealden settlements. Villages such as Rodmell and Southease in the Ouse valley, or Houghton and North Stoke in the Arun valley, were compact and tiny. The populousness of many of the wealden parishes, on the other hand, emerges clearly from the Protestation returns of 1642. These suggest that several of the parishes between Lurgashall and Rudgwick may have had as many as between 500 and 600 inhabitants on the eve of the civil war.[3] The JPs response to a request for recommendations about common brewhouses in 1620 indicates where most people lived in east Sussex. They named a string of villages along the north of the division: Crawley, Lindfield, Uckfield, Lamberhurst and Ticehurst were all considered convenient places for brewhouses, 'respect beinge had to the nomber and condicions of the inhabitantes', as well as the market towns of the northern district.[4]

Although the distance between London and Sussex was not great, the notorious wealden roads constantly threatened to isolate the county community from the capital. 'The ways be soe durty and deepe as in winter that I hard noe waggons will goe to London', reported Anna Busbridge from Etchingham to her daughter in Warwickshire during the disastrous harvest-tide of 1648.[5] Earl Cowper's jaundiced view of the Sussex roads, after a visit to Horsham in 1690, has become celebrated:

> The county is a sink of about forteen miles broad which receives all the water that falls from two long ranges of hills on both sides of it; and not being furnished with convenient draining, is kept moist and soft by the water till the middle of a dry summer, which is only able to make it tolerable to ride for a short time.[6]

Daily life within the shire was often hindered by a spell of bad weather which ruined the highways. In 1640 the constable of Hawksborough hundred was unable to hold the usual April meeting for nomination of surveyors of the highways at Burwash, 'by reason of the great inundation of waters'. A Lindfield infant was baptised at Newick when, 'by reason of greate waters, they could not carry it to their own parish'. The grand jury at the March assizes in 1634 stated that the roads were in such an impassable state around Hailsham that it was dangerous for people to attempt to reach market.[7]

Highway repair, enjoined on all householders by the Marian statute, was much neglected. The flurry of presentments at quarter sessions, when the JPs harried the surveyors into action in the 1630s, is evidence enough of this.[8] Moreover, even when men were persuaded to labour on the roads, the job was usually done incompetently. For many years, explained a Duncton man in 1651, the practice in his area had been to repair the roads with chalk, 'which by the frequency of wagons passing that way being crusht to powder, and by wet weather dissolved into dirt, hath in many places made the ways worse rather than better'. The Duncton commentator was proud of the exceptional effort his parish had just devoted to

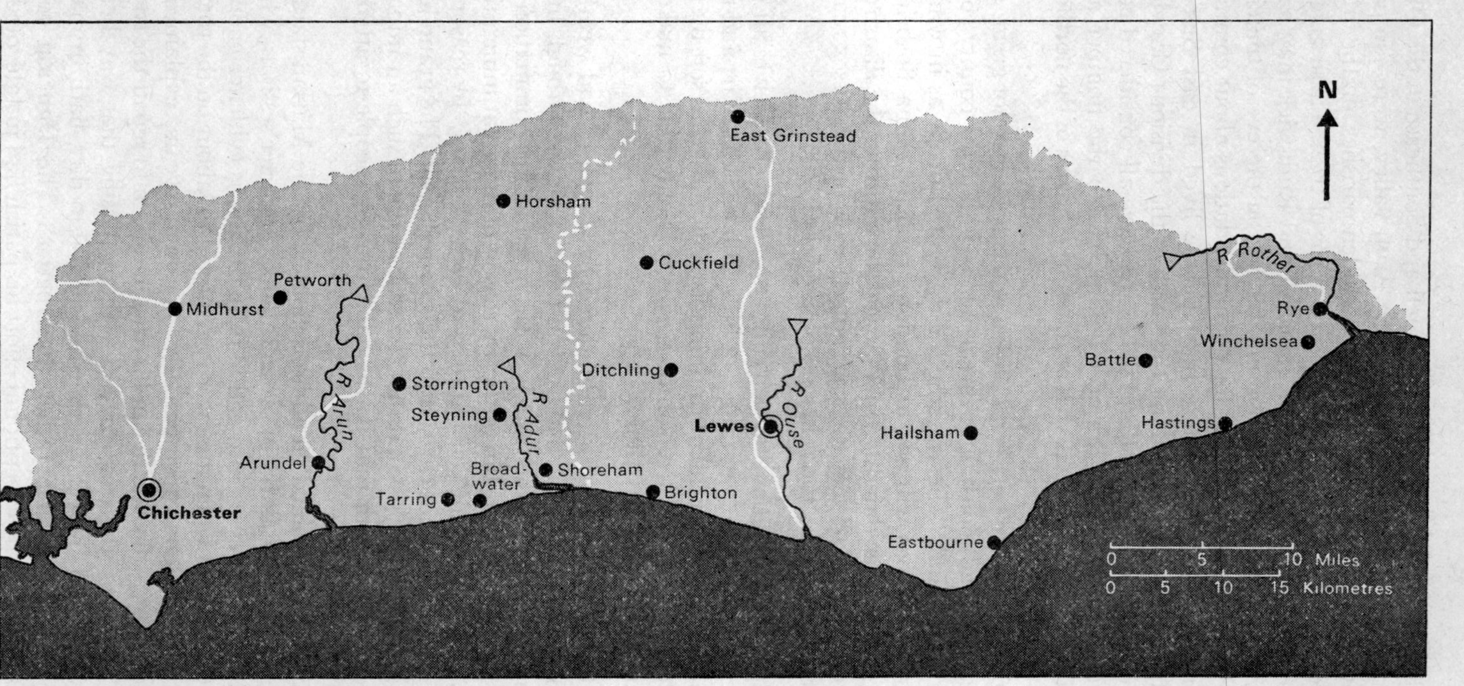

▷ Head of navigability on Sussex rivers in 1724

□ Ogilby's main roads (1675)

2 Communications and market towns

their section of the Petworth to Chichester road. There was not 'one hole left empty' by midsummer, he declared, after the road had been repaired 'onely with flints, fetcht very far, to the greater charge of the parish': 'and by the report of some ancient natives of the parish (of whom I enquired) the highwayes have not been mended so well these twenty years'.[9] The labour and expense involved in the process used at Duncton was enough to deter most parishes from ever undertaking it. The problem of communications became so serious in the wealden ironworking parishes during Elizabeth's reign that two statutes were passed to enforce obligations of road repair on the forgemen, whose heavy carts devastated the road surfaces every wet season. When the Privy Council found it virtually impossible to obtain ordnance and shot from the royal iron mills in Sussex in the summer of 1628, they reminded the justices of their duty to enforce these statutes and expressed their exasperation about gun carriages that sank and horses that would not move in the miry ways.[10] A campaign to improve the wealden roads followed. The justices appreciated that highway repair without the use of a stabiliser, such as cinders, flints or the 'rubbishe stone' that they insisted should be laid in the worst parts of Bramber rape in 1632, was virtually useless.[11] Several ironmasters were indicted for not laying down cinders in 1629. The grand jury named some of the more prominent offenders at assizes, including a Lamberhurst gentleman who, by carrying 200 loads of charcoal and 100 loads of iron to his furnace in a single summer, had played havoc with one section of highway.[12] The county Bench maintained pressure on the ironmasters throughout the decade before the civil war. A certificate of 1640, for instance, recorded that a Kentish forgeman had laid the quantities of cinders required of him on the road between Snape furnace and Burwash forge, through the parishes of Wadhurst, Ticehurst and Burwash.[13]

The comparative excellence of inland water navigation and the number of harbours and stades sited on a long coastline compensated to some extent for the appalling state of the roads. The Channel and the rivers Arun, Adur, Ouse and Rother, all of them navigable well inland, were the county's best highways. They were lifelines of its economy, always busy with traffic. For those who could afford to travel on horseback the best riding was along the coast. Daniel Defoe found that the shingle beach between Rye and Eastbourne provided him with a fine road. Lieutenant Hammond found that the crest of the Downs, where the turf was short and springy, provided a superb highway, dry and panoramic, from Eastbourne to Harting. He recorded how he left Eastbourne, after a night's lodging at the Lamb in 1635, and 'mounted unto a mill that stood in the clouds and so along on those high Downes, taking a fayre prospect of the deep and fertile wilds'.[14] The rivers alone thwarted a rider's coastal journey. Since there was no bridge on the Adur below Bramber, the Shoreham ferry attracted much custom; the Rye area was a maze of ferries. The traveller from Kent who wished to visit the decayed port of

Winchelsea first had to take the Rye ferry and then a further two ferries in his approach to the town. John Taylor, the water poet, found these ferries so muddy 'that they mir'd my mare and me'.[15] Rye itself was perched on a peninsular, overlooking the Rother estuary, commanding both land and sea.[16] The London road, which crossed into Kent by the Newenden causeway, was the lifeline of its economy. A Sandhurst gentleman, writing to the mayor about a gift his father had bestowed for the upkeep and improvement of this road between Rye and the Kentish border, noted the benefit that would accrue to the town thereby, 'for the exportation of your fish and all other comodityes towards London, as the accomodatcons and invitacons of the county towarde your markett'.[17] In 1637 the JPs, recognising the importance of the Newenden link with the Tenterden area, cooperated willingly with the justices of Kent in a scheme for rebuilding the bridge there, then in 'utter decay'.[18] Bridges that were swamped, destroyed by storms or unsafe were another hazard to travel in Sussex. Disputes about responsibility for repairs often delayed their being carried out. Midhurst and Chithurst bridges, for example, which were both 'ruinated and carried away by the violence of the water' at Christmas 1639 were not rebuilt until the following summer, and bridges that caused danger to the lives of those who used them regularly cropped up on the sessions agenda.[19]

Chichester was not a provincial capital of the importance of Norwich, Exeter or Canterbury, nor was it able to dominate the whole of Sussex from the western corner of the county, yet it was important as the ecclesiastical, administrative and trading centre for a large neighbourhood.[20] The city within the walls contained a medieval hospital, seven parish churches and numerous imposing timber-framed houses, some of which remain today behind red brick Georgian façades. Yet nothing on the Chichester skyline competed with the cathedral. Its spire overshadowed the lives of the citizens and its precincts occupied the whole of the south-western sector of the intramural area.[21] Most of the wealthier inhabitants lived along the four main streets radiating from the Market Place, which was then wide and open, extending up North Street and East Street. The only other residential areas were the Close and the Pallant. There were spacious gardens and orchards behind the main streets and there was almost no building at all beyond them in the north-western sector of the city. A lane ran across open ground from West Street to the city walls. In contrast to these salubrious living conditions the suburbs of St Bartholomew and St Pancras, beyond the west and east gates, were crowded huddles of cottages, housing the poor who could not afford to live within the city.[22]

Chichester in 1625 was a community of about 2,500 people, a thriving and bustling place and an important port, with its landing place at Dell Quay about two miles beyond the walls.[23] The market was held twice weekly under and around the octagonal opensided Market Cross, which Bishop Story had erected in 1501. The eastern half of the city was the most populous area and the focus of trading activity. Residents in East Street in 1625 included Nicholas Jordan, a barrister and senior member of the county Commission of the Peace, and William Cawley, the son of a wealthy brewer and sometime mayor of the city. Cawley's almshouse in the parish of St Bartholomew, for ten poor and aged men, was then in the course of construction. Leading aldermen like Henry Chitty, Thomas Farrington and George Greene also lived in the central area. Some of the county gentry, such as Richard Higgins of Bury and Sir John Morley of West Dean, had their own houses in the city.[24]

Social life, county politics, administration and marketing drew the inhabitants of the three eastern rapes, and to some extent of Bramber rape as well, to Lewes, a busy town with a population in 1625 probably well in excess of 2,000. The situation of Lewes between the Weald and the Downs had enabled it to become a more flourishing provincial capital than Chichester, although it lacked the prestige of diocesan leadership. The town occupied a naturally defensive site, above the first crossing of the Ouse, with sloping ground falling away from the walls on the northern, eastern and southern sides. Lieutenant Hammond found the 'fayre and strong castle', on the highest ground within the walls, 'now quite demolish'd'. But the town was 'reasonably well built, of that bignesse that in it are five churches'. The high-class suburb of St Anne's beyond Westgate, the industrial suburb of the Cliffe across the Ouse and the southern suburb of Southover were all well populated.[25] The High Street was both the principal trading thoroughfare and the most fashionable area for the gentry to have town houses. The Market Place was at the street's widest point: a provision market was held there daily and the Sessions House, erected in 1564, occupied the centre of the site. Among those who had their own houses on the south side of the High Street in 1625 were Sir John Shurley of Isfield, Sir Thomas Pelham of Halland and William Thomas, the clerk of the peace for the county. The following year Richard Amherst, a highly successful barrister and ironmaster and an assiduous JP, came to live at the Earl of Dorset's fine Elizabethan mansion, now known as Shelleys, on the opposite side of the High Street beyond Westgate.[26] Among others who regularly stayed at their houses in Lewes were Sir Thomas Springate of Ringmer and Walter Dobell of Streat. Cheek by jowl with these leading county gentry lived substantial townsmen such as Thomas Oliver and Thomas Traiton.[27] Caroline Lewes was a closeknit and well integrated community.

The largest concentrations of population in Sussex, apart from the county towns, were Rye, Hastings and Brighton. It is possible in fact that in the 1650s Brighton's population was greater than that of Lewes. In all there were twenty-one market towns in the county in 1640. Some medieval markets, like Alfriston whose Market Cross still stands, were already long extinct; others, such as Rotherfield, Burwash and Robertsbridge, had decayed more recently. Some markets still active were hardly more than villages: the survival of Ditchling, Tarring and Broadwater was precarious. The downland area was much better served than the Weald, despite the balance of population towards the north, and the deficiency of markets in the north-eastern corner of Sussex was notable.[28] Men living there certainly looked to Tonbridge, Goudhurst and Cranbrook, across the Kentish border, as well as to East Grinstead and Battle. The account book of the Sedlescombe gentleman John Everenden shows the use he made of the Cranbrook shops for household purchases.[29] Whereas both East Grinstead and Battle occupied hilltop sites, the western market towns in the Weald, Midhurst, Petworth, Horsham and Cuckfield, were situated on lower and wetter ground. Horsham, indeed, stranded in the midst of the clay vale, easily became totally inaccessible.

Petworth, with a population of around 1,000, was in many ways a typical provincial market and sessions town. A recent study of the inventories of the goods of its tradesmen has revealed the disparities of wealth common to such communities. Nicholas Warner, a versatile tradesman and farmer who died in 1645, was worth £1,539 according to the inventory taken by his neighbours; a bricklayer's goods came to a mere six pounds; there were many others too poor to have their inventories taken and wills proved. Whereas the leading townsmen occupied houses of seven or more rooms, the cottages of the poor were small and cramped. Nicholas Warner's main business was in wool and sheepskin gloves. He had his own oxen and horses, as well as sheep and lambs, grew his own wheat and barley for malting and probably did his own tanning. He was a reputable moneylender for the district. Warner was thus a typical urban entrepreneur with his feet firmly planted in the agricultural economy of his neighbourhood, a man with a comprehensive range of interests. Most tradesmen and craftsmen had at least a smallholding of land in addition to their business: a blacksmith left four acres planted with wheat; there were butchers who grew their own wheat and barley; a shearman had his own hogs, geese and poultry and grew his own hops; a shoemaker's goods included peas and oats in his barn, pigs and a lame mare in his farmyard, as well as thirty pairs of new shoes ready for sale. The inventories hint at the modest comforts of the more substantial Petworth families and provide glimpses of sophistication. A glazier's hall was adorned with a 'little perfuming pot of brass, books and glasses', a parson-farmer owned four pounds worth of books and a 'birding piece', a bricklayer had an hourglass in his bedroom, a physician, who rode on a gelding for his country visits, boasted a clock, silver spoons and damask tablecloths. This was a self-sufficient community, a town where trading and marketing relations were personal and intimate, a place where men paid their debts when they could. It had a firm economic base, quite apart from the employment opportunities of the Earl of Northumberland's mansion, which was then very much a part of the town, divided from it by a pale fence instead of the high and continuous wall which shuts it off today.[30]

The agricultural economies of the principal regions of Sussex dovetailed neatly and provided the county with a high degree of self-sufficiency. On the South Downs, and the arable foreland to the north of them, wheat, barley and rye were the main crops. The downland sheepwalks were an essential support for the farming in this area: the chalk soils were thin, the cornfields were shallow and the manure was vital. The large flocks were not kept primarily for wool, but to be folded on the arable lands. The larger farmers in this district were producers for the grain market, both inside the county and beyond it.[31] In the Weald, beef and mutton were the main market commodities. The barren uplands were given over to cony warrens and rough grazing. The surveyors of Ashdown Forest in 1650 recommended that it should be preserved as woodland and 'imployed for breeding of young cattle'. The wealden graziers used the rich alluvium soils of the Brede, Rother and Pevensey marshes for fattening the cattle and sheep which had been nursed in the higher country inland. The reclaimed levels were wholly enclosed by the seventeenth century. In this green landscape of ditches, dykes and irregular fields, the 'lookers' tended the livestock from their rough cabins; their masters, substantial farmers who made profitable bargains with the London cattle dealers, lived high and dry inland.[32]

The variety of terrain dictated a degree of specialisation. Yet this should not be overstressed. The wealden farmer, with the help of much marling, liming and ley farming, usually aimed to keep at least ten to thirty acres under the plough. John Roberts, a Ticehurst livestock farmer, for example, had wheat and peas in the ground at his death. As far as possible the wealden farmstead supplied its own needs: pigs were kept for the home, and all but the smallest farms had their own dairy house and cheese chamber. On the coastal plain towards Hampshire there was much mixed farming. Some inventories, for Goring, Barnham and Walberton for instance, suggest a leaning towards pasture farming, while others indicate a predominance of arable.[33] Mixed farming also predominated in the wealden clay country of Arundel rape. In the parish of Kirdford, the largest in West Sussex, a pattern of dispersed settlement had evolved from the process of gradual clearing of areas of forest around isolated farmhouses. Enclosure of the waste land had reached a climax with the partitioning of 1,700 acres of Shillinglee Great Park around 1600.

Henry Scutt, who died in May 1632, may be taken as a typical Kirdford farmer. He practised a four-course rotation of wheat, oats, peas and fallow on the fifty of his 120 or so acres which were arable, he had about forty-five acres of pasture and kept the remainder of his land as wood and furze. He kept six draught oxen, four cows and eleven young beasts,

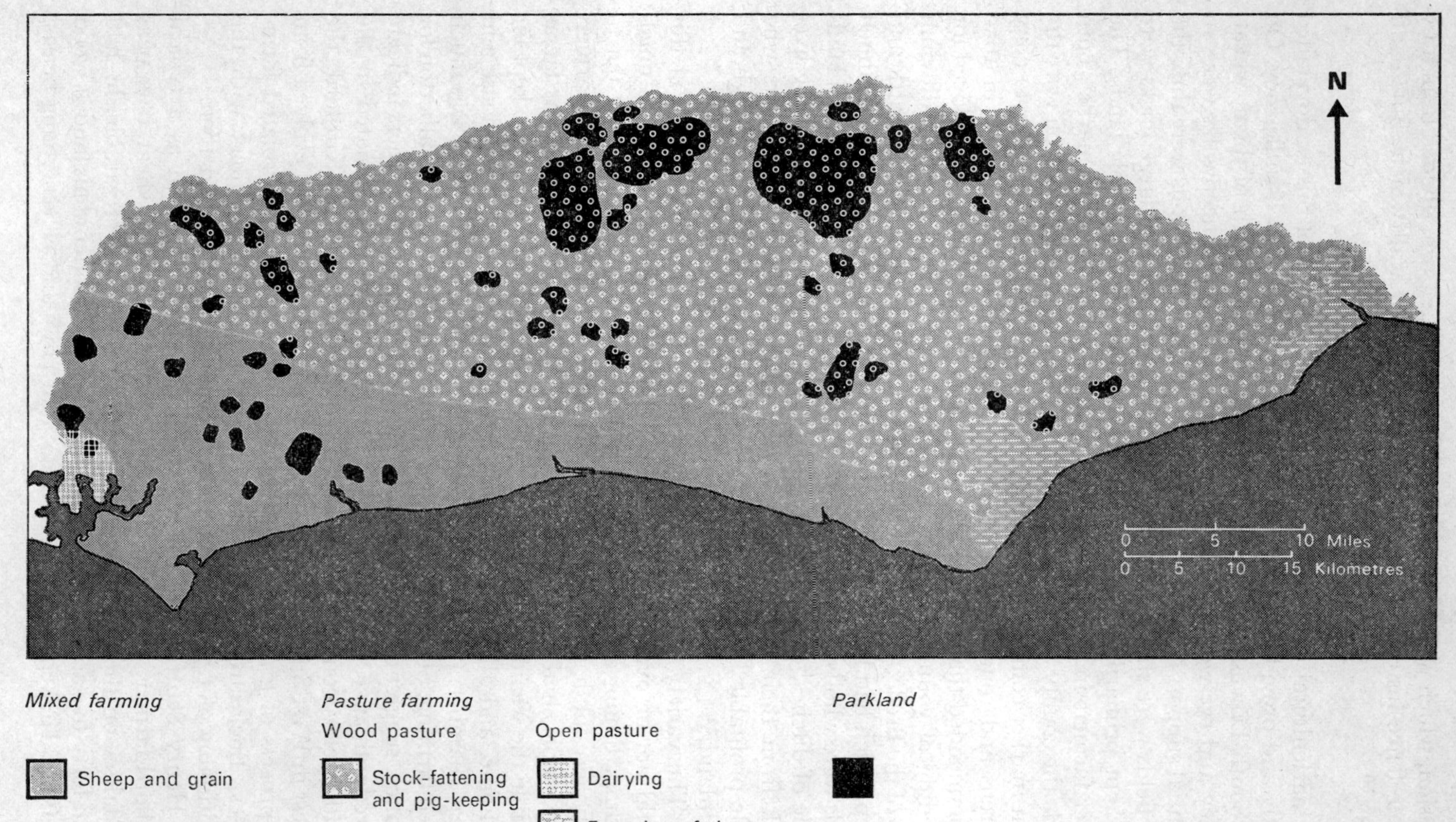
N
0 5 10 Miles
0 5 10 15 Kilometres
Mixed farming
Sheep and grain
Pasture farming
Wood pasture
Stock-fattening and pig-keeping
Open pasture
Dairying
Fattening of sheep with some cattle
Parkland

besides sheep, lambs, hogs and horses; there were ducks and poultry in his yard and fish in his pond. Henry Scutt owned his own wagons, dung-cart and plough. He improved his farming livelihood by working as a wheelwright. Scutt enjoyed the basic comforts a yeoman expected: there was a featherbed and ample linen in his chamber, an adequate range of cooking implements in his hall, plenty of pewter and brass in his kitchen. He made his own malt and butter. Two beehives stood in his farmyard. The inventory suggests the achievement of modest prosperity though a life of steady labour.

Henry Scutt was firmly established in the middle ranks of the Kirdford community. A few farmers were wealthier, many husbandmen and wage earners were much poorer. The outstanding family in the parish in the early seventeenth century were the Strudwicks. The house that Robert Strudwick of Crouchland left when he died in 1616 had ten rooms with lofts and a brewhouse and milkhouse attached; his parlour furnishings included a 'lyverie cupboarde with a carpet' and two 'wrought loome work cushions'; there were two psalters and a bible in his hall.[34] The Strudwicks had reached the borderline between yeomanry and gentry.[35] They lived in greater comfort than their neighbours and owned more land, but like them they were working farmers with their eyes firmly fixed on their fields of wheat and oats, on their meadows and their livestock.

Sir Thomas Pelham of Halland was a very different kind of man. He was a rentier with manors widely distributed across Pevensey and Hastings rapes, a large-scale industrialist, and he was a demesne farmer who took a vigorous personal interest in realising the profits of his lands. Pelham was a great magnate. His mansion and deer park, situated in the wealden vale seven miles from Lewes, occupied all the ground between the villages of Laughton and East Hoathly. In 1624, at the age of twenty-seven, he inherited a flourishing estate. His close attention to it during the subsequent thirty years, until his death in 1654, is recorded in a superb set of account books now in the British Museum. Pelham's accounts were kept on the new model being adopted at that time by nobility and magnate gentry, on paper rather than parchment, using arabic rather than roman numerals.[36] Three large volumes, one for income, two for expenditure, contain the full record of his financial dealings, except for the accounts of his ironworking interests and certain purchases of land from capital which he noted separately.[37] These accounts show that Sir Thomas was every inch a businessman. He was 'none of the least scrupulous of persons', remarked the Earl of Leicester, who found him exacting and suspicious in the negotiations of 1648 for the marriage between John Pelham and Lucy Sidney. Sir Thomas even sent his cousin and legal adviser Henry Pelham to question the Earl of Salisbury about the money he owed Leicester, and which had been assigned for the dowry. 'Though there were more distrust than discretion in it', commented Leicester about this inquiry, 'yet it may be pardoned in a man that never thinkes himself sure enough of money.'

Pelham's tightfistedness also showed itself in his pestering of his cousin Lady Elizabeth Wilbraham for money, in the midst of the distractions of the civil war, when their sons were on a joint trip abroad.[38]

Sir Thomas Pelham's rentroll fluctuated between about £1,500 and £2,700. The family could live very comfortably indeed within this income alone: in 1632–33 expenditure came to £1,694 and income to £2,039, in 1634–35 receipts dropped to £1,777 but a reduction in expenditure to £1,479 involved no hardship. The family's ironworks could be relied upon to bring in vast windfall profits. Periodic memoranda in the account books show that Pelham's cash resources were usually considerable. He recorded in May 1630, for example, that he had £2,500 'in one of my new drawers in the closett in new gould and another £1,000 or more in hand'. In 1634 he felt sufficiently confident of his resources to conclude a bargain for the purchase of extensive lands for £12,000. On his death his son noted that his father left him £3,000 in cash or bonds.[39]

The principal items in the Pelham rentroll were the Laughton and Bishopstone farms and the Crowhurst ironworks, which between them yielded about £650 a year. Sir Thomas dealt personally with important tenants such as the Newingtons of Bishopstone and Peter Farnden, who leased Crowhurst. But much of his income was made up of small sums from rents, perquisities of courts and other profits of the manors and hundreds which he held. This money was collected by his bailiffs, who held Sir Thomas's courts and accounted to him at Halland. The management of the demesne farm was the responsibility of the steward, Pelham's most trusted servant. When his steward John Vine left him after many years service in 1638, Pelham rewarded him with a parting gift of £40, whereas John the brewer and Roger the cook, who left the same year, each received five shillings 'at their going away'. Vine was responsible for buying grain and cattle, for hedging, ditching, railing and a multitude of other tasks in the upkeep of the estate; he ensured that the household was well supplied with wood for the fires and with all the necessities of daily life; he maintained oversight of Sir Thomas's large staff. Before he was made steward, John Vine had often accompanied Pelham when he was travelling, seeing that his master was well looked after, that the horses were fed, and that the coach was kept in good repair.[40] As steward he presented his accounts to Pelham at Lady Day and Michaelmas. They were carefully and accurately written up on the charge and discharge system. Sir Thomas's own accounts confirm his receipt and disbursement of the total sums noted by Vine.[41]

The Pelhams practised convertible husbandry on their Halland demesne.[42] It was only common sense to move the plough around the estate on the wealden soil and to allow arable land to regain heart under grass. But Sir Thomas went further than this. He was an unusually enterprising improver, denshiring an area of his demesne land year by year between 1634 and 1640. The process involved paring the turf with a breast plough, burning it and ploughing in the ash. Lime was spread at the same time.[43] Thus Pelham strove to maximise his returns from land that had previously been merely part of his deer park, just as the Earl of Northumberland had put commercial considerations before leisure facilities, earlier in the century, when he filled Petworth Great Park with cattle, sheep and ironworks.[44] Pelham also kept a substantial farm in his own hands at Bishopstone, where the deep combe running into the Downs from the Ouse estuary provided extensive arable land. This downland ranch played a crucial role in his farming system. Between 1629 and 1634 the Bishopstone farm was repaired and improved: the dog kennel and stable were thatched, repairs were completed at the mill, a 'provision house' was built and the farmhouse was enlarged and roughcast.[45] Besides supplying Halland with corn, Bishopstone was becoming a favourite resort of the family and their friends for hawking parties.

In theory, Bishopstone should normally have supplied the needs of the Pelham household for corn. The harvest year 1630–31 was so disastrous that expenditure of £124 on grain by the steward in the last quarter of it was predictable. But when in 1632–33, 1633–34, and again in 1634–35, the steward found it necessary to buy large quantities of grain from neighbouring gentry, like Francis Selwyn of Friston and John Gildridge of Firle, it became clear that the demesne farm had been left inadequately small by Pelham's leasing policy.[46] He escaped this dilemma by adopting a device, popular among magnate gentry at this time, for the supply of foodstuffs without the hazards and labour of oversight of a large arable farm. He bargained with his principal Bishopstone tenant to supply corn to the value of £50 per annum as rent in kind. Before long this arrangement had swung the balance in the other direction. In 1637 and 1638, John Vine accounted for 'Bishopstone rent wheat' that he had sold because it was surplus to the household's requirements.[47]

John Vine's real expertise lay in the buying and selling of cattle. The sale of such commodities as grain, conies, sheepskins, hides, tallow, wool, coal and brushwood were incidental profits of the estates. Livestock rearing was taken more seriously by Sir Thomas Pelham as a source of income. The aim was always to buy lean and sell fat. During the 1630s, there were normally between forty and ninety cattle and between thirty and 120 sheep on the Pelham farms. Most were 'country beasts', bred and bought locally, for resale ready for the shop to butchers of Lewes and other nearby towns. Nicholas Toke pursued the same kind of business in the Kentish weald.[48] The county's fairs were the landmarks of the farming calendar, occasions when Vine mixed with the crowd of wealden farmers, haggled and bargained and drove the beasts home to Halland at sunset. Heathfield, Pevensey, Framfield and Lindfield held their fairs in summer; the Cliffe, Rotherfield and Uckfield fairs were in the autumn; and in the High Weald towns of Battle and East Grinstead, safe from winter floods and storms, the fairs took place in January. For much of the year, some at least of the livestock were kept in the stall and grazed at Halland, where they could be watched by a single looker, who filled his time with odd jobs, molecatching and cutting the grass in the gardens. The inland estate was used flexibly with the excellent pastures within and around the ancient Roman walls of Pevensey castle and on the Bulverhithe marshes near Hastings, which Sir Thomas leased during the 1630s.[49] Pelham was prepared to look far afield for the kind of cattle he could rear most successfully. In 1626 Vine went to Bartholomew Fair and came home with ten runts and six heifers. During subsequent years Pelham regularly bought Cheshire cattle at the London and Uxbridge fairs. In selling his beasts he sometimes dealt with London and Kentish butchers as well as local ones.[50] He was an enterprising livestock farmer who, through some personal supervision and trust in an experienced steward, established a flourishing business.

John Everenden was a much less wealthy gentleman than Pelham, but he was an equally successful livestock farmer. His accounts cover most of the period from 1618, when he first established his stock, until 1658, when he handed over his farm to his son. In 1619, his second year of business, Everenden had almost 400 animals; by 1621, when he was in partnership with his brother Walter, they had a joint stock of 795 sheep and cattle; during the summers of the civil war years, more than 400 of his ewes and wethers were fattening on the rich marshland pasture below the ancient walls of Winchelsea.[51] Since his own estate was confined to the vicinity of his inland home at Sedlescombe, Everenden leased marshland pastures on the Brede and Pett levels. The upkeep of the innings there involved regular expenditure: Everenden paid his share, for 'waleing stuffe for the groynes', for instance, for 'makeing the salt dike' and 'for scouring the waterings in the Pett marsh'.[52] Unlike Pelham, Everenden kept his whole livestock business firmly in his own hands. He was down on the marshes inspecting the livestock so regularly from Easter onwards every year that it was worth his while to make a special arrangement with the Winchelsea ferryman, rather than pay him every time he crossed the Brede. Everenden took personal charge of the summer fattening and kept a keen eye on the efficiency of his lookers; he made his own bargains at the fairs; he took and recorded his own counts of the sheep and bullocks in the marsh each August.[53]

Until the mid-1650s, when steers, oxen and runts began to feature more prominently in his accounts than wethers and ewes, Everenden concentrated on the production of mutton rather than beef. But he had always had an eye for opportunities to purchase northern and western cattle from drovers. In the summer of 1648 he was able to make a handsome profit on nine runts he had bought from Fredrick the Welshman; in 1655 a Cheshire drover sold him six oxen.[54] He marketed some of his livestock virtually every autumn and winter. Two Battle men, Thomas Avery and Thomas Weekes, were among his most regular customers: 'our buchars' he called them in 1652, when he noted their purchase of 'the black crumple-horned cow and a branded haifer fatt and ten barren ewes'. The Battle butchers regularly supplied the Everendens' table with fresh meat and also, on occasion, their farm with lean sheep.[55] Everenden seldom sold at fairs, but preferred to deal privately with butchers in Rye, Winchelsea, Robertsbridge, Burwash and Hawkhurst, as well as Battle. His largest profits came from sales on the London market. Four seasons trading with one London butcher, between 1646 and 1653, brought him a total of £432 for wethers and steers. The butcher sent his agent down, or came himself, to negotiate the deal in the summer or autumn and an agreement was reached for delivery of the animals later in the year.[56]

As well as selling cattle and sheep for the table, Everenden made substantial profits from the sale of his annual wool crop. In the early 1640s his hop ground also yielded him twenty or thirty pounds a year on the market.[57] His labour costs were never high. He normally employed a couple of farm servants and his looker received three pounds or so a year for his many long and lonely days on the marshes. At sheepshearing, haymaking, harvest and hop-picking there was plenty of casual labour available locally to help him out.[58] Since he lived in the far east of the county, Everenden lacked a downland ranch. He grew his own flax and hemp but, despite some marling, liming and dung-spreading, his obstinate Sedlescombe lands seldom yielded sufficient supplies of wheat and barley for the household or of oats and peas for the stalls. He was forced to buy small quantities of grain in most years.[59]

Anthony Stapley was less systematic in his accounting than Pelham or Everenden, but he kept a memorandum book of the bargains he had made. Since coastal pasture was lacking near his home at Hickstead, in the clay vale, he put out his lean cattle on nearby farms when his own grazing was inadequate to support his herd. During the years 1642 to 1645, he kept up a regular marketing relationship with a London butcher, John Fleer, contracting to supply oxen at intervals between Christmas and Easter. He sealed the 1645 deal, which brought him £156, with a gift of a six gallon runlet of sack. Stapley specialised with more singlemindedness than Everenden. Cattle farming was his life and he was ready to purchase wheat, oats, apples, hops and other commodities from the substantial income which it gave him.[60]

The wealden iron industry steadily declined during the seventeenth century: in 1574 there were about 115 ironworks in Sussex, by 1653 the total had dropped to under sixty and only eight of them consisted of a furnace together with a forge. A grand jury petition to the county's MPs at Michaelmas 1661, stating that the ironworks were 'much decayed', stressed the employment in cutting and cording wood which the industry had previously brought to the Weald.[61] Some of the families who had built their fortunes out of iron withdrew from the industry before the

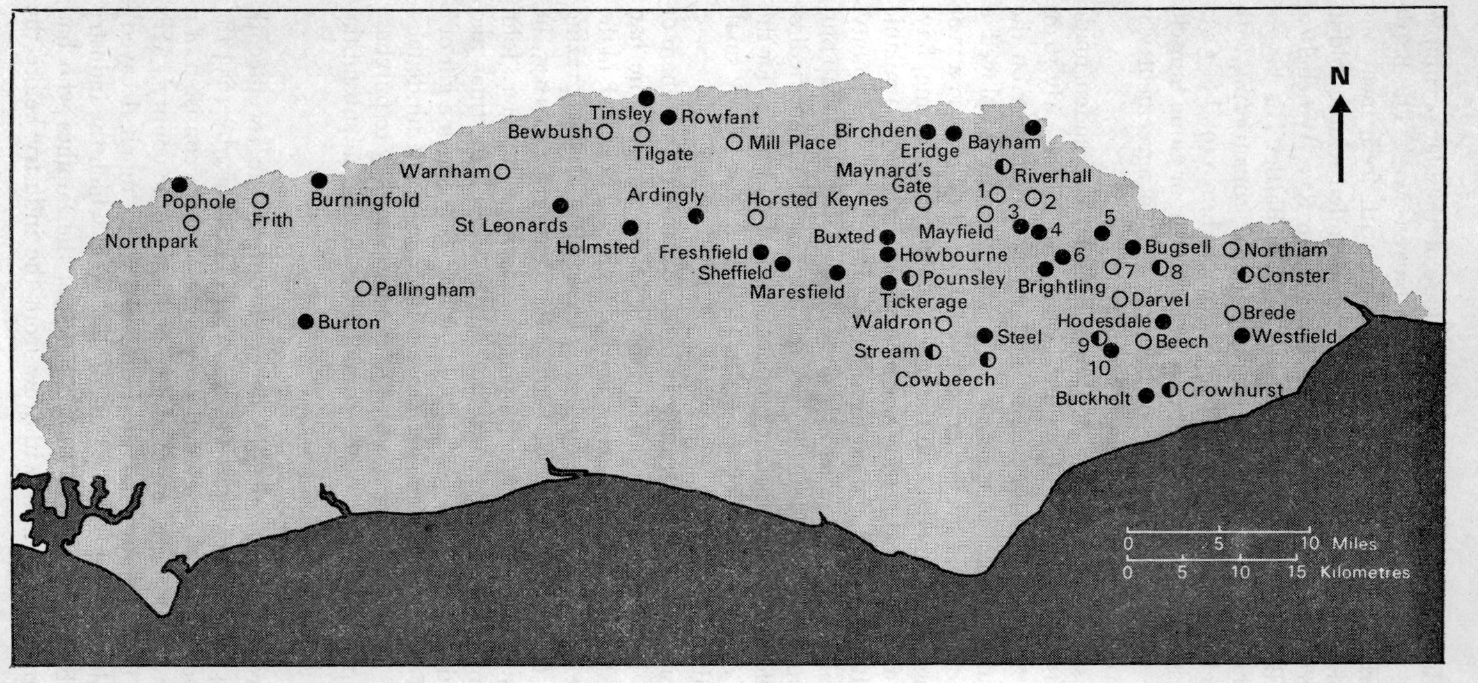

4 The iron industry in 1653

Restoration. Sir John Shurley, for example, sold Cotchford forge to a London gentleman in 1627, the May's furnace at Pashley was inactive by 1653; the Fowle's furnace at Riverhall was abandoned during the 1650s.[62] Yet the industry was still dominated by men who were established gentry in their own right. Most of the greatest ironmasters were county magnates. Stephen Pankhurst of Mayfield and Stephen French of Chiddingly were the only two men of merely parochial standing who made large enough profits from the industry for them to catch the eye of the gentry elite when it was called on to determine the highest assessments for forced loans to the crown.[63] A number of considerations, such as the state of the market, the availability of ore and of timber on their estates, and the proximity of their forges to furnaces and to water transport, influenced the policies pursued by gentry towards their ironworks. A short lease sometimes provided a useful respite from business, while woodlands matured. Obligations to keep tools and implements in good repair could be written into such contracts. Partnerships between gentry whose estates offered complementary resources were frequent. Thus Sir Thomas Dyke and John Fuller, close neighbours of French's, went into business together on the basis of a lease of his works at Streame in 1650. In 1644 Sir John Sackville and William White, as executors of Sir Thomas Sackville, went into partnership with the leading ironmaster of their neighbourhood, Peter Farnden.[64]

The military significance of the Sussex iron industry should not be overstressed. Only a limited number of the ironworks in the county were casting ordnance and making shot at any one time. In 1614 John Browne, the King's gunfounder, mentioned four furnaces with which he was dealing. In August 1653 the agent of the Ordnance office reported that he could only find six ironmasters prepared to supply great shot. Several of them were temporarily inactive for lack of water and one was 'straitened for workmen'.[65] The forges had a variety of specialisations. Some concentrated on elaborate firebacks and graveslabs, others on cooking equipment and utensils.[66] For most of the ironmasters transport of their products to the coast was a major problem and expense. Peter Farnden was exceptionally lucky in the easy access he enjoyed from Crowhurst to Hastings and from Westfield to the quay across the fields at Brede Bridge. He was an asute enough businessman to exploit his advantages to the full. When Walter Burrell was only asking £14 per ton for iron delivered from far inland to the Tower, Farnden undercut him by ten shillings, but insisted that this was his 'lowest price' and that he 'would not deliver it further from his furnace than Hastings or Rye'.[67] By this arrangement he virtually eliminated the heavy burden of transport costs. The accounts of the steward of his ironworks show how flourishing his business was in the early 1650s.[68]

Every mile up and down country lanes between an ironmaster's furnace and his forge involved considerable costs. Anthony Fowle's furnace at Maynards Gate and his forge at Maresfield were six miles apart. His other furnace at Rushlake was so inconveniently placed that he sold much of his sow iron from there to his colleague on the Bench Sir Thomas Pelham, whose Brightling and Bibleham forges were nearby.[69] Some gentry consistently engaged in one stage only of the industrial process. Sir William Goring's 'hot swarthy vulcans, sweating, puffing, hammering and drawing out those rusty sowes into bars', whom Lieutenant Hammond visited at Burton in 1635, had probably obtained their materials from a nearby furnace such as the Bartletts' works at Pallingham.[70] Since his Waldron furnace was six miles from his forges, Sir Thomas Pelham sold his sow iron directly; when he brought his Brightling and Bibleham forges into operation in the late 1630s they were largely separate enterprises, dependent on supplies of sow iron from friends. Both forges reached a peak of production in 1643–44. Carriage to Pevensey cost almost as much per ton as the hammerman's pay, but the profits of both works were substantial throughout the 1640s and 50s. The Waldron furnace was an equally successful business venture. With the price of sow iron rocketing to over £17 a ton, the annual income from it increased from £2,580 in 1643–44 to £3,408 the following year. In 1650 and 1651 Pelham's iron interests alone brought him around £4,000.[71]

The fortunes of the Sussex ports and fishing towns varied in the seventeenth century. Chichester by 1650 was on the brink of a very prosperous period as an entrepot for the grain trade. Shipments of wheat, barley and malt were increasing rapidly.[72] Lieutenant Hammond admired Arundel's 'convenient pretty haven'.[73] Newhaven's harbour facilities were sufficiently important by the 1640s for local merchants and shipowners to contribute to the clearing of the mouth of the Ouse undertaken by the sewers commissioners.[74] The pier at Hastings, on the other hand, was repeatedly destroyed by the sea, and Rye's harbour was caught in a process of ineradicable decay. Brighton, Seaford and Hastings struggled to make a living from the sea. Despite the hazards of French competition and Channel piracy, Hastings seems to have expanded its fishing industry in the 1620s and 30s and Brighton in the 1650s had a deep-sea fleet of fifty or more ships, the largest such fleet recorded anywhere in east Sussex between 1540 and 1660.[75] The Dunkirkers were a constant threat to fishermen and coastal merchants throughout the middle decades of the century. 'Non goeth oute but are taken', reported a frantic contractor for purveyance wheat from Shoreham in 1629, when he found that the masters of the vessels he had chartered would not put to sea without a convoy. The Hastings and Brighton fishermen were 'much dismayed' when the convoy provided them in 1656 for their voyage to the North Foreland mackerel grounds was taken by a Dunkirker off Pevensey. They were 'not willinge to stire out any of them except they have two convoys att the least', recounted the harassed captain in charge of the protection operation. In 1659 the Rye fishermen again sought a convoy for the mackerel season.[76]

The export of iron from Rye is an index of the decay of the port: 523 tons were shipped in 1633, fifteen in 1683.[77] In 1652 the corporation boldly claimed that theirs was still 'the best tyde harbor between the Downes and Isle of Wighte', but by then the choking action of sand and silt had in fact turned it into a tortuous maze of creeks. Bewildered by the fate that had befallen them, the Rye townsmen fought a long and useless battle to maintain their lifeline with the sea. Local JPs helped to promote a benevolence of 1628 towards repair of the harbour which was a dismal failure.[78] Rye doggedly opposed every attempt to reclaim marshland in their neighbourhood and to construct sluices on the Rother. The gentry with farming interests in the marshland were obvious scapegoats.[79] But the decay of the town's economy could not be arrested. In 1624 a hundred houses were reported to be empty. The town's fishermen clung to the outdated method of trammelling and gained nothing from a protracted dispute with the Hastings trawlers. There was much emigration of young fishermen to other towns.[80] Thus by 1653 the Rye fishing industry was heavily dependent on an ageing population: half of the thirty fishermen were over fifty, none under thirty.[81] Rye in the 1650s was a town with many troubles. There were endless problems in the maintenance of its water supply, walls and groins; disbanded soldiers and strangers infested its streets and alleyways. 'We are in a sore and deplorable condition', wrote the mayor in 1651, 'poverty and misery cometh upon us like an armed man'.[82]

Despite the decay of the iron industry, Sussex enjoyed a fair measure of economic stability in the period 1600 to 1660. The land provided an adequate subsistence to husbandmen and labourers. The gentry, from great magnates like Sir Thomas Pelham down to lesser men like John Everenden, assiduously exploited the resources of their estates. Industrial decline was not rapid enough, nor were harvest crises prolonged enough, to have major social and political repercussions. The economy of the county is in the main a backcloth to the drama of religious and political disruption in Sussex rather than the substance of the plot. Nevertheless it is significant for our understanding of administration and county politics, as are the facts of geography. Sussex's economy and situation carried much potential for disorder and unrest. The sea brought the danger of invasion and landings as well as a harvest of spoil. Rich arable lands tempted outsiders to rely on Sussex corn. The seasonal demands of both agriculture and industry, and the opportunities for casual work in the Weald, made it likely that there would always be a large number of people on the move. The JPs were sensitive to the implications of the economic pattern of the country, while central governments never fully understood or accepted them. There would always be an unresolved tension between the government in London and provincial gentry, immersed in the business of country life, who knew at first hand the problems of accommodating their countrymen to economic change, and of feeding and clothing families who in the last resort were dependent on them.

2

The gentry community

Believe it, Sir, you could not have found out a more effectual meanes to have gladded this whole contry (and especially your nearest endeared friends) then by marrying; nor in marrying then by soe happy an election of knowne and approved worth and vertue as you have made.
Nicholas Gildredge to Sir Thomas Pelham, 18 December 1637.[1]

Wish me two or three dayes this buck season with you.
Sir Robert Honeywood to Sir Thomas Pelham, 22 August 1644.[2]

I desire you may doe and receve all the good you can for soule and body, soe I could deny myselfe of my comfort for yours.
Anna Busbridge to her daughter Anna, 3 October 1648.[3]

Nobility and gentry

The Stuart gentry as a social class are hard to define. It is even harder to generalise about them. The 'gentry controversy' has now reached a stalemate: county studies have invariably shown great variations of economic circumstances, status and living standards within provincial gentry communities.[4] There was always social flux. Men who had acquired some of the accepted marks of gentility, a new and imposing house perhaps or a place in the administrative framework of the shire, were constantly claiming to be gentlemen. Their neighbours were sometimes surprised at the claim and took time to accustom themselves to it, as inventories of 'yeomen' who in their wills spoke of themselves as 'gentlemen' show. There were always some men climbing the social ladder, just as there were others slipping down it. Zabulon Newington, to take one example, was a cattle farmer who owned twenty acres of marshland at Pevensey and bequeathed a total of £1,300 in 1635 in portions to his eight children. He was content to call himself a yeoman. His son, Joseph Newington, became a JP in 1656 and entered his arms at the 1662 visitation.[5] Between the nobility and a man like Joseph Newington, who was stepping across the border to gentility, there were many kinds of gentry. A few magnate families constituted a ruling elite; many middling gentry owned estates in several parishes and exerted influence beyond their own village; other lesser men were essentially parish gentry, men who dominated their own tiny community but were of little account in the shire. The distinctions within the gentry community therefore are nearly as important as the vital distinction on which everything in seventeenth-century society was based, between the gentry and the people.

During the period of 1560 to 1640 a profound change took place in the balance of power between the Sussex nobility and gentry. In the first decades of Elizabeth's reign the Montagus, Arundels, De La Warrs, Lumleys and Sackvilles dominated social and political life. Five noble families was 'more than one shire can wel bear', reported Bishop Curteys of Chichester in 1583, 'specially if ill affected or doubted and agreeing all together and having often meetings'. But in 1569 Arundel and Lumley had been removed from the lieutenancy, and the power of the Protestant Sackvilles was steadily enhanced. In the 1590s, Elizabeth could enjoy the hospitality of the Montagus at Cowdray in the knowledge that Sussex was loyal to the crown.[6] By the 1620s the nobility no longer controlled the county. The parliamentary elections of that decade show how their influence had declined.[7] Pursuit of careers at court had led the Earls of Arundel and Dorset to become detached from county affairs, as their relationship with the deputies in the lieutenancy shows.[8] The Sackvilles had abandoned Buckhurst, inaccessibly situated in the miry vale, for Knowle, across the Kentish border, at the end of Elizabeth's reign. Francis, Viscount Montagu was resident at Cowdray but largely kept himself apart from county society.[9] Richard, Viscount Lumley had never established himself properly in Sussex, preferring his Durham estates. Algernon Percy, the Earl of Northumberland was on the Commission of the Peace in the 1630s, but played no active role in county politics until the outbreak of the civil war. Richard, Lord Dacre was a political nonentity, and his son Francis was a minor when he inherited in 1630. The contrast between noble power in Sussex and in a county such as Wiltshire had become striking.[10] Neither of the two new peers had succeeded in establishing a political ascendancy in any way comparable with that enjoyed by the ancient nobility in the previous century. The upstart Lord Goring was only concerned with exploiting his opportunities at court and his rental was anyway no larger than that of several magnate gentry. The Earl of Thanet, the son of a jumped-up peer who purchased his title for £5,000 in 1625, was enormously wealthy but of little account in Sussex outside the Kentish border country of Hastings rape.[11]

In the period from 1529 to 1558 the knights of the shire in the Commons had owed their places to the patronage of noble families.[12] As late as 1583 Bishop Curteys recommended that many 'illaffected, weak and indifferent' gentry 'that follow the noblemen' should be removed from the Bench.[13] Throughout the sixteenth century bastard feudalism characterised Sussex politics. Lord Montagu nominated a known Catholic as undersheriff and protected him from dismissal from the Bench in the 1570s. During the next decade, Montagu and Thomas Sackville, Lord Buckhurst, ran the county together. They successfully managed the 1584 county election. In 1588 Buckhurst extracted an assurance from the Privy Council that none of Montagu's 'servantes and reteyners employed in the countrye' would be withdrawn from their offices.[14] Together with noble dominance went gentry factionalism. Five JPs were omitted from the Commission in

1595, after the judges had reported that they were in the service of other gentlemen.[15] Yet there were some gentry who had escaped noble and magnate tutelage by the 1580s. The Morleys, Bowyers, Mays and Pelhams were among the families singled out by Bishop Curteys for their Protestantism and their independence. Such families constituted the core of the new ruling elite that emerged in Stuart Sussex.

Something of the atmosphere of the Tudor relationship between nobility and gentry survived in the next century, but a relationship that once carried crucial political force had become a matter of social etiquette. Sir John Sackville's remark to the corporation of Rye in 1630 that his friend Peter Farnden was 'a longe servant in our howse' no longer carried a commanding ring; it was almost a conventional courtesy.[16] Although the noble branch of the family was no longer resident in the county, the Sackvilles remained well integrated with east Sussex society. When the Earl of Dorset visited Buckhurst in 1617, 'all country gentlemen met him with their greyhounds' and there was feasting for three days. Richard, Lord Dacre and Sir Edward Burton were among the Sussex magnates who paid calls on Lady Anne Dorset at Knowle in 1619.[17] John Everenden waited on the fourth Earl of Dorset in London in 1626. It did not occur to Sir Thomas Pelham to omit a portrait of the fourth Earl, the lieutenant of the county whom he had served for fourteen years, when he furnished his long gallery at Halland in 1641.[18] Yet the Sussex gentry most closely attached to Dorset, as his men of affairs, were on the periphery of the county's ruling circle. Sir George Rivers, Richard Amherst and Edward Lindsey, who became his executors in 1624, all spent as much time in London or Kent as in Sussex.[19] When he made his will in 1630, Lindsey made a fulsome tribute to his 'especial good lord Edward Earl of Dorset'. He had seen, he declared, the 'excellence of his noble nature by entertaining small gifts proceeding from faithful minds, regarding the giver's affection above the gift'. He bequeathed to Dorset a piece of gilt plate, 'beseeching the eternal providence to blesse him and his noble house with longe contynuance in all prosperous estate'. Rivers, Amherst and Lindsey were a close-knit trio: both Rivers and Lindsey made Amherst overseer of their wills.[20] But the attachment of these men to the household of a courtier had distracted them from county affairs. Only Amherst, who had a house in Lewes and iron interests nearby, was a regular attender at quarter sessions.[21]

The men of affairs of the Earl of Northumberland show the same detachment from the community of county gentry. Sir Edward Francis pursued a career characteristic of such men: he was steward of the household at Petworth and then paymaster to the gentlemen pensioners at court, retaining in the meanwhile his borough seat at Steyning.[22] Edward Dowse devoted himself wholly to the Percy family. He was nominated as a JP and committeeman in the 1640s but was active in neither capacity. In the Commons he kept apart from the Sussex members. Dowse's will indicates the circumscribed world in which he lived, the world of his study at Petworth, his master's books and his master's estates. He gave his 'noble good lord' fifty pounds to buy a dozen silver plates and his lady the same amount to buy a ring, 'for a token of my thankfulness unto them both'.[23]

Sussex on the eve of the civil war was dominated by about ninety gentry families who exercised wide influence. These were the county families. Almost half of them could boast a more or less continuous tradition of administrative service going back to the Tudors. In this sense the county enjoyed a remarkable degree of social stability. Eleven of the forty-four families who may be regarded as of county status in both 1580 and 1642 could trace their ancestry in Sussex to before 1300. Nine more had been resident since the fourteenth century and another fourteen since the fifteenth century. Only ten of these families were Tudor newcomers.[24]

Although they were perhaps less preoccupied with genealogy than their Kentish neighbours, the ancient Sussex gentry shared their pride in ancestry and interest in heraldry.[25] Sir Thomas Pelham, for example, spent thirty pounds on an elaborate pedigree and engaged his Cheshire cousin Ralph Wilbraham to do research on his first wife's family history.[26] Confidence in their outstanding role in local society and the desire to perpetuate the memory of past generations, more than blatant ostentation, led to the gentry's demand in the early seventeenth century for large funeral monuments.[27] Richard Lewkenor had already made plans for a handsome monument to his grandfather, a distinguished judge, and his own parents before he made his will in 1635. He bequeathed £100 for its completion. Anthony May of Ticehurst requested his executors in 1636 to erect a tombstone with brasses to four generations of his family. Emphasis was often placed on a numerous progeny. The Selwyn tomb of 1613 at Friston has babes in swaddling clothes; the Lewkenor tomb was to include all the children born to Richard Lewkenor's father. The passion for heraldry was central to the fashion for impressive monuments. 'The armes of our familie with all their quarterings and bearings' were to be prominently displayed on the Lewkenor tomb.[28] At Isfield the family crest and arms surmount the deep coffered arch under which Sir John Shurley who died in 1631 lies in effigy, with his two wives on either side of him. The inscription speaks of his ancient family and of the marriages into families of good quality that his daughters had made. The arms of his own family and the Dacre family joined were an essential element of the design of the monument requested by Sir Thomas Parker in 1653. His motive, he declared defensively at a time when such monuments were coming to be thought superstitious, was to record his marriage into the Dacre family, 'for memoriall to be left to my posteritie for the better deciding of any controversies that in time hereafter may happen amongst them'.[29]

Some of the leading families of Elizabethan Sussex died out in the male line before 1642, such as the Bellinghams of Newtimber. Others, like the Onleys of Pulborough and Stanleys of Fittleworth, had lost much of their standing in the gentry community. Newcomers since Elizabeth's reign owed their advancement to various means. Perhaps the most painless entry to the ruling elite was an adroit marriage that brought with it a major mansion and estate. Thus Thomas Woodcock inherited the Bellingham estate at Newtimber and Sir Thomas Hendley obtained the fortunes of the Bowyers of Cuckfield.[30] Well established gentry might not accept such intruders at once, but, given an agreeable personality and some social graces, marriage could take a man of lesser gentry origin a long way towards magnate status. The influx of men of mercantile, metropolitan and professional backgrounds was not as marked in Sussex as in counties such as Northamptonshire, which experienced something of a Tudor and Stuart landed revolution, but it was nevertheless a significant feature of the social scene.[31] The *nouveaux riches* included the predictable crops of lawyers, men like Philip Jermyn who came of an Exeter family and founded his own estate at Racton, and of London businessmen. Robert Anderson of Chichester was the grandson of a sheriff and alderman of London.[32]

The most striking group among the parvenus were the ironmasters: families such as the Dykes, the Frenchs and the Pankhursts. The marriage portions they left their children in their wills reveal the extent of their wealth. Thomas Dyke left £1,200 each to two daughters and £1,500 to a third in 1632; John French, the previous year, directed that his daughter's portion should be £1,000 and that his two sons should receive £2,000 and £1,000 respectively.[33] This kind of generosity was well beyond the means of several gentry of county standing. Thomas Chown for example, a much respected JP, could only afford to leave a single daughter £300 in 1639; Sir Stephen Board, an ex-trained band captain and sheriff, had dug so deeply into his resources for his new home at Borde Hill that he could only promise his daughter £500 when he made his will in 1630.[34] Wealth by itself did not enable a man to leap up the social hierarchy. It was one thing for prominent landed families like the Pelhams to dabble in the iron industry as a sideline. But the man who was simply an ironmaster was not easily accepted into the county elite. The ups and downs of the Pankhurst family show why such men were treated with a degree of disdain and distrust. During the first three decades of the century, Stephen Pankhurst's success was spectacular. Sales of iron enabled him to buy estates in Buxted, Waldron, Mayfield and Wadhurst parishes. When the third highest assessment in the whole county was imposed on him for the privy seal loan in 1626, his business was at its most flourishing. But then the crash came. At his death in 1646, Pankhurst's estate was burdened by debt and his heir only succeeded in raising the portion that he had optimistically promised his granddaughter by plunging the family further into debt.[35]

The career of Thomas Dyke, on the other hand, indicates how the son of a successful ironmaster of parish gentry origins could, with patience and determination, establish himself as a leading figure in the shire.

Among the steps that he took up the social ladder were entry to St John's College, Cambridge, and the Inner Temple; marriage in 1639 to a daughter of the ship money judge Sir John Bramston; and the acquisition of a knighthood in 1641.[36] During the 1640s, Dyke was a regular visitor to Herstmonceux, sedulously attaching himself to the Dacres with gifts of leashes of pheasants.[37] In 1649 he offered Sir Thomas Pelham the services of his coachman to carry Lady Pelham to Godstone; in the 1650s he even found his way into the orbit of the Sidneys at Penshurst.[38] Sir Thomas Dyke became a JP and a man who mattered in Restoration Sussex. The gentry elite was thus not an entirely homogeneous group of men, and it was ready in time to absorb newcomers. Intrusions did not disturb the sense of continuity at the heart of county society, politics and government, since a core of families persisted who had ruled the shire much longer than anyone could remember.

Mansions and deer parks

No traveller through Sussex in the seventeenth century could fail to be impressed by the mansions and parks of the gentry. The rider on the Downs had a prospect of numerous fine manor houses; the vagrant traversing the wealden lanes found himself regularly diverted by the posts and rails of a deer park. Lieutenant Hammond saw or visited many of the major houses on his summer journey in 1635. He found Broomham and Burton 'fayre' and Firle 'sweetlie seated'. At Arundel he admired the long gallery and the orchard with its apples, pears and plums. At Petworth he wondered at the armoury, the 'stately, lofty, faire built stables', the bowling green, drawing rooms, library, chapel and parlour. Finally around Chichester Hammond found many 'goodly seats' of knights and gentlemen.[39]

At least twenty-five of the county's leading families built new homes or substantially rebuilt their houses between 1560 and 1640.[40] Only ruins remain of several of their finest creations, of Brambletye for example, of Slaugham Place and of Halland. Mansions that still stand, such as Borde Hill, Parham, Wiston and Danny have simple grids of mullions and transoms, a plain but careful symmetry. Such houses are characteristic of the sobriety with which the Sussex gentry accepted and expressed the Elizabethan Renaissance. It was the Pelhams who brought the Renaissance to east Sussex in the 1530s with their terracotta friezes and window-jambs on the tower at Laughton Place. Thirty years later, the Jefferays showed enthusiasm for classical allegory and detail at Chiddingly Place. But at no time in the next hundred years did the gentry become intoxicated with the new ideas. Their use of the classical orders was restrained and largely confined to porches and doorways. Gables and finials were the limits of their display. Wakehurst Place, for example, the mansion that Sir Edward Culpepper built at Ardingly in 1590, has some gaiety in the façade, but it also exhibits markedly conservative features.[41] The arcading that remains at Slaugham Place and John Thorpe's plan of the house suggest that Sir Walter Covert was the most enterprising builder of his generation. The entrance range towards the courtyard is reminiscent of Kirby Hall and the front garden with angle pavilions recalls the design of Montacute.[42]

In planning, as well as in style, the county was slow to adopt new fashions. Wakehurst, Halland and Slaugham, all built in the final years of Elizabeth's reign, were courtyard houses; so even was Brambletye, built by Sir Henry Compton in 1631. Whether its rib-vaulted undercroft is taken as a practical solution to the problems of a wet and low-lying site or as a piece of conscious archaism, it is clear that Compton, though by no means a country bumpkin, was having no truck with the innovations of Inigo Jones. The porch has a gothic rib-vault too. At Brambletye the symmetry was absolute, the style decisively Elizabethan, the taste backward-looking and gothic.[43] William Yalden's manor house at Blackdown, built in 1640, is another handsome but plain building which perfectly illustrates the attachment of the Sussex gentry to the Tudor style. During the century before the civil war they built no prodigy houses. They were content to marry the old and the new. Their manor houses were continually added to but seldom begun again from scratch. Yeomen and husbandmen shared the gentry's conservatism. The 'wealden' type of timber-framed house was adapted and improved as men found themselves able to afford better living standards.[44] The county has numerous fine examples of timber framing, but few really exuberant ones. The unemphatic progression from Wiston and Parham in the 1570s to Blackdown in 1640 has been described as 'a remarkable proof of how self-contained the county still was'.[45]

There were probably between seventy and a hundred deer parks in Sussex on the eve of the civil war.[46] Many of them had been carved out of the great forests of Stansted-Arundel, St Leonards and Ashdown, that formerly covered so much of the shire. A string of parks lay along the clay vale to the north of the Downs: Bignor, Burton, Wiston, Danny, Glynde and Firle were just a few of them. Some of the greatest magnates owned more than one park. Sir Thomas Pelham, for example, kept his parks at Hellingly and Halland well stocked with deer. Francis, Lord Dacre lived at Herstmonceux Castle in the middle of his home park, while his brother was keeper of his park at Bayly in Heathfield.[47] The Earl of Northumberland had two parks at Petworth.

It required all the magnates' vigilance to protect their deer parks from the marauding expeditions of neighbours who cast envious eyes upon them. The parks were everywhere a standing temptation. Deer stealing was endemic. Francis, Lord Dacre, not himself a justice, sought the co-operation of Sir Thomas Pelham in 1644 in checking it. 'My parke, and as I am enformed most parkes neere it, have suffered much', he reported, 'I doe therefore request you, that if there be any lawe on foote, you would be pleased to take the strictest course with them that may bee'.[48] A Jacobean statute gave the justices power to punish unlawful hunting in their parks and stealing of deer but it was difficult to enforce.[49] It was seldom, for example, that a JP was able to present as neatly packaged a case as that against the intruders in Broadhurst Park in 1639. On this occasion the Michelbournes' keeper heard hunters in the park at night, followed the tracks of their horses in the frost and obtained a confession from the culprits, who pleaded that 'it was but a cony or two' and tried to bribe him to say nothing.[50] Not all gamekeepers were so loyal or so alert. Moreover there were plenty of lesser gentry for whom hunting in their neighbours' parks was the best sport an idle country life could offer. They were bold and difficult to catch. Most satisfying of all was the chance to prick the complacency of a powerful recusant magnate. At quarter sessions in 1641, a Beeding husbandman testified to the boastful and audacious language of Thomas Bishe, who had

> protested that he would have two brace of buckes and two of dowes out of Sir Richard Weston's grownd yearely. And then said he had killed fower deere in one night there, besides the deere left killed by him and not carryed away. And said also that Sir Richard Weston beinge a recusant convicted he cold have noe remedy by law for itt. And he said he had killed a brace of deere in Mr Middleton's grownd.

Middleton's keeper related how, in any attempt to terrorise him into silence, Bishe had 'threatened to fyer his house over his head'.[51]

Gentry deer stealers were seldom indicted in the local courts since a Star Chamber prosecution usually offered a better chance of bringing them to book. Sir Thomas Pelham, Sir Edward Culpepper and several of the county's nobility initiated cases there in James I's reign.[52] But all too easily gentry who looked to Star Chamber for redress became entangled in the complexities of a wider feud with a neighbouring family.[53] It is hard to judge the effectiveness of the Bench's periodic drives to protect their private hunting grounds. A policy of severe fines at sessions for cony hunting was supplemented by attempts, in the 1630s and again in the 1650s, to enforce the statutes against unlawful possession of guns, bows, nets, greyhounds and ferrets.[54] In 1656 one man who owned a net fifty fathoms long forcibly resisted the constable's demand that he should part with it.[55] Poaching has always been a traditional rural activity and it was perhaps asking too much of constables to expect them to show diligence in searching their friends' and neighbours' homes for the means by which countrymen pursued it.

For the magnate gentry sport was the essence of country life and social intercourse. Thus the Pelhams had their own bowling alley at Halland, and at Petworth in 1635, Lieutenant Hammond found 'a company of his Lordship's owne gentlemen taking their recreations' in the bowling alley and on the tennis court.[56] The downland families of east Sussex traditionally enjoyed the pleasures of falconry. The Pelhams employed a full-time falconer and Sir Thomas gave the purchase of falcons and goshawks his personal attention on visits to London. Hawks were put in mew with those of Sir Edward Burton at Eastbourne, and Pelham's friend Nicholas Gildredge sometimes undertook to train them. 'He hath wanted noe caring, nor other rites that our skills afford, hee will now jump to the fist', reported Gildredge of a haggard that Sir Thomas had sent to Eastbourne in 1637. The open downland spaces above the Bishopstone farm were ideal for the family's hawking parties.[57] Their common athletic activities bound the gentry community together and civil war was not allowed to interrupt them. Sir Thomas Pelham hunted as usual during it with his friends at Forest Row; Francis, Lord Dacre devoted himself as usual to hawking, coursing and shooting. Stories of the chase were often more prominent in correspondence with kinsmen than political events. 'I have noe other newse to send you', wrote Pelham's cousin Walsingham from Kent, in a letter of 1644 which passed lightly over the Earl of Essex's most recent reverse, 'but I kild a buck which runn seaven mile an end and soe ended the best sport in the world with a leane deare'.[58]

Marriage and children

Since public actions have usually been more fully recorded than the private side of men's lives, the history of the family in England has been relatively neglected. Yet much correspondence relating to family affairs has survived, as well as account books and a few invaluable diaries. These sources, which mainly relate to the gentry, provide glimpses of the most important realities of men's lives: marriage and children, loving and quarrelling, births and deaths.[59]

Eldest sons and daughters at any rate normally had their first marriages arranged for them by their parents. Continuity of the estate and advancement of the family were the gentry's prime considerations in marrying their children. Marriage was seen as a partnership in household management. Although mutual affinity was coming to be taken more seriously, passionate love was still viewed by many with suspicion as the basis of a marriage. But arranged marriages sometimes faltered when the parties dragged their heels. John Wilson's son was reluctant to go to London to meet his prospective bride, the daughter of Christopher Swale, who, like the Wilsons, was a newcomer to Sussex from the north. Swale was put in an embarrassing position. 'For his sake I have kept off all other suitors', he told John Wilson, 'although for some I have been importuned for accesse.' A daughter's right of veto was coming to be generally accepted. 'Marriages', remarked Swale to Wilson, 'must be first concluded in heaven, before they can be consummated on earth.' The increasing willingness of fathers to leave their daughters portions free from any strings and payable at a certain age, rather than on marriage, is a mark of the gradual liberalisation of marriage customs. John Culpepper in 1607, for instance, and Zabulon Newington in 1635, directed that their daughters should have their portions at twenty-one. As time went on fathers were more often prepared to trust their daughters even younger. Thus William Thomas and Sir Thomas Gage in 1654 directed that their girls should have their portions at eighteen; and Francis, Lord Dacre's will of 1655 declared that both his daughters should enjoy their portions at marriage or sixteen.[60]

The most advanced ideas about marriage and courtship emerged in Puritan lesser gentry circles where negotiations were often personal, intimate and romantic. The love letters of John and Robert Pierson of Peasmarsh were full of exaggerated fancies and artful conceits. Anne Jeake's suitors often visited her and sent tokens. In 1650 Samuel Jeake indulged in an elaborate courtship of a twenty-year-old Kentish girl Frances Hartredge but found his suit refused. Jeake, who was deeply in love with her, was shattered. He asked her to 'rase out my lines and returne them to me in that mourning garbe', as a token of the finality of her decision. When he had 'embalmed' them 'with a few brinish drops', he promised, he would 'crave strength of the most High to bowe to his will'. But later Jeake heard from Christopher Blackwood, his close friend, who was Frances Hartredge's brother-in-law, that her uncertainty about the 'good title' of the jointure he had offered and certain other apprehensions about her independence of action as a married woman, rather than any fundamental dislike for Jeake, had caused her refusal. 'After a right understanding of things', they agreed to marry on Jeake's acceptance of a paper written by his fiancée, containing 'five propositions which I judge reasonable, which being granted I know not of any other thing I shall desire'. The paper amounted to a remarkable and unusual display of feminine individuality and Jeake apparently observed his promises faithfully. Three of them concerned property arrangements and a scheme for a Blackwood niece to live at Rye until the Jeakes had their own family; the other two concerned religious worship. 'I desire liberty of conscience', declared Frances Hartredge boldly. She claimed a right to return to the church of which she was 'a member' four times a year. She never it seems felt the need to invoke the further provision that 'if there should be such worship as my heart cannot close withall nor my bodily presence allow of without sin, that it may be no alienation of conjugall affection if I should absent herein'.[61]

Three happy marriages led Sir Thomas Pelham to develop an increasingly idealised view of love and marriage. His first wife Mary Wilbraham, the daughter of a Cheshire knight whom he married at the age of eighteen, was probably chosen for him, but he was deeply distressed at her death in 1635. He confessed to Nicholas Gildredge his 'distracted thoughts' in the 'unsetled course' of life that the loss of his partner in early middle age brought him. But he was soon looking for a new wife and within two years had chosen a widow, Judith Shirley. 'I cannot but claime and expresse my share of joy in this your soe blessed a way of quieting your minde', declared Gildredge in a letter of congratulation.[62] But within a year Judith Shirley was dead and Pelham was forced to turn his mind to courtship once more. He obtained the hand of Margaret Vane, the sister of Sir Henry Vane the younger. This auspicious match was celebrated in June 1640, at the Vane mansion of Fairlawn in Kent, with an enormous marriage feast, a gay social event in an otherwise tense summer season. But when, the day after the feast, Lady Margaret Pelham was taken ill the proud Sussex magnate who had been so ill-fated in his second marriage became the subject of a cruel jibe: 'Yt abated all mirth and caused a jealosye that Sir Thomas was the only kill weoman'.[63] Lady Margaret survived and Pelham became deeply in love with her. He lavished money on her throughout the remaining fourteen years of his life.[64] His arrangements for Lady Margaret's comfort after his death were meticulous. The family's town house in Lewes was to be her dower house and lands to support her in her widowhood were conveyed to her by deed. In his will Sir Thomas left her 'all the chamber plate marked with her father's arms', which had cost him several hundred pounds in the 1640s, her pearls and jewels, her portrait, a coach and six horses, £1,000 and much linen, 'shee ever having been a very loving wife to me and well deserving of mine'.[65]

Despite this generosity to his own wife, Pelham showed how tight-fisted he could be when it came to his son John's marriage. He was probably delighted at the prestige that his son's choice of Lucy Sidney brought to the family and approved John's determination to make a love match. But he did not allow his enthusiasm for the match to draw him into paying the excessively large jointure that the Earl of Leicester insisted on. John Pelham had to promise to make the jointure up to £1,000 when he inherited his father's estate in order to save the marriage.[66] Pelham's distrustful attitude throughout the negotiations led to a quarrel with the Earl of Leicester which lasted for more than five years. 'I went not thither', noted Leicester in his diary about an invitation to christen Lucy Pelham's child at Halland in 1652, 'and to put a civility upon Sir Thomas Pelham, which I thought would make him love the childe and use my daughter better then he had done, I desyred that the childe should be named Thomas, as so it was done'.[67] It was characteristic of Pelham that, before he gave his steward overall responsibility for the household as well as the estate, he should have expected his first wife to keep precise accounts for the house and the children, and for spinning, which he checked with her at intervals of a few months.[68]

Women were urged to seek the devotion of their husbands through obedience and deference. 'Endeavour to please him', Christopher Blackwood advised Frances Hartredge, 'and dwell with him with an amiable meekenes and contentednes of minde and doe not greeve his spirit with the least frowardnes'.[69] Gentlemen hoped their wives would bring continuity and stability to the family home. 'Swet hart thes are to ceartyfy you that I am cum well to London', scribbled John Busbridge in a hasty note in 1633, 'I pray remember my dutty wheare dutty belongs and love to alle'.[70] With a high death rate of women during or after childbirth, many gentlemen chose to remarry. Frances Hartredge only lived three years after her marriage to Samuel Jeake in 1651. John Everenden recorded, on one and the same page of his accounts for the year 1621, his wedding expenses and his payment 'to ringers and those that carried my wife to church when she was buried'.[71] Among the nobility, in the period 1558 to 1641, one of the spouses to over a third of all first marriages died within fifteen years.[72]

When gentlemen made their wills they had an opportunity to confirm and extend the provisions of the jointure for the ease of their widows. Only a few of the wealthiest families, such as the Pelhams, Coverts, Bishops, Gages and Springates, possessed a dower house.[73] The more usual arrangement at this level of society was for a widow to occupy a room or rooms in the family home. Some thought it sufficient to make a general provision about sufficient dwelling for their wives, after discussing the arrangements with the eldest son. Others sought to avoid any ambiguity by leaving precise directions.[74] Anthony May of Ticehurst, for example, listed the chambers that were to be his wife's and declared her 'free liberty of the use of the kitchen', her right to collect firewood and her use of the facilities for 'dressing meat and drink'. Occasionally awareness of tensions that might arise between an heir, perhaps by another marriage, and a man's wife lay behind specific testamentary provisions. 'I desire my deare wife and my sonne George to be aideing and assisting and comforting to each other that her love may appeare to him and his dutie to her', wrote Sir Thomas Parker in his will.[75]

Gentlemen saw their reputations living after them in the manner in which their wives kept up with fashion and social etiquette. Thus Sir John Gage, Sir Thomas Sackville and Herbert Hay ensured that their widows would have their own coach and horses.[76] Sackville also directed that his widow should have two men servants and three maids; John French and Thomas May of Rawmere were others who were explicit about servants. Bequests of treasured articles were marks of care and affection. Richard Lindsey, for example, left his wife his 'great blew bible'; Sir Walter Covert directed that his wife should have 'all the silver plate that usually standeth upon the cupboard in my bedchamber'.[77] In short, there is much evidence in wills that domestic tenderness was common. Marriage seems to have brought deep and lasting emotional fulfilment to many members of the gentry community. When he lost his wife in 1661, Sir William Wilson spoke of her as 'one of the best of women, being too good for me'.[78]

It is hard to say how often marital tensions occurred, but two documented cases suggest one cause of conflict. The hoary question of whether to live in town or the country seems to have brought about the estrangement of Sir Henry Compton and his wife in 1618. Lady Anne Dorset, Lady Compton's sister-in-law, achieved a reconciliation the following year, when she invited the pair to Knowle 'to sup here on purpose hoping to make them friends'. She later extracted a promise from Compton that he would keep his London house for a while longer, 'because my sister Compton might sometimes go to London'.[79] Francis, Lord Dacre was apparently another man who preferred a quiet country existence, with his yacht close at hand at Herstmonceux, to costly living in the metropolis. When he spent some months in London with his family in 1648, he found himself forced to borrow money to keep his head above water.[80] With such predilections, marriage to the daughter of a hugely rich London merchant, who had brought with her a tempting portion of £20,000, was perhaps unwise. When he made his will in 1655 he made no mention of his wife and made his brother-in-law, Sir Thomas Parker, guardian of his son Thomas. Later that year he was reported to have gone overseas 'upon some discontent with his lady'.[81]

While seventeenth-century family life remained authoritarian and patriarchal, a gradual humanisation of relations between parents and children was occurring. Sir Thomas Pelham's affection for his fifteen offspring, seven of whom he lost in his lifetime, is suggested by the presents he regularly brought down from London: a bonnet and drum for Henry, his firstborn by Margaret Vane, a muff for Bess or a looking-glass for Nan.[82] The Pelhams persisted in employing wet nurses in the 1650s, though at a time when, on emotional as much as nutritional grounds, this practice among magnate gentry was beginning to go out of fashion. Some mothers, Anna Temple for instance, undoubtedly found the old tradition of separation from their babies irksome.[83] From weaning to around ten years old parents normally exercised direct oversight over their children, although a boy whose parents died young, like George Courthope, might be expected to stand on his own feet at an early age. He was 'put to a grammar school' at four. In households such as Pelham's and Dacre's book learning began at home. It was generally accepted that children should spend much of their time away from home in adolescence, so that they might be disciplined by outsiders, who were not bound by the intimate ties of parent and offspring.[84] A few Sussex boys, like William Culpepper who went to Eton, attended the celebrated country boarding schools. London schools were also popular. Several of the Pelham children boarded in the capital: Frank went at eight, equipped with 'bed and furniture, silver spoon and porringer'; Bess boarded there from nine to thirteen, with a maid to look after her and a private lutemaster to attend her; Judith began her formal schooling there at ten.[85] Sir William Wilson and John Everenden were among other gentry who chose London schools for their daughters.[86]

Throughout England rural opportunities for education expanded considerably in the period from 1560 to 1640.[87] There were schools in a dozen market towns and schoolmasters licensed to teach in at least seventy villages in Leicestershire during the first four decades of the seventeenth century. South Cambridgeshire was also well endowed.[88] Schools of one kind or another seem to have existed in at least twenty towns and villages of west Sussex before the civil war.[89] Some of them no doubt were simple and informal. Thus the Everenden boys gained their grounding in letters at the vicar of Sedlescombe's petty school, before proceeding to the grammar school at Southover, where John Evelyn was so 'extremely remisse' in his studies between 1630 and 1637'.[90] The gentry enthusiastically patronised the local grammar schools: Robert Morley sent his son Herbert to Southover, John Stapley boarded his son at Cuckfield, John Pelham of Arlington started his son at Eastbourne when he was eight years old.[91] John French 'earnestly desired' his executors to see his children 'sett and kept to schoole for their better instruccion in learning'; Herbert Board settled lands in trust for the education of his sons and daughters.[92]

The next stages of the educational process took boys into the more rarefied world of the universities and inns of court. For the heirs of magnate families attendance at one or both of these institutions was virtually essential.[93] But lesser gentry like John Everenden were also aspiring to higher education for their eldest sons. He and his wife spared no cost on their trip to Oxford for their son's matriculation in 1632.[94] Rich relations sometimes helped a promising boy whose parents were of modest means. Thus William Pelham of Arlington's academic career from matriculation to a college fellowship and the rectory of Crowhurst was dependent on the patronage of his godfather Sir Thomas.[95]

Eldest sons were treated from the cradle as destined for the responsbilities of estate management. They were put through a strenuous upbringing and hurried forth into the adult world. Sir John Pelham was determined that his heir should be as much in fashion as himself. In 1659, when Tom Pelham was only seven years old, he was shaved and fitted with his first periwig. Sir John himself had undergone the standard training for the eldest son of a county magnate. From the age of eight he was tutored by a dancing master at Halland; a year or so later he had a writing master as well; at eleven he started boarding in London.[96] He was at school until 1640, when, aged sixteen, he matriculated at Emmanuel College, Cambridge. Late in 1642, as the country slithered into war, Sir Thomas Pelham paid his son's final Cambridge bills, equipped him with a satin cape, boots, spurs and a sword and paid his passage from Rye to Dieppe. For two years John Pelham travelled in France and the United Provinces with his Cheshire cousin Thomas Wilbraham. By the summer of 1644 the two young men had run through £650 and their repeated requests for bills of exchange made Sir Thomas restive.[97] John was sharply questioned about his expenditure: 'I will take a more exact account', he promised. Pelham's and Wilbraham's expenditure may seem heavy, but in fact it was modest in comparison with that of some sons of peers.[98] Gentlemen abroad expected to be properly attended, so they were bound to run through a large amount of money. John Pelham complained to his father about his difficulties in finding satisfactory servants. Sir Robert Honeywood, Sir Thomas's brother-in-law who was living at The Hague, had recommended a Frenchman to him, 'but I did not find him fitt for me, being neither barber nor having ever served as a waiting man. I hope that I may live very well with one man, though Sir Robert Honiwood tells me that I must keep a lacky'.[99] Among other young Sussex gentlemen who travelled abroad were Francis, Lord Dacre and George Courthope. Courthope provided a vigorous account of his escapades in Constantinople and Malta, as well as France, Switzerland and Italy, when he wrote his memoirs forty years later.[100]

Much was expected of eldest sons. They, in their turn, found it easy to fall out with fathers who kept them on leading strings. Sir Thomas Pelham doubted his heir's aptitude for the world of fashionable London society, which he himself was intoxicated by in the 1640s. His sister defended John in a gently chiding letter of July 1644. She found him 'stayed and descreet':

> You doe him wrong to say he is no courtier for I assure you I think him a greate one, though I think both he and I seek better a country life then to be courtiers. . . . we comfort ourselves often in descovring of the happiness of thos which enjoy that life.[101]

But this rift between Pelham father and son seems never to have gone deep. The provisions of some men's wills indicate the more persistent tensions that could mark this particular relationship. Sir George Rivers stipulated that his grand-daughters' legacies were bequeathed on the condition that his 'unkind son' did nothing to make his will void.[102] Sir Thomas Bowyer directed that, if his son died leaving any other wife than his present one, she was to receive an annuity from his estate. His son was to receive forty pounds per annum on condition that he continued to live at the family mansion of Leythorne and did not attempt to 'alter or overthrow' the testament.[103] Sir Thomas had earlier set about disinheriting his son and had refused to see or maintain him, when the young man chose as his bride a gentlewoman with a portion of only four hundred pounds. He had hoped, it seems, to clear the debts on his estate by his son's marriage portion.[104]

Thomas Wilson ascribed the gentry's attachment to primogeniture to their 'fond desire to leave a great shew of the stock of their house, though the branches be withered'. There were many laments in the seventeenth century about the plight of younger sons.[105] Yet Sussex gentry often made strenuous efforts to achieve the best of both worlds by leaving both an impressive estate for their heir and sufficient maintenance for their younger progeny. Sir Thomas Springate, Henry Bridger and Anthony May, for instance, pared off a few of their accumulated manors for their younger sons.[106] Others gave them substantial enough portions to purchase land, so that they might live in the manner to which they were born. Nicholas Eversfield was explicit that this was his intention. His trustees were to spend £1,500 in buying 'land to make dwellings', on behalf of each of his five younger sons, and were to manage the estates themselves until the young men were twenty-four. He did not intend, he declared, that they should labour with their hands, but that they should gain some maintenance from their rents. The same kind of aspiration probably prompted Sir Thomas Sackville to give two sons £1,000 each, Walter Burrell to bequeath £2,000 to a younger son, and Laurence Ashburnham to provide £600 for his younger son, on top of an annuity. The gentry realised, on the other hand, that it was neither practicable nor sensible to encourage their younger boys to set their hearts on an entirely comfortable and leisured country life. To secure their future further, Nicholas Eversfield desired his trustees 'to bringe upp my younger sons to some trade in London or to some honest vocation in the countrie, which they are most inclined unto, to keepe them from idleness which is the route of all evill'. If his younger sons were 'not capable of being scholars', they were to be apprenticed, declared John French. Thomas Chown left his younger sons portions of £100 each and made arrangements for their binding 'to some honest profession or trade'.[107]

Initiative and determination brought some younger sons status and prosperity, whereas others through their own helplessness fell by the wayside. Henry Chown, the fourth son of Thomas Chown, made a successful career in the East India trade. When George Courthope visited Smyrna, Chown entertained his countryman 'very magnificently'. Then, in the 1640s, Chown invested his fortune in estates near Horsham and, with a sound marriage to the daughter of the local magnate Thomas Middleton, established himself as a county gentleman in his own right.[108] The misfortunes of Francis Wilson offer a striking contrast. He was a drifter who battened on an indulgent father. 'I must study to get money to buy bread for my belly or starve', he wrote to John Wilson in 1631. To avoid paying his tailor's bills and a threatened arrest, he left London for Ireland, in the train of the Earl of Strafford, obtained admittance to the household of the Earl of Kildare, but soon fell out with his patron. His father remained hopeful that he would be converted to a sober course of life, while the young man experienced a series of captures, escapes, hardships and fevers in the Dutch and Swedish armies. He wrote about Francis to his eldest son:

> If it please God to grant him a religious harte, I would have him live like a gentleman, for the good of himselfe and the reputation of his family. Send him his bible, if you have it, which is the best history, and some other history fitt for a religious soldier.

The careers of most younger sons were less spectacular. The Church and the law provided a number with maintenance. A few, like William Wilson, gentleman of the horse to the Earl of Suffolk, became servants of the highest rank in a noble household.[109] Trade, of one kind or another, was a favourite occupation. 'Deare sister', wrote Thomas Busbridge to Anna

Farnden, in a hasty note when he was still bewildered by his new surroundings, 'my master likes me and I like my master. I ware bound one Wensday last and I ware not ashamed at all'.[110]

Teenage girls who were not at boarding school normally spent substantial periods of the year away from home, living with friends or relations, where they learnt domestic duties and the art of managing a household. Sir Thomas Pelham's daughter, Nan, for example, spent much of the time between her fourteenth and eighteenth birthdays with her mother's family, the Wilbrahams, in Cheshire.[111] Two families connected by marriage could thus provide each other with reciprocal domestic training for their daughters. The Busbridges of Haremere in Etchingham and the Temples of Frankton in Warwickshire cooperated in this way: in 1633 Susan Temple stayed with her married sister Anna Busbridge, five years later her younger sister spent some months at Haremere and in 1648 Anna Busbridge's daughter was old enough to be put under the wing of the Temples at Frankton. The point of these visits was both practical and spiritual, as the second epigraph to this chapter indicates. Both sides were expected to benefit. Anna Busbridge constantly reiterated to her daughter the duty she owed to her uncle and aunt: 'I perseve thair kindness to you which I hope you will acknowledge by any sirvis you can doe.' 'Take heed', she wrote on another occasion, 'of mispending pretious time.' Anna Temple's advice to her daughter was to make the most of her sister's presence in the household: 'If her company may bee any way comfortable or usefull to you I shall gladly spare hir and bee thankefull to you for hir'.[112] These exchanges did not always work out so satisfactorily. 'I fell out with Kate Burton and swore I would not keep her and caused her to send to her father', wrote Lady Anne Dorset in her diary for August 1619. Sir Edward Burton could only prevail on Lady Anne to keep the girl a further six weeks.[113]

Firmly attached as the gentry were to separation of parents and children in adolescence, mothers and daughters sometimes found the experience distressing and difficult to accept. 'I did not thinke that you would now have wept for want of a letter', wrote Anna Busbridge to her homesick daughter in 1648, 'knowing how often they miscarry and how constantly you have bin right to by one or other.' With a pen 'soe bad it hath weryed me to right' and an inkhorn that blotted the paper when the servant overfilled it, Anna Busbridge kept up a stream of cosseting advice and spiritual consolation to her daughter in Warwickshire. The girl was instructed about making her new gown, shopping on the way home through London, the amount she should tip the servants and prayer and striving 'against needlesse feares'. Letters from John Temple and John Busbridge to their daughters were as warm and affectionate as those between the mothers and daughters. The intimacy and trust between the parents and children in these families is evident.[114]

The marriage portions which a gentleman offered his daughters were taken to be a mark of his standing in county society as well as of his esteem for his progeny. Most men looked for the contentment of a happy and respectable marriage for all their daughters, rather than bid for a grand match for the eldest girl. Sir John Morley's discrimination to the extent of giving one daughter £2,000 and another £1,400 was exceptional. The marriage market was highly competitive. By mid-century most families with pretensions in county society aimed at portions of at least £1,000. Some men were already setting their sights high in the 1630s: Sir Thomas Springate gave two daughters £2,000 apiece in 1639, Thomas Dyke left two of his girls £1,200 and a third £1,500 in 1632. By the 1650s portions of £2,000 and more were becoming increasingly common, especially for single daughters. Thomas May explained in his will of 1655 that it was only the need to compound which had frustrated his 'earnest desire' to raise at least a respectable £1,000 for his daughter.[115]

Services and fashion

Major gentry households employed a considerable permanent labour force; even lesser gentry, like John Everenden and John Stapley, expected to keep a couple of maids and two or three farm labourers. The Pelhams and Dacres each had establishments of about twenty-five servants. At Petworth in 1635 there were nearly 160 gentlemen and servants on the check roll.[116] Magnates and their families lived among a throng of people in intimate and long-established communities. They undertook responsibility for the health and livelihood of those who served them. The Pelhams and Dacres regularly called surgeons to attend to servants or paid local women to tend them in their sickness.[117] In an age when most people could afford neither medicines nor doctors' fees, this was one of the more important benefits that accrued from membership of a gentry household. Service in such a household could offer a lifetime's security. Whatever sense of personal loss was felt at the death of a master, the break in a household's continuity was often imperceptible. Only the change of hand and the long list of funeral expenses mark the death of Sir Thomas Pelham in the family account books. For the steward the routine of accounting was the same though a new master had taken charge. The inheritance procedure was long planned and smoothly accomplished.[118] Gentry whose sons were not of age often took deliberate measures to ensure that the household persisted after their death. Sir John Gage, for example, in 1633 directed that, after the customary period of three months hospitality for the whole family, some of the older servants should be employed by his executors to keep the mansion and estate at Firle in good order until his son was of age to inherit.[119]

Families who served a gentry establishment for many years became bound to it in a close relationship of trust and dependence. Sir John Gage left ten of his servants wages for life. Millington, Sir Thomas Pelham's personal servant, who had often accompanied him to London and elsewhere, received £50 on his marriage; Mascall, another man who had served the family faithfully, was bequeathed a legacy of £40 in Sir Thomas's will.[120] Francis, Lord Dacre left one servant £100, another £500; Sackville Turner bequeathed £30 to the daughter of one of his servants and his watch and £20 to another; Sir Thomas Bishop provided a trusted servant with a £10 annuity. Others, like John French, added a small legacy to the customary bequest of a few months wages.[121] Occasionally gentry expressed themselves in exceptional detail with regard to their servants. Thomas Jefferay, meticulous in this as in everything he did, enumerated the legacies that his clerk, bailiff, 'paneful servant', dairymaid, cook, brewer and old servant were to receive and requested his executors to 'distribute amongst them some of my old coats and worst sorte of apparell'. A servant who had begun to work the seats of two chairs in linsey-woolsey was given possession of them. When he made his will in 1649, Thomas May of Rawmere explained the particular sense of gratitude with which he gave legacies to three of his most trusted servants. They had

> in these late great troubles, when my house was plundered and my goods wasted, consumed, carried away, lost and embeazelled from me, showed their fidelity and care in providing for my children and preserving them with God's help safe from danger, in which their duty and love to me and them was and is such acceptable service which cannot be by me and mine forgotten.[122]

By providing much of their own food, their own hops, hemp, flax, timber and sometimes iron implements as well, Sussex gentry households achieved considerable self-sufficiency. Magnates also looked to their own estates for lime, sand and stone when they engaged in building.[123] At the same time the mansions and estates of the gentry provided much employment for all manner of craftsmen and of trade for local businessmen. Wheelwrights, blacksmiths, glaziers, coopers, sadlers, masons, shinglers and thatchers were often busy with work for the Pelhams and Dacres. Truggers and basketmakers from the High Weald, and pedlars and tinkers on the road, called regularly at Halland and Herstmonceux. Basic household commodities were readily available from the general dealers and apothecaries of Lewes, whose business with the gentry was the foundation of a secure livelihood. John Everenden's younger brother Simon used his portion of fifty pounds to set up as a mercer there. He concentrated on groceries, spices and tobacco: sugar, licorice, pepper, starch, prunes, mace, nutmegs, cloves and cinnamon were among the items on one of John Everenden's bills from his brother.[124]

With a combination of enterprising farming and gardening and flexible shopping arrangements, the gentry were able to enjoy a high standard of living in their provincial backwaters. Cabbages, asparagus, cauliflowers, french beans, onions, radishes and artichokes were all grown at Halland in the 1640s and 50s, and John Everenden experimented with turnips. Wine and sack, brought in by French traders, were usually available at Hastings market. Eastbourne was renowned for the supply of wheatears, pigeons and bittern. The Dacres exploited the coastal markets, the marshes and their own ponds to indulge their passion for fish and wildfowl. Sprats, oysters, sole, crab, mullet, teal, prawns, lobsters, carp, ducks, herrings, mackerel, flounders, cockles and salmon trout were among the delicacies of their table. The whole county community exhibited an insistent demand for seafish. Sophisticated furnishings were available from the workshops of some of the county's more high class craftsmen. Giles Moore, the rector of Horsted Keynes, bought blankets, cushions, carpets and a 'coverlett with birds and bucks' from a Chichester upholsterer, 'living over against the Crosse', who travelled the country with his goods on horseback.[125]

During the seventeenth century the provision of medical care improved as the retailing of drugs and the craft of surgery gradually became absorbed into the profession of medicine. The general practitioner became a familiar rural figure.[126] William White of Midhurst, for instance, called himself a surgeon, but his will and inventory indicate that he was much engaged in prescribing and supplying drugs. At his death in 1632 he owned books on both physick and surgery, mortars, stills and 'urinalls and other glasses', as well as an incision knife, spatula, stitching quill, bodkin, lancets and syringes.[127] Doctors of one kind or another were well distributed across the countryside. In Bramber rape in 1640, for example, there were licensed physicians living at Steyning, Thakeham and Horsham, where two surgeons and two practitioners in bloodletting also resided. More than forty doctors were licensed in late Elizabethan Norfolk.[128] The gentry of much of east Sussex were served for more than thirty years by Nehemiah Panton of Brightling, himself an aspiring gentleman who had married into the well established Cruttenden family.[129] Panton charged about a pound a visit when he was summoned to Halland and it was seldom that months passed without his attendance on one member of the family or another. A sickly brood, the Pelhams poured out money on medical attention.[130] Sir Thomas's accounts confirm the truth of his testamentary statement of 1652 that he had already 'had so many summons' to death.[131] After a variety of illnesses in his youth, treatment for his hearing in 1629, and trouble with one of his hands in 1634, friends and lawyers hurried to his bedside in 1638, when he was first thought to be near to death. From the age of about forty onwards, Pelham was plagued with gout; he also came to suffer much from lameness and sciatica. In time he despaired of Panton and turned first to a French mountebank and then to two leaders of the profession in London, Dr Wright and Dr Bates. They charged ten pounds for a visit to Halland. In the 1650s Sir Thomas's doctors' bills mounted dramatically. He spent fifty pounds on medical care and a further fifty-six on a visit to Bath in 1652. Pelham also became obsessed with regular bloodletting, imposing it on his wife, children and servants. By the time his last illness came in 1654 the procedures were well oiled. The usual squad of doctors hurried down from London, but this time their efforts were in vain.[132]

Herbal remedies supplemented the skills of the medical practitioners. The Pelhams had local women gather wormwood and sorrel; they bought scurvygrass, aquavitae, oil of almonds and aniseed locally. An 'especiall water and diett drink' was available at Halland made from poppy blossoms, cowslips and other herbs.[133] Lesser gentry normally relied on their own preparations and anything the local apothecary could supply. John Everenden sent for two shillings' worth of physic from his cousin Panton, rather than pay for a full diagnostic visit, when his daughter was sick in 1645. When John Wilmsherst's mother was taken 'exceding sicke' with pleurisy in 1614 he hurried home to Burwash from Kent and, seeing her condition, himself rode to Cranbrook for physick for her. Three days had elapsed without treatment and two days later she died. 'Sure if shee had had some good meanes in time she might have recovered', wrote Wilmsherst to Anne Jeake.[134] Walter Roberts kept a note in his ledger of useful medicines for coughs, weakness in the back, colic and the ague and the Jeake family kept a large book of similar recipes. Roberts's cures included a 'salve to take ded fleshe out of a sore', 'a soveraigne medicine for a greate ach', 'a diet drink to take at the spring and fall' and 'an excellent ointment for strain'.[135] It is hard to say how much gentry resorted to magical healers, but it is quite likely that the Sompting cunning man George Sowton, who provided charms for sick people of his neighbourhood, counted gentry as well as husbandmen among his clients. Certainly the Rye cunning woman Susan Snapper sought to cure the mayor there with 'planett-water'.[136]

London offered a wider range of urban amenities than anywhere else in England. By 1600 the capital was the centre of the nation's commercial and professional life and the focus of all social intercourse.[137] Wives, as we have already seen, often yearned to exchange the tedium of a rural existence for its fashionable society. The development of the coach, which by the last years of Elizabeth's reign was coming within the means of many country gentry, had made regular visits to the metropolis a much more comfortable proposition. Once Ashdown or the Horsham vale could be negotiated in a showy vehicle wives were keen to visit London.[138] Business brought gentry of all kinds to London. Barristers who combined a town and country practice, like Richard Amherst who had chambers in Serjeants Inn and a house in Lewes, were often on the road.[139] Cattle farmers like John Everenden and John Roberts were attracted by the London food market. Opportunities for shopping were an additional draw. Roberts had his tailor send his suits down by the carrier in 1636, when they were tacked and pinned, for a fitting before they were made up.[140] Giles Moore regularly bought furniture, brass, clothes and books when he was in London each year.[141]

Sir Thomas Pelham's gradual intoxication with the metropolis between 1630 and 1650 provides a case study of a process that affected many families, but few so dramatically. In his youth Sir Thomas was content with country ways and dependent on the capital only for his best hats, shoes and clothes, for high quality silks, linens and woollens, for the more recherché wines and for the silver that such a magnate was expected to display on his table. His visits to London were limited to a few weeks in each law term. In 1635 and 1636 his stays became longer, the following year he bought a house in Clerkenwell, in 1640 he lodged with his third bride in Covent Garden. With the opening of the Long Parliament that autumn, Pelham became committed to long and regular spells in the capital. In December 1644 he took a house in the Strand, close to his father-in-law Sir Henry Vane's house at Charing Cross, where he and his family had lodged several times that year. For the first time the Pelhams spent Christmas in London and they subsequently adopted the regular practice of a long visit from December to about May. Living expenses edged upwards. Stabling alone cost forty-nine pounds during the 1644–45 visit and household expenses came to £276. The following year household expenses were £324, stabling cost seventy-nine pounds. During an eleven-week stay at Charing Cross in the spring of 1648 the family managed to get through £449, despite the fact that the Sussex carrier was bringing up loads of country produce week by week. The Pelhams gorged themselves and lavished on their guests the choicest goods of the markets: strawberries and cherries from Cheapside, oranges and lemons, caraway comfits and claret and Rhenish wine. They spent the decade buying their way into fashionable London society.

The influence of Margaret Vane probably accounts for the final conversion of the Pelhams to the metropolitan way of life. But Sir Thomas's increasing expenditure during the 1630s on silver, his bonanza of re-furnishing at Halland in 1638, his sudden interest the same year in having his portrait painted, his enormous expenditure in 1640 on his own clothes and his servants' liveries, all proclaimed his fascination with the world of fashion even before his marriage into the Vane family. The man who visited his silkman to buy wrought satin against his marriage in May 1640, and equipped himself with new points, gloves, spurs and a sword, had finally lifted his eyes from hawking on the Downs at Bishopstone and his furnaces and forges in the Weald. Pelham quickly learnt the ways to enhance his prestige in the world beyond his estates. Ostentation came easily to him, despite his Puritan turn of mind. During the next few years Pelham sat for several portraits; he gave portraits of himself to his brother-in-law Sir Robert Honeywood, his mother-in-law Lady Vane and his sister Judith, wife of the Earl of Dover; he had portraits of his wife, daughters, eldest son and Carey nieces painted; he bought pictures of great men with whom he or his county had personal connections such as the Earl of Dorset. He spent seventy pounds on new furnishings for his coach to take his new bride from Fairlawn home to Halland. The bills for the marriage bed and for new hangings and furnishings in the drawing room, parlour and long gallery at Halland in 1640 and 1641 were more than £220. In view of this outburst of conspicuous consumption, it is not surprising that Pelham's total expenditure, according to his own reckoning, increased from an average of £2,028 over the six years 1634–35 to 1639–40 to £4,152 in 1640–41. Thereafter it never fell below £2,500 a year and in 1645–46 was more than £3,500. During the years 1640 to 1654 Sir Thomas and Lady Margaret Pelham missed no opportunity to keep pace with fashion: clothes, coaches, hangings, upholstery, beds and silver were all discarded at regular intervals. From 1647 onwards the family acquired the habit of importing into the countryside the groceries they had grown used to in London. About fifty pounds worth of goods was transported by the carrier, or by sea to Pevensey, twice a year.

Sir John Pelham in the end proved as fashion-conscious as his father. He bought a new coach in 1655 and another in 1658. Soon after becoming mistress of the house, his wife Lucy chose new serge and damask for the drawing room furnishings and perpetuana for new curtains, musk-coloured in the hall chamber, grey in the parlour and green in the best chamber. Sir John lavished jewellery on his wife with an extravagance that put even his father's gifts to Margaret Vane in the shade: a necklace and two rings that he bought from the Countess of Sunderland cost £920, a ring and locket the same year £120 and a diamond bracelet a few years later £180. No expense was spared at Halland in the late 1650s. Only silver warming-pans and cotton-lined close stools reached the standards of comfort the family expected. Few Sussex families had the wealth to indulge themselves to this extent. Most lacked anyway the ambition and the pretensions to carry off the role in London society that delighted Sir Thomas Pelham and his son.[142]

Kinship and friendship

Gentlemen in Sussex revealed the same tendency as the gentry of Dorset, Leicestershire, Suffolk and Yorkshire to marry within their own shire. This tradition seems to have been most striking in counties that were geographically self-contained, such as Lancashire and Kent.[143] Sussex, with its long sea coast and marshland on the eastern border, had something of the same insularity. The testimony of Lucy Hutchinson, who came of the Apsley family, a clan which had spread its tentacles across the county in the sixteenth century, is supported by statistical analysis. 'It hath been such a continued custom for my ancestors to take wives at home', she wrote in her *Memoirs of the Life of Colonel Hutchinson*, 'that there was scarce a family of any note in Sussex to which they were

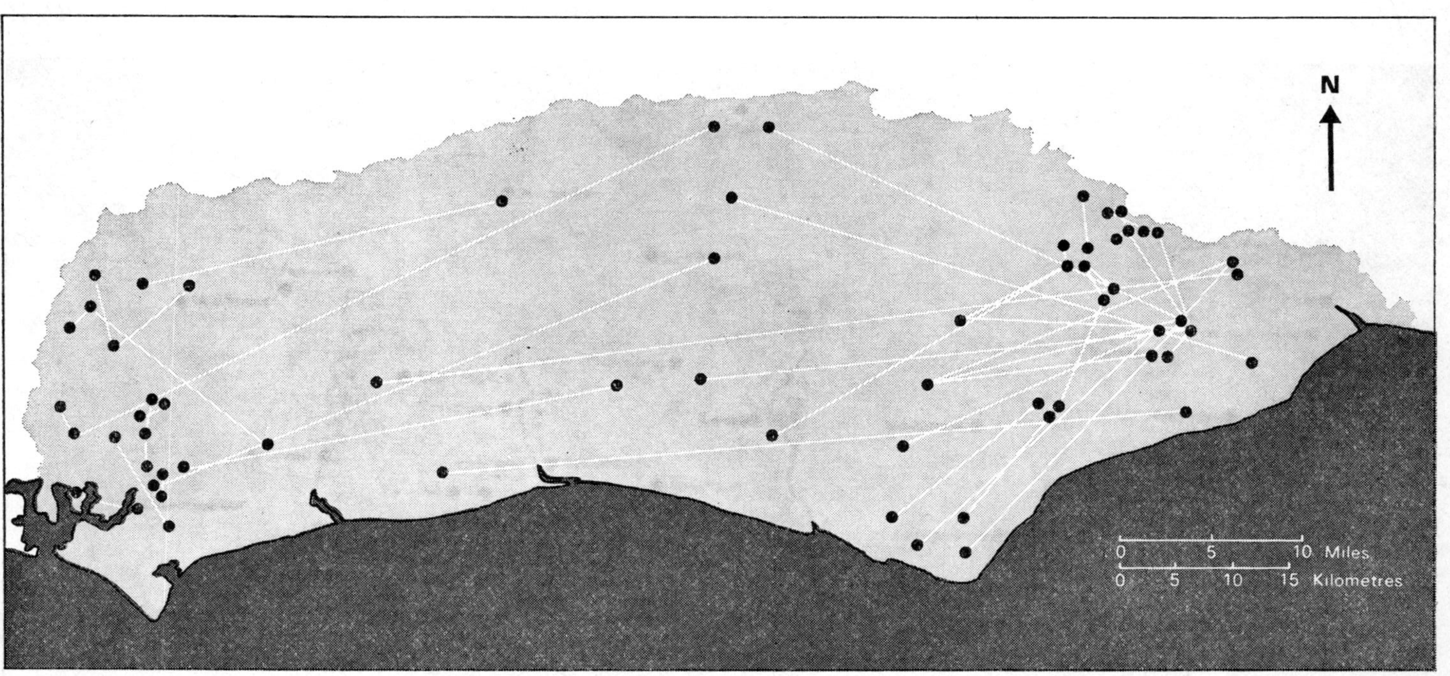

5 Marriages within the county of gentry of the Chichester and Hastings rapes, 1600–1660

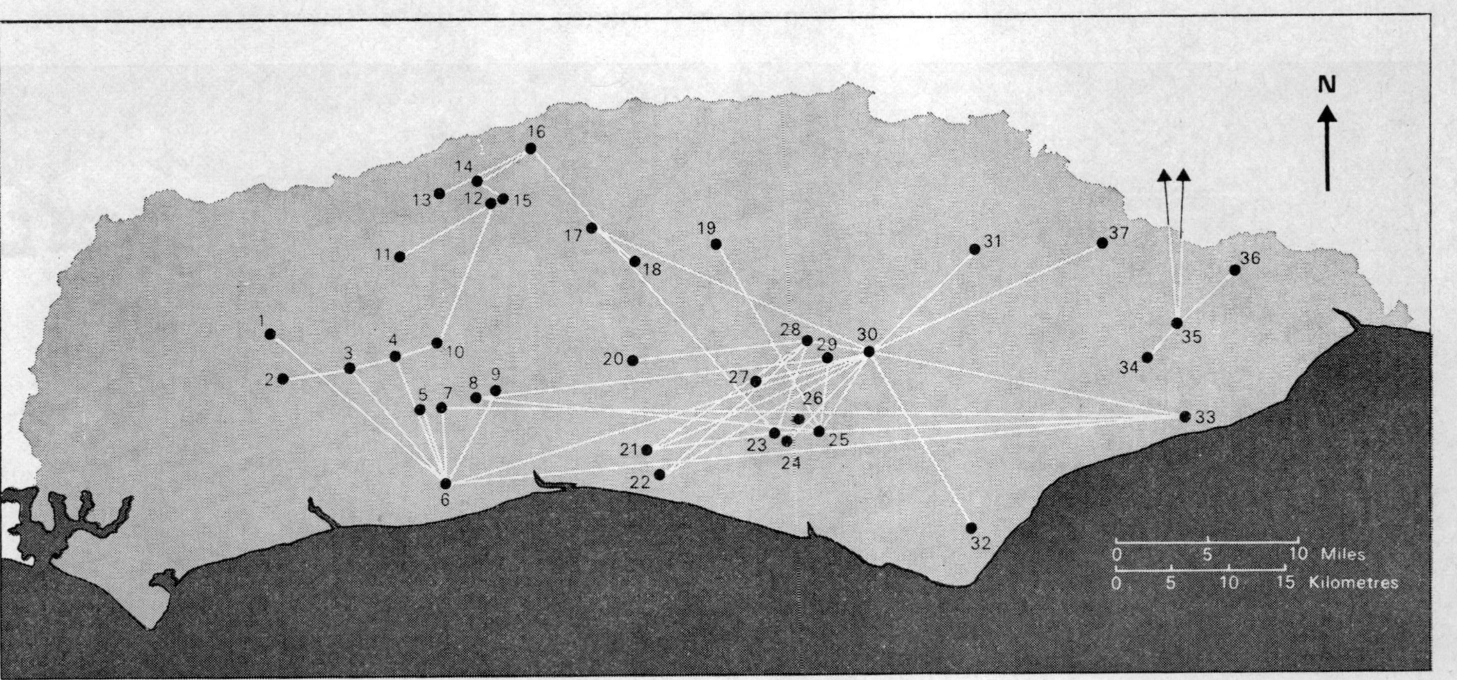

6 The friendships of some Sussex gentry, 1625-1660

1 Sir William Goring of Burton, *c* 1600–*c* 1670 (N)
2 William Pellatt of Bignor, 1594–1651 (N)
3 William Mill of Greatham, *c* 1580–1629
4 Nicholas Monck of Storrington, *c* 1595–1657 (N)
John Monck of Storrington, *c* 1630–1680
5 Edward Goring of Sullington, *c* 1600–*c* 1660 (N)
6 John Alford of Durrington, *c* 1590–1649 (N)
7 Henry Goring of Washington, *c* 1590–*c* 1665 (N)
8 John Fagge of Wiston, *c* 1620–1701 (P)
9 Sir John Leedes of Steyning, *c* 1595–1656 (N)
10 Henry Bridger of Warminghurst, 1586–1657 (N)
Richard Bridger of Warminghurst, *c* 1615–1698 (R)
11 Giles Garton of Billingshurst, 1588–1646 (N)
12 Hall Ravenscroft of Horsham, 1600–*c* 1673 (P)
13 George Churcher of Slinfold, *c* 1595–1650 (P)
14 Richard Yeates of Warnham, *c* 1600–1657 (N)
15 Thomas Sheppard of Horsham, 1626–73
16 Edward Michell of Horsham, 1568–1637
Edward Michell of Horsham, 1605–66 (P)
17 Sir Walter Covert of Slaugham, 1543–1631
18 Walter Burrell of Cuckfield, 1600–71 (N)
19 Herbert Board of Lindfield, 1602–48 (P)

20 George, Lord Goring, Earl of Norwich of Hurstpierpoint, 1585–1663 (R)
21 Anthony Stapley of Patcham, 1590–1655 (P)
22 Thomas Shirley of Preston, *c* 1580–1637
23 William Newton of Southover, 1564–1648 (P)
24 Henry Shelley of Southover, 1599–1654 (P)
25 Robert Morley of Glynde, 1577–1632
Herbert Morley of Glynde, 1616–67 (P)
William Morley of Glynde, 1621–79 (P)
26 Herbert Hay of Glyndebourne, 1591–1652 (P)
27 James Rivers of Hamsey, 1603–41
28 Sir John Shurley of Isfield, 1569–1631
29 William Hay of Little Horsted, 1594–1664 (P)
30 Sir Thomas Pelham of Laughton, 1597–1654 (P)
31 John Baker of Mayfield, 1589–1668 (P)
32 Sir Thomas Parker of Willingdon, 1596–1663 (P)
33 Sir Nicholas Eversfield of Hollington, *c* 1581–1629
Sir Thomas Eversfield of Hollington, 1614–49 (N)
34 Robert Foster of Battle, 1586–1663 (R)
35 Sir Thomas Sackville of Sedlescombe, *c* 1594–1639
36 William White of Northiam, *c* 1593–*c* 1660 (N)
John White of Northiam, 1599–1655 (R)
37 John Busbridge of Etchingham, 1611–*c* 1667 (P)

(R) Royalist
(P) Parliamentarian
(N) Neutral

not by intermarriages nearly related'.[144] The gentry community had become linked in a vast and intricate network of cousinage. Analysis of 137 gentry marriages between 1600 and 1660 shows that the pattern was at its most dense in Bramber, Lewes and Pevensey rapes. That was the area in which business contacts, administrative duties and the social round pulled men most strongly towards Lewes. The county town of east Sussex was bound to become a marriage mart. One match after another, generation by generation, locked the leading families in close bonds of kinship. The gentry of Arundel and Hastings rapes often sought through their marriages to integrate themselves with the society of the middle ground of the shire. The gentry of Chichester rape, on the other hand, on the whole kept themselves apart. Some looked over the Hampshire border, others found spouses locally. The cathedral city was too isolated to become a marriage market to anything like the same extent as Lewes.

The social isolation of the gentry of Chichester rape, their lack of the crucial kinship connections on which county society hinged, had considerable political significance when the gentry faced the crisis of the civil war. Kinship was the dominant principle of Sussex society. It was the basis of the ceaseless round of hospitality, of hunting and hawking, of christenings, marriages and funerals, of administrative business and above all of county politics; it encouraged the introversion and strengthened the cohesiveness of the gentry community; to some extent at least it guided and determined men's loyalties. In the eastern rapes the gentry were long acquainted and well integrated; the patterns of their social intercourse, which stretched to the Arun but hardly beyond it, confirm the remoteness of the gentry of the far west.

In a community where many of the men who moved on the same social plane were related by a marriage in one previous generation or another, stress on cousinage in correspondence and account keeping became a mere mark of courtesy. The tight circles of intimate friendship, which were more significant for the dynamics of county affairs, ran within the wider circles of blood. When men disposed of their estates and possessions, they looked to those in whom they had come to place most trust and confidence to act as overseers, executors and trustees. They also recorded their affection for their closest friends by testamentary gifts. Wills are the main source for the pattern of intimate friendships which has been adduced for the map on page 46.

The custom of giving rings in remembrance was a particular mark of love and a deliberate attempt to preserve the memory of friendships which had brought joy and fulfilment. John Alford specified that the nine 'loving and dear' friends, who he desired should wear rings in his memory, should have them inscribed '*morto il vive* J.A.'. Sir John Shurley requested his overseers to provide five 'very loving kinsmen and friends', three of whom were to be trustees of his estates, with gold rings with a death's head.

Anthony Stapley, who was one of the five, was also to receive 'my guilt rapier the blade whereof was his father's'.[145] Sir Thomas Pelham's capacity for deep personal attachments, already discussed with regard to his marriages, is confirmed by the pre-eminent place he occupied in the pattern of close friendships revealed by gentry wills. Both Alford and Shurley gave him rings; Sir Walter Covert bequeathed him forty pounds to buy 'a peece of plate in token of remembrance of the love I had borne him'; Sir Thomas Eversfield left him twenty pounds for a ring.[146] Many references in his accounts highlight other friendships that were important to Sir Thomas. Anthony Stapley and James Rivers were his constant companions in the 1630s. He was often at Stapley's home at Patcham; in 1636 he spent Christmas with the Rivers family at Hamsey; he gave silver saltcellars to both these friend's wives. He was frequently also at Ratton and Preston, the homes of Sir Thomas Parker and Thomas Shirley; Henry Shelley was another neighbour in whom he put special trust.[147]

A few of Sir Thomas Pelham's colleagues in county administration were close confidants. They were his equals, whereas many members of his social circle were men recognisably superior or inferior to him within the hierarchy of the gentry class. Sir Thomas sought the patronage of the Earl of Northumberland, who made available to him the breeding facilities of his stud at Petworth and whose friendship he particularly valued and cultivated. 'I must lett you know that the respect and kindnesse I found amongst you at my last being in that country ingages me to the uttermost of my power to serve you', wrote Northumberland to Pelham and his fellow-deputy-lieutenants in 1645.[148] Aspiring lesser gentry of Pevensey rape, in their turn, assiduously sought Pelham's patronage and company. Nicholas Gildredge clung to the fortune which brought him the favour of one of the greatest county magnates. He wrote Pelham an obsequious letter of congratulation on his second marriage in 1637. Although he counted himself 'altogether unworthy of soe hye a title' as one of Sir Thomas's friends, 'yet since by you soe highly favoured as to bee made acquainted', he added his voice to the chorus of 'reell expressions of your friends' affections . . . at this time of just rejoycing': 'Be pleas'd not to disdaine this empty appearance of his full joy at this your happy day and choyce, whose obligements to you are therefore more then others, because his merits lesse then any's.' The distinction between a magnate like Pelham and a parish squire like Gildredge counted for much in the intimate downland and wealden society. Francis, Lord Dacre, similarly, was a prince in his own little country of the Pevensey marshland and its interior. Men like Thomas Alchorne of Catsfield, John Dunke of Whatlington and John Thatcher of Westham enjoyed the hospitality of his table and attached themselves to him with their gifts.[149] Yet in a sense, despite his noble status, Dacre was never a county magnate. The difference between his standing in the shire and Pelham's is indicated by the maps showing the geographical range of their respective social contacts.

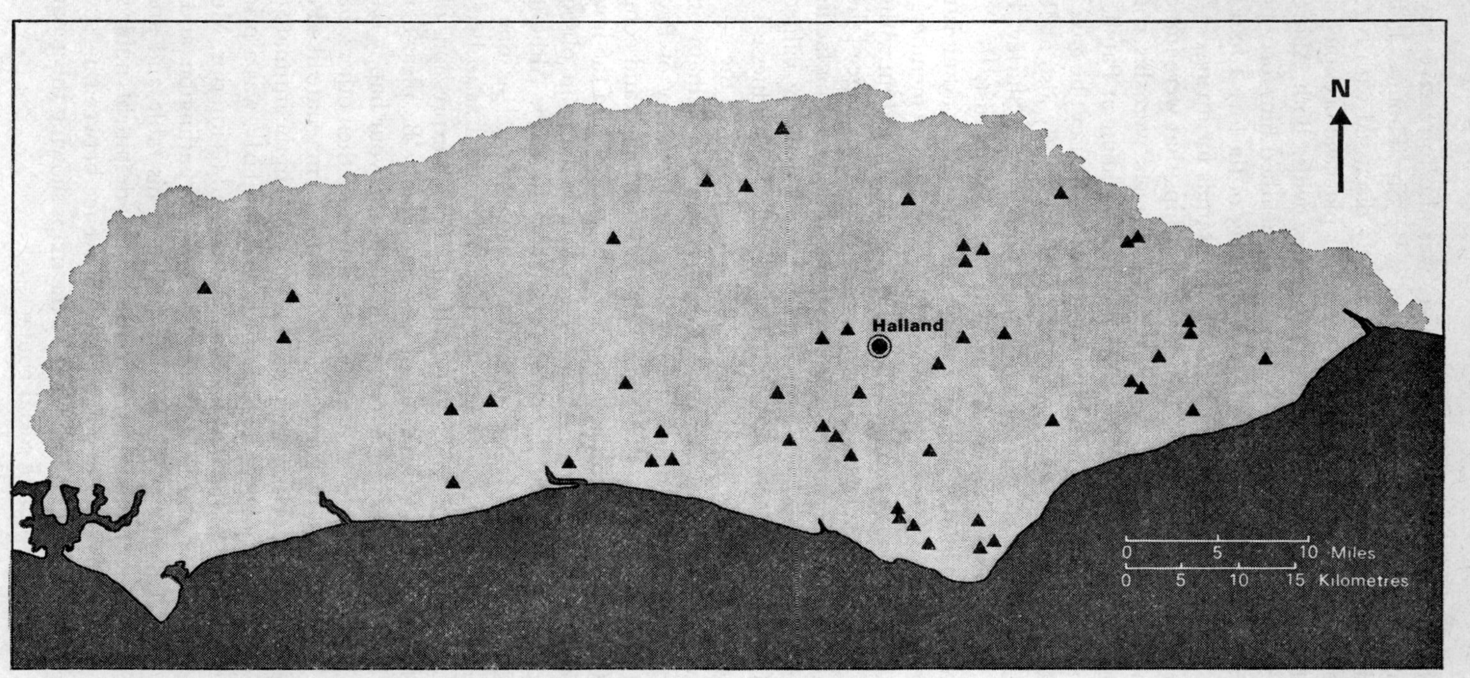

7 The social circle and the Pelham family, 1626–1660

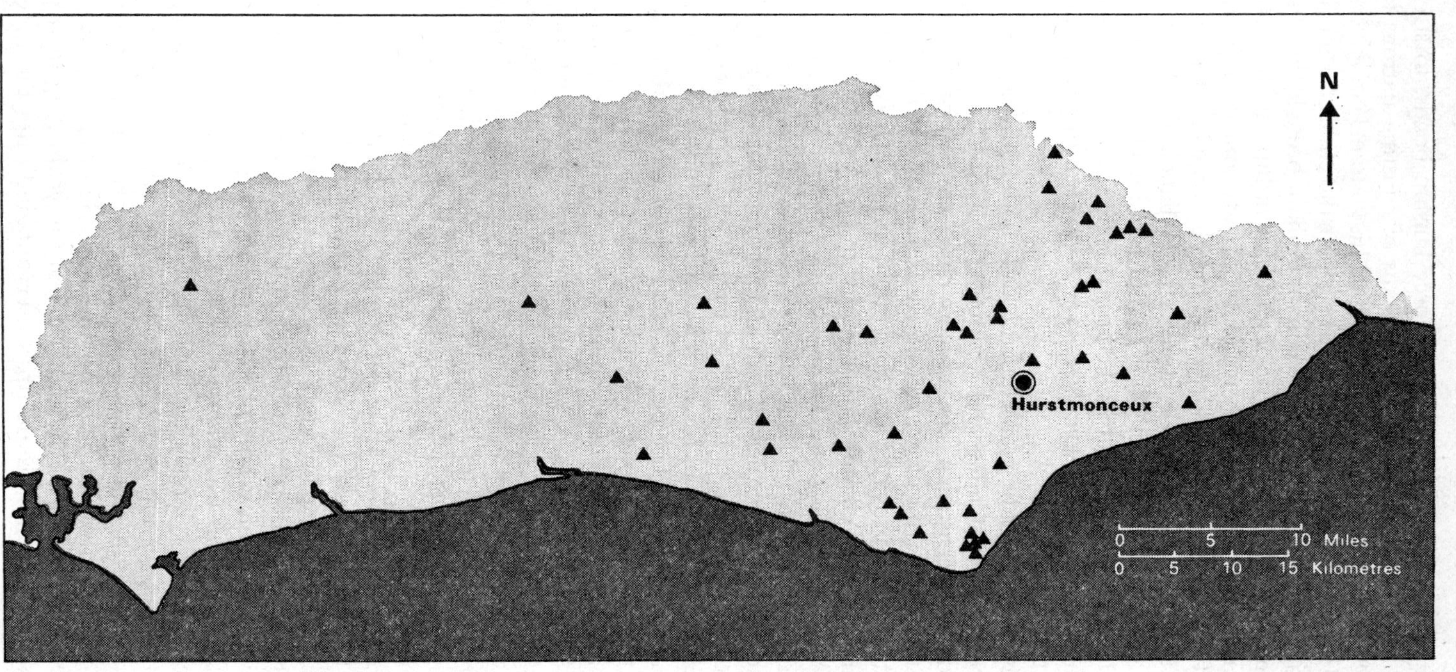

8 The social circle of Francis, Lord Dacre, 1643-1649

Godparenthood was used to reinforce kinship bonds, to strengthen the links between families and as a means of enlisting patrons in local society.[150] When Sir Thomas Pelham tipped his godson Tom Rivers on his visits to Hamsey, he was expressing his care for the child of a much loved friend; his concern for his godson William Pelham brought two branches of the family closer together; the tie of spiritual kinship with the Selwyns of Friston enhanced the link with a family already joined in cousinhood. Others of Sir Thomas's godchildren had merely come into his social orbit through the proximity of their families to Halland. Sir Walter Covert had so many godchildren of this kind that he refrained from listing them in his will, declaring instead that while the gentlemen's children were to have twenty shillings each to buy rings, the rest were each to receive a piece of gold worth ten shillings.[151]

Christenings, weddings and funerals were both family and neighbourhood events. At christenings and weddings the tradition of hospitality on the grand scale persisted. When a Dacre child was baptised in 1645, 450 prawns and 400 herrings were consumed at the feast.[152] The last tributes to a great magnate provided another kind of spectacular county occasion. When Sir Thomas Pelham's father died, Sir John Shurley, Sir Edward Burton, Anthony Stapley and Thomas Shirley were among the numerous gentry from all over east Sussex who attended. Sir Thomas spent eighty-one pounds on blacks for the children and servants when his first wife died and £150 on the funeral of his second wife. On the latter occasion, black baize was hired to deck out the church and Lady Judith's escutcheon was carried on a velvet pole. The poor of Laughton, East Hoathly and Lewes received the customary doles. When Sir Thomas himself died in 1654 he was embalmed while elaborate funeral preparations were made. Vast quantities of cloth, ribbon, serge and baize were purchased, there were black hatbands and livery stockings for servants and tenants, even the coach and horses were clothed in black. The final bill for blacks was £385. Sir Thomas had some sympathy with the Puritan reaction against excessive funeral opulence, yet his pride prevented him from forgoing this final act of honour and deference from the community. He sought the best of both worlds, directing that his burial should 'be without pomp and feast or heralds, having observed the abuse of them at such times, but to be accompanied with some friends, kinsmen and servants in mourning'. The mourning was certainly performed in a handsome manner, yet a minuscule bill for claret, the only hint of a wake, suggests that the spirit of Sir Thomas's instructions was observed.[153]

Whereas gentry largely confined their cross-country visiting to the summer months, servants were expected to travel the lanes at all seasons, fetching and carrying the constant exchange of presents and correspondence which the gentry community maintained. Some forty nearby gentry sent gifts to the Dacres at Herstmonceux in the years 1643 to 1649. The steward's large expenditure on tips to servants indicates the scale of the

Christmas bounty at Halland. Giles Moore received pigs, hops, capons, a fat goose and mead at Christmas 1656. His patron's son sent a pheasant. Wheatears were the favourite present of downland families like the Gildredges and Selwyns.[154] Ladies exchanged flowers in the summertime; wealden farmers sent each other sides of venison.[155] The courtesies of Sussex society were deeply rooted and they were reinforced by a tradition of mutual economic dependence. Sir Thomas Parker supplied his brother-in-law at Herstmonceux with malt and wheat.[156] Two of Sir Thomas Pelham's friends and colleagues on the Bench, Peter Farnden and John Baker, rented ironworks from him, and bought wood and ore in large quantities from his estates. Several other friends regularly bought loads of charcoal from Pelham for their households. He relied on Nicholas Gildredge for fish and birds; downland gentry such as Francis Selwyn, Anthony Stapley and Thomas Shirley supplied him with ewes and wethers. Much private dealing in colts and geldings went on between gentry friends and cousins. When men needed money they almost invariably turned first to relatives and close friends. When they were in London they did business for each other and employed each other to order the luxuries such as claret that provincial markets often lacked.[157]

The custom of marriage at home meant that the gentry's social contacts were often limited to within their own shire. Sir Thomas Pelham was certainly exceptional in the geographical range of his friendships, which were based on a longstanding connection with the Lincolnshire branch of his family, and his own marriages, together with those of his sister and his daughter Judith, into families outside Sussex. In the 1620s and 30s Pelham was regularly at Hunsdon visiting his sister's family, the Careys, and at the home of the Wilbrahams in Cheshire; he was also an occasional guest at Scadbury, the Kentish home of his mother's family the Walsinghams. Later he made the most of the Vane connection, frequently visiting Fairlawn, where he grew affectionate towards his wife's younger brothers and sisters.[158] Judith's marriage to the Grantham magnate Sir John Monson in 1647 provided him with a useful stopping point on his journeys to visit his north Lincolnshire cousins at Brocklesby. This was the home of two of his most intimate confidants, the lawyers Henry and Roger Pelham. In 1652 Pelham began negotiations for the marriage of another daughter to the prominent Northamptonshire gentleman Sir Justinian Isham. After several meetings with the girl in London, Isham expressed his willingness to 'wait on you at Haland about a month hence where I hope to make a further progress', but this time something went awry and Sir Justinian was shortly looking elsewhere.[159] Sir Thomas delighted in returning hospitality by entertaining his numerous relations at Halland. 'To complement with you for the noble entertainement I had would make mee sad and the loss of yours and the rest of the good companie has don that already', wrote his young cousin Walsingham after a visit there in 1644.[160]

Litigation and feuds

Country gentry were addicted to quarrelling and feuds. As their habits of open violence declined in the Tudor period they became increasingly litigious. Aggression against neighbours came more and more to take the form of pursuit through endless suits. The tedious processes of law consumed much time, energy and money, but they always held out the prospect of a final triumph against an adversary, which would be decked with all the trappings of justice.[161] Sir Thomas Pelham was one of those for whom litigation was a major pastime. Payments for fees of counsels and clerks, engrossment of bills and the opinions of distinguished lawyers occur frequently in his account books. In the 1620s and 30s he regularly spent more than £100 a year on legal expenses and occasionally, in the Michaelmas term of 1626 for instance and in the following Easter term, he ran through more than fifty pounds in a single law term. Papers relating to his interminable suits against his recusant neighbour John Thatcher of Westham take up more than forty pages of one of his memoranda books.[162] In these circumstances the legal profession flourished and there were always plenty of men willing to offer gentry their services.[163] Pelham relied heavily on his Lincolnshire cousins as well as seeking the professional advice of barrister colleagues like Robert Foster and Anthony Fowle. Many gentry had relatives in the profession to whom they turned. John Busbridge, for instance, employed his cousin Richard Tomlyns.[164]

It had become rare by the reign of Charles I for gentry openly to attack each other, but direct violence still occasionally occurred. The feud between the Chichester gentry Sir John Morley and Edward Higgins led to a brawl in 1638 in the cathedral cloisters. Morley used his riding stick to keep Higgins, the stronger man, at bay. He subsequently had to seek absolution and sue the King for pardon, when he was threatened with prosecution under a statute of Edward VI's reign against aggressive behaviour in a church or churchyard.[165] Two other incidents concerning Sussex gentry were more sensational. In 1627, the rash young Sir Edward Bishop killed the playwright Henry Shirley, by running him through with his sword in the course of a quarrel. The Shirleys were a distinguished Sussex family with whom the Bishops were on close terms. Sir Edward's father, Sir Thomas Bishop, indeed had given Henry Shirley an annuity of forty pounds. Sir Edward was convicted for the murder but was pardoned in 1628. For several years thereafter he went in fear of his life, since Thomas Shirley was known to be resolved to avenge his brother's murder.[166]

The origins of the feud between the Pelhams and their near neighbours the Lunsfords of East Hoathly are obscure, but a wrangle over some abuse by a Pelham servant about Thomas Lunsford the elder seems to have had something to do with it.[167] The jealousy felt by a somewhat insecure parochial family for the magnate whose parkland bordered their estate was probably at the root of an enmity that escalated when Herbert

Lunsford had one of his servants shoot and kill a hound of Pelham's, which ran into the Lunsford's territory one day in June 1632 when Sir Thomas was hunting near the border of his land.[168] Infuriated at the way Pelham had the law on them, the Lunsfords planned an attempt to kill him the following August. It was a foolish escapade and unlikely to succeed. But the manner of the attack, a dastardly interruption of a quiet family expedition to church, shocked the whole gentry community. Pelham was sitting, on the morning in question, with his intimate friend Anthony Stapley; their wives, Stapley's daughter, James Rivers and Sir Edward Burton were also in the coach. Thomas Lunsford the younger and his man leapt from a coppice, brandishing swords and pistols, and Lunsford discharged his pistol towards the coach. No one was seriously hurt.[169] But Lunsford was at once outlawed by Sussex society and the incident reverberated for years. In 1635, when he still languished in Newgate sick of a putrid fever, Lunsford spoke in one of his numerous petitions of his 'weakness of estate and want of friends' in his own county. Eventually, in 1637, Pelham's suit in Star Chamber came to trial. He obtained £3,000 damages and Lunsford and his servant were each fined £5,000.[170] When, in 1641, royal favour brought Lunsford the Lieutenantship of the Tower, Pelham and his friends ensured that the murder attempt was not forgotten. The City petitioners spoke of him as 'a man of decayed and desperate fortune, most notorious for outrages'; the Commons discussed his removal from office as 'a man wee cannot confide in'.[171]

Stuart gentry might think twice about simply contriving the murder of a witness to a poaching expedition, as Lord Dacre had done when his men were caught in the Pelhams' ground in 1541.[172] The use of servants as bully boys, though, was still accepted practice. Even allowing for the dramatisation normally injected into Star Chamber bills, there was undoubtedly a good deal of assault on the agents of feuding gentry in the early years of the seventeenth century. Henry Goring of Highden was accused of procuring an attack on a man carrying a letter which proved a debt of his; William Comber charged some men who destroyed his mill at Shermanbury with shooting at his servants; Sir John Caryll alleged assaults on his servants in Horsham market and at Denne, the home of Sir Thomas Eversfield, where his man was set upon by a dog. A gentleman servant of the Pelhams' was said to have been attacked at a Lewes inn over a quarrel with the Jefferay family; both Sir Edward Bellingham and Sir John Shurley, in their reciprocal suits about Cuckfield manor, declared that violence had been used against their servants.[173]

Gradually more sophisticated weapons of rivalry and intrigue were beginning to replace some of the violence traditionally inherent in gentry contention.[174] The subtle poison of gossip and slander became a popular means of expressing aggression against local enemies. In the village of Hurstpierpoint, Thomas Whatman, a JP and barrister of some standing, fell out with the minister Christopher Swale over some money owing to

Swale's orphaned niece. The quarrel was a conflict of personalities, compounded by a battle for status in the parish. The wives engaged in a public brawl about precedence in church. Swale employed his command of the pulpit to deliver reproofs for sin, which Whatman maintained were obviously levelled at him. In return, Swale alleged that Whatman scandalised and traduced his sermons, scoffed at him during services and spread slanderous accusations about him in writing. Swale maintained that he was jeered at as 'the talke of men, the laughter of youth and the songe of children'.[175] Another minister who provoked anger and malice among his gentry neighbours was Thomas Large of Hollington. Suspicions that he was popishly affected probably underlay the dislike felt by Nicholas Eversfield and Richard Alfrey. Eversfield, alleged Large, refused to pay his tithes and organised a general boycott among his tenants, offering to maintain them in suits at law. He persistently defamed the minister and threatened to 'make him worth a groat and undo him'. Alfrey, it was alleged, was a railer of false report with a talent for rabble rousing. He gathered about forty witnesses to testify slanderous matter against Large, in support of an indictment of him as a common barrator which he hoped to have presented at sessions.[176]

Expertise in the processes of the law enabled the gentry to dispose ruthlessly of any from outside their own class who challenged them or stood in their way. Sir Henry Compton, Sir Peter Bettsworth, George Gunter and Thomas Gray were among those who mobilised their superior resources in Star Chamber suits against men who had destroyed their enclosures. Bettsworth's tenants levelled and filled by night as he hedged and ditched by day. But at law the cards were stacked in favour of the landlords and even on the ground it was often in fact unwise to challenge them. Inhabitants of Fletching who threw down fences erected by Sir Henry Compton in 1624 were set upon by his servants and their dogs. One of them was shot in the chest and seriously wounded.[177] Any who slandered the gentry were also firmly dealt with. 'You knowe how irksome it is for a gentleman to be abused by a clowne', wrote Richard Amherst to Robert Foster, in support of his friend John Wilson's case against a slanderer in his parish. As a newcomer to Sussex from the north, Wilson was sensitive about his standing. 'As for this Wilson', the abusive neighbour had declared with a stream of coarse language, 'I am as good as he; nobody knows where he came from'. The man was convicted in the Court of Chivalry and made to make public submission of his calumny in the church at Fletching.[178] Gentry invariably stood by their own kind in such cases. In 1605, for instance, gentry commissioners appointed by the Privy Council cleared Sir Edward Caryll of the slanderous accusations of some countrymen: the slanderers were imprisoned for refusing to stand in Chichester, Arundel, Horsham and Steyning market places with papers in their hats declaring their perjury.[179]

The temptation for gentry who sat on the county Bench to bend their judicial authority in accordance with their personal enmities was considerable. Provincial government had been much disfigured by the abuses of bastard feudalism throughout the sixteenth century.[180] Cases of unscrupulous lobbying of colleagues against a local enemy still occurred in James I's reign. Sir Benjamin Pellatt, for example, procured the hands of two outstanding gentry, Sir Walter Covert and Sir Thomas Eversfield, in binding the curate of Bolney, Simon Wilkinson, to assizes. This was merely one of his expedients in a campaign against Wilkinson, which included intimidation, bribery and setting him in the stocks on his own authority.[181] Membership of the Commission of the Peace, at the very least, meant that a circle of leading gentry were disposed in a gentleman's favour when he ran foul of a neighbour. After the hunting incident with the Lunsfords in 1632, Sir Thomas Pelham ensured that two of his close colleagues were given the task of investigation and reporting to the Privy Council. There are signs, though, that JPs were showing increasing sensitivity over potential abuse of the law. Nicholas Eversfield was dissuaded from proceeding with the barratry indictment against Thomas Large by Thomas Aynscombe, one of the justices, since, with many on the Bench 'nearly allyed' to him 'or his very friend', Aynscombe thought the indictment might be misconstrued.[182] Standards of magisterial behaviour were gradually becoming established which excluded the pursuit of private malice.

The gentry community of seventeenth-century Sussex clung to its inner social life. Homes, hunting and local visiting preoccupied men, even in the midst of the Great Rebellion. Even then the Temple-Busbridge correspondence was primarily taken up with domestic trivia and family affairs, with the exchange of apricots, puddings or hops by the carriers, with the harvest, the weather, the doings of children and friends. Yet custom demanded that county gentry like John Busbridge and Sir Thomas Pelham should play a public role. In a time of peace and harmony, such men were the unchallenged rulers of the countryside. In a time of political and religious conflict and crisis such as occurred between 1640 and 1660, men from the whole spectrum of gentry society became engaged in argument and county politics. The collapse of unity at the highest levels of administration during the civil war left a vacuum which lesser gentry, and even men who could hardly claim to be gentlemen, were ready to fill. Dispute and disagreement shook the gentry class between 1640 and 1660, but its dominance of the shire was not permanently disturbed. Hierarchy remained, county society was jolted but not paralysed. During the Great Rebellion, as much as before or after it, county administration took its temper and pace from gentry attitudes and inclinations. The provincial history of the 'troubles in England' in the 1640s and 50s must inevitably be written in the context of their prejudices and preconceptions.

Part II

RELIGION

3

The Puritan mind

This is the manner of hir sickeness and death which as you said in your letter may be an instruction unto us . . . to spende all our time (which we can redeeme from the necessary affaires of this life) in such exercises as tend to our salvation and to wayt for death continully.
John Wilmsherst to Anne Pierson on the death of his mother, September 1614.[1]

Spying the finger of God in all these buffettings, I could even rejoyce to see how he hath made knowne to you the worth of mercy and deliverance and the freeness of grace in the mystery of the gospell.
Samuel Jeake 'to a drooping spirit to refresh it', 1647.[2]

To ly longe in bedd is neither for thy health, wealth nor for increase of godliness.
From the account book of John Everenden.[3]

The term Puritan was first used in the 1560s. It came to be widely applied in the subsequent hundred years as a term of abuse. During this time the Puritans were never an entirely homogeneous group of people, holding a common and consistent set of theological views and preconceptions about worship.[4] Even so it is possible to delineate a Puritan approach to religious experience and specifically Puritan attitudes to life, death and salvation. The purpose of this chapter is to explore these approaches and attitudes, among laymen and clergymen who were critical of certain aspects of the Church of England yet sought within it a more intense kind of spiritual experience. The differences between Puritans and other Protestants have recently been described as 'differences of degree, of theological temperature so to speak, rather than of fundamental principle'.[5] 'Those whom we ordinarily call puritans are men of strict life and precise opinion', wrote Henry Parker, the brother of the Sussex JP Sir Thomas Parker, in a pamphlet of 1641 which was intended to vindicate those who suffered by misapplication of the name. 'They cannot be hated', he added, 'for anything but their singularity in zeale and piety'.[6] An Elizabethan pamphleteer explained that the Puritans were 'the hotter sort of protestants'.[7]

In east Sussex the roots of Puritanism went deep. The Weald, with its large parishes and scattered farmsteads, was its heartland. Recent studies have suggested that dissent spread most easily in the peculiarly favourable conditions of areas such as the Weald, where the hold of the established Church was weakest, where there was a sense of insecurity through dependence on distant corn supplies, and where families were perhaps particularly closely integrated. The same kind of social and economic pattern has been found in the Pennine uplands of the Deanery of Doncaster, in Rockingham Forest and in the pastoral areas of Lancashire and Cheshire.[8] In the Weald Lollardy had flourished.[9] There heretics had been burnt in Mary's reign, three at East Grinstead and four at Mayfield. There that characteristic expression of Sussex Puritanism, the choice of fanciful Christian names, ranging from Be-thankful and Repent to Perform-thy-vows and Standfast-on-high, persisted from Elizabeth's reign until the Restoration.[10] At both Rye and Lewes Protestantism was quickly and easily established, nurtured by the longstanding heretical tradition of the neighbourhood. Charges brought by the conservative vicar of Rye against some of the poorer townsmen in 1537 'reeked of Lollardy and ribaldry'. Lutheran ideas about the priesthood of every christian man and denial of the necessity of penance were alleged to be circulating in the town. Eight men were arrested for holding heretical opinions.[11] On the death of Mary, Rye demonstrated its religious allegiance by demolishing the altar soon after the new Queen was proclaimed. An influx of Huguenots after the massacre of St Bartholomew strengthened the town's Protestantism.[12] Seventeen of the twenty-seven Marian martyrdoms in the county occurred at Lewes and a strident group of clerical puritans established themselves there in the 1570s and 80s.[13] By 1600 Puritanism had permeated many of the market towns, manor houses and farmsteads of the eastern rapes. The wills and correspondence of some of the most zealously Puritan families of this district provide the substance of this chapter. In the west the impact of Puritanism was muted and delayed, but in the long run attitudes that were the common coin of eastern families found adherents there as well. So that when Sir Nathaniel Brent visited Chichester on behalf of Archbishop Laud in 1635, he found that the aldermen were so 'puritanically addicted' that they would have no truck with him or his metropolitical visitation.[14]

'Have minde of deathe and fear to sinne.' This contemporary precept, inscribed on the wall of a chamber at the Jefferay family home in Chiddingly, was taken to heart by gentry of a Puritan cast of mind. In the preambles to their wills many of the Sussex gentry have left behind them a uniquely personal record of their final beliefs about salvation and life after death. The authenticity of these preambles is not in doubt, so full are they of individual quirks and phraseology. There were no standard formulas at this level of society handed on by a minister who acted as scribe. Whether in sickness or health, these men formulated the opening paragraph of their wills by themselves, in the knowledge that there was an account to be rendered.[15] 'The tyme will come', wrote Sir Thomas Springate, 'when this tabernacle of clay which I carry aboute me shall be dissolved.' It was a time for the abandonment of worldly ambitions and pleasures. 'I utterly cast away and renounce idle, vayne and fond desires of man's inventions, they having never so greate and goodly shew of godlynes', declared Sir

Richard Michelbourne.[16] It was a time above all to seek God's mercy and grace. Sir John Shurley, making his will on the day he died, expressed his assurance that God would 'assist and strengthen me at the hour of death with his holy spirit the comforter'. Richard Amherst, who was also close to death when he drew up his testament, beseeched God 'to comfort mee with his holy spirit duringe my life and at the tyme of my death'.[17]

Analysis of some seventy Sussex wills, made in the period between 1620 and 1670, suggests that the doctrine of justification by faith was universally accepted in gentry circles. Despite many variations of wording, the essence of every theological preamble was the same: that the testator relied wholly for his salvation on the merits, death and passion of Jesus Christ. Some gentry, whose outlook is known to have been decisively Puritan, gave no hint of their views beyond this brief justification clause. But a group of particularly zealous gentry distinguished themselves by three distinct emphases which provide an insight into the Puritan mind. Firstly, they expressed their trust in the fully fledged Calvinist doctrine of predestination, a doctrine which rested on the assumption of the rigorous exclusiveness of the godly.[18] Anthony Fowle, for example, expected to 'be partaker of eternal joy and happiness with his saints in heaven', Robert Spence to 'be made happy with the saints made perfect', John Wilson to 'remayne with the blessed saints world without end', and Sir Thomas Sackville to 'rest with his saintes in heaven for ever'.[19] Others, like William Mill, Edward Lindsey, Robert Morley and Edward Michel, spoke confidently of their place with the elect of God. John Board declared his assurance that 'I am and shall be one of the elect number written in the book of life'.[20] In making such predestinarian claims, these gentry were of course merely making explicit the orthodox teaching of the Church during the period from the 1580s to the 1620s.[21]

Secondly, the distinctly Puritan wills stressed man's total depravity and corruption. They show how thoroughly the gentry concerned had absorbed the thinking of William Perkins, who has been called the 'dominant influence in puritan thought' in the first four decades of the seventeenth century.[22] Robert Spence, Sir Thomas Pelham, William Hay, Sir Richard Michelbourne and Sir Thomas Springate were among those who emphasised their own vileness and sinfulness. Michelbourne proclaimed his hope that, through his salvation in Christ, the sins which weighed him down would be 'cast from mee as farr as is the east from the west'. Springate spoke of his 'body which hath been corrupted with sinne'.[23] Satan and his demons, the Devil as a tempter, was a literal reality to such men.[24] 'I beseech my good God . . . ever to defend mee from my cruell, subtill and malitious enemy the devill and all his wicked spirits', wrote Richard Amherst. 'Had I been left to Satan's malice my owne corruption, guilt and terror of conscience, the gulf of despair, had swallowed me up', avowed Philip Jermyn. William Newton embarked on a long dissertation on his own wretchedness:

> There be three things that hath greatly humbled me, first the guilt of my sins, secondly the promesse of my nature to commit sin and thirdly the grievances of this life which follow upon the former, but after my dissolution by God's mercy in Christ apprehended by faith, I shall be freed from them all, so that the combat between the flesh and the spirit will cease and be no more and all traces shall be wiped from my eyes.[25]

Thus fervent Puritans faced the Last Judgment with deep disquiet about their own worthiness yet complete assurance of God's intentions towards them.[26] Thirdly, their eschatology often included some kind of belief in physical resurrection. William Mill, William Hay and Robert Spence, among others, confidently expected their souls and bodies to be reunited at the last day of judgment. Sir Thomas Springate looked forward to receiving his body again then 'not as now it is a frayle and vile body but an imortall and glorious body clothed with the righteousness of my saviour'.[27]

The correspondence of a cluster of families who lived in Hastings rape shows how the religious convictions apparent in wills might colour every aspect of the daily lives of men and women who thought of themselves as belonging to the godly. How many families lived at the level of spiritual intensity of the Busbridges of Etchingham and the Jeakes of Rye it is hard to say. Among such families correspondence fulfilled an endless hunger for the reassurance of friends and kin of like mind. The Busbridge and Temple families mixed a stream of spiritual advice in their letters with family news and reports on the state of the roads. 'Espetially I desire you should seeke God constantly', wrote Anna Busbridge to her daughter Mary in 1648.[28] The same message was constantly reiterated in one form or another. Anne Pierson, who married Samuel Jeake, demanded that her mentor John Wilmsherst should regularly soothe her anxieties about the weakness of her spiritual estate. Her 'thirsting after grace and heavenly things', Wilmsherst wrote soothingly, was 'an evident signe that you have true grace in you, provided this thirsting be constant and continuing'. Samuel Jeake specialised in letters to friends and relations in need of spiritual consolation, the most inspired of which were written with singular imaginative power and persuasiveness. In September 1647, for example, he reminded his sister how much was offered to a 'believing soule' who trusted in God: 'here you may be secure in the greatest dangers, sheltered in the greatest stormes, shielded in the strongest assaults, shaddowed from the scorching heate, warmed in the shivering cold, yea lift your head to behold your redemption'. Moreover correspondence could be used as an aid to the introspection and self-examination that preachers and Puritan writers directed the godly should practise with regard to their moral and spiritual life. Samuel Jeake used his intimate friend John Coulton as a sounding board for his temptations and doubts, when Coulton was away from Rye with the parliamentary army in the 1640s. In reply he received a severe warning about the dangers facing his soul. 'I feare Satan hath gott you on the hipp', wrote Coulton, 'I beseech the nott to lett thy soule flag nor thy spiritt sinke'.[29]

Consciousness of the overwhelming burden of their sinfulness was a prerequisite for those who aspired to election with the saints. Preachers and correspondents constantly reiterated this theme. 'Labour to be more and more humble and sencible of your own vilenesse', urged John Maynard, the minister of Mayfield, in a fast sermon before the Commons.[30] John Wilmsherst rejoiced when Anne Jeake confessed the crookedness of her nature in 1629: 'doe you labour to see it more cleerely and to feel it more sensiblie, that you may feel it as an heavy burden pressing you down.' Family prayers stressed man's weakness in face of the devil's temptations. 'Make me able to descry an error and to detest it . . . gratiously deliver out of errors such of thine as Sathan houlds in snares', ran a passage in a prayer that John Everenden noted at the front of his farming account book.[31] Obsession with sin and worthlessness made complete subjection to Christ the only possible basis for life and salvation. 'When the Law of Christ is once lodged within a man', declared Maynard in the same fast sermon, 'written in his heart, fixed in his bowels, then is he a loyal subject of Christ, and goeth on in the way of holinesse with rejoicing.' The concepts of universal depravity and God's grace offered those who bent themselves to Christ an enormous injection of spiritual confidence. Yet the godly could never relax. Preachers sought to inculcate images of the life of the spirit as pilgrimage and battle, wayfaring and warfaring.[32] A state of permanent tension and awareness was required of predestined men and women. Christopher Blackwood described it to Frances Hartredge in 1651:

> Grow out of love with the world. . . . Remember Christ and all things goe together. Feare nothing but sin. Love God soveraignelye. Pray fervently and looke for answers to your praiers. Be affraid of decayes and tremble at declinings. Breath often towards Christ and let things bee on such good tearmes betwixt Christ and you that you may long for his appearance.

As John Wilmsherst put it in a letter of 1614, the world was for the godly a place of exile rather than abiding, of danger rather than safety, 'for the ship in the midst of the sea is not in greater danger then the Christian man or woman in this world'. How hard it was, he reflected in 1631, 'for the most religious and holy professours to keepe themselves undefiled'.[33]

Puritan laymen and clerics who had the guardianship of others less experienced in the school of Christ often expanded on the heavenly joys that awaited those who abandoned the vanities of the world and set their eyes on God's kingdom. John Wilmsherst became more and more convinced in his old age of the irrelevance of 'earthly felicitie'; as for earthly afflictions, they were 'not worthy of the glory of that blessed place: these are but light and momentary, the other are eternall and compleate'. On the eve of Frances Hartredge's wedding, Christopher Blackwood reminded her of the 'eternall joyes with Christ far beyond all the married joyes of this world'. Samuel Jeake advised his sister-in-law to disdain the things of this world, for when a saint dies 'he parts with a pebble for a pearle, he exchanges trouble for peace, griefe for glory, earth for heaven, a cross for a crowne'.[34]

Yet, since there was no escaping the earthly struggle, Puritan teachers also devoted much attention to establishing a philosophy of acquiescence in the fortunes of life, good or bad, here on earth. They promoted the quiet acceptance of God's mercies. The doctrine of providence, the essence of all Puritan teaching about worldly affairs, brought security and meaning to the lives of the godly. It became habitual for them to see God's hand in everything.[35] They saw it in the daily accidents and opportunities of life. Providence had offered her the chance to communicate with him, Frances Hartredge told her fiancé, when someone agreed to carry her letter to Rye. 'Since over ruling providence hath by your free election devolved upon me, I shall not resist a call from heaven', wrote Herbert Morley to the Mayor of Rye in gratitude for his place in the 1654 parliament. He would have attended the parliamentary election at Rye in 1661, Samuel Gott explained to Samuel Jeake, 'if providence had not hindered me by a casual blow on my knee with a stone'.[36] They saw God's hand in misfortune and learnt patience in adversity. 'God who is onely wise knowes what is best for his', reflected Thomas Housegoe, when he heard in 1626 that he was not generally welcome as minister at Rye. Perhaps there was 'another time in his secret counsell' more fitting for his ministry there. 'I need not write anything to stay your spirit from sinking at the disposal of these affaires, the soveraigne will and providence of God is the resting point for belevers', Frances Hartredge reminded Samuel Jeake, when she at first refused his suit in marriage. Jeake found it hard to accept the doctrine of providence on this occasion, but he struggled to do so.[37]

The godly saw providence at work in the trials of earthly life. Christopher Blackwood, about to set out on a journey, waited on God's determination; Frances Jeake, homesick for her sister and brother-in-law, sought to be 'content with the will of God . . . let him do what seemeth him good'.[38] Pregnancies, then so dangerous to life, brought a period of anxious waiting on God's will. 'Consider you are in the hands of a wise and mercifull father, who hath promised to make all things worke together for the best unto his, which you are', Anna Busbridge was advised by her mother in 1632, 'therefore it canot but goe well with you, come life or death, being the Lord's.' Safe delivery was always cause for thankfulness for God's mercy. 'The Lord was plesed to make her fullfill her month and att the apointed time gave in deliverance speedyly', related Ralph Gibbon to Samuel Jeake in 1657, with the news of his son's birth.[39] The quality of the harvest was seen in the same providential terms. At Mayfield 'it pleased the Lord in great mercy', the same day as a national fast in 1626, 'to send a comfortable sunshine and after that very seasonable and faire harvest weather'.[40] Above all political affairs were believed to reflect God's judgments. 'Man's ways are not in himselfe; he may purpose but God disposeth', noted Samuel Gott to his friend John Swynfen, in his desolation at Cromwell's refusal of the crown in May 1657. Anna Busbridge regarded the wet summer and pitiful harvest of 1648 as a mark of God's anger. Surely, she wrote to her daughter, 'his wrath is not all turned away', for all the victories of that summer season.[41] There was a general readiness, which was not confined to strictly Puritan circles, to see sudden death as a direct judgment. The clerk at Hastings, for instance, thought it worth recording that while one parishioner was 'slain by the hauling up of his father's ship upon Sunday', another 'fell down dead as he was playing a match at football upon the Sabbath day'.[42]

Misfortune acquired a positive and didactic role in providential thinking. Suffering was taken as proof of God's interest in the godly man. The correct procedure for a believer faced by illness or ill luck was to undergo a course of self-examination. 'Let the use of this triall', wrote Christopher Blackwood to Frances Jeake when she was recovering from a bout of sickness, 'bee to make you humble before the Lord . . . and to search for the sin which hath caused the Lord to break in upon you'.[43] When he believed himself to be on his deathbed in 1644, John Coulton 'with the liftedst up heart I could poured out my confession of those sinnes that Sathan and conscience had accused me of'. He made a covenant that, if God restored him to health, 'I would be his servant serving noe creature butt God onely'. Puritan correspondents invariably comforted their sick friends and kin by pointing out the spiritual opportunities that were opened up to them. 'We may see that it is good in the midest of prosperitie to feele some crosse and it is as you say a signe of God's love when by this meanes he restraineth us from wandering', declared John Wilmsherst to Anne Pierson, 'Surely friend', wrote Charles Nicholls to Samuel Jeake, commiserating with him over his ill health with the precept that God 'seekes rather to profit then to please us',

> no passage of his all disposing and most wise providence should be suffered to slip without an advantageous issue to our soules, whose rod hath a voyce and it is our duty to heare it. And afflictions are his love tokens and it is our duty to see it soe.

Thus sickness was a time for reflection and solemn vows, for promises which a believer once more in good health ignored at his peril, since, as John Pierson reminded his mother, there was bound to come a period of even greater necessity and dependence on God's will.[44] It was a time for the total abandonment of self and reliance on God's mercy, a time for the godly to immerse themselves in the fullness of God's love. Samuel Gott in his *Essay on the True Happiness of Man*, in which he devoted a chapter to providence, recommended his readers to reflect on their strange preservation from the dangers of life.[45] Samuel Jeake wrote in a letter to Ralph Gibbon of the strivings of Puritans to grasp all the meaning of their faith in the personal crises of their lives: 'Oh that in such extremities which our father makes oppertunities to discover his tenderness to his poore lambes we could with a sweeter repose of spirit acquiesce in his armes'.[46]

The godly were most in need of spiritual comfort and assurance when death suddenly deprived them of a loved one. Such misfortune was a signal mark of God's sovereignty. 'How vaine this life is, which many times is then neerest to an end when death seemeth to be farthest of', reflected John Wilmsherst, describing to Anne Pierson the sudden loss of his mother who had previously been in excellent health. 'So uncertayne is the ground of our hopes builded upon mortallitye, that when in our conceit wee thinke to rayse a most gorgeous pallace all cometh sedaynely to utter ruyne', wrote John Pierson in a letter to a friend about the death of his 'dearest sonne'. Puritans learnt fortitude as they mourned: 'this is brought to passe', declared John Pierson, 'by a superior power whose deelinge I must not contradict, nor in my hart call in question'.[47]

Inspiring deathbed scenes and courageous last words were treasured by Puritans. Nearly forty years after the death of her first husband Sir William Springate, Mary Penn related, in a letter to her grandchild, the story of her dangerous journey through the snowclad Weald to his bedside at Arundel. She recalled his words when she entered his chamber: 'Let me embrace thee before I die; I am going to thy God'.[48] The last words of Ninian Burrell, who died of consumption aged twenty-seven, were recorded by his family on his memorial: 'My flesh and my hart faileth but God is the strength of my hart and my portion for ever'.[49] Lengthy accounts of the death of relatives brought spiritual strength to the writer and were intended as instruction to the recipient. 'Although hir paynes were greate and allmost continual', wrote John Wilmsherst to Anne Jeake about his mother, 'yet was shee alwayes very quiet and patient and lay with as sweete and amiable a countenance as ever you saw hir in your life'. Samuel Jeake described his mother Anne Jeake's composure and preparation for death by reading, prayer and meditation to Wilmsherst's widow many years later:

> As she lay she read the 102 psalme, for the Lord seemed to hide himselfe from her, but he did not forsake her over long, in that night hee revealed himselfe to her in a sweet manner, so that her bruised bones leapt for joy; in the morning she revealed to us . . . that now she had found by experience what we have yet but by promise, that heaviness may endure for a night but joy cometh in the morning.

When Anne Jeake died several days later, 'she sweetly yeelded up her soule into her father's hands, catching up her hands together uttered these words Come Lord, but what more could not be heard'.[50]

If adversity provoked the believer to greater spiritual striving, prosperity contained the threat of overconfidence. The doctrine of providence had a dangerous self-confirming quality. It was tempting to interpret material success as proof of godliness.[51] Puritan correspondence in Sussex suggests that the snares of prosperity were often recognised. 'Then are we most prone to offend God', John Wilmsherst told Anne Jeake, 'when we prosper in all thinges, for hereby we are puffed up with pride'. 'O let us labor to have our harts low in time of prosperitie', insisted Frances Jeake to her sister.[52] There were various antidotes to pride. The Puritan's stricken conscience, persistent sense of unworthiness and continuing fear of God's displeasure was one. Industry was another. The precepts that John Everenden inscribed on the first page of his account book made the point succinctly:

> Frugallity and humility are thriving virtues: were a calling but to keepe a man from idlenesse, it were a goodnesse, for the industrious man is seldome at leasure to sinne, whereas the idle man hath neither leisure nor power to avoyed sinne.

Without the 'blessing of God', declared Peter Farnden in his will, 'it is in vaine to rise up early or to sit down late'.[53] It is not surprising in view of such thinking that economic achievement in this period has sometimes been identified with religious fervour and zeal.[54]

Household religion was the essence of Puritanism. Family prayers, catechising and repetition of sermons provided a framework of regular devotions.[55] Puritan gentry sought to ensure that from an early age their children imbibed an understanding of the faith. In their wills they often expressed concern for the continuance of the process of religious education which had preoccupied them. Thus Sir Thomas Sackville, for example, entreated his executors 'to take care that all my children may be religiously brought up in the knowledge and fear of God'.[56] The strict moral and spiritual upbringing provided by such men tended to produce young men and girls with a strong introspective streak and highly developed consciences. After indulging in a bout of gaming in 1630, John Wilson told his father he saw it as 'an affliction to make me thinke of myselfe the better'; the following year he agonised over visiting the dancing school attended by his friends among the young clerks and attorneys of the capital. Mary Busbridge fretted about the possibility that her mother might think she had spent money on frivolous pleasures, when she was away in Warwickshire, but after some hesitation she decided to defer writing home about it on the sabbath.[57] Instruction to children at home was normally complemented by education in the principles of religion at school. Puritan impetus often lay behind the founding of grammar schools; gentry and corporations imposed their assumptions on the local schools with regard to the place of religion in the curriculum. Home, school and parish church, indeed, were seen as a triangle of influences nurturing the godly child. When he founded Steyning grammar school in 1614, William Holland envisaged that the master would extend the household experience of the scholars, or replace it where it was lacking, by sowing 'the seed of religion in the hearts of children'. At Rye the corporation showed their expectation that parents would cooperate by insisting on ability to read both Testaments as a condition of entry. At both Rye and Steyning there was provision for attendance by scholars at Sunday services to take notes on the sermons preached.[58]

The Puritans set themselves an exacting programme of daily meditation and prayer, regular study of scripture and frequent attendance at sermons. 'Beware that you bee not slouthfull in these holy exercises of religion', John Wilmsherst warned Anne Jeake. Sussex homes were well equipped with copies of the Bible, the fountainhead of the faith.[59] Holy scripture was regarded as the godly man's antidote to the dangers of 'beinge amonge the people of this worlde'. It was the foundation of household religion. Mary Busbridge, who had been taught systematic study of the scriptures in her childhood, sent her mother a Bible with notes she had made on some passages of it from Warwickshire. Next to the Bible in its influence on the Puritan laity came John Foxe's *Book of Martyrs*. John Wilmsherst's mother spoke on her deathbed of how after hearing 'much reading in the booke of martyrs', at a time when she had been greatly troubled by her own sinfulness, she was 'somewhat comforted'.[60] Numerous other treatises were circulated and read in Puritan households. Robert Spence and the ironmaster vicar of Frant, William Dyke, were among those who owned copies of William Perkins's *Works*, an enormously influential exposition of Calvinist theology.[61] In 1628, at a time when he maintained 'many ungodly and erroneous conceites' had sprung up, John Wilmsherst recommended Anne Jeake to purchase John Downame's very popular book *The Sum of Divinity*.[62] Another popular work, Lewis Bayly's *Practice of Piety*, was owned by a Slinfold husbandman. An incident in 1643 in which he lent it to a widow, whose servant carried it off to read, pleading later that he had won the book in a wager from its owner, is an interesting indication that the readership of devotional literature went well down the social hierarchy.[63] For a few laity, as well as for Sussex divines such as Christopher Elderfield, writing as well as reading was part of the search for spiritual maturity. 'As meditation is the glass of the soul so writing steals it and strengthens the reflection', declared Samuel Gott, explaining his motives in presenting to the public his book *An Essay on the True Happiness of Man*.[64]

Puritans hungered for sermons. They regarded regular parochial preaching as the best means of rooting out superstitition and building a Protestant society.[65] 'Except it be about Lewes and a little in Chichester', it was reported in 1569, 'the whole diocese is very blind and superstitious for want of teaching'.[66] Apart from Bishop Curteys, whose prophesyings must have done something to remedy clerical ignorance, the Elizabethan episcopate never tackled the problem of providing the county with an educated preaching ministry. Anthony Watson's requirement of monthly instead of quarterly sermons in his visitation articles of 1600 was a tardy recognition of the importance of preaching, but it was a pious hope rather than a purposeful policy. The Puritan gentry remained dissatisfied. Edward Lewkenor spoke in parliament about the survey of clergy in east Sussex made by a clerical pressure group about 1584, which revealed gross inadequacies in many parishes. The demand for a 'learned, godly and resident ministry' was the main impetus behind the gentry's petitioning campaign at the accession of James I, which was led by William Newton of Southover, Henry Apsley and the Brightling ironmaster Thomas Collins. Many leading magnates, including Sir Walter Covert, Sir John Shurley, Sir Thomas Pelham, and Sir Nicholas Parker, backed the campaign.[67] By the 1620s and 30s sustained local pressure seems to have made an impact. Many parishes had a licensed preacher and a well-established weekly or monthly sermon, yet there were still cases of scandalous neglect. The Binderton churchwardens, for instance, alleged in 1623 that their minister preached 'not hardly one tyme in five years'.[68]

It was the drive and initiative of town corporations and zealous gentry that brought a number of well-educated and highly competent preachers to Sussex between 1560 and 1640. As early as the 1570s, Rye corporation was giving the minister there a yearly stipend to augment a pitifully small allowance from the leasee of the vicarage.[69] The Rye townsmen developed a critical attitude towards the occupants of their pulpit. A skilful and learned preacher like Christopher Blackwood became popular with the community. 'The Lord make you and the whole towne thankfull' for his ministry, wrote a Kentish correspondent of Anne Jeake's in 1633.[70] On the other hand, the corporation reacted stridently against anyone who threatened their independence to support whoever they wished. The quarrel between Thomas Warren, the first occupant of the Rye lectureship founded in 1617, and James Whitaker, a new curate who arrived in the town six years later, shows the corporation at its most assertive. Whitaker attempted to prevent Warren from occupying the pulpit of the parish church. In seeking to end a controversy which 'the further that it runs the more infamous it seemeth to be', the town authorities naturally threw the weight of their prestige in favour of their own preacher. They persuaded Lord Zouche, who as Lord Warden of the Cinque Ports had supported the establishment of the lectureship in the first place, to take up the case. Under pressure from him, Bishop Carleton agreed to discharge Whitaker and install Warren as curate as well as lecturer, despite the fact that Whitaker was one of Carleton's own chaplains.[71]

Establishment of a lectureship was a favourite device among those who desired to extend the availability of sermons in market towns.[72] The Lewes lectureship in the late 1620s was organised and supported by a group of gentry living in the neighbourhood. Anthony Stapley and Sir Thomas Pelham were among the initiators of the project and they probably drew in other members of their social circle such as James Rivers and Herbert Hay.[73] The vigorous preacher they appointed, Anthony Lapthorne, later found himself before the northern Court of High Commission when he declared that 'preaching was the only means to salvation'.[74] The lectureships established at Horsham in the 1630s and Midhurst in 1642 seem to have had the same kind of basis of interest among the gentry of the vicinity.[75]

Initiatives of this kind were merely an extension of the long-established control exercised by gentry over many of the advowsons of the county. Though there were few of the large concentrations of benefices in the hands of individuals that occurred elsewhere, 120 parishes out of 250 were impropriated in 1603 and a few families like the Pelhams and Coverts had for many years controlled appointment to several livings.[76] Rights of patronage were often the foundation of lasting friendships between gentry and clergy. In 1633, for instance, Sir William Goring presented Christopher Elderfield to the rectory of Burton. His estate virtually comprised the tiny parish. Elderfield, the son of an illiterate yeoman farmer from Berkshire who had studied at Oxford, in fact became a private chaplain to the Goring family. For twenty years he lived in seclusion, becoming known in the meanwhile in academic Puritan circles as the author of *The Civil Right of Tithes* and *Of Regeneration and Baptism, Hebrew and Christian.* In his will of 1652 Elderfield acknowledged his debt to the family that had given him succour: Sir William, his wife and children were to have rings in remembrance of him. His bequest of five pounds to be distributed among the servants at Burton is a mark of the status that the Puritan divine had held in the household. Yet the relationship had a final bitter twist. Elderfield left almost all his wealth to found a charity for the poor of his native village of Harwell and gave no legacy to his patron. So, although he had requested that he should be buried in the chancel at Burton, Sir William Goring directed that he should lie in the nave instead.[77] Other instances suggest relationships of similar intimacy. The Yorkshireman John Abbot, who was vicar of Hollington in the 1630s and early 1640s, bequeathed five pounds to his 'honourable patron' Sir Thomas Eversfield for his 'singular love to me'.[78] John Maynard enjoyed the friendship of a leading Puritan JP, John Baker. He dedicated a volume of sermons to the Baker family and the parishioners of Mayfield. An inscription on his tomb there recorded that, as 'a preacher of the greatest piety and learning', he 'shone for forty years the light and ornament of his flock'.[79]

Gentry wills also illuminate the friendships that blossomed between laymen and clergy. Sir Walter Covert, for instance, left five pounds to Simon Aldriche, the rector of Slaugham whom he had presented to the living. John Wilson bequeathed forty shillings to his 'kind and loving friend' Mr Roote, the vicar of Fletching. Thomas Springate gave John Vine, the minister of Plumpton, all his books, his lease of Plumpton parsonage and his silver watch. John French and Thomas Jefferay were others who made bequests to a local minister.[80] The funeral sermon, a practice which often appealed to gentry despite the disapproval of it expressed by some Puritan writers, offered the chance for a final act, charged with emotion, in the relationship between a cleric and his lay patron.[81] Some men, like Anthony Fowle for example, were content to request a sermon from a 'godly minister'. Others, such as Thomas Jefferay, specified the individual who should preach.[82] It was seen as right by all concerned that Benjamin Pickering, the minister of East Hoathly who had benefited so greatly from the patronage of Sir Thomas Pelham, should have made the solemn panegyric before the large company at Pelham's funeral in 1654. Sir John Pelham gave him four pounds and a mourning cloak for this signal service to the family.[83]

Whereas a good deal of clerical nonconformity had been detected in late Elizabethan Sussex, only a few clergy appeared before the ecclesiastical courts for nonconformist practices during the period between 1610 and 1640.[84] There were occasional presentments for failure to wear the surplice and use the sign of the cross in baptism early in the century.[85] Ministers in hotbeds of Puritanism like Lewes and Rye in particular were sometimes in trouble. The minister of St Michael's Lewes was presented in 1638 for using extemporary prayer.[86] Thomas Warren was alleged to administer the sacrament to men sitting rather than kneeling at Rye. His successor Christopher Blackwood abbreviated the prayer book service to a point where it hardly counted: 'sometimes he omitteth one of the lessons, the litany and the ten commandments altogether', reported a churchwarden. Instead he preached interminable sermons.[87]

These few hints of nonconformist practices that reached the diocesan authorities through churchwardens hardly gave cause for alarm. Bishops Montagu and Duppa indeed were optimistic about the state of the diocese in their reports to Archbishop Laud. From 1634 to 1636 Montagu remained confident that the clergy were basically conformable, despite the efforts of Puritan JPs who had 'awed some of the clergy into like opinions with themselves'. In 1639 Duppa found the diocese 'not so much troubled with puritan ministers, as with puritan justices of the peace, of which latter there are store'.[88] It is hard to say whether the bishops of Chichester had the measure of the situation in Sussex, or whether they were the victims of an administrative machine too rusty to reveal clerical nonconformity that was in fact rife. Some resistance at least to the surplice, the sign of the cross, standing at the reading of the Gospel and bowing at the name of Jesus must surely have gone unpresented. Churchwardens may often have been in sympathy with ministers' initiatives over such matters. Yet it was quite possible, of course, for a Puritan minister to conform to the prescribed ceremonies, without compromising his fundamental religious stance.[89] Many Puritan clergy were undoubtedly conformist throughout the first four decades of the seventeenth century.

Bishops Richard Montagu and Brian Duppa were certainly correct in assigning the leadership of militant Puritanism in east Sussex to laymen rather than clergy, though they probably exaggerated the role of a few JPs, whose activities were widely known and discussed, at the expense of the many lesser gentry and substantial householders who were the backbone of the godly in communities such as Rye and Lewes. Lay prejudice against vestments, such as has been found in other counties, is discernible behind some of the presentments that were made by Sussex churchwardens. 'Hee had as leefe see a sowe weare a saddell as see a minister weare a surplice', a Catsfield gentleman, Herbert Pelham, was alleged to have declared in 1611.[90] Some ceremonies were disliked. There were cases of neglect of the churching of women, for instance, because of lay objections to it. 'God deliver us from such a malicious priest', railed a Hove woman against a minister who was strict in observing the prescribed form of churching.[91] The use of the term priest in this instance was presumably a deliberate slander. But in general Puritan gentry did not appear before the diocesan courts because they were well able to protect themselves from ecclesiastical censure. They were content to tolerate the institution of episcopacy so long as it did not press too hard upon their consciences. Their social supremacy in their parishes and the inviolability of their households enabled them virtually to escape surveillance.

Puritanism before 1640 was therefore a movement for zeal and godliness within the Church. The Puritan gentry led a campaign to stress evangelical religion. Until the rise of Arminianism, they were not fundamentally at odds with the ecclesiastical establishment. In the meantime much was achieved. The general reaction among the gentry, which was most marked in Puritan circles but was not confined to them, against the traditional paraphernalia and pomp of death and burial is one example of the power of the currents of reform within local society. Puritan criticism of funeral ceremonies undoubtedly helped to undermine the fashion for the tolling bell, large companies of mourners and huge wakes.[92] Catholic gentry like Sir John Gage in 1633 and Arminians like William Nevill, who directed in 1640 that his burial should be 'without any funeral pompe or solemnity', took up the fashion for simplicity.[93] Many of the Puritan gentry echoed it: William Newton declared in 1645 that he wanted 'no mourning or ceremonies', John Board directed in 1648 that there should be no pomp, doles to the poor or blacks, Roger Gratwick set a limit of ten pounds on expenditure for his funeral when he made his will in 1653, Robert Spence wanted no 'blacks, ostentation or show' in 1656, William Dyke wished his body to be interred in 'as private a manner as maybe' in 1659.[94]

The new dislike of ostentation showed itself also in the shift in taste away from the ambitious figured tombs of the Elizabethan and Jacobean eras.[95] The tomb of William Thomas, with two kneeling figures and columns, which was erected about 1640, was the last of its kind in Sussex for many years. When Sir Thomas Parker desired an elaborate monument in 1653, he took care to stress that his motive was 'not for any cause of superstition'. His request was so old-fashioned that its execution was long delayed.[96] The first examples of a new style of memorial in east Sussex were the frontal busts of Sir William Springate, who died in 1643, at Ringmer and of John Nutt, who died in 1656, at Berwick.[97] But any kind of representation of deceased gentry in fact became uncommon in the 1640s and 50s. The aged Anthony Cruttenden, who had been born fifteen years before the Armada sailed, expressed the new mood when he made his will in 1659. His request was straightforward: for a 'good fair tombstone' over his wife and himself, 'with a piece of brass with letters and words'. Cruttenden had become something of a patriarch in the Burwash neighbourhood, where his daughters had married into several prominent Puritan families. Moreover his wife was a daughter of the fiery Puritan JP Herbert Hay of Glyndebourne.[98] Anthony Cruttenden's last appearance on the Bench at midsummer in 1648, in the company of men like Sir Thomas Pelham, Anthony Stapley and the Spence brothers Robert and William, thus symbolised both the continuity and the strength of the Puritan tradition in the eastern rapes of Sussex.[99] The presuppositions of the Puritan mentality which have been examined in this chapter are crucial to an understanding of gentry responses to the Arminian campaign to transform the church between 1628 and 1640.

4

The enforcement of Arminianism

> Mr Staply at Michaelmas sessions last (our churches being well and peacibly composed before) possest the people in his charge that the altering of the communion table alterwise was an innovation detracting from God's glory.
> *Edward Burton to Archbishop Laud's chaplain, 27 January 1640.*[1]

> For as much as I finde in your church of Heathfield one pewe of late times erected . . . very unseemly for height and situation and which incroaches upon the middle part of the church and is an annoyance to those that sit neare, thes are therfore . . . to admonish you and either of you forthwith to remove the said incroachment.
> *Christopher Dowe to the churchwardens of Heathfield, 8 September 1640.*[2]

The emergence in the 1620s and the subsequent ascendancy in the 1630s of the English Arminians brought to an end a period of harmony in the Church when Puritans had been left relatively undisturbed. The triumph of Arminianism replaced Calvinist predestinarian theology, which had been the national orthodoxy for around sixty years, with a belief in God's universal grace and the free will of all men to obtain salvation. It involved the capture of the episcopate by William Laud and his associates. It led to a programme of reform based on ceremonialism and sacerdotalism.[3] The gentry's response to the campaigns of the Arminian bishops to impose the new orthodoxy parish by parish is crucial to an understanding of their mood and of provincial politics on the eve of the civil war.

From 1628 until 1638 the diocese of Chichester, which was coterminous with the county of Sussex, was governed by Bishop Richard Montagu.[4] The community found itself under the direct spiritual overlordship of the man whose book, *New Gagg*, had as a test case provided the first triumph of the Arminian party, the man who, while he was hounded by the Commons, had received the personal protection of Charles I, the man whose writings were the substance of the debates at the York House conference in 1626, which proved a substantial rebuff for Calvinism. Montagu was bound to be fundamentally at odds with many of the Sussex gentry since he defined all predestinarian Calvinists as Puritans. It was this divisive spirit that MPs had particularly resented in Montagu's writings. When Montagu was translated to Norwich in 1638 he was succeeded at Chichester by the

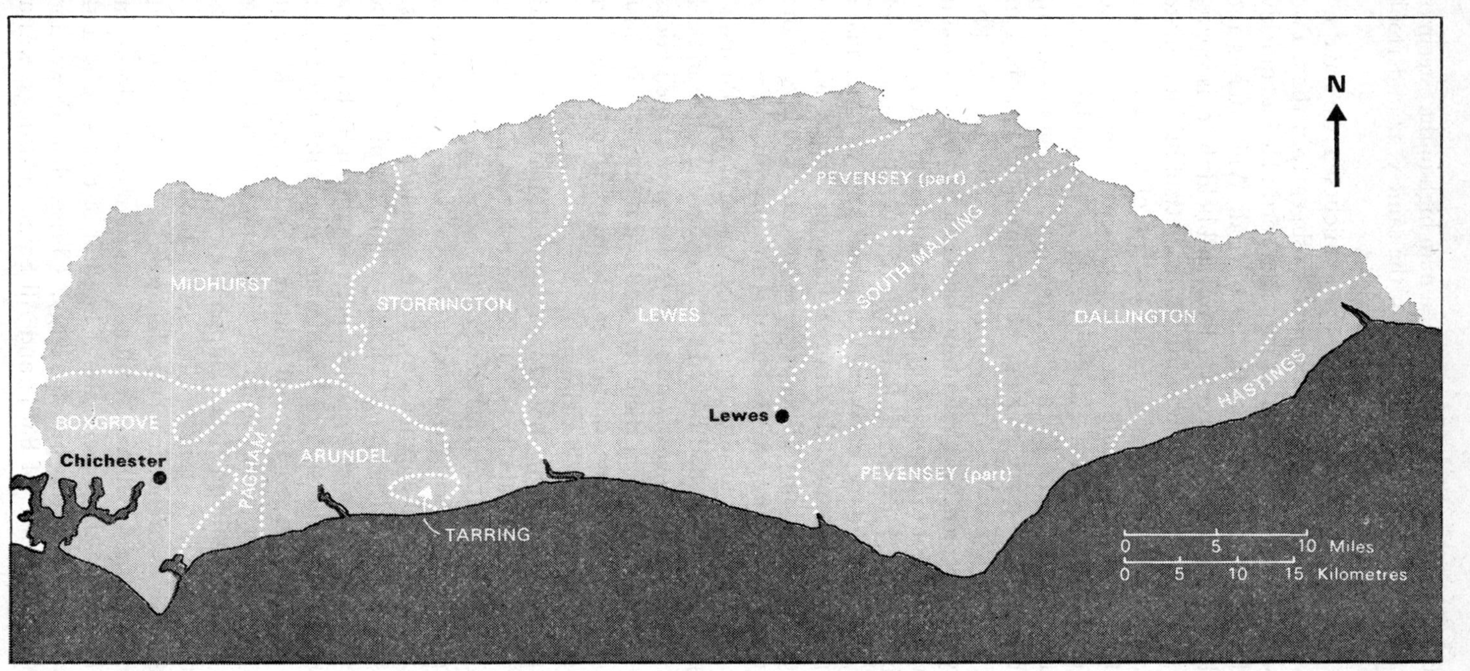

Rural Deaneries

Archdeaconry of Chichester	Boxgrove, Midhurst, Arundel, Storrington
Archdeaconry of Lewes	Lewes, Pevensey, Dallington, Hastings
Archiepiscopal Peculiars	Pagham and Tarring, South Malling

9 The diocese of Chichester

Dean of Christ Church, Oxford, Brian Duppa, a man high in the esteem of both the King and the Archbishop and who in the same year undertook the tutorship of the eight-year-old Prince Charles.[5]

'In Sussex I am a stranger as yett . . . att Chichester we have no great interest', wrote Montagu to his friend John Cosin early in 1625. Two years previously he had acquired the rectory of Petworth. He had quickly grown attached to the rural seclusion that it offered. While across the Downs his theological opponent George Carleton still held the episcopate, Montagu was tentatively feeling his way into the society of his immediate neighbourhood. He made the acquaintance of a few of the gentry who served the Earl of Northumberland, men like Edward Dowse, but he remained unknown, except for his extreme views, in the wider county society.[6] Montagu still had scarcely any influence at Chichester when, after years of indefatigable place seeking, he acquired the bishopric in 1628. Moreover a closed capitular corporation like Chichester could not be quickly or easily transformed by a reforming bishop.[7] In 1632 Montagu was thwarted in his attempt to acquire a place as canon residentiary of the cathedral for his kinsman John Scull. Relations between the bishop and William Hicks, the prebendary of West Wittering who was the main contender against Scull, were already strained through Hicks's failure to fulfil the traditional responsibility of his prebend to teach theology in the cloisters. Residing at Southampton, Hicks had sent 'any riff raff who he can light upon, shifters, unconformitants, curatts, young boyes, Puritans' to teach in his stead. Montagu had lacked authority in the Close to deal with him, until, at his triennial visitation in 1631, he had charged Hicks with extreme negligence, but even then he could not oust him.[8] It must have been a bitter blow to Montagu that this recalcitrant and difficult man grasped the vacant canonry from his kinsman.

It was not until the mid-1630s that Montagu established a substantial Arminian party in the cathedral city. Then Richard Steward, a friend of John Cosin's who apparently shared his views on the necessity for salvation of confession to a priest, succeeded Francis Dee as Dean; Montagu's friends Robert Bostock and Laurence Pay became residentiary canons, and Pay was also made archdeacon of Chichester; John Scull crowned a spate of vicarages and prebendaries obtained since 1629 through Montagu's nomination with the chancellorship of Chichester cathedral.[9] Finally, in 1637, Montagu had the learned vicar of Sutton, Aquila Cruso, his and Cosin's longstanding friend, admitted to the important West Wittering prebend, on the death of William Hicks. Duppa likewise infiltrated friends and relations into important posts in the diocese. His brother-in-law James Marsh succeeded Pay as archdeacon of Chichester in 1639; his friend Richard Chaworth replaced William Nevill as chancellor of the diocese in 1640.[10] By the late 1630s there were also a handful of enthusiastic and eminent Arminians among the parish clergy. Christopher Dowe, for instance, who held the livings of Battle and All Saints, Hastings, was a vigorous controversialist who defended confession as 'agreeable to the constant and resolved doctrine of this church' and questioned whether any of the Popes were Antichrist.[11] Edward Burton, a friend of Dowe's, who held the royal livings of Sedlescombe and Westham, was epitomised on his memorial inscription at Broadwater as 'always a hater and smiter of presbyterians'. Christopher Swale, who like Burton was a JP and gentleman of some standing, urged his parishioners to bow at the name of Jesus 'uppon paine of damnacon', and highly extolled the Book of Sports.[12] Parish clergy who inclined to ceremonialism were able to be much bolder in the new climate of the 1630s than during James I's reign and some adopted the Arminian insistence on parishioners receiving communion only at the altar rails.[13] Arminianism seems to have had a particularly strong appeal to men with a sense of social inferiority, anxious to establish their prestige, who found attractive its stress on the dignity and special role of the priesthood. Laurence Pay, for example, came of a humble Shropshire family.[14] The notebook of the London merchant's son John Nutt indicates his meticulous concern, as rector of Berwick, for the preservation of all his rights.[15]

Despite his appetite for academic controversy, Bishop Montagu had no liking for public affairs. A victim of the stone, aged over fifty, he preferred to cosset himself in the remoteness of his palace at Aldingbourne than to live in the midst of the rough and tumble of Chichester's factional politics. Unlike his predecessor Bishop Carleton and some other Arminian bishops such as William Peirs at Bath and Wells, he took no part in local government.[16] However, he did take an interest in his episcopal estates which he found 'miserably depopulated'. Montagu set to work 'to pick holes in the leases to void them' and was soon offering new leases to friends at court such as Endymion Porter. The implementation of Arminianism, meanwhile, fell on the shoulders of the chancellor of the diocese, William Nevill, the archdeacons of Chichester and Lewes and their working bureaucracy.[17] Montagu himself did no more than proclaim a programme in his visitation articles which, if it was enforced, would translate the new theological fashion into an administrative reality. He set out his version of Arminianism in his episcopal visitation of 1628; he reiterated it in his visitations of the whole diocese in 1631, 1634 and 1637; the impact of his ideals was reflected in the archidiaconal visitation articles of Laurence Pay in 1635.

Comparison of Montagu's visitation articles with those of two predecessors, Thomas Bickley and Anthony Watson, issued in 1586 and 1600 respectively, is instructive. His programme was based firmly on the canons of 1604, yet it carried the impress of his own personality. The questions were much more searching than those of the Elizabethan bishops. Does the minister stand at the reading of the gospel and creed? Is baptism administered according to the 'prescript forme expressed' and the sign of the cross used? Is the bread and wine consecrated 'with those words that are set downe'? 'Is the wine as it should be, representing blood; not sacke, white wine, water, or some other liquor?' Are all the prescribed rites and ceremonies used in the visitation of the sick and the churching of women? Does the minister ever omit to wear his surplice? Does he 'admonish and exhort' parishioners to confess and receive 'ghostly counsell and comfort', together with 'the benefit of absolution', before they take communion? Montagu omitted the Elizabethan article about the frequency with which the minister preached or procured sermons and ignored the stress of the 1604 canons on this aspect of the priestly office. Instead he included a detailed set of questions about contentious preaching. One of them, referring to the 1622 Directions to Preachers, was a direct challenge to any who dared controvert the new orthodoxy.

> Doth your minister preach or teach any thing contrary to His Majestie's late injunctions, about predestination, falling from grace etc, to trouble men's minds with those deep and darke points, which of late have so distracted and engarboyled the world?[18]

Sacerdotalism was the essence of Montagu's ecclesiastical policy. The stress on ritual implied it; articles about the minister's involvement in trade 'contrary to the honour of his calling', and about reproachful words against him by laymen 'to the scandall of his vocation', asserted it. Montagu gave relatively little attention to the setting of worship. Apart from articles dealing with profanation of the communion table and the placing of the font at the church door, he confined himself to the standard questions about church ornaments and furniture. It was the quality of ceremonial in the parish churches that concerned him. He set before the churchwardens the ideal of a reverent and obedient congregation, their lives ordered and enhanced by the rituals their minister provided Sunday by Sunday and by the *rites de passage* that it was his spiritual function to administer. Churchwardens were not merely to keep an eye on blasphemers, drunkards and fornicators; they were to report men who failed to kneel during the general confession, the litany, the ten commandments or other prayers, above all any who sat to receive communion. Any who omitted to bow at the name of Jesus, to stand for the creed and the Lord's prayer, to keep their hats off throughout the service, to babble, talk or walk around during it were to be presented. Montagu hoped to root out lay Puritanism and recusancy. He asked about nonconformist practices such as gadding, attending church for the sermon only and parental insistence on nomination of themselves as godfathers and godmothers to their children.[19] He required special attention to be given to the conduct and regular attendance at church of schoolmasters.

The writer of a memorandum composed at the time of Archbishop Laud's trial, which argued that Montagu was one of 'the chief promoters of his innovations', based his case partly on quotation of the 1628 visitation articles at Chichester.[20] It may well have been there that the authentic voice of Arminianism as an ecclesiastical policy was first heard. Montagu's 1628 articles were probably at that time the fullest statement of the intentions of the group of clerics who were in the process of capturing control of the Church and who made the same kind of programme familiar in other dioceses in the course of the 1630s. Virtually identical wording in several passages suggests the influence Montagu's articles may have had on Laud, when he came to formulate the programme for his metropolitical visitation of 1635. Laud's aim was to turn individual initiatives such as Montagu's into a national policy, to impose a uniform pattern diocese by diocese.[21] His metropolitical articles became the most comprehensive declaration of Arminianism in action. They touched on many points that Montagu had neglected and they were in many respects more inquisitive than Montagu's articles had been. They in their turn influenced Montagu's programme. He adopted an article of Laud's in 1637 about schoolmasters in private houses, in elaboration of his earlier enquiries about masters who taught without a licence. Under Laud's influence he also expanded his interrogation about altars. It is clear that Montagu and Laud were largely at one in their vision of spiritual order and fulfilment, although the Archbishop failed to adopt all Montagu's crotchets. Montagu's objection to Puritan ministers who conducted fasts to exorcise the devil, for instance, his concern about the form of marriage service used by recusants and his campaign against 'ignorant persons' who abused the people by the practice of physic or surgery were omitted in the metropolitical articles.[22]

Bishop Duppa's visitation articles of 1638 faithfully mirrored the Archbishop's of three years previously. The two archdeacons in their turn, James Marsh at Chichester and William Hutchinson at Lewes, reissued Duppa's articles without alteration for their own visitations during the following three years. In the sphere of church fabric and furnishings, Duppa greatly extended his predecessor's programme of reform. He directed the churchwardens to report about broken windows, paving, the depth of graves, the condition of lead roofs and the state of brasses and monuments. 'Is your church swept and cleansed', he asked, 'at least once a weeke, the walls whited, the windowes and roofe kept cleane from cobwebs?' Practical as well as aesthetic considerations lay behind his inquisition. Pews of varying heights prevented some of the congregation seeing the minister, some people could not hear if pulpits were badly placed. Duppa required the ten commandments to be set upon the east wall, 'where the people may best see to reade them'.[23] Until his campaign to beautify the interior of churches, improvements in furnishings and even essential repairs had largely depended on the public spirit of incumbents and gentry. For instance, Thomas Vicars had the two east windows in the aisles of Cuckfield church painted and glazed in 1627; he persuaded Dorothy, Lady Shurley to pay for a gallery 'for the schollars and to the adorning of the church' a few years later.[24] Such initiatives were unusual. Bishop Duppa in fact set before the churchwardens an ideal of startling novelty. Responsibility for a high standard of seemliness, order and decency, he suddenly insisted, rested with them.

Bishops Montagu and Duppa sought to impose an enormous and exacting task on the Sussex churchwardens. The whole weight of detection fell on them, yet there must have been much in the new articles that baffled them. They were suddenly forbidden to allow the petty school to be kept in the parish church, a practice established in some places as long as anyone could remember. They were immediately expected to purchase a table of the forbidden degrees of marriage, something no bishop or archdeacon had stressed before. The close surveillance of their minister demanded by the Arminian episcopate involved such matters as whether or not he wore 'long haire, deepe ruffes, falling bands down his shoulders'. Eternal vigilance and systematic record keeping were necessary, if churchwardens were to produce the kind of full report required of the behaviour of the parishioners in church and in the precincts of the churchyard. Moreover the Arminians were attempting to revive social and religious customs that had fallen into disuse in many places. Beating the bounds at Rogationtide by the whole congregation, with prayers and reading of psalms and the gospels, was by the 1630s much neglected. The use of the veil in the churching of women was omitted in some places. The passing bell was only tolled in many villages if the sick person or his friends desired it; at Guestling it had not been tolled 'in any man's remembrance'.[25] The churchwardens thus found themselves faced, on top of everything else, with enforcement of a pattern of life that was at least partly obsolete.

Compiling a presentment on seventy or more articles was a tiresome and difficult business for the husbandmen or craftsmen taking their turn in office as churchwardens. Friends and neighbours were ready to persuade them to omit misdemeanours that would land the defaulters in a journey to court and ecclesiastical censure and fees.[26] Awareness of the weaknesses of the system led the Arminian bishops to enquire about parishioners who gave the officers evil words for doing their duty and who tempted them to leave matters unpresented or to 'dispense with your oathes by using equivocation'. Yet, despite the pressures on them, some churchwardens acted diligently. They bought the book of articles as the 119th canon of 1604 directed they should, perused it, if necessary with the assistance of someone more literate than themselves, and made a presentment which showed a care and concern commensurate with the detail of the questions. Thus the Horsham officers, in 1640, informed Archdeacon Marsh that they had precisely an acre of consecrated ground in their churchyard; the Wisborough Green churchwardens responded to his curiosity about the felling of trees with the information that the churchyard's single ash tree was as healthy as ever. A highly responsible but illiterate Binderton churchwarden, insisting that all the articles should be distinctly read out to him, admitted that the worship of the parish did not meet the standards required in numerous particulars.[27] But returns of this kind were exceptional. Much more often the bishop and archdeacons were kept in the dark for months or years on end about gross omissions and dilapidations, until a man of unusual diligence told the truth. *Omnia bene* was returned by Aldrington, for example, at four visitations in 1637 and 1638. Then, as if it had all occurred overnight, the churchwardens declared that their church 'wants paving, is unhealed, no font, no Bible of the last translation, no communion table, no cloth for it'. At Ovingdean and Maresfield the presentment implied on four occasions that the churches were adequately paved, then the officers suddenly admitted that they had not been all the while. Ministers occasionally sought a remedy for neglects of this kind by making their own presentment. A catalogue of complaints by the minister against the churchwardens of Ticehurst in 1639, for example, included their 'suffering the parrishe church to go to ruine and much decayed in lead and timber work at least in a dozen places'.[28]

By and large the rough and ready approach of the churchwardens was distinctly at odds with the ideals of the Arminians. They were puzzled, for instance, by the ecclesiastical authorities' sudden obsession with the uniformity of pews. Several of them sought to justify the status quo. Their pews were 'not all of one heigh, yet soe that they are noe hindrance to the rest', confessed the churchwardens of Warnham. 'Our pewes are decently built without any hinderance one to the other as we conceive but not uniforme', explained the Horsham officers. At North Mundham the churchwardens dodged the issue by insisting that they found 'no inconvenyence'; they declared that a pew remaining in the chancel did not encumber it. The North Mundham officers were in fact bolder than most. They also resisted Archdeacon Marsh's strict precepts about the use of consecrated ground, maintaining that the minister 'usually had the herbage of the churchyard' and they knew of 'no offence done by swyne to the graves'. They scathingly rejected the Archdeacon's suggestion that the parish clerk might have acted corruptly, with the comment that he could hardly 'medle above his office' since he could neither read nor write. West Wittering was another village which showed itself reluctant to give up the economic exploitation of the churchyard: 'cattle sometime depasture in our churchyard and so have beene usually tyme out of mind'.[29]

The unwillingness of churchwardens to abandon their low standards in the care of the church and churchyard, standards which had served for generations, enormously hindered the enforcement of the Arminian reform programme. The slackness evident among many churchwardens was deeply rooted. An additional reason for the failure of the visitation system to provide effective remedies was the collusion of the ecclesiastical bureaucracy in the abuse of the established procedures. Instead of making a personal return, churchwardens could go to court and face the perfunctory questioning of a clerk, who was anxious to collect his fees and dispose of the queue of men who had come in from their farms and fields.[30] Most churchwardens naturally took this easy way out. So rigid and formalised had the system become, that there was little chance of their being troubled to think seriously about or even grasp the meaning of every article. By the 1630s some of the clerks had established a procedure that enabled them to concentrate on the few articles most likely to elicit positive individual responses. Model presentments were prepared beforehand and numerous copies made. Thus the clerks could begin their interrogation with a presentment in front of them running to several pages, which already contained a full sentence saying that all was well in reply to more than 100 of the 115 articles. There was no pressure on churchwardens to search their minds. The blanks left open for routine matters, such as the status of the minister, the names of physicians, schoolmasters, recusants, sectaries and excommunicates, and cases of sexual immorality, were quickly filled in. The queue of churchwardens was rapidly despatched.

Between 24 September and 17 October 1640, officers from eleven parishes in Boxgrove deanery put their signatures or marks to presentments identical in format and in the same hand. These documents, together with the Storrington deanery presentments which although written by several different clerks kept close to a single model, show how adept the clerks had become at inserting such matters as the churchwardens mentioned spontaneously in the spaces they had left. When they were caught out for space, they were quite ready to make a final note which made nonsense of an earlier declaration. Thus at Compton, where Archdeacon Marsh was informed 'our church is in good repayre in every part', 'our chancel in decay', he was also told, 'is not yet repayred'. A similar contradiction cropped up at Singleton. At Birdham the assurance that all the parishioners duly attended church appeared on the same page as the presentment of a man for seldom doing so. The impact of the articles thus depended on the discretion of the bureaucracy, on men who treated writing presentments as a means of secure employment but who were not fired by enthusiasm for uniformity and reform.

Some clerks certainly were more conscientious than others. Whereas one in Storrington deanery usually asked the officers about the frequency with which parishioners had received communion, another stated before they had arrived that 'all receive accordingly'. Some were brazen in their failure to check their statements against the facts parish by parish; others ingeniously acquiesced in the increasing disuse of certain customs by tempering their confident assertions with such compromise phraseology as 'the passing bell goeth for the most'.[31] Taken as a whole the evidence is conclusive. The churchwardens themselves grossly undermined the visitation system, but it was finally made farcical by the practices of the men who wrote the majority of the presentments. The breakdown of the system was not peculiar to Sussex, though it remains uncertain how widespread were the bureaucratic abuses to be found there. In 1636 Laud received a long lament from a Buckinghamshire partisan, who stated that 'such visitations have we kept ordinarily that one may break every canon and preach against every article of the church and yet escape with commendation for it'. Two years previously, the same commentator had told the chancellor of Lincoln diocese that the churchwardens 'present usually *omnia bene* whereas there is nothing almost in order'.[32]

The earliest surviving presentments for the archdeaconry of Chichester show that in 1579 the visitation procedure was working efficiently. Virtually every parish had something to report and most parishes spontaneously presented half a dozen or so items. The records of the 1597 visitation of the diocese of Norwich indicate a similar level of effectiveness.[33] By the 1620s it was a very different story. In both of the Sussex archdeaconries the proportion of presentments containing a positive report of one or more defaults had sharply declined. The decline continued. The issue of Bishop Duppa's articles in September 1638 brought only a marginal increase in the number of positive presentments, although several new articles dealt with matters that were undoubtedly amiss in many parishes. Nor did repeated visitations within a few weeks improve the officer's response. The ecclesiastical authorities merely found themselves landed with little more than a crop of stale sexual misdemeanours. The archdeacon of Lewes only brought to light fifteen new matters requiring judicial proceedings from 150 parishes when he followed Duppa's September visitation of 1638 with his own at Michaelmas.[34] Neither the chancellor of the diocese of Chichester nor the archdeacons seem to have made any serious attempt to drive the cumbrous and rusty machinery of ecclesiastical discipline harder in the cause of Arminian reform. Elsewhere there is some evidence of more energy. Edward Mottershed, the archdeacon of Nottingham, for instance, attempted to tighten up the examination of churchwardens there in the late 1630s. But from 1639 onwards his pressure apparently met with increasing resistance from the churchwardens themselves.[35]

If reform was to be achieved, the churchwardens clearly had to be circumvented. In 1636, Bishop Montagu, using his powers under the eighty-sixth canon of 1604, issued commissions for surveys of the churches in the Chichester archdeaconry. Churchwardens' presentments, made a few weeks earlier, survive for twenty-one of the churches surveyed by the bishop's visitors. The visitors reported 202 items amiss in these churches, only a single one of which, the decay of the shingling of St Botolphs steeple, had been mentioned by the parish officers.[36] The inertia behind the endless *omnia bene's* of the previous decade is fully revealed by the 1636 church inspection book. The visitors told of dilapidation in structures, disrepair of furnishings, ragged vestments and old and torn books. Seven churches were reported to be in a serious condition: the visitors predicted the collapse of the steeples of Chidham and Stoughton and the chancels of Funtington and Washington. Twelve fonts were unusable. Numerous flagons were 'unfitting': Cocking's, Parham's and Wiggenholt's were all

D

condemned as 'like an alehouse quart pott'. At Wisborough Green the flagon was 'but a glasse bottle wherein they fetch the wine from the tavern'.[37] Few altar clothes were of the silk or 'faire cleane linen' envisaged by the bishops. They were variously described as old, moth-eaten, rotten, very unseemly and worn out. Surplices were in little better condition. Many pews were described as 'ruinous' or needing planking; some churches needed paving, plastering or their walls whiting; in others new Bibles, service books, chests for alms or even pulpits were lacking. Few parishes escaped without at least half a dozen matters to be remedied. The inspection made plain the gulf between the Arminian ideals and the rough furnishings and utensils cheerfully tolerated by the Sussex countrymen.

Their tour of inspection provided Bishop Montagu's visitors with plenty of opportunities to be caustic. At Compton, the visitor reported, 'the reading place and the pulpett stand soe weakly that the minister cannott stand steddy in either of them'. At Rogate, he noted disapprovingly, 'the minister goeth up into the pulpett upon a ladder' and at Westhampnett 'they christen in a buckett'.[38] But the way the churchwardens saw it was that repairs or replacements of any kind cost money. Faced by a torn register book, a poor surplice, a floor made uneven by graves sunk in it, they found it tempting to let the matter go another year rather than trouble themselves with the likelihood of exceeding their account and having to raise extra church rates, which never made a man popular. Windows were particularly likely to be neglected because of the expense of glazing. Churchwardens at Climping and Midhurst admitted that windows had not been repaired, 'to save charges'. Yet broken windows began a process of decay and defilement. Pigeons, let in by a smashed chancel window, were breeding in Lancing church and polluting it with their dung in 1636. The visitors directed that new windows should be made in such dark and dingy churches as North Mundham and Warningcamp, but the work and materials involved were bound to impose a considerable charge on a small parish population.[39] There were exceptions to the general slackness in upkeep of churches revealed by the 1636 inspection. At Billingshurst, for instance, the churchwardens accounts show steady expenditure during the early 1630s on repair of windows, paving and furnishings. Even here, though, the visitor's thorough survey brought to light matters needing attention. The ivy and shrubs growing in the steeple wall were seen as a potential danger to the structure; hogs were managing to squeeze between the churchyard fencing.[40]

From all over the archdeaconry churchwardens trooped to Chichester in November 1636 to answer the charges of neglect that followed the bishop's inspection. The chancellor held a long series of special sittings to enforce the improvements suggested by the visitors. Many parish officers dad hastened to put at least some of them into practice since the visiting cleric had lectured them on the new standards required. Many of them were diligent in ensuring that repairs were completed within the time allotted by the authorities until the following February. At West Chiltington, for instance, the churchwardens faced the village community at Easter 1637 with a bill for ten pounds more than the usual annual expenditure, after they had paid for a chest for alms for the poor and for rewriting the ten commandments which had been reported as illegible. Parishes that were recalcitrant in fulfilling the visitors' demands were pursued in the archdeaconry court between 1637 and 1641.[41]

During the same period the Lewes archdeaconry court was attempting to enforce the comprehensive programme of reform adumbrated in an inspection of the churches of Lewes deanery, which had also been made in about 1636. At Cowfold, where two men did four days carpentry in 1637 and further work the following year, a special landscot of five pounds for 'charges extraordinary' was imposed. Even then the court was not satisfied. The churchwarden was cited for 'default of reparations' in 1638 and for 'the default of the pannells' the next year. More money was spent on repairs to leading and windows and for paving in 1640 and 1641.[42] Much was certainly achieved in enforcing the adornment and beautifying of church interiors in the western deaneries before the collapse of ecclesiastical jurisdiction on the eve of the civil war. Archbishop Neile of York used the same processes with striking success in the restoration of Nottinghamshire churches between 1635 and 1640. In the archdeaconry of Buckingham also, considerable improvements in church fabric and furnishings were achieved at this time by a combination of inspections and court proceedings.[43] In the far east of Sussex, on the other hand, the implementation of the inspection procedure seems to have been so long delayed that glaring deficiencies must have remained at the fall of the Arminian regime in the church. Only a few months before the Long Parliament met, Christopher Dowe was still busy visiting churches in Hastings and Dallington deaneries.[44] Arminianism crumbled at the centre as he tried to bring the churchwardens of the Battle district to heel.

In so far as the county resisted the Arminian restoration of churches it did so largely on grounds of cost. The same kind of economic realism lay behind its stubbornness in the face of the attempt, initiated by the Elizabethan and Jacobean bishops and persisted in by the Arminians, to eradicate the profaning of the sabbath and of holy days by agricultural labour. Men were regularly presented in the church courts for ploughing, driving beasts, cocking hay, turning peas or reaping wheat on the sabbath, and there were probably many other offenders to whom the churchwardens turned a blind eye.[45] No disrespect was usually intended. Indeed sabbath workers were seldom alleged to have missed the day's services. But the Worth man who, looking to the skies, took his servants out to bring in a load of oats on an uncertain and rainy Sunday evening after the service acted from simple common sense in refusing to wait for the morrow. A Yapton man rationalised this sort of attitude in 1623 by maintaining that 'the people need not to bee so strict and careful in keeping the sabbath day, for it is abolysed, and that every day in the weeke is a Christian's sabbath'. So far as holy days were concerned, the opinion seems to have been generally held that these irritating interruptions of the working week could be safely disregarded, particularly at the busiest times of the farming year such as harvest. Three substantial Chichester mercers who regularly kept open their shops on holy days defied the ecclesiastical authorities in the knowledge that the community supported them.[46]

The habit of regular churchgoing was never successfully inculcated into all the poorer inhabitants of Stuart England. Moreover when they did appear the more religiously apathetic members of society tended to turn public worship into a travesty of the ideal that Montagu and Duppa set out in their visitation articles.[47] There were Sussex worshippers who spewed and farted, who played cards and scales, who jostled, pinched and stuck pins in each other and who talked or sang rudely and out of turn. A Slaugham man beat his wife during divine service; a Balcombe man let his bitch give birth on the pew beside him. Numerous parishioners slept their way through prayers and sermons and some did not take kindly to being awoken: a Ewhurst girl picked up a paving stone and hurled it at the person who nudged her, a Catsfield man requited the youth who caused him to stir 'with a sound blowe ment at his head with a cudgell'.[48] Schoolboy behaviour, in this kind of unruly atmosphere, was liable to run riot. The churchwarden of Laughton related the disgraceful behaviour of two youths one Sunday in 1637. They

> did seate themselves in the seate of Sir Thomas Pelham baronet, being the upmost seate in our church, and there in a very uncivill and jearing kinde of manner, did in time of divine service take upon them one to be the master and the other man, and so lay peeping over the top of the seate, till prayers were ended, to the offence of the congregation. And as soone as prayers were ended, they in a very uncivill and violent manner did fling open the seate dore, and came grinning and laughing out of the said seate, as it were vaunting themselves in theire uncivill acte.[49]

Churchwardens did what they could, by presenting incidents of this kind, to combat irreverence and rowdiness on holy ground. But the ecclesiastical sanctions could not change the life style of the lower orders. Substantial householders sometimes turned to the secular arm, in the hope that fiercer punishments would tame men's boorishness. Thus, in 1616, some Lindfield parishioners called in the local JPs to have a man who disturbed their minister by 'singing unreverently' put in the stocks.[50] There is no evidence that the Arminian episcopate achieved any more than its predecessors in raising standards of behaviour in church.

Nor were Montagu and Duppa any more successful than their predecessors in eliminating pluralism and non-residence in the diocese or the neglect by clergy of certain of their spiritual duties.[51] The reading of the litany on weekdays, for example, was still often omitted.[52] They were less concerned than some Elizabethan and Jacobean bishops to enforce monthly sermons.[53] Yet Montagu could not eradicate the Puritan practice that he heartily disliked of a sermon on Sunday afternoons as well as Sunday mornings instead of a period of catechising. John Pym noted punishment 'for preaching on the Lords Day in the afternoon' as one of the innovations resented by the gentry in his speech at the opening of the Long Parliament.[54] Nor could Montagu and Duppa enforce the uncritical response to sermons they envisaged in their visitation articles. Provocative or boring preachers were likely to find themselves openly challenged. A Treyford man told the minister his sermon was 'nothing but of a dead hog'; a Fittleworth man told the village priest he 'cared not a fart for him'.[55] The cumulative weaknesses of the Church were too formidable, the independence of Protestant parishioners was too deeply ingrained, for the Arminian bishops to achieve more than a fraction of what they intended between 1628 and 1641.

It remains to assess the overall clerical and lay reaction to the enforcement of Arminianism in Sussex. So far as matters of worship were concerned, the clergy showed deference, but no enthusiasm, when Sir Nathaniel Brent visited Chichester, Arundel and Lewes in the course of his metropolitical visitation of 1635. At Chichester, the chapter agreed to buy new copes, and William Speed, the rector of St Pancras, who 'confessed his error in being too popular in the pulpit', undertook to have the gallery in his church removed. At Lewes, four Puritan ministers declared, against their consciences to be sure and only in order to escape suspension, that they would observe the law of the Church over bowing at the name of Jesus. At Arundel, Brent inhibited three Puritan ministers from preaching. But these were merely temporary intrusions. John Albery's 'violent extemporary prayer' in the street at Arundel, that the town 'should be delivered from the persecution that was now coming upon them', was unnecessary. It was easy, once the metropolitical visitation was over, for clergy to resume their old ways. The tastes of local gentry, the inclinations of parishioners and the conditions of local society remained the decisive influences on the forms of worship employed from village to village. At Rotherfield, for example, a large and dispersed parish with a populace intent above all on hearing the preaching of the word, John Large accommodated himself to the people by providing a 'double taste' in the morning: he 'seldome or never', he said, 'preached lesse then neare two houres whereby those which dwelt farre off might have benefitte of the whole dayes exercise as well as those neare adjoyning'.[56]

The Sussex gentry are unlikely to have taken Brent's orders any more seriously than men of rank did in Buckinghamshire. When a JP there learnt from an Arminian cleric that it was intended that the Archbishop's orders should be 'duly and punctually and generally kept', he expressed amazement: 'for', he declared, 'I doe assure you neyther clergiemen nor laymen (if they bee gentlemen, or men of any wealth) do keepe them, but laugh and jeere at them'.[57] The gentry were well placed to undermine the Arminian reform movement. If they ignored directions about bowing and kneeling, the parish would probably follow their lead. The powerlessness of the church courts against county magnates who as lay rectors failed to fulfil their obligations in the repair of chancels is an example of how things stood. Thus in June 1637 the archdeaconry court was still trying to bring Sir Thomas Bowyer to book over the dilapidated state of Hunston chancel, which had been reported the previous autumn. Other defaulters over chancels, who had been noted in the 1636 inspection, included Sir John Leeds, Sir Edward Bellingham and Sir William Goring of Burton. At Billingshurst the communion table stood at that time in Mr Goring's chancel. The recommendation by the bishop's visitor suggests that he expected difficulties with the lay patron: 'it were fittest to remove it into the parish chauncell, except Mr Goring will give way to have it sett at the upper end of his chauncell and to remove his seats which stand about it'.[58]

Interference with private pewbuilding also brought out the gentry's latent anticlericalism. Elaborate pews were a much cherished public expression of gentry opulence and prestige, and an ostentation which parishioners generally accepted, though when a Maresfield gentleman removed some public seats to erect his own pew which he subsequently kept locked there was a parish outcry.[59] Yet Sir Edward Bishop was directed to reduce the size of the pew for his servants at Parham, merely because it was too close to the communion table. The survival of Christopher Dowe's order to the Heathfield churchwardens to make Thomas Taylor's pew uniform with the rest in the sessions rolls suggests that the Bench may have discussed the challenge to lay independence which it implied.[60] In Buckinghamshire some gentry capitulated to the demand for uniform pews while others showed firm passive resistance.[61] The question of secular uses of consecrated ground raised the same kind of issues. 'Wee cannot conceive or imagin', wrote Mark Thomas the deputy mayor of Rye in 1637, seeking to justify the use of consecrated ground for the town's arsenal, 'that any would be so bold to adventure to sequester to use and employ the chancel, but by order from some Lord Bishop of Chichester . . . for good cause and consideration then shewed for the sufferinge and allowinge of it'. Besides, he pointed out, when Bishop Lancelot Andrewes had visited Rye some years previously he had made no objection. Thomas shrugged off a further charge that the church was profaned by being used as a place of punishment with the explanation that it was a convenient place for the whipping of the town's unruly servants and boys. He gave no undertaking that the practice would cease.[62]

The placing of communion tables altar-wise, behind rails at the east end of parish churches, became the touchstone of Arminianism, and it was this which in the end brought open conflict in Sussex between the gentry and the episcopal party. The furore over altars was still in the future when

Montagu issued his 1628 articles. He merely directed that the table should be 'placed conveniently'. It was the metropolitical visitation which brought the Privy Council's 1633 ruling that parishes should adopt the new altar-wise arrangement, by then general in cathedrals, before the nation as a whole.[63] At Lewes, in July 1635, Sir Nathaniel Brent 'willed all the churchwardens to looke upon the rayle which incompassed the communion table in the sayd church of St Thomas in the Cliffe, where they were, and to take that for their pattern, telling them that it was very comely and decent'.[64] Bishop Duppa and his archdeacons reiterated the new policy in their visitation articles between 1638 and 1641.

The churchwardens complied slowly and grudgingly with the new requirements. The clutter that filled chancels was a disincentive to action, and there were vested interests in some places behind the status quo. At Wartling, for instance, the Hart family, who claimed to own 'two great joyned seats' which encumbered the chancel, held up its final conversion to the new dispensation until at least 1638. The expenses of carpentry, and particularly of the turning of a 'hansome raile', tempted parish officers to drag their heels. 'Worke about the communion tabell' at Cuckfield in 1637 cost the parish more than six pounds.[65] When the survey of 1636 was made, at least thirty-four parishes in the Chichester archdeaconry had not even accomplished the first step towards the Arminian ideal, the clearing of chancels of irrelevant furniture. At West Chiltington and Greatham large chests were still as prominent as the table itself; at Horsham the seats surrounding the table used by communicants were still in place; at Itchingfield seats remained behind the table, against the east wall. Moreover thc visitors found twenty-four altars without satisfactory railing and they complained of tables which were still wrongly placed or were rotten and unseemly.[66]

A good many parishes seem to have been driven to complete the work by the judicial campaign following the 1636 inspections. The Billingshurst and West Chiltington churchwardens in the Chichester archdeaconry and the Cuckfield and Cowfold officers in the deanery of Lewes recorded the relevant charges in their accounts.[67] In the far east of the county, where no inspection of churches was held until 1640, there was undoubtedly more protracted resistance to the moving and railing of communion tables than in west Sussex or than in some other counties such as Buckinghamshire. Churchwardens in the Lewes archdeaconry presented sixteen altars that were not railed between Easter 1637 and Easter 1639. A few parishes may even have been holding out against the Arminian altar policy when the Short Parliament met. At Udimore, for example, the table was not even placed as late as March 1639.[68] Certainly this aspect of the Arminian revolution was barely completed in Sussex by the end of the decade.

Sheer inertia accounts for much of the resistance to the Arminians' policy over placing and railing altars. Some villages prevaricated, others provided a range of ingenious excuses. 'Wee have not a raile but wee will make one against Easter', promised Falmer early in 1638, a year later nothing had been done. 'Wee purpose to have all things orderly done with all convenient speed', declared Whatlington at Michaelmas 1638, yet the following February, appearing before the archdeaconry court, the churchwardens merely repeated their assurances.[69] Beckley took its stand in 1639 on the 'want of fitting and seasonable materials'. The railing would be undertaken 'as soone as we can get timber convenient for the same', pleaded Iden in September 1638. The Brede churchwardens maintained disingenuously the same month that they were 'willing to new raile the table about, so soone as wee shall have order from the court for the manner of doing it'. The same court heard a long tale of woe about the cost of making the changes from the decayed port of Winchelsea. There was not even an ascent for the altar there since the seats for the mayor and jurats stood between it and the east end of the chancel. The charge, apologised the officers, 'in removing the seate, placing the altar, severing the chancel from the church and paving and beautifying the chancell wil bee so great, besides the annuall charge, that the parishe is neither able, neither willing to undergo it'. They had the audacity to request time to obtain a brief for a charitable collection to cover the work.[70] In certain Puritan parishes the procrastination was probably quite deliberate. 'Our communion table stands in the midst of the chancell and without rales', admitted the Chiddingly churchwardens in 1638. 'Our communion table standeth where it formerly stood tyme out of mynde', the Rye churchwardens had stated defiantly two years before. Balcombe, which was dominated by the Puritan Spence family, was another village where no attempt was made to comply with the visitation articles. The churchwardens' plea that in any case they had 'no roome' to rail the altar about was hardly convincing.[71] One churchwarden, John Parmely of St Michael's, Lewes, offered the authorities open defiance. Chancellor Nevill, holding court in Parmely's church in July 1637, had the table placed in the Arminian position and declared that 'no man should presume to remove or alter the same'. But Parmely later visited the church at night and moved the altar back to its old position. He seems to have lacked the general support enjoyed by the Beckington churchwardens in Somerset, since, when he was charged before Nevill, he apparently accepted the court's ruling.[72]

The stress laid by the Arminian bishops on the leadership given to the Puritan movement in Sussex by a group of JPs has already been noted. In 1636 Archbishop Laud heard the same story of lay initiative behind resistance to Arminian policies from a Buckinghamshire correspondent, who complained that his clerical colleagues were 'wonderful timorous', because 'the clergie in theyse parts are overawed by the justices and lay gentry'.[73] Although there was no sustained Arminian campaign against Puritan nonconformity in Sussex of the kind that occurred in Cheshire, East Anglia and the diocese of York, the Puritan gentry were shocked by the programme of Montagu and Duppa into a total rethinking of their attitude towards episcopacy.[74] A radical party emerged on the Bench and among the gentry in the late 1630s determined to counter the Arminian innovations in the Church. Their first initiative, a dramatic one, came in 1639. James Rivers, John Baker and Herbert Hay, the ringleaders of a Puritan clique, persuaded Anthony Stapley of Patcham, who shared their bitterness against the Arminian episcopate, to include an outspoken attack on the ecclesiastical establishment in his opening speech as chairman of the Michaelmas sessions. Stapley used the sessions platform to challenge Laud's altar policy. 'Some prelates in this kingdom', he maintained, showing that he was well informed about the stand taken by Bishop Williams of Lincoln, 'did not approve of it'. But Stapley was on delicate ground. He had no authority to interfere in a matter of ecclesiastical jurisdiction. His colleague William White, indeed, at once questioned 'what he meant to meddle with those businesses ther, which the Bench had nothing to doe withall'.[75]

Stapley's outburst merely heightened the tension between the factions on the Bench. In February 1641 the radical Puritans, led by the knights of the shire Sir Thomas Pelham and Anthony Stapley, presented a root and branch petition to parliament in the name of the county.[76] Although it is likely that there were many gentry who at this stage disapproved of so extreme a measure as the abolition of episcopacy, there was no open conflict between gentry factions over the petition of the kind that occurred in counties such as Nottinghamshire, Cheshire and Somerset.[77] There was at least general support among the gentry community for the way things were moving. The Arminians were removed from the Bench by a parliamentary order of August 1641 and during 1641 and 1642 the diocesan administrative machine ground to a halt.[78] The abolition of the Court of High Commission, which had recently excommunicated two Sussex gentlemen for assaulting a priest, was greeted by the MPs for Rye as a move that 'cannot be but of great contentment to the subjecte'.[79] The death of Richard Montagu in April deprived the Commons of the chance to pursue him along with other notorious Arminians such as Matthew Wren. In February 1642 the Sussex gentry expressed their gratitude to the Commons by petition for its dismantling of the Arminian regime and for 'the much freedome we enjoy in our consciences and livelihoods, defending us from the violent cruelties and formidable power of the prelates and their courts'.[80] Arminianism, probably more than any other single issue, had hardened many gentry, particularly those of a Puritan cast of mind, against Charles I, his court and his régime.

5

Catholicism and fear of popery

There is now of late come to our towne to dwell one Mr Abington with his wife sonne and daughter all papists . . . wee desire not the company of any of that religion, if possibly we may lawfully avoid them.
The Mayor and Jurats of Rye to the Lord Warden, 10 March 1624.[1]

Our humble desires are that . . . papists may be totally disarmed, their persons confined, their subtile conveyances of their estates discovered and presented . . . the masse utterly abolished.
The Sussex Petition, February 1642.[2]

Catholicism in England between the accession of Elizabeth and the Restoration was essentially a seigneurial religion. Its survival depended on the unity and independence, the traditions of hospitality and the social dominance of a neighbourhood of numerous gentry households which were geographically scattered but linked by bonds of kinship and spiritual affinity. Elizabethan Catholicism has been characterised as 'a set of ingrained observances which defined and gave meaning to the cycle of the week and the seasons of the year, to birth, marriage and death'.[3] After 1603 there was a movement within the Catholic community, based on these habitual household devotions, 'towards the monastic, the contemplative and the quietistic'.[4] At the same time, as a precaution against conviction for recusancy, the husband often continued to attend services in the parish church.[5] The Catholic gentry of Elizabethan Sussex had exhibited a bewildering variety of kinds of occasional conformity: some attended church 'once a moneth or nowe and then', but refused to take the oath of supremacy, communicate or have their children baptised in church; others took the oath and came to church regularly but would not communicate, others again observed 'all thinge commanded but yet are feared that they be notable papists, howe they be dispenst withall God doth know'.[6] Between 1581 and 1640 many Catholics capitulated to government pressure. Only six of the eleven leading Catholic gentry families of late Elizabethan Sussex appear to have remained devoted to the old faith on the eve of the civil war.[7] The Catholic community certainly became more clearly identifiable between 1603 and 1640. It became a clustered community with a fringe of ageing couples and widows who were isolated but faithful. Yet occasional conformity still persisted and while it did so the extent and power of the popish clique within the county remained uncertain and alarming. There were still Catholic gentry in these decades who regarded attendance at church as a mere formality, something that did not properly associate them with the Protestant Church; they saw it as a social duty that did not conflict with the religious routine of their households.

From 1603 churchwardens had a statutory duty to report cases of recusancy to both the diocesan authorities and to the JPs, while constables also retained their standing orders to present recusants at sessions and assizes. Moreover a Jacobean statute compelled attendance at communion as well as matins.[8] Despite an inducement of two pounds for every conviction obtained through their information, many churchwardens were as inert in this matter as in everything else required of them and constables were often scarcely more energetic. A Buckinghamshire minister who reminded his churchwardens of their obligation to collect fines from those wilfully absent from church found himself derided: 'they sayd the would not incurr the hatred of the gentlemen and neighbours for any priest's sayings whatsoever'.[9] Presentment was an erratic and uncertain business, apart from during the periodic anti-Catholic drives by the JPs. Analysis of presentments for the archdeaconry of Chichester and its associated peculiars to five assizes between 1624 and 1628 reveals that 552 individuals were reported as recusants, yet the highest total on a single occasion was 300 people and the average was only 249.[10] There were obviously many Catholics living in western Sussex during these years who escaped presentment on several occasions. The inefficiency of the presentment system was partly due to uncertainty, perhaps deliberately propagated by the Catholics themselves, about the precise legal definition of recusancy. While gentry hoodwinked them with excuses, the local officers groped after an interpretation of recusancy in terms of actual refusal to attend divine service. There was a general hesitancy about making presentments and a desire to clarify their meaning. The Wisborough Green gentleman Thomas Smith and his family, explained the churchwardens in 1640, neither attended the public services nor received communion. In the same year the Racton papists were said 'never to come to church' and the East Grinstead Catholics were presented 'for that they totally absent themselves from church'. 'He hath not received the sacrament for five years, whether a recusant or not I refer it to your judgement', noted the tithingman of Stedham in 1625 about William Coldham.[11]

Erratic enforcement and the persistence of occasional conformity make it hard to assess the incidence of recusancy in Sussex. The map on page 96 showing major and minor centres of recusancy is based on the 1620s assize lists, the 1626 subsidy certificate and presentations in the sessions rolls for 1625, 1641, 1657 and 1658. At the major centres at least

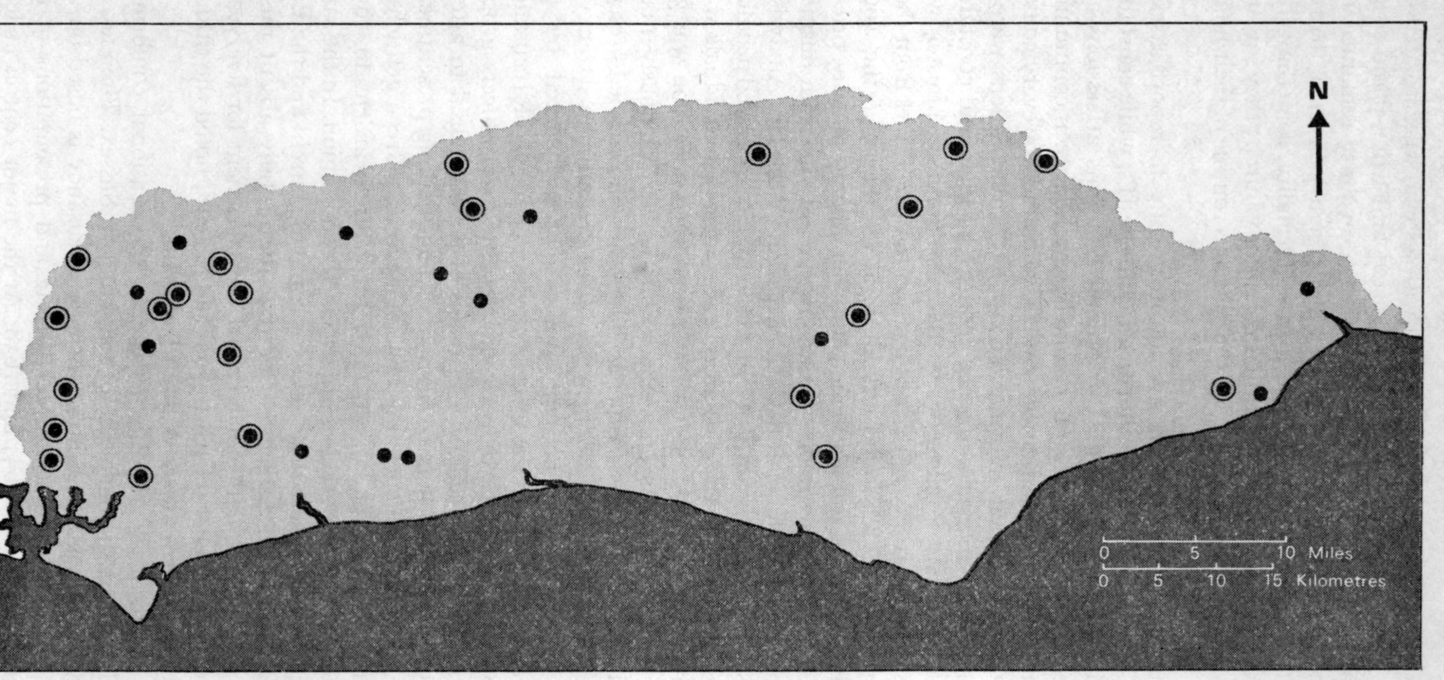

10 Centres of recusancy, 1624-1658

ten recusants are recorded, at the minor ones at least four. The sources used for this map are not exactly comparable, but they provide some indication of the distribution of the Catholic population. The subsidy references relate to men who had been previously convicted as recusants, whereas the sessions presentations were the immediate outcome of a series of campaigns by the JPs to eradicate popery in the county.[12] The drive of 1657 and 1658 represented a rapid and vigorous response to the act of 26 June 1657 which put the conviction of recusants on a new basis, a basis which had been foreshadowed as long previously as 1643.[13] The constables were charged with presenting men 'suspected or reputed to be papists or popishly affected'; the Bench then summoned them to appear and take the oath of abjuration, which was more strongly worded than the Jacobean oath of allegiance and included denials of the main points of Catholic doctrine as well as the Pope's supremacy. On their failure to do so and the oath of the constable that the warrant had been duly delivered they were convicted.[14] By receiving the initial presentments at petty sessions and issuing warrants for the next quarter sessions the justices were able to complete the procedure in a few weeks. The Catholics presented invariably defaulted and were convicted. Thus the abandonment of compulsion to attend church enabled the tangles of occasional conformity to be cut through by the adoption of a new criterion of recusancy. In Sussex 222 recusants were brought to book in less than a year. How rigorously the new Act was enforced there and how far it was enforced at all outside Sussex is not clear, but its importance has certainly been unduly neglected. By and large the map confirms the established view that west Sussex remained much more strongly Catholic than east. In some downland villages of Chichester rape, such as Up Marden, Catholic households may have accounted for up to forty per cent of the population.[15]

Some Catholic families isolated themselves totally from the parish community, others kept a stake in it, seeking to maintain contacts, exert pressure and protect the religious inviolability of their homes. On the one hand there were families like the Lewkenors of Slinfold, 'whoes names' reported the churchwardens in 1640 'wee knowe not neither can wee learne', the Thatchers, whose servants' names were unknown to the local officers, and the Crispes, whose servants' surnames neither the subsidy collector in 1628 nor the headborough in 1641 could discover.[16] At the other extreme there was Sir Henry Compton of Brambletye. Compton was the head of a household celebrated in the neighbourhood for its Catholicism, yet with remarkable aplomb he maintained his personal immunity throughout the period, from the early 1620s until 1642, when he was active as a justice and deputy lieutenant.[17] In both 1640 and 1641 his wife, children and servants were presented as recusants. Finally, in the tense atmosphere of the summer of 1642, Sir Henry himself was presented for failure to attend communion for a whole year, while his family were once more reported as recusants. Even then he was an audacious man who dared to imply that such a pillar of the county establishment was a Catholic at heart.[18]

The case of Sir Garrett Kempe, which was investigated at length by the County Committee in 1649, illustrates the difficulties faced by the authorities in convicting a slippery church papist. Kempe had escaped presentment at Slindon ever since, aged twenty-one, he inherited his father's estate in 1597. He had regularly attended matins, and villagers recalled that he had once or twice received the sacrament around 1620. Nevertheless 'the general report of the countrey is that he is a papist', declared a Slindon woman in 1649. It was thought 'by most that he did goe to church to save his lands', admitted John Newland, who had been Kempe's servant for forty years. The Committee at Chichester sequestered Kempe's lands in 1643 and insisted that as a popish delinquent he was one of those exempted from composition. They noted that Kempe, as they believed, resorted to church 'to avoyd the penaltie of the lawes', that 'he hath bene alwayes reputed a church papist' and that he 'hath bred up all his children papists'.[19] They were wrong in fact about the education of his heir Philip Kempe. Despite pressure from Catholic kin and friends, Sir Garrett had sent him to school in Chichester and elsewhere 'under several protestant ministers'. 'His father did very often urge and perswade him to goe to the protestant churches', testified Philip Kempe and the servant Newland remembered how he had heard his master 'often in discourse with Mr Cox the minister of Slindon wish that his said sone would be brought to come to church'.[20] Sir Garrett Kempe hoped to maintain the family tradition of occasional conformity, although after the 1620s this practice was coming to be looked on with increasing disfavour within the Catholic community.[21] His achievement in maintaining his own immunity for so long was remarkable. The Committee's case came to rest on the slender evidence of alleged failure to attend communion for thirty years, a failure which had never led to his indictment, and on the fact that he had been charged double as a reputed papist in the taxes of 1642. The force of this evidence was reduced when John Newland, who paid his master's taxes for him, admitted that he could neither read nor write 'but that he ever payd what was demanded'. In 1650 Sir Garrett was discharged from sequestration 'not appearing to be a papist'.[22]

Sussex Catholicism was concentrated around the estates of families like the Kempes at Slindon, the Thatchers at Priesthawes in Westham, the Gages at Firle, the Shelleys at Michelgrove in Clapham and the Carylls at Ladyholt in Harting.[23] Once gentry support was lacking in a parish the recusant tradition quickly failed. Thus at Battle, a hotbed of popery in the 1590s when Lady Montagu made it a vigorous centre of Catholic worship, a mere six recusants survived in 1626.[24] When they moved, recusant gentry gravitated to each other. The Threeles, for example, abandoned their lonely outpost just outside the Puritan town of Rye in the 1640s in favour of Rotherfield, where the Marsh and Middlemore families were long established as Catholics.[25] Of the 168 people presented as recusants in the eastern division of the county in 1641, 139 lived in one of the centres of rural Catholicism that appear on the map on page 96.[26] Time and again a pocket of recusancy turns out to have consisted of a large gentry establishment with its village dependants. At Harting in 1625, for instance, Sir John Caryll and his wife were presented with eleven servants. The Whithingtons at Slindon, who were constantly presented, were gentry dependants of Sir Garrett Kempe.[27] The only urban community where any kind of persistent recusant tradition flourished in the seventeenth century was Chichester. Twenty-seven people were treated as convicted recusants in the assessment of the 1626 subsidy there.[28] This tight-knit Catholic group enjoyed the leadership until 1627 of the celebrated and much respected doctor John Bullaker and thereafter it retained the support of the substantial Peacock and Lewkenor families.[29]

Elizabethan Catholicism in Sussex had taken its strength and inspiration above anyone else from the leadership of the first Viscount Montagu who lived at Cowdray Park. Here Queen Elizabeth herself had been entertained by a man whom the Queen held in complete trust despite his papist beliefs.[30] Although Montagu's heirs never enjoyed the national or local standing he had obtained, their patronage kept a flourishing Catholic community alive in the village of Easebourne and its market town of Midhurst across the Rother. Furthermore the significance of Cowdray in providing protection and regular opportunities for sacramental worship to Catholics of the wider neighbourhood emerges strikingly from the map of recusant centres. The total number of recusants presented in the two parishes between 1620 and 1660 was invariably higher than anywhere else in Sussex: 123 at Midhurst alone in 1625, 120 in 1628 and 129 in 1641, eighty-one at Midhurst and Easebourne together in 1657.[31] There alone in the whole county a group of sixteen people actually refused in 1641 on principle to make any contribution whatever for the relief of the Irish Protestants.[32] The Oath of Protestation, which the recusants living in and around Cowdray Park found themselves faced with the following February, was designedly a political test aimed at pockets of potential disaffection just such as this. All males over eighteen were to swear acceptance of 'the true protestant religion expressed in the doctrine of the church of England against all popery'. At Midhurst fifty-four men initially refused to take the Protestation on 18 February, but two days later thirty-five of them capitulated, perhaps at the persuasion of John Phage, a qualified doctor of some influence in the town whose moderate views on Catholic cooperation with the Protestant state are suggested by his having taken oaths in the church courts for the practice of medicine.[33] At Easebourne fourteen recusants who could not in conscience take the Protestation oath as it stood swore to it in a modified form without the religious clause.[34]

The secular clergy in Sussex were numerous and well organised. A letter of 1631 carries the signatures of the archdeacon, two rural deans and six other priests.[35] The rapid expansion of the Jesuit mission after 1600, together with the emergence of an English Benedictine mission, made it easier for leading Catholic gentry, especially those who lived near the south coast, to acquire the services of priests for their households.[36] The Carylls certainly had a resident chaplain for some while during James I's reign. The churchwardens at Midhurst did their best to keep track of priests who slipped quietly in and out of Cowdray. Mr Oxenbridge 'thought to be a priest' was presented in 1625 and 'George Fortescue whome wee suppose a priest' was mentioned in the presentment of 1628.[37] The Lancing churchwardens presented a suspected priest in 1625, living with Sir Richard and Lady Mullenor 'under colour of teaching her children French'.[38] Catholic gentry often made special provision for the secular clergy on whom their household devotions depended. In 1634 John Arismendy, a servant to Viscount Montagu, left twenty pounds for the maintenance of a priest to administer the sacrament to the 'poor catholikes of Midhurst', with the obligation 'to say two masses every weeke for my soule and my Lord's auncestours'.[39] John Thatcher set aside money in the 1640s for the education of seminarians, for the upkeep of the family chapel at his remote marshland home at Priesthawes and for a chantry priest there.[40] John Caryll specified in 1671 that one of the priests supported by £600 he had put aside was to be chaplain at the family's West Grinstead home, while the other two were to be 'riding missionaries' from village to village in Sussex and Hampshire.[41] Although these resident and peripatetic clergy provided the children with a grounding in the faith, most Catholic gentry expected to board their sons and daughters for much of their youth. Sir Garrett Kempe, for instance, sent his second son to be educated at Harting in the home of the boy's grandfather Sir John Caryll, his third son he placed with the Jesuit schoolmaster Mr Polwheele and his daughters he lodged with papist kin in London.[42]

From about the 1570s Catholic magnates began increasingly to choose wives of their own faith. In the long run this practice was to cut them off from the mainstream of the English landed classes. Sir Garrett Kempe's mother was a daughter of Sir Edward Gage of Firle; he himself, as we have seen, married a daughter of Sir John Caryll. The children of the second Viscount Montagu married into the Paulet, Arundell, Petre and Somerset families.[43] The paucity of Catholic gentry at home led Sussex papists to look further afield. Thus Sir Thomas Gage married into the Chamberlaynes of Sherborne Castle, Oxfordshire, and his sister married a Petre. One of the Thatchers, a grandson of Sir Edward Gage, found his wife among the recusant Treshams of Rushton, Northamptonshire.[44] There was also a tendency among Catholics to entrust their estates and the care of their children to men of their own faith. Sir John Gage, for example, handed over responsibility at his death to a group of Catholics which included his 'noble friend' Sir Henry Compton, John Thatcher, John

Caryll, the Buckinghamshire recusant Augustine Belson and the Kentish recusant Thomas Pordage.[45] Yet it would be a mistake to assume that a man like Gage was totally ostracised by his magnate neighbours. The Pelhams, indeed, did not disdain him. In the summer of 1630 Sir Thomas called the local fiddlers to Halland when Lady Gage paid a social call; soon after he bought a goshawk from Sir John Gage.[46] Nor were Catholics entirely excluded from local government. Sir John Caryll was active with his Protestant colleagues in assessing the 1626 subsidy for Dumpford hundred and in 1628 he was nominated to a commission on martial law.[47] Sir John Shelley and Sir Garrett Kempe were commissioners for sewers in the 1620s.[48] Whatever suspicions the gentry community may have harboured against the Catholics in its midst, it was normally ready to put class solidarity before anti-Catholic sentiment. In 1652 John Apsley of Pulborough, a Protestant barrister whose father and grandfather had been staunch Catholics, confessed that he had been a 'familliar friend' to Sir John Shelley and had acted for his papist neighbour over his son's marriage agreement in 1634.[49] When Thomas Threele became the centre of rumours of a popish plot in 1640, the local JP William White warmly commended him to the government in London as a man known in the locality for his 'faire and honest carryage'.[50]

The ravages of fortune brought about by sequestration in the 1640s faced Catholic gentry with a dilemma. Some, holding firm to their faith, sought to cling ever more closely to their papist kin and friends. 'When he was forth of London' during the 1640s, Sir Garrett Kempe's servant related, his master had 'bin at the houses of Sir John Caryll and the Lady Shelly two notorious papists'. It was Caryll's son in fact who, by putting in security for £3,000 and by petitioning, eventually secured the release of Kempe's estates from sequestration. John Caryll also led a campaign to obtain the release of the lands of the Gages of Framfield from sequestration, after the Committee attempted to stay the rents of William Gage's widow.[51] The other possible response to economic difficulties was to make some compromise over questions of faith in the interests of the security and continuity of the family properties. Thus Sir Thomas Gage broke decisively with his family's practice by appointing Protestant executors and even a Protestant guardian for his eldest son and heir. Through his friendship with the influential downland gentleman Francis Selwyn Gage assured his son a strong voice at county level, at the cost of the abandonment of the tradition of an exclusively Catholic upbringing.[52]

In general the county community managed to live in peace and even friendship with its Catholic members in the decades before the civil war. The anti-Catholicism on which men had been bred since the Armada and the Gunpowder Plot was normally latent but in a political crisis it was easily awakened. Englishmen had learnt through homilies, sermons and pamphlets that Catholicism was 'politically seditious, morally evil and doctrinally damnable'. England, in the Foxeian tradition, was the Elect

Nation; the Pope was antichrist; the battle was seen in apocalyptic terms.[53] Every 5 November the bells of parish churches from the Downs to the Weald rang out a reminder of the country's survival and of its manifest destiny.[54] There were particular reasons for the Sussex JPs to be sensitive to the Catholic menace. In the first place, there were more Catholics there than in most counties. According to one list there were 960 convictions for recusancy in Sussex between 1625 and 1641. This record must surely be incomplete, but it probably provides a fair indication of the ranking of counties. Only Hampshire, Middlesex, Monmouthshire and Warwickshire convictions exceeded those for Sussex.[55] When certain counties 'most stored with papists and in that respect most dangerous' were selected for immediate attention in the disarming of recusants in November 1641, Sussex was among those chosen.[56] Secondly there was the obvious vulnerability of the county to foreign invasion. Fear of attempts at invasion in conjunction with domestic plots was an important element in the coastal population's dread of Catholicism. Panics about Catholic activity along the coast in 1596 and 1619 were related to invasion rumours. In the first instance a servant of the recusant Darells of Scotney Castle went through Sussex and Kent 'with an alarum that the Spaniards were landed at three places in Sussex, had burned Bourne and Pemsey—and could not be stayed'.[57] The Council showed its awareness of Sussex's accessibility to invaders in 1615 when it reminded the lord lieutenantss that it was a county that 'ought above all others to be sound and inhabited with people best affected'.[58] Finally, gentry with responsibility for order in the shire could well appreciate the dangers inherent in the pattern of estate recusancy. The identity of magnate householders and their dependants, the ease with which clergy could pass unnoticed as tutors or servants, the physical isolation and impenetrability of estates such as Firle, Ladyholt and Brambletye made the Catholic presence more alarming than mere numbers would suggest.

Despite all these good reasons for anxiety, men in authority generally proved cool and level-headed when alarms occurred. The arrest and imprisonment of John Isack of Firle, who had been foolish enough to say in public that 'he would sooner take the part of the Pope or the King of Spain then of the King of England', was a sensible precaution against the circulation of treasonous talk. The Lewes JP Richard Amherst took the subsequent story that the Gages had 'six or seven cart load of arms in their house in a secret place' for the idle tale that it was, but the mayor of Hastings, treating the news more warily, sent the Lewes butcher who had carried the story along the coast before the Privy Council.[59] Neither the mayor of Rye nor the neighbouring justice William White gave credence to the 'timorous fantasies' of three boys who reported seeing thirty-one men armed with muskets driving up kine, shooting at conies and drilling in the fields below Thomas Threele's house at Leasam outside Rye in September 1640. The colourful imaginations of lads who had imbibed the anti-Catholic propaganda of the time had turned the servants and tenants of a local recusant gentleman into popish conspirators. The Puritan town buzzed with rumours about the activities of a man who lived less than a mile beyond the walls, but kept himself and his family apart from its affairs. But the mayor acted quickly to scotch the rumour-mongering, with a proclamation that all the stories were untrue 'whereby we conceive Mr Threele is grievously injured'. 'I am confident that there was no such thing', declared White in a letter to the Earl of Arundel. He explained that Threele's fields were clearly visible to townsmen crossing the Rye ferry, which had been busy on the Saturday evening in question, and no one gave support to the boys' tales.[60]

The county community was altogether more suspicious of papist newcomers than of Catholic families well known and long respected in the shire. In 1615 the deputy-lieutenants drew the attention of the Council to the arrival of recusants who had recently 'planted themselves' near the coast, such as the Crispes at Ore and the Roots family at Guestling.[61] The intolerant reaction of the corporation of Rye to the arrival of the Abington family in 1624 is an extreme example of the fear and animosity generated by papist intrusions into an entrenched Puritan community. Rye was certainly exceptional in the degree of its anti-Catholicism. The minister's use of the words 'dear sister' at the burial there in 1641 of Anne Threele provoked a vehement reaction from Samuel Jeake. 'What fellowship hath righteousness with unrighteousness? what comunion hath light with darkness? what concord hath Christ with Belial?', demanded Jeake of his friend John Coulton, who had attempted to justify the minister's humane tolerance:

> Are not all the tenents of the papisticall religion for the most part egregious and pernicious errors, derogatory to the honour and dignity of Christ and that in a high degree . . . nay she was an infidell being a papist, for they deny the faith of us Christians and cleave to the covenant of workes which is now abrogated and no man is able to performe, neither is any man justified by it.[62]

To some Puritans Catholics were utterly beyond the pale. Yet the fact was that both the strangers and the old established Catholic gentry were entirely quiescent in their political attitudes. Their reaction to the outbreak of the civil war was supine.[63] Moreover on the few occasions when JPs entered the homes of recusants and had an opportunity to assess their military potential, they were surprised to find that the reality in no way accorded with the popular expectation that Catholic estates contained well stocked arsenals for rebellion. At Cowdray in 1625, for instance, four JPs and Bishop Carleton were unwilling to accept that the miserable collection of wormeaten pikes and old bills, lances and gauntlets presented to them was the sum of Viscount Montagu's armoury, but a search revealed nothing else. The disarming of the county's leading recusant proved a remarkable anticlimax.[64]

The heightened political tension of 1640 brought the latent anti-Catholicism in Sussex to the surface.[65] The Bench responded with alacrity to the Commons' order of Christmas Eve that JPs should 'make strict inquiry after recusants': Christopher Dowe forwarded the order to the constable of Foxearle hundred on 4 January and Laurence Ashburnham, William White and Peter Farnden met at Westfield the following day to initiate a drive for comprehensive presentments in Hastings rape. The constables responded energetically. By 10 January Farnden had received a presentment for the six parishes of Baldslow hundred.[66] The anxiety of the county's MPs during 1641 is indicated by their insistence that it should receive priority over the disarming of recusants.[67] Anti-popery references in the Sussex petitions of February 1642 confirm that the gentry there shared the general obsession of the time with Catholic conspiracies. They requested the Lords to ensure that 'none popishly affected' had 'any place of trust in the kingdome', they acknowledged the endeavours of the Commons in defending them from 'the destructive plots of papists and the power of the popish lords' and they demanded a severe programme of anti-Catholic measures.[68]

Although the Catholic gentry exhibited little positive support for the King in Sussex when the civil war broke out, the county remained highly susceptible to popish scares. In the summer of 1644, for example, the committeemen Laurence Ashburnham and Peter Farnden initiated discreet enquiries after they had received persistent reports about 'often and greate meetings of papists and men evill affected' at the homes of Mr Threele, Mr Roots and Mr Harrington, who had taken over the Crispe's manor at Ore. A belief was current that James Roots's house on the cliffs at Fairlight was being used as a base for landing papists, who watched for the lights he set up towards the sea. The mayor of Rye's hasty reply the same day as the committeemen wrote to him from Broomham promised 'diligent inquire' amongst the town's fishermen. The previous week, reported the mayor, a parliamentary captain had searched Thomas Threele's home for priests and Jesuits and found no one.[69] The dread of Catholicism became obsessive in the minds of Puritan gentry who were constantly involved in maintaining the parliamentary cause. Herbert Morley's misinterpretation of the picture found in the *St James* in 1644 was based on his rapid emotional reactions to anything that carried the faintest whiff of popery. In the early seventeenth century the Sussex gentry had accustomed themselves to the presence of scattered Catholic families as a permanent feature of the social scene. But the political crisis of the 1640s brought out the full force of their deeply emotional loathing of the Catholic faith and its adherents.[70]

6

Achieving the millennium

Be pleased to receive inclosed a peticion from diverse well affected to the service about their minister, and this let me say that parish is very populous and hath not had a good minister in it in man's memory.
Herbert Morley to Speaker Lenthall, 23 May 1643.[1]

You are as a city set on an hill, labour to hold forth an holy life, least it be said what doe you more then others.
Christopher Blackwood to Frances Jeake at Rye, 9 August 1652.[2]

The time is drawing neere when we shall see the father plainly, and know him as we are knowne of him, and though now we read God in the language and similitude of the creatures, we shall then make exchange and read of the creatures in the language and similitude of God.
Samuel Jeake to Ralph Gibbon, 7 March 1656.[3]

In the 1640s and 50s millenarianism was in the mainstream of English Puritanism. Across a wide spectrum of creeds from Presbyterianism to Fifth Monarchism, men shared an optimistic belief in a perfect society that would be established through divine intervention.[4] Puritans fought the civil war inspired by this belief. John Coulton wrote home to his Rye friends in June 1643 about the stark terms in which he saw the war:

> Such is my corage that if my hart deceive me nott I will either se King Charles at his parliament or myselfe in heaven; what have I fought for this thirty-two yeares but assurance. I blesse God I have it more than ever I had. Duty compeles me to discover my soule unto you who are so deare unto me; take notice of it; and I charge you before God the judge of all the world, that if you heare of my fall, never shed one teare for me, rather joy the Lord hath freed me from this body of sine, and answer my enemies in my name.

After the taking of Arundel the following January, Coulton's religious excitement was at fever pitch. 'You se answered praiers comes home crowding', he wrote to Samuel Jeake, 'unto your praying soules heaven begins to be gratious; the Lord awakes as a man from his wine'.[5] Others gained support from their millenarian beliefs when they found themselves defenceless. 'God hath begun to accomplish that which he gave my farther and mother faith to beleeve', declared Mary Temple to her sister Anna

Busbridge in Sussex, when she was living in fear of royalist attack at Frankton in Warwickshire in the summer of 1642.[6]

Meanwhile in the House of Commons' programme of fast sermons Sussex preachers joined in the chorus of apocalypticism. Benjamin Pickering, for instance, assured MPs in 1644 that 'the Lord hath promised great things, and spoke of glorious dayes which now hasten concerning his church . . . you are ingaged in the greatest worke that ever lay upon the children of men'.[7] Edward Haughton, the lecturer at Horsham, described the civil war as 'part of the battel you read of in the 16 and 19 chapters of the Revelations'.[8] In the letters of men like Samuel Jeake the millenarian theme was constantly reiterated. An ecstatic letter written early in the civil war urged his friends that as men they might 'be faithfull, as souldiers couragious, as Christians gracious and as saints glorious': 'I desire victory for you against yours' and the Lord's enemies. I desire you may (as I heare you are) be couragious, having so good a cause call and captaine'.[9] Nor did the millenarian vision fade, among the most zealous of the godly at least, in the later 1650s. 'Where now are all your God damn me's?', demanded the fiery John Pellet of the royalist Henry Woodcock in 1656 when Woodcock was poking fun at Puritan soldiers who had gone into battle mouthing pieties: 'hath not the Lord trampled them all as mire in the street under the feet of the present power?' Pellet still saw Marston Moor and Naseby as 'signal testimonies' of God's power against the King's party.[10] Millenarianism was the common coin of Puritan thinking during and after the civil war: some saw it in cataclysmic terms, others expected the achievement of the millennium to be a gradual process.

The breakdown of ecclesiastical administration, the abolition of episcopacy and the subsequent emergence from the lengthy deliberations of the Westminster Assembly of the 'lame Erastian presbytery' brought a situation in the localities in which everything depended on the energy and initiative of the governing classes.[11] The clique of Puritan gentry in Sussex who dominated the Bench and the County Committee, which subsumed the role of the local Committee for Plundered Ministers, concentrated on securing an adequate preaching ministry, inculcating morality and ensuring that churches and churchyards were still cared for. For eighteen years men like Robert Spence, Herbert Morley, John Busbridge and Anthony Stapley of Patcham exercised as firm control over the religious as over the secular life of the county.[12] The close relationships built up between Puritan gentry and clerics bore fruit in these years. MPs advanced their protégés both at Westminster and on county commissions. Thus men like Benjamin Pickering and John Maynard gained their chance to participate in the fast sermon programme: in 1646 Anthony Stapley thanked Maynard on behalf of the House, in 1654 John Fagge was deputed to give Francis Cheynell notice that the Commons requested him to preach.[13] A close-knit group of Puritan ministers, which included Nathaniel Hilton of Billingshurst, John Chatfield of Horsham and John Tredcroft of West Grinstead colonised the commissions for ejecting scandalous ministers.[14] The new atmosphere enabled ministers such as William Speed of St Pancras and John Maynard, who had been in trouble with the Arminian authorities, to exercise considerable initiative.[15]

Francis Cheynell was outstanding among the Puritan clergy of Sussex for his millenarian zeal and for the bitter and violent spirit in which he pursued his goals. He was undoubtedly a narrow and revengeful man.[16] His fierce interrogation of the vicar of Rotherfield, John Large, about his practice of breaking a cake over the bride's head, a harmless enough country custom but one that to Cheynell merely reeked of superstition, was characteristic.[17] But no one was more vigorous in working for sound preaching and morality throughout the county. Cheynell was an active member of the Westminster Assembly and he entered the articles of faith which were enshrined in the ordinance of 20 October 1645 in the Petworth parish register.[18] He served for a time as chaplain to Anthony Stapley's regiment.[19] He was indefatigable in ejecting ministers he thought disloyal to the parliamentary cause.[20] He organised a petition of Puritan ministers to the Bench in 1644 for a monthly fast throughout the county. He led a series of campaigns in the 1650s for the augmentation of ministers' salaries. His name headed the new ejection commission of 1654.[21]

A loyal and fervent ministry was the first priority in the eyes of the Puritan gentry and clergy who took control of Sussex in 1642. They envisaged a positive propagandist role for the clergy. Constables were submitted to a constant barrage of warrants and letters which were to be read by ministers to their congregations. Days of public thanksgiving for parliament's victories were strictly enforced.[22] Moreover in January 1644 the leading committeemen embarked on a scheme of general subscription to the National Covenant, after a period of instruction from the pulpits about its political and religious importance. They told Speaker Lenthall that they thought the Covenant was 'of speciall use for uniting of the minds and hearts of men to stand firme for the comon cause'.[23] The Covenant was certainly taken in eastern parishes and in some parishes at least the Solemn League and Covenant was also subsequently administered.[24] To the most zealous Puritans the dissent on this issue within the ranks of the committeemen was proof that binding the people by oaths was the only sure way of combating the prevalent spirit of malignity and neutrality. Thomas Middleton strove to overthrow his colleagues' scheme: he objected to Nathaniel Hilton and John Chatfield as preachers for the Covenant, on the ground that they were too 'round', and refused to order the ministers of the Horsham neighbourhood to deliver it to their parishioners.[25]

The severe measures enforced by the Puritans against Arminian and allegedly royalist clergy must be seen in the context of their awareness of backsliding among parliamentary gentry.[26] Using a straightforward political test, the County Committee bent parliament's orders on investigation of scandalous and insufficient clergy to the purpose of eliminating royalist propaganda from the pulpits. The ejections were arbitrary and they often involved the use of force. Benjamin Blaxton alleged that he was 'put out by force' at West Thorney.[27] The curate of All Saints, Hastings, John Hinson, lay in the common gaol there for three weeks after Colonel Morley's troop had taken command of the town in July 1643.[28] Richard Tanton was ejected at Ardingly in November 1643 by a company of dragoons sent by the command of Captain Simon Everenden. Others like William Carr and George Heath avoided violence by abandoning their benefices. Sometimes a committeeman appeared in person to carry out an ejection. Thus William Cawley himself removed the parish register at Boxgrove when he sequestered Samuel Hill in 1648.[29] The political atmosphere of the 1640s gave full rein to personal animosities. John Large at Rotherfield, for instance, was the victim of a design by three men to obtain the living for a kinsman. A testimonial signed by more than 200 parishioners and a lengthy and persuasive defence could not save him once Francis Cheynell's animus was turned against him. Occasionally the influence of the more moderate committeemen or of the London Committee for Plundered Ministers saved a cleric from destitution when he was being hounded by the fanatics. Christopher Swale was thus restored in 1645 to the rectory of Westbourne, which had no cure of souls, since he was aged and of 'great desert and eminence in the church'. Another aged man who escaped through his learning was Aquila Cruso of Sutton, who in 1655 was able to furnish the triers with an account of his faith in Hebrew and Greek and a testimonial from his parish of his sober life and good learning.[30]

At least 76 of the 272 Sussex benefices came under sequestration at one time or another between 1643 and 1660.[31] In most villages in fact ministers were able, by adjusting themselves to the times, to sit tight and survive. The best security lay in possession of a living where the advowson was in the hands of a parliamentarian magnate. John Swan told Sir Thomas Pelham in 1644 that he feared nothing from those who questioned his right to Burwash rectory 'so long as God shall preserve me from malignancy' and 'so long as I shall enjoy the favour and honour of your noble patronage'.[32] Swan's apprehension was understandable in view of the tendency, in the disrupted conditions of the civil war, for vociferous parishioners to take matters into their own hands. Thomas More, who owned the tithes of Wivelsfield, refused to provide maintenance for an 'unlearned and unordayned maultman' whom the parish chose as their minister. At Steyning a Baptist hatter of the town was alleged to have procured the living for a coachman in 1642, superseding the patronage of Lord Goring.[33]

Between 1642 and 1645 the more fanatical committeemen ruled the roost: those who were concerned about social order could do little to check the excesses of soldiers and parishioners. On the day that Colonel Morley's troops arrived in Hastings to eject John Hinson a common soldier preached from the pulpit. The Lewes Committee appear to have been powerless to stop the 'violent and outrageous behaviour of divers ill affected persons' who hindered Mr Braine, the new incumbent at Ardingly, in the exercise of his ministry. Braine was eventually driven from the parish.[34] The Grand Committee did what they could to check on the ability of men put forward by parishioners to the Committee of Plundered Ministers in London. Herbert Morley supported petitions in favour of men he knew to be both 'able and honest'.[35] But adequate control was impractical while there was so much else to distract and preoccupy committeemen and JPs. By 1645 there was general dissatisfaction with the anarchic parochial situation. The inhabitants of Chichester and Arundel rapes complained to the Committee about 'orthodox ministers cast out without cause and never heard, mechanickes and unknowne persons thrust in who were never called by Aaron but by a committeeman, whereby God and the parliament are dishonoured and the people grieved'. The remedies proposed were the restoration of men in orders, the removal of laity from the ministry and the protection of patrons' rights. No one was to be removed at a committeeman's displeasure, but only after lawful conviction before the Grand Committee at Lewes.[36] The moderation and good sense of the Puritan clique as a whole was seen as a counterweight to the whims of the fiercest and most bitter spirits.

In the decade following the end of the civil war much was achieved in response to the 1645 demands. The County Committee in the later 1640s and the commissioners subsequently appointed in 1654 and 1657 energetically tackled the problems of ensuring an able and adequately maintained ministry.[37] The revenues of the Dean and Chapter of Chichester were used to bring numerous livings up from only a few pounds to between fifty and a hundred pounds a year.[38] Men eminent for their zeal and spirituality were given special commendation by the clerical pressure group. 'This pretious man (unlesse you take compassion on him) must be either starved or removed', declared Cheynell to the Protector in a petition on behalf of Nehemiah Beaton of Wiston, who was suffering from the Earl of Thanet's failure to pay the yearly maintenance of forty pounds he had promised when he compounded.[39] Samuel Wilmer was certified to be 'studious and pious, zealous in prayer, diligent in preaching' in a petition supporting the proposed union of the benefices of Clapham and Patching, which would increase his livelihood.[40]

Above all it was a preaching ministry that the Puritans sought. The Committee at Chichester oversaw a scheme of 1646 by which three learned divines, paid handsomely from the sequestered cathedral revenues, were established in the city and assigned accommodation in the Close.[41] One of the men appointed, William Martin, had held the important and well endowed St Antholin's lectureship in the city of London during the

1630s.[42] In 1657 the scheme was put on a more permanent footing by amalgamations of benefices which reduced eight parishes to two. Martin remained minister of one of the new parishes until his ejection in 1662.[43] The union of benefices was a commonsense solution to the problem of finding adequate maintenance for ministers. Stanmer and Falmer, for instance, were united in 1645 being 'very neere and the livings very small'. After investigations by JPs, and discussion where necessary before the Trustees for Maintenance of Ministers, at least nine more amalgamations were approved between 1656 and 1658. They were sensible rationalisations such as the merging of three families at Ovingdean with Brighton.[44]

The unprecedented religious toleration of the 1640s and 50s provoked derision among some conservative clerics and laymen. John Chatfield, the Puritan minister at Horsham, was told by the father of one man to whom he tendered the Covenant

> that he wondred what religion the roundheads would have, and that he knew a minister that compared the parliament's religion to a sunder pole, that was groundles, rootles and fruitles, having a weathercocke on the top that would turne with every wind.[45]

The Protestant Church in England had never before been so comprehensive; it was never to be so comprehensive again. Nearly three-quarters of the ministers who had been episcopally ordained before the civil war retained their livings, yet benefices were also held by Congregationalists, Baptists and even Fifth Monarchists.[46] Samuel Wilmer of Clapham, Robert Parke of East Lavant and John Stonestreet of Lindfield were all Congregationalists.[47] Samuel Wilmer was typical of those who were able, within the broad Cromwellian church, to combine the pastoral care of the godly of a neighbourhood with a parish cure. The petition of 'the gathered church at Clapham . . . with the well affected inhabitants of adjacent parishes' explained that he had been 'zealous for and successful in the gathering and uniting of scattered saints into one body, that they might enjoy all the ordinances of God according to gospell order in faith and love'.[48] Some Fifth Monarchists attacked parochial livings as contrary to the voluntary principle, but Walter Postlethwaite, who held the rectory of St Michael's Lewes from 1649 to 1660, was one of those who ignored this dictate.[49]

Even among men such as Francis Cheynell who could exhibit remarkable bigotry, great tolerance and extraordinary patience were sometimes displayed towards men believed to possess some godliness.[50] Nicholas Smith, the Tillington shoemaker who published an account in 1653 of the vision he had experienced thirty years previously in which Christ himself had appeared to him, related how he had badgered Nathaniel Hilton, Francis Cheynell and other west Sussex ministers to interpret the prophecies he had heard spoken. The ministers, it seems, dealt gently with the deluded shoemaker.[51] By and large the Sussex ministers showed a willing ness to further any scheme that would promote zeal and sound religion. In 1656 Stephen Street told Richard Baxter of the success of his campaign for catechising: he had 'at last prevailed with many godly ministers . . . to subscribe to that work'.[52] There was little impetus towards a fully worked out Presbyterian classical organisation of the kind that flourished in some other parts of England, but a group of ministers moved tentatively in that direction when they set out a blueprint of a voluntary Presbyterian association in 1653. It was, they announced, 'the best expedient that they could think on for the present to unite in love those that professe Christ in these dissenting and distracted times'. The scheme, formulated in the hope that unity might be preserved and 'yet dissenting brethren not offended', is evidence that the Cromwellian compromise, of a church that retained the parochial structure but provided no articles of religion or common liturgy, was seen by some clergy at least to be bound in time to be found wanting. It seems to have arisen from the disputes which were common to many counties about how far ministers could or should impose discipline upon their parishioners. It was drafted at a time when alarm in the provinces at the tide of religious radicalism was at its height.[53]

In worship the variety of practice which had existed in the 1630s persisted and was extended under the approving eyes of JPs and committeemen. During the 1640s and 50s the gentry fully realised the long hankered for autonomy of their parish churches. The *Directory of Worship*, which the Cowfold churchwardens bought as soon as it was available, probably proved acceptable to most of them, but in practice the *Book of Common Prayer* could still be used without much danger of reprisals. Only in Hastings rape, where Puritanism was at its most strident, is there any evidence of a campaign to eliminate prayer-book worship. Thomas Sharpe of Beckley related in 1642 how 'my zealous defending and maintayning and using the *Book of Common Prayer* hath drawn the envy of all the schismaticks of the country round about me, who traduce me as a malignant, a popish priest and invent and spread abroad all manner of horrible untruths against me'.[54] More characteristic of the positive initiatives of Puritan gentry was the expansion of the lecturer movement. In market towns like Horsham and East Grinstead extra-parochial preaching became a regular feature of urban life.[55] Attendance at lectures at Lewes and Battle became part of the routine of an active committeeman like John Everenden when he was there on business and the Committee sometimes entertained the lecturer in one of the inns.[56]

The little town of Rye became something of a model Puritan commonwealth during the Interregnum. It was a community in which the more substantial citizens set their hearts on achieving the millennium: 'a city set on a hill', a minister who had served there called it, which should be a light to the godly of the surrounding marshland.[57] The town was served by several outstanding ministers. In the early 1640s John Beaton held the vicarage. He was a man, said Francis Cheynell, 'who lived in much honour amongst us for his workes sake'.[58] Then, from 1653 until his ejection in 1662, the vicarage was held by John Allin, a Suffolk man who had emigrated to New England with his father to escape the persecution of Bishop Wren of Norwich. He had returned to England, after graduating at Harvard in 1643, to hold a London lectureship.[59] The Rye Puritans liked Allin's style when he came down to preach to them. So, finding him a man 'able and fitting for the place', they informed their MP, William Hay, that 'at a vestry he hath beene approved and chosen by the parish to be our minister'. The appointment of Allin came as a relief after two false starts in replacing the previous minister. A chaplain in Commissary General Whaley's regiment, who was 'generally approved of', had proved unavailable, despite a plea by the corporation that he should be released, and then Mr Benbrigge, 'who most of us pitcht upon for a minister', had suddenly died.[60] Rye insisted on choosing its own pastoral leaders and the townsmen were used to applying high standards. They showed the same meticulous care in finding masters for the free school. A testimonial signed by five Staffordshire ministers of Richard Hartshorne's skills as a teacher and his 'temperate and unblameable conversation' helped convince them of his suitability in 1659.[61] The town was fortunate in enjoying the patronage of two prominent gentlemen, Herbert Morley and William Hay, who shared its Puritan zeal. A fruitful relationship was based on unanimity of religious interests. Hay was in regular correspondence with the corporation during the 1640s and 50s. It was he who recommended Allin to them and who was instrumental in securing exceptionally large augmentations of the minister's maintenance. Hay's election as a burgess became almost a foregone conclusion. Praying for 'an assisting strength from God' to accompany him in 1656, the mayor announced that they had elected him in view of his 'faithfullness and ability in the like employment'.[62]

The atmosphere of Puritan Rye nourished an intense and energetic kind of spiritual experience. The passionate clinging letters of Samuel Jeake and John Coulton, separated by the demands of war, provide an insight into the religious milieu of the town. In June 1643 Coulton referred to the last fast that the Jeake circle had 'kept in our chamber: my master praied two houres, Joseph Relphe one, Thomas Carew and myselfe five houres'.[63] The services in Rye parish church were by no means to everyone's taste. John Evelyn was shocked when he visited Rye in 1653 to meet his wife off the Channel boat: 'I was displeased when I came home that I was present at it; having hitherto kept my eares incontaminate from their new fangled service'. He particularly disapproved of 'one of their canters who dismiss'd the assembly rudely and without any blessing'.[64] There was little else but listening to sermons in the way of stimulus on the sabbath in Rye. The corporation maintained a strictly sabbatarian régime. The constables were on the watch for any who danced, sang, drank or tippled, for boys who loitered or played in the streets, for men 'working in their callings, selling wares or merchandise or travelling by land or sea'.[6]

Many fines were imposed for offences against the sabbatarian code, for drunkenness and for profane swearing.[66] This was the town where a travelling musician had been told by an innkeeper in 1610 that 'we have a Puritan to our mayor and therefore you may play as long as you will at his door, but he will give you nothing'; where the corporation had decreed in 1631 that elections of officers should be held on a Monday rather than a Sunday, since the sabbath 'ought wholely to be employed and spent in the service and worshippe of God'; and where three lads who went out to slide on the ice one Sunday in 1654 found themselves in court for breaking the sabbath.[67]

Sabbatarianism was the essence of the Puritan's religious and moral code. General attendance at church and abandonment of secular pursuits on Sundays were seen as prerequisites for the building of a godly society. Francis Cheynell led a group of six Puritan ministers who petitioned the western Bench in 1644 to take action for 'the strict observation of the ordinances of God':

> notwithstanding the just and pious ordinances of parliament for the strict observation of the Lords day, and the monethly fast, the looser sort of people in this county doe grossely profane the Lords day and refuse to observe the monethly fast.[68]

Ordinances of 1644 and 1650 and a new statute in 1656, following up Caroline sabbatarian legislation, gave the justices plenty of scope in this matter, but there seems to have been no sustained drive to root out profanation of the sabbath.[69] Individual initiatives brought a few men to book, but they could make no significant impact on a problem that had defeated diocesan administrators for decades.[70] Cheynell presented a man for travelling in 1652; five more men were indicted for 'profanation of the Lord's day by travelling' in 1658; Herbert Morley fined a Glynde man for breaking the sabbath in 1659.[71] In 1657 James Butler and Richard Knowles directed churchwardens in the hundred of Rotherbridge to buy a copy of the recent sabbatarian act, 'to be kept in the parish and to be reade upon the first Lord's daie in March every year'. Presentments were not forthcoming.[72] At the lower levels of society resistance to the new sabbatarian legislation was probably intense. A jury at the western sessions in 1659 discharged a Steyning feltmaker whom a JP had presented for travelling on a Sunday.[73]

It was impossible suddenly to eradicate habits that were ingrained in the life of the countryside. Sunday labour was one of these, Sunday drinking another. Alehouses and churches were in direct competition. One man stated the case succinctly: 'heere I cane have a cup of beere and if I should goe to the church there I should gett none'. 'Unlesse he might have beere brought him he could not come to church' he declared to the churchwarden. When this reluctant churchgoer was driven to attend, reported the churchwarden, he 'stayeth there but a very small tyme, since we have had a pious minister there placed by the parliament'.[74] The sermons were probably too long for him. No wonder Puritan JPs were so prejudiced against alehouses.[75] A petition to the Bench of 1654 from some Heathfield inhabitants summarised its own attitude:

> They are the nurseries of all licentiousness whereby God is dishonored and his sabbath many times much profaned, for by the extreame remissnes and connivance of officers, these houses on that day also become the receptacles of loose persons where they practise folly to as great a height as at other times.[76]

Puritan opposition to churchales, traditional occasions for drunkenness, disorderly behaviour and sexual licence, was reinforced by the tendency for them to be held on a Sunday.[77] As early as 1614 the wealden parish of Buxted had decided to hold its parish feast on St James's day only so long as it did not fall on a Sunday.[78] In 1641 the JPs, using their authority under the Caroline statute forbidding unlawful pastimes on the sabbath, cancelled the annual churchale at Hartfield.[79] Four years later, after the ordinance of 8 April 1644 had specifically mentioned churchales as a profanation of the sabbath, they issued a general order terminating others throughout the country. When the Bench heard about an intended churchale on a July Sunday in 1652 at Herstmonceux, they issued a sharp reminder of their own and parliament's policy.[80]

The concern to eradicate immoderate drinking was part of the general obsession of Puritan JPs with popular morality. In Sussex, as in Hampshire, this also showed itself in the justices' concern to enforce the statutes against bigamy, rape, buggery, incest and adultery.[81] Some JPs also strove to eliminate profane swearing, although this was probably a hopeless task in an age when expletives and curses were the common coin of everyday speech.[82] A campaign by Edward Cooke, for instance, led to eight convictions of men from the coastal parishes from Angmering along to Shoreham.[83] Paying the graduated penalty reserved for gentry convicted of swearing, the notorious royalist and troublemaker John Goring of Greatham suffered a severe fine when he was indicted by James Butler.[84] Fines for swearing occurred sporadically throughout the period from 1640 to 1660.[85] But there was no sustained or coordinated drive to inculcate the moral code. Even when Major-General Goffe arrived in 1655 the initiative was left with individuals.[86] It is highly doubtful whether moral standards in Sussex significantly improved during the Interregnum. The greater involvement of the magistracy in matters of personal conduct, however, was a pointer to the future. In the long run the JPs were 'the true residuary legatee' of the church courts as disciplinary agents over the lower ranks of society.[87]

The additional administrative tasks that fell on an already overworked Bench with the collapse of ecclesiastical government in 1641 provide a partial explanation for the failure of the JPs to effect a more thoroughgoing programme of moral reform in the 1640s and 50s. The civil war brought a hiatus in the care and repair of churches in many parts of the county. In 1646 the Bench remarked on 'the great decay and ruine of parish churches'.[88] The impact of the Arminian programme of refurnishing and rebuilding had proved shortlived. The work of the churchwardens was already integral to secular administration before the civil war: they shared with the overseers the obligations of poor relief, they collected the village payments to the county funds.[89] The justices were bound to extend their control over every aspect of the churchwardens' administration once ecclesiastical oversight was removed. They began at midsummer 1645 by dispensing, through a general order, with the oath of office, since some men were refusing to serve on the grounds that they had not been sworn. Then they initiated a vigorous campaign to ensure that appointments were made, taxes were collected, repairs were carried out and accounts were presented in every parish.[90] The matters covered by the ordinance of 9 February 1648, which authorised the role of the justices in parish church administration, had already been firmly taken in hand in Sussex during the previous three years.[91]

By the 1650s full oversight of the work of churchwardens had slipped smoothly into the routine of the Sussex magistracy. Accounts were checked and signed by the justices in each rape.[92] At quarter sessions, meanwhile, the Bench took every opportunity to promulgate and reinforce its ultimate authority in all matters of ecclesiastical administration. A Stanmer churchwarden who made an unequal tax without the agreement of his colleague in 1657 was called to order. An appeal by the parishioners of Alfriston in 1655 caused the sessions to overrule the churchwardens nominated by the local JPs. The report of Herbert Morley and Anthony Stapley into the dispute over the election of the parish clerk at Worth in 1656 led to an order that the right of election belonged to the minister.[93] This important decision, which was in line with a similar one in Warwickshire in 1653, illustrates the determination of the gentry to stamp on any democratic tendencies that emerged in the parish during the Interregnum.[94] As for ministers, the justices did not attempt to interfere with matters of worship, but they did claim to support or admonish them as they thought fit over financial issues. They tried in 1650 and 1651, for instance, to enforce an agreement brought to their notice by William Cawley and Stephen Humphrey by which the parishioners of Funtington were to make a voluntary payment of four pounds a year to their minister over and above his normal maintenance. On the other hand they also directed in 1651 that the minister of Oving should pay over to the parish twenty pounds he had pocketed that was due to the church and poor rates.[95]

In a number of ways the JPs proved a good deal more efficient than the diocesan administrators had been. In the first place churchwardens accounts suggest that the fabric of the churches was in as good repair in the 1650s as it had been after the Arminian inspection programme, in some cases even better.[96] Between 1656 and 1660 the Bench also took in hand, under the pressure of numerous presentments, the thorny question of the repair of churchyard fences.[97] The customary system in most villages, by which each parishioner had responsibility for so many feet and inches of fencing, was hard to enforce.[98] The JPs initially tried to do their best with it. Defaulters were indicted, just as they might have been for failure to carry out bridge or highway repairs, and were ordered to complete the necessary work on pain of a fine.[99] But when there was confusion about where responsibility lay, churchwardens were authorised to make a general assessment on the occupiers of the parish lands to cover their expenses.[100] Thus, at a stroke, judicial procedure cut through the shackles of tradition. The Bench were also prepared, if necessary, to indict gentry who held rectories for their failure to repair their chancels. For example, the JP Herbert Board's widow and son were indicted about Lindfield chancel in 1659.[101]

Another extra duty was imposed on the JPs by the act of Barebones parliament which handed over to them the solemnisation of marriages.[102] Some justices, grasping the chance to perform so exalted a function, enthusiastically involved themselves in the new system. Thus at Glynde Herbert Morley saw to it that the parish elected a registrar on the date specified and he was soon busy marrying couples both from the downland parishes and from more distant wealden villages like Buxted and Mayfield.[103] In Puritan centres such as Rye and Lewes the new style of marriage became firmly established: the registrars there were still publishing banns and receiving fees during 1658 although the 1653 Act had actually lapsed in October 1657.[104] Yet the secular marriage procedure does not seem to have been generally popular.[105] Delays in the appointment of registrars and the scarcity of active JPs forced people to travel considerable distances for their weddings.[106] There was anyway a deep attachment to the traditional religious ceremony. News that the minister of Chiddingly was willing to conduct marriages in defiance of the parliamentary ban spread quickly: in 1654 he married thirty-seven couples.[107] The Sussex Bench, like that of Somerset, found it difficult to stamp out church marriages. They persisted at Slaugham, Ardingly and elsewhere as well as Chiddingly, either in addition to or in place of the bare secular rite. At midsummer sessions in 1655 the JPs ordered that the minister of Chiddingly should be bound over to appear at the next sessions, but no more was heard of the case.[108] The Commons debate of April 1657 revealed the opposition of many gentry to the Barebones experiment.[109] Secular marriage gradually petered out in Sussex between then and 1659: no one challenged the minister of Cuckfield for reclaiming his role in marriage before the statute lapsed in October 1657. Nor for that matter did anyone challenge Herbert Morley for performing a final magisterial marriage, of a couple from Firle, in November 1657.[110]

Though the English Church in the years following the civil war was remarkably comprehensive, there were some radical Protestants who felt an overwhelming desire to separate themselves from the unregenerate, to worship with the saints alone. Congregationalism, it has been suggested, was a development 'implicit in the processes of the English Reformation'. The meetings of the godly of Elizabethan England 'pointed unmistakably to voluntarism and independence'.[111] The religious liberty of the 1640s and the Cromwellian period checked these tendencies but it could not eradicate them. The emergence of separatism in Rye provides a case study of processes that were the logical conclusion of the puritan stress on every man's freedom to interpret the Bible for himself. The Rye godly had always shown an exclusivist streak: they appreciated the dangers of mixing with sinners. John Wilmsherst had warned Anne Jeake in 1614:

> O remember to have a care of your selfe for you are gotten into a towne which is given to much prophaneness, as I have bene certified: swearinge curseing whoredome skolding and many such sinnes they say doe there abound. Whearefore take heede to your selfe, easily may you decay in goodness but hardly will you recover agayne that which is once lost.[112]

In a town such as Rye a minister who combined zeal with tact might hope both to retain the goodwill of the godly and to maintain at last a minimum spiritual oversight of the rest of the community. Christopher Blackwood, who was later to become a Baptist, achieved this in the 1630s: the Puritans rejoiced in his ministry and private prayer meetings flourished to supplement Sunday worship in the parish church. Yet controversy erupted among the young men of Rye in 1641. It centred around the speculations of Samuel Jeake, who though still in his teens was ready to hold forth before credulous townsmen, and of the messianic young John Coulton, a newcomer to the town who had left his wife and was lodging with a Puritan family. Jeake had serious doubts about whether it was proper for Coulton to live as he did. 'I thinke it occasion of scandall', he told him, 'for a professor and his wife to live at variance'. But he found Coulton a powerful influence. He had even been heard to say that Coulton 'was more able in gifts' than the new minister of Rye, Mr Harrison, 'wishing that he could pray as well as' Coulton did. The views of and differences between these two young men quickly became the subject of gossip among those 'whose glory and practise it is to run prateing from house to house'.[113]

Samuel Jeake recounted in his letterbook how his 'tender yeares and apprehensions tooke offence' at two incidents that occurred in 1641. His letters reveal the development of his strict opinions. Firstly, he reacted vehemently when a woman who was dangerously ill bearing a bastard child was publicly prayed for in the parish church after she had requested the minister to make prayers on her behalf. Jeake took a harsh view of the woman and her motives. He held against her the 'vile words' she was known to have 'spoken to one that professt godlyness'. He was convinced that 'she had no love nor liking to the waies of God, neither to humiliation nor prayer but onely to have her sickness removed (which many an honest woman endures more in the comon disease of childbearing)'. He concluded, in a letter to Coulton, that

> its true we must judge charitably . . . but for to be praied for in the publique congregation before she had testified her humiliation and repentance and before she had beene soundly reproved I cannot thinke to be lawfull, since her fault was so sandalous, lest it were a countenancing of her in it.

Secondly Jeake objected most strongly to the minister's burial of a papist, one who had followed 'dumbe idolls' and 'joyned unto a false church', with the words 'deare sister'.[114]

During 1641 and 1642 Jeake and his friends were troubled souls searching, through long and serious conversations and continual resort to their well-thumbed Bibles, to resolve their scruples about the practices of their minister. Jeake and Coulton quickly made up their differences and became 'loving friends'. Matters came to a head in 1642 over their decision to leave the parish church whenever the minister baptised the children of 'visible unbelievers'. Predictably in so intimate a community, this behaviour raised a storm of gossip which the young dissenters attempted to quell by visiting the new minister John Beaton to argue out the whole question. It was the failure of this meeting, which merely produced 'vaine janglings' and futile swopping of texts, which caused the dissenters to set down on paper a full statement of their views. The letter sent to Beaton by Samuel Jeake, John Coulton and their immediate friends provides an unusually detailed illustration of the mental processes of a group of men who were moving towards a separatist standpoint. The lengthy argument, backed throughout by extensive biblical citations, sought to prove three propositions:

> First: That the Churches instituted by the apostles in the primitive times are onely particular Churches and not nationall.
> Secondly: That the faithfull onely and their seed being in Church communion are the proper subjects of baptisme.
> Thirdly: That it is high sacriledge and a profanation of the name of God and his ordinances for either Church or officer to dispense baptism upon any other subject save onely the faithfull and their seed.

The dissenters began by arguing that the covenant made with Abraham and his seed was 'not legall but evangelical and so continueth unto the end of the world'. The New Testament, they maintained, taught that 'none but visible saints were the subjects either of Church membership or of baptisme'. A further series of texts, they argued, proved that 'repentance goes before either admission into the Church or baptisme'. It seemed logical to these men that a minister like John Beaton, who withheld communion from wicked men, should also withhold baptism from those who had not shown visible signs of faith. The dissenters had developed an obsession with keeping the godly inviolate, apart that is from the 'incestuous persons . . . and covetous persons, idolaters, railers, drunkards, extortioners . . . we have in our assemblies'. They were bitter about the impact of the ungodly on the Church: 'visible wicked men whatever in words they professe makes a church a synagogue of Sattan nay Babylon, an habitation of devills and a cage of all foule spirits'. They ridiculed the whole theory of 'feederall successive holyness running as through a channel unto many generations', which supported infant baptism. The whole drift of the paper indeed was towards adult baptism and complete separatism. The compromise which Jeake, Coulton and their friends pleaded for with Beaton, for him to give his blessing before baptising 'or else not to be offended at us if we go out of the assembly', was logically absurd. But these men, radical as they were, could not yet in 1642 make the imaginative leap necessary for the realisation of their exclusive intentions. 'Some of us afterward seeing further into the point of baptisme', related Jeake, 'laid by the baptisme of all infants as well those of the immediate, as remote believing parents, and onely annexed baptisme to believers making profession of their faith'.[115]

The atmosphere of religious contention in Rye which was provoked by the questionings of Jeake, Coulton and their clique on the eve of the civil war set the pattern for the following twenty years. Once harmony among the Rye godly had been broken it was found to be impossible to restore it. Conventicles had for some time been rife in the town. Gossip and recriminations increased as some of them gradually took on a sectarian tone. Samuel Jeake himself, as the leader of an independent congregation, became much engaged in controversy. He deeply disliked the bitterness and strife which had marred the peace of the town; he was ready to defend himself against those who charged him with seducing the people; he sought to calm those who were censorious; he held out friendship to his critics.[116] His wife Frances Jeake found the religious factionalism of Rye equally distressing: 'we looke for peace and behold trouble, for rightuousness and behold opression' she told her sister in a letter around 1653. In another letter shortly before her death in 1654 she reflected on Christ's precept, 'by this shall all men know that ye are my disciples if ye love one another', and regretted that 'this is much wanting amonst the saints and instead division, which brings much dishoner to the truth'.[117]

The quest for the millennium in Rye had become entangled with the personal strivings and animosities of a declining port. The decision of the mayor in 1647 to arrest and imprison the Baptist Nicholas Woodman at a prayer meeting in a private house was perhaps a genuine attempt to reduce religious strife by removing one of the principal factional leaders, or it may have been no more than spite against a personal enemy. Whatever the purpose, it probably increased tension. The action was of dubious legality anyway, as Christopher Blackwood pointed out in a strong letter of remonstrance to the mayor and jurats. The ordinance of 31 December 1646 only forbade preaching by the unordained in a public place: Woodman was not preaching but praying and his congregation was meeting in private. Blackwood appealed for charity towards 'a member of Christ', towards a man of godly life and preaching ability. He sought to use his reputation to quench the factious spirit of the town:

> I looke upon you right worshipfull and beloved as persons in all or divers of whose affections I have formerly lived and I am confident, setting my judgment about baptisme aside, I do yet live . . . neither do I thinke that all of you but some did consent in this act.

In this letter Blackwood summarised the dilemma with regard to attendance at the parish church of those dissenters who felt an overwhelming urge to hold to and communicate the truth as they saw it:

> They shall either deny Christ by suffering a fundamentall error to go for sound doctrine when they are able to witness in the behalfe of Christ and his truth or else they shall be in danger to partake in the seducement of a whole congregation, when they by a word speaking were able to informe.[118]

The same kind of processes of incipient separatism that evoked so much debate and discord in Rye were occurring elsewhere in England during the period 1600 to 1660, usually with much less disturbance.[119] In a small village it was sometimes possible for a group of dissenters quietly to give more and more of their attention to private meetings and less and less to public worship, until they had effectively cut themselves off from the parish. Thus in 1640, for example, the churchwardens of West Wittering presented as 'Anabaptists' a group of eight men and women who attended their own conventicle instead of the parish church.[120] But it was also possible for radical religious groups to flourish near the periphery of the state church yet within it. In Lewes in 1655 the Fifth Monarchist Walter Postlethwaite had the largest congregation at St Michael's, where he held the rectorship from 1649 until after the Restoration.[121] Postlethwaite held some extreme views. He rejected the legality of the Protectorate and he feared that God would abandon the apostate English nation and go to America and the East Indies to 'set up the government of Jesus Christ among the barbarous places'.[122] Yet his preaching was not too extreme for Major-General Goffe. Having heard him twice one Sunday in November 1655, Goffe commented to Secretary Thurloe on Postlethwaite's moderation. The hold this Fifth Monarchist had on the godly of Lewes is indicated by Goffe's report that 'the generallity of the professors of religion in this town' were dissatisfied about the continued imprisonment of the leaders of the sect Christopher Feake and Major-General Harrison.[123]

The impact of Quakerism on Sussex between 1655 and 1660 was startling and dramatic. Quaker doctrines were first preached in Horsham market place in March 1655. George Fox's tour of the county that spring led to the establishment of regular meetings at Ifield and to numerous conversions in such villages as Steyning and Beeding, where leading Quakers lived. At Southover, which Fox also visited, a Seekers' meeting was rapidly converted to the new doctrines.[124] The dissemination of Quaker literature during 1655 and 1656 greatly assisted the spread of the movement.[125] Thomas Leycock, the first Quaker to be imprisoned in Sussex, became a martyr for the cause. In March 1656 Major-General Goffe reported to Secretary Thurloe how the multitudes flocked in to him at Horsham gaol. From his cell Leycock distributed copies of a Quaker book 'with many desperate words in it', several hundred copies of which had been 'brought on horsebacke in a sacke . . . since the assizes'.[126] The Quaker campaign had quickly attained a solid basis of popular support: the adherents of the new doctrines ranged from lesser gentry and yeomen to blacksmiths, weavers and labourers.[127]

The Quakers challenged ministers of parish churches with varying degrees of vehemence. One tactic was to evangelise before people had time to leave the building at the end of Sunday worship. At Ifield in 1658, for example, Thomas Patching stood up on a pew and, as the minister's servant put it, 'delivered with an audible voyce a greate deale of nonscence concerninge a newe light as he sayd he would hold out to them'. This kind of approach was appropriate when a Quaker was confident of some support from the congregation, as Patching was in 1658. Neither the tithingman nor the churchwarden would arrest him.[128] More common in the initial stages of the Quaker campaign in Sussex were direct attacks on 'hireling priests'. Thus Thomas Leycock reviled John Chatfield, the minister at Horsham, in 1655 'before he was come out of the pulpit and poynting to him sayd Thou lyar and that he was a ravening wolfe in sheepes cloathing'. Later that year Leycock was engaged in fierce controversy with John Beaton, the ex-minister of Rye, whom he called a murderer. John Pellet, at Westmeston two years later, questioned the minister when he had 'done his sermon' about the doctrines he had preached. This kind of public intervention became characteristic of the sect.[129]

It is hardly surprising that the gentry were alarmed by the spread of Quakerism in Sussex. The attitudes of the sect struck directly at the foundations of order and authority in Church and state.[130] At midsummer sessions in 1655 Thomas Leycock told Herbert Morley, Sir Thomas Parker and other pillars of the county establishment present on the Bench 'that they sate there to maynteyne those lawes that maynteyned priests and false wayes'. During the next few years, Quakers frequently refused to acknowledge the jurisdiction of the quarter sessions court. Ninian Brockett, chosen as a constable, would neither doff his hat nor swear his oath of office.[131] Moreover Quaker evangelism led to alarming disturbances among the populace of Lewes. When the Quaker John Pellet, a man celebrated for his quarrelsomeness, was brought before the Bench in 1657 and stated that 'he was not convinced of any ill behaviour that he had comitted', the Lewes rabble 'violently haled him from the barr' and riotously dragged him to the house of correction. The following year the opponents of the Quakers began to interrupt meetings of the sect by throwing water, dirt, fire or cowdung into their homes. Some Quakers meeting on Castle Green were attacked by a mob armed with guns and pikes. In 1659 further discord was provoked when the Quakers reacted to Ralph Akehurst's violent treatment of his wife, after she had testified to her conversion by intervening in a service at St Michael's, by publicising his cruelty in an appeal to two JPs which was affixed to the post of the market house.[132]

The policy of the JPs was to keep behind bars those Quakers whose influence appeared to threaten the social and religious stability of the shire. They were driven to a variety of expedients in order to attain this end. The Bench's initial reaction to Thomas Leycock's defiance in 1655 was to keep him in gaol until he found sureties for his good behaviour; they showed themselves ready thereafter to recommit men from sessions to sessions on this basis.[133] The JPs once made use of the blasphemy statute but they more often invoked that of Queen Mary's reign which gave them authority to impose three months' imprisonment on men convicted of disturbing licensed preachers in their sermons.[134] Edward Michel, making his own idiosyncratic interpretation of the Act, committed the Ifield Quaker Thomas Patching in 1658 for making a public disturbance 'contrary to the statut made for the better observation of the Lord's Day'. Some JPs also imprisoned Quakers for owning books which they took to be seditious.[135] The mayor of Arundel committed Leycock to the house of correction as a vagrant in 1656 and then disposed of him by offering him the unpalatable choice of working at his bidding or being sent from parish to parish to his Yorkshire birthplace.[136] The Alfriston Quaker John Willett was 'to be sett to hard labor and to be dealt withall as a disorderly person' in 1657, for his disturbance in church and other unspecified misdemeanours.[137] There is no doubt that the legality of the Bench's proceedings was often questionable and a group of Quakers languishing in Horsham gaol in 1656 did their best to exploit this fact. They were vindicated by the referees who reported to the Protector on their examination of the prisoners, justices, gaoler and mittimuses in the case. The referees found the commitments illegal on four counts: the crimes were insufficient, the mittimuses did not provide for delivery by course of law, several of the Quakers had not been brought to trial at the next sessions, and the 'whole process seems to be for matter of opinion in worship'. The outcome is not entirely clear, but it seems that the magistracy bowed to superior authority and Horsham gaol was cleared of at least these particular Quakers during 1657.[138] Usually though the JPs were able to impose a harsh and intolerant policy against the Quakers, free from outside interference.

Achieving the millennium proved no easy task. The collapse of the shortlived Puritan unity of 1642 brought disillusion to gentry like Herbert

Morley, who had taken up the parliamentary cause in the full flush of their millenarian enthusiasm. Yet the practical achievements of the years 1642 to 1660 should not be underrated. More able and better paid preachers brought a higher standard of spiritual leadership to many congregations; the churches were efficiently administered; some moral reform was attempted. At the Restoration the evangelical impetus of Puritanism, which had been the mainspring of reform within the Church since the accession of Elizabeth, was finally excluded from the Church. The Anglicanism of St Bartholomew's Day 1662 made the Protestant Church in England narrower than it had ever been before. In Sussex a new generation of county magnates, lacking the Puritan zeal of their predecessors, came to regard the Prayer Book and uniformity as the symbols of the return to moderate ways, the touchstones of the settlement which the gentry community had so long hankered for.[139] Thus the clerical leadership of Puritan Sussex was in its turn ejected and men who had been removed from their livings in the 1640s came back. During the summer of 1660 the petitions of sequestered ministers flowed into parliament. The new generation of JPs backed the movement to restore men to the benefices they had lost. Robert Tomlinson, for instance, had his petition to be readmitted to the rectorship of Trotton certified by Henry Goring of Burton, John Byne, Henry Peckham and Edward Blaker. Samuel Hill, who regained his benefice and parish register at Boxgrove through the support of John Farrington a 'loyal JP', noted 'how confusedly' entries had been made of christenings, marriages and burials for thirteen years and sought by annotations and corrections to put straight the record 'done by others in the time of my persecution'.[140]

A few noted Puritans conformed. One who did so was George Vinter, who had acted in the 1640s as Francis Cheynell's right-hand man. His career of tacking was long remembered in the county. In 1716 a correspondent told John Walker of how Vinter had 'acted the zealous loyalist' before the civil war, had then 'tacked about to the strongest side', and had finally 'zealously disuaded' neighbouring ministers from conforming at the Restoration, while he himself 'conformed kept Cowfold and together with it got in time the fat benefice of Rotherfield'.[141] Others employed their control of the pulpit to defy the new régime. Nehemiah Beaton said in a sermon at Lurgashall that 'the late King caused his own death by marrying with an adulterous woman, and a harlot, whereby he adulterated his whole generation'. In a sermon at Ditchling church in September 1660 Nathaniel Jones declared that 'the people and parliament had broken the Covenant, because they had covenanted against bishops and now we had bishops'.[142] A small group of Puritan gentry themselves became dissenters: they gave protection and support to some of the men who lost their livings. Nathaniel Beaton lodged under the wing of Herbert Morley at Glynde, while his brother John was received by Sir John Fagge at Wiston; Zachary Smith, the vicar of Glynde from 1644 to 1662, ended up as a chaplain to William Morley; William Wilson, who was ejected at Billingshurst, was befriended by Sir Henry Goring. Fagge sent his two sons to a school at Steyning run by William Corderoy, the ejected minister of Duncton.[143]

When the religious census of 1676 was taken there were sizeable nonconformist groups in more than twenty parishes in the archdeaconry of Lewes. Conventicles flourished in towns such as Rye, Lewes and East Grinstead, and villages such as Maresfield, Warbleton and Salehurst.[144] At Rye, where half the adult population were nonconformists in 1676, Samuel Jeake pursued his career as a dissenting minister, astrologer and religious controversialist until his death in 1690.[145] Thus in the east particularly the Puritan tradition survived, cut off from its roots in the national Church but still informing and enhancing the spiritual life of the households of the godly. Seen in the retrospect of a hundred years since the accession of Elizabeth I the impact of Puritan zeal and evangelism on the religious life of the county was incalculable. Moreover without Puritanism the politics of Elizabethan and Stuart Sussex would undoubtedly have been entirely different. Religion in the last resort was dearer to the Puritan gentry and townsmen of the county than politics or economic interests. Their faith called for constant striving in their daily lives. When they were convinced that the cause was good, it also sustained them in the hazardous decision to challenge their sovereign in the civil war.

Part III

GOVERNMENT

7

The framework of government

This devision of sessions beinge a thinge so singular to yourselves, as but in your shire onlie, we doe not know of the like elsewhere nor can find anie cause that can approve the same with you.
The Privy Council to the JPs, 24 May 1584.[1]

I have a further sute unto you in the behalfe of my verie good neighborr Mr Ashburnham. . . . I desire that he may be put in againe or that I may be spared, for onely two of us cannot well dischardge the busynes of these parts.
Peter Farnden to Sir Thomas Pelham, 15 April 1644, regarding the Commission of the Peace.[2]

Wheras I was formerly presented for not scowering a dike . . . and received a promise from you that in case you should receive a note from me with on or two of my neighbors hands that it is well and soficiently performed you would give me a discharge these are therfore to satisfy your desire.
Ralph Dale to the clerk of the peace, 29 September 1649.[3]

Accounts of the institutions and procedures of county government in the seventeenth century already exist.[4] Another one would be superfluous. On the other hand, some discussion of how justices of the peace were appointed and of the modes of government peculiar to Sussex is a necessary preliminary to an assessment of the effectiveness with which order was maintained in the county. Throughout the period from 1600 to 1660 the Sussex justices were experimenting with forms and methods, moulding the institutions and adapting the procedures inherited from their predecessors, as the exigencies of administration required. They enjoyed a remarkable degree of autonomy, one reinforced by the cousinage, the social relations and the common assumptions of the county families. This chapter is about the composition of the Commission of the Peace in a period of political crisis, the role in the total framework of government of the main office-holders—the sheriffs, clerks of the peace and constables—and the curious mixture of formality and informality that gave local administration its particular temper and atmosphere.

The Commission of the Peace

Ninety-eight commissions of the peace were issued for Sussex between the accession of Charles and the end of 1660. Deaths, shifts of power within the county and government purges necessitated frequent renewals. The commission was invariably headed by local nobles, privy councillors, and the judges of assize, but none of these was active in the day-to-day government of the shire. One hundred and sixty-three resident Sussex gentlemen were members of the Commission of the Peace between 22 December 1625 and 30 July 1660.[5] These were the men on whose shoulders every aspect of local administration rested in a period of political turmoil and disruption. By the reign of Elizabeth a place on the Bench had become a prerequisite for a gentleman keen to find his way in county affairs. 'If thou hast not some command in the contry', Sir John Oglander of the Isle of Wight advised his grandchildren, 'thou wilt not be esteemed of the common sort of people, who have more of fear than love in them'.[6] The prestige of the office of JP and the ambition of country gentry to 'bear rule' led to an invasion of the rural Benches. There were seventeen gentry on the Norfolk Commission in 1562 and fifty-two in 1608. The distension of the Commissions of the Peace was general. Ninety-seven Kentish gentry were JPs in 1608.[7] There were twenty-three resident justices, excluding the dignitaries, in Sussex in 1570, thirty-nine in 1604 and fifty by 1621. The tradition that knights had an outstanding claim to inclusion, given the Jacobean inflation of honours, exacerbated the situation. Seventeen titled men were justices in Sussex in 1604, twenty-two in 1622.[8]

The ideal size for Commissions of the Peace was a matter of dispute. Enormous variations in the length, breadth and shape of counties certainly made generalisations impossible. Lord Burghley was adamant that a small Bench, working with 'herculean courage', was normally the best recipe for good government. For almost forty years by regular piecemeal weeding of the Commissions, he tried to prevent the tide of gentry ambition from hampering the efficiency of local administration. Six times between 1561 and 1595 he purged the Norfolk Bench.[9] His charge, shortly before his death in 1598, to the assize judges to reduce the many justices who 'do so swarm that they trouble and molest the Bench, yea, some justices be ashamed to sit with such companions as some of them be' was an admission of failure.[10] From 1598 until 1625 the policy of systematic exclusions was abandoned, though there was a shortlived attempt around 1605 to tighten up the nomination system. The underlying problem during the whole period from 1558 to 1660 was finding able, loyal and energetic men to staff the Commissions. Elizabethan and Jacobean Lord Keepers were well aware of the difficulties of separating the wheat from the chaff, the responsible men from the turbulent, indolent and socialite magistrates. Sir Thomas Egerton in 1608, for instance, lamented that young knights 'come in their bravery and stand there like an idol to be gazed upon, and do nothing'.[11] In theory the circuit judges, whose twice yearly visits to the counties gave them a chance to hear about and report on individual JPs and gentry, should have been able to control the size of the Commissions and provide sound information about who should be appointed or dismissed. But such were the pressures imposed on them by factions and powerful magnates, and so adept were magnates at circumventing the judges through lord-lieutenants and patrons at court, that purges when they did occur were often thoroughly hit and miss. Sometimes they were no more than reflections of the temporary ascendancy in a shire of a particular faction. A Sussex commentator on the recent purge of the Bench in 1587 noted the inadequacies, in terms of capacities or age, and the religious dissidence of many of those who had retained their places, in comparison with the good qualities of some who had been omitted.[12]

The Tudors made systematic use of assize judges, lieutenants and bishops as sources of intelligence about the magistracies; after the Restoration much initiative was again given to lieutenants in reshuffling the Benches. Between 1600 and 1660, however, the initiative in nominations was grasped by well-connected county magnates. The role of judges and lieutenants became largely formal: the control of the composition of the crucial institution in provincial government fell into the hands of the gentry themselves.[13] The reason new appointments had been delayed, the lieutenants of Sussex explained to their deputies in 1619, was their desire for so many new justices. Sir Walter Covert and Sir Thomas Bishop had sent in one long list of nominations, while Sir Nicholas Parker and Sir John Shurley had sent in another. The lieutenants were concerned to regularise the procedure and put a stop to any tendency to factionalism, not to reduce local participation in appointment. 'We shall desire you therefore', they wrote, 'as wee knowe the course formerly hath bene in all busenes of this nature and of the countrey, that you will advise together and then joyntelie together comende your desires to us'.[14]

Sir Thomas Coventry, appointed in 1621, was the first Lord Keeper in the seventeenth century to make a systematic purge of the Commissions of the Peace. There had been pressure for reform in the parliament of 1621. In Sussex his drastic pruning, carried out in December 1625 'without rendering any cause', reduced the Bench of resident gentry from forty-eight to twenty-seven.[15] During the next fifteen years he ensured that it did not exceed about thirty-five members.[16] The Council imposed another nationwide purge in 1637, when it insisted that JPs should take the oaths of supremacy, allegiance and office at assizes, on pain of removal from the Bench.[17] Among those omitted were two Sussex justices who showed no inclination to stir themselves on county business: the courtier Sir Thomas Farnfould and Sir Thomas Pelham's intimate friend John Alford. Coventry was quick to sack men whom he heard were difficult or inert. Richard Higgins, the Chichester lawyer of 'fierie ambition' who was dismissed in 1635, had neglected out-of-sessions work; perhaps more significantly he had also been at odds for years with the corporation of Chichester who may have pressed for his removal through the court connections of their recorder Christopher Lewkenor.[18] Sir Thomas Bowyer, dismissed at the same time, had played some part in out-of-sessions work but had seldom been seen on the Bench at sessions.[19]

It has been suggested that during the 1630s the balance of advantages and disadvantages in holding magisterial office was changing.[20] However there is no clear evidence of Sussex JPs resigning or of men showing reluctance to take on the tiresome and time-consuming work involved. Sir William Culpepper, who inherited an outstanding county estate in the 1630s, was merely one of a group of knights overlooked in the restrictive and competitive conditions of Coventry's Lord Keepership.[21] Others in the same case were Sir Thomas Springate, who had to content himself with his captaincy of the Pevensey rape trained bands, and Sir John Chapman, who was eventually appointed and proved an energetic justice in 1644. No one was appointed to the Sussex Bench between 1625 and 1640 under the age of thirty, and the average age of sixteen of the men who joined the Commission was forty-five. One of the effects of Coventry's policy was the domination of the Bench by senior county magnates.

Some aged men, tiring of travel and long meetings, gracefully accepted the chance to retire in both 1625 and 1637. Sir Edward Bellingham, Sir George Shurley, Sir Richard Michelbourne and Sir John Wildgoose were all in their middle to late fifties by 1625. Only Michelbourne sought reappointment, though Bellingham and Wildgoose also had been active in the year before the purge. Sir Benjamin Pellatt, another old man pushed into retirement in 1625, was excused from his trained band captaincy a few weeks later on account of the infirmity of advancing years. Richard Blunt, marked as *senex* on a 1625 assize role, received the same treatment.[22] In 1637 another crop of old men was disposed of. Sir Richard Michelbourne, who died the next year, may simply have been too unwell by then to ride the few miles from his home at Horsted Keynes to the assizes at East Grinstead. John Middleton, who died the same year, was also probably in declining health. Others who made no attempt to rejoin the Bench included Anthony Apsley, who was nearly seventy, and Christopher Swale, who was around sixty.[23] Michelbourne, Middleton, Apsley and Swale had all worked hard at petty sessional business during the 1630s. Their acquiescence in retirement indicated awareness that there was no room for idle justices on the compact Commissions of Charles I.

Sir Thomas Pelham and his associates in the deputy-lieutenancy had no difficulty in filling vacant places on the Caroline Commission. Pelham's wide circle of friends afforded a convenient reservoir of talent. Moreover, most of the younger men purged by Lord Keeper Coventry in 1625 were keen to regain their places. Twelve were restored in due course, five were back on the Bench within a year. Coventry's vigorous pruning indeed had gravely prejudiced the effective government of the shire, leaving whole districts, such as the Midhurst neighbourhood, with no resident justice. Even after Pelham's nominations there remained a definite tendency for Lewes and Bramber rapes to be undermanned. Appointment never became sufficiently systematic for considerations of an even distribution of JPs to weigh heavily. The successful nominations of the period 1625 to

1640 represented instead the tug of war between the magnates and the clergy to secure control of such vacancies as occurred. There had been moves to appoint cathedral clergy, ecclesiastical administrators, and even in some cases parish clergy, to the county Benches during James I's reign.[24] John Tichborne and Christopher Swale appeared on the Sussex Commission shortly before the King's death.[25] They were joined between 1625 and 1640 by William Nevill, Richard Steward, Laurence Pay, Edward Burton and Christopher Dowe, five of the county's leading clerics. Burton was responsible for Dowe's appointment in February 1640: 'I confesse ther being a defect of justices at this time in that division wher Dr Dow lives', he wrote to Archbishop Laud's chaplain on 27 January, 'and none soe fitt ther for that place as himselfe, I could hartely wish he weare in, that he and I might be assistants one to the other'.[26]

The influence of Sir Thomas Pelham on the composition of the Sussex Bench was gradually overshadowed during the 1640s by that of his friend Anthony Stapley and the thrusting young Herbert Morley.[27] But they, like Pelham, regarded social rank as an important qualification for office.[28] Later even Major-General Goffe was ready to recognise the claims of rank. When he arrived in Sussex in 1655 several county magnates gathered in Lewes urged him to make new appointments from their own social circle. John Stapley hastened to visit Goffe at his lodgings with protestations of loyalty to the Protector and a few days later entertained him at Patcham: shortly after he was appointed *custos rotulorum*, putting an end to fears and rumours that the office would go to Francis Lord Dacre, and his brother Anthony joined the Bench. Goffe subsequently nominated Sir John Pelham, assured by one of the magnates whom he trusted that he was 'a very honest man'. Anthony Shirley was another of his nominees, after a show of hospitality at Preston had allayed his fears about the political stance of a man who had married a daughter of Cromwell's Surrey opponent Sir Richard Onslow. Goffe was also instrumental in the restoration of George Courthope.[29]

The re-emergence of Herbert Morley in national politics in the summer of 1659 accelerated the return to the Bench of magnates who had remained in seclusion for two troubled decades. He called on men from the old county families, such as John Hay, John Byne and John de la Chambre. The Bynes and de la Chambres had supplied Jacobean justices, but had been unrepresented since Lord Keeper Coventry's purge of 1625. Francis Selwyn, who after several busy years in office in the 1640s had spent the 1650s in seclusion, came back.[30] In 1660 men of this kind flooded back into county government. Whether by chance or design, an even distribution of justices across the whole county was achieved at the Restoration. A new magnate caucus came into being and the system of local nomination, under the patronage of the new lord-lieutenant, the Earl of Northumberland, was confirmed.[31]

Before the civil war there was no magisterial strike in Sussex; during it there was merely some sign of increasing sensitivity to the burden of office. Peter Farnden, who had earlier appealed 'to be spared or at least to joyne and goe alonge with' his 'verie good neighborr' Laurence Ashburnham, wrote as follows to Sir Thomas Pelham in April 1644:

> I lately here that Mr Busbridge and my selfe are putt into the Comission of the Peace and that he is left out (which I know he will well like of) but the contry soe well approving him and beinge soe well beloved besides the necessitie of his assistance, I desire that he may be putt in againe or that I may be spared, for onely two of us cannot well dischardge the busynes of these parts.[32]

Farnden's fear of being overworked was well founded. During the previous twenty years there had usually been at least four active justices in Hastings rape. The situation was remedied by Ashburnham's reappointment at the age of sixty-five in October 1644. The policy of the parliamentary clique at that stage was to seek to engage men with great estates or kinship connections who were loyal, however aged and decrepit they might be. Anthony Cruttenden, for example, was seventy-one when he joined the Bench.[33] This kind of appointment was obviously no solution in the long run to the problem of governing the county.

But once the magnate caucus had accepted that they would have to cast their net wider and draw on families of lesser standing, there was no difficulty in staffing the Commission during and after the civil war. They could afford to choose the most trustworthy and able men from a large pool of aspiring lesser gentry. The caucus brought in parliamentary colleagues like Roger Gratwick, Herbert Board and William Cawley; friends and relations like John Fagge, William Hay and William and John Spence; administrative careerists, like the treasurer for sequestrations at Chichester, Stephen Humphrey, and Thomas Marshall, the collector of customs and agent of the town of Rye; and Puritans like the barrister and divine, Edward Polhill, and the ironmaster rector of Frant, William Dyke. The Bench in the 1640s was held together by a multitude of kinship connections, spiritual affinities, and business and administrative relationships.[34] The parvenu ironmaster Nathaniel Powell, for example, as a newcomer to the Bench in 1657 was in the midst of negotiating a lease from Herbert Morley of Hawkesden forge.[35] Above all the Commission of the late 1640s and early 1650s was a body of men who had worked together for victory in the civil war. Of the new magistrates between 1649 to 1653, nine had served an apprenticeship as committeemen. The military careerists also, including two colonels, two majors and four captains, came into local government in force under the Rump.

Recruits to the Bench between 1644 and 1660 came to magisterial duties with a variety of administrative experience behind them. A few men had fulfilled tasks, such as the examination of parish disputes, delegated to them by the JPs at sessions. Nathaniel Studley, for instance, had investigated and reported on the circumstances surrounding a petition over a bastardy charge at Buxted in 1648, the year before he was appointed as a justice. Several gentry had acted as treasurers of one of the county funds or expenditors for bridge repairs.[36] Arthur Bettsworth, for example, organised bridge repairs in Chichester rape shortly before his nomination to the Bench in 1652.[37] The committee experience of many of the recruits included responsibility for taxation, sequestration and public order. Richard Yates earned himself a favourable reputation in magnate circles by his energetic response to the Horsham commotion of 1648.[38] Others had held more humble offices long before they raised their eyes to the Commission of the Peace in the 1650s: John Albery had been collector for the assessment in Arundel rape, Nathaniel Powell surveyor of the highways at Ewhurst in 1640.[39]

Writing to the deputies in 1619, the lieutenants of Sussex stressed that 'a speciall care' should be taken to recommend men suitable 'as well for their fashion of lyfe as for the vallue of their estates, knowinge they are noe waie fittinge excepte both be good'.[40] The roots of political obedience were seen to lie in social deference. The 1634 visitation of Sussex, a roll-call of the magnate families, included the majority of the Caroline JPs.[41] During the upheavals of 1642 to 1660 some drop in the status of the county magistracy was bound to occur, despite the efforts of the ruling group to preserve its social standing. Many of the new JPs hastened to confirm their place in county society when the Clarenceux herald returned in 1662. William Yalden was a parvenu ironmaster, Arthur Bettsworth a London merchant, John Fagge the son of a Rye merchant who had acquired an important county estate, James Butler a London cloth merchant who bought Amberley Castle for his retirement in 1648.[42] John Albery, who had reacted so violently to Sir Nathaniel Brent's visit to Arundel in 1635, was typical of the assertive townsmen who as mayors crept on to the Benches at this time in Sussex and elsewhere.[43] Albery's legacies in 1655 to a London haberdasher and grocer indicated his connections with metropolitan trade; his lands in Bognor and Westergate had been purchased with the fruits of his business. Yet Albery's wealth was modest: his brothers and sisters received legacies of ten to thirty pounds, his daughters were to content themselves with twelve pounds a year for their board and diet, his nephews were to receive eight pounds to clothe them and bind them apprentices 'to some handicraft trade'.[44] In economic status such a man was worlds away from the magnates who regarded it as their prescriptive right to govern the shire. Yet there were fewer such men on the Sussex Commission than on some other Benches.[45] Only briefly in the late 1650s did lesser gentry and merchants on the Sussex Bench outnumber the magnates.[46] Even then it was prestige and experience rather than numbers that set the tone of county government.

The shift in the social complexion of the Commission in the 1640s and 50s involved some decline in higher educational experience among JPs and in family continuity on the Bench. Though they were not as highly educated a body of men as the justices of such counties as Kent, Norfolk or Northamptonshire, in Sussex about three-quarters of the JPs in the period 1625 to 1642 had attended either a university or an Inn of Court or both.[47] The proportion of JPs whose father, grandfather, uncle or great-uncle had served the county increased during the 1630s and reached more than 50 per cent in 1642.[48] The stability of the years 1625 to 1642 was striking: twenty-five men served for ten or more years during this period. Four Elizabethan justices, Sir Walter Covert, Sir Edward Culpepper, Sir Thomas Bishop and Sir John Shurley, were still active after Charles I came to the throne; eleven of the gentry in the commission of 30 March 1625 had already been there for sixteen or more years.[49]

This remarkable record of continuity could not be matched in the 1640s and 50s. The proportion of JPs who had experienced higher education dropped to around half; less than a quarter of those named in the commission of 2 July 1657 had close relatives who had been members of the Bench in the two previous generations. Four times between 1644 and 1660 substantial reshuffling of membership took place. First in 1644 the royalists were excluded in a massive purge: twenty-seven gentry were omitted, twenty-four were restored or appointed, only ten serving JPs survived. Next, in February 1649, eleven justices were dismissed and ten new men came in.[50] Then, in July 1659, eight men were replaced. Finally, through the new commissions of March and July 1660, thirty-five JPs lost their places, eight men were restored with twenty-seven newcomers. The clean sweep at the Restoration left only sixteen men in office. On the face of it four purges suggest an unstable institution. In fact there was always in office a solid body of men, many of them leading magnates, with a decade or so of experience behind them. A core of seven conscientious members of the Caroline magistracy soldiered on from the 1630s into the 1650s. These stalwarts—Anthony Stapley, John Baker, Sir Thomas Parker, Sir Thomas Pelham, Philip Jermyn, Ralph Cowper and Henry Goring of Highden—were distributed across five of the six rapes. Sir Thomas Parker, in a remarkable feat of service to his county, was active throughout almost the whole period from 1625 to 1660. The Restoration Commission enjoyed the advice and expertise of seven men who had sat in the 1640s.[51] At no time between 1600 and 1660 were the foundations of sound government in Sussex less than adequate.

Courts and procedures

Sussex was unique in having a single Commission of the Peace which for most practical purposes acted as two separate Benches. The practice of holding sessions in both the eastern and western divisions of the county at Epiphany, Easter and Michaelmas, and a full county sessions at midsummer only, was well established by the 1570s. The Elizabethan Council issued a severe reprimand about it in 1584. They had found that the lack of opportunities for 'generall conference and resolucion' made the shire unresponsive to conciliar demands. A muster certificate, for example, had been delayed while a prolonged argument was conducted by messages and letters. Besides, they pointed out, 'the whole assembly of justices by theire aucthorytie and presence shall much better both discerne and judge of causes then the one half of them maie or can'.[52] It was easy for privy councillors to scoff at the Sussex justices for their 'privat respect of a litle ease to yourselves by savinge travell of a fewe miles farther'. But the position of the two shire towns provided a peculiarly awkward problem because the leading western JPs were simply not prepared to tolerate the long ride to Lewes, any more than the eastern ones were ready to come all the way to Chichester. Lewes was in fact the only town at all conveniently situated for the county as a whole with the facilities to serve the throng that sessions brought. It was the obvious venue for the midsummer sessions, though East Grinstead and Horsham were occasionally chosen. The justices of the western division tried meeting at Steyning and Arundel in Elizabeth's reign, and Arundel rather than Chichester became their regular Epiphany sessions town in the seventeenth century, but neither market town was equipped to entertain justices and litigants from all over the county. The choice of Arundel reflected the state of the January roads rather than the number and quality of its inns. The Elizabethan Council's attempt to make the Sussex magistrates fall in with the practice of other counties failed. In fact the system of autonomous divisions worked well enough, despite the occasional dispute. The clerk of the peace riding the road between Lewes and Chichester, with the order book of all the county's sessions in his charge, did much more than keep the record in a single volume. He was a messenger and linkman between those justices who lived in the east and those in the west. He alone was able to hold all the threads of county business in his hands.

As time went by the autonomy of the two divisions became more complete. The summer court at Lewes was always dominated by the eastern JPs and it never really became a county assembly dispensing justice and administration to all six rapes. By the 1650s men from the west bound over to the midsummer sessions almost invariably lived in Bramber rape. One or two justices from Bramber rape made a habit of attending, but it had become unusual for any to come from further west. The attitude of the western JPs is indicated by their custom of requiring defaulters at their Easter sessions to attend in the west at Michaelmas, rather than travel to Lewes at midsummer. In 1654 they even directed that 'no amerciaments shal be sett or estreated upon any of the constables in the west part of this county for not appearing at the generall quarter sessions'. Attendance by the western constables at the midsummer court had come to be much neglected; the western JPs were satisfied if 'a competent number' appeared to make up a jury.[53] Their lenience led to more constables staying at home. The JPs in the west had in fact decided to content themselves with three sessions instead of four, and in 1687, when the grand jury at Chichester sessions complained that Lewes was too remote for the inhabitants of the western rapes, their plea was accepted by the whole Bench and the annual joint meeting was abandoned.[54]

Assizes were normally held at Horsham or East Grinstead, since the judges were unwilling to suffer the hazards of the wealden roads any further from London. The Lent and Summer assizes were the most important legal, political and social occasions of the county's year. Any assiduous justice regarded it as in his interest to attend. Sir Thomas Pelham, for instance, had a regular arrangement with an East Grinstead woman to provide him with a chamber. If his expenditure and that of John Everenden were at all typical, the hostelries did good business for a few days each March and July.[55] Clerks, constables, bailiffs, attorneys and informers to assizes attended from across the county. Gentlemen and yeomen rode in to pursue their suits. A sleepy market town became a throng of people, a place of bargains, of the discussion and airing of grievances as well as of gaol delivery and punishment. The judges, outsiders epitomising the pomp and majesty of central government, brought their own awe to a court which was otherwise very similar in procedure and atmosphere to quarter sessions. The two courts were indeed complementary. The grand jury in each instance presented the same kind of offences: decayed bridges, impassable highways, unlicensed alehouse-keepers and obstinate recusants were regularly on their agenda.[56] Grand larceny—the theft of goods valued at over one shilling—made up a high proportion of the criminal business at both assizes and sessions, and both courts were lenient in their interpretation of the borderline between it and petty larceny.[57]

Assizes provided an opportunity for JPs to improve their knowledge of the law. When Lambarde and Dalton failed them, they could take advice from men of greater legal understanding and experience. The judges could be asked to bring their learning to bear on tricky administrative problems: in 1637, for example, a man was found fit to take an apprentice after 'a full hearing of the cause' before them and in 1654 they considered a complicated settlement case involving a bastard child.[58] They could also be expected to intimidate and inculcate obedience into men who were particularly refractory, pressed men who had deserted, for instance, recalcitrant unlicensed publicans and irresponsible fathers of bastard children.[59] Disputes involving people from both divisions of the county could conveniently be examined at assizes. Thus the JPs directed that the inhabitants of parishes in Bramber and Lewes rapes who were at loggerheads in 1643 over the settlement of a madwoman should be heard there.[60] Whereas the midsummer sessions never attracted sufficient support to become an effective meeting of the whole county Bench, the two assize courts neatly fulfilled that role. Moreover the judges could adjudicate and bring harmony when there were differences between the eastern and western justices. It was they, for example, who insisted that the whole county should contribute to the rebuilding of the Horsham gaol. The judges were the overseers of county magistracy, yet they were not simply the justices' masters. 'Ye are above them in power, but your rank is not much unequal', warned Lord Keeper Bacon in 1617, adding a reminder that they should not be 'imperious and strange to the gentlemen in the country'.[61] They depended on the JPs to enforce their orders, and could do no more than exhort them. Their charge to the grand jury was nevertheless seen by the government as a potent means of propaganda. Thus in the 1630s assizes were used to stress the importance of the *Book of Orders*, of ship money and of the enforcement of Lent at inns and taverns; in the following decade the parliamentary régime laid particular emphasis on the evils of alehouses and on their requirement of strict sabbath observance.[62]

In a few counties before the end of Elizabeth's reign petty sessions courts began to be held in each neighbourhood, between the quarterly meetings of the county Bench. In Elizabethan Norfolk the new court became institutionalised when justices began regularly to attend the high constables' hundred sessions.[63] Wiltshire was another county where some kind of petty sessions was established before 1600.[64] In several more counties, including Essex, Hampshire, Warwickshire and Worcestershire, petty sessions were set up in response to a Privy Council order in 1605 for four such meetings to be held annually.[65] The Northamptonshire system established in the first decades of the century may well have provided the model promulgated in the 1631 *Book of Orders*.[66] JPs were instructed to meet monthly in their own neighbourhoods to receive the presentments of constables, churchwardens and overseers.[67] The six rapes of Sussex were the obvious units of administration below the county and divisional level. A report of 1587 had noted that JPs were 'apoynted severally to the charge cheafly of some one of theas rapes'.[68] Moreover the rapes were the accustomed units of Tudor militia administration and subsidy assessment.[69] In two at least petty sessions proper were held before 1631. 'We have in our division before the publishinge of the Kings Majestie's orders and ever since kept our monthly meetings att Uckfield, viz. the first Tuesday of every month' reported the wealden justices in Pevensey rape in May that year. Again, in 1633, they reiterated that they had met 'according to our wonted custome'.[70] In Chichester rape, according to a statement made after the Restoration, the JPs 'did sometimes keep their monethly meetings in the Close' between 1618 and 1622, in a period when the city was exempt from their jurisdiction.[71]

During the 1630s petty sessions were held monthly throughout the county. The justices showed flexibility and cooperation in sharing out the work involved, since in many ways the rapes proved to be awkward administrative units. It was often convenient, for example, for JPs living in the Horsham area of Bramber rape to look after the affairs of Rudgwick and Slinfold, the two north-eastern parishes of Arundel rape. Inhabitants of the large parish of Worth, in a part of Lewes rape with a dearth of justices in the 1630s, found themselves on occasion before the licensing sessions of the Pevensey rape justices and the petty sessions in Bramber rape.[72] Sir John Leedes, who lived in the centre of Bramber rape, spent many of his working hours in the adjacent rape of Arundel, where JPs were lacking in the southern hundreds.[73] The 1605 conciliar order had envisaged a scheme of administrative units within counties so that 'none be driven to travel above seven or eight miles'. The Somerset JPs worked out a plan which gave them twelve compact units; in Essex there were only six, but these were much more practical units than the Sussex rapes.[74] Only Hastings rape could offer a petty sessions town approaching the standard of convenience contemplated by the Council in 1605. Most of the villages there were within a ten-mile radius of Battle. When petty sessions were held at Chichester, Arundel, Petworth or Lewes, JPs and parish officers faced long journeys. But in Pevensey rape, the largest of all, the justices never attempted to conduct administration from one town. The establishment of separate downland and wealden units there was an obvious practical step immediately out-of-sessions work became institutionalised. In the north the JPs found Maresfield and Uckfield generally acceptable meeting places; in the south they usually chose Alfriston or Hailsham. The attempt to hold petty sessions at a single centre for the whole of Bramber rape soon ran into difficulties. A number of officers had 'of late defaulted in theire appearance', the Council was told in May 1633. In November the justices issued warrants for the refractory constables to attend 'to become bounde to answere it at the assizes'.[75] Soon after this however, they faced up to the impossibility of forcing unwilling officers to make long monthly journeys throughout the year to appear before them at one centre. Separate meetings in the wintertime were established for the downland and wealden hundreds. In 1639 even the general summer meetings were abandoned.[76]

A long period of piecemeal, almost haphazard, experimentation preceded the establishment of the fully fledged petty sessions of the 1650s. The civil war interrupted the final stages of the process. In Cheshire, it has been demonstrated, the power exercised by JPs at the local level declined and the development of petty sessions was checked after the civil war; in Sussex the new court had come to occupy a vital role in the framework of government. Quarter sessions agendas had grown alarmingly. The new court eased the burden facing the Bench at the quarterly meetings and brought a new tempo to out-of-sessions administration.[77] Whereas in the 1630s the petty sessions had been limited to the oversight of local officers and the summary trial of misdemeanours, twenty years later it had become a court that debated the details and precedents of central issues of county government, such as bastardy, settlement, apprenticeship and local taxation.[78] Much business which had previously involved a special assignation between two justices for a private hearing was then more conveniently brought before the next monthly meeting. Cases which by statute a single justice might have heard, such as wage disputes, were also often referred to the local court. Judicially as well as administratively, the scope of petty sessions expanded enormously during the period between 1630 and 1660. As early as 1636 it was being used in place of the special sessions normally summoned for the purpose to enquire into a forcible entry. In 1657 the justices of Pevensey rape were directed to make a preliminary examination of so important a matter as the death of a Maresfield husbandman who had been 'beaten and wounded'.[79] Petty sessions in short were recognised as convenient, necessary and effective.

When a fully developed system of petty sessions had taken over many of the administrative chores that JPs had previously handled at home, the main part of their business that remained private was the informal examination of men under suspicion for criminal offences. These examinations continued to be held in the intimate surroundings of a manor hall, with a personal clerk normally at the magistrate's elbow, yet they often had an inquisitorial air. The intention was to provide the basis of the case against the accused at the sessions.[80] The occasion was one for direct and personal confrontation, for discovering the truth and obtaining a confession if possible.[81] Sir Thomas Parker's investigation of a characteristically inept cattle stealing partnership in 1625 illustrates the procedure at its most effective. William Marriner, a Chiddingly husbandman, and Thomas Brooke, a butcher from Goring, had met near Chichester and travelled together along the coast 'with an intent to gett worke'. At Jevington, Brooke took a shop 'with an intent to sett up his trade there', but, lacking any means to start a business, the men stole a bullock, killed it and sold the meat and hide. Brooke disingenuously maintained that he and Marriner had bought the bullock at 'a place in the wilde of Sussex' from 'a tall man, a yeoman in shewe by his habit, browne haired and of a middle age'. Marriner, on the other hand, denied going into the Weald and produced a quite different rigmarole. The tanner who bought the hide testified that it was marked with the initials of the Firle gentleman who had reported losing an animal.[82] The offence was a common one: forty-six butchers were accused of driving away cattle from commons and roadside greens in Elizabethan Essex.[83] Sir Thomas Parker, with some skilful questioning, was able to tie up the case as neatly as any Bench could wish.

The diary of the Surrey justice Bostock Fuller illustrates this continuing tradition of private hearings.[84] JPs recognised that there were various matters, administrative as well as judicial, which required their immediate attention at home. Villages often demanded quick action to fix at least some of the responsibility. The story of an irresponsible father, who was lucky enough to have the support of a sympathetic constable, is a case in point. A justice issued a warrant in 1652 for Thomas Baldee to be carried to the gaol unless he paid half a crown weekly for the support of his bastard child. The constable instead took Baldee before John Fenwick at Warminghurst Place,

> where he advised the said Baldee before Major Fenwick and the officers of the parishe to pay the said money or to agree with the parishe for a certayne some for the bringinge upp the said child, whereuppon the said Baldee offered to pay to the officers six pounds if they would putt out the said child and discharge him, which Major Fenwicke obiected against and said it was to litle.

Bargaining continued at a nearby alehouse, with the constable still in the role of referee and the overseers determined to acquire a proper maintenance for the child thrown into their care. The referee's bias was obvious: 'Wilt thou not obey the constable', he demanded when the overseer was reluctant to negotiate further, 'and asked him if he would have a man to the gaole for nothing'. In the end Baldee escaped lightly with a down payment of thirteen pounds, but not as lightly as he had hoped earlier.[85] In fact it was sometimes in the interest of parishioners to accept the full burden of a bastard child rather than have a reputed father sent to gaol and his wife and children become a parish charge. 'The chiefe of the parish of Hailsham', with this in mind, persuaded the constable to release a man accused of fathering a child in 1643. They ignored the letter of the law, abrogated the constable's authority and even flouted the *mittimus* of Sir Thomas Parker in order to do the least pecuniary damage to their own community.[86] Such intimate glimpses of the way things were done are rare. But the importance of personal relationships in day-to-day administration is often clear. Friends and neighbours frequently might settle a bastardy case or a village brawl with the help of a JP who lived nearby. At the magisterial level close friendship and the trust that came of years of cooperation oiled the wheels of local government. Everywhere their patronage mattered. 'Had I not bin hindred by illness I had intended to have weyted on you and spoken for him', wrote Nathaniel Studley to Herbert Morley in 1649, about a maimed soldier to whom he desired the Bench to grant a pension. Morley received the letter in the middle of the sessions, when he himself was back home at Glynde tending his sick mother. He forwarded it with a scribbled postscript to his 'cosin Hay': 'you see Mr Studley's letter: the bearer is the person concerned, pray further his request'.[87]

Relations between the Sussex Bench and the justices of the contiguous counties and the independent jurisdictions of the Cinque Ports and Chichester were for the most part amicable, though tensions did occur from differences of approach to complicated administrative problems such as settlement.[88] Rye, Winchelsea, Hastings, Pevensey, Seaford and Chichester all had their own JPs, yet politically, socially and economically their boundaries with the county had little meaning.[89] There was need for mutual compliance between the town and county authorities. Rye and Chichester were the most assertive and troublesome corporations in their relations with the county Bench. An incident in 1627, recorded in a correspondence that remained icily polite, provides a hint of the determination with which the Rye oligarchy sought to protect its independence of action. Sir Thomas Sackville and Robert Foster found themselves frustrated in their dealings with a disorderly alehousekeeper, who insisted that his house lay in Rye parish, although, according to their information he had 'not soe mutch as any fireroome' within the Cinque Ports liberty. Yet the mayor of Rye maintained his right to license the man, alleging that the publican had paid taxes to the town and kept watch there.[90]

The anomalous situation whereby the inhabitants of Rye Foreign came under the jurisdiction of the county, yet paid their poor rates to the town, was still causing conflict in the 1650s. The local JPs sided with the countrymen in their battle to escape the high assessments that the town's overseers, moved by the needs of their poor, sought to impose. When John Busbridge refused to sign the tax book in 1655 the mayor suggested that he should, 'with some of my brethren', entertain him to reconcile their differences, but further and more acrimonious correspondence shows that if a meeting took place it failed to bring about harmonious relations during the late 1650s.[91] At Chichester the merchant oligarchy was aggressively independent. They used their new charter of 1618 to prevent the county Bench from holding quarter sessions within the city precincts.[92] For three years county sessions were held instead in the Close, until, by the charter of 1621, the JPs were able to reassert their long-established right to meet in the city.[93]

The ancient leet and hundred courts survived alongside the structure of magisterial government.[94] In such matters as the repair of highways and bridges their work complemented that of the JPs. The improvement in communications in the wealden part of Pevensey rape in 1633 was accredited by the justices there to the many indictments and presentments that had been made at leets as well as assizes and sessions.[95] The sheriff's tourn also continued to meet, whereas in Somerset it had 'quietly expired', but its single mention in the sessions records suggests that its decrees might need magisterial backing before they could be enforced.[96] John Rowe's memoranda book is a monument to the intricate web of custom and tradition within which these ancient courts subsisted and which they perpetuated. As steward to Lord Abergavenny he held the courts in the barony of Lewes between 1597 and 1622.[97] But for gentry like Sir Thomas Pelham these ancient courts were little more than a useful source of cash. The profits were regular and substantial.[98] The decay of the court leets was a gradual process. More and more of them failed to perform their single vital function, the appointment of local officers. The Bench had to intervene over appointments of constables on fourteen occasions between 1625 and 1640, on thirty-four in the 1640s and on forty-nine in the 1650s.

Nominations of headboroughs and tithingmen at sessions, which were unusual before the 1650s, became frequent during that decade. The JPs took action to fill vacancies in every hundred, except three in West Sussex, at some time over a thirty-five-year period in the middle of the century.[99] Only a few hundreds, on the other hand, required persistent attention and even the most notorious lapses in the holding of the leet, such as Patching's in the 1640s, were ended after a period of years.[100] A Restoration statute authorised magisterial intervention when leets were not held, but left their powers of appointment intact. The system of overlapping powers of appointment between leets and sessions thereby established was bound to be unsatisfactory. A rumpus at Horsham just before the Restoration is a case in point. Unable to produce a satisfactory set of accounts, the two constables due to end their term failed to appear at the leet called by the mesne lords, the bailiffs and some of the burgesses of the town. Instead they pretended at the sessions that the leet had not been called. The Bench slipped up by failing to demand their accounts and replaced them. A few days later George Hussey and Henry Onslow, holding their petty session at Horsham, were faced by the bailiffs, who put their case in high dudgeon. The justices had no choice but to resummon the leet and let them begin the whole process over again.[101] Such was the jealousy with which towns men might guard the small degree of autonomy that the procedures of county administration still permitted them.

Offices and officeholders

Until 1636 a joint sheriff for Surrey and Sussex was appointed. Si Richard Evelyn was the penultimate man to occupy the joint office and h was also one of the last to attempt a style of hospitality that had once bee common: 'he had 116 servants in liverys, every one liveryd in green sattin doublets; divers gentlemen and persons of quality besides waited o him in the same garbe and habit.' 'He could not refuse the civility of hi friends and relations', declared John Evelyn, seeking to explain his father ostentatious expenditure.[102] But the diarist's excuse does not quite rin true, since in the 1620s and 30s it looks as if a decisive break with pa practice had occurred. The shrievalty had been opened to gentry of mor modest means and pomp and display had declined accordingly. Evely himself admitted that thirty or forty men comprised the usual retinue of sheriff in the 1630s. The magnate families, who had monopolised th office during the reigns of Elizabeth and James I and had engaged i prodigious expenditure, found its labour and expense increasingly di agreeable.[103] The office had landed with monotonous regularity on a sma group of men: those two stalwarts of county administration, Sir Walt Covert and Sir Thomas Bishop, had each borne it twice between 1583 an 1601. Such families, anxious to shift the burden, were ready to see t prestige of the shrievalty decay. Sir Richard Evelyn's lavishness may not i fact have gained him prestige with the kind of men in the middle ranks of gentry society who were likely to have to follow him. For a man to revive the former licentious custom of splendour and extravagance could be seen as a betrayal of his fellow gentry, Sir Thomas Wentworth pointed out to his Yorkshire neighbour Christopher Wandesford in 1625, announcing his intention to execute the office with moderation and sobriety.[104]

The fact is that the sheriff had anyway become a mere servant of the magistracy. In the Caroline period men with no experience of county administration were more likely than JPs to be pricked for the office. Herbert Hay was on the list in 1640 and 1641 but as a diligent justice escaped both times; nor was Sir William Goring, another energetic magistrate, chosen in 1641.[105] Instead the shrievalty fell on Giles Garton, whose family had not been represented on the Bench since 1606. Anthony May of Ticehurst, George Churcher and Anthony Foster were equally untried when they were appointed as sheriffs. Knights who were not JPs were particularly liable to be pricked: Sir Stephen Board, Sir John Chapman, Sir William Culpepper and Sir Edward Bishop all served between 1628 and 1637.[106] The parliamentary régime made no attempt to entice magnates back into the shrievalty. Men of even more modest status began to occupy the office, such as Thomas Collins, a careerist militia captain and committeeman, and Thomas Luxford, a man of no standing outside the few parishes surrounding Pevensey marshes where his estates lay.[107] The wealthier men chosen in the 1640s and 50s tended to be relative newcomers to the shire, like Peter Courthope, the purchaser of the Goring mansion of Danny, Sir Thomas Hendley and William Wilson. Whereas the Elizabethan sheriffs had invariably been members of the social elite of the county, only ten of the thirty-four resident sheriffs between 1625 and 1660 were even JPs. A new group of men had an office that was generally recognised to be unprofitable thrust upon them.[108]

Most of the humdrum duties of the office were usually performed for the sheriff by his undersheriff or deputies. Thus Thomas Collins employed two minor gentlemen, Robert Shoebridge and Lewkenor Middleton, as his deputies in 1655.[109] The crucial figure in the shrievalty was the undersheriff. A conciliar circular of 1609 warned sheriffs to beware of men 'bredd in nothing but craft, extorcon and corruption' who might put themselves forward for this office, yet a gentleman appointed as sheriff for one year had little choice but to trust the man who had established a working bureaucracy of clerks and bailiffs.[110] It was a better proposition to contract with a powerful but unscrupulous undersheriff, who had a group of bailiffs under his thumb, than to start from scratch. How far the Sussex undersheriffs were generally corrupt is not clear. The only documented career is that of Thomas Henshaw who held office from 1643 until well into the 1650s.[111] His dealings with the unruly gaoler of Horsham, Richard Luckins, shed a dubious light on his character. Luckins was a notorious drunkard, quarreller and blasphemer, who kept a thoroughly disorderly house at the George Inn near the gaol. He was accused in 1645, among other things, of extorting unjust fees, of putting debtors in irons 'upon the least discontent given him', of allowing prisoners to escape and of dabbling in black magic.[112] His ill-famed career only ended when he was indicted at sessions two years later for the forcible exclusion of the sheriff, Sir Thomas Eversfield, from the gaol. It seems that by this time he was endeavouring to remain in office by force.[113] Henshaw throughout had been Luckins's immediate superior. Moreover he had procured a reconciliation with men who had intended to present bills against Luckins for fighting and breaking the peace. Luckins's survival for so long in such an important office suggests at least a degree of collusion between him and the undersheriff.

We have already seen how the autonomy of the Sussex divisions gave the clerkship of the peace special significance. The whole central bureaucracy of county government at both Chichester and Lewes was under the clerk's management. He was the majordomo of the sessions, arranging the agenda, collecting the fees, helping poor men with the wording of their petitions, putting the decisions of the court into proper form and producing the final record.[114] Only two men held the office between 1615 and 1660: William Thomas and William Alcock were cousins and close friends.[115] Thomas's career from 1615 to 1640 well illustrated the opportunity that the clerkship provided for social and economic advancement.[116] An ambitious newcomer to the county, he invested the profits of his office in an estate at Westdean, which his son, who became a JP, added to in the 1640s.[117] The few remnants that are preserved of the vast correspondence of the clerks indicate the importance that men attached to keeping on good terms with them. The clerks' relationships were easy and familiar with high and low alike. The clerk of the peace acted as an intermediary between the Bench and the public. Ralph Dale, who is quoted in the epigraph to this chapter, entreated William Alcock, with protestations of his service, not to be unmindful of his word. Two Lamberhurst gentlemen asked the assistance of William Thomas in stopping up a dangerous plank footbridge over a millgate in their parish, which had led to a man being drowned:

> We desyer your assistance herein that it may be presented as a nuisence our neighbours that are to serve the sessions will further inform you, if they be impannelled, otherwise they wil be unwillinge to stay about it so with our harty well wisheinge to you and all yours we rest your assured lovinge cosens.[118]

Private clerks to justices worked in cooperation with the clerk of the peace. Kept indoors for a month after being lamed by his horse in 1643, Sir William Goring's clerk had not been able to give his master's affairs his usual diligent attention. The day before the sessions he wrote anxiously to Alcock about a recognisance he feared had been lost or overlooked:

> for as I remember the wife of George Rouse was bound to the peace as well as her husband . . . sir if you please to add a salve to this sore and (if she were bound) to draw the recognisance assure yourselfe I shall ever endevor to deserve it and rest your lame but ever faithfull freind to serve you.[119]

Other private clerks are mentioned in the records but how many Sussex justices had the services of one is not clear. A dozen or so JPs in Elizabethan Norfolk and at least twenty-two in Caroline Somerset had clerks of their own.[120] The trust that developed between these clerks, the clerk of the peace and the justices helped the machinery of government to run smoothly.[121] The clerk of the peace was the obvious intermediary between a JP unable to attend sessions and the Bench. In 1628 Thomas Gray wrote to William Thomas asking him to discharge two men he had bound over for wounding a woman while they were 'strivinge for a gunne' in a casual brawl, since the woman was 'past all danger'. On another occasion Sir Richard Michelbourne sent his 'very loving friend' William Thomas a full report on the cases that would arise from his activity since the previous sessions.[122] Michelbourne's letter was a mixture of personal impressions of the people he had bound over and sent to gaol, notes on their misdemeanours, and advice on how they should be dealt with. For instance, in a case where the defendant was ill, he suggested that three witnesses should be further bound 'to the next sessions or to what other time the justices think fitt'. The Bench, he indicated, might think it appropriate either to admonish or bind to good behaviour a man 'much defamed' for harbouring vagrants in his barn.

It has been suggested that the seventeenth century saw a 'radical change, amounting almost to a revolution' in quarter sessions record keeping.[123] The process was not uniform throughout the country; nor were the new types of record that emerged identical in format and content, since clerks of the peace enjoyed considerable freedom to experiment.[124] Until 1642 the sole memorial of each court held in Sussex was the sessions roll, a working file of recognisances, presentments, indictments, depositions, petitions and so on wrapped in the large parchment membrane, which was used to record orders and judgments of the Bench on one side and attendance of bailiffs and constables on the other. But the membranes were clumsy and unsatisfactory as a means of reference to previous decisions of the court. With increasing pressure of business and complexity of the case law of matters such as settlement, precedent hunting became a regular duty for the clerk.[125] Moreover more administrative cases dragged on from one sessions to another. A paper order book, devoted entirely to the final record of each sessions, was an obvious aid to efficient business. After two years accustoming himself to the routine of his office, William Alcock began such a book in 1642. Four years later he abandoned the otiose practice of entering the court's administrative decisions on the outer membrane. William Alcock also began a separate book for certioraries, estreats of fines and highway defaults. His innovations mark a new consciousness of the importance of careful record preservation. They contributed substantially to the maintenance of administrative continuity and stability in Sussex during the Great Rebellion.

The Sussex hundreds consisted of bewilderingly irregular patterns of parishes, with outlying members sometimes far distant. Each hundred was divided into tithings in the western division and into boroughs in the eastern division. Tithingmen and headboroughs, the officers of this smallest unit of government, were immediately responsible to the constables of the hundreds, who acted at the command of the justices.[126] Near the coast, where parishes were generally small, a borough often consisted of two parishes: in the Ouse valley, for example, Southease and Telscombe formed one borough and Newhaven and Piddinghoe another.[127] On the other hand in the Weald, where farmsteads were well scattered, huge parishes sometimes contained several boroughs. The Bench sought to ensure that the local offices were filled by reliable men from the middle ranks of society. They were prepared to discharge gentry who pleaded that the constableship was degrading, or allow them to execute it by a deputy; they refused to accept a Newtimber hired servant as headborough or an Easebourne recusant as tithingman. They excused the old and infirm and men with other responsibilities. An ensign in the militia, a provost marshal, a monthly-assessment commissioner and a clerk in the Exchequer all escaped the constableship.[128] But they could not avoid the web of custom, which produced awkward and absurd situations. It was ridiculous that Richard Greenfield, an old and sick man, whom the court dismissed in 1649, should have been expected to serve as tithingman for Apslee in West Grinstead hundred because he occupied 'certayne lands called Swallowsnest' which 'ought to beare the sayd office for halfe a yeare'.[129] Custom sometimes played into the hands of men reluctant to bear office, until a steward of the leet or the Bench found a way round it. John Rowe was deeply imbued with respect for customary ways, but he had the good sense to recognise when they were inequitable. He was perplexed to find in 1615 that in the hundred of Swanborough, where the constableship was traditionally held in turn by men from Kingston and Iford, there was only a single suitable man in the latter village. His solution, 'not thinkinge it reasonable and fittinge that the said Steven should execute the said office every second yeare and yet desirous to observe the anncient custome', was to appoint a man who lived in Kingston but held extensive lands in Iford. When the appointee complained to the sessions of a breach of custom, the JPs, '*una voce*', supported John Rowe, declaring that 'custome was not broken'.[130] By decisions of this kind the Bench sought to ensure that the ablest rural inhabitants, whether yeomen, husbandmen or craftsmen, played their allotted role in the processes of local government. Without their active service the county could not have been governed.

8

The enforcement of order

It bordereth south on the sea and north on the wyld; in which towe places comminly the people be geven mutch to rwedness and wyllfulness.
Report to the Privy Council concerning Sussex, 8 October 1587.[1]

I cannot see howe it cann stand with the conveniency of the country for me . . . to suffer these privat persons to export this corne nowe in ther possession.
Sir John Leeds to the victualler of the navy, 24 February 1638.[2]

If we should be less industrious then our neighbours in keepeing out those wilde conditioned people from amongst us, not only the publique but every particular man of us would soone finde the inconvenience of it.
The Earl of Northumberland to the Sussex JPs, 23 April 1647.[3]

The essence of the magistracy's task was the preservation of order in their shires. The Sussex JPs recognised that adequate supplies of grain in all parts of the county and strict control of alehouses were preconditions for peace and harmony. They realised that order depended on the effective working of the parochial machinery for the relief of the poor. They regarded the stability of the social hierarchy, the maintenance of sexual morality and the permanence of the family unit as their proper concerns. They took notice of every aspect of men's behaviour and drew no distinction between private and public spheres, since order rested on the patriarchal family and only as a last resort on the parish. In two areas of Sussex continual watchfulness was particularly necessary: the wealden economy attracted a huge vagrant population and on the coast there was a long tradition of wrecking. This chapter explores the various kinds of aggression, exploitation, misfortune and strife which disturbed the normal relationships and the day to day lives of Sussex communities. It is about the poor, the weak and the vulnerable as well as the violent, quarrelsome and irresponsible members of society. How effectively did the justices relieve and control such men?

Harvests and dearth

Sussex was normally self-sufficient in grain supplies. Every rape except Hastings had its own cornland on the Downs and the coastal plain. Yet the quality of the harvest was the most unnerving factor in county government, since the Sussex grain markets were constantly and vigorously exploited by outsiders. London, the West Country, the navy and the King's household in varying degrees all made use of the county's corn.[4] With a run of good harvests, farmers were pleased to unload the excess in their granaries. They were hampered in doing so though by a complicated and inflexible system of proclamations and licences. At Michaelmas 1628, for example, the JPs reported to the Council the many complaints they had received from farmers, who could neither sell their new crop nor their 'great quantityes of corne of the last year's growth', because of the ban on export that the government had nervously applied when heavy rainfall had been expected to ruin the harvest in the summer.[5] On the other hand, the licensing system was sometimes used recklessly in favour of an outsider whom the government was anxious to please. It was a dangerous gamble on the new harvest, for instance, to give the Dutch ambassador a licence, in June 1629, to export 5,000 quarters of corn from any ports in Hampshire and Sussex.[6] Nine months later the general scarcity of grain in the kingdom caused the Council to deprive the United Provinces of a large proportion of the promised consignment, which was still being loaded in Sussex, so that other parts of England might be adequately fed.[7] The presence of two Dutch ships at Chichester and one at Arundel had meanwhile attracted suspicion and rumour along the coast. Peter Cox of Chichester, the factor for the Dutch consignment, was attacked in petitions to the Council as an engrosser for private gain. In fact, the alarm was unfounded. The JPs found no evidence that prices were being inflated and plenty of corn was available. But this case shows the Caroline government's lack of delicacy in handling the licensing system and it illustrates how easily it could appear to be supporting private interests against the public good.[8]

The sensitivity of the community towards the activities of a man with an outside contract is understandable in view of the pressure on the county's granaries. The operations of outsiders could bring real hardship to the poor. The JPs knew well that nothing was more conducive to riot and disorder than the desperation induced by hunger. Thus, Sir John Leeds took the initiative in staying all transportation of corn from Shoreham in February 1638, when he found that the shipping of 130 quarters of wheat and the engrossing of a further 320 quarters by the navy victualler had left the local markets almost bare. A single sack of corn had been sent to Steyning in two market days and the Shoreham populace was threatening to break open the granaries of corn ready for lading. Moreover, Leeds found an error in the licence he was shown which made him doubt whether it was duly authorised. In these circumstances he was bound to put his own neighbourhood first, though his discomfort in flouting the government's licence is evident in his lengthy explanation of the local situation to John Crane, the victualler of the navy. He had taken action, he reported, 'for prevention of a further mischeefe', following the 'outcry of the poor that they could neither have corne in the marketts nor at farmers' houses'. Leeds continued:

> I shall present as a petition on the countrye's behalfe that my consent may not be further pressed for, but that you wil be pleased to make triall of me and my respects towards you by some other commands, wherin I may be so much master of myself that I may shewe my love by my willinge obedience, which in this I cannot do, if I shall discharge that duty to my country which I owe.[9]

Sir John Leeds had acted to prevent any attempt forcibly to seize the grain. Incidents of forcible seizure and minor riots had occurred in Hampshire in 1631 and in a number of counties, such as Kent and Essex, during the harvest crisis of the 1590s.[10]

The fiercest competition for Sussex grain in the decades before the civil war occurred in the winter and spring of 1630 and 1631. The exceptional rainfall in the previous season is well documented. 'Wheat could not be sown in many places', noted Sir John Oglander in the Isle of Wight, 'and that which was must prove ill'. The 1630 harvest was predictably disastrous everywhere, but it was even worse in many other counties than in Sussex.[11] Faced with a national catastrophe, the Council ignored the reports of Sussex JPs about the county's lack of grain to spare.[12] They licensed a London baker to transport large quantities of wheat to the capital and the royal purveyors obtained 462 quarters of oats from the county.[13] Crown purveyors were of course obvious scapegoats, but the county was probably right in its surmise, reported by Sir Thomas Sackville and Robert Foster, that they were 'a greate meanes to raise the prise of oates to two shillings the bushell, it being a rate before that tyme unhard of in these parts'. The justices, meeting in their own rapes, were unanimous in attributing the difficulties they faced in preventing the starvation of the poor to the demand in the adjacent counties. The Pevensey rape JPs spoke of the great quantities of wheat and barley 'drawne from hence' to London and elsewhere. The justices of Arundel rape explained how the draining of the Surrey markets by the purveyors of the city of London put pressure in turn on theirs and caused prices to reach an 'extraordinary rate'.[14]

The moral consensus of opinion of the community favoured paternalistic intervention by the JPs and a responsible policy to ensure that the poor received bread in time of dearth.[15] Scarcity of grain made men watchful and suspicious of the activities of all corn dealers who might be tempted to put their own profit before the public good. After the deficient harvest of 1637, some of the Ouse valley farmers were accused at sessions of buying and engrossing wheat in private transactions. Corn had been seen being carried to the river from Rodmell in carts and on horseback. The quantities involved were small, but any dealings, however tiny, outside the open market were thought to encourage the rise in prices. There was perennial suspicion that millers would exploit a situation of dearth, so they came under close scrutiny. In the midst of the run of bad harvests from 1646 to 1650 the Lewes constables presented five millers, who were generally unpopular because they took 'mutch moore tolle in these deear times then is thear due'. Farmers and tradesmen were expected to respond generously to the needs of the poor when the harvest failed and there is much evidence that they did. Farmers throughout Sussex cooperated readily with the JPs' enforcement of the government's *Book of Orders* in 1631 by releasing small weekly proportions of their stocks of grain for sale on the open market. The Lewes maltsters agreed with the constables in 1649 to keep in hand sufficient unmalted barley 'to searve all the poore of this burow iff they requiar it'.[16] In the end it was the gentry and wealthier yeomen who were obliged to see the county through the harvest crises of 1631 and 1650 by generous subsidies to the parish poor rates. These rates suddenly had to support much larger numbers than usual. In 1650 Sir Thomas Pelham gave three pounds to East Hoathly 'to buy corne for the poore'.[17] In the earlier crisis the justices of Pevensey rape made a systematic appeal to those who had the means to support their neighbours:

> Wee dealt with the most substantiall inhabitants of those parishes where the poore did most abounde to afford some liberall helpe to theire poor people, who partly by the perswasions of us and of their ministers and of theire owne charytable disposition have laid down in some one parish about thirty pounds, in another twenty pounds, some lesse, accordinge to the extent and abilitie of theire parishes, above their assessments.

The JPs appointed badgers to buy corn and sell it at a subsidised rate. This procedure, they declared in May 1631, 'hath yeelded greate releeffe to the poore and we hope will hould out in that measure till harvest'.[18]

The Elizabethan government's 1586 *Book of Orders*, reissued in the dearth of 1631, commanded that all corn should be sold in the open market; it emphasised magisterial supervision of the markets as the best protection of the poor from exploitation.[19] In the reports of their practice only the JPs of Lewes rape stressed their enforcement of such supervision. In Lewes and Brighton markets, the justices explained, no corn was sold until eleven o'clock, when the people of the remotest parishes had been able to come in, and then only small quantities until one.[20] But the Sussex justices, like those of Norfolk, Nottinghamshire and other counties, in general preferred to rely on the willingness of the comparatively wealthy to help their poorer neighbours at home, 'upon reasonable prices and upon trust'. 'Every town knows their own poor and their own wants', declared the Norfolk Bench in a statement of the 'reasons against the general sending of corn to markets' in 1631.[21] Moreover the Sussex JPs found it practical to maintain surveillance over a system of parochial distribution of corn through overseers of the poor, who accounted to petty sessions. On several occasions they pointed out to the Council the advantages of the parochial system. The JPs of Arundel rape found attendance at market 'much prejudiciall to the labors of poore labouringe people'. Those responsible for Hastings rape expounded the same point more fully. It was fitting to allow those with a little extra corn to sell it to the poor at home:

> who beeinge farre from markett wil be much more disabled by losse of time, neither have they money to buye in time of the markett, but are constrayned by reason of theire necessity to buye when they have money, besides we finde those who have any corne to spare sell it better cheape at home to their poore neighbors then in the markets.[22]

The Norfolk JPs put the same arguments, adding that, besides losing a day's work, the labourer was attracted to the urban vices of 'drinking, disorder, and idleness'. Country gentry knew the temper of their counties better than the Council and were not afraid to ignore directions from London that would only hinder their efforts to keep stomachs full and men quiet.

The consequences of a deficient harvest were always most serious in Hastings rape which did not have 'a corne country or wayes to bee made passable for carrieinge any greate quantitie in the winter tyme'.[23] Hastings and Rye depended principally on coastal imports of grain from the western rapes, though mealmen travelling the wealden roads also did something to help them out.[24] When the mayor of Rye heard rumours that the town's mealman had been complained against as an engrosser after the deficient harvest of 1637, he appealed to the JPs of the county not to deprive him of his licence. The mealman's trade, explained the mayor, succoured 'the poorest sort' of Rye, who bought 'some a peck, some a gallon, some more, and some lesse according to such quantities as they were able'.[25] The dearth of 1631 brought about an open conflict of interests within the county between the east and the west. In November 1630 the Rye purveyor shipped a substantial consignment of wheat from Chichester. But by the end of the year the western Bench was enforcing a strict restraint of coastal trade in grain, basing their policy on the *Book of Orders* and the exigences of the situation in their own rapes. Import by sea into Hastings rape ceased and the JPs there gloomily concluded in February 1631, after a survey of barns and granaries, that there was not even half the corn available to sustain the rape until the new harvest.[26] The government's response to this report, and to a direct approach to the Council through the Earl of Dorset's cousin Sir Thomas Sackville, showed blank incomprehension of local transport conditions. They merely reiterated that it was not their intention by the *Book of Orders* to prevent farmers from selling corn outside their own neighbourhood so long as it was transported by land. It was not until the end of April that the Bench was directed to lift its ban on shipment of grain to Rye, after the corporation had explained in a petition how, with 'little or no corne growing thereabouts', they had always been provided for by purveyors. Hastings was relieved a month later after a similar petition.[27] The Council only acted when the plight of the eastern corner of the county had become desperate. On 9 May Sir Thomas Sackville and Robert Foster had expressed their fear that, despite the charity of the more wealthy, corn might soon be 'soe deere that the poore will not be able to live', unless free passage by sea was allowed. The people of Rye must have seen it as an act of God when, in March, a ship carrying corn from Hull to London was blown by a strong wind into the Channel and against Dungeness, where, floundering and leaking, the captain willingly sold off much of his cargo.[28] In short, the justices strove, successfully on the whole, to protect the county from the worst effects of harvest failure, despite insensitive responses by the government in London to provincial conditions.

Control of alehouses

A general consensus of opinion among gentry, substantial householders and ministers regarded alehouses with suspicion and disfavour. However, there were some differences in the motivation behind the numerous petitions for the limiting of alehouses that were presented to the Bench. The minister of Eastergate, who organised a petition there in 1606 alleging that an unruly publican had sold at least three tons of beer since he was suppressed a few weeks previously, presumably saw the matter in more directly moral terms than the licensed publicans of Boxgrove, who resisted the competition in 1625 of the village tailor, who had extended his lines of business without a licence but with 'great bragges and bosts'.[29] But the general pattern of complaint was invariably similar. Alehouses were seen as nurseries of potential crime and immorality. The Eastergate petition claimed that they encouraged theft and quarrelling; a Lindfield petition concluded that the suppression of three or four alehouses in the village would 'give a great stroke at iniqty'; the inhabitants of Heathfield spoke of the corruption of youth

> who havinge so many snares before them and the alluringe insinuations of alehouskeepers, are easily englangled, so that it is much feared that there may be a foundation of loosnes laied in the succeedinge generation and heerby this parish retaine too justly the old repute of licentiousness.[30]

JPs knew from experience the truth of such allegations. Time and again their interrogations led them back to a chance meeting at an alehouse, where a sheepstealing partnership had been founded or a quarrel had begun with rash drunken words.[31] Furthermore, the sabbatarian concerns of Puritan JPs also prejudiced them against alehouses. Numerous presentments in the church courts confirm their impact on church attendance.[32] There were other practical considerations. In periods of dearth a check on maltsters and an abridgement of alehouses was an obvious step to conserve grain supplies, as the Council regularly pointed out. Inns assisted the spread of infectious diseases: a Brighton publican who continued to trade when he had smallpox in 1653 caused an epidemic involving many deaths in the town.[33] Most serious of all, in the eyes of the leaders of the community, was the distraction of the people from a sober, industrious course of life. A memorandum listing the likely causes of the 'destruction and ruine' of Rye included 'the suffiring of soe many younge people to draw beer licensed and unlicensed who have or may find other callings, to the better improvement for themselves and good to the town in generall'. The Heathfield petition maintained that the frequenting of alehouses by the poor caused 'the wastinge of theire strength, time and mony untill such time as they become a parish charge'.[34]

The policy of the Bench was only to license alehouses in the places where there was a regular demand for food and lodging. In the market towns they favoured establishments which were commodious for commercial transactions and administrative business. A Lewes alehouse, for example, was suppressed in 1658 when the landlord refused to lodge strangers; a Petworth man stressed his 'convenient house and good stable rome' in an attempt to obtain a licence to sell wine.[35] In regard to rural alehouses the Bench paid attention to the proximity of main roads. Some smallish villages could make out a special case. West Wittering emphasised the needs of travellers on their way to the ferry to Hayling Island; the parishioners of Wartling argued persuasively that a victualling and alehouse at Boreham, on the busy thoroughfare skirting Pevensey marshes, would serve many people.[36] Analysis of the licences issued in Hastings rape between 1627 and 1640 shows how, such considerations aside, the JPs there sought to confine rural alehouses to the larger villages such as Ticehurst, Heathfield and Burwash. Regularly they refused to renew licences to men in the less populous parishes.[37] Sometimes the Bench made it clear at sessions that no alehouse was henceforth to be licensed in a particular village: Goring, for instance, suffered this fate in 1605 and Rodmell in 1647.[38] There were, nevertheless, considerable variations from rape to rape in the attitudes of justices towards village establishments. The justices of Arundel rape reported that they had allowed every parish which was not a market town one alehouse only in 1631. In Chichester rape magisterial policy at that time was much stricter: 'we have putt downe all alehouses in villages unlesse it bee neere a creeke or haven and suppressed them for the most parte in the markett townes', the Council was informed.[39]

How effectively were the justices able to enforce alehouse regulation? The 1631 reports came at a time of maximum activity, after a drive to close unlicensed establishments and abridge licensed ones which had revealed fly-by-night tippling houses in village after village. They reflect the optimism of men who had completed a purge. But in town and country alike mushrooming alehouses were a problem that required constant attention. With the competition for licences as intense as it was in Hastings rape in the 1620s and 30s, it is not surprising that for many the temptation to sell beer on the quiet, when they were unlucky with the Bench, was overwhelming. At least twenty-eight villages in the rape had a licensed alehouse at some time between 1615 and 1642, but the publicans of the smaller villages seldom managed to retain their licences for more than a year or two at a time. It is hard to believe that the publican of Peasmarsh, for example, who was successful in 1627 and 1638 yet deprived of a licence in 1636 and 1640, let his friends and neighbours go thirsty when his house sign was down. Although unlicensed alehouses appeared on the serious agenda with monotonous regularity, suppression was in fact a haphazard business.[40] The weakness of the statute 3 Charles I, c. 4, which gave a single JP authority to close an unlicensed alehouse on 'view and sight', was that it did not require him to certify his action to the clerk of the peace. There was no adequate procedure for ensuring that the constable had seen the doors finally closed. Closure of the numerous tippling houses that infested back streets depended in the last resort on the initiative of parishioners. They recognised the need for a systematic approach. A ban was imposed at Lewes in 1598 on the issue of licences except at sessions and at the request of the constables and the company of the twelve; in 1628, and again in 1651, it was necessary for the leading inhabitants of the town to draw the attention of the Bench to the neglect of this ban. The Heathfield petition of 1654 demanded 'some well disposed and active persons in some way and power for a full search and discovery' of the back street establishments.[41]

Coordination was the essence of the problem. So long as each justice granted and withdrew licences as and when he thought fit, there was a chance for men to play JPs off against each other and for corruption to occur.[42] Comprehensive and systematic oversight was gradually achieved between 1600 and 1643. As early as 1605, the justices of Arundel rape held licensing sessions in their northern and southern divisions. In Hastings rape the clear policy which has been discussed coincided with close cooperation between men long used to working together. Licensing sessions were also held in Bramber and Pevensey rapes during the 1620s. Yet the necessity for a drive against alehouses in the early 1630s suggests that licensing was still erratic in some rapes and that it was not fully coordinated before the general campaign to reform local government, enshrined in the government's *Book of Orders*, began. The large numbers of certificates of recognisances in the sessions rolls for the years 1636 to 1643 indicate that comprehensive licensing was then established.[43] There was a partial breakdown of the system in the war years: in 1644, for example, a Burwash man got a licence 'upon undue information', after another justice had convicted him of keeping an unlicensed house. Back street tippling flourished in Arundel when it became a garrison town. Thirty alehouses were open there in 1645. The previous year the churchwardens of Horsham had reported twenty-seven publicans without licences in their town.[44] It was not until the 1650s that alehouse licensing became fully integrated into the month by month procedures and petty sessions of the JPs in each rape.

Charity and poor relief

With the Reformation the tradition of charity towards the poor was reinforced by the exhortations of Protestant preachers and pamphleteers. The Elizabethan poor law merely gave statutory form to a generally recognised social and moral duty.[45] Had they provided for the poor of the parish 'according to God's word', Bishop Bickley asked the churchwardens in his visitation articles of 1586?[46] The poor box in church was a constant reminder of the needs of the less fortunate members of the parish. The gentry had always given a lead in charitable giving and during the years 1600 to 1660 there was no sign of a slackening of their responsibility. Christmas was customarily the time of greatest generosity: at Sedlescombe John Everenden gave a few shillings to the poor of his parish; at Herstmonceux in the 1640s Francis, Lord Dacre in the style of his ancestors distributed beef, loaves and money to forty-four poor people; at East Hoathly and a handful of neighbouring parishes Sir Thomas Pelham gave in a similar fashion. In both 1626 and 1627, Pelham accounted for more than thirty-five pounds spent on Christmas doles. Lady Pelham unloaded her cast-off gowns on the villagers and men living beyond the immediate circle of the family's bounty knew that they could expect bread and money at the Halland gate.[47] At other seasons of the year the gentry's charity was more erratic, but it often sustained parishes or individuals in time of need. During the civil war Thomas Whitfield gave large numbers of coats, waistcoats and other garments to the numerous poor of Worth. Sir Thomas Pelham frequently responded to the plight of a poor boy by providing the money to bind him out as an apprentice, or of a parish stricken with smallpox or plague by a gift of money.[48]

Despite a Puritan reaction against funeral doles, many gentry continued to direct in their wills that money should be given to the poor of their parish. Great magnates often recognised a wider obligation: Sir Walter Covert, for instance, bequeathed five pounds each in 1631 to the poor of nine parishes in the vicinity of Slaugham. William Fettiplace, more unusually, specified in 1656 that his legacies to the poor of Slaugham and Cuckfield should be used to buy corn in time of famine.[49] Charities founded by gentry in their wills took many forms. Thomas Jefferay's in 1663 was for the succour of forty of the poor of his parish of Chiddingly. William Holland sought to ensure that after his death in 1614 six poor men and women of Chichester should receive the same benefit every Sunday that they had done in his lifetime. His executors were to arrange the distribution to each of them of a piece of boiled beef, a pot of pottage, a loaf of bread and a quart of beer. Holland also established a stock to bind poor children apprentice, 'whereby they may gett good trades for the better maintenance in tyme to come for the avoydinge and suppressinge of idlenes'.[50] But such bequests, like the county's almshouses, were haphazardly distributed. Chichester was well endowed with almshouses: there was St Mary's as well as William Cawley's new foundation of 1626 in the suburb of St Bartholomew's. So was East Grinstead, where Sackville College gave shelter and board to thirty poor people. In Arundel rape, on the other hand, whereas Petworth had four useful charities including an almshouse for twelve people, only nine of the other fifty-seven parishes could rely on any regular source of charitable funds.[51]

The charity of the gentry was too erratic, too indiscriminate in its geographical distribution, too dependent on the whims and initiative of individuals to support by itself the growing numbers of poor people in Sussex between 1600 and 1660. During the first three decades of the century parish after parish was forced to fall back on taxation for the aid of its poor. The enforcement of the 1601 poor law was gradual and piecemeal. Disputes about rating to the poor tax, a significant new feature of the sessions rolls for the 1620s and 30s, suggest that by then most parishes had resorted to taxation. A few of the surviving overseers accounts go back further: those for St Andrew's, Chichester, for instance, begin in 1618.[52] Analysis of the numbers of poor relief cases coming before the Bench between 1625 and 1660 shows why it had no choice but to confirm and enforce taxation as the permanent basis of care for the poor. The increase in the scale of poor relief ordered by the JPs was not as dramatic in Sussex as in Warwickshire, but the pattern was the same. The numbers requiring help steadily increased throughout the period and cases multiplied fastest in times of dearth.[53] Harvest failure always pushed some of those on the edge of subsistence below the poverty line. It sometimes made increases in taxation necessary. 'Wee have ordered that the impotent poore in some parishes should have their weekly allowance dobled, in all parishes increased', reported the justices of Bramber rape in the harvest crisis of 1631.[54] So, when the civil war broke out, the poor rate had become a fact of life. Men's charitable impulses had been straightened and directed into a system of regular parochial relief of those unable to support themselves.

How much men had to pay depended largely on where they lived. Taxation was heaviest in the wealden parishes of the east. At Rotherfield, an ironworking parish with a large but dispersed population, receipts in 1658–59 totalled £119 and disbursements £111. The next year £156 was collected and the following year £173. At Worth, said in 1638 to be 'full of poore people', the assessments raised between forty and fifty-seven pounds in the mid-1640s.[55] The Fittleworth overseers, on the other hand, only reckoned to raise about twenty pounds, the Cowfold overseers about ten pounds and those of St Andrew's Chichester about five pounds.[56] The normal qualifications for assistance from the poor rate were childhood, age or sickness. Most of the money was spent on the weekly dole to individuals, many of them widows. Except in periods of dearth, there is no sign of any broadening of the concept of the deserving poor such as took place in Salisbury and perhaps other towns.[57] Able-bodied single men were expected to support themselves whatever the local employment situation. Special circumstances were necessary to bring a family with a breadwinner within the system, such as the disabilities of the whole of a Kirdford family of four or the madness of a Ringmer housewife with five small children. The financial support given to families was roughly graded according to the number of children and was gradually increased with the rising cost of living. The Sussex JPs seem to have been rather more generous in fixing people's doles than those in Warwickshire.[58]

The poor rate was also much used to give partial and temporary support to those in need. The Bench frequently responded to overseers' petitions for licences to erect cottages for the poor without the statutory four acres of land.[59] Surgeons' fees and bills for physic were sometimes paid for people who in good health scraped a living on their own. Laconic entries in the Worth accounts provide fleeting glimpses of the realities of life for those on the borderlines of subsistence: a man was bought a pair of hose or a smock, a woman was assisted with a 'fortnight's bording and washing when she could not helpe herself', a child's 'grave and knell' were paid for.[60] After the catastrophic harvest of 1630, the JPs in Chichester, Arundel, Bramber and Hastings rapes all enforced the usually disregarded provision of the 1601 statute that stocks of materials to set the poor on work should be provided. In some areas, Bramber rape and parts of Hastings rape for instance, the stocks were kept going and the work was supervised well into the decade. Sir Thomas Pelham contributed to a special 'scott for a stock to the poor at Burwash' as late as 1636.[61] But the task of overseeing the business was tiresome and time-consuming for the parish officers, and there was a strong temptation to return to total reliance on the dole once the harvest crisis was over. In Pevensey rape the Kentish clothiers were ready to put out so much work to poor women and children, and the employment opportunities in the ironworks were such that the expedient of provision of stocks was never implemented. It was essentially an emergency measure and an unpopular one with those expected to administer it. When ninety pounds was raised for setting the poor of Petworth to work in 1650, the achievement reflected the tireless campaigning of the Puritan divine Francis Cheynell more than any general enthusiasm for the scheme.[62]

One of the most striking reforms achieved through the government's *Book of Orders* was the magistracy's drive to make the apprenticeship system play its proper role in poor relief. The system was already well established in some places. The Worth apprenticeship indentures run from 1616 and a standard printed form was in use from 1625.[63] But the inflated numbers of apprentices put forth in 1631 suggest that overseers had become slack about raising the covenant money and about persuading their neighbours of their duty and obligations. In Arundel and Chichester rapes 130 children were put to masters in a single year; in Arundel rape, moreover, the JPs took a note 'of all children above the age of eight years, which are yet unfitt to be put forth, with the names of the ablest inhabitants in every parish which are fitt to receive them', as a record to check future action.[64] During the 1630s apprenticeship of poor children was made systematic in every rape and so continued after the civil war.[65] The Bench insisted, taking as their authority the ruling of the judges in 1633 that no occupation was excluded from receiving apprentices, that the whole community should cooperate in the scheme. Sometimes a threat of binding to assizes was necessary to drive men to fulfil their responsibilities; more often persuasion worked. In 1626, for instance, the mayor of Arundel informed the clerk of the peace that a reluctant master had, 'uppon better consideration', received his apprentice again and so should not be called to the sessions.[66] There were sound practical reasons for the Bench's careful attention to the working of the apprenticeship sytem. One lad explained to Sir Thomas Bishop 'that he was inforced' to steal 'three or fower pudinges for want of meate for that his master keepeth him so hard without victualls that he was not able to live'.[67] In cases where there was clear evidence of maltreatment the JPs put compassion for the child before insistence on a man's obligations. Harsh masters were sometimes permitted to buy their way out of the system, with a payment towards the apprentice's maintenance or towards his putting forth to a new master.[68]

Whereas men became accustomed to the obligation to relieve the poor of their own parish, they found it hard to accept the provision of the poor law statute 39 Elizabeth, c. 3 that in an emergency they could be taxed towards the relief of a neighbouring parish. The Bench encountered the utmost difficulty in enforcing this clause of the statute in favour of St Pancras, Chichester. St Pancras was an extramural suburb of Chichester in which poverty was endemic at the best of times. After its devastation in the siege of 1642 it became a slum: 'by reason of the burninge and pullinge downe of their houses, the chiefest of the inhabitants are gone, and the poore increased, beinge twice soe many as formerly have bine', related a petition of 1651.[69] The sale of the church bells yielded a paltry eight pounds.[70] In 1649 the JPs faced the fact that special rates would have to be imposed on nearby parishes. The assize judges confirmed their order but, even so, the officers of seventeen neighbouring parishes which were called upon to help St Pancras were not prepared to cooperate. In fact they dragged their heels throughout the 1650s. Parish after parish badgered quarter and petty sessions to let them off the charge. There was no willingness to help the miserable community of shack dwellers who clung to Chichester's city wall. In 1655 Bersted managed to show that its own poor had increased; at the next sessions North Mundham put in a petition; in 1658 East Lavant and Westhampnett complained; the following year Boxgrove was discharged. Sixteen orders of sessions concerning St Pancras were made between 1649 and 1660 and at the end of it all the problem of this parish, which had been deserted by the wealthy and invaded by the hapless and unemployed, remained unsolved.[71] In general the reaction of the county community to the problem of the destitute was sympathetic and constructive, but the case of St Pancras shows how narrowly parishioners could regard their responsibility.

Contention and conformity

In pre-industrial village communities, everyone assumed that they had a right to know what everyone else was doing. There was little or no privacy. Eavesdropping may technically have been an offence—in 1648 a Horsham husbandman and his wife were in fact fined for it at sessions—but it was habitual and ineradicable. Villagers were constantly prying into each other's affairs.[72] When a Steyning lad saw a stablehand in the act of buggery of a mare in 1610 'looking in a hole', he quickly called a passer-by, who in turn called his dame. Others were called 'uppon this rumour' and later testified. A Westbourne cordwainer told a JP in 1655 about how he had witnessed a married woman of his village in bed with another man.[73] Both informal and judicial means were used to enforce social conformity. Cuckolded husbands or wife-beaters were mocked with the procession of 'riding the skimmington', scolds were punished with the ducking-stool, contentious men and women and those who offended the moral values of the community were presented before the ecclesiastical and lay courts.[74] The Bench used sureties for good behaviour, charges of barratry and the house of correction as punishments.[75] Churchwardens sometimes complained bitterly when a minister admitted to the sacrament offenders against established mores. At Westhampnett in 1625, for instance, it was thought intolerable that a man who was an 'open contender', one who 'will not reconcile himself, though it hath been sought by some of the parish', should be admitted; in 1639 the curate of Mountfield was presented for giving communion to two notorious sexual offenders.[76] Tudor and Stuart rural society was rigid and intolerant. Those who failed to conform were often relentlessly pursued.

The values of village communities are well documented. Concern to enforce a rigorous sexual code as well as anxiety over maintenance of bastard children lay behind the endless presentations by churchwardens for sexual activity outside marriage.[77] But the breakdown of the church courts in the 1640s forced villagers to concentrate on sexual offences punishable at assizes. Eight men came before the assize judges in the 1650s accused of the longstanding felonies of bigamy, rape and buggery; three others were accused of incest as it was widely defined under the 1650 Act.[78] With determined sexual offenders villagers were already turning to the JPs, rather than the impotent church courts, before the civil war. A Ringmer couple, alleged the parishioners in 1641, had 'for many yeares lived together in a scandalous manner and have ben often presented by the churchwardens of Ringmer uppon a common fame of adultery and fornication into the ecclesiasticall courte'. The Bench ordered that they should cease to cohabit, binding the man to good behaviour, and the minister repeatedly admonished them, yet by the following Easter their infamous life was said to be as notorious as ever, not only to the Bench but to 'the whole countrie'.[79] The efforts of churchwardens to secure punishment of adulterers and whoremongers shows their concern for the cohesion and stability of the family unit. The activities of a man like Peter Soane of Henfield were seen as a threat to the foundations of society and a provocation to the whole village. Despite the churchwardens' warnings and a previous presentation in the archdeaconry court, Soane continued to keep company with another man's wife 'in time of divine service upon Sondaies in a scandalous and suspicious manner'. The behaviour of the Hailsham shoemaker who caused 'publique scandall and offence' by keeping three young women in his house was equally provocative. So was that of the Arlington man who, according to the churchwardens, ran after eleven whores as soon as his wife was dead.[80] There is no evidence that the death penalty for adultery in the Act of 1650 was anywhere enforced, but one Sussex couple were sent before assizes for adultery in 1659. In the same year another couple were bound to good behaviour at sessions after they were reported as 'persons of ill name and fame' who lived together unmarried.[81]

Discord and quarrelling within the family were regarded as proper matters for public concern and intervention. Once a man had a reputation as a drunkard and swearer, gossip was particularly liable to circulate freely about his family affairs. Thus, taking their lead from the stories of the village busybodies, the churchwardens at Hamsey in 1637 presented William Young for his ill respect towards his mother. Young, it seems, habitually called his mother, in whose house his family lived rent free, an old whore. Moreover, his wife had been heard to hope 'that the divell would shortly breake her necke'. What scandalised the village was the couple's lack of gratitude for the maintenance the mother had given them, without which, it was thought, 'theire children would have sterved before this tyme'. On another occasion, at Framfield in 1627, a group of parishioners took the initiative in requesting the Bench to investigate the 'unkinde differences' between the vicar and his wife. Numerous husbands and wives were presented in the church courts for living apart.[82] The breakup of families often had the serious practical implication of increasing the parish charge, as parents evaded their responsibilities towards children. It was seen as the root of disorder within a village community. Feuding between families was taken equally seriously. Sometimes the JPs, responding to pressure from a village, persuaded the parties at odds to participate in a public reconciliation. Thus, at the sessions in 1625, the minister of Warbleton and two parishioners with whom he had fallen out took each other by the hand as a mark of their desire 'to live in amity'.[83] No such solution was achieved in the case of Francis Pelling, a Chailey man who for twenty-six years plagued the local and national authorities for redress of his grievances against a group of neighbours. 'Unless your lordshipps wil be pleased to stay his course', wrote Sir Walter Covert and Sir John Shurley wearily after the fourth full hearing of the case in 1630, 'he will still be troublesome to this most honourable boarde and the country whilst he liveth'.[84]

Men who disturbed the harmony of village life by their contentious ways were colourfully described in the petitions and presentments of parishioners. A Burwash man was 'a common sower of discord and debate among his neighbours . . . full of evill and foule wordes'; a Storrington man was 'a makebate amongst his neighbors using all meanes he can to sett them to law with each other'; a Bodiham man was 'a malicious, contentious, uncharitable person, seeking the unjust vexation of his neighbours'.[85] A few of the troublemakers were clearly deranged. A Hardham husbandman who threatened to fire the thatch of his landlord's house, declared 'that he served the devill and that the divell must have him' and ran down the street naked at night turned the whole village in terror against him. It is hard to know what to make of the behaviour of the choleric Selsey vicar Henry Kent, who managed to make enemies of most of his parishioners. He rode off leaving women waiting to be churched, told those who would not play cards with him in the alehouse that they would be damned, and preached in 'such kinde of doctrine and in such outrageous words and rayling manner spoken that it rather affrighteth and feareth most of his hearers than edyfieth them'.[86]

Quarrelsome people often came to the notice of the substantial men of a village because they offended against the principles of social deference. The chief inhabitants of Lamberhurst were highly indignant that a forgeman's wife was not only 'of very evill behaviour by hir comon brawling and untamed rude speeches amongst hir equalls but also to divers of the better sort'. The Burwash troublemaker mentioned above provoked 'not only his equalls and inferiors but also his superiors' and boasted that he had 'made his betters to buckle under him and to lett him have his will'.[87] In other cases blatant idleness generated suspicion and brought tensions with neighbours to the surface. A Fletching tailor, 'of very evill and lewd behaviour, usually drunck, a blasphemer and curser', followed neither his vocation 'nor any honest labor or meanes for his maintenance'. A Steyning man, always idle by day, was believed to live by filching at night.[88] Hard dealing was regarded as equally reprehensible. Articles against a Mayfield yeoman painted him as the stereotype of the vicious self-interested sheep-farmer, engrossing, enclosing, rackrenting, maiming any who 'find fault with his hard dealing', perjuring and harassing poor men at law. The Storrington 'makebate' mentioned above was reported to open his gates and fences to take his poor neighbours' cattle to impound them, 'till hee very neere starveth them and breaketh some of their swynes leggs'. The unscrupulous self-advancement of an Eastbourne quack doctor and usurer was set out in twenty-eight articles exhibited against him in 1614. He was accused of lending money on bond and then extorting huge sums by refusing to deliver up the agreement, and of taking out suits against his enemies as a means of terrorising them into paying him money or giving him land. Posing as a physician, he charged 'simple people as much as the best phisihon in Sussex': he had demanded fourpence it was said, for looking on the urine of a child who, despite his confidence, had died within an hour.[89] Even when allowances have been made for pique and personal animosity, a pattern of what was seen as antisocial and offensive behaviour emerges. Fair dealing, honest labour, respect for social superiors, mild language and kindliness towards neighbours: these were the ideals that sustained village communities in the seventeenth century.

Contentious, isolated, non-conforming members of the local community were the most likely to be accused of witchcraft. The helpless old woman who had fallen out with her neighbours was an obvious scapegoat when others were in distress. For the rejected, witchcraft, like arson and cursing, was a means for expressing hostility against society. Yet, in comparison with many other counties, Sussex was hardly touched by the witch craze of the sixteenth and seventeenth centuries. In the whole period 1558 to 1736 only seventeen persons were indicted for witchcraft at the assizes, whereas in every other south-eastern county at least fifty individuals were charged with the crime. Most of the Sussex prosecutions occurred in Elizabeth's reign. Such evidence as there is about witch beliefs in the county fits the pattern that has been described from the material relating to other counties.[90] Accusations of malevolent witchcraft invariably emerged after a period of rumour-mongering. The master of a ship becalmed at Pevensey in 1656 blamed an old woman of the village, who was alleged to have prophesied that he would not get the wind he needed for three months. While he kicked his heels in the village, he absorbed the gossip about the witch's evil tongue and the harm she had done to parishioners and their cattle. When a Brightling family were the victims of diabolic possession about 1660, John Busbridge and Thomas Collins held responsible a woman living nearby who was already suspected of witchcraft.[91] The activities of the Rye cunning woman Susan Snapper, who frequently communicated with spirits and on one occasion was taken in a vision to meet the Queen of the Fairies who 'would give her a livinge', began harmlessly enough. In 1607, indeed, she attempted to help the mayor in his last sickness with some 'planett water'. But Susan Snapper was too keen a publicist about the power of the spirits she commanded. Awe turned to suspicion among her neighbours and in 1608 she was found guilty and condemned for witchcraft.[92] Nearly forty years later there was another flurry of activity in Rye when suspicions centred on a woman who was supposed to have visited a neighbour at night, arriving and vanishing through a pane of glass. A sore place on her body, which grew wider and redder, was taken to be the mark of her profession and she and another woman were ordered to undergo the ordeal of 'swimming'.[93]

The depositions about a dispute at Dallington in 1617 indicate a neighbourly conflict of the kind that was particularly likely to produce a charge of *maleficium*. An aggressive couple had quarrelled endlessly with their neighbours since arriving in the village, about the boundaries and fencing of land, assessments to the King and county and financial dealings. Slights and envy turned to threats and malice as the feud consumed the minds of both parties. When cattle were 'strangelie taken' and 'could not be recovered by the skyll of bullocke leaches', it was easy to blame the unpopular intruders. The woman was seen with 'a white thinge in her hands of the bignes of a little chitt or younge catt which she did earnestly looke uppon'.[94] Piece by piece a case to take to court was built up. The circumstances which led one deviant or isolated individual to be accused of witchcraft and not another remain obscure. There were certainly plenty of contentious individuals in Sussex who were vulnerable to charges of witchcraft and who might have been accused in a county such as Essex with a stronger tradition of judicial proceedings. The Horsham husbandman mentioned above who publicised his attachment to the Devil is one of the recorded examples, and the Warnham woman who threw dirt on her neighbours from her gate, reviled them and even prepared a 'posnett of scaldinge water' to do them harm is another.[95]

The late Elizabethan bishops of Chichester enquired in their visitation articles about men known to 'tel destenies, to helpe men to thinges lost' or who used charms or sorceries.[96] But churchwardens were unlikely to present cunning men unless some fradulent practice was suspected. The magical profession was generally tolerated, when engaged only in white magic, since it fulfilled a useful role in rural society.[97] But, more than most professions, it was open to swindle and deceit. The Bench, believing that George Sowton, the Sompting butcher and magician, had by 'the invocacon of spirits and other dyvelise artes' deceived many people, had him bound over in 1605, yet nearly twenty years later the demand for his services in healing the sick seems to have been as great as ever.[98] Whether the JPs had evidence that Sowton habitually overcharged or cheated his clients, or whether they merely distrusted his particular brand of faith healing is not clear. A much more likely case of deliberate fraud occurred in 1614. A Suffolk man had returned home leaving a certain Mary Loveall pregnant and with a promise of marriage. She was persuaded by an acquaintance William Matchwick to give him money and goods, so that he could pay a cunning man called 'Jacke of Nubury' to fetch the man from Suffolk 'wheather he would or noe'. She later gave Matchwick a sheet worth eight shillings, when he told an elaborate story about how he had drunk with the cunning man at Newbury, who had promised to 'cause the devell' to bring the irresponsible father of her child 'agayne upon his back'.

The magician was probably fictitious and Mary Loveall had fallen prey to a trickster.[99] The Bench kept a wary eye for corrupt practices of this kind in connection with white magic.

Bastardy, the consequence of the Bench's and the ecclesiastical courts' inability to check a degree of sexual activity outside marriage, probably created as much work for the JPs as any of the tasks entrusted to them. Churchwardens regularly presented women for having illegitimate children, but the ecclesiastical sanctions were of little use once the child had been conceived.[100] The responsibility for securing maintenance for the unfortunate children who were not born into a stable family fell on the justices. Precisely how many bastard children they dealt with cannot be ascertained, since this was out of sessions work and there was no obligation on JPs to certify their paternity orders to the court. In Somerset, where certification was properly established, an average of more than four cases was recorded per sessions between 1625 and 1638.[101] The high bastardy rates evident from Sussex sessions records can be related to abuse of one particular element in the marriage customs of the time, the private marriage contract. Sexual intercourse was assumed to be permitted once an engagement had taken place.[102] Men of substance would hardly allow an espousal to take place until a firm agreement had been reached between the two families and, in the middle ranks of society at least, there was likely to be insistence on some public act of contract. At the poorer levels of society, on the other hand, engagement was often interpreted as no more than a man's rash and foolhardy promise that he would marry the girl he currently desired to seduce. There were many like Mary Loveall who were abandoned by their insincere suitors. Time and again mothers of bastard children told JPs about their naïve acceptance of wild promises from men they hardly knew.[103]

The justices' first concern in bastardy cases was to save the parish by fixing responsibility on an individual. They showed ingenuity in finding relations who could be made to bring up the child or contribute towards its maintenance. They insisted, following a ruling of the judges in 1633, that masters should retain covenant servants who had become pregnant until a month after delivery. On occasion they even held responsible constables who had allowed a putative father to escape.[104] The Sussex justices regarded the punishments authorised for bastardy in the statutes of 1576 and 1610 primarily as a means of securing adequate maintenance for the child. A spell in the house of correction was used to extract a confession from the mother or enforce responsibility on the father.[105] Yet the Bench reacted angrily to the 'fowle abuse' of a master of the house of correction in 1617, who 'purposelie whipped' a woman 'to make her confesse an other father' three years after the first man she had named had run away to avoid the charge of the child.[106] So tangled did the business of paternity accusations become, even without this kind of cruelty, that the JPs were sometimes cautious in imposing regular weekly payments on a single individual for the support of a child whose fatherhood was in doubt. A Heathfield man, for example, was 'discharged of all further charge or trouble' concerning a bastard on payment of five pounds, since the mother had also accused another.[107] Girls could be terrified by the father into making a false accusation, though they often broke down under the midwives' interrogation at the delivery. Warned by four midwives to wrong no man, Elizabeth Hooke 'tooke up her hands' during her labour and asked God's forgiveness for the false accusation she had made. The father, she later told two JPs, had 'charged her divers tymes that upon her lyfe she should not lay yt to him'. An Arundel gentleman, desperate to save his reputation, mingled threats with blandishments to make his maidservant hold her tongue. After he had failed to abort the child with pills and by hand, he named the man she was to accuse. Eventually the girl blurted out the whole story to the mayor.[108] The truth was often less simple than this and there was undoubtedly a good deal of rough justice in the imposition of affiliation orders, despite the Bench's attempts to be fair. Richard Browne was one who might have expressed a grievance. After he had been bound to support Mary Barber's child, it emerged at her confession in labour 'that Pont lay first and last with her and Richard Browne once and Pont three severall tymes and the said Browne once and that all was done within one weeke'. The niceties of responsibility between these two men did not bother the JPs. A father had already been secured and that was what mattered.[109]

Vagrancy and settlement

There was a long tradition of lawlessness in wealden Sussex. In Ashdown and St Leonard's forests gentry were few and far between and manorial custom was weak. Society here was very different from that in the static nucleated villages of the downland. Churches were often remote. 'Some of the poore of St Leonards forest resort to our church', reported the churchwardens of Slaugham in 1638, since their own parish church was nine miles from their homes.[110] Many others in these forest communities must have attended church seldom or never. Moreover the economy of the wealden area made for a substantial mobile population. The JPs of the downland area of Bramber rape explained that they had found no vagabonds there in 1638 because their neighbourhood, unlike the Weald, had 'no iron works nor other places for employmente'.[111] But mobility was not confined to the northern parts of the county. There were always many men, women and children on the road in all parts of Sussex. An examination of immigration to Canterbury, Faversham and Maidstone between 1580 and 1640 has shown the popularity of the south coast tramping ground.[112] Some people had come considerable distances. Among the vagrants apprehended by the constables in Hastings rape in 1638 and 1639 were a man and his wife with three small children from Yorkshire, a woman with three children from Northamptonshire and men from as far away as Norfolk, Wiltshire, Glamorgan and Devon.[113] Tinkers and chapwomen travelled the county's lanes and did business with all classes of society. The decay of trade in Rye in the 1640s was attributed to 'the sufferinge of strangers, as clothiers, chapmen and pedlers to come into the towne with their wars and sell thm privatly in evry house'.[114]

The wayfaring population created enormous problems of order. There were respectable migrant labourers who scraped a living through seasonal work or who earnestly followed the rumours about where there might be a ready market for their craft. But in law there was no distinction between them and vagabonds. In practice every poor labourer on the roads was likely to be tempted to beg or steal when hard times came. Much of the larceny investigated by the JPs was committed by vagrants and a deficient harvest invariably increased the number of cases of petty theft at sessions.[115] There were always too many casual labourers infesting the shire, too many men like Thomas Brooke and William Marriner, whose cattle-stealing partnership had emerged from a vague hope of finding work and then had quickly come to grief.[116] The bareness and insecurity of the vagrant's life is evident in numerous depositions. For example, a Kentish husbandman had worked in Surrey and Hampshire, and Mayfield, Falmer and Rodmell in Sussex, in the two years before he was taken begging, after breaking his arm 'with a fall out of an oake as he was cutting wood'. Richard Walegrave, who was whipped for stealing a shirt at Lewes in 1625, had lodged during the previous fortnight at Rye, Hastings and Ripe. A Battle man who was accused of stealing some clothes declared that he was returning home after going to Sandwich to seek work as a glover. William Perkins, 'travelinge in the countye of Sussex to gett some relieffe', found the temptation to steal overwhelming when he saw a pot of meat and porridge inside an open cottage door. A Kentish labourer, who 'wrought by the day', stole a piece of cloth and bargained with it for a 'potte of beere and a penny white lofe', at a house on Burwash Down. A discharged soldier returning home to Kent in 1645 took a napkin and handkerchief from the hedge of the Courthopes of Whiligh.[117]

During the civil war conditions played into the hands of the vagrant population. It was easy for a man to pretend that he was a soldier and that his company was a couple of villages away.[118] The drive in the early 1630s to rid the countryside of vagrants might just as well have never taken place. By 1647 the Surrey JPs were so thoroughly alarmed that they requested the Earl of Northumberland, when they discussed with him 'a course to suppresse the multitude of vagabonds and other idle people that swarmed' in their county, to gain the cooperation of the Sussex Bench in a new attack on the problem.[119] The most serious aspect of vagrancy was the tendency of gangs of unemployed ruffians to roam the countryside. A band of 'wandering people', who slept in barns and were led by Black James, menaced the iron-working district around Horsham in 1614. 'They are such as breede a terror in the country heerabout', reported Sir Richard Michelbourne of another band which infested the Horsted Keynes neighbourhood in 1633.[120] In the war years the number of gangs of rootless men greatly increased. A Shropshire collier apprehended in Sussex in 1644, explained how he had been taken while travelling into Devon, 'with thirty-six more with him by the scouts belonging to the armies, but whether the King's or parliament's he knoweth not'. The same year a man was eventually arrested at Rye, after he had successfully deceived the townsmen into feeding and boarding several gangs of men, by showing a forged pass and declaring that he was 'the conductor and leader of the said company'. Another marauding band, brought before the assize judges in 1644, had 'counterfeited passes to the terror and disturbance of His Majestie's subjects'.[121]

Strict enforcement of watch and ward and general searches for vagrants by parish officers were the foundations of the Bench's policy for the control of vagrancy. Regular watching was particularly important at much frequented entry points to the county, but the byways also required attention. A footway by a mill in Lamberhurst parish, noted the gentry there, enabled rogues to escape the watch set on the nearby bridge.[122] The JPs recognised the need to keep a firm hand on public occasions such as fairs, which encouraged vagrants to congregate. In 1657 they suppressed the two-day fair planned at Fletching, 'without authority and contrary to lawe to the disturbance of the publique peace'. Cases in the sessions rolls show how country fairs provided a heyday for cutpurses and for wandering rogues to sell stolen goods. A rogue taken at Rudgwick fair, for instance, confessed that he had 'hadd no certaine place of dwelling' for two years and told an unlikely story about how he had obtained the pewter he was trying to sell. Another man, in his company, had 'wandered about the countrey' for six years since his master, a Brighton fisherman, had died.[123] The Bench experimented with a system of provost marshals to combat vagrancy, which was also tried in Worcestershire. A minor gentleman in each rape was appointed to the office of marshal at various times between the 1620s and 1640s.[124] The provost marshals thus had authority over a much wider area than the constables. The JPs seem to have been well pleased with the experiment: no vagrants had been apprehended in the previous months, they reported from Bramber rape in 1639, because the provost marshals had 'rid the country of such wanderers'.[125] In view of their effectiveness in Sussex, it is surprising that the JPs in both Essex and Hampshire resisted the Council's pressure to use marshals, maintaining that constables were more satisfactory.[126]

Houses of correction for the idle and disorderly were set up before the civil war at Lewes, Battle, Chichester, Horsham and Petworth.[127] Three bridewells soon proved too great a burden on the county funds in the western division, so they were replaced by a single one at Arundel.[128]

The Lewes house of correction, under the mastership of Nicholas Shelley in the 1650s, became a model of good order and careful management. Shelley regularly presented to sessions notes of his expenses and repairs.[129] The houses of correction were convenient dumping grounds for those who plagued the countryside. 'I pray sir', wrote Sir Richard Michelbourne to the clerk of the peace about the ruffians he had sent before the Bench in 1633, 'if they be quitted moove the justices that they may goe to the howse of correction there to remayne untill further order'. But hard labour and regular whippings did nothing to deter from further thieving a man who had taken to the road, and despaired of finding employment. Black James had already been twice committed to the Chichester bridewell when he was arrested in 1614. One of the wanderers taken at Rudgwick fair had just been delivered from the house of correction.[130]

Vigorous enforcement of settlement was the only real solution to vagrancy, but there were enormous difficulties. Settlement of unemployed people needing financial assistance in their birthplace or last dwelling-place was highly unpopular with village communities and it was resisted with increasing unscrupulousness and cunning. During the 1640s and 50s overseers showed a new zeal in reporting the arrival of families in their village who were 'likely to become chargeable', in persuading JPs to grant them warrants to remove such families, and in direct action of their own to avoid any increase in the number of their poor. The overseers of Ebisham in Surrey argued at length, through their counsel at assizes, that a family whom they had managed to have sent to Lindfield should stay there. The assize judges were not persuaded that the family would become a parish charge, indeed they found the father had 'lands of his owne and is able to live of himselfe' in Ebisham. Seeing a man beginning to build a cottage in their parish and knowing that it might soon fall to them to support his family, the Clayton officers gave him forty shillings 'to provide for himselfe elsewhere'.[131]

The callous shuttlecocking of unwanted sick people from place to place, which became a feature of the eighteenth-century poor law, had already started in Sussex before the Restoration. A Westham man, who became lame while visiting relations in Eastbourne, was rapidly delivered home in a cart. The constable of Rudgwick, armed with a counterfeit warrant, did the same with a dangerously ill vagrant and her three-year-old child. When, at Ockley, 'she was no sooner layd downe but she imediatly dyed', the chief inhabitants there told the Rudgwick officers that 'they had don more then they could answere in sending a dying woman away in that case'. The officers were persuaded to take the child back again and he was disposed of to a vagrant, who agreed to 'carry him away' for a consideration of forty shillings. 'The childe', it was reported, 'was never heard of since'.[132] Other less harsh methods against an increased burden of poor were also used. Overseers sometimes took security from newcomers against their becoming a parish charge. The JPs, responding to demands for security, evolved a new type of delayed settlement order. In 1640, for example, they recorded that a nailer's sojourn at Easebourne, where he had found work, should not constitute an inhabitancy. A miller's widow and her children, who had gone to live with her brother at Bosham, were to be 'sent back to New Fishbourne there to be as inhabitants if they shall hereafter become chargeable to the parishoners of Bosham'.[133]

The 1662 Act of Settlement finally cleared up the ambiguities of the 1597 poor law about the length of residence establishing inhabitancy. In the interim the resolutions of the judges in 1633 were the only guidance available to JPs. The judges were quite emphatic about what constituted a lawful settling: 'every one who is settled is a native householder; (and a) sojourner, an apprentice or servant for a moneth at least without a just complaint made to remove him or her shall be held to be settled'.[134] The Sussex Bench, like the Hampshire one, based their practice on this resolution and were careful to check that complaints against new arrivals were made within the stipulated time limit.[135] But in some other counties JPs applied different tests. The Surrey justices were particularly susceptible to pressure from overseers who deliberately turned inhabitants into vagrants. Their warrant for the removal of a Charlewood man to his birthplace at Rusper declared that 'hee was not for the space of fower yeares now last past' an inhabitant of Charlewood, but interrogation revealed that he had in fact lodged in barns and outhouses in Charlewood parish doing casual work for most of that time. The Sussex justices sent him back over the county border, just as they did 'a poor lame and impotent' man from Albery, who, they established, had lived in the Surrey parish for ten years.[136]

With children there was no clear guidance from the judges, though they did rule that bastard children should be sent to their place of birth, even if this meant separation from their parents. The Sussex Bench's application of this rule brought further disputes with neighbouring jurisdictions with different practices. They clashed with the Hampshire magistracy in 1636, for example, over a child aged nine, born at Bishop's Waltham, whose mother had married a poor labourer of Selsey. They supported the inhabitants of Lurgashall in their attempt to unload a girl of eight on Cranleigh in Surrey, where she was born, but were unable to enforce their order.[137] Within the county they applied the judges' ruling generally to all children. Though this procedure split up families, it sometimes enabled the JPs to spread the charge of a family over several parishes. Thus in 1657 the Bench sent a vagrant, his wife and three-year-old daughter to Cuckfield and his sons of thirteen and eight to Horsted Keynes and East Grinstead respectively.[138] Another cause of confusion was the contradiction between the 1589 Cottages Act, which enabled overseers to bring inmates to the notice of the court even if a month had elapsed before they were detected, and the judges' ruling that inmates, as sojourners, were lawfully settled after a month's residence. From an overseer's point of view, it was creeping multioccupation rather than the more easily detected establishment of new households that posed the most serious threat to the parish. The JPs recognised that inmates were likely to escape detection. A general order at sessions in 1651 was an attempt to clarify the situation: inmates were not to be 'prejudiciall to any parish to make them inhabitants notwithstanding their habitacon or continuance for moneth or longer'.[139] This order was overturned by the Act of Settlement, which applied a forty-day settlement rule to all mobile poor. The justices, then, did have a coherent policy over settlement and struggled to make it work. The 1662 Act gave statutory backing to their procedures and added little that was not already established practice.[140] Vagrancy was perhaps the most intractable problem of county government. The time and energy that the JPs devoted to it are an indication of its significance as a threat to good order in the shire.

Wrecking and plunder

Storms and gales brought Sussex a substantial harvest of wrecks. Moreover, victims of Channel warfare, left battered and helpless before the winds, were often driven on to the coast. Plunder of ships cast ashore was habitual. News that a ship was being driven towards the coast travelled fast. When a Dunkirker came ashore at Shoreham in 1629, following a Channel engagement with some Hollanders, 'the country people thereabouts, perceiving their distress came down in numbers (according to their inhuman custom) first taking away the goods of the said bottom and afterwards cut and spoiled the same'. A shepherd on the Downs above Seaford heard about a wreck just before sunset one day in January 1633: 'he putt his sheepe in fold', he later deposed, 'and went down to the said shipp all alone, but at his comeing he found the cuntrie alreadie come in'. By sunset a hundred men or so were gathering spoil from the ship. The shepherd's booty included a velvet-lined red cloak, knee tops lined with red taffeta and a silk garter. The mainsail was taken down that night. Squabbling and violence broke out as the ship was ravaged in the gathering dusk.[141] Another Dunkirker, rammed ashore at Brighton in 1630 to escape its pursuer, was only two days out and provisioned for two months at sea. Before anyone in authority reached the scene, the ship was 'pulled all to peces and the goodes all distributed amongst the people in the towne'. The previous year the Dutch ship *St Peter*, the victim of attack by the Dunkirkers, had been systematically looted near Arundel. The mayor of Arundel told some of the Dutch mariners, who had survived the engagement and rowed ashore, that he had seen barrels of tar and herrings, copper kettles, brass pans, the carpenter's chest and the sails carried into houses in the town.[142]

In short, the tradition of wrecking was well entrenched in Sussex and hard to eradicate. Yet in theory all rights of wreck belonged to the Lord

High Admiral, who sought to maintain them on each section of the coastline through a vice-admiral, his staff, and a court presided over by the local ecclesiastical judge.[143] When the administration was in the hands of a local gentleman of standing, served by efficient underlings, a substantial measure of control over wrecks and prizes could be achieved. The partnership in the late 1620s between Edward Alford, the receiver of admiralty droits in Sussex, and his agent Richard Streater, for example, appears, from the reports submitted to Secretary Nicholas, to have been effective in controlling some of the worst excesses in west Sussex.[144] The earliest surviving records of the Sussex vice-admiralty jurisdiction, for 1638 to 1640, show that courts were held annually at Chichester or Brighton, that seamen and fishermen in the littoral hundreds were summoned and that all admiralty offences were covered. Minor wrecking regularly cropped up in the jury presentments, beside fishing with unlawful nets and dragging of oysters. Masts, anchors, wire, topsails and an iron gun seized from wrecks were mentioned over a two-year period. Some Hove men were presented 'for taking up of the apparrel and stripping of certaine men which was found by the seaside'. Admiralty officers were normally ready to sell to the salvors the useful odds and ends that came ashore on the beaches, for about half their actual price.[145] This system was deliberately employed to gain the cooperation of the local populace, so that when a substantial cargo came ashore in west Sussex their help could be more cheaply bought. Edward Alford's account of the proceeds of the cargo of the *St Michael* of Dunkirk, which was worth £226, show that the local salvors received less than five pounds reward.

From Seaford to Dungeness the Lord Wardens of the Cinque Ports claimed maritime jurisdiction. Although seamen from Exceat and East Dean were cited to appear on the juries of the vice-admiralty court for the county, ships cast against the notoriously dangerous cliffs of Seaford Head were invariably taken to lie in his jurisdiction.[146] The case of the *Rose* of Amsterdam, which drifted ashore at Seaford with a cargo worth about £2,000 after being pillaged in the Channel in 1637, shows that the Cinque Ports' admiralty jurisdiction could be effective. Forty-eight countrymen of the Seaford neighbourhood were interrogated within about ten days of the wreck. After full inventories and valuations of the contents of the ship had been made, the Lord Warden obtained judgment in his own favour in his own admiralty court. The local inhabitants on this occasion were to receive a quarter of the profits.[147] This decision was a resounding defeat for the Seaford bailiffs, Sackville Porter and Thomas Elphick, who had vigorously campaigned for half the goods in kind for the locality, 'according to former usage in like cases there and elsewhere within the Cinque Ports and their members'. The bailiffs argued that such a reward would encourage them and their neighbours to venture their lives on future occasions. Their dramatic story of the affair contrasts strikingly with the matter of fact account from Thomas Paynter, a county officer in the vice admiralty, of what actually happened. The bailiffs spoke of the *Rose* being 'driven ashore upon the rocks and there beaten all too peeces' and of the 'great perill and danger of many of their lives' in saving the goods in her. In fact the *Rose* was beached in front of the town, not dashed against Seaford Head. The salvage operation was begun with boats, when the ship was 'grownded ffar of uppon a low water' and the next tide and a southeast wind then conveniently 'brought the shipp to the gravell'.[148]

But those who were sent to investigate the whereabouts of goods mysteriously spirited away, and to take custody of what was left because the men of the locality had no time or means to move it, faced problems. Thomas Paynter's urgent request for a warrant to seize goods from those known to be holding them in the Seaford hinterland, and to make quick payments for salvage, shows his awareness of what he was up against. If the goods were left in the hands of the local inhabitants, he warned, they would surely be embezzled. The Lewes customs officer left the ten ordnance of the Dunkirker rammed ashore at Brighton in the hands of the constable there, while he requested his superior in London to have an immediate 'course taken for the levyinge of those goodes which otherwise wil be lost'.[149] Local society was more than likely to close its ranks against those in authority who sought to rob them of the harvest of the sea. Men remained bold despite official intervention. Edward Alford concluded that two musketeers should be appointed to watch the masts of the *St Peter* at night if theft was to be prevented:

> for about ten dayes past one of them in the night was drawne over the beach (as appeared by the track of horses) and belike some shipp ready and carryed yt away for it cannot be heard of, and an other cutt into short peeces.[150]

The pattern of maritime jurisdiction, broken up by the claims of corporate bodies such as the Cinque Ports, was further complicated by the determination of private individuals to maintain rights of wreck founded on precedent or ancient grants. For landlords such rights were regarded as a gamble with wars and weather in the Channel. The Burtons' right to 'wreck of sea by the space of four myles' at Eastbourne, it was noted in an account book, 'may happen to be worthe £10,000 in an hower, as it hath beene in other places on the coast, but in the meanest year we have it is worth twenty or thirty pounds'.[151] Sir Thomas Pelham's accounts include details of windfall profits made from naval stores and goods driven ashore in Pevensey and Hastings rapes: 1635 was a particularly good year in this respect. Pelham received eighteen pounds 'for anchor and cable at Bishopstone come aground in my liberty' and more than twelve pounds 'for the wine that came in'. Bailiffs and tenants who saw to the enforcement of their landlords' rights were well rewarded. Occasionally the Pelhams considered it worth while to challenge the Lord Warden in the High Court of Admiralty. In 1624 the family's steward was much occupied with gathering information and organising witnesses at Eastbourne, Birling Gap and Seaford for a case to be brought in London.[152] Others who tried hard to maintain their rights included the Earl of Arundel and a redoubtable lady, Mary Thompson, both of whom were involved in the protracted case of the *St Peter*. Edward Alford, who acted for Arundel in the business, in the end concluded that a case could not be made out to entitle the Earl to the goods of the ship. Mary Thompson, however, was more determined. She alleged that twenty-eight masts which came ashore on her land at Felpham belonged to her by right of wreck granted by Queen Elizabeth. After she had wrangled with the Amsterdam owners of the *St Peter* in the High Court of Admiralty for a whole year, they gained a writ of restitution, but she remained determined to prevent them from acquiring the masts. In July 1640 the crown agents reported their reception at Felpham to Secretary Nicholas:

> She demaunded of us what fleet the King was setting forth that there was such present occasion for them and that shee was sure the King would not take any man's goods without paying for. . . . The next day we gott eight or tenn men with shovells to digg them out of the shingle but she was there ready, with her tennants being three of them with staves and pitchforks, and told us wee should not touch a mast there and that she would indict us for comeing on her land.[153]

It is indicative of a vital weakness in the admiralty jurisdiction that two JPs told the crown's officers at Felpham that Mary Thompson might indeed 'bring an action of trespas for comeing on her land'. The most they could do was to attempt in vain to persuade her to submit and to assure the crown officers that 'they would be ready to assist us to keepe the peace'.[154] JPs had no authority to act on behalf of commissioners sent from London or of admiralty officers in the county. Admiralty jurisdiction formed a separate compartment of county government. Yet justices, with most power and influence on the spot, were the obvious men to lead a campaign against plunder and looting of ships cast ashore. Sometimes a JP living near the coast did intervene when he heard about a wreck, although an interfering local gentleman could not be sure of the respect he normally expected in the melée of the spoil of a ship. Thomas Chown's son, sent by his father to investigate the wreck at Seaford in 1633, returned home with his head bruised and the news that he had been prevented from entering the ship.[155] Two years later, Thomas Chown acted promptly to prevent things going so far again, when a ship with goods thought to be worth about £10,000 was forced ashore at Seaford after being chased by a Dunkirker. He organised a rapid salvage operation and saved the cargo. Chown took meticulous care of the goods, until he received what he regarded as sufficient discharge, in other words, a bond from the merchants who owned them. Meanwhile, he wrote nervously to Secretary Nicholas about the responsibility fallen on him and fussily apologised for his 'want of knowledge and judgement in matters wherein I am altogether unexperienced'.[156]

Edward Burton was another JP who took the initiative himself, when survivors from the *Fortune* told him of their being cast away off Beachy Head in 1636. He employed local men to salvage the cargo and subsequently acted as a principal witness in the High Court of Admiralty.[157] If the Bench had been given a definite role in admiralty matters the clumsy jurisdictional machinery might have been made considerably more effective. On the other hand, although the Sussex countrymen's habits of coastal plunder shocked stalwart administrators like Sir Walter Covert, occasional activities of this kind did not threaten the foundations of society and stability in the shire in the same way as unrestrained vagrancy, unchecked contentiousness or prolonged hunger and starvation.[158]

9

The exact militia

But wheras in his princelye wisdom his Majestie observeth that the manner of trayninge and arminge hetherto generallie used in this kingdom is not soe exacte and serviceable as the course held both by all straingers and his owne subiects being in forraigne ymploiement, he hath therefore resolved oute of his royall care to provide and aplie those remedies whereby that defecte maie be fittlie and effectually redressed.
The lieutenants of Sussex to their deputies, 7 July 1623.[1]

I praye you faynt not though the labour will be greate now in the conclusion to ridd them fayrely out of the country, so as his Majestie's service may be accomplished and yourselves freed and discharged from all future molestacons in this kinde, the which I know hath bin so greate as it hath allmost taken you upp from all your private occasions and pleasures.
The Earl of Dorset to the deputies concerning billeting, 30 March 1627.[2]

When Charles I ascended the throne the government was already talking about the need for an 'exact and perfect militia'. The military reforms were proposed by veterans of the wars against Spain, such as Lord Compton, Sir Edward Cecil and Sir Edward Conway, and supported by the Duke of Buckingham. One of the courtiers who took a particular interest in the improvement of the nation's defensive equipment was the Earl of Arundel, who was one of the lieutenants of Sussex. In 1620 he put a motion before the Council concerning the unequal bores of muskets and the unequal lengths of pikes; the next year he spoke in favour of a Bill in parliament specifying uniform standards for the weapons of the trained bands.[3] In the years 1625 to 1628 the government campaign for an exact militia reached its climax. The purpose of this chapter is to examine the impact of that campaign on Sussex. The government's intentions during a few years of intensive military activity must be put in the wider context of its attitude towards the county militias over the whole period 1612 to 1642.

The gentry and the militia

Sound leadership and management of the county militias depended on co-operation between those local nobles who held office as lord-lieutenants and the leading gentry who acted as their deputies.[4] The obvious men to be trusted with responsibility for the Sussex militia during the 1620s and 30s were the Earls of Dorset and Arundel. The Earl of Arundel served from 1612 to 1642; the fourth Earl of Dorset was appointed in place of his brother in July 1624.[5] Both became members of the Caroline Privy Council, Dorset in 1626, Arundel in 1628.[6] During the years from 1625 to 1628 Sussex had only these two lieutenants, although it was more normal for the county to have three or more. From 1612 to 1624 Lord Howard of Effingham had acted in partnership with Arundel and the third Earl of Dorset.[7] In 1635 the Earl of Northumberland was appointed alongside Arundel and Dorset and the following year Lord Maltravers, the Earl of Arundel's son, joined them. Maltravers was already a privy councillor and a lieutenant of Norfolk, where he had some practical experience of militia matters.[8] Thus there were four lieutenants until the Militia Ordinance of March 1642 broke this partnership.[9]

The original warrant of 1585 authorising a commission of lieutenancy for Sussex stipulated that nomination of deputies would rest with the Privy Council. In 1608 this power of nomination was handed over to the lieutenants and they retained it thereafter, except between June 1623 and May 1625.[10] At the accession of Charles I the senior deputy was Sir Walter Covert, who was then aged eighty-two. He had served on the commission of November 1569, and when the lieutenancy became a permanent feature of county government in 1585 he was reappointed.[11] Covert was one of a handful of gentry who had carried the brunt of the organisation of mustering and the defence of the coast in the Armada crisis. The bound volume which provides an invaluable record of the Sussex militia over the period 1584 to 1631 is essentially his letter book.[12] In the week that the Armada reached the Channel, Lord Buckhurst, the county's lieutenant, wrote of his utter dependence on Covert and his colleagues.[13] Covert's long experience was a welcome asset to the new generation of deputies who faced the demand in the 1620s for an exact militia. Sir John Shurley and Sir Thomas Bishop had been his associates for much of James I's reign. In July 1624 these three deputies were joined by Sir Henry Compton and Sir Thomas Parker.[14] Parker's father, Sir Nicholas, himself a deputy until his death in 1620, had held important military offices in France, the Netherlands and the West Country in the latter years of Elizabeth's reign.[15]

A new commission of 9 May 1625 authorised Arundel and Dorset to appoint and discharge their own deputies.[16] More appointments came early in 1627 when the unusually onerous demands of the new government's military programme were weighing heavily on the four remaining deputies.[17] Sir Thomas Pelham and Sir Thomas Sackville had both served already on the martial law and billeting commissions of 1626. Richard Lewkenor and Edward Alford, from the west, had both sat regularly in parliament.[18] Alford's appointment is somewhat surprising since he was evidently still out of favour with the government in the autumn of 1626, when he was omitted from the Commission of the Peace.[19] It was an odd and unusual situation for a deputy-lieutenant not to be

JP, as Alford was until December 1628. The power of the leading deputies to co-opt whom they wished is perhaps reflected here. Five deputies died during the 1630s and two men gained office, Robert Foster and John Alford.[20] Thus when the war against the Scots brought new demands on the deputies' time and energy there were still enough active men in office.

Although the lieutenancy bore ultimate responsibility for the defence of the county, all justices were expected to share in organising musters. The JPs were an essential link in the chain of command, ensuring that the constables in their own rape received the details of the muster arrangements.[21] They were in trouble if they failed to play their part. In an angry letter of 1615 the lieutenants remonstrated with the justices in Chichester rape over their 'undutifull neglecte' of muster orders and threatened them with conciliar reproof.[22] A number of other gentry were intimately involved in the control and command of the militia, since few JPs were willing to take on the additional burden of a militia captaincy. Only seven of the captains of the footbands in 1606 appear in a *liber pacis* of 1604; only six magistrates held captaincies in 1618.[23] Twenty-five men were needed to fill the captaincies of foot companies alone. Each rape provided four bands, while Chichester had a band of its own; each rape also mustered a cavalry company, normally commanded by a knight. The captains of foot were mainly parish gentry, many of whom do not even appear in the 1634 visitation.[24] The Stapleys of Hickstead were typical of the unassuming hardworking farming families who set their sights on this office.[25]

There was little reward, save honour in a man's own neighbourhood, for the work involved in a foot company captaincy, yet there is no sign that in Sussex men were slow to take it on, as it seems they were in some other counties at this time, or that they were anxious to retire without good reason.[26] On the contrary, the wrangle that took place in 1616 over the replacement of Captain William Comber shows the deputies supporting Comber in his desire to retain his captaincy despite advancing years. Dorset upbraided them for their impertinence in insisting that Comber was 'verie sufficiente for the place'. Arundel and Nottingham on the other hand showed some sympathy for the deputies' point of view.[27]

Trust that developed between the deputies and the lieutenants over a period of eighteen years brought about the abolition of the practice by which the lieutenants appointed captains from a list sent up of suitable gentlemen.[28] In 1616 the deputies' nominations for two vacant captaincies were readily accepted by their masters.[29] So two years later they were bold enough to claim, when some further vacancies occurred, that the choice might be left to them. Arundel commented in a letter to Dorset:

> For the choice of the captaines I leave it wholly to your lordship, who are neere at hande to receave informacon of the abilletie and fittnes of the men herin presented to your choice; or if your lordship thinke rather fitt to comitt the matter to the deputie lieutenants, as is

propounded, I shall concurre with your lordship anie waie, and I doubt not but my lord of Nottingham will doe the like.

'I cannot doe the countrey better service', wrote Dorset subsequently to Covert and his colleagues, 'then to referre it to your discretions who beste knowe the fittest for that service'.[30] Thereafter it was as a matter of courtesy that the deputies consulted the lieutenants about captaincy appointments. Thomas More of Wivelsfield's letter of appointment in 1626 was written from Dorset House in London, after a meeting between the deputies and the Earl, but it came from the deputies rather than the lieutenant.[31] Another replacement in 1630 was left by Dorset entirely to Pelham and Compton.[32] Once the deputies had obtained the authority to nominate captains themselves they were careful to preserve it.

Numerous gentlemen were called upon to assist with militia business in the years of exceptional governmental activity from 1625 to 1627. In August 1626, for example, following instructions from the Council, the deputies formalised the county's pioneer units into companies and appointed a captain of pioneers for each rape.[33] The men chosen were of parish gentry status. Two of them came from armigerous and rising families, the Blakers of Shoreham and the Bridgers of Warminghurst, both families represented by the next generation on the Commission of the Peace.[34] Sixty-two men in all, besides the deputies, held militia appointments of one kind or another in the first two years of Charles I's reign. Leading justices who lived near the coast were joined with the deputies in the commission to impress mariners in 1625 and 1626.[35] Special commissions for billeting and martial law were issued in 1626 and 1627. The 1627 martial law commission included eleven gentry, two of them knights, not on the Commission of the Peace.[36] Other men undertook particular tasks. The collection of billet money was delegated by the deputies to one man in each rape: four of those chosen were colleagues on the Bench, the other two were senior trained band captains. In December 1624 and August 1626 provost marshals were appointed.[37] Three of them, George Churcher, Anthony Cruttenden and Thomas Jefferay, became prominent in county affairs as magistrates during the civil war. All were well into middle age by 1624. Indeed Anthony Cruttenden was fifty-three when he was appointed a provost marshal. Thomas More achieved further office more quickly. His efficiency in controlling vagrants and billeted soldiers led to his trained band captaincy in Lewes rape in 1626.[38] Militia business enabled men with ambition, who had previously stood on the sidelines, to achieve notice and to make useful contacts with the most powerful men in the county.

Musters and training

The leading figure in the Sussex lieutenancy between 1615 and 1624 wa[s] the third Earl of Dorset. 'My Lord of Arrundell and my Lord of Notting[ham]

ham have made declaracon and are both well pleased', he announced to the deputies in 1619, 'that such directions as I from tyme to tyme shall give to you our deputie lieutenantes for the furtheringe of his majesties service shall be as effectuall as if their lordshipps did joyne with me'. The other two left things very much to Dorset. When the deputies sent their report to Arundel in 1618 he directed it unopened to Nottingham who lost it.[39] As early as that year Dorset was harping on the need for exactness in the militia. King James, he wrote on one occasion, would require 'a speedy and exacte reformacon of the generall neglecte of his service in the provision of armes'.[40] Attempts to reinvigorate the militia after the doldrums of the early Jacobean years had begun in 1612, a few months before Dorset joined the lieutenancy.[41] In a letter of 30 May, Arundel and Nottingham reminded the deputies of their duty to ensure that vacancies in the captaincies were reported and defects in arms were supplied, during a period when there had been no muster for 'divers yeres last past'.[42] Musters were held in a number of counties in 1613 and 1614, but neither the Council's letter of 13 September 1614 for musters, nor any letter from the lieutenants about musters that summer, appears in the Covert lieutenancy book.[43] 'Special notice hath byn conceaved by their lordshipps of your remissenes in taking the general musters as well of foote as of horse', warned the lieutenants in June 1615.[44] The deputies were urged into action, 'for the honor of the kingdom and your owne safety, as for avoiding censure in the pointe of neglecte in you above all the countyes of this realme'. Under pressure from the centre the system of mustering and certification creaked into action again.[45] By October 1615 musters had been held in five of the six rapes. There was delay however, and the deputies had to be reminded to send in the muster rolls.

Subsequently pressure from the centre intensified.[46] Each year the lieutenants added their own words of encouragement to the directions of the Council. In 1617 there was a sharp reminder of the need for 'dutifull reguard and dilligent assistance' from certain gentry whose 'contempte' the previous year had been noted.[47] The lieutenants' general exhortation took on a new tone of asperity in 1619:

> Thoughe wee are perswaded that this declaracon of his majesties expresse pleasure, together with the presente occasion of the tymes, wilbe a forceable inducement to the countrye to quicken their obedience, yet you maie lett them withall understand before hande that, though matters have bene suffered heretofore to passe with some more conivence then hath bene well taken, yet may they not hereby take courage to dispense with their duties in the presente service, but rather endeavour by their willinge conformetie and forwardnes at this tyme to repaire their former faultes, or otherwise expecte a heavier weighte of punishement to fall upon them, as well for their contemptes and omissions paste, as muche more for their obstinate persistinge in such their disobedience.[48]

Dorset followed this up with a personal visit to the muster of Lewes rape. He was well pleased with the standard achieved and gave 'a very good accompt' to the Council of the conduct of the muster. Lady Dorset noted in her diary that the county's performance was 'in so much better fashion by reason of their affection to him, which was as much as my Lord hath in any county or can have'.[49] The Lewes muster of 1619, an occasion when the county town entertained the lieutenant with fireworks, marks the beginning of a new confidence in the relationship between Dorset and the deputies. 'We see not what remaines to be added', he wrote in 1622, forwarding a conciliar letter for musters which was an almost exact replica of that of the year before, 'but care in the performance, which wee might reasonablie conceave that yeerly contynuance and your former paines had by this tyme made easie both to yourselves and the countrie'.[50] The next year he spoke approvingly of former directions which had been 'dilligentlie observed and performed'.[51] Captain Mathew Parker, the muster-master, seems to have been adept at easing tensions. In April 1619 Sir Walter Covert entreated his help over a delay in the return of the certificates of the bands, which were 'allmost finished'. 'Yf their lordshipps should require to see them', suggested Covert, Parker might 'make some excuse and delaye untill you shall receive them from us which wee will hasten with all conveniente speede'.[52]

From September 1624 onwards, a fuller and more rounded view of the activities of the Sussex deputies and their subordinates becomes possible, since the 'Book concerning the Deputy Leiuetennantshipp' was begun in that month. It is a more formal and detailed record than Covert's letter book and contains both material about enforcement of government policies for the defence of the county and reports to the lieutenants from their deputies. The first two pages were taken up with the long letter of advice and instruction in which the new lieutenant, the fourth Earl of Dorset, announced to the deputies his intention of attending musters.[53] But later he excused himself, on the grounds of the bad weather and 'the feare I had to receave but little content in the present view'. Dorset warned that his standards would be high: 'there were few spectators', he pointed out to the deputies, 'but would confesse that proportion for proportion the armye of the States were nether better equipaged nor disciplined' than the militia of Middlesex at the end of his lieutenancy there. Men's vanity, he believed, could be a means towards the achievement of an exact militia. No one should be allowed to serve by servants or others, since men could be taught to 'take pride and delight to apeere hansomly beinge as well the wearers and ownors of theire owne furniture'. In all matters of assessment and business the deputies were to 'uncloth yourselves of all private respectes and partiality'. It was a lengthy lecture little of which Covert, Shurley and Bishop had not heard before. The following March the deputies received more precepts from Dorset, together with a detailed set of instructions which he had drawn up with the help of the Earl of Arundel.[54] Several of their proposals were already established practice, for instance the payment of muster-master's wages to the clerk of the band to avoid wasting the muster-master's time.[55]

The muster system worked smoothly during the first years of Charles I's reign. In 1626 the deputies met and agreed the arrangements a fortnight before they received the Council's letter for the holding of musters.[56] In their anxiety about the supposed threat to the coast, which had been dramatised in the government's letters, and their confusion about the intentions of the Council and the lieutenants, the deputies held musters three times that year. Although the Council's letter of 10 July specifically stated that musters should only be held 'if the same be not alreadie donne upon former direccions', they at once ordered the third muster within two months.[57] In 1618 Dorset had put forward a scheme to enable the muster-master to be present in every rape and carry out preliminary training the day before the muster.[58] The normal practice, based on this, was for musters to be held at two-day intervals starting with Hastings rape. Each rape had its traditional places for musters: Ditchling Common was convenient in Lewes rape; Broyle Heath, outside Chichester, was usually chosen for Chichester rape, though it meant a long journey for men from the northern parishes; Pevensey rape normally mustered at Berwick Common, but sometimes the deputies allowed the wealden parishes to muster separately at Uckfield. The horse companies normally mustered at two centres only. Bury Hill and Piltdown were favourite venues.[59] In 1625 the deputies experimented by convening the footbands at three centres only, two rapes at a time. But they only tried this once, presumably because it proved too difficult to secure an adequate attendance when such long travelling distances were involved. The Dorset scheme was exacting enough, yet in 1627 the lieutenants directed the deputies to set aside three instead of two days for the musters in each rape. 'All or most' of them were urged to be present 'at the mustering of every company'.[60] The county magnates soon balked at the prospect of spending nearly three full weeks of the summer away from home and in the saddle. Next year they abandoned the Dorset scheme. The invasion scare was over, the whole business was too burdensome. The 1628 musters were completed in a mere four days.[61]

How many men attended musters, how well were they armed and how effectively were they trained? These are the important questions about a county's response to the exact militia programme. The problem of defaulters was never solved. At a meeting in May 1626 the deputies decided in future to choose one defaulter from each band, who would be sent before the lieutenants as an example to the rest.[62] This said, there is firm evidence that the numbers in one band at least were considerably improved between 1619 and 1627. The 1619 muster roll of Captain Walter Roberts's unselected band in Hastings rape shows that it was in a decrepit state: about 130 men were under some kind of obligation, but many were only required to provide a pike or half a corslet or musket. The number of men who could be expected to muster was well under one hundred.[63] The previous year Captain Parker, the muster-master, had noted that each band was supposed to number 168 men.[64] Walter Roberts's band therefore was acutely deficient. Until 1625 the four companies in each rape had been divided into two selected companies, regarded as the front line of defence, and two unselected companies. Much more care had naturally been given to the former than the latter. 'The selected bands are compleete for the most part with corslets and musketts', reported the deputies on 3 October 1625, but the unselected bands, they admitted, were in a sorry state, 'and cannot by supplyed with strong weapons'. To meet this situation the deputies proposed a radical restructuring of the militia.[65] Within a few months they had worked out a new policy with the concurrence of the lieutenants and in February 1626 they explained it to Captain Roberts:

> All the bands shal bee scelected and noe more unscelected and everye captayne shall have but a hundred or fewe more in his band. Wee have therfore sent you a rowle of those souldiers allotted unto you, which we have taken as near as wee can out of those hundreds that lye next unto your habitacon, for the better ease of yourselfe and your soldiers.[66]

The system of downland and wealden bands in each rape was thus abandoned and captains were allotted hundreds according to the situation of their homes. Captain Roberts was made responsible for Hawksborough, Foxearle and Bexhill: his muster roll in September 1627 listed 118 men.[67] Of course, under the new system, a captain of a previously unselected band benefited from the superior strength of the selected band in the hundreds he took over. Nevertheless it seems clear that an immediate improvement in the county's military strength was achieved through the enforcement of the deputies' rationalisation. Moreover, in this Hastings rape band at least, the improvement apparently continued into the 1630s. Another muster roll for this band, when John Roberts who was captain from 1632 until 1639 had taken charge, lists 140 soldiers.[68] In 1638 the Sussex footbands were returned as consisting of 2,804 men in all, so, although John Roberts's company appears to have been rather larger, the average for the twenty-five companies in the county was still, shortly before the civil war, over the one hundred mark set in 1626.[69]

Not only were the Sussex trained bands more complete in 1638 than twenty years earlier, they were also better armed. The drive towards this had begun in the latter years of James I's reign. The deputies received a long lecture in 1618 about the replacement of calivers, which 'the moderne use doth altogether exclude as unserviceable', by muskets. The Council returned to the question in 1623 and demanded that arms 'decaied or broken' should be replaced by arms of the 'beste moderne forme'.[70] The deputies were consistently pessimistic about enforcing the government's requirements. Most of the arms were of the 'olde fashion', they told the lieutenants in 1624, 'which we feare we shall hardely reforme uppon the sudden by reason of the greate charges they are dayely to undergoe'. Two years later few had yet renewed their arms. 'Theire excuses', reiterated the deputies, 'are that there are so many dayly payements required as that they are not able yeat to make this new supply'. The deputies' demand in 1625 that 'all the armes throughout the county be forthwith reduced to the moderne fashion' was totally impractical.[71] It was too much to expect men with weapons that were serviceable but outdated to replace them. Yet there is evidence that both the quantity and condition of arms was improved as a result of the exact militia campaign. The Roberts muster rolls show a steadily increasing proportion of muskets to corslets and pikes between 1619 and the 1630s. By the late 1620s every militiaman was expected to provide either a musket or a pike and a corslet. Bare pikes, which were the limit of many men's obligation in James I's reign, had been eliminated.[72] In 1638 over 1,800 of the Sussex militiamen had muskets reported as serviceable.[73] Some county magnates set an example by sending tenants well armed to musters. In 1623 the armourer did six days' work at Halland 'about mendyinge the armor'; in 1626–28 Sir Thomas Pelham recorded payments for five more visits by the armourer. Pelham bought 'two horsemen's arms compleat' in 1626 and 'foure foote armes' the following year.[74] Sir John Shurley's well-furnished armoury at his death in 1631 probably owed something to the imprecations of the lieutenants in the latter years of his deputyship. He listed in his will a stock there of 'twelve muskets furnished, twelve corselets furnished, two horsemen's armours furnished, twelve bills'.[75]

The essence of Dorset's scheme for musters was a two-day programme of training in every rape. The teachers of each file, together with the corporals and sergeants of the companies, were to be given four hours training by the muster-master on the first afternoon, 'whereby they may be the next day the better able to instruct the rest of the file'. Letters sent to the constables in 1619 and 1622 indicate that the scheme was enforced.[76] In their orders of March 1625 the lieutenants extended the system. Captains were to institute regular training of their bands 'by small numbers' in each neighbourhood during the weeks previous to the annual muster. The deputies, forwarding these instructions to the captains, suggested that the training should be in groups of not more than twenty.[77] This move implied a considerable additional burden for the captains. It must have been tempting to summon the whole band to one centre, convenient for all concerned and get the matter over quickly. The choice of Hurst Green as a venue for training in Hastings rape suggests that this may have happened.[78]

The experienced officers on leave from the Low Countries, who were sent into the counties in February 1626, were intended to provide a short period of intensive training for the national militia.[79] Sussex received three sergeants, so each was given two rapes to attend to. They spent a week with each company. In a letter introducing the sergeant to Captain Roberts, Sir John Shurley and Sir Thomas Parker stressed that it was the officers and leaders of files who should receive most of his attention. Cadres of non-commissioned officers were to be trained so that they could instruct raw countrymen in the military arts after the sergeants had left the county. Training arrangements were left to the captain of the band and he and the sergeant were given discretion to call before them 'soe manie of your band as you shall agree upon'. The captains were expected to provide the sergeants with a horse and with board and lodging during their progress through the shire. Shurley and Parker also mentioned the royal direction that the sergeants should receive some 'reasonable allowance'.[80] According to Henry Chitty, who entertained the sergeant sent to Chichester rape, he was paid fifty pounds.[81] The impact of this experiment and the value for money obtained is hard to judge. It must surely have done some good. Thereafter the pressure on the captains to drill their bands in their own rapes was maintained at least until 1628.[82] In February that year the Council's letter about the King's personal review of the Home Counties horse at Hounslow Heath, which in the end proved abortive, led the Sussex deputies to undertake the unusual expedient of winter training.[83] Sir Thomas Pelham paid his man 'for going three days to the muster'.[84]

There is little evidence about the state of the Sussex militia in the 1630s beyond John Roberts's muster roll and the 1638 statistics. There was certainly no longer the bustle and energetic activity of the first years of the new reign. The Council was apparently complacent. The lieutenants expressed themselves well satisfied with the 'great paynes' taken by the deputies when they forwarded the last conciliar letter that appears in the deputy-lieutenancy book in 1631.[85] There is no reason to doubt that musters, and perhaps even training, continued to take place as the Council required. The speed with which John Roberts was replaced on his death in 1639 with a new captain in Hastings rape hardly suggests a militia sunk in inertia.[86] The contrast with the previous decade makes it easy to overlook the achievement of deputies in Sussex and elsewhere who kept the trained bands up to scratch at a time when pressure from the centre had been relaxed.[87] The Jacobean and Caroline drive for an exact militia left a distinct mark on the county. Nevertheless, at the end of it all, the trained bands were only half reformed. A number of reasons may be suggested for this. The government can be blamed for attempting far too much too quickly. The lieutenants must also bear some responsibility. In their own eyes their duty began and ended with exhortations. The fourth Earl of Dorest and the Earl of Arundel remained on more distant and formal terms with their deputies than the third Earl of Dorset had: even an occasional appearance at musters would have been a useful stimulus to those inclined to shirk their obligations. More seriously, there is a strong suspicion that, from 1624 onwards, the lieutenants were failing to give adequate support to their deputies' efforts to check muster defaults. Why otherwise is there no record of any Sussex defaulters being summoned before the Council after 1623? In their report of 7 October 1625 the deputies directly requested that Arundel and Dorset should 'take some strict course' with defaulters, so that 'by your lordshipps power they may be reduced to better order'. This request was apparently ignored.[88]

The performance of the deputies in reorganising and managing the musters of the footbands was impressive. They were much less successful in improving the condition of the cavalry companies. This was a delicate business and a matter of considerable embarrassment to the county magnates, who disliked imposing military charges on their social equals. The Earl of Dorset's opinion was that every man worth two hundred pounds per annum 'should be compelled to find a horse', since they were bound to have a horse for their own use anyway.[89] At a discussion in the Council in December 1638, at which Dorset was present, his opinion was adopted as government policy.[90] In theory each rape of Sussex had a company of fifty horse, but it is doubtful whether there were fifty gentlemen in every rape whom the deputies could confidently regard as members of the category Dorset had determined.[91] Even if he had a suitable horse a man so charged had to spend over five pounds on a complete horseman's armour.[92] In 1616, after the horsebands had been found generally defective, the deputies produced a list of men they regarded as fit to be charged. The lieutenants were delighted and congratulated them on their discretion, which would avoid 'the clamour of the countrey'.[93] But the deputies did not take kindly to enforcing the charge on their friends and neighbours. In 1621 they reported that there had been a number of defaults at the horse muster, since it was held while some gentlemen were in London for parliament. The lieutenants at once ordered a special second muster. When some of the gentlemen defaulted again, the deputies sought to shelter them from the wrath of the lieutenants by suggesting that 'by such for bearance they would be drawne to redeeme their former faults'.[94]

After 1622 the lieutenants made little further attempt to invigorate the horse companies. 'They are as we have often signifyed unto your lordshipps', reported the deputies in 1625, 'very weak in number and many meane horses and ill furnished'. The total cavalry strength of the county in 1638 was only 160.[95] Despite their talk of efforts to put the matter right, the deputies must bear the main responsibility for the failure to effect a major improvement. The suspiciously large number of gentry defaulters at the musters of foot also reflects on their difficulties in dealing with men of the same status as themselves. Both the men who appeared before the Council in 1617, John Tichborne and Henry Bridger, were gentlemen; a list of defaulters in 1623 included Sir Edward Bellingham, a JP, and his brother-in-law Sir John Chapman.[96] The weakness of a system of government so dependent on the leaders of the local community is evident. The Council was dealing with a group of independently minded men ready to block proposals that clashed with their own interests. When, in 1626, it directed that a special regiment was to be created to repel attack on the coast, commanded by some of the 'best experienced and fittest' gentry, the deputies replied that no one experienced in war and fit for such a command was not already an officer.[97] The scheme was ignored.

A fundamental reason for the failure to effect thoroughgoing reforms was their cost, the stumbling block in the way of both the replacement of arms and the equipment of cavalry companies. Resistance to the cost of the exact militia centred on the muster-master, a cause of dispute in Sussex, as in many other counties, since Elizabeth's reign. When muster-masters were first established in the maritime counties in the 1580s, the Council had paid their salaries; when the counties themselves were made to pay, the new burden was at once resented as an unconstitutional practice. The dispute about payment of the Wiltshire muster-master, which came before parliament and the Council in 1606, may be seen, it is suggested, 'as a minute part of the great antagonism to prerogative government and taxation that was the central issue in the gathering crisis'.[98] In 1613 the Sussex deputies received a curt letter from the Council about the arrears still owing to Master Humphrey Covert, 'an ancient servitour and nowe growen old'.[99] He can never have received much financial support from the Council, since as early as 1588 the county owed him £1,800, which the deputies had contracted to pay off in instalments of a hundred pounds per annum.[100] They neither fulfilled Covert's contract nor showed any readiness to receive Captain John Panton, his replacement in June 1615. Four months later Panton arrived with a letter from the lieutenants informing the deputies that 'it is requesitt he be sent down'. There was further correspondence before his salary was agreed.[101] By 1620, when Panton's successor Captain Matthew Parker received £88 of the £103 due to him, most parishes had grudgingly accepted the new tax for his salary.[102]

From 1625 Captain Parker acted as muster-master to the Cinque Ports as well as Sussex. He once told Edward Nicholas, secretary to Buckingham, the Lord Warden of the Cinque Ports, that he was thinking of giving up the Sussex post, so that he might 'wholy dedicate my service unto his Grace', but in the end he kept it but probably neglected it, since opposition to paying his wages increased after 1625.[103] From 1625 Parker lived at Canterbury, where he was much better placed to train the Cinque Ports than the Sussex militia. So the deputies may have sympathised with those who were reluctant to reward him. Certainly they did little to persuade the county to settle the arrears that mounted from 1626 to 1628. They conspicuously failed to mention the matter in two letters to captains and justices in this period.[104] The lieutenants rebuked them in April 1627:

> We take it in ill parte that our often wrighting in Captayne Parker's behalfe for the collecteing and due payeing of his entertaynement should be so slighty regarded as that for these two yeares past it hath not pro-

> cured him one penny of what is in arreare. We therefore once more praye and require you to give strict order for the speedy collecteing of the same.[105]

The following November, the Council criticised the deputies for their neglect, and the trained bands for their obstinacy, in hindering the execution of the muster-master's office.[106] In the delicate matter of militia charges and taxes the deputies were simply not prepared to fly in the face of county opinion. They were anyway powerless to do so since they depended on the cooperation of their colleagues on the Bench in enforcing royal policy.

Confusion over the whole legal basis of militia obligations underlay the recalcitrance of the provinces. The lieutenants themselves were aware of the problem: 'Wee wishe all thinges to be still contynued without anie inovation, which without very urgent cause wee would have carefullie avoided', they wrote in June 1622 in reply to a query from the deputies as to whether or not captains of horse should be charged towards equipping the foot and vice versa.[107] In this case some of the leading gentry were attempting to cast doubt on what was, in theory anyway, established practice. When Sir Thomas Pelham, Sir John Shurley and Robert Morley wrote to the constables of the hundred of Dill about musters on 1 July they emphasised that 'their lordshipps pleasure is, that the captaines of the horsehandes shall find furniture in the foote companies and the captaines of the foote companies shall find furniture in the horse companies according to former order and directions in the behalf'.[108]

More often than not cases of default involved fundamental questions about the legality of the deputies' actions and the scope and extent of their discretion. The notorious John Bishe of Brighton, for instance, who failed ever to appear at musters for thirty years, 'stood to defende' in 1620 that 'there was no law to enforce him'.[109] Strictly Bishe was quite correct: since the 1558 statutes had been repealed at the start of James I's reign, military obligations had rested on prerogative.[110] The gentry resisted the lieutenants' demands that horsemen should attend musters with the most up-to-date weapons and armour on the ground that 'there is no late order setled for their arminge after the moderne use'. Dorset's ruling about who should be liable to provide a horse lacked even conciliar authority from 1625 until 1638. The lieutenants admitted the weakness of their position on the question nearest to the pockets of the gentry, the equipment of cavalry, when they pointed out in 1622 that the absence of a declared national policy 'cannot serve them for excuse of not shewinge their horse and usuall armes untill orders be gyven for an alteracon when the tyme serves, the charge wherof the presente estate of the countrie will not admitt'.[111] The basis of assessment, as well as the scale of militia obligations, lacked definition. Bishe was charged with a musket and corslet since he had 'money at use' as well as lands worth two to three hundred pounds a year, but in some other counties he would very likely have been treated differently.[112] Assessment raised all sorts of problems. Accurate information about men's sources of income was not easily obtainable and deputies often had to rely on secondhand reports.[113]

The question of the authority by which the deputies acted became increasingly a matter of public controversy between 1625 and 1642. Their ability to enforce a reform programme was gravely weakened by the lack of any machinery to bring defaulters to book within the county. The Norfolk deputies discussed this problem in correspondence with their lieutenant, the Earl of Arundel. They suggested that they might be given power to bind defaulters to good behaviour and from assizes to assizes. 'Publique and bitter reproofe' to men made an example of by the judges at assizes would act as a deterrent to the whole county. They also pleaded for measures to 'free us from pursute in law or parliament by the offenders'.[114] Anxiety about the lack of sufficient grounding in law for the actions they were called upon to perform must have been common among deputies. Awareness of this vulnerability lay behind the open hostility to them, expressed in parliament in 1628 and 1640–41 and which was common in those counties most prey to faction in the 1620s and 30s.[115] So dispirited did the Norfolk deputies become that when in 1628 their authority was challenged not only among tavern gossips but in quarter sessions, they pleaded with Arundel to accept their unanimous resignation.[116] Sussex escaped both this kind of crisis and the squabbles which affected the Somerset militia, but its militia also undoubtedly suffered because both the deputies and the county knew very well that the legality of much of what they did could very reasonably be questioned. The constitutional basis of the militia was one of the first problems tackled by the Cavalier Parliament after the Restoration. The 1662 Militia Act removed the ambiguities which had debilitated the Caroline militia. The powers of lieutenants and deputies were defined and rules were laid down for the imposition of arms and the raising of military taxes.[117]

Defence of the coast

When the Council asked the deputies to make a survey of the coastal defences of Sussex in 1625, Sir Walter Covert was able to refer them to the splendid 'plott in cullers', which he himself had helped to make in the year of the Armada. 'We cannot better certify your lordshipps therein then the deputie lieutenants did in 88', wrote Covert and his colleagues.[118] But they were optimistic to assume that all the various defensive arrangements marked there were still in good repair. From Chichester harbour to beyond Brighton the beaches were low and open; from Brighton to Eastbourne, and again from Hastings to Winchelsea, the cliffs provided some protection, yet even here there were havens such as Cuckmere and Birling that might tempt men to land. Effective defence of the Sussex coast, ninety miles in length, required regular oversight and expenditure. Defence thus raised exactly the same kind of financial problems as the maintenance and training of the militia.

Between 1625 and 1630, when England was at war with Spain and France, Sussex countrymen had good reason for fear. The mayor and jurats of Hastings told the Lord Warden of the Cinque Ports in 1627 how 'fourteen saile' of Dunkirk pirates had pursued a Hollander, which 'fledd to their towne for reliefe':

> They shott throwe diverse howses in the towne to the terror of the inhabitants that were much endangered therby. Sittence which tyme a fisherman of their towne laden with iron and bound for London was taken by the said Dunkerkes, who questioned him concerninge the strength of their towne, and tould him, that if it had been two houres flood, as it was fallinge water, they would have battered downe the towne.[119]

The following year Edward Alford, in a letter to the lieutenants requesting two ships to guard the coast, described how three French ships and a pinnace had taken a bark at Shoreham haven. The people of the neighbourhood had been forced to fetch ordnance from Brighton to defend the town.[120] Nor did piracy cease with the end of the war. Thirty men, 'taken to be sailors', landed at Brighton from a Holland man-of-war anchored offshore in 1635. The town, declared its petitioners to the Council, was 'subject to much danger of an enemy, haveinge bin twice taken heretofore by the French'.[121]

There were at least ten occasions, in the war years alone, when foreign seamen landed in numbers on the Sussex coast. In March 1629 thirty-three Spaniards came ashore between Rye and Hastings; in November of the same year sixty-six men landed from a Dunkirk pinnace driven ashore at Worthing; in the following February seventy-eight men were stranded at Brighton.[122] Such landings raised serious problems of law and order. JPs did their best to ensure that the seamen were taken into custody, but there could be delay before the county disposed of them. The authorities at Rye found themselves responsible for several weeks in 1627 for a company of 'Portingalls', whose ship had been taken by a Hollander. They implored the lieutenant of Dover Castle, in whose harbour the Hollander then lay, to insist that the victors of the Channel engagement should provide means to support the shipwrecked crew, 'who otherwise are like to perishe for want of sustenance, for our serjeant who hath the custodie of them havinge disbursed some money to provide them victualls, not knowinge how to be replued refuseth to disburse any more'.[123]

If it was impossible to stop the victims of Channel warfare from seeking refuge on the southern coast of England, a proper system of defence could at least prevent raids on fishermen and coastal property. Reports of raids usually contained requests for more ordnance.[124] When Charles I came to the throne, it seems that the eastern end of Sussex was better defended than the west. There were at least four guns at Lewes, six each at Eastbourne and Hastings and three or four at Rye. Two pieces were added to the Rye munitions in 1627 through the good offices of the Lord Warden, the Duke of Buckingham.[125] But, as the Shoreham incident showed, guns were useless unless properly mounted. The Brighton ordnance 'were well mounted and rescued many shipps from the enemye' during the 1620s, since the wooden carriages had been repaired in 1619; by 1635 they were 'all rotten and broken' again.[126] The deputies failed to respond to a plea from the inhabitants, who could not afford the cost of the repairs needed. In 1626, though, they had been energetic in repairing the Eastbourne gun carriages and had raised forty-two pounds to cover the cost.[127] The expense then explains the reluctance of the deputies to do anything about the Brighton carriages, when raids on the coast were no longer as frequent or serious as ten years previously. The matter raised awkward questions of the apportionment of taxation between coastal and inland hundreds, for which the precedents were uncertain. In 1626 the solution agreed on by the deputies at a general meeting had been to impose one-third of the tax on the hundred of Eastbourne and two-thirds on the rest of Pevensey rape. They had acted decisively then under the impetus of the government's invasion propaganda.

The government gave the county little help in strengthening its defences. During the late 1620s the well-built Henrician bastion of Camber had been considered an essential defence for the vulnerable Rother levels. In 1627 it was said that it merely needed the repair of the platforms, but by 1643 the castle was 'soe greatlie ruinated and broken that any man may goe in there and purloigne and take from thence the tymber and lead'.[128] The gun house at Seaford was also out of repair by 1640.[129] Moreover, when a Dunkirker was wrecked at Brighton in 1630 with ten pieces of ordnance, the Council insisted, despite the protestations of Sir Walter Covert, that the guns were shipped to London.[130]

The county's stocks of gunpowder needed periodic inspection, since the powder became unserviceable with age.[131] It was not until 1619 that, prodded by the government, the deputies replenished the county's store. A postscript to a letter from Dorset to Covert in 1619 about the arrangements for the purchase of gunpowder show that the deputies were expected to send and pay for the powder Dorset's servant had bespoken before it was sold elsewhere.[132] When they next looked into the question in 1625 this powder was useless. At this stage the deputies still hoped to get new stocks of powder free. 'We know not how to be supplyed but by your lordshipps goodd meanes, for agaynst 88 the Queene most graciousely pleased to furnish the county', they wrote wistfully to the lieutenants.[133] The next year the deputies faced up to realities and ordered a tax to be levied throughout the county for ten barrels of powder for each rape.[134]

The deputies' efforts to obtain sixty barrels of gunpowder in 1626 led them into the administrative web surrounding the monopoly of manufacture held by John Evelyn of Godstone in Surrey. Evelyn was not allowed to deliver powder without authority from the Council, and anyway was failing to produce the quantities stipulated in his contract. Sir Henry Compton arranged for ten barrels of powder apiece to be sent to Hastings and Pevensey rapes, but then found Evelyn would not supply any more.[135] Eventually, meeting at Lewes in July 1627, the deputies wrote in exasperation to the Earl of Dorset, complaining that in the four westernmost rapes they were still altogether destitute of powder for both defence and training.[136] In this instance it was undoubtedly the lieutenants' and the Council's fault if training suffered, as it must have done, since there is no record of powder being supplied. In 1639 three lasts, that is seventy-two barrels, were finally obtained.[137] The refusal of five men, led by the trained band captain Sir Thomas Springate, to pay the tax for this powder is evidence of the increasingly pervasive opposition to all military taxes in Sussex. The sums were small: Sir Thomas Pelham, for instance, only paid four shillings for his very extensive lands in Laughton parish.[138] It looks as if those who resisted took a stand on principle. The threat of a summons before the Council did not deter them.[139]

The essence of the defence of the coast was the system of beacons, which was reinvigorated by the deputies in 1625. Braziers and poles which had rusted and rotted since the Elizabethan war were to be replaced by new beacons 'in places accustomed'. Minute instructions for procedure were laid down. The watchmen's immediate responsibility was to 'five of the discreetest howsehowlders' living nearby, two of whom were always expected to be at home in case they were called to climb to the beacon site and give judgment on what action should be taken. In the case of an imminent landing by one or two ships, church bells were to be rung from village to village, 'from the sea costes to the skirts of the hill and no further'. The nearest justices were to be informed, so that they might ensure that men of the locality hurried to the coast 'with armour and weapons'. In the case of a larger landing, both beacons were to be fired at all the sites on the section of downland immediately inland from the threatened part of the coast, to indicate where the trained bands should go, but one beacon only was to be fired on the neighbouring downs. The system was not foolproof. In 1619 some burning furzes near one Sussex beacon had led to 'a great alarm . . . by the firing of almost all the beacons in Sussex and Kent'.[140]

From 1626 until at least 1628 the deputies renewed their warrants annually for beacons to be repaired and for watches to be set throughout the summer months.[141] Beacon watching was so unpopular that it required considerable enforcement. The cooperation of colleagues on the Bench was obtained in binding to sessions anyone who neglected his watch. The court also intervened in disputes about the liability of particular parishes to supply watchmen: in July 1627, for instance, it ordered that Patcham, Withdean, Preston and Hove should provide one of the watchmen nightly for Brighton beacon.[142] The task of watching, avoided by the more substantial men, tended to fall on the old and inadequate. In August 1627 the Earl of Dorset wrote to the deputies, when he was staying at Wiston, to rebuke them for the neglect of beacon watching, which 'I see myself since my comeing into the country'. He particularly criticised the choice of men 'unfitt for it, in regard of theire yeares, want of experience in the use of their weapons and other imperfections'.[143] In a general order at Epiphany sessions in 1628, which attempted to tighten up the system, the Bench reminded the county that recalcitrant men might be bound over or even sent to gaol.[144]

Opposition was concentrated against the taxation involved. In order to spread the burden of beacon watching, both the taxes for payment of the watchmen and the service itself were imposed on inland as well as coastal hundreds. The case of Edmund Freeman of Billingshurst, which came before the Council in 1627, illustrates the kind of grievance which arose. Billingshurst residents claimed that Freeman, by all accounts difficult and insolent, was 'the man that causes all the tithing of Fewer to be back in this and all other services'. But his case was sound. He lived twelve miles inland from the beacon for which he was responsible and he claimed that he could not defray his charges, in travelling this distance and back plus his night's watch, for the fivepence a day he was to be paid, nor could he find anyone else who would do it for that.[145] In Elizabeth's reign eightpence had been considered a normal wage for a twenty-four-hour period of watching, and the quarter sessions confirmed this as a standard wage in January 1628. It was the reluctance of the county as a whole to pay for beacons to be tended that made it impossible for Freeman to be offered an adequate wage. The Bench's repeated directions for tithingmen to collect the taxes set for proper payment of watchmen, and its order for a special tax in hundreds where watchhouses needed repair or to be erected, are indications of the way in which the beacon system foundered. Again the actual sums involved were paltry. Sir Thomas Pelham paid a shilling for beacon watch in 1628.[146]

The defence of the Sussex coast in the early seventeenth century was thus a makeshift and haphazard affair. A burst of energy at the height of the exact militia programme was not enough to provide a permanent improvement. Without due attention and expenditure, guns, powder and beacons all decayed rapidly. Even so, an impressive amount of ordnance and a significantly large supply of gunpowder became available in Sussex when the crisis came in 1642. The defence of the coast then temporarily became a secondary consideration and the ordnance and powder intended for it were needed to determine the county's internal affairs.

Impressment, billeting and martial law

Fundamental reasons for the disastrous outcome of the three major English military expeditions of the years 1624 to 1628 were the limitations of resources and the difficulties of keeping an army in being from one voyage to the next.[147] Jacobean and Caroline governments lacked the means to fulfil their undertakings. They were unable to raise enough able men or to equip them properly. By August 1627 shortage of money had forced the Council to excuse the counties from providing the reinforcements pressed for Rhé with arms or coats. 'Pray provide cassocks and hose for I thinke it will suffice', wrote Dorset to the Sussex deputies.[148] Levies arrived at Portsmouth hopelessly ill-equipped.[149] An examination of impressment, billeting and martial law in Sussex in the years 1624 to 1628 and in 1640 will exemplify the weaknesses of the country's military machine and the strains imposed on the southern counties by the government's policies.

The county's special commissioners pressed 1,150 footmen and 550 mariners between 1624 and 1628.[150] It was never easy to find men not members of the trained bands who were yet fit for the wars and could be spared from the support of families. It was tempting to fill the pressed bands with rogues and vagabonds, the scum of the county. When reinforcements for Rhé were required at the height of the harvest in 1627, the deputies decided that they should be recruited entirely from the wealden hundreds, where masterless men abounded.[151] Moreover, impressment was notoriously open to abuse. A justice, in a warrant to constables, attributed the repeated calls on the county for the Rhé expedition to their 'suffering notice to be given to those that were fittest to be ymployed in this service whereby they have kept themselves away'.[152] In 1628 a man was presented at quarter sessions for 'temptinge the king's majestie's officers with money to permitt him to escape after he had received his presse money'.[153]

Timing was crucial. Once rumours of the press had reached the county, it was best for it to be carried out quickly, before men had a chance to take measures to escape it; once pressed, they had to be paid or they would run away. The deputies always acted immediately when they received the Council's letter for a press. They normally allowed only a few days for the constables to press the men required in each hundred before they held a county rendezvous for the whole force.[154] In 1625 and 1627 the deputies handed the pressed men over to the conductors, drew up the tripartite indentures required and saw the companies marched across the county border to Plymouth or Portsmouth straight away, since, by the time the lieutenants had taken a week to forward the Council's letters and the rendezvous had been held, the men were either almost due to be at the port of embarkation or were already late in arriving.[155] But the Council's directions for impressment for the Mansfield expedition in 1624 were vague about the date of the rendezvous at Dover. The men were merely to be ready to march by 30 November.[156] Sufficient warning was given and the four hundred men required were duly ready. Yet it was not until mid-December that the deputies were told to hand them over to their conductors for the march to Dover. They finally left the county on 22 December: for four weeks constables had been required to pay out eightpence a day to each of the men in their charge.[157]

Whereas in 1624 the deputies' task was made more difficult by the imprecision of the government's orders, in 1640 it was made harder by its feverish changes of plan. Initially the 600 Sussex men for the army against Scotland were to be at the county rendezvous on 20 May and to leave the county for Gravesend, after ten days' training, on 1 June. The deputies wasted no time when they received the Council's letter about the beginning of April. By the last week of the month, the men were in readiness and were being exercised weekly in companies of 100 as the Council required. But on 6 May the Council ordered a delay of ten days in the whole programme.[158] The deputies were caught with the pressed men on their hands until mid-June. Day by day the charge mounted. By 22 May it was nearly £4,000. 'We beseech you free us from the soldiers as soon as possibly you may because we have had them upon the country's charge one month already', wrote Dorset to the Earl of Northumberland, the Lord General, at the end of May. It is not surprising that the Sussex men billeted in Stroud, prior to sailing later in the summer, proved 'especially ungovernable'. The government's mismanagement and delays had led to their being away from home, frustrated, bored, and probably unpaid, for weeks on end. The deputies had done all that was expected of them: 'I heare that other countryes are not so forward', noted Henry Pelham in a letter to the Earl of Rutland on 14 June. In Warwickshire, Northamptonshire and Herefordshire the deputies were unable to obtain the coat and conduct money or make the soldiers march.[159]

Delays in the repayment of coat and conduct money were normal. In the case of the Mansfield expedition the Council talked first of it being repaid out of the subsidy, before its proceeds were sent to London, but this was not done.[160] In the autumn of 1625, when several hundred pounds remained unpaid, the clamours of the county increased. Some constables were owed twenty or thirty pounds in all for the expenses involved in equipping and paying the men from their hundred. 'We are mutch called upon', declared the deputies in a letter to Arundel and Dorset on 7 October 1625:

> Wee doe humbly beseech your lordshipps that som present course may be taken that these monyes may be speedely payed, otherwise we shall not be able heerafter uppon like occasions to command the constables the furtherance of his Majestie's service.[161]

This warning brought a reassuring reply from the Council.[162] Yet there were again long delays after the Cadiz expedition and the coat and conduct account was only finally settled out of the forced loan fund early in

1627.[163] When it came to the 1627 press the deputies sought to ensure speedy payment from the Exchequer by an efficient accounting procedure within the county. Despite this, it was not until the summer of 1629 that Sussex was reimbursed from the Exchequer for the sum of over £300 which had been spent since April 1627.[164] Coat and conduct money had all the signs of another military tax. There was open resistance to it in 1625 and 1627: in 1625 the deputies attempted to use the impressment rendezvous before the Cadiz expedition to confront those who had refused to pay the winter before; in 1627 the receiver for Hastings rape was unable to obtain thirty-eight pounds of the money due from the hundreds of Robertsbridge, Shoyswell and Goldspur. The names of the constables of the recalcitrant hundreds in 1627 were forwarded to the Council, but no action appears to have been taken.[165]

Soldiers were billeted in Sussex from September 1626 until June 1627 and from the following November, when they returned from Rhé, until July 1628. In the first period about 800 men were lodged in the county.[166] The deputies and commissioners for billeting received precise instructions about how they were to proceed. Companies were to be billeted close together, so that officers could keep an eye on their men and carry out regular training. The deputies were to oversee the training and they, together with the commissioners, had the sole authority to allow officers or soldiers to leave their quarters. Permission was to be given only 'upon very necessary occasions'.[167] Billeting, in short, was to mean more than occasional diversion from the deputies' hunting and estates. Dorset, as the epigraph to this chapter shows, recognised the fact. The immediate problem of finding suitable homes for the soldiers was made harder by the Council's insistence that they should be billeted in the maritime parts of the county, where the population was thin. In several rapes the deputies had no choice but to spread companies through a number of villages and towns: in Chichester rape they concentrated the soldiers in the Bosham and Fishbourne area, in Lewes rape they chose the downland triangle between Brighton, Lewes and Newhaven, and in Pevensey rape they lodged the men in the villages between Alciston and Eastbourne.[168]

The county quickly felt the cost of billeting. The initial levy of forty pounds in each rape lasted a mere fortnight. The King's demand for a forced loan came in the nick of time for the deputies. They at once saw in it a solution to their problem. On 29 November 1626 the Council granted the deputies authority to discharge billeting expenses from the loan money. 'I have not bin slack', wrote Dorset shortly after, 'to hasten the accomplishment of what I undertook for the good of the country at my last being there'.[169] So the deputies had good reason to urge their countrymen to contribute to a tax which in reality was merely the previous summer's abortive free gift in another form.[170] In Lewes rape, presumably through pressure exerted by Sir Walter Covert, nearly £1,000, a sum equal to about five full subsidies, was collected between September and January.

In Pevensey rape, on the other hand, there was open resistance to the loan, based it seems upon doubts that the government would in fact allow the money raised to be used for the county's billeting expenses. When Dorset heard about people's grumbling, he was affronted: 'I hope heerafter they will add more fayth to theire soveraigne's word and believe I am one on whom no such digrace shall be layed as to be made the instrument of deception', he wrote to the deputies on 17 January 1627. In the same letter Dorset spoke sharply of his determination that the county should bear the charge of the billeting out of the loan money, which was to be raised forthwith:

> It is high tyme to dispatch and to make your conclusions suteable to your beginnings. I cannot doubt of the one when I remember the other. And yeat may not omitt to tell you that when I fynde denyalls or delayes I have order imediately to place all the sowldiers within the sheere in that rape so that the difference may apeere betweene the refractory and obedient.[171]

At this threat, the recalcitrant commissioners for the loan in Pevensey rape hastened to appoint collectors.

In general the need to discharge the continuing cost of billeting undoubtedly proved a massive incentive to the commissioners to drive forward the collection of the loan. When the men were marched to a rendezvous at Chichester, there was enough money left to give them decent clothing and a month's allowance for food. There was not enough though to pay all the officers, who at first refused to march their men with arrears of pay since the previous October. Dorset suggested that the trained bands should if necessary be called out to 'make the soldiers march in spight of theire teeth'.[172] In a spate of letters Sir George Blundell, the Sergeant-Major of the Forces, bitterly attacked the Sussex gentry for their failure to raise through the loan sufficient funds to satisfy the officers. His attempts during April to reorganise the survivors of the Cadiz expedition, together with the raw levies, into new regiments were frustrated by the officers' refusal to cooperate until they had been paid. 'It is a shame they should be so used in that county, where there is money if it could be gotten', he wrote to Edward Nicholas on 16 April.[173] But was this a fair charge? The total cost of billeting 800 men in the county for seven months, at a minimum of three shillings a week per man, cannot have been less than £3,500. Money was also spent on their clothing and equipment. Furthermore the sum required to satisfy the officers was £3,000.[174] It can be argued that the deputies and commissioners for the loan had done well to sustain the cost of billeting, let alone those officers' salaries that they had managed to meet. The loan after all, in its original form, had met with a blank refusal in Sussex. A subsidy at this time raised under £1,400 from the county. It was a considerable achievement to have raised a sum equal to at least three subsidies when the tax had no parliamentary authority.[175]

To Blundell, faced with the appalling task of forming an army out of the scarecrow troops sent by deputy-lieutenants from all over southern England, the deputies themselves were the obvious scapegoats. Confessing himself 'almost out of my wittes to see how thinges are carried', in a letter to Buckingham on 28 April, he concluded: 'Thus the deputy lieutenants will use you in every shire. Until some of them be made an example, the King will be at charge and the service overthrown'. On another occasion he avowed that the King had 'been cozened by the collectors, commissioners, treasurers and constables in those five shires above £10,000'.[176] Such comments ignored the fact that the Caroline government was hopelessly out of its depth. It is no surprise that the relationship between overwrought councillors and conscientious but exasperated deputies creaked under the strain.

At the end of June 1627 the Rhé fleet at last set sail. In November the soldiers were home again, weary, defeated, ragged and many of them sick. The decision to retain the army under its colours at this stage was lunatic.[177] The government's policy over the distribution of regiments was erratic and confused. First, on 16 November, the Sussex lieutenants were informed that Colonel Courtenay's regiment, which had been billeted in Chichester rape in May and June, would return to their old billets; on 22 November this order was countermanded, when it was learned that there were already two other regiments billeted in Sussex. Finally, on 17 December, admitting that they were unable to control the situation from London, the Council gave the Hampshire deputies authority to distribute the soldiers that remained there as they thought best. At this stage the intention was that five counties, including Sussex, should bear an equal charge. A month later the Council decided that thirteen counties should billet one regiment each.[178] This decision led to a general post just as it seemed the matter was sorted out. The Sussex deputies jumped at the opportunity to march off 300 men of Colonel Sprye's regiment into Gloucestershire but were chastened to find themselves landed in return with the same number of Colonel Courtenay's regiment, who had somehow ended up in Surrey.[179]

About 600 men were billeted in Sussex from November 1627 until the following September. This time there was no loan money to pay those who quartered the troops. Instead there were merely honeyed words from Dorset about the army paymaster's imminent arrival in the county.[180] Both the county and the deputies were less cooperative. The deputies did their utmost to shift part of the burden elsewhere, by suggesting to Dorset that 100 men might be billeted in Hastings. The mayor and jurats reacted to news of the proposal with a desperate plea that Buckingham should free their 'weake ympoverished towne of that heavy charge'. All inhabitants 'of any ability', they declared implausibly, would move away rather than accept soldiers in their homes.[181] In view of Dorset's direction that the men should be billeted in whole companies 'so as uppon all occasions their captaynes and commanders may have them in reddiness', the deputies decided to concentrate the soldiers in the larger towns, a policy that soon brought protests.[182] Plague spread rapidly in Chichester during December and naturally the presence of large numbers of soldiers was held to blame. Some citizens refused the heavy rates imposed to defray the billeting charges there.[183] The inhabitants of Lewes complained directly to Dorset at the 'unjust' imposition of 140 soldiers on them. The relationship between Dorset and the deputies was tense in the last weeks of 1627. There was a good deal of pique behind the Earl's conclusion to the letter in which he directed that one of the companies in Lewes should be moved to the Eastbourne and Hailsham district. If he had known the number of soldiers in the county, he declared,

> I then showld know whether they be more than is fitting. And accordingly should take order to have redress from hence, besides I showld then compute what the monthly charge wowld amount unto and accordingly judg how your county can supporte it, but if it be for your ease and the countryes to keepe me heere in ignorance I shall rest contented.[184]

The deputies were perhaps ill-advised to billet two whole companies in Lewes but in general they had tried to follow their instructions. Dorset may have taken a hard line because he expected trouble. His initial letter about the new period of billeting contained the old threat that if any refused to contribute to the billet money they should have men billeted on them in reprisal, 'though it be in the inmost parts of the county'.

In July and August 1628, prior to the sailing of Willoughby's expedition to La Rochelle, the western end of the county again bore the brunt of the billeting. Courtenay's regiment was brought together there from the other rapes and companies from other counties were found lodging on the coastal plain.[185] When, after the expedition had sailed, the government tried to billet two companies of Sir John Meldrum's Scottish regiment, who had arrived too late, anger turned to open resistance at Chichester. Led by the city's two MPs, Henry Bellingham and William Cawley, who had returned from Westminster that summer with all the arguments about the illegality of billeting at their fingertips, some townsmen threatened to shut the gates of the city against the soldiers.[186] The government was already 'fundamentally at loggerheads' with the gentry of the Isle of Wight, who had had their fill of uncontrollable Highlanders since 1626, about these particular companies.[187] So it dared take no more punitive action in face of Chichester's 'insolence' than summon Bellingham and Cawley to London and then immediately release them.[188] With the crises surrounding the Petition of Right and Buckingham's assassination only just behind them, and huge outstanding bills for the billeting of the previous months still unpaid, it was no time for confrontation with the gentry of southern England.

The aftermath of billeting in the southern counties in 1627 and 1628 was a long period of wrangling over the payments due to householders. In April 1628 Captain Mason, the army paymaster, received a paltry £2,000 towards the billeting expenses that had mounted along the south coast since the previous November. It appears that he received more money about August, since he was able to pay some money to those who lodged soldiers in the Chichester area immediately prior to the sailing of the fleet.[189] But for much of Sussex, as for Essex, Dorset and Somerset, and the Isle of Wight, billeting amounted to one more form of unparliamentary taxation.[190] Numerous men who had entertained soldiers and supplied services for the expeditions of the years 1624 to 1628 were left unpaid. The Chichester merchant Henry Chitty was one of them. Sir James Bagg recommended him to Buckingham in 1628, as one who could supply corn for the fleet and who had already provided one ship. In 1633 he listed the services for which he was still unrewarded: two ships, 200 quarters of wheat and 'apparelling His Majestie's soldiers billeted at Chichester', which had cost him £300.[191]

The same group of gentry who were appointed to the billeting commission of August 1626 received a commission to execute martial law upon soldiers and mariners lodging in the county. It gave them extensive powers to use 'such summary course and order as is agreeable to martiall law' against offenders.[192] There is no evidence that they ever used them. Indeed martial law was included in the Petition of Right despite the fact that only a handful of soldiers and sailors and, so far as is known, not a single civilian suffered execution under it in the 1620s.[193] It was associated in men's minds with arbitrary government and so generally disliked. The Hampshire deputies used special commissions of oyer and terminer to expedite punishment of murders committed by soldiers, and thus avoided recourse to their powers under the martial law commission. It was only in conditions of riot and spoil, such as at Dover before Mansfield's expedition set sail, that martial law became a necessary expedient. The most that the Sussex authorities had to deal with was the odd case of larceny or manslaughter. The normal processes of quarter sessions and assizes were quite adequate to control the soldiers billeted in the county. Some soldiers who were involved in a tavern brawl that led to a civilian being wounded at Eastbourne in 1626 were bound over to the next sessions. A Kentish barber who deserted the press at Chichester and was arrested some weeks later at Arundel also appeared before the Bench.[194]

Martial law was overshadowed by the permanent institutions and generally accepted legal procedures of county government. So was the office of provost marshal. Marshals with powers of summary execution had been active in the 1590s when the coast was infested with penniless starving soldiers returned from abroad. Their particular task was to clear the district of soldiers, though other riffraff naturally came into their net.[195] But when the Council directed a marshal to be appointed in Sussex in 1617, it specified the reason as the multitude of rogues and beggars in the ironworking region of the Weald.[196] In 1624 the military aspect briefly reappeared: watch was to be kept on soldiers being conducted through the county to the rendezvous at Dover as well as on other 'idle and loose' persons on the highways in the winter season. On this occasion the justices appointed a marshal in each rape.[197] The military aspect had in fact become incidental and the marshals had become poor law officials. In 1626 a marshal was again appointed for each rape.[198] Regular re-appointment in the 1630s shows the importance that the justices attached to the office in their drive against vagrancy.[199] The transformation of the provost marshal from a military official to an administrative subordinate illustrates the pragmatic, experimental way in which provincial gentry bent the institutions of Tudor government to serve their own ends in the localities.

The exact militia was an impracticable programme for a government which lacked agents other than independently-minded gentry to enforce its will. Every aspect of the programme broke down, sooner or later, because men were not prepared to bear the charges that arose. Musters were purposeless unless men brought proper arms and armour, training meant remuneration for the muster-master, effective defence depended on the repair of ordnance and purchase of gunpowder, men would not spend long cold nights watching beacons unless they were properly rewarded, overseas expeditions involved coat and conduct money, householders could not be expected to billet soldiers for months on end unless they were paid. Contributions to the taxes involved appear as merely incidental and minor expenses in the account book of Sir Thomas Pelham. His assessment for 'powder and raising of ordinance' at Eastbourne in 1626 was eight shillings, and he paid the same amount 'for press and conduct money' in 1628.[200] Many ordinary householders could afford the few pence that were demanded of them. But the demands were so frequent in the years 1625–28 that they had a cumulative effect on men's minds. The pent up anger that emerged in the stormy parliament of 1628 and again in 1640–41 had its roots in a thousand farms and manor houses. It was the deputies in the end who were made the scapegoats.[201] The Earl of Dorset had foreseen the troubles that the exact militia programme would run into as early as 1624. He did not minimise the difficulties the deputies would face:

> Innovations in most things quadrates with the opinion of the multitude, who ever meete it with gladnesse and wellcome, onely this rulle howldes not in such things as bringe along a new charge, as perhapps in the accomplishment of your imployement in this particular may arise; wherein I doubt not but you shall allmost undergoe a dispaireinge taske, did I not withall rest assured that your love to his Majestie's

> service, and the common good of your country, will make you indefatigable, and so overcome the difficulty.[202]

In fact deputies were indefatigable. But it was hard for them to square their duty to the King with their concern for the good of the county community. The emergency posed by the government between 1625 and 1628 can never have seemed anything like as real to Sir John Shurley or Sir Walter Covert as the crisis of the Armada and the war of the 1590s. The deputies were men with a strong sense of duty to the new King. Yet they must often have found his Council's priorities hard to accept. Moreover their relationship with the lieutenants was too formal, too often uneasy, for it to influence the policy made in London. Cooperation on matters that seemed crucial, such as muster defaults and the supply of powder, was not always forthcoming. On the other hand, the Council proposed grandiose schemes of training and mounted expensive foreign expeditions. The fate of the exact militia exemplifies, perhaps better than any other of the projects of the Caroline government, its failure to work in tune with the men who administered the provinces of England.

10

The taxation of the county

By the Lordes woundes, yf he did not sursease to medle about the sesse, he would cudgell his coat.
William Roberts to the minister of Warbleton, August 1625.[1]

The full and speedy retorne which the rape of Lewis hath made . . . condems the remaynder both of cowldness in them that showld paye, and mutch remissnes in those that are trusted either to see it collected, or certfie where the impedement lyes.
The Earl of Dorset to the deputy-lieutenants concerning the forced loan, 17 January 1627.[2]

The failure of the Elizabethan government to maintain the yield of the subsidy, its principal means of taxing the country as a whole, in a period of massive inflation exposed a fundamental source of weakness in the Tudor state.[3] Nothing was done to correct this in the early seventeenth century, so James I and Charles I were driven to supplement parliamentary subsidies with a variety of fiscal expedients, which included forced loans and compositions for knighthood.[4] Ship money and the new style parliamentary subsidy of 1642 were experiments in national taxation designed to remedy the chronic deficiencies of the Tudor subsidy. The new taxes were imposed on householders who were already accustomed to paying various local rates: for the poor, the upkeep of the parish church, bridge repairs and militia expenditure.[5] Taxation was a fact of life, but at every level of the taxpaying classes men were constantly trying to shift the burden elsewhere. Thus taxation tested the delicate relationship between a county's magnat gentry and the central government to the uttermost. It revealed their self interest and made them face their conflicting responsibilities towards th county and the nation. Fiscal issues illuminate the realities of count government with peculiar intensity.

Subsidies, ship money and the Act for £400,000

Analysis of the decline in the yield of the subsidy is set out in appendi V. In Bramber rape for instance it yielded 31 per cent less, and in th city of Chichester 38 per cent less, in 1628 than it had done in 161 Inefficient methods of collection do not account for the progressive co lapse of the subsidy. The high collectors tended to be ambitious minor gentry, anxious to prove their administrative capacity. Hall Ravenscroft did this so successfully that he jumped from a high collectorship in 1628 to a commissionership in 1640.[6] The strict timetable set out in the statute for payment of the money into the Exchequer was normally closely adhered to. Thomas Ball, for example, presented his account for the third Chichester payment in 1628 just over three weeks after starting work.[7] Once the assessment had been made by the subsidy commissioners, the procedure was well worn and worked smoothly. Assessment itself was less straightforward. Indeed it was often a matter of disputes, adjourned meetings and long drawn out haggling between the assessors for a particular hundred and the gentry appointed as commissioners.[8] The commissioners were thus often somewhat behind the schedule set out in the statute in making up their certificates. When subsidies came thick and fast between June 1628 and February 1629, the delays became cumulative. By the time it came to the fourth payment the commissioners in Hastings and Bramber rapes were running a month late.[9]

The yield fell because assessments were constantly reduced. For decades magnate families who provided the subsidy commissioners had set an appalling example. 'The rich', remarked the Elizabethan JP James Colbrand, 'were often rated, in fixing their tax, much too low, at not a fortieth part of their wealth'.[10] The average assessment of seventy leading Sussex families between the 1540s and the 1620s dropped from sixty-one pounds to fourteen pounds.[11] Rural magnates, here as elsewhere in England, were engaged in blatant collusion to defraud the state. They had spoken with some JPs who were assessed at less than twenty pounds in lands, reported the Lincolnshire commissioners to the Council in 1621,

> who think it too burthensome for their small estates to be so rated considering the daily charge they undergo by their pains in his Majesty's several services. And therefore submit themselves to your lordships' pleasure for the continuance of their places.[12]

JPs held the whip hand. The Council needed their service in the provinces and they knew it. When the Sussex commissioners met at Shoreham in 1621, they agreed that four of them should be taxed at less than the twenty pound minimum for justices that the Council had attempted to impose. Thus as wealthy a man as Robert Morley of Glynde escaped at a mere ten pounds. Sir Thomas Pelham headed the 1621 list with an assessment of fifty pounds, a farcical sum for a man with a landed income of around £2,000 a year. Sir Walter Covert was the only other gentleman who was to pay on a fifty pound assessment.[13] Five years later the commissioners agreed that Pelham and Covert should both have ten pounds lopped off their assessments.[14]

Lightening the burden of colleagues and friends was normal practice.

On his retirement from the subsidy commission in 1626 Nicholas Jordan was handed a reduction in his assessment from twenty pounds to six pounds. In 1628 Thomas Traiton and Richard Shelley, commissioners in Lewes rape, assessed themselves at three and four pounds respectively. In the same year, Sir Benjamin Pellatt, Sir Edward Bellingham and Laurence de la Chambre, all of them ex-JPs, had their assessments reduced; so did Sir Edward Culpepper, Anthony Fowle and Sir Richard Michelbourne, who were still on the Bench. Occasionally someone showed faint susceptibility to the government propaganda about setting a good example. Sir Thomas Sackville's assessment was raised from seven to ten pounds when he became an active commissioner in 1628; Richard Amherst accepted an addition of four pounds when he was involved in making the 1626 assessment, but he willingly joined in the general move to cut the magisterial tax burden two years later, when his assessment went down from twenty to eight pounds. In view of proceedings of this kind it is hardly surprising that assessors saw their appointment as an opportunity to join in the game and ease themselves. Sackville Turner and John Wilson, for example, hastened to do so in 1626.[15]

The magnate gentry must bear full responsibility for the collapse of the subsidy as an effective fiscal instrument. Not only did they constantly cut men's assessments. They made little serious attempt to ensure that men once on the subsidy books stayed there. The decline in the numbers of subsidymen, viewed hundred by hundred and parish by parish, was certainly very uneven, yet the trend was almost always in the same direction: Shiplake hundred lost five taxpayers between 1626 and 1628, Eastbourne hundred two, Avisford hundred eleven. Not a single hundred in Bramber rape maintained its complement of subsidymen over the two year interval, only two hundreds in Hastings rape did so. Sometimes the eliminations were drastic. Steyning almost halved its taxpaying population in 1628; the little villages of Tarring and Patching lost seven subsidymen between them in the same year. Neither mortality nor mobility can account for the scale in the reduction of men liable to contribute. Nor did a core of men recur from year to year in each hundred. Mobility is unlikely to account for six additions to the subsidy roll for Broadwater or three new men out of the seven Lancing subsidymen in 1628. Replacements were also found for men who were dropped between the second and third payment of the 1628 subsidy in some parts of Bramber rape. Undoubtedly there was always a large pool of men who could reasonably be taxed on land worth one pound a year. There was much chopping and changing since men put pressure on friends whenever they could do so and a primitive concept of spreading the burden in a rough and ready fashion applied.[16]

Comparison of the trends of assessment on lands and goods provides further insight into how the yield of the subsidy was reduced. The fall in the crown's income from the city of Chichester was due more to progressively lower assessments on subsidymen who paid on their lands than any alteration in the numbers or change of men liable to pay on their goods. In Bramber rape, on the other hand, the sharp decline in the number of people paying on goods was a more important factor in the overall reduction in the yield of the subsidy. The figures for Bramber rape conceal many transfers of assessment from goods to lands: the minimum assessment on goods was three pounds, which normally meant an actual payment of eight shillings, whereas the minimum qualification on land was one pound which usually cost the taxpayer only four shillings. Thus in the country, where it was much simpler anyway to ascertain the landed income of minor gentry and yeomen than their real property, assessment on land commended itself to both assessors and taxpayers. The number of men paying the subsidy on goods in Bramber rape decreased by 60 per cent between 1626 and 1628. Increasingly, land dominated the subsidy and there was a levelling downwards towards the one pound minimum. By 1628 the vast majority of subsidymen paid a mere four shillings. In Shinglecross hundred for instance, by 1628 69 per cent of those taxed were on the base level of payment; only four of the forty-eight subsidymen were assessed at four pounds or over.[17] The sabotage of the subsidy was thus achieved by a combination of reduction of numbers, reduction of assessments and exploitation of the dual basis of assessment to the advantage of the taxpayer. The wrecking process was led by the magnate gentry, who, as the King's servants in the county, acquiesced when the community at large followed their example and put the protection of their own pockets before the financial needs of the central government.

Seen against the fiscal catastrophe of the subsidy, the resounding success of the successive ship money writs is unquestionable. In all, the Sussex assessments yielded around £28,000 over a period of only six years, whereas the total yield of twelve subsidies granted by parliament in the 1620s can hardly have been £16,000. Ship money tapped the wealth of the countryside far more effectively than the subsidy had done. The subsidy payments in Arundel and Hastings rapes in 1628 had been only 4 and 14 per cent respectively of the 1635 ship money yield. The impact on Chichester was less dramatic, since the 1636 assessment was lower than the subsidy yield in 1610, but even there the decline of the 1620s was halted.[18] In general the Sussex evidence, like that for Essex, supports William Prynne's claim that the sums demanded by the 1635 writs were equal to four subsidies and more.[19]

It is probable that the weight of the increased tax burden fell on the middle ranks of society. Customary assessments for poor rates and purveyance were generally adopted as the basis for sharing out the sums to be levied on towns and villages. Thus the bulk of the money came from the pockets of landowners, according to the number of yardlands they possessed. The North Stoke subsidyman Thomas Harmewood, for instance, who had paid four shillings on an assessment of one pound in lands in 1625, contributed eleven shillings and sixpence for his two yardlands in 1635.[20] But the Council's directions to tax men of ability as well as landowners, enforced by the Sussex sheriffs, also caught numerous tradesmen and craftsmen in the new tax net. Some magnate gentry seem to have dodged any swingeing tax increase. Sir Thomas Pelham paid roughly the same amount, about eight shillings, towards each ship money assessment as he had done towards each subsidy in the previous decade. The forty-eight pounds, for which he accounted in ship money payments between 1634 and 1639 hurt a man of his wealth no more than the £100 odd he had handed over to the crown in the 1620s.[21] Yet in Chichester, where the corporation was faced in 1635 with finding more than £120 from the city excluding the Close, men found themselves paying two or three times the amount they had contributed to each subsidy in 1628. A surviving assessment of South Street and the Pallant indicates that every effort was made to extend the scope of the tax to poorer men, but, although fifty-six men paid in these two principal residential areas as against nineteen in 1628, substantial increases had to be imposed on gentry and merchants. Typical cases were Henry Chitty who paid £1. 4*s* instead of 13*s* 4*d*, George Greene who paid £1. 4*s* instead of 8*s* 4*d* and Thomas Farrington who paid £5 instead of 26*s* 8*d*.[22]

Two innovations transformed the effectiveness of national taxation in the 1630s. A fixed sum was charged on each county under the ship money writs and a single individual, the sheriff, harried remorselessly from London, was given entire responsibility for the collection in a particular year. The success of the ship money experiment in Sussex rested on the shoulders of six sorely tried men. Five of them took great pains to fulfil the responsibility thrust upon them. They exhibited the same kind of devotion to the government's service as most of the Somerset sheriffs. The task undertaken by Sir William Culpepper was one of the heaviest imposed on any of the men employed in the ship money business. He was held answerable for the collection of Sussex's share of the 1634 writs to the coastal counties as well as for the first nationwide collection, under the writ of August 1635, in both Surrey and Sussex. In fact it was his recognition of the burden on Culpepper and a few others that led Secretary Nicholas to propose in the Privy Council 'that the Judges take into consideration the dividing of all the counties where one sheriff serves for two counties'.[23] Considering the difficulties he faced, Culpepper acted with efficiency and despatch. By 8 March 1635 he had paid in to the Treasurer of the Navy a higher proportion of the 1634 assessment than any other sheriff except Cornwall's.[24] At the end of August the arrears due from Sussex and Kent were the lowest in the country. In January 1636, six months after the issue of the second writ, Culpepper had paid in £4,574 for Sussex, 78 per cent of the tax on the county.[25]

After some chivying of corporate towns and recalcitrant parishes Culpepper's successor Sir William Morley completed the collection und the 1635 writ in Sussex in July 1636.[26] The collection of arrears for 1635 in Surrey, where many taxpayers were absentees for much of the year, faced Morley with formidable problems which he never entirely solved, but this was not through want of effort. 'The trouble to finish it wil be very much', he wrote to Lord Treasurer Juxon in July 'and I feare it must be my owne worke to doe it, for I finde all men (and my owne officers alsoe) unwilling'.[27] Anthony Fowle moved swiftly to enforce the writ of October 1637. He called a meeting of mayors and bailiffs at the Bull Inn at Lewes on 3 November; within a fortnight after it he had completed his rating of the whole county.[28] Neither he nor his successor Anthony Foster seems to have had any great difficulty in collecting the full sums. Sussex was one of only four counties with no default at all on the 1638 writ. With the taxpaying nation as a whole on strike, Edward Apsley, the sheriff given the impossible task of collecting £5,000 under the 1639 writ, did remarkably well to bring in as much as 44 per cent of the Sussex tax.[29]

The unsatisfactory performance of Sir Edward Bishop, who was given the oversight of collection of £5,000 under the 1636 writ, contrasted sharply with the industry of those who came before and after him. In the first place, he did his best to shift the work on to others, by appointing a gentleman in each rape as grand collector. The choice of Sir John Shelley as collector for Arundel rape, although he lived over the border of Bramber rape, has a hint of personal enmity about it. Shelley was a recusant incapacitated by gout and largely out of touch with the affairs of county government. A warning from the Council that they took this move as an attempt 'either to hinder or trouble the business' and that he should find a more 'able, careful, diligent man' did not, it seems, awake in Bishop a livelier sense of his duty.[30] He received another sharp note from the Council in May 1637, when his dilatoriness was reported to have delayed the payment of money raised to the Treasurer for the Navy. Peter Farnden, the collector in Hastings rape, had appealed to Secretary Nicholas for arrangements to be made for him to be relieved of £877, which had been in his hands for two months. He had heard nothing from Sir Edward Bishop, who 'can comand the strength of the county, to assist him to convey it, which I cannot doe, neyther dare I adventure the charge of carrying soe greate a some'.[31] The ship money arrears from Sussex in the summer of 1637 tell the story of Bishop's inertia. He finally produced £422 of the £522 outstanding, under threat of attendance before the Council, but left arrears of £31 uncollected.[32]

The distribution of the sum charged under a ship money writ on towns and villages was entirely at the discretion of the sheriff. The procedure provided an unusual opportunity for partiality, which some sheriffs employed more blatantly than others.[33] Sir Edward Bishop, for example, eased his own rape by transferring £104 on to the neighbouring rape of Chichester. Bishop made numerous other adjustments to Sir William Culpepper's apportionment of the charge, shifting the weight of the burden away from the Downs to the populous parishes of the Weald. Thus in some northern parishes the increase in the tax burden from the 1620s was startling: Petworth paid £106 instead of £18 for a single subsidy in 1628, Kirdford £44 pounds as against thirty shillings; Billingshurst, Rudgwick, Beeding, Worth, Framfield and Ticehurst were among others assessed at a high level. Some southern parishes escaped lightly in 1636 compared with 1635: North Stoke paid £4 instead of £8, Bosham £22 instead of £50. In general, Bishop's scheme was probably more closely in line with the distribution of wealth than Culpepper's. But his campaign to spread the load by demanding a multitude of modest contributions from inland also reflects the self-interest of the gentry class, who dominated the south and middle part of the county. The excessive disparities between payments from different rapes, which had become increasingly glaring in the subsidies of the 1620s, were corrected in the ship money apportionments. Even Hastings rape, the most politically and religiously obstructionist district which had been exceptionally ruthless in reducing subsidy assessments, began once more to pay something like its fair share of the county's tax burden in the 1630s.[34]

Resistance to ship money in Sussex was less determined and slower to emerge than in many other counties, not so much because the gentry made responsible for collecting it were more dutiful than average, but because the situation and conditions of the county made the whole community aware of the importance of a fleet to protect the coast. The ostensible purpose made sense to Sussex men. The dangers their countrymen faced were well known. There was no initial disposition to question such a purposeful tax.[35] It was not until late in 1639 that men began to refuse to pay their ship money rates in Sussex, as the county became fully informed about the mood of neighbouring counties such as Kent and Surrey. Even then the representatives of the corporate towns took their stand on 'a mistake of the sum', rather than the principle of the tax. At a meeting with Edward Apsley, they were incensed that the Council was again demanding £5,000 to furnish a smaller ship than in previous years.[36] During 1640 a critical attitude turned into adamant obstruction. A conciliatory letter from the Council offering to reduce Sussex's charge from £5,000 to £4,000 if the sum was paid in full by 2 March, fell on deaf ears. Yet so much did coastal defence matter to towns like Rye and Winchelsea, that they were among the very few provincial communities that continued to trust the government on this issue during the tense spring and summer of 1640. Rye paid in £40 of its £50 under the 1639 writ and Winchelsea all but £5 of its contribution before the collection of ship money finally collapsed in the autumn.[37]

It was predictable that there would be pressure from the start to shift the burden of a tax that was recognised as necessary elsewhere within the county. In 1634 £2,700 was paid by the 'maritime places' of the county so the following year the Cinque Ports urged Sir William Culpepper to relieve the coast which, they maintained, was 'fullest of poor inhabitants and more eminent to dayly dangers and subiect to losse and dayly burthened with charges then th iner parte of the countie'. They recommended distributing the £5,000 charged on Sussex at £16 each on the 329 parishes. Culpepper saw that this simple solution would not be equitable, but he agreed to ease the towns of Hastings, Rye, Winchelsea, Pevensey and Seaford so that they paid only £250 between them. Further pressure on Anthony Fowle two years later led to another reduction to £230. The meetings between the sheriff and the officers of the corporations produced hard bargaining. One surviving certificate shows that the Arundel and Shoreham assessments were reduced in the course of the meeting at the Bull in 1637.[38] Chichester's contribution had been cut from £150 to £70 in 1635.[39]

The same kind of haggling certainly went on between and within parishes. Numerous discrepancies in the amounts paid by Sir Thomas Pelham for his Hellingly, East Hoathly, Dallington and Brightling lands suggest that chopping and changing of rates was common.[40] Much of the opposition to ship money in other counties took the same form. Contention was particularly likely where rating for local taxes was already in dispute. This was the case at North Stoke, where two parties set about the collection of rival rates early in 1635. Richard Freake, the largest landowner in the village, was assessed at six yardlands in one case and eight in the other. His fight for the nine shillings at stake was examined at length by two JPs who resolved in his favour. But meantime, his enemies, armed with a warrant to arrest him, had 'laid at him with bills and staves' as he was leaving his boat at Arundel. They 'carried him by force (foure of them on horsebacke and one with a long staffe in his necke on foote) along the country to Horsham gaole'.[41] Neither in this case, nor in another one at Bosham, is there any indication of objection to the principle of ship money.[42] Such cases, together with the quarrel between the Chichester townsmen and clergy over rating the Close, merely illustrate how easily a new tax became a catalyst to well-established enmities. Men were bound to grumble about their own ship money assessments, just as they did whenever their pockets were raided, but by and large the Sussex response was moderate and acquiescent.

The new style parliamentary grant of 1642 applied the ship money principle of a fixed charge on each county, but preserved the old subsidy procedure of collection through gentry commissioners, assessors and high collectors. The Act for £400,000 was a triumph for the group of responsible opposition MPs led by John Pym and Oliver St John who, as long before as the 1620s, had recognised the need for some kind of permanent reform of royal finances. The proposal to deal with the falling yield of the subsidy by the proportionment on the counties of a fixed sum, which Pym put forward on 19 November 1640, was the linchpin of a constructive programme for settling the King's revenue.[43] Sussex was to pay £10,914 in two payments by 20 June and 20 December 1642. The commissioners responded energetically but the problems of organizing so large a collection were immense. The statute required the assessment for the first payment to be completed and high collectors to be appointed by 20 May. In Hastings rape the commissioners did not even meet the representatives of the corporate towns until 2 June, and it was 14 July before they drew up their certificate; the Pevensey rape assessment was ready on 6 June; in Chichester rape the commissioners completed their part on 15 July. The collectors worked almost as fast as they had normally done under the old subsidy procedure: William Cooke, for example, took exactly a month to obtain £863 due from almost 2,000 scattered inhabitants of Bramber rape.[44] The money was raised without difficulty and in a single year the King received from Sussex well over half as much as he and his father had received from the county in the whole of the 1620s.

Each payment of the Act for £400,000 represented a substantially increased burden compared with the ship money assessments. Again it was the north of the county that suffered most. In Bramber rape, for instance, the tax fell heavily on the wealden hundreds of Burbeach and West Grinstead; in Arundel rape, Rotherbridge hundred paid £299; in Chichester rape Easebourne hundred was hit hardest. Within each village the tax was divided among the inhabitants by a method which departed from both the subsidy and ship money procedures. The village quotas were made up by a poundage rate on the occupiers of lands, which in Bramber rape was initially set at ninepence. Thus a great landowner such as Sir Thomas Pelham paid numerous small sums for the land he farmed in different parishes and he also reimbursed his tenants for the multitude of payments made for lands they leased. It is hard to say how far this system dug deeper into the pockets of the magnate gentry, but it seems likely that it was a bitterer pill for the middling sort than for them. Samuel Locke of Steyning and John Bowrer of Warnham, for example, were charged with sums that were eight and twelve times respectively their 1628 contribution as subsidymen at one pound in lands. The tax was spread heavily through the middle ranks of the communty. Merchants like Thomas Botting of Tarring and Samuel Newington of Kingston Bowsey, who had escaped lightly on their lands in the 1628 assessment, were taxed on their goods. Thus they paid more than two pounds instead of a few shillings. More than a third of the Steyning men who paid did so on their goods and a few Bramber townsmen were charged on both their land and stock. The commissioners also ensured that the harsh regulations about double taxation of recusants were strictly enforced.[45] In 1642, for the first time in a hundred years, the Sussex community as a whole began to face up to the implications of realistic taxation of the wealth that had accrued to it during a century of rapid inflation.

Fiscal expedients 1603–42

Financial expedients to supplement parliamentary subsidies became inevitable between 1603 and 1642. It was not merely that MPs were reluctant to vote enough subsidies. Some of them just did not understand the magnitude of the sums which were needed.[46] Thus, in 1604–05, 1611, 1614, 1621, 1625, 1626 and 1627, the Stuart government attempted to raise various kinds of loans, voluntary contributions and benevolences. Finally in 1630 another extra-parliamentary expedient of dubious legality, the scheme for taking compositions for knighthood, was implemented.[47] Faced with these demands, the Sussex gentry prevaricated, excused themselves and occasionally put up outright opposition.

The most favoured response among independently minded country gentlemen who received a request for a loan was to ignore it until the Council exerted further pressure. This was what men did all over England in 1614 when James I asked for money after the disastrous Addled Parliament.[48] When the Sussex magnates felt obliged to respond at all to demands for extra-parliamentary taxation, they invariably dragged their heels in doing so. 'Thorough the shortnes of tyme it is not possible for us to execute your comaund' by the date stipulated, explained eighteen JPs on 3 May 1622. They had received the conciliar letter about a voluntary contribution on 31 March but had been busy since with the sessions 'at severall places farre distant'. There was no inclination to interrupt the Easter social round with business of this nature. On 21 September 1625, the deputy-lieutenants heard that the Council wanted a book of names of men of ability for receipt of privy seals to be sent up by 8 October. Politely but firmly, they explained to the Earl of Dorset that they were meeting at Lewes about militia business early in October and would put it on their agenda then. Dorset's entreaty in reply 'by the trust we repose in you immediately (setting aparte what occasions soever) to assemble yourselves and accomplish the command' fell on deaf ears.[49] The justices were equally slow the following summer when the King demanded a free gift after the failure of a stormy parliament. At Horsham assizes and the July sessions there was plenty of opportunity for the eleven JPs who had spent such an unsatisfactory spring at Westminster to report on the debates they had attended.[50]

Under pressure from London, the Bench went through the motions of collecting the free gift during August 1626. At a meeting at Lewes on 15 August, which was attended by six of the disgruntled MPs, all the deputies and a good many justices, the magnates formulated their report to the Council. Their conclusion was stated succinctly in the deputy-lieutenancy book: 'the whole county of Sussex would not give above £120 and that they did crave a parliament by a general concent'.[51] Writing to the Council the Bench put the matter more circumspectly, seeking to square their consciences and spare themselves further molestation. They had 'not failed according to our duties as well in generall as in particuler to move . . . the ablest of the inhabitants' at meetings held in each rape. As instructed, they had tried to avoid misunderstanding by not propounding the supply 'by way or soe much as name of subsidie or fifteene'. Yet they had found that the people generally answered

> that their wants and poverty, occasioned by the late greate expenses in many publique charges, have been such, that they are not willing to give as is required, but in a parliamentary course they will straine themselves beyond their abilities.

The Bench shrugged off the paltry collection they had made as 'under your honourable favours not worth the presenting to his royall Majestie'.[52] The plea of poverty was insidious and hard for the government to answer. The Bench had adopted the same tone of hollow protestation the previous year over privy seals: 'we finde our country much decayed but we trust your lordshipps will accept our endeavors heerein'.[53]

Time and again the sums raised from Sussex through the Jacobean and Caroline fiscal expedients failed to match the government's expectations. In 1614, only £772 was extracted.[54] The knighthood compositions only raised about £1,600.[55] £3,650 from the privy seal scheme of 1625 was not nearly as impressive as it might have been although it was the sixth highest county contribution.[56] The readier response to the 1626–27 forced loan can be accounted for by the permission given to use it for the county's outstanding billeting, coat and conduct and impressment charges.[5] Parish gentry and wealthy yeomen, rather than the great magnates, bore the brunt of the Stuart fiscal projects. Most of the 255 privy seals of 162 were directed to minor gentry who paid ten pounds each. Only in Suffolk Norfolk and Devon were more men asked to pay. Richard Lewkenor' list for the western rapes of men liable to compound for knighthood comprised a single baronet, ten esquires, nineteen gentlemen, twenty-five yeomen and an alderman. But there was at least little overlap between the privy seal and knighthood lists. In neither 1625 nor 1630 was there any serious attempt to report all eligible men. The magnates merely dipped into the pool to provide a respectable showing.[58] Thus the royal project were undermined by magnate halfheartedness. If the JPs had made detailed investigation of the subsidy rolls, freeholders book, muster roll and books of collectors for the poor and had gathered information from the undersheriff, escheator, feodary and constables, as they were directed they must have come up with more than 120 names of men liable t compound for knighthood. Their slackness is clinched by the ease wit which they produced a further 111 names under government pressure The commissioners showed little vigour in pursuing reluctant compounders. Colleagues such as Anthony Apsley and Robert Morley wer let off at once when they alleged they had tallies from the Exchequer Only the doddering Sir Walter Covert, making one of his final publi appearances after more than sixty years of service to the Tudor and Stuart crowns, was at all stalwart in the business. Seven men had refused to compound in Lewes rape, he declared, 'not withstanding they are fitt and able men'.[59]

The JPs put their own pockets first, their county second and the interests of the crown third. Their extreme partiality affords further proof of their untrustworthiness as the King's servants and explanation of the failure of the royal projects. In nominating men for privy seals, the Earl of Dorset directed, the justices should rate the wealthy highly, by showing impartial judgment 'of your neighbours abilityes'. On the contrary they displayed blatant prejudice, picking on four Catholics, Sir John Caryll, Sir Garrett Kempe, Sir John Shelley and Sir John Gage, as scapegoats for the King's financial needs. Caryll paid £100. Sir Thomas Pelham, the only JP rated at more than forty pounds, was originally charged with the same sum, but pressure in London secured him an abatement. His actual payment was forty pounds. While the leading Catholic magnates were treated harshly, JPs who were just as well off escaped with fifteen or twenty pounds. Some, like Walter Bartlett, Anthony Apsley and Sir Thomas Sackville, paid no more than mere parish gentry.[60] The instructions for rating compounders for knighthood stipulated that JPs were to pay at least twenty-five pounds 'it beinge presumed that they are all of good estates' and that subsidymen assessed at more than three pounds in lands were to pay at least three and a half times their subsidy assessment. The first precept was ignored, the second was followed in the case of only two justices. Yet the subsidy rating of one of them, Robert Foster, was so low that, despite paying seventeen pounds and ten shillings, he was nowhere near the level demanded of magistrates. Most JPs paid their subsidy assessment or a bit more: Henry Goring and Ralph Cowper, for instance, agreed to a charge at the same level, Walter Bartlett paid three pounds more than his patently absurd subsidy rating of seven pounds. No one except Sir Thomas Bowyer, whose composition at seventy pounds was an eccentric gesture, compounded at over twenty pounds.[61]

The east was more obstructive towards the royal expedients than the west. Fifteen of the twenty-three loan refusers in 1622 were eastern gentry; those refusing in 1627 all lived in the east.[62] The same pattern of stubborn defiance by the eastern gentry emerged when Charles I requested voluntary contributions for the Scots war in 1639.[63] Hastings rape contributed nothing to the free gift of 1626 and Pevensey rape less than four pounds. In Pevensey rape there was open resistance to the forced loan of the same year.[64] The Cinque Ports refused to have anything to do with the knighthood composition scheme: 'none of them came or offered to make any composition' reported the commissioners after their meetings at Battle and Buxted.[65]

The period of Stuart fiscal projects coincided with the last years of purveyance. By exploiting the ancient right of the crown to provision the royal household below market rates, James I and Charles I were able to impose an annual tax on Sussex of well over £1,000. Purveyance was 'a chronic rather than an acute grievance', but it must be seen in the same context as the other expedients.[66] It was a constant irritant to men at all levels of society above the very poor and it undoubtedly helped to alienate public opinion from the Stuart monarchy. Until 1622, when the Bench agreed to compound with a lump sum, they themselves acted as undertakers for purveyance. The business of organising contractors to deliver the goods charged on the county was tiresome and burdensome.[67] Separate taxes were imposed for provision oats, charcoal, wheat and flesh. The sums involved were small: Sir Thomas Pelham paid rather more than a pound a year in all, John Everenden up to four shillings.[68] Provision taxes for Worth and Sedlescombe show that most people only paid a few pence.[69] Nevertheless disputes about the distribution of the charge were common.[70]

The taxes themselves did not create hardship, but the activities and abuses of purveyors sometimes did. Great distress was caused in 1605 when the purveyors took 395 of the 400 loads of charcoal due from the county from the northern part of Bramber rape on the grounds that it was convenient for the royal palaces they were supplying and 'that they found there a greater store of coles then they understood to be in the rest of the shiere'.[71] In 1625 some poor sawyers, supported by the entrepreneur glass-maker of Billingshurst, Isack Bungar, appealed to the Bench about the way they had been treated by two purveyors for timber. They had been paid on very low piecework rates in arrears, forced to make their own pits and threatened with gaol or impressment as soldiers if they refused the terms offered:

> They have been constrained to worke in the depth of winter in open weather, where theire pitts not howsed. Through extremitie of raine snowe and suche like and the ladinge out of water to make drye theire pitts, they have loste manie weekes two or three daies worke togeather in a week.[72]

Purveyors often made themselves thoroughly unpopular. At Rye there was longstanding enmity between the fishermen and certain London fishmongers who, through holding the office of the King's purveyor, were able to pre-empt the market for the crown.[73]

Predictably, there was contention over some aspects of purveyance between the magnates and the first two Stuarts. The county made objections to a demand for 400 loads of charcoal instead of the customary 240 loads in 1605. After a long argument over this Sussex agreed to supply 250 loads a year, but wrangling continued until 1616 over charcoal alleged to be in arrears. The deputies only grudgingly complied after they had been threatened with the charges of purchase on the open market and with summonses to London.[74] In the 1620s, though, composition agreements for provision of charcoal seem to have worked more smoothly.[75] Carriage of timber for shipbuilding and the repairs to St Paul's Catheral under the direction of Inigo Jones made onerous demands on Sussex in the 1630s.[76] Pressure from the county may have lain behind the attempt to shift part of this burden on to Kent.[77] The JPs had the last word. In 1650 some money retained by Anthony Stapley from a tax for provision of flesh was allocated, at the direction of the Bench, to ridding the county of a pirate captain and his company who had been captured by the fishermen of Brighton.[78]

Local taxation

The twin pillars of local taxation were the poor rate and the church rate. These were supplemented by a variety of *ad hoc* taxes for hundred charges, bridge and highway repair and emergencies such as the relief of plague and militia charges.[79] The JPs, sensitive to county opinion, were the final arbiters of local taxation. They determined the distribution of the charges and enforced collection, clinging to precedent and accepting that there were limits to their power. Thus when the public spirited gentleman Lewkenor Middleton spent seven pounds on building a 'cage for the safe keeping of prisoners' at Chailey in 1643 the Bench granted an order for his reimbursement by the hundred of Streat, but when some of the neighbourhood failed to show their appreciation by paying him, Middleton was told he would have to pay the balance himself.[80] Since the same men organised both national and local taxation, the methods and procedures of each became intertwined. In the 1630s poor rates provided a convenient basis within villages for ship money assessment; in 1651 the Bench directed that repair of the Rother bridges should be paid for according to the proportions of the monthly assessment.[81] In 1653 the JPs' schedule of parish payments for the gaol fund reflected the general recognition among justices, after two decades of ship money and assessment oversight, that the northern district should bear a proportionately large share of taxation.[82]

Two innovations in local taxes between 1600 and 1660 were conducive to greater equity and efficiency. Firstly, assessment and collection by tithings and boroughs, which had been customary for the subsidy, was abandoned in favour of the parish. Secondly, rating came to be based on the value of a man's lands, the poundage system, rather than on the number of yardlands he occupied. Abandonment of yardlands as the basis of the poor rate was only achieved after much contention. A trickle of sessions cases about landscots for the poor in the reign of James I grew to a steady stream in the 1640s and 50s, when the east Sussex justices alone handled forty disputes.[83] Taxation by yardlands could produce obvious unfairness, since it took no account of the quality of a man's lands: this was usually the fundamental issue at stake. By the 1630s magisterial opinion strongly favoured conversion to the poundage system. One JP inscribed his interpretation of the ambiguously worded 1601 statute on a petition from

Angmering: 'that the taxacion according to lands is not according to law, for by the law the taxacions ought to be by abilitie and valew of the land and not otherwise'.[84] In Sussex, as in Hampshire, Hertfordshire, Kent and Warwickshire, the abandonment of the old type of landscot was a gradual process between the 1630s and the 1650s.[85]

As the justices became accustomed to the increasing stress laid in national taxation on ability as well as or instead of lands, they became keener on the same approach to the poor rate. Whereas in a case in 1638 they had directed that assessment should be by lands 'and not otherwise', they took a different view after the civil war, when they heard a complaint from Petworth about townsmen with 'great personall estates' who had abated themselves. They ordered that 'goods and chatells as well as lands' should be rated.[86] In another case regarding Selmeston their judgment was that the poor rate should be 'by lands or ability and not both'.[87] Taxation of tithes was frequently a matter of lay-clerical dispute. A general order of 1657 reiterated established magisterial policy by insisting that occupiers of tithes that were leased should be taxed for them.[88] The Puritan Bench was generally sympathetic to the claims of ministers over questions of taxation. In response to pressure from Francis Cheynell in 1655 they investigated the whole question of taxing ministers towards repair of the highways.[89]

A general increase in poor rates evident in account books such as John Everenden's was inevitable in the mid-seventeenth century.[90] Hardly anyone actually refused to pay.[91] When there was acrimony and dispute, it often reflected longstanding animosities. In a row at a meeting in Warbleton church in 1625, for instance, Herbert and William Roberts, gentlemen of the neighbourhood, took the chance to challenge the minister over the taxation of the parsonage. 'Thou arte a lyar and the devil is the father of lyes, thou arte a knave and a base knave, a firebrand of hell', Herbert Roberts told him in a torrent of abuse.[92] When the Bench found villagers hopelessly at odds they normally ordered an entirely new assessment of the lands concerned.[93]

Bridges in sound repair were essential to the daily life of the county, yet, because everyone was so anxious to avoid paying for the work to be done, use of them sometimes became dangerous.[94] Repairs to major bridges could be costly. £730 was the estimate for work at the four principal crossings of the Adur in the 1650s.[95] Towns naturally kept a wary eye on precedents being established against them. A note was made that it would be 'no prejudice nor president to them for the future' when the constables of Lewes and Ringmer hundred agreed to spread gravel on Lewes bridge, which had been 'built at the charge of the country'.[96] Arundel lost a crucial case in 1642 about repair of the town bridge and thereafter it was the only town with sole responsibility for upkeep of an important bridge. Three years later the townsmen, sullen that the decision had gone against them, refused to pay fines and amerciaments for failure to carry out repairs.[97] The heavy taxes necessary in the west during the 1650s proved highly unpopular. In a general order of 1657 for binding over defaulters, the JPs explained that, through the extent of the arrears, 'some of the surveyors and expenditors are out of purse and have expended more than they have received and some of the bridges are not yet finished'.[98]

Enforcement of the assessments for the county funds, for charitable uses, the gaol and maimed soldiers, caused the JPs persistent trouble throughout the years 1600 to 1660. The funds were established under the 1601 poor law statute. From the first, as in other counties such as Wiltshire, money came in grudgingly and belatedly. In 1615, the local officers were accused of 'carelessness and negligence' in collection.[99] Despite a new schedule of rates, approved by the Bench in 1624, widespread arrears were still endemic in the 1630s: in 1636 forty-one parishes were behind with their maimed soldiers payments and in 1639 three parishes were reported to have failed to pay their gaol assessments for fifteen years.[100] In 1653 confusion still persisted about the sums due and much money was unpaid: 'it is not certeynly knowne what every parish ought to pay' declared the preamble to a general order of the western Bench which attempted to put collection for the funds on a rational basis.[101]

The maimed soldiers tax in the eastern division yielded just over eighty pounds annually, the charitable uses tax fifty-nine pounds and the gaol tax twelve pounds.[102] The maimed soldiers fund gave some scope for generosity. Several of the sixty-seven men who were granted pensions between 1642 and 1660 received extra assistance. Sometimes a man was helped by an advance to 'travell to the bath for cure' or to provide a dwelling for his family; widows were assisted after a soldier's death.[103] The gaol fund, on the other hand, was totally inadequate for its purpose and the JPs had to subsidise it heavily by drawing on money intended for charitable uses. Victims of calamities who benefited from the charitable uses fund included men who had lost their goods through fire or shipwreck and a man whose house had blown down.[104] Grants to such men of briefs for collections in parish churches were used as an alternative to charitable payments.[105] Thus the Bench showed flexibility in its management of the money available for county purposes. The creation in the 1650s of a genuine county stock, which was funded by arrears of maimed soldiers, charitable uses and gaol payments, was an important step towards a more sensible basis for county finance.[106] As the Bench saw it, they alone had the power and responsibility to put the money coming in to the best use they could. It was common sense, for instance, to raid the maimed soldiers fund in 1636, the charitable uses fund in 1640 and the surplus of the monthly assessment in 1655 for essential repairs to county bridges.[107] In managing local taxation the magnates were spared the dilemmas thrust upon them with regard to national taxes. The sums involved were small, the needs of the county obvious to the whole community.

11

The administrative achievement

We present Henry Cox barber of Steninge for reviling and railing against John Grome constable of the same by calling him rascall and moreover he said that he alltogether lived by deceit and cosseninge and he saith he wold prove it.
Presentment of the jury of constables, 12 July 1626.[1]

That wee have in the east part of the Downes of Sussex and the parts adioyning within the divition wherein wee dwell, indeavoured with all diligence the performance of those directions given by his Majestie's proclamacions and books of orders.
Sir Thomas Parker and Thomas Chown to the Privy Council, May 1631.[2]

The burden of work

The 226 sessions rolls that have survived for the period 1594 to 1660 leave a forceful impression of the quantity of work undertaken by JPs in the mid-seventeenth century, in comparison to the load borne by their Elizabethan predecessors. The record of administrative business transacted sessions by sessions confirms that the Bench found itself under considerable pressure. In the first two decades of the century the JPs normally made a coupe of orders or sometimes none at all; between 1625 and 1628 the western justices made an average of six orders per sessions; between 1632 and 1641 this number doubled, and by the 1650s the western Bench was making, on average, seventeen orders per sessions.[3] The assize judges faced the same kind of increase in business.[4] At the same time the complexity of many of the cases adjudicated at sessions made them extremely time consuming. The clerk of the peace often recorded the 'debate' or 'full hearing' of a settlement or bastardy dispute in the 1650s which had preceded the judgment of the court. There were also new tasks to be taken care of and emergencies to be dealt with. The Jacobean programme of taking recognisances from innkeepers and victuallers that they would not allow meat to be prepared or sold in Lent, which reflected the King's staunch support for Lenten fasting, implied lengthy and tiresome annual sittings in market towns.[5] The clerk of the peace returned 176 recognisances into the Exchequer in 1619.[6] An outbreak of plague in Arundel and

Pevensey rapes in 1637 made necessary measures for watch and ward, licences to travel and extraordinary taxes for relief of infected families.[7]

Thus the evolution of petty sessions was a response to the exigencies of the administrative situation. Extra and longer formal meetings of justices at the level of both the rape and the county division became essential. Quarter sessions came to mean several days away from home for JPs, especially for men who lived remote from sessions towns. Single day sessions, normal in the 1590s and quite usual in James I's reign, gave way to two-day sittings, except at midsummer when sessions fell close to the assizes. The tiresome recurrence of long agendas even caused the eastern justices to extend their sitting to a third day five times between 1642 and 1660. The Bench did what it could to improve the despatch of business. The western JPs issued a general order that, in order to avoid 'new hearings and trouble to this court', notice should be given by disputants to all the parties concerned before the sessions. They were exasperated by having to repeat examinations of disputes, when they had issued a parish or individual with an order in their favour before they had full command of the facts.[8]

As the justices grew ever busier an ever increasing load of work and responsibility fell on the clerks of the peace. Besides his manifold judicial and administrative duties, William Alcock took control of the new county fund, formed out of maimed soldiers and charitable uses arrears in the 1650s, and acted as treasurer for the assessments for the whole county. In fiscal matters centralisation and reliance on trusted professionals were sound moves, relieving the justices themselves, yet conducing to continuity and efficiency. The appointment of the assiduous servant of the Committee, Thomas Collins, to oversee the special fund for the rebuilding of the gaol in the 1650s is another example of the expanding role of such men in local government.[9] There was in fact a serious attempt from the 1620s onwards to find trustworthy outsiders on to whom the Bench could unload tasks that an earlier generation of magistrates would have expected to undertake themselves. Once the appointment of non-magisterial treasurers for bridge repairs, tried in 1628, was seen to work satisfactorily it became normal practice.[10] In 1640 the western Bench decided to appoint gentry not on the Commission to the treasurerships of the county funds; in 1643 the eastern Bench followed suit.[11] The justices also grew fond of handing over trivial wrangling to gentry of known worth and integrity. Differences over wages and poor taxation and between masters and apprentices, even a bastardy case on one occasion, were referred in this way.[12]

Despite these expedients, the core of stalwart JPs clearly worked much harder in the mid-seventeenth century than they had done in the Elizabethan period. Though the record is defective, it appears that fifty-three of the magistrates of the period 1625 to 1660 attended more than half the sessions where their presence was obligatory, three in their own division and one joint sessions annually; another forty-four men were present on at least one occasion in four.[13] Many of these men must sometimes have had pardonable excuses of sickness, chronic ill-health, distance or barely passable roads. Eastern justices were more willing attenders: thirteen of the twenty men who notched up twenty attendances between 1625 and 1660 were resident there.[14] But every commission named more eastern gentry anyway, a reflection of the way the eastern gentry dominated county politics and society. Moreover Chichester was awkwardly placed for many JPs and the social life and hospitality to be found in the alternative sessions town of Arundel during January was hardly an alluring prospect.[15]

Sussex miscreants did not have to face the large assemblies of more than twenty justices who sometimes crowded the Benches of counties such as Essex, Hampshire, Kent and Somerset.[16] Indeed, it was rare for more than fourteen JPs to be present. Huge attendances, though, were not an index of efficient and equitable government. A small, well-informed and conscientious Bench was just as effective. Considering the peculiar circumstances in Sussex of a single Commission acting independently in two divisions for most of the year, there was almost always an adequate showing. At 135 out of 189 recorded sessions between 1625 and 1660 at least ten magistrates sat; on only six occasions, all of them in the disrupted war period, were fewer than four justices present.[17]

At least eighteen barristers served on the Sussex Commission between 1625 and 1660, bringing their valuable legal expertise to the affairs of their county. Eleven of them were active over a period of some years and, as elsewhere, they tended to be outstandingly industrious. Robert Foster, Nicholas Jordan, Thomas Chown, Henry Peckham and John Spence were all exceptionably diligent in attending sessions.[18] Whenever possible a barrister took the chair: Philip Jermyn, Henry Peckham and William Spence were among those who did so regularly.[19] Otherwise an experienced justice acted as chairman, though occasionally, as for example at Michaelmas 1639, a thrusting junior member of the Bench grasped the chance to lecture his colleagues and the court by delivering the charge.[20] In general, the justices seem to have been well enough supplied by colleagues with the knowledge necessary to unravel complex problems of law and precedent, although neither division of Sussex at this time enjoyed the services of a single indefatigable presiding officer like John Harington of Somerset.[21]

Shirking out-of-sessions work was often less excusable than failure to attend the quarterly courts. On top of it, inertia at home implied total dereliction of the duties of the magisterial office: 29 of the 163 Sussex justices between 1625 and 1660 can be charged with this. They were mostly Caroline courtiers, royalists appointed in 1642 whose good intentions were probably swallowed up by the civil war, moderate gentry who shunned public affairs in the 1640s or staunch supporters of the parliamentary cause who joined the Bench in their dotage. A few justices, like William Yalden and Thomas Bettsworth, appeared at sessions now and again, but managed to avoid entirely the drudgery of work in their own localities. A good many more were busy at home but seldom seen in court. Old men like John Middleton, Anthony Apsley and Sir Richard Michelbourne were still issuing warrants, binding over and holding petty sessions long after they had abandoned regular journeys to sessions.[22] Once he was past his mid-sixties, Sir Edward Culpepper of Ardingly was only tempted out to summer sessions nearby at Horsham. Meanwhile his colleagues frequently heard the cases of the men he sent before them. Younger men too, who were disinclined to face the roads and the weather, were often conscientious in their own neighbourhoods. John Busbridge, whom Major-General Goffe found 'very unapt' for county militia business in 1655, had long enjoyed a reputation for readiness in local administration, although he could be waspish to deal with.[23] Hall Ravenscroft sent in recognisances over a period of ten years, but only once attended sessions. Richard Porter and Edward Polhill, justices living far from Lewes, were only active out of sessions. Edward Michel returned recognisances to twenty-six western sessions and six eastern ones between 1651 and 1660, yet, curiously, never sat with his colleagues at Lewes, Chichester or Arundel. His lack of opportunity for discussion and consultation with colleagues might have gravely impaired his knowledge and standing had it not been for his close partnership with Richard Yates, who was more diligent about attendance.[24]

Local officers gravitated to the homes of JPs known to be energetic and dutiful. So to some extent business became concentrated in the hands of the most industrious men in each rape. Five men, four of whose families had served Elizabeth in the government of the shire, were outstanding in their performance. They all lived in the east and they all attended at least forty quarter sessions. Sir Thomas Parker was aged about twenty-four when he replaced his father in 1620; he was briefly omitted after the King's execution and finally retired in 1660.[25] The wealden ironmaster Anthony Fowle served from early in the 1620s until his death in 1647.[26] An opportune move from Rotherfield to Newick shortly before the outbreak of the civil war enabled the Bench to impose on him the main brunt of work from Ditchling northwards to Ardingly, an area which had for some years lacked a resident justice.[27] With a single brief interruption, Anthony Stapley served from 1633 until he died in 1655, carrying sole responsibility in the first half of his career for the southern district of Lewes rape. Thereafter he did not neglect county government despite other preoccupations. He was much involved in out-of-sessions work in the west when he held the office of governor of Chichester from 1643 to 1645; he still managed to attend sessions at Lewes when membership of the Council of State between 1649 and 1653 kept him often in London.[28]

It was a mark of the esteem in which his family was held that Sir Thomas Pelham was added to the Bench in 1622, two years before he inherited the Halland estate, and that he was at once placed in the commission immediately under the knights and above twenty-six men senior to him in their appointments.[29] Pelham remained a JP from the age of twenty-three until his death at fifty-seven. The recognisances he returned in the 1620s for villagers from Eastbourne to Fletching and Burwash indicate the broad area over which a magnate of such renown exercised jurisdiction.[30] Out of sessions his services were always much in demand; at sessions he enjoyed a pre-eminent reputation. He was a grave loss to the Bench when, following the King's execution, he decided to play no further part in county administration. Yet in a way the most remarkable performance was that of Thomas Jefferay since he was well over fifty when he took up his duties in 1644. During the next sixteen years he attended forty out of sixty quarter sessions; almost three-quarters of the sessions rolls for the years 1649 to 1660 reflect his vigour out of sessions.[31] Jefferay's very first report on some disputes at Hailsham, neatly penned in his own hand and systematically listing the points at issue, was typical of his approach to personal and public affairs. His will showed the same meticulousness. When he made it in 1663 he had already handed over to his son-in-law Anthony Fowle, who replaced him on the Bench in 1661, some of his legal works. Jefferay bequeathed to Fowle the rest of his 'books concerning the lawe and office of a justice of the peace' and 'such printed statute books as I have in my studie' as well as his Holinshed. The trust which he had so attentively fulfilled in his old age remained with his family by prescription.[32]

On the early Caroline Bench the record of Sir Walter Covert was unequalled: he had served the county since the middle of Elizabeth's reign as an MP, deputy-lieutenant, JP and twice as sheriff. Between 1625 and 1632, Covert showed remarkable tenacity for a man in his mid and late eighties. He was often busy taking recognisances, he was regularly at sessions, he undertook tiresome out-of-sessions tasks such as the investigation of abuses by purveyors in Buttinghill hundred and the disputes of the contentious Francis Pelling with the parish of Chailey.[33] He reported to the Council in 1630 that he had met with his lifelong associate Sir John Shurley over the Pelling affair 'as soon as health would permit'.[34] When he made his will in July 1631 Covert emphasised the tradition of service which his family owed to the county. His books were to remain in his study 'as standerds in my house to be and inure to the sole use and benefit of my next heir'.[35] In October 1660 his intention was at last fulfilled: his nephew Sir John Covert, who inherited Slaugham Place, newly created a baronet, rode to Lewes for his first public appearance as a justice of the peace.[36]

Others were indefatigable over short periods of time. Laurence Pay, George Oglander and Thomas Springate had impressive careers cut short by death. Between 1651 and 1653 William Morley was energetic in riding between Lewes and Arundel or Chichester, appearing five times on the Bench in both divisions. John Fagge also, with his home at Wiston as a convenient overnight stopping place, sometimes did the same. So did Richard Boughton, which helps to explain how Major-General Goffe found him an 'understanding person' who knew 'as much of the present temper of Sussex as any man that I am acquainted with'.[37]

The participation of humbler men in local government was extensive and the burdens imposed on them were also considerable. Much was expected of the husbandmen, tradesmen and craftsmen who acted as constables and tithingmen. The Bench regularly fined those few, a small proportion of the total, who failed to take their oath, refused their responsibilities, neglected to execute warrants or omitted to set watch and ward.[38] When the unfortunate constable of Holmestrow hundred let the suspected father of a bastard child escape from his charge in 1643, he found himself ordered to pay sixpence weekly for the child until he produced the man.[39] By and large though, negligence and inefficiency seem to have been the exception rather than the rule among the parish officers.[40] A more jaundiced view, however, must be taken of the sheriff's bailiffs who usually served for several years on end. The execution of writs depended on them, and their attendance at sessions was therefore important, but it was often slackly performed particularly in the late 1650s. Twice, in 1658 and in 1659, four of the five bailiffs in the western division failed to appear at sessions.[41] Bailiffs were notorious for their rough treatment. When a Racton woman tried to prevent two of them carrying off some pewter and brass, she was struck on the arm with a hatchet. In 1655 the bailiff of Rotherfield hundred admitted that he had employed as bully boys two labourers accused of making arrests without warrants. The labourers 'weare unreasonable in causinge men to spende their moneyes when they weare arrested' confessed the bailiff.[42] In 1645 the bailiff of Arundel rape and his deputy were both charged with extortion.[43] Another officeholder who faced temptation was the coroner: in 1654 the Bench dismissed Richard Aylwin from office after he had confessed to extortion.[44]

During the 1640s and 50s local government offered new career opportunities. The bureaucratic structure of the magistracy was supplemented by a parallel secretariat for the Committee in each rape; receivers of the assessment were appointed in each rape; the Committees needed treasurers for sequestrations. The careers of men like Thomas Collins, William Alcock and Stephen Humphrey show the opportunities for professionals.[45] Many others served as clerks, assessors and collectors. For those who worked hard enough the rewards were substantial. William Alcock recorded that the total salaries, at fourpence in the pound, for the assessments from 1647 to 1660 amounted to £5,794. Yet from such men also much was demanded. Clearing accounts at London could be exasperating, as William Alcock learnt by bitter experience: 'we have a very troublesome business here and all is not yet over, much money turned back . . . what will be the issue I know not', he wrote to Richard Burdett, who held a receivership of the assessment, in May 1657. When Burdett broke his ankle in an accident, riding to London, the Committee showed their appreciation of his services by an *ex gratia* payment of twenty pounds; later they supported his claim for arrears of salary.[46]

The relationship between the gentlemen who governed Sussex and successive régimes seeking to impose their will from London must be seen in the context of the problems faced by the county. The gentry were highly responsive to the exigencies of the local situation. They can be credited with a sustained and vigorous enforcement of order, defence and taxation and with the evolution, within a settled framework, of new procedures and expedients in the face of new and more exacting problems. But they were not susceptible to outside pressure unless it was in line with the purposes of government as they saw them. When demands were made whose force they did not acknowledge, the cards were stacked in favour of the country gentry. No seventeenth-century government resolved the contradiction between a scheme of local administration which was loosely organised and largely in the hands of amateurs and the achievement of domestic policies through close supervision of the localities. Various kinds of central pressure and persuasion were attempted, through the judges of assize, lord-lieutenants, MPs, conciliar letters to JPs and summonses before the Council Board.[47] None of them proved a reliable instrument of policy throughout the nation.

Twice in our period, in 1631 and 1655, pressure from London became more intense than usual and the imposition of a degree of centralisation was attempted. In the case of the major-generals experiment, the reform of local government was merely one of the tasks set before the men sent to integrate the counties more closely with Whitehall. Other concerns preoccupied them.[48] Major-General Goffe was on the Sussex Commission of the Peace from 1655 to 1659, but he never attended sessions or intervened in the processes of county administration.[49] The 1631 *Book of Orders* involved no new men. It was more a question of encouraging the use of new and systematic methods to deal with old problems. From the government's point of view the scheme was a daring and novel one, intended to provide permanent effective oversight of the rural Benches.[50] In Sussex, as in Essex, the *Book of Orders* gave impetus to several developments which made good sense to the JPs. Petty sessions were nudged into a full and regular life in those rapes where they had not yet been properly established. Alehouse licensing was put on a firmer footing. Apprenticeship of poor children was systematised.[51] There was certainly an acceleration in the tempo of Sussex government in the early 1630s, a drive for more thorough enforcement of the law which, by making certain procedures customary, left a permanent mark on the administration of the county. In this limited sense the *Book of Orders* was a success.

The Caroline programme of reform, it has been claimed, 'lasted for almost a decade with remarkably slight diminution of intensity in its application'.[52] Sussex material does not support this view. It was one thing for justices to show willing, when they received the *Book of Orders*, by initiating drives to improve the highways and eradicate vagrancy, but it was quite another for them to work to the same high standards year after year. The first reports were complacent. Vagrancy, declared the JPs in Pevensey rape, had been 'soe well looked into that wee thinke the countrey hath noe cause to complayne of theire number'. 'There are few (if any) that now wander', boasted the justices of Bramber rape.[53] The campaign against vagabonds had a brief effect, but the rogues soon crept back again once watches on the highways and bridges were less strictly kept or abandoned. Whereas in April 1634 there were still 'very few' vagrants to be seen, in Bramber rape at least, by 1636 they were once more infesting all parts of the shire.[54]

The close and continuing supervision envisaged in the *Book of Orders* scheme, through quarterly certificates to the Council, was never achieved in Sussex. Quarter sessions never attempted to oversee the certification system, but left the petty sessions to report independently. All of them were highly erratic in doing so. Some rapes reported direct to the Council, others through the assize judges. The convenience of the latter system led to its being generally adopted from 1636 to 1639. Their participation in the execution of the *Book of Orders* has been called the apogee of the administrative power of the circuit judges, yet they only managed, unless some reports failed to reach the state paper collection, to extract sixty-three certificates in all from the eight petty sessional divisions of Sussex between 1631 and 1639.[55]

The Sussex certificates quickly became stereotyped. As early as the autumn of 1631 the tendency to repeat previous formulas became apparent.[56] Thereafter in the western rapes the certificates conformed by and large to a set pattern: a page of reassuring phrases was concocted to satisfy the Council in London. The characteristic tone was *omnia bene*. In Arundel rape the justices employed virtually identical wording in 1631, 1632 and 1633; Chichester provided straightforward repetition of earlier affirmations.[57] The justices in the east were blunter. After 1631 they contented themselves with sending succinct statements of apprentices put out and rogues apprehended. In 1632 six justices of Pevensey rape signed a perfunctory note, drafted for them at assizes, to the effect that the *Book of Orders* was being enforced and they found 'a good effect lykely to ensue'.[58] Thus, in virtually no time at all, the government's scheme of communication with country justices lost in Sussex such power as it had ever possessed to drive the machine of local government harder. In 1633 Anthony Apsley and George Courthope expressed their hope, in a report from Hastings rape, that, through their 'care and diligence', they would be able to bring 'the country about us to better conformity and more agreeable to his Majestie's orders and directions then now it is'.[59] Their declaration of intent was entirely sincere. There was much unanimity of purpose between the Caroline Council and rural JPs. Good order in the localities mattered to both of them. Yet the magistracy stubbornly insisted that they were the best judges of the pace of local justice and of the measures that suited the conditions of their own county. Their vigour in enforcing the settlement legislation in the 1640s and 50s, for instance, reflected their concern at the increasing seriousness of the threat of vagrancy.[60] The JPs held a consistent county viewpoint, which guided their response to every intervention by a government agency.

The response of the county

Government in local communities was conducted in an atmosphere direct and intimate. Time and again the sessions records illuminate the interplay of personalities and the provocative or aggressive behaviour of men who came up against the law. The extent of lawlessness must not be exaggerated. Most men worked rather than stole, sustained their families rather than abandoned them. By and large, men showed respect for the officers of the law, whether justices or constables. The tradition of deference ran deep and this, much more than the stocks, the whipping post and the house of correction, was the foundation of the authority of rural magistrates. To a large extent a JP's standing in his neighbourhood determined the degree of respect and obedience which he was shown. Reputation was all important. Even justices were not immune from criticism. It was intolerable that a Rusper gentleman should escape with the remark about Thomas Middleton that 'he is noe honest man but a knave'. Quarter sessions fined him ten shillings.[61] Although gossip went largely unchecked, a man could run himself into trouble through it, as an incident at Heathfield in 1608 illustrates. Some villagers were discussing why an alehouse which Sir Edward Culpepper had suppressed was still open. 'Mr Colepeper's warrante is not regarded this much for other justices will not allow of it', said a labourer Thomas Pettite, who went on to call Culpepper an 'olde dotishe who in some accons was as wise as one's arse'. The Bench's informant stoutly maintained that on the contrary Culpepper was 'as wise a man and hath bene as longe in Comision as any that he knew'. When the informant called witnesses Pettite added 'that he mente he was as wise as his own arse', which hardly extenuated his remarks.[62]

The men chosen to serve in the local offices by no means automatically commanded respect. Depositions in the sessions rolls show how easily men's distrust of authority could flare up in the face of a neighbour or a man apparently no better than themselves who claimed, as the sheriff's officer, constable or headborough, to interfere with them or their livelihood. A Slaugham yeoman, finding himself forcibly impeded by a watchman whom he had refused to answer, dismounted from his horse, assaulted the watchman, 'and did strike upp his heeles'.[63] A Steyning man was presented for 'reviling and railinge against' the constable there; the headborough of Tarring Neville related how a man 'did assault and abuse him in the execucon of his office upon his demand of his tax for Lewes bridge'.[64] When the Eastbourne headborough told one who took from him a hog that he was driving to the pound that he should heed what he did or he would forfeit five pounds to the king, the man 'answered that he did not care for the kinge'. The churchwarden of Little Horsted, accused by the parish clerk in 1642 of failing to bring in his accounts according to law, replied 'what care wee for his Maities lawes and statutes?'.[65] Sometimes men were tempted to take their revenge on the unfortunate officer when a friend had suffered under the law. The execution of a warrant to convey a Nuthurst man to the house of correction in June 1660 led the headborough into an angry confrontation a few days later with one of his neighbours, who vowed that he would have rescued the man if he had had a chance to do so. Pressing the point, the headborough asked the quarrelsome neighbour

> if hee would have turned the sayd Wood backe again. Hee replyed veryly I would have done it and held up a spade staffe and shooke it at this informant and sayd againe I would have done it, and answered it and the justices should have done what they could.

Officers were particularly likely to come in for abuse when they attempted to exert themselves against men in their cups. A drunken blacksmith, for example, was presented for calling the constable a 'proud rogue' and for telling him roundly to 'medle with what he had to doe withall'.[66] They were most likely to meet outright opposition when they executed warrants to distrain men's goods. In 1655 the Warnham tithingman was pelted with stones by two neighbours as he was leaving a butcher's house with goods worth ten shillings forfeited for profane swearing. The pots and pans were grabbed from him by one of the neighbours. 'What hath the kinge to doe with me? if he have nothing else to doe he is an asse to send such rogues fleeceinge about my ground', the under-sheriff's deputy was told when attempting to distrain in 1627.[67] An East Blatchington man went out at night in 1643 and collected the ten wattles that the overseers had distrained because he refused to pay eight shillings towards the poor rate.[68] The Bench dealt firmly with those who defied their agents. Indeed they took a severe view of any kind of subversive talk, even if it was outside the context of administrative enforcement. In 1637 John Wilson sent before the Bench a West Hoathly man who, in an altercation with a sawyer of the parish who boasted that 'he had served the Kinge three severall times in the face of the enemye', had declared 'God's wounds there was none served the Kinge but rogues'.[69] The justices were bound to take seriously an undercurrent of disaffection towards authority which could have threatened the very foundations of their political and social control of the county.

Part IV

POLITICS

12

Opposition and conflict 1603-1642

I colde never yeat be drawne to put a little finger into the fyer of Chichester, thoughe many coles have been kindled, and much smoke blowne up and downe.
Bishop Harsnett to the Earl of Arundel, 12 September 1617.[1]

When I first attended his Grace, I acquainted him that the Puritane faction was growen strong amongst the justices upon our Bench for the eastern part of this county: steered rather by humor and faction then justice.
Edward Burton to Archbishop Laud's chaplain, 27 January 1640.[2]

Mr Eversffield hath sent three letters to the freemen . . . and not to the maior and jurates, thereby giving them occasion and countenaunce to side against the said maior and jurates and to be att distance with them.
The mayor and jurats of Hastings to Robert Read, 7 April 1640.[3]

The gentry and the House of Commons

Few counties were as fortunate as Sussex in the number of seats in the House of Commons potentially at its gentry's disposal. Two county, eighteen borough and six Cinque Port seats within the shire made a total of twenty-six possible parliamentary places. In the early sixteenth century all these seats had been dominated by the nobility. But before the end of Elizabeth's reign noble interests had been successfully challenged on several fronts; by 1628 the era of noble patronage was definitely waning. The Sackvilles were able to nominate one of the knights of the shire in 1603 and 1621 and the ninth Earl of Northumberland obtained one of the county seats for his son Lord Algernon Percy in 1624, but from 1625 onwards families like the Pelhams, the Shurleys, and the Coverts were able to monopolise the leadership of the county's parliamentary delegation. 'In times past', the Duke of Norfolk had boasted in the 1530s, he 'could have made burgesses' at Horsham, Shoreham, Steyning and Lewes, as well as Arundel itself. The Howard interest also extended to Bramber and at times Chichester.[4] Step by step this monopoly of a single noble family over a handful or more of boroughs was broken. Early in Elizabeth's reign local gentry took it for granted; by the 1620s they resented it. At Steyning local gentry managed to intrude in the 1570s and a double nomination by the Earl was flatly turned down in 1624; Bramber was captured from the Howards in the last years of Elizabeth's reign; Shoreham consistently returned local men from 1621; at Arundel and Horsham, the towns where the Earl was most tenacious, the breakthrough came in 1624 with the election of William Mill and John Middleton.

Other boroughs ceased to accept the double nomination of the outsiders recommended by noble patrons during the 1620s: Richard Lewkenor sat for Midhurst, where the Montagu interest had long been supreme, and at East Grinstead Thomas Pelham's parliamentary debut in 1621 marked the end of a long period of undisputed Sackville influence.[5] Chichester normally elected its recorder as one of the borough's MPs in the 1620s, but the merchant gild remained susceptible to the persuasions of a variety of outsiders anxious to grasp the other place. The election of two townsmen in 1628, William Cawley and Henry Bellingham, was a sharp break with tradition. Lewes was perhaps the borough most favourable to local men during Elizabeth's reign, yet even there both seats were not regularly grasped by county gentry until the 1620s. The Lord Warden exercised an almost prescriptive right to choose one of the burgesses for each of the three Cinque Ports from the 1580s until 1640.[6] The Sussex gentry competed vigorously with their Kentish neighbours, who had fewer seats at their disposal, for the remaining Cinque Port places. Nicholas Eversfield obtained a firm hold on one of the Hastings burgess-ships in the 1620s. Sir Alexander Temple, on the other hand, failed in his 1624 bid to wrest control of a Hastings seat by having the return of the Kentish gentleman John Finch invalidated. He won the case in the Committee of Privileges but was defeated in the subsequent by-election.[7]

In 1603 eleven Sussex gentlemen sat in the House of Commons, in 1624 fourteen and in 1626 and 1628 eighteen.[8] Furthermore, the county's delegation became increasingly vocal. In the sessions of 1606–07 and 1610 the rank and file Sussex members seem to have been virtually silent, apart from a motion and a speech by Sir John Shurley.[9] In the stormy parliament of 1621, on the other hand, five Sussex men, Thomas Bowyer, Richard Amherst, Edward Alford, Sir George Goring and Thomas Whatman, made contributions to the debates. Goring, Buckingham's creature treading the stairs to further office and court favouritism, was the Duke's agent in putting the motion that brought about this parliament's undoing. The others were typical country members, ready to make their move when the opportunity arose. Thomas Whatman spoke up in the discussion of the notorious gold thread patent and gave the House the benefit of his knowledge of medieval statute law. Richard Amherst spoke several times. Thomas Bowyer requested free coastal transport of corn 'withoute pleadeing licence and such troubles', a plea that was directly related to the peculiar economic conditions of Sussex.[10]

Edward Alford of Offington sat in every parliament from 1603 until 1628, apart from that of 1626 when the government pricked him as sheriff. He was always the outstanding figure in the Sussex delegation. In the session of 1606–07 Alford was already prominent. He was quick to comment on points of procedure, highly sensitive to the House's rights and privileges, ready to stand firm whenever he saw a grievance against the crown. It was his initiative, for instance, which secured a ruling that all matters which touched the privileges of the Commons should be perused by the Committee of Privileges before the clerk entered them in the journals.[11] By 1610 Alford's prestige was such that he was one of a 'select number of the Lower House' whom the Earl of Salisbury sought to lobby. In 1614 and during the 1620s Alford regularly distinguished himself by his oppositionist stance. In 1625 he vigorously opposed the granting of money and was one of those who led the attack on Montagu; in 1628 he was consistently vocal in the Petition of Right debates.[12] Time and again Alford showed himself capable of articulating the frustration felt by friends and colleagues on the Bench. He spoke for them as well as for himself when, at the opening of the second session of the 1621 parliament in November of that year, he stated the obligations he felt to his Sussex countrymen:

> I did desyer that in regard we had given away our two subsidies and donne no good for our countrie that we might have some care saving our reputacions, for I was ashamed that it should be bruted that we should do nothing but give away their moneyes, and doe nothing for them.[13]

If his fellow MPs were relatively silent it does not follow that they were apathetic. In June 1626 Nicholas Eversfield organised and paid for the copying of the remonstrance to the King which brought another unhappy parliament to its dissolution. He wanted something positive to take home with him. Secretary Conway's desperate attempt to round up copies of the remonstrance in the hands of various members on the day that the parliament was dissolved was apparently unsuccessful.[14]

The obstructionism that Edward Alford displayed towards Stuart policies was based on his experiences as a country gentleman and justice of the peace. In 1621 he was frequently on his feet: he spoke in favour of a Bill against scandalous and unworthy ministers, warning that 'if we looke not to them' the bishops would 'incroach upon all men's rights and lands in England'; he demanded that there should be no innovations in the method of assessment for the new subsidies voted and that the Bill should contain 'a preamble to give satisfaction to the country'; he condemned the law courts for their delays, relating that he had been party to a suit that lasted twenty-four years; he attacked the proclamations prohibiting the killing of flesh in Lent as 'a troublesome thing to the country', which raised the price of 'butter, cheese, herrings etc., which is that which the poor man must live by'.[15] Proclamations and monopolies were twin obsessions with Alford, because he saw both as instruments through which the central government interfered with the local authority of JPs and deprived his Sussex countrymen of their livelihoods. His parliamentary papers include an extensive collection of proclamations including some on the subject of Lenten fasting dating back to 1549, and a list of monopolies.[16]

Urban politics and factionalism

Economic difficulties, more complex administrative processes, polarisation of wealth and fear of social disorder all encouraged a narrowing of the political framework in Tudor and Stuart towns.[17] The tendency towards oligarchy is evident in several Sussex towns in this period. At Arundel the small clique who controlled the town's affairs sought to diminish the number of burgesses during the reign of Elizabeth; at Lewes the Twelve, a society of 'wealthier and discreter sort of townsmen', sought to tighten their grip on the government of the town; at Seaford, a corporation though it was scarcely urban, a small group of families, who had for some time monopolised the bailiff and jurat offices, confirmed their exclusive domination by a ruling in the assembly in 1650 that the number of freemen should be permanently limited to eighteen; at Hastings the election of the mayor was removed in 1603 from the public view of the multitude in the open hundred place to the Court Hall, a place more decent, apt and secret.[18] By 1600 Chichester and Rye were under the power of tight-knit merchant oligarchies: in the former control was exercised through the common council and aldermanic Bench, in the latter through the mayoralty and juratships.[19] A crucial stage in the gradual reduction of the democratic element in the government of Rye had been the establishment by the general assembly in 1575 of 'a common council of twenty-four of the ancient and discretest commoners to joyne with the maior and jurates in the publique affaires of the towne'.[20]

The urban situation bred intense loyalty and stubborn defensiveness. If provincial society was everywhere intractable, it was nowhere more so than in its urban communities, which, while they themselves were prey to internal faction, needed little provocation to come into open conflict with other sections and interests of the county community. Chichester and Rye guarded the western and eastern approaches to the county. The politics of these two towns between 1600 and 1640 are particularly important because they provide the context for analysis of their roles during and after the civil war. For much of this period the merchant clique at Chichester was at odds with either the clergy of the city or the county gentry of the neighbourhood. The city's exempt jurisdiction was a bone of contention with the west Sussex justices. In 1617 Bishop Harsnett reported to his patron the Earl of Arundel 'the sparkes of a late emotion, which, without your lordship's hand, is likely to breake out into a tumultuarie combustion'. He explained how two county magnates who were members of the county Bench, Richard Higgins and Nicholas Jordan, had 'lately crept into their comision, without notice, love or liking of their Bench . . . tending to the utter subversion of their exempt jurisdiction'. Both had residences in Chichester. Higgins was the leading adversary of the townsmen, Jordan was a 'grave, stayed and temperat gentleman, stepping in (as I ghesse) to balance the other's fierie ambition'. The intervention of the Earl of

Arundel, who held the High Stewardship of the city, brought the aldermen a new charter in 1618. 'I am more then fullye satisfyed touchinge the charter of Chichester', declared Harsnett in a further letter of December 1617.[21] The new charter confirmed their jurisdiction and authority and gave the mayor and common council power to elect a recorder. The next round in the struggle between magnates and merchants went to the city: they interpreted the ambiguous phraseology of the new charter to their own advantage and managed for three years to exclude the county gentry from holding their sessions in the city, forcing them to meet in the Close instead.[22]

The clash at Chichester between the corporation and the clergy fits a pattern of urban animosity and conflict, characteristic of cathedral cities in this period, which also occurred at York, Salisbury, Worcester and Gloucester.[23] Bishop Harsnett was on amicable terms with the city fathers; Bishop Carleton, who was regularly present on the county Bench when it sat in Chichester, was probably more detached from them; Bishop Montagu's staunch clericalism provoked them to open hostility.[24] The Close occupied nearly a quarter of the area within the city walls. Such a large enclave was bound to provoke resentment, all the more so because it was 'all waies separated by a distinct wall and inclosure of its own'. Deliberate measures had in fact been taken to insulate the vicars' buildings in South Street from the daily life of the city. The statutes of the cathedral forbade the vicars choral, under the penalty of deprivation, from letting any of the tenements to 'citizens or mechanicks'. Covenants in the leases of the tenants prevented them from using any part of the buildings as shops, taverns or alehouses. No doors or passages were to be made into South Street. The leading merchants found this situation of a city within a city intolerable. Thus, alleged a petition of the cathedral clergy after the Restoration, 'under pretence and under colour of the large and comprehensive expressions' in their Jacobean charters, the mayor and aldermen 'have hereupon inferred and concluded the Close as part of the city to be within their liberty and have by degrees attempted to bring the precinct of the said Close . . . under their government and jurisdiction'.[25]

By June 1635, when Sir Nathaniel Brent visited Chichester, relations between the corporation and the cathedral clergy were tense. The mayor and his brethren, whose addiction to Puritanism he noted, would not visit him 'because I lodged in the Close, there being some difference between them and the Dean and prependaries'. One of the issues of the moment concerned a piece of ground, formerly used by the scholars of the Dean and Chapter school for games, which an alderman, Peter Cox, had taken over for his own use.[26] The attempt to impose heavy ship money contributions on the Close in 1635 was seen, when the whole tangled story was unravelled after the Restoration, as 'the first great and notorious incroachment made by the said city upon the church'. The mayor, faced with a charge of £150 on the city, exceeded his jurisdiction by including the Close in his apportionment and exhibited blatant prejudice against the Arminian clergy. Whereas substantial aldermen like Henry Chitty and George Greene escaped with a tax of £1. 4*s*, the Dean Richard Steward was charged £3 and the Chancellor William Nevill £2. 10*s*. The mayor hoped to extract a total of £14. 3*s* 4*d* from six Arminian residents of the Close. But the clergy called his bluff. They reported his proceedings to Archbishop Laud, who took the matter to the Council. In January 1636 the Dean and Chapter were directed from Whitehall to pay their ship money to the sheriff alone. Meanwhile the mayor received a severe reprimand:

> We have thought good to . . . lett you knowe that wee doe conceive our former direccons touching this busines were full and effectuall for preservacon of the rights and liberties of the church, yett wee have againe given direction to the said Deane and Chapter to pay their monies to the high sheriffe of that county, they being noe part of your corporacon.

A few days later, the sheriff, Sir William Culpepper, wrote to the mayor from Wakehurst refusing to reduce the tax of £150 on Chichester in view of the Council's decision. Culpepper taxed the Dean and Chapter at £7. 13*s* 4*d* instead of the mayor's £11. 13*s* 4*d* and the following year Sir Edward Bishop reduced their contribution to a mere £5 in all. William Nevill paid £1 for 1635 and 1636 and only eight shillings in 1639.[27] The bid to victimise the Arminian clergy over ship money was roundly defeated.

The dispute over ship money rating brought the whole Chichester quarrel to the ears of the government. Exhaustive hearings of the differences between the merchant and clerical factions were subsequently held before the Attorney-General and, in June 1636, before the King himself. The corporation was ably represented by its recorder Christopher Lewkenor, who may be said to have led the campaign to bring the Close under the city's jurisdiction during the 1630s. After the King's judgment that the corporation should surrender their charter and receive a new one finally excluding jurisdiction over the Close, Lewkenor did everything he could to frustrate its enforcement. First he wrote sycophantically to Secretary Nicholas. He disingenuously took the liberty 'to put you in mynde what I conceaved the order to be', whilst craving a copy 'in the way you apprehend it'. The flattery was undisguised: 'to entreate favour from you is in vayne for I know you to bee an equall man and not to be biased, but not to desire your frendlike care were supine negligence'. The tactics were unscrupulous: on the central question of the government of the Close, Lewkenor proposed a compromise which would have left effective power with the merchant oligarchy. The Close might 'remayne still part of the citty', declared Lewkenor, skilfully suggesting that right and precedent had all along been on his side, with the Bishop and Dean as justices by charter; but they would be outnumbered by the *ex officio* aldermen on the city's Bench. When nothing came of this initiative, Lewkenor surrendered the charter of 1621, but, instead of taking out the new charter promised by the King, he encouraged the corporation to encroach on the rights and privileges of the Church as vigorously as ever by virtue of the earlier ambiguous charter of 1618.[28]

Overall, the victory of the Caroline government was a hollow one. The King's failure at the June 1636 hearing to pronounce decisively on the provocative issues of seating in the cathedral and the carrying of maces played into the hands of the Chichester townsmen. After the hearing Lewkenor brazenly claimed that, apart from 'the Deane beinge first placed', 'the maior and citizens shal bee placed in the church where they desire'. Tension over maces went back to the Deanship of Martin Culpepper in Elizabeth's reign. It seems he had obliged the sergeants who processed with the mayor to put their little maces, 'with which they used to arrest persons', under their gowns immediately on entering the Close. It was Lewkenor himself who revived the argument by giving the mayor a new great mace. This was carried before him into the cathedral, in defiance of Dean Steward who petitioned the King about this innovation.[29] Stalemate on this issue meant that the Chichester oligarchy were able to continue their weekly display of lay pomp and pride in the cathedral precincts from 1636 until the 1640s.

Whereas the Chichester oligarchy kept itself apart from the gentry community of the western rapes and, by relying exclusively on the counsels of Christopher Lewkenor, put its trust in a single local magnate, the ruling clique at Rye took more trouble to cultivate its friendships with gentry of the vicinity. As at Chichester there were tensions arising from the town's exempt jurisdiction, yet men such as Sir Thomas Sackville of Sedlescombe and William White of Northiam were generally good friends to the merchants. When rumours of plague there caused 'the country to forbeare to resort' to the Rye markets in 1636, for instance, the corporation turned to Sackville to quash the false gossip.[30] Rye was certainly more anxious than Chichester to send men with an understanding of local conditions to parliament in the 1620s, but in part this was merely a reflection of the greater economic stresses under which it laboured. The decay of their harbour was the obsessive priority in the minds of the Rye oligarchy in the early seventeenth century. Much was hoped for from burgesses at Westminster. The Earl of Dorset's peroration of 1628 in favour of his cousin Sir John Sackville, the brother of Sir Thomas of Sedlescombe, was thus on the face of it well timed:

> He is your countryman, borne near you, his father lived noblely many yeares in the country wee be loved of all, and now his brother doeth noe less. And though hee lives not neare you, he lives heare neere the court, and uppon all your busyness ready to be imployed by you.

Yet Rye rejected Dorset's nomination. Sackville had made a poor showing on the town's behalf when he was elected to the two previous parliaments, since he was preoccupied with military service in the Low Countries. The corporation turned instead to another member of a noble family with local interests, Richard Tufton.[31] During the 1630s the activities of gentry who sought to reclaim saltmarshes and improve communications in the Rye district caused constant suspicion between the urban and rural communities. 'Nothing can be hurtfull to the harbor of Rye that is not likewise hurtfull to our wett marshes', insisted the gentry sewers commissioners in 1634, answering a panic-stricken letter from the mayor about their plans for a ferry at Kent Wall.[32] The townsmen found such reassurances hard to accept. Their negative reaction to the olive branch that Sir John Sackville held out in 1630, when he tried to further Peter Farnden's suit with the town for compliance in his plans to reclaim some saltmarshes, indicates how defensive they had become. Sackville protested that Farnden's work would not prejudice the town and promised to take the mayor's petition for a new benevolence for the harbour, which had recently been discussed by a delegation that had visited the Lord Warden, personally to the Lord Keeper. It appears that the offer was not taken up.[33]

Discord and factionalism were endemic within the walls of both Rye and Chichester between 1600 and 1640. Controversy and division over religious issues broke out at Rye in 1624 and 1640.[34] Feuds at Chichester necessitated the intervention of central government agencies in 1626 and 1633. The allegations of the Chichester clique who, at a caucus meeting of the common council in 1626, removed Thomas Whatman from the recordership, illustrate the opportunities that existed for a meddlesome and ambitious intruder to divide and rule:

> For his owne ends he hath raised faction and sedicon betweene the mayor and aldermen and betweene the aldermen and common councill, as latalie in perswading the mayor that he had power of himselfe by lawe, as clerke of the markett, to remove the butchers shambles or standinge from one street to another and then underhand anymating and persuading divers of the aldermen to contest with the mayor therein affyrming to them that the mayor's doinge therein were not warrantable By which meanes there grewe much combustion in the cittie.[35]

A trivial incident sometimes provided the chance to pay off old scores Thus in 1633 when Isaac Thornbury, the vice-admiral's deputy, heard that the mayor, Henry Chitty, was entertaining at his home a sea captain who was renowned to be a Dunkirk pirate, he threatened to report Chitty to the lords of the admiralty, unless he called off a Star Chamber action which a friend of his had taken out against Thornbury over a slanderous and bawdy rhyme.[36]

Henry Chitty was a man to be reckoned with in Caroline Chichester His captaincy of the city's trained bands gave him considerable power which he was ready to use against those with whom he was at odds

Isaac Thornbury, whose scandalous practices as customs officer caused general resentment in the merchant community, had been his enemy ever since Chitty had reported him 'for refusall to doe his Majestie service and for the contempt of his Majestie's officers military'. The speed and efficiency with which he mobilised a chain of powerful men, which included Christopher Lewkenor, John Ashburnham and the Earl of Dorset, against Thornbury in 1633 illustrates Chitty's ability to ingratiate himself in magnate society.[37] His angry response to the Council's demand in August 1626 that he should appear before them in connection with the Whatman affair, in which he was a ringleader, illustrates his stubborn independence. He would not go up till 'after harvest'.[38] The Star Chamber cases in which he was the defendant hint at unscrupulous dealings towards other townsmen. He was alleged, for instance, to have seized cloth and other wares from the shop of John Exton, an alderman and mercer, in the course of a quarrel about some land in Bosham.[39]

Joseph Benbrigge, who was mayor of Rye in 1629, was a man of a similarly factious temper. His family was at the centre of a series of disputes in the 1630s which involved suspicions of his plans to reclaim some marshland that he owned near the town. Allegations were also made that he had counterfeited gold. Many Rye inhabitants accounted the Benbrigges to be 'base rascally knaves'. Joseph Benbrigge was undoubtedly a choleric man. 'They had more neede to present themselves for being drunkards, adulterers and fornicators', he scornfully told a churchwarden who cited him to the archdeaconry court.[40] Benbrigge's isolation from the Rye oligarchy by 1640 is indicated by his decision to support the freemen candidates against those of the mayor and jurats in the Long Parliament election.[41]

The contrast between the political situation of Chichester and Rye on the eve of the civil war is instructive. Both towns were a prey to faction but Chichester's divisions were the more serious. The cathedral city was divided against itself and the merchant oligarchy was largely isolated from the magnates of the neighbourhood. Chichester's dissensions made the city ripe for exploitation. At Rye, on the other hand, there was no clerical party. Puritanism indeed was a powerful cohesive force, although it gave rise to religious controversy. Despite distrust over the activities of some gentry in the marshland, relationships between the merchants and several local magnates were secure and should a crisis occur these personal ties held the promise of fruitful cooperation.

The emergence of county factionalism

Clearly Sussex gentry felt the pull of the metropolis. Some men like Sir Thomas Pelham had the wealth and energy to combine a London social life with a rural one.[42] To take on a career at court whilst pursuing an active role in county politics and administration was more difficult. Sir

William Morley's fate in this respect is instructive. He was removed in 1635 from the clerkship of Star Chamber, which he acquired in partnership with Sir William Uvedale four years earlier, because 'he lives remote and has not disposed himself in a way fit for the execution of the said place'.[43] But there were other gentlemen who did manage to keep a foot in both camps. Sir Henry Compton, the crypto-catholic Custos Brevium of Common Pleas, was assiduous as a JP and deputy-lieutenant. George Courthope enjoyed the office of Deputy Commissioner for Alienations, while maintaining his local prestige by regular attendance at sessions and a responsible role in the government of Hastings rape.[44] Such instances, together with the evidence of magnate visits to London, are a reminder that the court–country dichotomy, which has recently been seen as the key to the conflict between crown and parliament, was by no means absolute. It is worth noting that Sir Thomas Pelham, the man who epitomised the country interest in Sussex, had aspirations for his heir to be a 'courtier'.[45]

Nevertheless, it is certainly true that those gentry who devoted themselves wholeheartedly to careers at court generally paid the price in terms of their influence at home. Through his attachment to Buckingham, George Goring of Hurstpierpoint amassed numerous offices and became the greatest customs farmer in the land. He added to the knighthood he obtained in 1608 a peerage in 1628 and the earldom of Norwich in 1644.[46] After his marriage to the wealthy heiress of a Chichester alderman, John Ashburnham spent some of his time there and in 1639 he was dabbling in corn exportation from Chichester, but most of his interests and dealings revolved around his court associations.[47] Neither Goring nor Ashburnham sat on the Sussex Bench in the 1630s; when the 1640 elections came neither was able to wield effective power in the county contests. 'Though I failed', wrote Ashburnham to Secretary Nicholas in March 1640, 'yet I have nothing to blame but my own negligence in looking after it'.[48] Two other courtiers, Sir Selwyn Parker and Sir Thomas Farnfould, were absentee JPs and men of no account in county affairs. Parker, a gentleman pensioner to Charles I who obtained the revived office of Aulnager of Linen Cloth in 1635, probably spent little time at Eastbourne. Farnfould owned a house in Westminster as well as Gatewick in Steyning. He kept his hawks at Colebrook, rather than in Sussex, while he pursued a chequered career in London.[49]

The hallmarks of the country viewpoint in the parliaments of the 1620s were suspicion of the corrupt and extravagant Stuart court, concern for provincial interests, public spiritedness and independence.[50] Edward Alford, as much as any MP in that decade, was the representative of the country against the court. So Alford's attitudes were the common property of the Sussex magnates. Their response to fiscal demands between 1603 and 1640 and to the exact militia programme of the 1620s shows their stubborn insistence on putting the county before the state.[51] At home prevarication became the keynote of the magnates' policies. No confrontations were sought. Positive opposition, of the kind displayed at Chichester over the prospect of further billeting in the autumn of 1628, was rare. The magnates' protestations of loyalty were persistent, their resistance to Stuart policies was subtle and underhand. The emergence of county factionalism in Sussex during the 1630s should be seen against this background. Political attitudes were relevant to it, but there was much more to the story of how a clique of JPs and gentry came to impose themselves so effectively on county politics and government that their triumph in the 1640 elections was almost a foregone conclusion.

The eastern gentry were socially well integrated. The commanding presence of Sir Thomas Pelham, whose home at Halland was within easy reach for many leading men, from the late 1620s became the pivot of magnate society in the eastern rapes.[52] Sir Thomas himself shared the Puritan outlook of friends such as Anthony Stapley, James Rivers, John Baker, Herbert Hay, John Busbridge and Peter Farnden. All these men joined the Bench through his nomination between 1633 and 1640.[53] The recalcitrance of members of this Puritan clique over royal demands for loans is some indication of their political stance. Pelham refused to contribute in 1622 and 1639, Stapley, Rivers and Baker in 1639, Hay in 1627 and 1639. But on each occasion the Puritans were in the company of other eastern gentry in their reluctance to help out the Stuart kings by dipping into their own pockets.[54] Even men with court connections like Sir Henry Compton and George Courthope refused the King loans. The most important distinguishing mark of the clique was its determination to pursue an anticlerical, and particularly an anti-Arminian, policy at quarter sessions. Early in 1640 the Arminian JP Edward Burton explained to Archbishop Laud in an interview with him in London the way things were going in Sussex. He put his allegations on paper to the Archbishop's chaplain on 27 January:

> When I first attended his Grace, I acquainted him that the Puritane faction was growen strong amongst the justices upon our Bench for the eastern part of this county: steered rather by humor and faction then justice, growen soe strong that such as are moderatly disposed weare not able to withstand it: that Mr Stapley, Mr Rivers, Mr Baker, Mr Hayes were the ringleaders . . . as for the swaying of temporall affayres in open sessions their owne way with difference and distinction betweene other men and those of their own character it weare endlesse to mention particulars; wee are most sensible of it that see it and feele the burden.

Burton went on to suggest that the Archbishop should ask Robert Foster, 'but newly gone from us' since he had been made a judge, to wait upon him and provide further information. He had 'groaned under the burden of that faction soe long', declared Burton, 'that he could noe longer endure the country'.[55] In the absence of corroborative evidence it is hard to judge the precise impact of this Puritan factionalism on county government, but the allegations of a preacher at the summer assizes in 1640 hint at the kind of anti-clerical practices that the Puritans probably encouraged. He criticised 'impropriators who defraud the tithes from the priest' and

> also taxed with foul corruption the whole county of Sussex, and all the jurors of that county who served from time to time, laying it to their charge that when any poor priest commenced any suit for recovery of his tithes out of the lands of the laity they delivered their verdicts before the priest had given in his full evidence.[56]

Bishops Montagu and Duppa had recognised the challenge which the Puritan JPs posed to their authority and policies.[57] The outright attack on the Laudian altar policy at Michaelmas sessions in 1639, planned by the fiercest spirits who persuaded Anthony Stapley to be their spokesman, reflected the growing confidence of the Puritan clique engaged in a campaign of lay assertiveness. The men responsible were well aware that they were stepping onto dangerous ground: 'I was not there present', confessed Burton, 'for it was ordered and plotted betweene three or four of them to be acted in this manner before the rest of the justices being more remote could come thyther'. In fact one moderate JP, William White, did question Stapley's right to raise a matter of ecclesiastical jurisdiction at sessions. Sir Henry Compton and George Courthope were probably among those JPs who were expected to disapprove of the Puritan initiative and who did arrive after Stapley's charge.[58] There seems to have been no coherent faction in opposition to the Puritans, but merely a collection of individuals who stood apart from them. The Arminian Edward Burton, the church papist Sir Henry Compton, the careerist lawyer Robert Foster and the country gentleman William White were men of widely different views and temperaments. They shared a dislike of the aggressive policies of the Puritan clique. The effect of Stapley's anti-Arminian outburst was merely to heighten tension on the eastern Bench. The outbreak of factionalism in a previously harmonious magnate community was painful to all those involved. Burton felt it keenly: 'God who knowes my hart, knowes that they are not the men I accept agaynt but their condition: and it was the peace of the church and commonwealth that moved me to move his Grace', he wrote to the Archbishop's chaplain. He feared the possible consequences if the great men of the county heard that he had spoken to Laud: 'to be brought forth as an informer agaynst them will cause an implacable cloude of hatred to hang over mee not to be undergone'. Yet at the same time he was so distraught about the consequences of the domineering attitude of the Puritans that he boldly suggested that the Lord Keeper Sir John Finch, who had just been appointed, should counteract the threat they posed to the Arminian church by a purge of the Sussex Bench. This was 'a thing done out of course by his predicessors', he argued, citing the precedent of Lord Keeper Coventry.[59] The advice was not heeded.

During the 1630s the eastern and western Benches drew apart

ceasing to do business together at an annual midsummer meeting. To save travelling this had sometimes been held immediately before or after the July assizes. In 1626 when thirteen JPs in all had attended the joint summer court at Horsham, six of them were resident in the west; but in 1636, 1638 and 1639, when the sessions was held in conjunction with assizes at East Grinstead, not a single western justice was present; and in 1637 at Horsham only one JP on a Bench of seven men represented the western rapes.[60] The sudden acceleration in the 1630s of the process by which the autonomy of the two magisterial divisions became more complete was probably due in large measure to the capture of the eastern Bench by the Puritan caucus. It was also based on a general recognition that the gentry at the two ends of the county mainly moved in separate social circles.[61] Thus two interwoven aspects of factionalism in Sussex on the eve of the Short Parliament are of profound significance in relation to future political developments in the county. First, a small group of men of outstanding social prestige in the east, led by the formidable partnership of Sir Thomas Pelham and Anthony Stapley, a group who were strongly motivated by Puritanism, held the county in their grip. Secondly, the magnate gentry were divided by geography and social relationships into two camps, and they lacked any regular opportunity to discuss and argue out administrative and political problems.

The 1640 elections

The King announced his intention of calling a parliament on 6 December 1639. The very next day the Earl of Suffolk, as Lord Warden, wrote a curt note to the corporation of Rye to signify his intention of making a nomination and 'to prevent your ingagements otherwaies'. It was generally appreciated that competition for places would be stiff.[62] Sir Thomas Pelham and Anthony Stapley, cousins and close friends, put themselves forward for the knightships of the shire. Pelham's pre-eminence in the gentry community was such that he was unlikely to be seriously challenged. He had held the knightship in both 1624 and 1625. Yet, taking no chances, Pelham and Stapley lavishly entertained the freeholders at Lewes on 12 March and Stapley engaged in a vigorous campaign there. The bill for food and drink came to £130.[63] Despite the absence of serious competition the election brought an air of political tension to the county. 'I must be in Sussex at the election', wrote Sir John Sackville to Sir Henry Vane from Knowle on 6 March.[64] Choosing the knights of the shire had become a matter of the utmost importance, when there were so many grievances to be remedied and such great hopes were placed in the parliament which had at last been called.

In the boroughs the elections were far less straightforward. At Horsham, where Thomas Middleton and Hall Ravenscroft were elected, and at Shoreham, which elected John Alford and William Marlott, men without parliamentary experience quickly snatched the available burgess ships. Elsewhere the gentry were forced to fight. At Chichester, Midhurst and Bramber court candidates successfully claimed one of the places. Moreover Sir Thomas Farnfould, who again sat for Steyning, was first and foremost a courtier: he could not be counted on fully to understand or to support the country viewpoint. Nevertheless a strong team of fourteen county gentry attended at Westminster when parliament opened on 13 April. If the Short Parliament had outlived its three week span, the ambitious young Herbert Morley, elected at Lewes when Stapley waived his burgess-ship in favour of the knightship, and Henry Garton, who obtained the Arundel place vacated when Lord Maltravers went to the Lords, would have joined the Sussex delegation.[65]

The honours in the fierce contests between court and county candidates at Bramber, East Grinstead, Lewes, Hastings and Rye were roughly even. The borough campaigns were marked by libels, threats, chicanery and bribery. Never before had the political atmosphere in Sussex been so intense at election time. Edward Burton, in his letter to Dr Bray, Archbishop Laud's chaplain, expressed his apprehensions about the outcome at Lewes, where the town as well as the Sessions House was 'tainted' with Puritanism:

> Not withstanding my Lord of Dorset's and my Lord Goring's letters and intimations for their creatures to be parliament men; yet Mr Stapley and Mr Rivers have a strong party in the towne, and it is much feared they will be chosen burgesses for the towne of Lewes: God forbidde the greater part of a parliament should be of their stampe: if soe, Lord have mercy upon our Church.[66]

Religion was bound to be a prominent issue in the Puritan east. By and large though, the borough conflicts revolved around clashes of personalities and personal influence. Sir Edward Bishop's sinister reputation following his conviction for murder in 1627, the opprobrium which easily attached itself to ship money sheriffs and a period of absence abroad in the late 1630s all may have contributed in some measure to his double failure.[67] He was thwarted both at Steyning, where his previous seat and the other place were quickly grasped by rival gentry of the neighbourhood, and at Bramber, where Sir John Suckling intervened, armed with a letter from the Earl of Dorset and the support of other influential courtiers. Bishop later alleged that Suckling threatened the 'better sort' of burgesses and 'by offering money to the meaner sort persuaded them to vote for himself'.[68]

Looming over many early Stuart election contests was the crucial political issue of the extent of the franchise.[69] In many cases the motive of country gentry who attempted to widen it was the breaking of the stranglehold of aristocratic patrons. The Earl of Dorset's long control of East Grinstead, for example, was based on his ownership of a majority of the burgage tenements. When in 1640 Robert Goodwin, who had sat for the town in 1626 and 1628, found himself challenged by John White, Dorset's secretary and nominee, he sought to retain his place by appealing beyond the burgageholders to the townsmen. White brought a petition against Goodwin's election to the Commons. Goodwin subsequently appeared before the Committee of Privileges, where he produced a series of Tudor indentures to show that the right of election rested with the inhabitants. He also charged Dorset's bailiffs with threatening his supporters. He alleged that they were told that if they voted for him their servants would be pressed for the Scots war and their carts would be commandeered by the royal purveyors. Predictably the House found Goodwin properly elected and resolved to examine the bailiff's misdemeanours.[70]

Nowhere in Sussex did the issue of the extent of the electorate emerge so dramatically as in the celebrated Hastings election.[71] At an assembly of jurats and freemen called by the mayor, John White, acting for the Earl of Dorset, boldly promised the corporation that, if the court nominee Robert Read was elected, the town would receive twenty pounds plus ten pounds a year during Read's life and 'two barrels of powder yearly for the exercise of youth'. White's public announcement came as a bombshell in an already tense situation, since several other men had been nominated. One of them was John Ashburnham, who lived nearby. Thomas Eversfield, who lived just outside the town and whose father had sat for Hastings four times in the 1620s, was also preparing to make a bid for a place through his control of a vociferous faction among the freemen, some of whom were his tenants. The mayor and jurats were clearly proceeding cautiously and had been initially well disposed to electing a local man. 'They inquired much after me and resolved to have chosen me', explained John Ashburnham to Secretary Nicholas.[72] But Eversfield, the obvious local candidate, seems to have gone out of his way to alienate the ruling oligarchy: he slighted them by never writing to them to declare his candidature, he encouraged his party to engage in house to house and tavern campaigning, he sought to have the corporation's ship money accounts questioned, and he became embroiled in the quarrel between the town and an insolent London fishmonger Robert Underwood. In view of all this the mayor deliberately ignored Eversfield's candidature and at a second assembly proceeded to elect Read, in the absence of about half of the freemen, who had left the hall after they had been threatened with fines and the wrath of the Lord Warden.[73]

The mayor of Hastings saw himself as defending the privilege of the most substantial townsmen to control the borough's affairs. The central issue in the campaign became the question of social order. The 'abler discreeter and soberer sorte of inhabitants' might be forced to leave the town, warned the mayor and jurats in a letter to Read about the commotions which followed his election. They saw Eversfield as one who had deliberately provoked an open struggle for power between a faction among the freemen and the jurats:

> The cause of all this is their intent of opposicon against us, for they make such distinctions between themselves and us as if they were not of us and will neither our counsell nor advise, but think themselves of power to have all things as they lyst and so they souldfaine have it and us to be ordered by them and not they by us.[74]

Perhaps Eversfield saw an effective freemen franchise as a matter of principle. If so he may have been fighting a battle that he had inherited from his father in a new and, as it appeared to the corporation, more dangerous way. Between 1624 and 1628 Nicholas Eversfield had plenty of opportunity to imbibe the ideas of the parliamentary pressure group which sought to widen the electorate.[75] Moreover, it is possible that he did his own research into the records of the borough since one of the corporation's charges against Eversfield in 1640 was that he refused to return the 'many writings belonging to this towne' which his father had borrowed when he was one of its barons in parliament. Defeated in the spring, Eversfield resolved to fight the same battle again and he kept up his campaign for popular support for several weeks after the election was over. On one visit to Hastings he was to be seen proceeding through the streets with his supporters beside him and two fiddlers back to back on a horse before him. The mayor found it comic that the frightened horse 'flung one of the fidlers' when 'a drume was beate up at a sudden'. But this kind of campaigning was a portent. It marked a new political awareness on the part of the gentry, which in time was bound to communicate itself, with consequences they did not dream of, to less substantial men. Meanwhile Thomas Eversfield related the scandalous behaviour of the Hastings corporation to his many influential friends in the county. When John Ashburnham was in Sussex at the end of March he found the gentry community buzzing with the story. He did his best to undo the harm done by 'Mr White's impertinences and over-busying himself in that place', by assuring Sir Thomas Parker and some others who talked of questioning the election that Robert Read had been maligned.[76]

In so far as national political issues arose in the Sussex contests there was a strong tendency for them to be seen in the local context. Thomas Eversfield raised the ship money question at Hastings, it seems, more as a way of casting doubts on the probity of the town's officers than as a grievance against the crown. He 'would know what is become of the shipmony'. He appears to have been much more interested in exploiting grudges and animosities between the freemen and jurats and raising a general campaign against court intruders than in educating the Hastings electorate about the issues at stake when parliament met.[77] As preoccupied as ever with the decay of their harbour, the corporation of Rye set out to secure local representatives who understood their problems. Within days of receiving the news of the parliament from the Earl of Suffolk on 7 December, they had entered into discussions with neighbouring gentry such as William White. On 18 December Laurence Ashburnham, whose home was a mere five miles from the town, wrote declaring himself to have been 'many yeares a neighbour and a well-wisher to the good and prosperous estate of your towne', although he had enjoyed no occasion to become acquainted with the leading townsmen. He declared his readiness to serve, having heard from his Cousin White 'and other of my good friends of your love and forward inclination towards me'. Ashburnham's appeal held out no extravagant promises: it was a straightforward one of 'some reall performance'.[78] In normal times he would probably have succeeded, but on this occasion the mayor and jurats found themselves besieged by courtiers who made nominations and by local gentry anxious to go to Westminster. Between December and February nine candidates were proposed or proposed themselves to the town.[79] In the end, Rye rejected the Lord Warden's nomination for the first time in the seventeenth century and chose the Kentish gentleman, Sir John Culpepper, together with the Earl of Dorset's secretary John White, whose brother William White of Northiam was influential with the townsmen.

Sir John Culpepper was for a while uncertain about his chances of election at Rye because of the slurs of opponents among the Kentish and Sussex gentry. In January 1640 he wrote at length to 'cleare a jealousie (which as I heare) some have fancied' that he intended to use his place, if elected, to reclaim some saltmarshes he owned near the town. On the contrary, Culpepper protested, he had 'bin an actor in head and purse to lay open 1500 acres of salts for the benefitt of your harbour, but never inned any'. 'I have often declared my opinion', Culpepper assured the corporation, 'that the inning of salts hath produced (as a necessary consequence) the decay of your outfall'. The letter was a well-calculated and effective piece of electioneering, which undoubtedly weighed heavily with the mayor and jurats. They had too long an experience of men imposed on them from London who did little for the town. It was also a good move of Culpepper's, in the heady atmosphere of early 1640, to remind the Rye electors that their election was free and that they would always command his 'ready service' whether they chose him or not.[80] Almost everywhere in Sussex during the Short Parliament elections there was a firm desire to acquire local representatives who had the county's interests at heart. Where local candidates were defeated, such as at Bramber and Hastings, it was through chicanery or because class issues cut across the court–country division.

The Sussex delegation must have found their brief sitting at Westminster an unhappy and frustrating experience. Sir Thomas Bowyer, a seasoned parliament man, and Christopher Lewkenor were both appointed to the Committee of Privileges; Lewkenor also had an opportunity to produce the notes he had made at the time when he was nominated to the committee for establishing the facts of the violation of the privilege of parliament on 10 March 1629.[81] Otherwise the Sussex members had no chance to distinguish themselves. Between May and September 1640 a series of incidents aggravated their hostility towards the Caroline government. Three deputy-lieutenants who sat in parliament in April and May, Sir Thomas Pelham, Sir Henry Compton and John Alford, returned home to find themselves at once embroiled in the tangled situation brought about by the Privy Council's changes of plan on the embarkation of the county's pressed band for the army against Scotland. While the soldiers kicked their heels, the county felt the cost in coat and conduct charges. Meanwhile the sheriff, Edward Apsley, received a new demand for the payment of the large outstanding balance of the ship money account by 24 June, a demand the county ignored.[82] The gentry were also shocked and angered by the assertively clerical sermon preached to them at the summer assizes by the son of Lewis Bayly the late Bishop of Bangor. Taking as his text the words 'justice exalteth a nation', the preacher adopted a line of argument that was thoroughly offensive to the lay community. It was alleged that some passages in the sermon were 'to the great scandal of the laws and statutes of the realm', others were 'against the propriety of the subject'. Yet the judges refused to admit a grand jury indictment against Bayly. While they contained their own discontents, the JPs sought to prevent treasonable gossip and unfounded rumour from going unchecked. One man was sentenced to a fine of £2,000, after the Bench had sent him before the assize judges for scandalous and seditious words against the King.[83] At Chichester the authorities had for some while been keeping an eye on the Berkshire clothier Henry Spier, who regularly visited the city. As early as 1638 he had questioned whether the Scots were in fact rebels and traitors in a conversation with an innkeeper. In August 1640 Spier brought the news that the Berkshire deputies and justices had 'commanded the soldiers pressed thence that they shall not take shipping' and commented 'that he wondered that the soldiers would fight against the Scots, for they shall ere long prove the best subjects'. He also gave forcible expression to his dislike of cathedral churches and spread rumours that 'a bloody time' lay ahead. Christopher Lewkenor committed Spier to prison, informing the lieutenants about his 'language on matters above him'.[84]

The elections for the Long Parliament were no less competitive and acrimonious than the spring elections had been. Local candidates again started with an enormous advantage. Gentry who were known and respected as countrymen did well everywhere. The county election, which was held at Lewes on 22 October, was bigger and more expensive than in the spring. The bill this time was £193.[85] Not that there was any question about the re-election of Sir Thomas Pelham and Anthony Stapley as the knights of the shire. The signatures on the election return show that they enjoyed the overwhelming support of the magnate gentry of their neighbourhood. Herbert Morley, John Baker, Herbert Hay, John Busbridge, Peter Farnden, Thomas Eversfield and Henry Shelley were among those who were there. The election was entirely an east Sussex affair. Indeed the roll call of eastern gentry on the election return demonstrates the extent to which at this time they held the county in their power. Virtually no one of magnate status from the western rapes came to have their say.[86]

Eleven other men held on to seats they had won for the Short Parliament: Herbert Morley and James Rivers sat for Lewes, and Shoreham and Horsham remained faithful to the newcomers they had chosen in March. Four men gained places that had previously been occupied by courtiers and nominees of noble patrons: old Sir William Morley, a pillar of west Sussex society, was chosen at Chichester, William Cawley obtained a burgess-ship at Midhurst, William Hay took the place of the expelled monopolist Sir John Jacob at Rye in January 1641 and Thomas Eversfield gained the seat at Hastings for which he had been campaigning since the spring. At Steyning Sir John Leeds retired in favour of his son Thomas. Seaford, restored as a parliamentary borough in February 1641, elected Sir Thomas Parker, a leading county magnate without previous experience in the Commons, whose brother Henry Parker was rapidly emerging as a prominent parliamentary apologist. Only two county gentry lost their places and in both cases they gave way to men who had strong local connections, although they were not actually resident in Sussex: John Alford's brother Sir Edward obtained Henry Goring's Arundel burgess-ship and Lord Buckhurst claimed Sir Henry Compton's place in the Sackville borough of East Grinstead. The Sussex boroughs proved less sympathetic to court nominations than in the spring and where courtiers were successful they were helped by the propinquity of their estates to the borough in question. Steyning could hardly refuse Sir Thomas Farnfould, any more than Hastings could neglect John Ashburnham this time, when a strong word from the Lord Warden compensated for his failure to nurse the town. The grievous loss of James Rivers, who died of the plague in June 1641 and had been an intimate member of Sussex's Puritan clique in the Long Parliament, was made good by the election of another friend of Pelham and Stapley's, Henry Shelley; Henry Garton, who died in October 1641, was replaced at Arundel by John Downes, a resident, though a comparative newcomer to the county. Thus the Sussex delegation, which by 1642 consisted of nineteen resident gentry, was in the end a rather stronger one than in the Short Parliament.[87]

Control of a wider effective franchise than was traditional in certain boroughs undoubtedly helped some Sussex candidates. At East Grinstead, where Robert Goodwin successfully challenged Sir William Culpepper's election by the mayor and burgesses, Goodwin's election return was signed by about fifty of the inhabitants, some of whom made their marks.[88] At Hastings once the slander that Robert Read was a papist was sedulously spread in London and Hastings by the corporation's inveterate enemy Robert Underwood, and had stuck, the court candidate had no real chance. This time there was no chicanery. The assembly of 20 October was a triumph for Thomas Eversfield and the principle of freeman participation. First John Ashburnham was unanimously elected by the mayor, seven jurats and twenty-two freeman; then Eversfield was elected with the whole body of freemen voting in his favour.[89]

At Rye, William Hay might have ridden to Westminster on the band-wagon of the freeman franchise at once in November 1640 if it had not been for the skilful trickery of the town clerk, Samuel Landsdale and some of his friends among the jurats. The re-election of John White was acceptable to the jurats and freemen; John Fagge was a popular candidate with only minority support; the real battle was between the customs farmer, Sir John Jacob, and William Hay. The traditional procedure by which the freemen elected two men from nominations presented to them was normally susceptible to management by the oligarchy in favour of their own candidates. On this occasion, however, instead of waiting for a lead, the freemen insisted that White and Hay should be the members for the town. The mayor and jurats, dissatisfied with their choice, 'would not joyne in the same'. In an effort to convince them that their decision was quite clear, the freemen 'did there divide themselves and draw sides': thirteen were for Hay and White, three were for Jacob. Wherupon, alleged Hay in a petition to the Committee of Privileges, the clerk 'did invent and put in practise a new waye for the chusing of burgesses never before that tyme used in that place'. He declared that every freeman should give his voice for two of the candidates and then added the names of some absentees as supporters of Jacob, pretending 'by such indirecte meanes' that he had 'plurallity of voyce'. Although two of their own number defected, the mayor and jurats were thus able to secure a final tally of eighteen to fifteen votes in favour of Jacob. Richard Cockram, in a letter to Samuel Landsdale of 13 November 1640, spoke of the many falsities in Hay's petition, but, whatever the precise merits of his case, the underlying class conflict is clear.[90] The struggle for power between the freemen and jurats of Rye produced the curious situation of the town's oligarchy supporting a court monopolist against a local gentleman who shared their religious predilections, their political aims and their county interest. The whole affair illustrates the primacy in Rye politics of internal social conflicts and personal animosities on the eve of the civil war.

In general, the Committee of Privileges proved sympathetic to local gentry in disputed election cases. There is little doubt that, had the House not disposed of Jacob in January 1641, William Hay could have unseated him through the evidence of sharp practice that he had gathered. William Cawley secured his place at Midhurst after he had challenged the bailiff's return of the Arminian friend of Bishop Duppa, Richard Chaworth, who may have been supported by Viscount Montagu. Only in the case of Bramber did the Commons censure a resident Sussex candidate, but Sir Edward Bishop's foolish offer of a ten pound bribe was such a crude attempt to buy his way into the House that it could hardly be overlooked. He was debarred from seeking election again.[91] The full extent of the Long

Parliament's hostility to noble patronage became evident when the news that the Earl of Arundel had nominated his secretary as a burgess at Arundel in place of Henry Garton led to the Commons' vote that letters from peers should not be allowed to influence free elections. Sir Simonds D'Ewes commented in the debate of December 1641 on this issue that 'there was a simonie of favour as well as of monie'. Drawing a parallel with Bishop's bribery at Bramber, he stressed how 'a poor borough towne' might be 'awed by a great man's letter'. Oliver Cromwell had proposed that the Speaker should direct the borough of Arundel to make a free election.[92] Thus the spring and autumn elections of 1640 revealed an unprecedented degree of interest in gaining seats and in the political debate. Sir Thomas Pelham and Anthony Stapley led the cohort of Sussex MPs who rode up to Westminster in November 1640 in a mood of determination to see the grievances of eleven years remedied without delay.

Parliamentary politics 1640–1642

The first months of the Long Parliament were a period of optimism, almost of euphoria, for all those who opposed the Caroline court and the policies of the Caroline government. 'God be praysed the parlament goeth one cumfortablely and like to prove a happy parlement', wrote the Rye jurat Richard Cockram to the town clerk ten days after the knights and burgesses had gathered at Westminster. Speeches and proclamations were enclosed in numerous letters bringing the provinces up to date with events in London.[93] It was a heady, exciting time: 'Wee shall see idolatry and superstition rooted out and God's ordinances sett up in the puritie and power of them; altars begin to goe downe apace and railes in many places', reported Anna Temple from Warwickshire to her daughter in Sussex.[94] Until the summer of 1641 there was a substantial unity of purpose, both within the Commons and in the relationships between MPs and those whom they represented. The correspondence of John White and William Hay with the mayor and jurats of Rye was friendly and co-operative. The MPs helped the corporation obtain a lease of the vicarage tithes; they freed the town of the subsidies parliament voted, 'although not without some difficulty'; and they kept the townsmen informed about the progress of a Bill concerning saltmarshes. White and Hay were model representatives. They were eager to report each victory for the subject's liberties: the abolition of High Commission and Star Chamber, they declared in July 1641, would content the nation 'for as they were used, were a terror to all menn'. The Rye members lifted their eyes from the Sussex fields, they became aware of the national issues and of their wider responsibilities. Their parliamentary experience made them intolerant of Rye's studied self-interest and parochialism. The town, they insisted, could expect no relief from the poll money, since it was intended for 'the distressed people in the north' and 'all are comaunded by God to have a fellow feeling of one another's miseries'. Rye responded readily to parliament's bid to bind the nation through the Protestation Oath. It was taken at a general assembly, called by the mayor immediately he received a copy from White and Hay, by 'almost all of the inhabitants . . . to the number of 200 men'.[95]

Sir Thomas Pelham missed only a few weeks of the Westminster debates between November 1640 and August 1641. Then he joined the general exodus to the country after the long summer of political argument. During May and June, when Lady Pelham also was in town, the family took a house at Charing Cross.[96] Pelham led a group of Sussex MPs who were wholeheartedly in support of the programme of the parliamentary opposition to the King. In December 1640 he, Anthony Stapley and James Rivers were nominated to the committee on the establishment of a preaching ministry. Sir Thomas Parker, Herbert Morley, Robert Goodwin and William Hay were other energetic country members ready to take their share in committee work. Sir Thomas Bowyer was particularly diligent, sitting on a total of twenty-three committees between November 1640 and June 1642.[97] He was the only member of this group who lived in west Sussex and the only one who drew back to the King's side when war broke out. The rest of the Sussex MPs whose dissension from the parliament's proceedings eventually led them into neutralism or royalism were largely inconspicuous during 1641. Sir William Morley, Thomas Middleton, Hall Ravenscroft and Thomas May were hardly heard, Christopher Lewkenor's prestige is evident from his immediate appointment to the Committee of Privileges but he may have been rarely in the House after the opening weeks, Thomas Eversfield failed to fulfil his promise as a champion of the people's liberties.[98] By and large the existing factional division of the Sussex gentry on geographical and religious lines was carried over into a split within the parliamentary delegation between the activists and the rest.

Robert Goodwin, Herbert Morley and Sir Thomas Bowyer were appointed to the committee which sat every Tuesday and Saturday during the parliamentary recess from 9 September to 20 October 1641. Goodwin, whose startlingly bold motion on evil counsellors led to a fierce debate on 28 October, and Morley, who was an articulate and aspiring member, probably attended at least some of the committee's meetings.[99] Whether Bowyer attended is more doubtful: he may well have been coming under some pressure by this time from magnate friends of the Chichester neighbourhood, who were dubious about the course that parliament was steering. Others of the Sussex delegation, enjoying a respite from national politics, were able to turn their attention to county business. Sir Thomas Pelham, Sir Thomas Parker and Anthony Stapley were all at the Michaelmas sessions, where they had a chance to test the opinions of their colleagues on the Bench. Two new recruits, William Thomas and Francis Selwyn, both of them downland nominees of Pelham's who had been appointed as JPs in August, were sitting for the first time.[100] They made their debut at a time when political issues, more than routine administration, must have preoccupied the magnates gathered at Lewes.

The uncertainty of the political future made secure relationships with the nobility an immediate priority, yet since 1625 the deputies had never communicated easily with the county's courtier lieutenants the Earls of Dorset and Arundel. In the tense summer of 1641 contact with them could hardly be fruitful. The Earl of Northumberland, on the other hand, was known to have been dissatisfied with royal policy towards Scotland and when bad health caused him to spend July and August 1641 at Petworth there were rumours in London of his increasing alienation from the court. 'With the Houses', it was reported, 'he stands very well'.[101] Sir Thomas Pelham visited Northumberland at Petworth during the summer. For some while he had been cultivating the Earl's friendship; it now took on an unexpected importance. The visit must have occurred around the end of August, when Northumberland wrote a despondent letter to Sir Thomas Roe: 'we never were fuller of jelousies then we are att this present, nor lesse hopefull of avoideing a confusion'.[102] Against this bleak outlook the bonds between the two men, each so powerful in his own end of the county, were tightened. Northumberland's informal and friendly letter to the deputies the following May, when, predictably, he had become the county's lieutenant under the Militia Ordinance, set an entirely different tone from the correspondence of the previous years with Dorset and Arundel.[103]

Sussex gentry joined in the general move to petition the parliament in the first months of 1642. A delegation from the county presented petitions to both Houses on 17 February. They were in the name of the 'High sheriff, Knights, Esquires, Gentlemen, Ministers, Freeholders and Inhabitants' of Sussex.[104] The characteristic concerns of the leading Puritan magnates, who presumably formulated and organised the petitions, emerged strongly in the catalogue of requests:

> that the lawes of God be truely maintained, government and discipline so setled, that we may be conform'd therein to the perfect rule of God's word, able, learned, and painful ministers bee incouraged, scandalous speedily displaced, pluralities and unwanted orders and dignities of the clergie taken away, that the probats of wills and testaments may be reserved to the cognizance of the temporall courts . . . the clergie, and other disobeying your late orders, in our cathedrals and other churches questioned, the universities thoroughly purged.

The virulent attack on popishness and the enthusiastic support for the parliament's attack on Arminianism were other characteristic notes.[105] The political programme envisaged was essentially that of Pym and the parliamentary leaders. The punishment of delinquents, the prevention of the sale of 'honour and offices', the rooting out of evil counsellors and the further relief of Ireland were all stressed as prerequisites for the restoration of harmony between King and parliament. The Lords were urged to join in a 'general taking of the Protestation many reporting it a thing discountenanced by some of your honours'. The petitions display a firm grasp of the national issues. Local matters, in so far as they appeared, were secondary: seamen should be 'encouraged', fishing should be 'maintained'. The overriding local issue was the defence of the county, 'more than seventie miles naked to the sea', which the petitioners insisted required speedy attention 'by sea and land'. As in so many of the county petitions of 1642, the concluding statement propounded the vision of unity that men clung to as the nation slithered towards war: 'that the glory of God may be by your zealous and loyal intention propagated, the honour and safety of his Majestie and his kingdome advanced, the privilege of parliament and every member thereof maintained'.[106]

13

The county at war 1642-1648

Wee heare there are both foote and horse come from the King into the citty . . . divers houses are threatened to be plundred within and without the citty, the sherife beinge abetted by the gentlemen before named is extreame violent in the comission of array . . . all this hath befallen us through the base neglect of the deputy lieuetennants.
Edward Higgins, William Cawley and Henry Chitty, from Chichester, to Speaker Lenthall, 21 November 1642.[1]

This aproaching clowd I feare may raise a storme in Sussex, which county is full of newters and malignants and I have ever observed newters to turne malignants upon such occasions.
Herbert Morley to Speaker Lenthall, 16 September 1643.[2]

Prize your fireside comforts, you know nott the hardshipps of warr naii though it be in a flowing county as is Sussex.
John Coulton to Samuel Jeake, 8 January 1644.[3]

The struggle for the county

Between July and November 1642 civil war broke out by fits and starts all over England. The multitude of local conflicts from which the full scale war eventually emerged centred around the enforcement of parliament's Militia Ordinance and the King's commissions of array.[4] It was not until November 1642 that a Sussex gentleman received a commission of array. But active steps to take control of the county for parliament were initiated by the Earl of Northumberland on 26 May. He ordered that general musters, 'att such places as you shall thinke fittest and for the ease of the countrie', and training of the bands should be held in the first fortnight of June. There is little doubt that the Earl's trust in his deputies' 'care in the performance of this publicke and important service' in the east was fulfilled. What sort of showing Sir Thomas Pelham, Sir Thomas Parker, Anthony Stapley and Herbert Morley managed to obtain in the western rapes is more uncertain.[5] During the summer the parliamentarian oligarchy imposed a firm hold on the eastern end of Sussex. The Act for £400,000 was efficiently administered.[6] The defence of towns such as Lewes and Rye was treated as a pressing necessity. On 1 July Herbert Morley obtained permission to buy twenty barrels of powder for the county's defence. His intervention also lay behind the Commons' order of 29 August that the ordnance, muskets and powder in Camber Castle, 'exposed to the surprise of any ill-affected or malignant persons', should be removed to Rye 'for the use and service of the county'.[7] Four large pieces of ordnance were brought up from Newhaven and Brighton to Lewes.[8] Not that the coast was forgotten: in April the Bench had directed that the vulnerable communities of Brighton, Rottingdean and Newhaven should each receive a barrel of gunpowder from the Lewes stock.[9]

The sympathetic response of eastern parishes to the voluntary collections of March and April 1642 for the relief of the Irish Protestants hints at the mood of commitment and exertion there which made the deputies' task an easy one. In the large parish of Mayfield, for instance, a 'libberale and free contribution' raised forty-five pounds. The gentry and minister gave a lead: John Baker found five pounds for the Irish cause, John Maynard matched his patron's sum, and the ironmasters Stephen Pankhurst and Thomas Aynscombe were generous. At East Hoathly the minister, Benjamin Pickering, was sharp enough to insist that each man should state his contribution in his presence. Sir Thomas Pelham, who had already 'given in parliament', led off with fifty shillings; James Temple who was staying with him gave a pound; even the men and maid servants of Halland contributed their mites. At Burwash the total collected was thirty-nine pounds, after Edward Polhill and Anthony Cruttenden had volunteered five and three pounds respectively. Etchingham, Sedlescombe and Brightling were other parishes where Puritan gentry set a firm example.[10] The campaign for Propositions money in June and July, based on meetings of freeholders in the market towns of the eastern rapes, went almost as smoothly.[11]

There was enthusiastic backing for the parliamentary cause in the Puritan towns and villages of east Sussex. Those who were out of tune with the prevailing mood got short shrift. The minister of Beckley, Thomas Sharpe, found that he was the odd man out when he declined to engage in the Propositions scheme at a meeting at Battle. He told William Newton in a letter how

> I went in the simplicity of my hart (God knowes) speaking plainly and modestly what I thoughte of the businesse, and being pressed thereunto, gave also the reasons of my opinion, never suspecting it woulde be imputed a crime to any man, to have dissented. This gayned me the repute of the greatest anti-parliament man in these parts.[12]

Investigation of the views that John Wilson, the Arminian vicar of Arlington, was propagating there led the justices to indict him at the midsummer sessions as a common barrator, a shrewd means of checking the dissemination of royalist propaganda. The argument between Wilson and the tailor Samuel Andrewes shows that one Sussex craftsman at least, and doubtless he was not the only one, grasped some of the central issues in the national crisis of 1642. Andrewes boldly confronted his minister, with biblical quotations at his fingertips. The dispute began with some talk about the disagreements between King and parliament and the Scots invasion in 1640. Andrewes claimed that he had seen a recent declaration from which he understood 'that the Scots wold have the same religion established that was in Queen Elizabathe's time'. 'What if the King will not have the same?' Wilson was provoked to reply. There followed a lengthy argument about the role of heathen and Christian kings and emperors. Wilson, quoting scripture, sought to prove that if 'Moses had powre from God to make lawes' and the apostles had been obedient to heathen emperors, Christians ought much more to honour a Christian king who was God's anointed. Andrewes denied that Charles I deserved the degree of honour that Wilson insisted he should be given and questioned the *jure divino* claim with a piece of bland rationalism: 'he was not God's annointed for God did not annoint him'. Wilson's assertiveness probably did the royalist cause no good in Arlington. He was too ready to feud with parishioners reluctant to attend his services. 'It is no marvell that thou art a rebell', he told one of them, 'the parliament are rebells and do rebell against the King setting forth lawes contrary to his will'.[13]

The inertia of the western gentry in the summer of 1642 was in marked contrast to the response of the east to parliamentary preparations for war. The justices did as they were asked in administering the Protestation Oath, and thus revealed a dangerous pocket of disaffection at Midhurst and Easebourne.[14] But the reaction to financial schemes such as the contributions for Ireland and the Propositions indicates a general hesitancy and inertia. The sums raised for Ireland were meagre in most places, strikingly so when they are compared to the generosity of the east. Few gentry, apart from the recusant Sir John Caryll who in an eccentric gesture gave ten pounds, provided much of a lead.[15]

Outsiders played a waiting game towards west Sussex. The eastern oligarchy neglected it, so much so that when a crisis came in the autumn they invited the wrath of the Chichester parliamentarians.[16] The King was curiously unmindful of the Hampshire borderland, a fruitful ground for a strong royalist movement. The potential loyalty of Portsmouth, under the leadership of George Goring, gave the area particular strategic significance. The one initiative that Charles I did take towards Sussex in the summer of 1642 shows that his information about the magnates there was sound enough. A new commission of the peace, issued from Beverley on 20 July, brought in eight gentry, all of them moderates susceptible to royalist pressure. At a stroke, it deprived the parliamentarian administration in the east of the services of Anthony Stapley, Herbert Hay, John Busbridge, John Baker and Peter Farnden, all men it could ill afford to lose. Edward Higgins of Bury, who was also omitted, was probably the only JP in the west whose allegiance to parliament was clear at that stage. The Beverley commission was a clever tactical move, but it was not drastic enough to dislodge county government from the hands of the roundhead clique.[17]

The first spark of open royalism in Sussex was Robert Exton's publication early in July 1642, as mayor of Chichester, of the King's proclamations concerning military activities. The proclamations of 18 and 20 June forbidding levies of forces without his consent and informing subjects of the lawfulness of the commissions of array were probably the ones concerned.[18] When the Commons summoned Exton to answer his contempt, he fled to join Charles at York.[19] Chichester's tensions came fully into the open with Goring's declaration in favour of the King at Portsmouth and the ensuing siege of the town.[20] Predictably in view of their Puritan spirit and their wrangle with the Council during the 1630s, the merchant oligarchy inclined to parliament. Theirs was a parochial parliamentarianism, made up of resentment against the crown, which was identified in the merchants' eyes with the Arminianism they had been forced to tolerate in their midst, and fierce corporate independence. The Close inclined to the King, led by its residents Sir John Morley and Joseph Henshaw, who sent a load of wheat to the besieged garrison of Portsmouth. Thus the alignments of the previous decades formed the basis of civil war allegiances in Chichester, except that Christopher Lewkenor detached himself from his mercantile allies and turned royalist. He joined Goring in the defence of Portsmouth.[21] The alliance between Arminians like Henshaw and the magnates with residences in the city like Sir John Morley had its origins in the distrust felt by both parties for the merchants after the dissensions of the previous thirty years. The only magnate who threw in his lot decisively with the merchants and parliament was Edward Higgins, who, perhaps significantly, had been involved in a prolonged feud with Sir John Morley.[22]

George Goring's declaration for the King put the gentry of the western rapes in a quandary. Sir William Morley, Sir Thomas Bowyer, Thomas May and John Alford were already under some suspicion, due to their long absences from Westminster.[23] Others, like Sir William Goring, had so far been able to cling to the detachment of their estates. If Portsmouth held out and the royalist cause gathered strength in the south-east, these men would be tempted to espouse the King's cause; if Portsmouth fell and they found themselves pinioned between the roundhead east of the county and a parliamentary garrison in Hampshire, they would be grateful for the chance to avoid the charge of malignancy by adopting a neutralist standpoint. The game they chose to play was a tricky one. They took care for both possible futures by writing a 'resolute letter' to Goring. They demanded why he had betrayed parliament's trust concerning Portsmouth and threatened to 'raise forces against him', unless he showed the commission by which he acted. When Goring sent them copies of his royal commissions of June and July to hold the fort and raise a regiment, the western magnates forwarded them to the Speaker of the Commons, with a request that the Chichester magazine might be delivered into their hands.[24] It was a disingenuous move. A group of men who at best were inert neutrals, at worst incipient royalists, expected the Commons to allow them, instead of the energetic parliamentarian Captain Henry Chitty and his townsmen, to control Chichester, a key town on the south coast. The eastern MPs ensured that the Commons' reaction was a sharp one. Herbert Morley accepted responsibility for writing to Chitty to require him to secure the magazine for parliament and to resist any who should attempt to take it. Chichester was close to bloodshed during August. The gentry's letter was regarded by the merchants as a plot to betray the city, the cathedral clergy preached in favour of the King, the royalists of the Close even drilled a body of light horse within their precincts. Yet the aldermen maintained control. 'The city of Chichester', reported a newsletter of 24 August 'stands now in a good posture of defence and have declared their resolution to the parliament'.[25]

Strenuous efforts were made by the Commons during September, October and early November to achieve effective control of west Sussex whilst avoiding any resort to arms. The declaration taken by every MP present on 10 August, that they would 'maintain, assist and adhere unto' the Earl of Essex 'with their lives and estates', was used as a political test of the loyalty of Sir William Morley, Sir Thomas Bowyer, Thomas May, John Alford, Thomas Leedes, Hall Ravenscroft and Sir Thomas Eversfield. None of them balked at it; yet all of them remained inert.[26] On 3 September a new Committee was appointed for receiving money and plate upon the Propositions in Chichester rape: it consisted of three Chichester aldermen, two gentlemen who lived near the city, Sir John Chapman and George Oglander, and Sir Gregory Norton, the only fully trustworthy JP resident in the rape at that time. This Committee achieved something but not enough. In October the House thought it necessary to send Herbert Morley down to urge forward the contributions and on 1 November further gentry and merchants were added to the Committee for Propositions in the western rapes. On the same day seven gentlemen from Chichester rape, including Sir John Morley and George Gunter, who had allegedly refused to 'contribute to the public charge in this time of common danger', were summoned as delinquents. In the meanwhile the Chichester alderman led by the indefatigable Henry Chitty were busy. Their plans to improve the fortifications of the city were given full backing by a Commons order of 2 November. Chitty had obtained seven pieces of ordnance from the governor of Portsmouth; ten barrels of powder were also to be despatched from there to Chichester.[27]

The advance of the royalist army towards London after Edgehill brought a surge of optimism to those manor houses of west Sussex where men sympathetic to Charles I had held their hand through the summer. It seemed the chance had at last come to secure the south-east for the King, or at least to seize a base in Sussex for a spring campaign. Edward Ford, the heir to the grand estate of Uppark on the Hampshire border, hastened to the court at Reading, where on 7 November he obtained a commission of array for Sussex.[28] Shortly afterwards he was pricked as the new sheriff of the county. Ford made his plans to take control of Sussex as the King advanced to Brentford. The proximity of the royal forces gave him confidence: 'They had great assurance given them', it was reported in one newsbook, 'that the King would come into those parts with his army'.[29] But Ford appreciated the hesitancy of his countrymen. His plot to seize Chichester, which was hatched in conjunction with a group of magnates and gentry resident in the city and its neighbourhood, was shrewd tactics. There was to be no declaration for the King until the city was in their hands. Instead Ford hoped, by exploiting rumours of an intended invasion by Prince Rupert, to call forth the trained bands on the basis of the defence of the capital of the western rapes. It is hard to assess the size of the clique implicated in Ford's plan. When sequestration stared men in the face the next year, gentlemen hastened to dissociate themselves from all knowledge of it, pleading that they had misunderstood the sheriff's purpose.[30] Among the rural magnates, Christopher Lewkenor was almost certainly involved; *The Kingdomes Weekly Intelligencer* referred to him as 'the fomenter of the distractions' in Sussex.[31] So were George and Thomas Gunter, who had also shown their colours at Portsmouth, Nicholas Wolfe, who accepted the captaincy of the trained band for Chichester rape when the roundhead George Oglander was deprived of it, and Thomas Leeds, who took charge for the King of the horse of Arundel rape. Within the city the key man was Sir John Morley.[32]

The planning of Edward Ford and Sir John Morley was carefully coordinated. The sheriff issued his warrant to Arundel rape to come in to the town of Arundel on 14 November.[33] The following day the gentry in Chichester put into practice a premeditated coup. Edward Higgins, William Cawley and Henry Chitty later related to Speaker Lenthall how that day

> wee called all the inhabitants of the citty of Chichester togeather there to lett them understand wherefore we had fortified the citty which was to defend ourselves from beinge plundered by the King's army and to know yf they would all joyne with us to secure one another from beinge distroid by them, there was a generall consent in yt not one contradicting but with severall vowes and protestations resolved to live and die in yt uppon which agreement wee went out of the Towne Hall where the meeting was. When wee came into the streete wee perceived some swords drawne at the north gate of the cittie (where one of the gunns wee had from Portsmouth was placed) which swords were drawne against the gunnes . . .

While most of the substantial citizens were debating in the Town Hall, the gentry party, led by Sir John Morley, had provoked a section of the poorer inhabitants to possess themselves of the guns on the walls and at the gates. Having raised the mob, Morley then used the need to 'allay the fury of the comon people' as an excuse to insist that twenty gentlemen should watch that night. The conditions of an uneasy truce were that twenty citizens under Edward Higgins should watch beside the gentry under Morley 'and that the keyes of the citty should be delivered to the maior'. But when the evening came Morley, with around thirty gentlemen and fifty 'of the meaner sorte of people' at his back, overawed Higgins and gained the city's keys into his own hands, which, he declared, 'should be kept for the Kinge'.[34] Thus at last the merchants and the gentry were face to face. The gentry acted with the assurance of support from members of the clerical community in the Close, such as the newly consecrated Bishop Henry King's brother Robert and son John. Factionalism had been transformed into a conflict between cavaliers and roundheads.

Edward Ford's arrival before Chichester with a hundred horse and several hundred men on the morning of 16 November was exactly timed. 'In regard the forces which he brought were countreymen, the city did not suspect any treachery and let them into the town', reported *A Perfect Diurnal*. Morley had hinted at his true intentions the night before; the next morning, as the trained bands swarmed through the gates, the full truth came out. Some of the royalist gentry 'drew their swords, crying, For God and the King, and so shut up the gates and seized the ordnance'. With 'pistolls against his brest', the mayor was forced to read the King's proclamation of pardon to the county at the market cross.[35] Ford's deception had secured Chichester for the King. Many of the gentry who had responded to his warrants by sending horsemen did so in good faith that he was acting for the county, not for King or parliament. Some of them, like George Churcher and Sir John Chapman, were parliamentarians at heart. How could he be justly questioned for his action, Chapman replied when it was alleged against him later, seeing it was in the name of the sheriff and 'on pain of death'? Calling out the *posse commitatus* was a time-honoured emergency procedure: it was his authority as sheriff rather than as a commissioner of array that Ford stressed and that men respected.[36]

Chitty, Cawley and Higgins fled to Portsmouth on 16 November. In their haste they left their homes without money; Higgins had 'noe goods or clothes at all with him'. In their letters to John Pym and Speaker Lenthall they emphasised the violence of the royalists in Chichester and their need for help, 'otherwise the country will be ruined'.[37] They were bitter about the way the eastern gentry had neglected them. The seizure of Chichester certainly startled the east of the county and parliament, but a week or two revealed the narrow social and geographical basis of Edward Ford's support. His warrants had brought in many frightened countrymen. A lieutenant sent to negotiate from Portsmouth, whose garrison lacked the resources to besiege the city, reported 'there were eight hundred or a thousand soldiers' there, yet the sheriff failed to breathe life or energy into a popular royalist cause. 'The countrymen', Speaker Lenthall was informed, 'express they have no hearts to the service, but they are kept in with hopes that there will forces come from the Kinge and yt is given out the citty shal be made a garrison'. Gentry support for Ford was largely confined to the city of Chichester and to scattered manor houses in the immediate vicinity. Sir Garrett Kempe, for instance, encouraged the two servants he had sent, horsed and 'armed with pistolls and swords', to come and go freely between Slindon and Chichester. This kind of open association with the sheriff after he had revealed his royalist purposes was exceptional among gentry from beyond Chichester rape. Further west Thomas Leeds was probably one of the few men he could wholly rely on. Neutral gentry who had sent servants allowed them to stay with Ford only because they were afraid of being plundered. The fate of Sir John Chapman was an object lesson. When his man, riding back from an expedition to Steyning, told him that some of the company had broken in and taken boots and shoes from the shoemakers' shops and hats from the haberdashers', he stoutly declared that, 'if this bee the doings', his servant should desert Ford's army. In reprisal Ford sent a raiding party to seize all the horses in his stable.[38]

In the face of Ford's coup the east faltered. 'The country is willing to joyn with other auxiliary forces, but they want a head to lead them', it was reported on 26 November. At Lewes there was hectic activity to defend the town led by Ambrose Traiton, a gentleman of some standing in Lewes itself but of little account in magnate society. The rural gentry did not offer him support. The 2 December issue of *England's Memorable Accidents* carried gloomy news from Sussex: Herbert Morley 'had bin long expected' from London, Anthony Stapley 'stirs not at all', there was a 'want of men whereupon many there fall off from the parliament and are providing upon any termes to make their peace with the King'. Traiton, it seems, had lost his nerve when he saw a copy of the King's proclamation.[39] Things were probably never quite as bad as this newsbook made out, since on 1 December Morley was able to inform the Commons that at least two trained band captains, Herbert Springate and Edward Apsley, were raising forces to oppose the royalists.[40]

Yet Ford undoubtedly missed an opportunity to catch the eastern rapes unawares. When he did invade in early December, with the intention of making a base at the Earl of Thanet's house in Lewes, he was too late. A skirmish near Haywards Heath showed that the west Sussex levies had no heart to fight their countrymen. Morley's forces reached Sussex just in time to help repel the royalists before Lewes, 'well provided for with ordnance and ammunition', came under attack. Ford himself, according to one report, 'conveyed himself away and left his men in the lurch to shift for themselves'.[41] Once across the Adur, Ford was in territory where his name counted for little and no party existed in his favour. His agent in the east, Limming Dickenson, made no useful royalist contacts except a single minor gentleman Robert Heath of Piddinghoe. Dickenson's 'assiduall labouring and officious intelligence' to assist the commissioners of array appears to have consisted largely of jeering at those who contributed to the Propositions money in his own village of Beddingham and picking quarrels with any who showed sympathy for the parliamentary cause. His reputed ambition was 'if all the parliament men's hearts were reduced in one and he had the same in his custodie or power, that then he would cutt or shredd the same as small as herbes to the pott'. This vociferous royalist spy rode busily to and fro between the Ouse valley and Chichester but achieved nothing.[42]

Once the forces of Sir William Waller and Colonel Morley had converged on Chichester on 20 December the royalists had little chance of holding out for more than a few days. Over Christmas the parliamentary journalists entertained the capital with derisive accounts of their plight: 'the papists and malignants there are now all at their witts end . . . they have now no way to escape unlesse they leap into the sea, which would prove but a mad Christmasse gambole'.[43] The derision of the Sussex cavaliers was well deserved. It was absurd to choose Chichester, a city open to attack from all sides defended only by a low wall, as a winter stronghold in preference to Arundel, which could have been made more impregnable. In fact it was left in such a feeble state of defence that 100 of Waller's men took it without difficulty. Waller's siege of Chichester was well organised and methodical. On the second day he beat a hole through one of the gates and was shooting into the town. Once he had gained control of the suburb of St Pancras and its church, 'from whence we galled the enemy extreamely, so that they durst hardly any of them appeare upon the wall', the royalists recognised they could not survive for long. Their surrender after seven days forestalled plans to 'batter downe' the East Gate, fire the West Gate and petard a back gate in the Deanery garden, measures which would almost certainly have enabled the parliamentarians to swarm into the city.[44] 'The constant duty', recorded Clarendon, 'was performed by the officers and gentlemen of quality, who were absolutely tired out'.[45] Above all the brevity of the siege was due to the divisions within the city. The political and Puritan traditions of the merchant oligarchy ran counter to the whole course of Edward Ford's campaign to establish it as a royalist base. The citizens regarded his coup as a betrayal; it confirmed in their minds an identification of royalism with gentry as well as clerical intrusion. On 28 December Waller despatched Ford, Sir John Morley, Christopher Lewkenor and other royalist prisoners to London. Meanwhile parliamentarian troops pillaged the cathedral and its library.[46] Early in 1643 Anthony Stapley was appointed governor of Chichester. The initial struggle for the county was over.

The Arundel campaign

Charles I's proclamation of pardon to Sussex of 7 November 1642 excepted two men: Henry Chitty and Herbert Morley.[47] Chitty, we have seen, was an irascible merchant with a long public career behind him who had probably done much to stiffen his Chichester friends against the crown. Herbert Morley, by contrast, was a young man of twenty-six who until he won a burgess-ship at Lewes in 1640 was hardly known outside the vicinity of his home. His family, who had been Tudor ironmasters as well as landowners, was well connected in east Sussex; his grandfather, the builder of the imposing Glynde Place, had served as MP, sheriff and JP; his father Robert Morley had sat in parliament on three occasions and had been an energetic justice. The Morleys showed the strict Calvinist Puritanism of their kin such as the Pelhams, Stapleys and Boards.[48] Robert Morley had spoken in his will of October 1631 of God receiving his soul 'into that endles glorie prepared for his elect'.[49] Thus Herbert Morley was well qualified to lead the parliamentarian movement in Sussex. From the first his commitment to the cause was wholehearted. Morley had the militancy and zeal of youth: he was nineteen years younger than Sir Thomas Pelham, exactly half the age of Anthony Stapley. Francis Cheynell noted his 'nimble apprehension and vigilant spirit'.[50] He saw the struggle in uncompromising terms. Obsessive fear and hatred of popery was an important element in his motivation, as his misinterpretation of Gerarde de la Valle's picture of the betrothal of St Ursula shows. The picture, intended for a church in Seville, was in the *St James* which was driven ashore at Heene in 1644. Morley took the principal figures of Ursula, her fiancé Conanus and a bishop, to be Henrietta Maria, Charles I and the Pope. The deep political significance he saw in the picture was entirely the product of his own fervent imagination. Explaining his horror at its 'gross idolatory', he wrote to Speaker Lenthall:

> On the Pope's right hand stands the Queen accompanied with her ladies, the King tenders his sceptre to the Queen, she accepts it not, but directs it to be delivered to the Pope. . . . I look upon this picture as an hieroglyphic of the causes and intents of our present troubles, and the opinion of neighbouring nations concerning them and if the House please to command the picture to London and there permit it to the public view, I conceave it would very much convince the malignants and open the eyes of all that are not wilfully blind.[51]

Herbert Morley was in many respects typical of the men who emerged as the county bosses of the 1640s. Sir John Gell in Derbyshire, Sir William Brereton in Cheshire, John Pyne in Somerset were others in the same mould.[52] 'Spent at Battle when Colonel Morley sent for me': an entry in John Everenden's account book summarises his authority.[53] Morley increasingly dominated county patronage.[54] During 1643 he had under his command four score horse and 100 dragoons; the only other standing force was a regiment of foot under Anthony Stapley.[55] Morley saw his military role in a wide context. His grasp of the importance of regional strategy made him the driving force behind the informal associated brigade for the protection of Hampshire, Surrey and Sussex, which was formed during 1643, before there was a sufficient sense of urgency to shake the south-eastern counties into forming a fully-fledged association.[56] The abortive resolution of the Commons on 18 July in favour of a South-Eastern Association probably reflected his pressure. So in all likelihood did the appeal of the Sussex Committee in August to Speaker Lenthall for an association between London and the south-eastern counties.[57] Herbert Morley regarded vigorous mutual cooperation between Sussex and adjacent counties as a necessity, for their own interests besides the crucial protection of the capital. During 1643 his troops were always on the move, as he boldly set an example to other commanders like Sir Michael Livesey of Kent who remained stubbornly insular in their approach to the war.[58] In June his adventurous spirit brought him into conflict with the Earl of Essex, when a detachment of his regiment, venturing beyond the Thames valley, fell prey to one of Prince Rupert's sorties. Captain Gratwick, John Coulton explained to Samuel Jeake on 29 June, 'posted to his Excellency for help to redeeme his twelve men butt was denyed which made the Colonell lay downe his armes . . . resolveing never to beare armes more in this cause'.[59]

Everywhere he went Herbert Morley was tireless in his zeal and vehement in his hatred of those who opposed or hindered the parliamentary cause. Summoned to attend Morley at Lewes and finding him gone to Arundel, Thomas Sharpe, who had declined to respond to the Propositions in 1642, sought the advice of two of the Colonel's friends. Herbert Hay suggested that, with Morley's return uncertain, it was reasonable for him to return home; James Temple promised to make Sharpe's peace for him. But Morley was furious that Sharpe had gone home and sent Captain Cockram after him with a troop who rifled his house, illtreated his maidservants and carried Sharpe himself off to Rye 'as if I had been the vilest catiff alive'.[60] Morley quickly acquired a reputation for his implacable pursuit of malignants and his readiness to wink at disorderly behaviour by his troopers. The descent of the 'crooked rebel of Sussex' on Hastings in July 1643 was described by *Mercurius Rusticus*:

> The Colonell being entered the town, scattered the body of his horse into severall parts, to intercept all passages out of the town, and having secured the ports, he summons the mayor and jurats and demands the arms of the town, to which he found ready obedience.

Morley left Hastings with a wagon furnished him by one of the fearful jurats.[61]

Activists of Morley's stamp saw the civil war in terms of black and white. Informing Speaker Lenthall that he had confiscated the barque of the Brighton man who had transported the Earl of Thanet into France in April 1643, he remarked that he thought it 'noe smale crime to transport those that have made war against the parliament without your warrant'. The following month he requested parliament's authority to inflict 'corporall punishment by martiall law' on the ringleader of a riot at West Hoathly fair, when 'some of the country in a tumultuous manner' set upon the recruiting officer, 'his serjeant and drummer, wounded them all, beat out the head of the drum'. In May 1643 he was also active in promoting severe measures of retaliation on royalist prisoners in consequence of parliamentarians being illtreated at Oxford; in July he urged the Lords to be more diligent over the impeachment of the Queen.[62]

There were limits to what Morley could achieve through his own zeal and the number of other gentry as fully engaged as he was in the drive to maintain a tight parliamentarian grip on Sussex during 1643 remained small. The Committee did what they could to drive forward assessments and sequestrations.[63] Nevertheless lack of money was a real anxiety, particularly in the west. When the Commons forbade him to seize the rents or estate of the delinquent Sir William Morley in November 1643, Anthony Stapley protested to Speaker Lenthall. Excusing his 'playne dealing', he wrote bitterly: 'You will I hope give me leave to provide for myselfe and men as I can, and to quitt the employment, when I cannot longer serve you in it'.[64] Nor did the state of the trained bands give cause for confidence. The Earl of Northumberland wrote of their inadequacies to the deputies in February 1644. They had failed, it seems, to keep them up to their prewar strength during 1643, when the keenest soldiers joined Morley's and Stapley's regiments.[65] Yet they had done their best to keep the militia up to scratch. In Hastings rape at least four musters were held during the summer; at one of them Captain John Everenden sought to put heart into the business by providing a barrel of beer.[66] Such measures were necessary. The sullen reaction of the West Hoathly neighbourhood to Morley's recruiting drive in May was discouraging. Furthermore the undercurrent of disaffection revealed by the Bench's interrogation of two East Grinstead men at the Michaelmas sessions was alarming. A West Hoathly yeoman had told them of his belief that 'none but rogues or rascalls would goe or serve under the comaund of the Earl of Essex'.[67]

It is not surprising that the Committee remained nervous about a royalist invasion throughout 1643. Study of the appeal for support by Edward Ford found in the hands of one of his agents in February 1643, they told Speaker Lenthall, 'and many other pregnant circumstances', made the parliamentarian caucus 'very sensible of our more then approaching danger'. The sheriff's statement, hinting that assistance would soon be forthcoming from the Oxonian royalists, was well calculated to touch waverers' hearts.[68] In September, Morley's patrol of the Hampshire border failed to prevent the conjunction of several royalist troops in the

Winchester area. 'You may now see', he declared to Lenthall, 'how necessary it was for the associated brigade to stay in these parts, without which or some considerable force instead of it these southerne counties wil be all lost, then London cannot but be in danger'. The next month the cavaliers captured twenty of the Earl of Northumberland's best horses in a raid on Petworth. Lady Northumberland decided to spend the winter in London where, she wrote to her husband on 4 November, 'I should be happy to meett you and peace'.[69]

The royalist invasion of Sussex in December 1643 was a bold attempt, dangerously late in the year, to pursue the King's strategy for an advance on London from the south-east. Sir Edward Ford, knighted at Oxford on 4 October, again took the initiative. It was he who importuned Sir Ralph Hopton to support the plan to take Arundel Castle and to make it a winter headquarters for a spring movement into Kent. The plan was foolhardy.

> It was a general misfortune and miscomputation of that time (commented Clarendon) that the party in all places which wished well to the King . . . had so good an opinion of their own reputation and interest that they believed they were able, upon the assistance of a few troops, to suppress their neighbours who were of the other party.

It was one thing for raiding parties to reach Sir John Caryll's house at Harting or Northumberland's park at Petworth; it was quite another to hold so distant an outpost as Arundel through the long winter months.[70] Initially west Sussex was again taken by surprise. A hard frost enabled Hopton, Ford, and their forces to make a swift march across the Downs. Harting, Stansted and Petworth were garrisoned, Arundel town and castle quickly fell. On 9 December, the day after John Pym died, the royalist campaign in Sussex appeared triumphant.[71] The weakness of the parliamentarian control of the western rapes had been revealed. This was still a neutralist, even an incipiently royalist, countryside. The loyalty of JPs and committeemen was uncertain. Thomas Middleton, an MP and committeeman who had already clashed with the activists on several occasions, did his utmost to discourage resistance to the December invasion.[72] No resistance was offered by the native gentry because there was still no substantial group of gentry in the west prepared to act openly for parliament. Since Colonel Edward Apsley's troop from Bramber rape, the only reliable one in the west, had been put into Cowdray House to check the royalists, Hopton had simply bypassed Midhurst.[73]

For the eastern gentry the river Adur became a frontier. Weeks before Hopton invaded, when Colonel Morley was sending alarming reports of cavalier activity in Hampshire, they had begun to defend it. At the end of October John Everenden spent ten days with his whole company at Lewes and Shoreham.[74] Within forty-eight hours of the arrival of the royalists at Arundel, the eastern levies had begun to converge on Bramber, where the castle guarded the main river crossing, and on Shoreham. When Colonel

Apsley reached the Adur on 8 December, after attempting to rally support at Horsham, he found several militia captains, such as Simon Everenden and John Fuller, already there. Herbert Morley at first pinned his hopes on regaining Arundel without help from outside the county but skirmishing on the Downs above Parham, where he quartered about 400 men on 9 December, and intelligence brought by spies, convinced him that the only sound tactics were to hold the Adur. Moultbridge above Bramber was destroyed: inland from it were the deep and miry wealden ways which would become clogged as soon as the winter weather broke.[75] A fierce engagement at Bramber on 12 December, which thwarted the royalist march for Lewes, showed that Morley's tactics were right. Captain James Temple led the defence of the bridge at Bramber, which was protected by earthworks quickly completed by the pioneers. Francis Cheynell recorded that his bravery was 'the wonder of all the countrie', but 'I did not marvel at it for he is man that hath his head full of strategies, his heart full of piety and valour and his hand as full of success as it is of dexterity'. John Coulton told the story in apocalyptic language to his friend Samuel Jeake:

> The enemy attempted Bramber bridge butt our brave Carleton and Everenden with his dragoones and our Collonel's horse welcomed them with drakes and musketts, sending some eight or nine men to hell (I fear), and one trooper to Arundel Castle prisoner and one of Captain Everenden's dragoons to heaven.

Yet the country behind the Adur remained at the mercy of the royalists. Wiston House was seized and raiding parties for food and forage penetrated northwards towards Horsham.[76] Only outside intervention could resolve the renewed struggle for the county.

The dormant South-Eastern Association ordinance was hurriedly resuscitated and promulgated in November 1643.[77] Alton fell to Sir William Waller on 13 December; a week later he was in Arundel; the royalists surrendered the castle after a seventeen-day siege on 6 January. Waller gathered overwhelming forces at Arundel, some 10,000 men in all. Kentish regiments under Sir Michael Livesey and Sir William Springate, Hampshire and Surrey forces, twelve troops from the Earl of Essex, even some of the city of London trained bands: all joined the Sussex militia, which by Christmas was mustered in and around the town.[78] Herbert Morley was temporarily overshadowed; the glory went to Waller. 'It is worth noteing', John Coulton wrote to Samuel Jeake on 8 January 1644, 'to se how our easterne gentry comes to comfort our power Collonell: and to shew theire thankfulness to noble Waller'. Lewes gave him fifty pounds in gratitude. Coulton described the campaign in a mood of religious exaltation: 'Bleeding harts cheere up', he wrote to his friends at Rye, 'your God will worke for you and fight both for you and us'. He hoped parliament would 'provide gallows for Ford and Bishop'.[79] In fact Ford, who Hopton left as governor of the castle, might have held out considerably longer if he had taken proper precautions against a massive siege. When Waller arrived, Clarendon recorded, he found the garrison 'as unprovided as he could wish'. 'Instead of increasing their magazine of victual by supplies from the country, they had spent much of that store which the Lord Hopton had provided for'.[80] By 22 December the soldiers were rationed to half a pound of bread a day. An ox fell into the best well, making it unfit for drinking; then by draining some pounds beyond the walls Waller emptied the castle wells altogether. 'They were driven into that necessity for want of salt that they made use of powder instead of it', reported the *Weekly Account*. The royalists were forced to release oxen and horses for want of fodder; each soldier, the story went, 'had two spoonefulls of soden wheat a day'; they began to parley, it was reported, 'extremely pinched with famine'.[81]

'We have fortified Arundell as strong as ever you saw a thing', reported John Coulton in January 1644. Nevertheless the Sussex parliamentarians were unnerved by Hopton's campaign. They panicked easily and continued to feel vulnerable for the duration of the war. When the King's forces were at Newbury in October 1644, the Committee for Arundel rape, who had made their headquarters in the Castle, asked to be allowed to demolish the strong houses of the west as a precaution against a repetition of 1642 and 1643.[82] In December of the same year, George Goring, armed with a new commission as Lieutenant-General for Hampshire, Sussex, Surrey and Kent, made a lightning advance along the coast, reaching Hampshire early in the new year. The Committee of Both Kingdoms responded to Sussex's alarm by directing Morley and Stapley to call the trained bands into Chichester and Arundel. But it soon became obvious that Goring had overstretched himself and he fell back on Salisbury. Like Ford before him, Goring was over confident about the 'many well affected persons' who would rise in his own county.[83] The expedition proved a naïve escapade. The Committee remained apprehensive, particularly about the vulnerability of Cowdray, into 1646, but by 1644 the war was in fact won within the borders of Sussex.[84]

The aftermath of war

The realities of the civil war for the ordinary soldier were not principles or politics but cold and hunger. 'Wee endured a long and tedious seige', reported one of them who was at Arundel over Christmas 1643, 'the weather was cold, the nights long, and the season of the yeare troubled us who lay in the field extreamly with high windes and extraordinary showres of raine.' John Coulton described a scouting expedition in pursuit of Sir Ralph Hopton across the Downs to Petersfield with 'no meat but a peece of bread and cheese'.[85] Only the chief officers ate well: fowls, eggs, veal, pork and mutton were on their tables, supplied by the country tradesmen who made handsome deals with Sir William Waller's commissariat.[86]

Injuries sustained in the haphazard warfare of the seventeenth century were not invariably the work of the enemy. The sergeant of the Rye company shot off his own thumb with a carbine on Christmas Day 1643.[87] Herbert Morley showed responsibility and compassion towards those who were wounded. He ensured that a surgeon and his staff were attached to his regiment on campaign; he bought a new surgeon's chest, for which he was later reimbursed, for use at the siege of Basing House; he supported the petitions of incapacitated soldiers to the Bench. 'He hath much suffered by want already and if not now relieved like totally to perish, you charity to him will much oblige', he wrote to his colleagues on one occasion. Most of those assisted from the maimed soldiers fund had served outside the county in engagements at such places as Donnington, Portland and Basing.[88]

The civilian inhabitants of west Sussex suffered much more from the war than their eastern countrymen. On eastern estates such as Herstmonceux and Halland the pattern of rural life was hardly affected. The Dacre household went through its accustomed routines: the moat was mown, the cattle were killed and dressed, new chamber pots were purchased and new coal baskets for the kitchen, the mercer of Boreham provided a new suit for the footboy, the tinker still called and mended the warming pans, rabbits, eggs and fish were in as plentiful supply as ever at the Eastbourne market, there were cherries on the parlour table in July 1645 brought from Maidstone. The Pelham accounts tell the same story. Everything was much as usual, except that taxes had sharply increased and the Cambridge carrier did not bring down John Pelham's bed after he had left the university in 1642 until 1645. Even John Everenden, a busy committeeman and militia captain, was largely preoccupied with his farming tasks.[89] If the eastern community suffered directly at all it was through the war at sea. 'I pray sir be ernest with the Committee about the safetie of the Cinque Portes', wrote the mayor of Rye to Herbert Morley in desperation after one of the King's men-of-war had ransacked the Dieppe passage boat in the summer of 1644. He requested that a parliamentarian man-of-war should lie between Rye and Dieppe, otherwise the cross Channel vessels 'dare not adventure out'. The following winter Rye had five barques, 'some of them richlie laden with goods', taken by royalist privateers. Other ports along the coast experienced similar losses.[9]

For those unfortunate enough to find themselves in the midst of the campaigns at Chichester and Arundel the war brought severe personal hardship through the destruction of property. Some of them owed 'great sumes of money, and are not able to pay them', others were 'broughte very low', declared the merchants of Arundel to the Committee at Billingshurst in 1645:

> Humblie sheweth: that which your eyes have heretofore seene, and your eares heard, the sad and distressed estate of us, the poore, plundered

> robed, and spoyled inhabitants of the said burrough, whoe were driven by the King's forces from house and habitation, to secure our lives, and, in our absence, robed and spoyled of all outward comforts to mayntayne a livelyhood; some of our houses being burnte, and others made stables of, and some pulled downe, and all our goods imbeasled, and taken away, to our great impoverishing.

The total losses of thirty-eight individuals were alleged to amount to £3,772.[91] The destruction of the Chichester suburb of St Pancras in the siege of 1642 exacerbated the poverty of a community that was already a problem to the county authorities. The losses of some Chichester gentry were also substantial. Richard Williams, for instance, reckoned that the 1642 campaign cost him £350: he had a house outside the West Gate burnt and a barnful of peas and oats and seven horses taken; he was also compelled to billet soldiers for seven weeks.[92]

Most of the inhabitants of west Sussex were sullen and apathetic about the war. In frustration at their obstructionism, Sir William Waller issued a warrant against neutrality in April 1644, which bitterly attacked the negative and defensive mentality of the county. 'We shall take them for no other then enemies to the State, and men accordingly to be proceeded against', he declared of the neutrals, intending 'that all may know how detestable such persons are' that did 'not shew themselves forward for the maintenance of the common cause, tending to the advancement of God's glory, the parliament's service and the kingdomes good'.[93] The impressment, free quarter and high taxation enforced by the committeemen had a cumulative impact. Examples of the abuses of Committee rule came to the notice of the Earl of Northumberland, who in August 1645 forwarded some warrants which he thought 'very strange' to the leading magnates on the Grand Committee. He questioned the authority of the Chichester Committee to 'issue out any such warrants' and to delegate power to one Stonham 'who goes by the name of Mr Channell's provost marshall and one Anthony Smith a fidler being now in great imployment at Petworth'. These were men, he declared, 'of soe base a condicon as renders them unworthy of such trusts'. He feared that by their 'unnecessary oppressions and insolent behaviour' they might 'make the people desperate that by plundering and sequestring these fellows may raise some benefitt to themselves'. On another occasion the Grand Committee decided to overturn an order of the Committee at Billingshurst for searching the homes of papists and malignants and confiscating their arms. 'It was more power then any Committee ought to have or then the parliament could give', declared Thomas Middleton, who made vigorous use of his prestige in magnate circles to hinder the harshest proceedings of his colleagues on the Committee at Horsham.[94] Enforcement of parliamentary ordinances was often high-handed, resentment built up, the local Committee became the focus of all discontents. In the end the community revolted. When it did so the traditional rulers of the county who controlled the Grand Committee were the focus for its complaints.

By 1645 disillusionment with parliamentarian government was widespread, but the form in which it was expressed varied from county to county. In Lincolnshire, for instance, Colonel Edward King became the spokesman for a popular movement at quarter sessions. The principal outlet for discontent in the southern counties was the clubmen movement.[95] The Sussex rising came at the end of a series of demonstrations in Somerset, Dorset and Wiltshire. It began with a meeting on Duncton Down on 17 September 1645 and was crushed only four days later: the governor of Arundel, Herbert Morley's militant brother William, sent out a party of ten horsemen and forty footmen who dispersed the clubmen encampment at Walberton and thus prevented a major rendezvous at Bury Hill. As a challenge to committee government the outbreak was insignificant. Those who assembled were described by a gentry witness as a 'vulgar multitude ignorant of manners'. There were only a handful of minor gentry and yeomen ringleaders, one of whom was the son of the Chichester royalist Francis Shallott.[96] Yet there was general sympathy at all levels of west Sussex society with the grievances that motivated the clubmen. The petition to the Grand Committee at Lewes, which some western gentry formulated after the abortive rising, spoke for Chichester and Arundel rapes, the district which the clubmen had sought to unite. Bramber rape was on the fringe of the movement. This petition was presented in the name of 'the not ingaged as well as the ingaged party' in the rising and it apologised for the countrymen's late assembly. Gentry would have no truck with clubs, staves and disorganised downland meetings. Instead they appealed directly to the magnates who, they noted, 'have bin pleased to propose an orderly way to heare and have engaged themselves to endeavour to redresse the insupportable agrievances and oppressions amongst us'.[97]

Resistance to the harshness of committee rule smouldered on in many counties through 1646, 1647 and 1648. A run of disastrous harvests increased discontent in many parts of the provinces.[98] Against this background the full extent of the intense localism of the Sussex community became apparent. The decision of the Committee at Horsham to move the town's magazine to Arundel, in the midst of the south-eastern revolts of 1648, indicates the ability of the radical committeemen to grasp the regional implications of the crisis of that summer. They feared that the magazine might 'be in danger of surprisall by a malignant party'.[99] The townsmen saw the matter very differently. They mounted an armed demonstration, which lasted for almost a month before Sir Michael Livesey swept down on Horsham with his Kentish regiment.[100] Arundel was only seventeen miles away, its garrison was crucial to the security of the whole coastal district, yet the men of Horsham regarded county defence as someone else's responsibility. 'Our countreymen rose with one consent and two or three hundred appeared in an instant, leaving their mattocks and plowes to rescue the swords and musquets', related a Horsham correspondent. From 9 to 28 June watches were set every night on the arms in the market loft. The sequel shows how the Committee's new policy was the spark that set alight the latent discontent of several years standing over the arbitrary government of a narrow and isolated political clique:

> At a full assembly in the market place it was voted unseasonable, unreasonable to watch them any longer, and resolved upon the question, that the day following, being Wednesday, at the sound of drum and ringing of bells those men both in towne and countrey who are resolved to fight for the King and the liberties of the county against the encroachments of one Freeman and his followers should come in and take what they pleased.[101]

During the first week of July, the Horsham commotion took on a wider dimension. It looked as if the worst fears of the Committee at Lewes might be realised. On 29 June Sir Thomas Pelham, Herbert Morley and other principal magnates had warned Speaker Lenthall of the danger of a county wide rising. 'Wee feare we shall be imbroyled in blood in this county', wrote a Steyning correspondent, reporting the massing of support for the Horsham demonstrators around Pulborough and towards the Hampshire border. Some of the trained bands were implicated and there were rumoured to be 600 armed men training at Horsham, yet, the letter-writer confessed, they were 'most countreymen, none of any great quality assists them'. The clubmen protest in fact had been revived in a new form. There was talk of seizing Arundel or Chichester. The Steyning correspondent described how a geographical polarisation had begun with the Adur once more as a frontier and Bramber as a stronghold:

> They intend to make good all on that side the water, we understand that those at Horsham are speedily to joyn with them, if not prevented, and so to keepe together in a body . . . this is a very malignant county and they will soone be a strong party . . . the well affected gather together about Lewes.[102]

The rising that Livesey's regiment nipped in the bud was tinged with royalism. The Horsham men threatened to 'ryse as one man against all such as have not ioyned with them' in the semi-royalist Sussex petition of June 1648. But essentially the whole affair was a protest against the policies of the County Committee. William Freeman, Richard Yates and Nicholas Shepard, the activists on the Committee at Horsham who fled to Lewes in the company of the Puritan minister of the town John Chatfield, were the scapegoats. The demonstrators even dared to defy a warrant for removal of the magazine signed by both Herbert Morley and Anthony

Stapley, who assured them that they acted under the directions of the Earl of Northumberland.[103] Committee rule had alienated county opinion and generated a distrustful parochialism. Even the magnates on the Grand Committee were tarnished by the actions and carriage of their colleagues. *The Moderate* summarised the situation:

> A right understanding between the soldiers and the countreymen would have prevented this turmult . . . the countrey were loath to part with that which they say was bought by the county, and if the soldiers want ammunition, let the parliament supply them.[104]

The western rapes suffered the tramp of armies and in 1642 and 1643 became one of the seats of the war; they bore the burden of the quartering of troops and the provisioning of garrisons on top of an unprecedented level of taxation. In districts where these conditions prevailed the parliamentarian administrators were bound to face resentment and obstruction.[105] The assessments were naturally most resented in the areas where men were also being called on to contribute much in kind to the cause. 'Litle or noe satisfaction' had been given, the Grand Committee were reminded in 1645, for the 'great store of provisions of all sorts' sent into the county's garrisons. Earlier the same year the Committee of Both Kingdoms had considered the petition of Rotherbridge hundred against the exactions of Sir William Waller's commissaries.[106] In 1644 Pulborough twice refused to raise its assessment contribution. On one occasion the inhabitants 'stood upon their guard and would not admit of his entrance', when Colonel Morley arrived with a troop of horse. He lost one of his men in forcing his way into the village to disarm them.[107] In the autumn of 1645 the clubmen of Chichester rape brought taxation there to a temporary halt. William Cawley reported on 13 October that he and his colleagues had only managed to raise £100 of the assessment for more than £4,000 then on foot, 'it being one of their articles to pay such taxes only as they please'. The Horsham townsmen refused to pay taxes in 1648.[108] The 1645 petitioners complained about abuses of the sequestration procedure to grasp money from men's purses, the excise and inequitable rating for the weekly assessments. They pleaded for 'noe more sett upon us then we are able to beare'. The 1648 petitioners boldly demanded freedom from all taxes and impositions.[109]

Free quarter, like the provisioning of garrisons, was one of the exacting yet unpredictable ways by which a subject countryside was made to carry the cost of the civil war.[110] For three years, expostulated the 1645 petitioners, their daily labour had not brought them the 'fruite of the earth', since 'by free quarter and plunder of soldiers our purses have bin exhausted, corne eaten up, cattell plundred'. So great had been the soldiers' demands, they insisted, that they could not pay their rents or maintain their families. They pointed out the lack of any procedure for complaint or relief.[111] Anthony Stapley had been more responsive to these grievances during the war than the western gentry allowed in the misery of its aftermath. After the Arundel campaign he had refused to let Waller quarter any men in Chichester where he was governor. He had also engaged in an acrimonious correspondence with the Earl of Essex and the Commons, seeking to have Waller's troops removed from the county altogether. In 1645 he succeeded in having the horse quartered on the Hampshire border moved over it.[112] Despite these measures many villages in Chichester, Arundel and Bramber rapes were for longer or shorter periods at the mercy of the soldiers, who were usually alien to the neighbourhood in which they lodged. Mutual fear easily brought a vicious circle of recrimination, violence and plunder.[113] The 1645 petitioners alleged that they had sometimes been frightened from their homes and put in fear of their lives. The inhabitants of Nuthurst killed two soldiers in 'defence of their town' in 1644; in reprisal some of them were imprisoned in Arundel Castle. This incident must have contributed to the tension which eventually exploded in the 1648 tumult at Horsham. In 1644 and 1645 the Commons considered complaints about the behaviour of soldiers in Sussex; in the latter year they were accused of rapes and other outrages.[114]

Despite Herbert Morley's campaign to awake the community to a sense of its wider responsibilities, the neutralist gentry and countrymen of west Sussex held stubbornly to a narrowly self-interested approach to impressment and defence. The 1645 petitioners pleaded for relief from impressment in proportion to other parts, which did not face the danger of invasion by sea or lie upon a county boundary. They suggested that a county association for mutual defence should be formed 'against all parties whatsoever', through which, with the assistance of the trained bands where necessary, 'the frontiers may be preserved without further charge to the county'.[115] Impressment was a constant drain on able-bodied men. Families were left unprovided for. In September 1645 the clubmen forcibly rescued some pressed men on their way to Chichester. The following month William Cawley related from Chichester how men impressed were taken away with violence, 'sending sometimes a constable or tithyingman with the blood running about his eares, soe that of sixty-seven to bee imprest in this rape were brought in but twenty-seven'.[116]

In the aftermath of the war the parliamentarian caucus of gentry were desperately afraid of civil disorder.[117] Their ready response to a petition of January 1646, from 'a considerable parte' of the county, for the dissolution of the Chichester garrison reflected their awareness of how close to the brink the civilian population had been driven. The dissolving of the Chichester garrison would release some sequestration funds for repayment of money lent towards the £200,000 for the Scots advance. Thus it was earnestly desired by the countrymen. The dissolution at Chichester would encourage them to undergo the services and payments desired of them, declared Anthony Stapley and his colleagues, since the country had 'bin much impoverished and are highly charged for the parliament's service'.[118] In fact the question of maintenance of garrisons became caught up in the wider debate in the Commons during 1646 and 1647 over disbandment, a debate in which national party issues became intertwined with vital questions about the balance of power in the localities. The decision to dissolve the Chichester garrison was finally taken in March 1647. Cowdray had been dissolved in the interim.[119] Thus the burden of providing for the county garrisons was gradually eased. Yet Arundel, with its 100 foot, remained as a thorn in the county's side and an unpleasant reminder of a decade of economic hardship. The decision in March 1647 to restore some of the ordnance brought to Arundel from Hastings and other eastern ports indicates that the Committee was beginning to think once more in terms of external instead of internal defence. But it clung to Arundel which thus became the focus of the county's discontents. The call of the neutralist and crypto-royalist gentry in their 1648 petition for a full return to the old pattern of county defences exemplifies the yearning felt in Sussex for the closing of an unhappy chapter in its history:

> That no garrisons within the said county be any longer continued and that the ordinance and ammunition taken from the sea townes may be returned for the better defence of them and the whole country from forraign invasions.[120]

Royalists, parliamentarians and neutrals

Political ideas, religious convictions, and social and familial relationship all contributed to men's decisions about which side to support in the civi war. The gentry did not split along class lines.[121] On the contrary the behaved as a collection of individuals. Loyalty to the county and their own community cut with varying degrees of force across the basic allegianc which men felt able to give to the King or parliament. Indeed there were many different degrees of royalism and parliamentarianism. Whateve their private thoughts, the desire to avoid too open a commitment was a compelling emotion for many gentry. Thus neutralism had a stron appeal.[122] The problem of what constituted allegiance is so complex and the evidence is so inadequate that it is hard to define the boundaries wher decisive commitment shaded towards neutrality. But if the record of thei actions is taken as a whole, it seems that the ninety or so leading count families, those under most pressure to take a firm stand, were divide roughly equally into royalists, parliamentarians and neutrals.

Sussex royalism was largely the product of events and circumstance in the county in 1642 and 1643. Hardly a dozen royalists by convictio showed themselves before the Chichester campaign. John Ashburnham the King's intimate friend who had joined him at York in the spring c 1642, was the first Sussex MP to be questioned by the Commons fo delinquency. Ashburnham had made plain his attachment to the King' interest. In the tense debate in the early hours of 16 December 1641, fo instance, he had acted as teller for the noes in the vote on the printing of the Grand Remonstrance.[123] Such influence as Ashburnham exercised was on western gentry with whom he had been engaged in commercial dealings. He may well have helped to pull Christopher Lewkenor and the Chichester gentleman Nicholas Monck into the royalist camp.[124] They were members of a small group of western gentry who attached themselves to the King on principle. This group, which included men like Edward Ford, Sir John Morley, George Gunter and Robert Anderson, grasped the political issues at stake.[125] Ford undertook the Chichester campaign confident that the core of a royalist party existed in west Sussex. Sir Henry Compton was the only member of the administrative caucus of east Sussex prepared to defect to the King as soon as the war began. His royalism was probably the spontaneous response of a crypto-catholic married to a Sackville with connections at court.[126]

Only a small proportion of the western gentry who took part in the Chichester campaign were more than lukewarm in their royalism. The real test came after it. About thirty men in all were prepared to leave their homes and fight for the King's cause outside the county; but several of them lost heart and came home before long. William Rishton, for instance, who had been arrested by Colonel Stapley as a 'very violent incendarie' during the Chichester campaign, admitted that he went into the King's quarters the following July until April 1644 'about which time totally dislikinge the proceedings of the army . . . returned to his house neere Chichester and ymediatly submitted to the Comittee there'. Had the eastern gentry been less fiercely vindictive after the fall of Chichester there might have been fewer royalists still. Men like Francis Shallott and the town clerk Richard Williams, whose house was occupied by Sir William Waller, fled in face of the harsh treatment they received. Gentry who had complied with Ford, however unthinkingly or reluctantly, were alienated by heavy fines.[127]

The Chichester campaign brought the internal logic of war, the pattern of repression and victimisation which Herbert Morley had already established in the east, to the west as well. The case of Sir Edward Bishop is instructive. It is not certain how fully implicated he was in Ford's plan to seize Chichester. He later insisted that he was one of the few western gentry who had no arms, horse, or foot in Chichester when it was taken. Whatever his initial royalist leanings, the course and outcome of the campaign certainly made him think again. Despite some special pleading, the gist of his later account of how he became a royalist may well be accurate. Finding himself 'between two armies and our country likely to be made the seate of warr', he decided to leave home as 'the best and saffest way for many respects'. His actions were those of a desperate neutral. He went not to Oxford, but into Kent with his pregnant wife and then to London. Yet, as soon as he heard of Bishop's return home, Herbert Morley sent a troop of horse to seize him. The soldiers interrupted a service in Parham church and, not finding Sir Edward there, broke into and searched his house. Bishop attempted to treat with Morley by letter, but he was quickly sequestered and plundered. 'Findinge noe redresse, I was constrayned through necessitie ever for present means and mayntenance to followe the wars, and confesse I was made a Collonell, thereby to gain maytenance'. Sir Edward Bishop's final commitment to the King was the only possible response to the harshness and intransigence of his opponents. In their eyes, on the other hand, Bishop had already become 'a principall instrument in formeting and nourishinge the miserable calamities and afflictions' which befell Sussex in 1642. Bishop's conduct during the Arundel campaign fulfilled the Committee's worst expectations. He became a hot-tempered and implacable cavalier. His vicious threats that he would burn Horsham scandalised the county. He had 'ever bin a malitious opposer of the proceedings of parliament and a zealous persecutor of all well affected persons', the Committee concluded in 1645.[128]

So war brought bitterness and venom to county society. Since delinquents' estates were the means allowed by parliament to maintain the garrison of Chichester, Anthony Stapley was bound to look for delinquents. Men were sequestered during 1643 on the slenderest evidence of support for Ford the previous winter. Those who had not shown themselves for the cause were often assumed by the militants to be resolutely against it. Stapley was furious when Sir William Morley, as hesitant a royalist as any of the western gentry, obtained release from sequestration at Michaelmas 1643, perhaps through the friendship of Stapley's colleague William Cawley. 'This gentleman', he told Speaker Lenthall, 'I doubt deserves not that favour you wer pleased to shewe him'.[129] The very name of Lewkenor became so closely identified with royalism, and thus with betrayal of the county, that Christopher Lewkenor's nephew John, a harmless lad of nineteen, was 'causelessly pillaged of his goods, stripped of his clothes, violated in his person and threatened with wounds and torments', when in 1643 he admitted his name to a party of soldiers. In this case the Committee expressed 'much sorrow for the accident'.[130]

Concern for the preservation of their estates may have prompted a number of magnates, who secretly sympathised deeply with the King's cause, to hold back from positive action. In a county where active royalism meant the abandonment of home and territory, the royalist cause particularly appealed to the young and adventurous who were free of landlord cares. Thomas Leeds, whose father's Wappingthorne estate was encumbered with annuities and mortgages by 1640, was an ardent royalist who was eventually killed in the King's service near Oxford.[131] Whereas both Sir William Goring of Burton and Henry Goring of Highden maintained a wary neutralism, their sons were active cavaliers. Sir John Caryll refused to join in Hopton's dash for Arundel in 1643 but his son was in the castle when it was taken. Although both William Coldham senior and junior in the end compounded for delinquency, only the son had gone into the King's quarters. John Busbridge's younger brother Robert, who with an estate worth a mere forty pounds had little property to lose, engaged in both the war and the Horsham insurrection of 1648, breaking with the Puritan and kinship ties which pulled him towards parliament. Thomas Sackville of Sedlescombe explained to the Committee for Compounding how, 'being a younger brother and a soldier of fortune', he had thrice listed at Guildhall for service in Ireland and on being left out had joined the King at York, until his brother died 'which made him consider that he had an interest in this kingdom'. He had done nothing against the state, he insisted, since his estate fell to him. Richard Rishton, who fought for the King from April 1644 until he was taken prisoner at Newbury in November, was a younger brother with no estate except an annuity of forty pounds.[132]

Predictably the eighty-one men who compounded for delinquency in the war were concentrated heavily in the western rapes. Fifteen of them lived in Chichester. In the west obedience to Ford and rumour about a man's political attitudes were enough to procure his sequestration. In the east the case was very different. The decision to make a clean break with the common viewpoint of neighbours and friends required more positive commitment. By and large the scattered eastern royalists were men already isolated, to some degree at least, from county society. Robert Foster had cut his links with the county in 1639, the Gorings of Hurstpierpoint had been remote from it even longer. Thomas Lunsford had put himself beyond the pale by his feud with Sir Thomas Pelham. Sir Nicholas Selwyn of Preston, a gentleman pensioner to the King, was as much an absentee as John Ashburnham. William Levett of Maresfield was another who had made his life and career at court rather than in the county. As a sworn servant of Charles I, who had 'performed the duty of his place' for eight years, he naturally gravitated to Oxford.[133] No resident gentleman of any prominence followed the lead given by the stalwart JP and deputy-lieutenant Sir Henry Compton, who turned his back on two decades of close cooperation with families like the Pelhams, Morleys, and Parkers when he threw in his lot with the King.

At least a dozen or so of the clergy were sufficiently convinced about where right lay in the civil war to offer the King firm support. Five ministers of the Lewes district gave their parishioners an immediate lead by refusing to contribute on the Propositions.[134] The rector of Bignor read the homily of rebellion from the pulpit. Christopher Swale, the prominent Arminian JP, did his best to dissuade the men of Hurstpierpoint from taking up arms against the King. He laughed at those who read the orders of parliament in parish churches, said 'that the parliament is noe parliament', and told his parishioners that 'they must beare what ever their sovraigne please to lay uppon them though to the death'. John Wilson, the notorious vicar of Arlington, echoed his words: 'whatsoever the King commands, we are all bound to obey, whether it be good or evil'. He

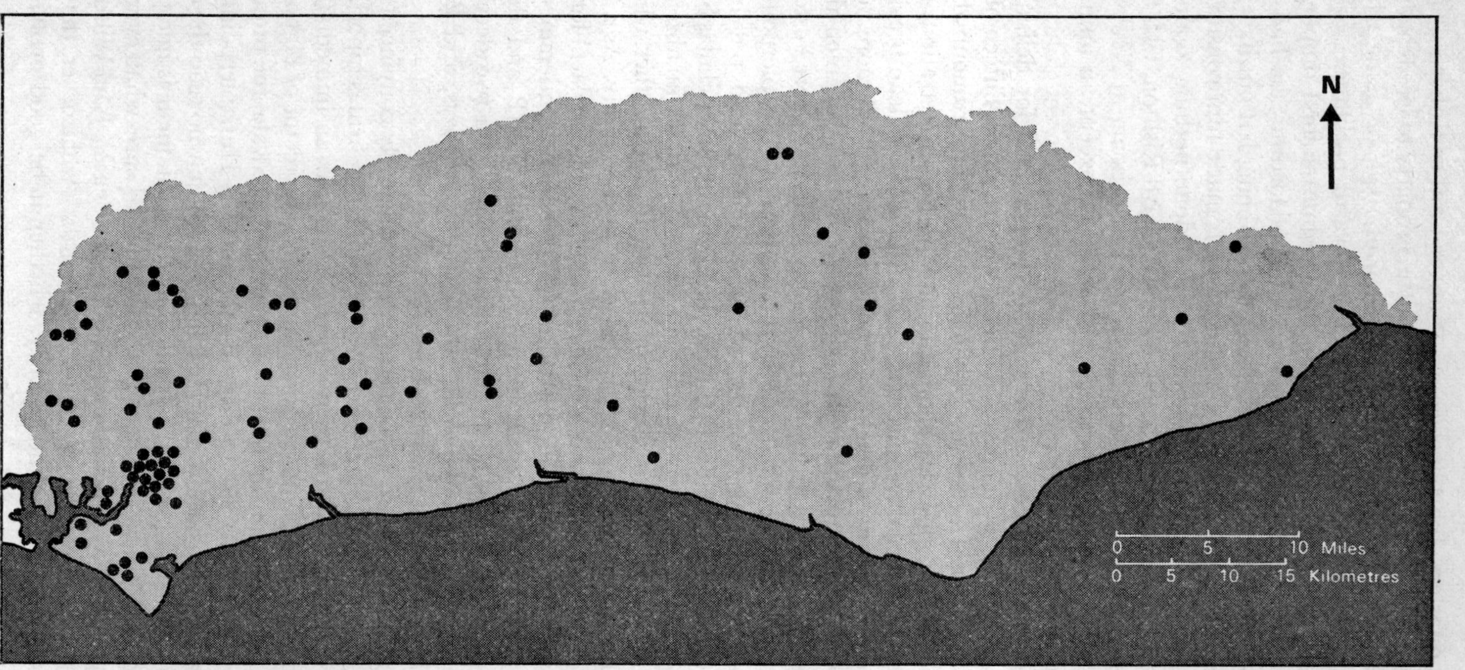

11 Men who compounded for delinquency or as papists, 1645-1656

accused parliament of endeavouring 'to starve the King'. Richard Goffe, vicar of East Grinstead, assured his parishioners 'that he cared not a figg for the parliament'. A royalist sermon preached by James Graves, vicar of Eastbourne, included the analogy that 'as Jacob crossed Jordan with his staff, so the King went forth with his standard'.[135] George Edgley, the minister of Nuthurst, managed to stimulate a good deal of royalist gossip in the Horsham area by circulating pamphlets against parliament. One of those who read them was the Horsham gentleman Robert Tredcroft who was later heard to declare that as soon as the King's forces reached Sussex they 'would kill such roundheaded rogues as did hold to the parliament'.[136] The recusant gentry, by contrast, contributed little to the royalist cause. Only three men showed any signs of exertion: Sir Garrett Kempe was fully implicated in the Chichester campaign; Thomas Kempe and John Caryll were in Arundel Castle during the siege of 1643.[137]

Sussex parliamentarianism had its roots in a smouldering distrust of Caroline government, a distrust which was based on both the political and religious policies Charles I had pursued. The parliamentary initiatives of the period from November 1640 until the spring of 1642 were not sufficient to allay the fears and doubts of many gentry, particularly in east Sussex, about their monarch's aims and intentions. Parliamentarian strength was based on the east. There, political dissent had showed itself most forcefully in the 1620s and 1630s. There, Puritanism had flourished since the middle of the reign of Elizabeth. There, tight bonds of friendship and kinship knit together both magnates and certain groups of lesser gentry. Sir Thomas Pelham, the greatest magnate in the eastern rapes, embodied all these traditions. When the Bench was remodelled by parliament in 1644 he was able to pack it with relatives, friends and gentry neighbours: men like Henry Shelley, William Hay, Thomas Jefferay, and Herbert Springate. Several of the newcomers joined cousins already on the Commission of the Peace: James Temple, for instance, whose family's intense correspondence with the Busbridges indicates their close ties, sat with his cousin from the same village, John Busbridge.[138] The Grand Committee was colonised by the same group of men. In Hastings rape Thomas Collins, who became a committeeman and a captain in the parliamentary forces, was a key figure. His marriage in 1619 to Mary Cruttenden had linked him to a family with important connections in Pevensey and Hastings rapes. His father had organised one of the Puritan petitions of 1603. He himself had opposed the forced loan. In Pevensey rape William Newton of Southover Grange was a key figure. He also had been involved in the formulation of a Puritan petition in 1603. He made Puritan marriages into the Rivers and Polhill families for his children. As an octogenarian in the 1640s, he busied himself with matters of Committee administration.[139] Such men were the backbone of the parliamentarian party in Sussex.

Herbert Morley's social status and family connections gave him every opportunity to organise a strong parliamentarian party in east Sussex. Two clans in particular whose energies he exploited were the Hays and the Boards, both of them as Puritan as the Morleys themselves. In 1618 the Hays had settled at Glyndebourne, which one of the daughters of the builder of Glynde Place had taken as her jointure on her marriage to John Hay of Herstmonceux. Glyndebourne was less than a mile from the Morley mansion. From 1605 to 1612 Robert Morley was guardian to Herbert Hay, whose brother, William, also came under Morley influence. These two men became active parliamentarians: their friendship with the young Herbert Morley was marked by affectionate references and generous legacies in their wills. The Board connection went back to the marriage of one of Herbert Morley's aunts. Its strength is indicated by Robert Morley's choice of Herbert Board as an executor of his will in 1632. Both Herbert Board and his brother John became stalwart committeemen and JPs in the 1640s.[140]

The most significant relationship of all for Sussex politics in the civil war was that between Sir Thomas Pelham and Herbert Morley. In 1632, when he had just entered Emmanuel College, Cambridge, Herbert Morley lost his father. He came under the guardianship of Pelham and his friend Anthony Stapley.[141] When the war came ten years later his approach to it was similar to Stapley's; but their approach and Pelham's were poles apart. Herbert Morley's militancy has already been discussed. At Westminster he belonged to the war party. His view of the war transcended family ties and considerations of property. Pelham's standpoint is harder to define precisely, but basically he was a moderate, a peace party man. Pelham moved in a social circle which included a broad spectrum of political opinion. He regularly lodged and dined at the Vanes' in the Strand. 'Your chamber shal be readie for you', wrote the elder Sir Henry Vane in June 1644, when Sir Thomas and his family were back at Halland after a visit to the Vanes' country estate at Fairlawn in Kent. Pelham corresponded regularly with his father-in-law, who sometimes brought him up to date with the debates at Westminster and the campaigns in the provinces.[142] By and large, though, and with the notable exception of Anthony Stapley, Pelham's closest friends were very moderate and cautious parliamentarians or neutrals. Writing to him in July 1644, Henry Shelley confessed that the rumour that the King intended to write to the Earl of Essex, expressing his readiness 'to condiscend to a good accomodation', chimed in with his own hankering for peace. Most of the members of Pelham's circle who gave their unqualified support to parliament held a limited conception of the war. They saw it in terms of a demonstration against the King which would persuade him to govern with greater respect for the desires of men of property. Such men saw the military action in terms of its local implications; they began to look for peace at an early stage. Reporting that the ordinance for a new impressment had been passed in July 1644, Shelley commented to Pelham that, 'now that we have had soe great a victory in the north', he hoped it would not need to be executed. 'I am glad that they draw off soe far from our county', he declared, retailing the news that the King had gone into Leicestershire. Letters from cousins such as the Wilbrahams of Cheshire made Pelham well aware of the threat that military strife posed to great landowners. 'Pittie your friends, and pray for them, and a happy accomodation, and I harttily wish that you may be freed from what wee daylye suffer', wrote Elizabeth Lady Wilbraham in 1644.[143]

During the civil war Sir Thomas Pelham combined his usual social and sporting round at home and in London with a positive but limited public role in Sussex on behalf of parliament. His pattern of activity reflected the nature and degree of his commitment. He regularly attended both quarter sessions and the Grand Committee.[144] He was conscientious in organising musters of the trained bands, but this was the limit of his military activity. On several occasions Sir Thomas played a mediatory role between the fiery spirits on the Committee and the fellow magnates whose interests he sought to protect. He secured the release of John Alford from the threat of sequestration in 1644, for example.[145] The same year he obtained a breathing space, during which his tenants were not to be molested for nonpayment of their rents, for the Earl of Dorset, while he pursued his suit with the Commons: he was 'desireous to give your honor satisffaccon as farr as our trust will permitt'.[146]

Tension between Sir Thomas Pelham and Herbert Morley was inevitable. Pelham's county militia in the eastern rapes remained firmly in the hands of gentry, lesser gentry perhaps, but men with names like Gildredge, Everenden, Fowle and Springate that were well respected in county society.[147] In Herbert Morley's and Anthony Stapley's county regiments, on the contrary, the captains who led troops at such sieges as Basing and Donnington were most of them obscure men, who had seen that the war offered military careers open to talents, who put the cause before the claims of rank and property.[148] Morley's army, one where yeomanry could become officers, challenged the fundamental assumptions of the magnate world. Pelham's ambiguous stance and his well-known attachment to the peace party in turn provoked suspicion and distrust, not so much on the part of Morley himself, who must have understood Pelham's priorities if he did not share them, but among the men he had at his back. Whether Morley himself colluded in the campaign during 1643 and 1644 to discredit Pelham and destroy his influence in Sussex is not clear. It seems unlikely that he did so, more likely in fact that his relationship with his former guardian was strong enough to bear the strain imposed on it by their divergent attitudes during the war, and that his influence prevented the open breach in the magnate ranks which was necessary for the campaign to succeed. The first hint that a party was working against Pelham was the division in the Commons on 7 March 1643 on the question 'whether Sir Thomas Pelham shall be sent in Sussex to advance the service of the weekly assessments', possibly a war party move against a known moderate when the House was thin. When twenty-four voted for Pelham and twenty-eight against him, he was directed to send the books for the assessment to Stapley and Morley. Then, in July 1643, Pelham was at first omitted, together with Sir Thomas Parker, who seems to have pursued a similar political path, from the committee for securing the county. They were added three days later. Finally, in October 1644, a group of Sussex ministers and freeholders presented a petition in the Commons against Pelham and Parker, charging them with being 'backward in the service of the parliament'.[149] This proved abortive, probably because Pelham had plenty of friends in the House ready to rally to his support. Thereafter the campaign collapsed.

Pelham's voice remained authoritative in the counsels of the Grand Committee at Lewes throughout the war. On one occasion at least a direct clash between the Committee and Herbert Morley almost certainly reflected the unresolved rivalry between him and Pelham. 'Some difference is betweene our Collonell and Lewes Committee', wrote John Coulton to Samuel Jeake in October 1643, 'they will give us noe pay if we stay nott in the county. Sir William Waller desires us with him, what will be done the Lord knowes'. Whereas Morley was keen to work with Waller, his colleagues sitting at Lewes exasperated the major-general of the South-Eastern Association by their heel-dragging and their clamours for the release of county forces for defensive duties. Cancelling a commission to Edward Apsley in 1644, Waller declared that he did it willingly 'because I would not have anything to do with the gentlemen of Sussex from whom I have received nothing but constant incivilities'.[150]

Sussex neutralism tended to fall into three categories: the neutralism of self-interest, that of apathy and that of bewildered moderation. In the parliamentarian east neutralism was an attractive refuge for gentry whose careers had brought them into contact and sympathy with the court. Walter Burrell had enjoyed a place in service to Queen Henrietta Maria; Sir John Sackville, a cousin of the Earl of Dorset, had busily collected contributions for the King in 1642; William Wilson had engaged in the Scottish expedition of 1639; George Courthope had hurried to Wolverhampton when his father died in 1642 to obtain his place in the Alienations Office.[151] By remaining neutral, such men secured their estates and salved their consciences. In Sussex as in other counties there was also a strong tendency for recusants to remain neutral. Viscount Montagu spent much of 1643 and 1644 in France. In September 1642 Sir John Caryll obtained a licence for himself, his wife, and four servants to cross to France. The following month William Gage of Bentley requested a similar licence, 'to go into France until things are quieter'. Caryll was back at Harting the following December when the royalists garrisoned his house, but he appears to have been unwilling to play any active part in the campaign.[152] Other leading recusants, like Sir Thomas Gage of Firle, Sir

John Smith and Thomas Threele, also sat tight on their estates. They were sequestered for recusancy but their delinquency could not be proved.[153]

Numerous gentlemen simply lacked the political or religious motivation to become engaged. Nothing would stir a retired justice in his dotage like Laurence de la Chambre from the comforts of his Ouse valley home. Many a lesser gentleman like Anthony Stapley of Hickstead was content to pay the taxes asked of him and escape public burdens.[154] The farming life of east Sussex was after all little affected by the war. For a time in 1642 the normally reclusive Francis, Lord Dacre took an active interest in the proceedings of the Lords, tending to a hard line against the King, but once war broke out he preferred his yacht and the seclusion of the Pevensey marshes. When the Lords summoned him to attend in January 1643, he excused himself on the grounds that the highways were 'extremely clogged by a very deep snow'. His coach, he insisted, would never reach London and his health would not permit him 'to endure the rigour of journeying on horseback in such exceeding cold weather as now it is'.[155] Dacre's neutralism was probably motivated by a combination of laziness and reluctance to face the stark test of allegiance which the war posed. He was by temperament a moderate, who saw no need to take sides and who recognised the yearning for reconciliation felt by propertied men throughout the civil war. Friends and relations were welcome at Dacre's table during the 1640s, whatever their political views. His guest-lists were a remarkable demonstration of gentry solidarity. In January 1644 his cousin Sir William Waller visited Herstmonceux with a party of about twenty officers and gentlemen; Sir Thomas Pelham, John Busbridge and James Temple were occasional visitors, as were the Kentish parliamentarians Sir Isaac Sedley and Sir Philip Stapleton; in September 1644 Viscount Montagu spent three weeks at the castle; Lady Campion, the wife of the royalist governor of Boarstall, was there several times in 1643; in 1646 and 1647 other royalists, like Sir Selwyn Parker, Sir Nicholas Selwyn and Sir Edward Filmer, mixed with the horde of local gentry who frequently enjoyed the Dacre hospitality.[156]

A number of those who were sequestered for their part in the Chichester campaign were quite clearly neutrals who had innocently obeyed Ford's warrants. Thomas May, Christopher Lewkenor's brother-in-law who had held the captaincy of the horse in Chichester rape since 1634, had at once dissociated himself from Ford when he made his intentions plain. Ford deprived him of his command and kept him in Chichester against his will. For the rest of the war he remained at home, hastening to grasp opportunities to ingratiate himself with the Committee, by a loan for the Scots advance and by taking the National Covenant immediately the chance was offered. In the calmer atmosphere of 1646 magnates on the Committee rallied to support May. Herbert Morley, Edward Apsley, Thomas Middleton and William Hay were among those who certified his innocency to the Compounding Committee at Goldsmiths' Hall. Anthony

Stapley interrogated him in December 1646 and subsequently added his support to the case for leniency.[157] How many of those who later pleaded that they had acted in 1642 under menaces and threats were as unspotted in their neutralism as they pretended is hard to determine. But it is undoubtedly the case that men were implicated on the flimsiest charges. Henry Barlow, or instance, was given a pistol by Captain Wolfe which he disposed of as soon as he could, but the story that he had carried it in the street was enough for him to be sequestered. The unfortunate man eventually paid a fine of £120, although the Committee at Chichester, noting that the quality of his offence was 'as small as any that was ingaged in that accon' and that he had contributed 'freely' upon the Propositions, hoped to discharge him on the basis of a private deal in the shape of a 'valuable consideration for his estate'.[158]

The outbreak of the civil war brought agonies of heartsearching and personal decision to many manor houses, where the pressures of friends and kin and the promptings of conscience and political idealism locked men in conflict with themselves. 'I did not rashly or unadvisedly put myself uppon this service', wrote the royalist Sir William Campion in 1645 to his friend Herbert Morley, 'for it was dayly in my prayers for two or three months together to God to direct mee in a right way, and bedsies I had conference with diverse able and honest men for advice, who confirmed mee in my judgement'.[159] Some gentry, particularly men who were moderate by inclination, adopted a neutral stance as a solution to their unease in feeling themselves pulled in both directions.

John Alford's hesitant and uncertain political course reflected the ponderings of a troubled mind. He was a Straffordian and he appeared to be lukewarm to parliament in 1641; he was summoned to attend the House in November 1642; the following September he was removed from the County Committee; in October 1644 the Committee at Arundel reported 'the resort and great meetings of people ill-affected at his house'; his only subsequent public appearance was at the meeting of magnates, strictly a meeting of the Committee on which he no longer sat, in September 1645 which considered the petition of the western rapes about the hardships of war.[160] John Alford made his will in July 1643. Among the 'loving and dear friends' to whom he gave rings were four prominent neutrals: Sir William Goring of Burton, Edward Goring of Cobden, Henry Goring of Highden and Sir John Leeds. He was at the centre of a circle of magnate neutrals living in Bramber and Arundel rapes. Yet he also had intimate friends on both sides. Sir Thomas Pelham, he declared in his will, was his 'real and faithfull friend'. Royalists with whom he was on close terms included Thomas Mill and the young Henry Goring of Burton, his brother Sir Edward Alford, his brother-in-law Henry Bishop and his Oxfordshire cousin John Fettiplace.[161] No wonder John Alford was a man perplexed by the times. He attempted to steer a safe course, without commitment, without giving displeasure. But in July 1644 his balancing act almost failed when his son came under the suspicion of the Grand Committee. Alford hurried to see Sir Thomas Pelham in London but, missing him, wrote to him at Halland instead. His appeal for help is a classic expression of the emotional stress that was imposed on magnates caught up in the intensity, prejudice and personal strife of the civil war:

> I am sorry you suddaynly left this place, I was to waite on you with my acknowledgment of your friendly respect which how highly I have ever valewed, God knowes my hart: for the particulers of my sonns business, as exprest by you, and of his miscarriage therein, I must crave leave to plead my absolut innocency, of any least thought, of trespass, or contempt, to the proceedings of the Committee att Lewis, in so much, as my directions went with him. If his owne will have otherwise misguided him, and his indiscreations, either in language, or action have over ruled him, to his great prejudice, by the displeasure of the Committee, hee must stand, or fall to his owne affections; which I hope, and wish, may be suche as may to the full, give the Committee ample satisfaction, yett I shall not pass by the assuered hopes of your frendly quallefication of the business: I may not forgett your frendly advice, but the miseryes of the times are such, as what was black yeasterday, is white today; and so in this particuler, am I, cleere, and unspotted: but if such bee my fate; that by the indiscreation of anothers actions I must perish; tis as sadd as what the times can produce: Gods will be done: If your advice can prevayle to his preservation, itt is the uttermost of a friend; and in requitall, I hope nothing of ingratitude will appeere: I am most certayne, not from him, who hath long since vowed himselfe yoor most affectionat freind and servant.

No more was heard of the Committee's proceedings.[162] Sir Thomas Eversfield of Hollington married John Alford's daughter in 1638. His will indicates his intimacy with his father-in-law, as well as his attachment to Sir Thomas Pelham. He was also related to the Gorings of Burton and Highden. Eversfield pursued a similarly wavering course to Alford's. He obtained leave of absence in the middle of the debates on Strafford's attainder; he was summoned to attend the Commons in May 1643; he was removed from the County Committee in September 1643; yet the sequestration with which he was threatened in September was never carried out.[163] Pelham's hand was probably once more at work.

Whereas Alford and Eversfield made an immediate retreat from public activity when war broke out, other neutral gentry like William White and William Thomas were busy as JPs until the 1644 commission gave them a chance to retire. Such men were torn between their duty to the shire and antipathy to the parliamentarian régime. Laurence Ashburnham's disillusionment got the better of him in 1644. In 1643 he was sometimes at both sessions and the Committee at Robertsbridge.[164] His energy led to his approval by the Commons in July as a deputy-lieutenant. But by the next spring Peter Farnden was reporting to Pelham Ashburnham's desire to be rid of public burdens. In June 1644 the Sussex MPs informed the Commons that his lethargy made him unacceptable after all as a deputy.[165]

Others like Sir William Goring and Henry Goring, both of them fathers of royalists, were prepared to maintain a distinction between traditional local peace-keeping and the national struggle against the King, so long as the parliamentarians required their services. They were dropped from the Bench in 1644, but resumed their duties with alacrity in 1646 when they were restored. Sir Thomas Eversfield of Denne, Henry Goring's brother-in-law, was another man ready to undertake magisterial office and even the shrievalty, but unwilling to show himself on the County Committee.[166] Two men who adopted a continuing public role despite their inclination to neutralism found themselves in trouble when their waverings were taken as evidence of delinquency. Edward Apsley was active in raising forces for parliament in the western rapes in 1643 and 1644. He was implicitly trusted by the ruling clique and he was made a deputy-lieutenant as early as December 1642. Yet in 1644 he became so apathetic that, when the Committee at Arundel exhibited articles against him in the Commons, he was sent for as a delinquent. He seems to have been frightened into line and the next year he entered the House as a recruiter.[167] Thomas Middleton was active as an MP, JP and committeeman throughout the period 1642 to 1648, although his heart never seems to have been in the parliamentary cause. No action followed the presentation of articles against him in 1644, probably because he still retained the confidence of the Grand Committee. Finally, though, in 1648 the strength of Middleton's neutralist and crypto-royalist aspirations emerged when he took a leading role in raising and maintaining the Horsham tumult.[168]

The 1644 articles afford some insight into the underhand role that Thomas Middleton played in the heart of the crisis. During the 1643 campaign, it was alleged, he discouraged the Horsham townsmen from defending the town, sent countrymen home who came in to be quartered there and dabbled in secret discussions to raise royalist support in the north of Bramber rape. When a group of royalist conspirators was arrested, Middleton had them released 'notwithstanding a letter shewd him from Captain Temple requiring them to be sent to Shoram'. He also refused to take up complaints against royalist ministers, who used the pulpit for anti-parliamentary propaganda, and objected to assessments set on neutrals by other Horsham committeemen. His control of the Committee at Horsham enabled him to protect Mrs Michel of Stamerham, although she was 'knowne to be a woman ill affected to the parliament'. Middleton had her arms restored to her and procured the hands of Sir Thomas Eversfield of Denne and others to a certificate that she was well affected, 'as the said Sir Thomas Eversfield hath confessed expressing sorrow for being so misled'.[169]

Only a minority of the Sussex gentry made a wholehearted commitment to the King or parliament. Parliament's pursuit of victory, which required divisiveness in the cause of financial strength, was constantly hampered in the county by the predilection of gentry to put personal ties and class solidarity before singleminded effort towards the defeat of Charles I. But the desire for reconciliation and a return to harmony could also work the other way. The climax of the war in Sussex came in December 1643 when Sir Edward Bishop and his family, Sir Edward Ford and members of other magnate clans were under siege at Arundel. The division of the gentry community symbolised by the siege was intolerably painful. Yet the courtesies of polite society, even in this tense moment, offered a way of damping the blaze of war. Once negotiations for a treaty had been opened by the royalists on 5 January 1644, Sir William Waller invited Lady Bishop and her daughters to dine with him. They emerged from the castle and received 'noble respect and good entertainment'. The final surrender was a triumph of gentry cohesion over political division. Henry Goring's wife and daughter came over from Highden to visit the Bishop contingent at Waller's camp, 'which visite', reported a parliamentary journalist later, 'gave a speedy accomplishment to our designe'. For the previous year Frances Bishop, at the age of sixteen, had married the heir to the Goring estates at Highden. The young couple had joined the royalist army, while Henry Goring himself, a pillar of county society, remained passive. 'After some conference with her mother-in-law', Frances Goring, 'returned to her husband in the castle; and shortly after, the enemy sent a drum . . . to treat for a finall agreement'.[170] In pressing for a quick surrender the Gorings put the county, which was suffering terribly from the siege, before the rights and wrongs of the national political conflict. There were few Sussex gentry with the vision and daring of Herbert Morley and Sir Edward Ford. Most of them were strongly tempted to put harmony and order within their own county before the decisive resolution of the crisis in the state.

14

The search for settlement 1648-1660

Wee doe humbly pray that our sad differences and divisions may be happily composed, all misunderstandings between princes and people timely removed, his Majestie according to our solemne engagement rendred glorious.
The Sussex Petition, June 1648.[1]

I doe not know the hearts of men; but I bless God I have not wanted the civil respects of all sorts of persons with whom yet I have had to doe.
Major-General Goffe to Secretary Thurloe, 13 November 1655.[2]

I was very glad to understand that Sussex remaines quiet and in a good posture; the carrying things with moderation is the only sure way to serve the King and to mentaine the countrie in peace.
The Earl of Northumberland to Sir John Pelham, 6 February 1661.[3]

Regicide and the Rump

Once the civil war was almost over, Sussex gentry were anxious to heal the breach in their society. Men in the King's quarters made contact with friends and kin at home to help them in their negotiations with the Committee. Thomas Mill 'sente to some of his ancient acquaintance', including his father-in-law Ralph Cowper, about September 1645; Henry Bridger obtained a pass for his son Richard's safe return from the borders of Cornwall the following month.[4] There had been much anxiety among her Sussex relations that summer about the wellbeing of Lady Campion, who was a daughter of Sir Thomas Parker. Her husband was the royalist governor of Boarstall in Oxfordshire. Pressed by other gentlemen, Herbert Morley agreed to assist her to return home. In a letter of 28 July, in which he promised to procure a pass for her, Morley assured Sir William Campion that he wanted bygones to be bygones: 'old acquaintance neede noe appollogy; all your Sussex freindes in health and continue their wonted affections towardes you, equally valewing your welfare with their owne'.[5] The desire for settlement was general, but the political developments of 1646 and 1647 brought it no closer. Then in 1648 a series of risings threatened to plunge the nation once more in blood. In a letter of 5 August Samuel Jeake reflected on his fear of the political outcome: 'times are eminently sad and have runne into excesse . . . evil spirits are exalted, some men's hearts faile them for feare the foundations are shaken'.[6] County politics became more intensely polarised in the summer and autumn of 1648 than they had been at any time since the Arundel campaign. On the one hand, the Puritan militants tensely waited for the millennium; on the other hand, the moderates sought to unite the gentry behind a petition for a personal treaty with Charles I.

In south-east England the troubles of the summer of 1648 were sparked off by petitions to Parliament from a ring of counties. The Sussex petition was along similar lines to those of Essex, Kent and Surrey. It set out a programme for the removal of the 'miserable effects' of the war: disbandment of the army after the payment of its arrears, government 'by the known lawes of this kingdom', reduction of taxation and dissolution of the Arundel garrison. There were royalist undertones in its demand for a 'well grounded peace both in church and commonwealth', which took account of the King's 'most just rights as of the rights of parliament'. Yet in general the mood of the petition chimed in well with that of the middle group leaders in the Commons, whose minds were becoming set on a final settlement based on a renewed trust of the King. The Lords and Commons expressed their approval of the Sussex petition, which was presented on 9 June without the tumults that had accompanied the Surrey petition.[7]

The petition had been formulated at a meeting in Lewes on 30 May. The initiative seems to have been taken by a group of neutral gentry including George Courthope and Sir William Culpepper, who carried the petition to Westminster. The sons of Thomas Middleton and Sir Thomas Parker were among the others who went to London.[8] The signatures attached to the petition show that it attracted much support in the four eastern rapes and a fair showing of names from the rapes of Arundel and Chichester. This geographical spread probably reflects the predominant influence of the gentry whose organisation lay behind it. Anyway, the petition's programme appealed to a broad spectrum of gentry opinion. Royalists like John Goring of Amberley and Robert Tredcroft of Horsham signed it; so did men who had all along been sympathetic to the King without showing their hand, like William Wilson and Edward Burton of Eastbourne; leading neutralist magnates such as John Alford, Sir William Goring and Sir Thomas Eversfield of Denne found its demands agreeable; so did parliamentarian militia captains like John Fuller, Nicholas Gildredge, and John Everenden; so even did a few of the more moderate committeemen such as Anthony Fowle, Francis Selwyn and Thomas Jefferay.[9] But the petition's royalist undertones alienated most of the parliamentarian group of the 1640s: Sir Thomas Pelham, Anthony Stapley and Herbert Morley would have no part in it.

The petition amounted to a direct challenge to the Grand Committee. To men like Pelham and Morley it was a dangerous and divisive move, identified with men like Thomas Middleton and George Courthope whose political stance had long attracted rumour and suspicion. It was organised with a boldness that affronted the county's bosses. When on the way to Westminster Courthope and his friends lodged at East Grinstead, it was later alleged, 'he appointed other persons of the same party to meet him; and there was a guard set by them in that town, to the terror of the honest party of that county'. Courthope's 'many threatenings against all that should oppose or discourage a general subscription' were held against him by a correspondent of Major-General Goffe's as late as 1656. So angry was Anthony Stapley at the petitioners that he threatened to proceed against them. Not far short of 10,000 signatures had been collected. The petition spoke for the 'knights, gentry, clergy and commonalty' of Sussex and its presentation with the full panoply of a gentry delegation at Westminster suggested that it represented the real voice of the county. It was a nasty jolt, yet, apart from a few defections, the Committee stood firm against it. There was no breach in the ruling group before Pride's Purge. The new militia commission, passed in the ordinance of 2 December, included the usual names: Pelham, Parker, Stapley, Morley, Temple were all there together with their stalwart henchmen like William Freeman and Nicholas Shepard.[10]

The outcome of the summer's military actions convinced the most zealous Puritans that the millennium was at hand. In a letter for which he collected signatures among his Rye friends during November, Samuel Jeake hailed Lord General Fairfax as the saviour of the nation. After a paean of thanksgiving for the summer's deliverance, Jeake urged Fairfax, as one who challenged 'the foremost place', to the vigorous pursuit of the harvest of victory. An exceptional opportunity might so easily be lost:

> Yet is it not unknowne to you that the kingdome yet groanes (for liberty as waiting for the manifestacon of the sonnes of God) for shall a nation be borne at once or in one day delivered from the monstrous molas or conceptions its wombe hath inclosed and hatched these many ages? Our miseries were breeding many generations agoe, we must turne over yeares and reignes ere we read their original, yea runne and rowle beyond the Norman Conquest, and there finde some seeds of our divisions sowne, some men's wills made lawes, some publique persons act to privat ends, and judgment inverted into gall and wormwood, this we know what it meanes by wofull experience.

So far from releasing the nation from bondage, declared Jeake bitterly, the outcome of the war showed that 'our physicians have beene of no value, our remedies have been our diseases'. His mind was now set on retribution, his vindictiveness was turned with full force against the King and his advisers. 'We desire', he wrote, 'that no delayes (as conceiving them altogether unsafe) may be admitted' on the *Remonstrance of the Army*. He suggested that commissioners should be appointed 'to find out the actors and formentors of the late warre and bringing in of the Scots and being found to secure them'. Jeake was obviously closely in touch with members of the Rye garrison. He wanted condign punishment for all those who cast aspersions on the army's proceedings 'to the execution of justice and righteousness'; he asked Fairfax to set up a more effective network of communications between remote garrisons and the army headquarters, so that all the soldiery could contribute more freely to its political programme of action. He also requested that County Committees, which he spoke of as 'the seminary of many evills', should be purged and the corruptions over free quarter and taxation of public servants should be examined.

Jeake's letter exemplifies the explosive nature of the mixture of Puritan fervour and army radicalism which was a feature of provincial as much as of national politics in the autumn of 1648. The zeal of magnate Puritans like Herbert Morley was waning by this time, as they took fright at the emerging identification of millenarianism with social and political radicalism. Thus the ruling clique was poised uneasily, at the moment when Colonel Pride purged the Commons, between the mass of the neutralist gentry searching for monarchical settlement and the minority of Puritan militants seeking blood and the millennium.[11]

Between 6 December 1648 and 30 January 1649 the consciences of Sussex MPs were tested by the most revolutionary events of the seventeenth century. The crisis stirred Edward Apsley, William Cawley, John Downes and Sir Gregory Norton from their homes. They came back to Westminster although they had missed nearly all the sittings in 1648.[12] A fracture in the gentry community was inevitable. The dividing line, blurred though it was by the contortions of men prepared to conform to, but not to create, the new régime, was largely predictable. Sir Thomas Parker, Sir Thomas Pelham and his son John, their friend John Alford, Thomas Middleton and his Horsham colleague Hall Ravenscroft were all excluded immediately the army took control of the House. Herbert Springate, a recruiter who had never appeared on the parliamentary Bench and had scarcely shown his face in the committee room, was also excluded; so was another lukewarm recruiter, Samuel Gott. On 20 December Herbert Hay, who had committed himself much more wholeheartedly to the parliamentarian régime in the country during the previous years than the men who had already departed, left London for Glyndebourne. He had balked at the political test imposed by the dissent from the vote of 5 December in favour of the Treaty of Newport negotiations. One other MP, Henry Shelley, was not apparently secluded, but he never sat in the Rump. His relationship with Pelham was close; he probably followed his lead.

At the other extreme from these men who opted out of the army's proceedings against the King were the five Sussex regicides. One of them, the timid and querulous John Downes, is celebrated for his reluctance to see the King judicially killed. First he refused to be made a commissioner, but 'through weakness and fear' was ensnared; then he interrupted the trial and urged his colleagues to let the King be heard, until he broke down in tears before Cromwell's anger and scorn.[13] The other four regicides

—Anthony Stapley, William Cawley, James Temple and Sir Gregory Norton—were tougher. They saw the business through without flinching. Herbert Morley, on the other hand, lost his nerve after attending the trial for three days. John Fagge and Roger Gratwick were also nominated as commissioners: Fagge was present in the early stages; Gratwick never appeared at the trial but he took his seat in February 1649. He had made no recorded appearance in the House during the previous thirteen months.[14] Gratwick was one of the final group, those who hovered uncertainly between revolution and retreat until the trial and execution was over. This group of conformists included John Baker, William Hay, Robert Goodwin and Edward Apsley, as well as Morley and Fagge. They all took the dissent to the vote of 5 December during February.[15]

The rift in the gentry community at Pride's Purge was painful. In Sir Thomas Pelham the sober constitutionalism of a great landed magnate triumphed over Puritan idealism. Herbert Morley fell back from the revolutionary deed, but there was still enough youthful millenarian enthusiasm in his breast for him to seek his political and moral aims through the Commonwealth. When the moment of decision came, Anthony Stapley proved the boldest of the three. The course pursued by the Sussex MPs lends some substance to the view that the more firmly established and propertied a man's family, the more likely he was to draw back from revolution. Stapley was the only regicide with an impeccable county background, Cawley was hardly established in county society, Temple was the careerist younger son of a recently settled family, Downes's background remains bafflingly obscure, and Norton was clearly an upstart.[16] Furthermore, several of the regicides were men with a stake in the revolution. Downes and Temple had claims of more than £1,000 on the state, Stapley and Norton were purchasers of Church lands. If social conservation held some men back, material considerations as well as religious ideology may have driven others on.

A strong band of eleven Sussex MPs sat in the Rump, but eight of them were rarely present at debates. The most active members were William Cawley, who sat moderately regularly, Herbert Morley, who was present as often as not, and John Downes, who immersed himself in political and administrative commitments. Morley was the key man. The historian of the parliament has called him' one of the ablest parliamentary managers of the Rump period'. From the summer of 1649, Morley became a major political figure at Westminster. So efficiently did he control and organise his Sussex friends and colleagues that they became a pressure group to be reckoned with, despite the tendency of most of them to prefer their country estates for much of the year. He could also count on frequent support from Sir Henry Heyman and his father-in-law Sir John Trevor. The records of the Army and Navy Committees, the Committee for Indemnity and the Committee for Plundered Ministers all show the effectiveness of the Morley connections. In the November 1651 elections to the Council of State Morley's prominence emerged most strikingly: he himself topped the poll of those newly elected, and three other Sussex men, Anthony Stapley, William Hay and John Downes, also gained places. The following year, when his protégés were dropped, he just failed to get John Fagge elected. On domestic issues Herbert Morley was moderate and conservative. In November 1651 he was a teller against Cromwell's motion for a deadline to be set for the Rump's dissolution. His success in the elections shortly afterwards was an indication of the reactionary mood of the House at that time. Morley, as much as anyone, represented the landlord interest. In commercial and diplomatic matters, though, he joined forces with the Marten-Chaloner group in pursuing an ambitious policy designed to increase national prestige.[17]

The Rump did everything it possibly could to bind country gentry to the new régime. In the provinces it was bound to depend on the active service of many who only learnt to stomach regicide when the deed was done. The first consideration was the Commissions of the Peace.[18] Herbert Morley, Anthony Stapley and William Cawley all sat on the Rump committee, set up in February 1649, to consider them.[19] Many of the county Benches were not remodelled until the following summer, but the presence of three Sussex men enabled the committee to dispose of the rearrangement of its Bench with speed. Eleven JPs were dismissed and ten replaced them at the end of February. Three of the secluded members—Sir Thomas Parker, Herbert Hay and Thomas Middleton—were among those despatched and the chance was taken to dispose of other moderates like Francis Selwyn, George Courthope and Henry Peckham. These men, shocked to one degree or another by the King's execution, probably accepted their seclusion willingly. Only Sir Thomas Parker swallowed his doubts and came to terms with the régime. He was readmitted in March 1650.[20]

There was no shortage of willing recruits to the magistracy. Captains, committeemen and careerist administrators swarmed in to replace the men who had withdrawn. Twenty-one new JPs in all were appointed between February 1649 and October 1652.[21] The degree of continuity varied. With John Busbridge and Peter Farnden still ruling the roost in Hastings rape, both as JPs and as committeemen, nothing had apparently changed. Elsewhere too, there were experienced men who were as unstinting as ever in their service to the county. Sir Thomas Parker, once he was restored, Henry Shelley and Edward Apsley all remained assiduous justices.[22] Yet the complexion of the Commission of the Peace had subtly altered. The absence of Sir Thomas Pelham from quarter sessions, despite the efforts of the Bench to secure his cooperation, was symptomatic of the new régime's failure to secure the loyalty of the whole county establishment.[23] Some magnates who were willing to continue in service as JPs would on the other hand have nothing to do with the Rump's local militia, which was based on a new assessment on all persons with over £10 a year or £200 in personal property. It may have reflected the initiative in parliament of Herbert Morley.[24] Morley, John Fagge, John Baker and John Busbridge, all of whom enforced the 1650 Act, were able to draw in a few trusted men of stature from the key families, but had to find most of their captains from among the minor gentry and aspiring townsmen. William Morley retained the crucial post of Governor of Arundel, one of Anthony Stapley's sons accepted a captaincy, James Temple remained in command of a troop of dragoons.[25] But the colonel of the horse in the western rapes was Richard Boughton, an ambitious newcomer who had worked his way into the gentry orbit during the 1640s, through the solicitorship of sesquestrations.[26]

How loyal was Sussex to the Commonwealth? There was undoubtedly much that troubled moderate men who had withdrawn from public affairs. Upstarts were feathering their nests. At Chichester, for instance, John Downes acquired most of the Close, demolished the Chancellor's house and established himself in the Deanery. The new sequestrators arrogantly busied themselves over the estates of their social superiors who had still not been able to compound.[27] Yet so long as men of their own standing were in charge, magnates like Sir Thomas Pelham, however much they resented the Rump's constitutional nakedness and dependence on high taxation, were hardly likely to make trouble. Pelham was content to live out his advancing middle age in the traditional social pattern to which he was accustomed. He was not alienated from friends like Stapley and Shelley who had chosen a different path.

How far the Sussex moderates allowed themselves to become entangled in the contortions of the Engagement controversy is hard to judge. One man who undoubtedly read the pamphlets of John Dury, Francis Rous and Anthony Ascham with care and thought was Samuel Gott, the secluded ironmaster and lawyer who had settled at Battle.[28] Gott found himself plagued by London friends for advice. He confessed to John Swynfen early in 1650 that he was 'in a cloud not knowing what to doe or say'. Nevertheless he provided a precise summary of his views. In the first place he was convinced that many were 'held in the snares of needles scruples', over such questions as the payment of taxes and the finding of arms. Declaring that while he could 'never consent to any thing which may bee a justification' of the Commonwealth, he would 'yeild as farr as may bee to anything which is not', he took his stand on the Calvinist and providential case made out by Rous. Yet he also accepted Ascham's secular case, which fully answered the problem of contrary engagements. Gott concluded as follows:

> There could be no preservation of men and humane society which is the end of government if inferiors should bee bound immutably to a mutable authority and not follow the visible possession of the supreme power.

Similar sentiments may well have animated many of those who were content to live quietly under a régime whose origins they abhorred. He himself admitted that he was not 'so much troubled for myselfe, intending to live privately and out of business, as for my neerest friends'.[29] Gott employed his leisure in putting together, from his 'loose papers' now 'digested into method', a book under the tital *An Essay of the True Happiness of Man,* which he published in 1650. It exemplifies the contentment of a country gentleman in retirement from the passionate exchanges of national politics. 'Though I know writing of books to be a very mean employment, and of no great efficacy', confessed Gott in his preface, 'yet I am content to make use of it, because I have no better antidote against idleness'.[30]

The Rump, anxious to secure a broad basis of support, was in general slow to push forward the Engagement, but, with Stapley and Morley behind it, it may well have been more energetically enforced in Sussex than some other counties. In December 1649 Stapley had his faithful adjutants Stephen Humphrey and Richard Boughton 'added to those that are to give the Engagement in Sussex'.[31] The following April Morley reported the taking of the Engagement in the Ashdown Forest area.[32] Only the Rye Engagement has survived. There, on 6 March 1650, 168 heads of households swore their obedience to the Commonwealth 'without a King or House of Lords', seventy-seven of them making their mark. Fishermen, brewers, coopers and blacksmiths took the oath alongside the freemen and jurats.[33] But there is little sign that the Commonwealth acquired anything more than halfhearted tolerance from the country people. In 1651 the churchwardens of Cowfold at last paid a painter for striking out the King's arms and setting up the State's in the parish church; at Billingshurst and Tillington the work was not done until 1652.[34]

Throughout the period from 1649 to 1653 the ruling clique remained anxious and jumpy in face of a sullen community. Herbert Morley was uncompromising towards men who dared challenge the republican régime. When the Hurstpierpoint gentleman William Hippisley, who was the Earl of Norwich's agent in Sussex, appeared before the Bench in 1649 charged with seditious words, Morley treated him fiercely. Hippisley reported to the Earl that it was only the intervention of another magnate, 'your good friend', that 'brought me clearely off and that with much gallantry and like a gentleman'.[35] The Rump's régime remained blatantly military. Security was maintained by patrolling troops of horse which, together with the temporary presence of certain foot regiments, bore heavily on the county Sir Michael Livesey's regiment, quartered in Sussex before embarkation for Ireland in 1649, was reported to be 'a great burden, both by their free quarter and their disorderly behaviour'.[36] Alarms the following December led the Council to order a new troop of horse to be raised; in the flurry of activity when the royalist army marched south to Worcester urgent measures were taken to make up the troops of horse.[37] The local authorities' feelings of insecurity are indicated by the pressure they applied through the county MPs to retain the Arundel garrison in 1651 and by their reluctance to disband Colonel Temple's troop of dragoons the same year.[38] Arundel was too useful as a political prison to be readily dissolved: an outsider who attracted suspicion in 1651 was rapidly despatched there.[39]

But in fact, though, there was no serious trouble in the county. A royalist agent was apprehended in February 1650; five malcontents were made to take the Engagement in open court in 1653.[40] The Amberley alehousekeeper deposed in 1651 that John Goring had 'kneeling downe drunke a health to Prince Charles, and to the confusion of this present parliament', which was made up of 'rogues, knaves and upstart gentlemen'.[41] Two yeomen told Herbert Morley the tale of the seditious conversation of another gentleman who spread a rumour in February 1652 that 'the parliament's ships were all lost'. He had apparently declared that around Framfield, the home of one of the yeomen, 'were many roundheads and now was a tyme that the king's bloode would be requited'; he also spoke of 'the plagues and curses of God's word' following rebels and rebellion.[42] This kind of wild talk was about as far as resistance to the Commonwealth in Sussex ever went. Yet it was easy to smuggle a king through the county. The story of the escape of Charles II by boat from Brighton, too well known to be retold here, shows that royalist families like the Gunters were ready to do him any immediate service they could.[43] But royalist conspiracy in the south-east at this stage was no more than aspirations and paper plans. When the royalist agent Thomas Coke visited Sir Edward Ford at Harting in 1650, Ford spoke hopefully of those who would 'engage in that end of the countie'.[44] No plan materialised.

Besides the question of internal security, there was the constantly unnerving presence of royalist privateers in the Channel. The period of the Dutch war, from 1652 to 1654, was exceptionally hazardous. Pirates and pickeroons prevented Sussex fishermen from making their way in safety to the North Sea fishing grounds for the summer season; they also frequently brought coastal trade in commodities such as corn and iron to a standstill.[45] Any boats daring to leave their havens were liable to be taken instantly. In August 1652 the Dutch fleet, in its progress down the Channel, took one barque and pillaged another near Hastings, 'carrying her with the fishnets and men along with them'. They plundered and chased ashore another fishing boat near Brighton. The following summer three ships were taken by pickeroons.[46] Furthermore landings also occurred. The Council was sufficiently alarmed at the news of 'considerable numbers' of Frenchmen 'going up and down the country to beg' in May 1652 to instruct the county's troops of horse to be used against them. In December the same year, 800 Dutchmen were reported to have landed in Sussex and Kent, 'which drove away abundance of cattel and sheep and plundered divers houses and so consequently put the country in a lamentable fear'.[47]

The Sussex coast had not been so seriously threatened since the wars from 1625 to 1630. The Privy Council had been deaf then to the pleas of the county for convoys and effective protection for fishermen. The deputy-lieutenants had to rely on ordnance and beacons; they were dependent on their makeshift defensive arrangements.[48] A general order at the Easter sessions in 1649 required beacons to be made up once more at the ancient sites. Watch-houses were to be repaired and watches duly kept.[49] But the beacon system merely provided warning in the case of landings. Only the government had the means to tackle the more persistent problem of depredations at sea. The protection given to the Sussex coast between 1649 and 1653 reflected the power of Herbert Morley's voice in the Rump and the exceptional degree of harmony which pervaded the relations between the local governors and the central government under the Commonwealth. Morley marshalled Hay, Fagge and Gratwick as an effective pressure group on the Navy Committee; Baker and Hay pressed for convoys in the Commons; the fishermen of towns such as Brighton and Rye pestered the Council with petitions. Pressed by its Sussex members, the Council regularly reiterated to the generals and captains at sea that they should offer their services at the Sussex ports and drive away the pickeroons 'that lurk under Beachy and thereabouts annoying poor fishermen'.[50] Disruption was thus kept to a minimum. Trading communications and fishing were never totally halted for more than a few weeks at a time. The Rump showed greater sensitivity to the livelihood of Sussex's coastal community than did any other government between 1600 and 1660.

Cromwellian government

In 1653 Sussex lost its voice at the centre of national affairs. In this important sense the year of the Barebones parliament was a turning point for the county. Whereas for four years the ruling caucus had enjoyed a strong voice at Westminster, the expulsion of the Rump brought a general sense of disillusion to the Sussex MPs. Herbert Morley, already Cromwell's opponent in the Rump, could not condone his betrayal of the cause.[51] His cousin William Hay was another rumper who joined him in retirement from national politics. John Downes and William Cawley went into even more complete oblivion, abandoning their role in county government and politics when they were secluded at Westminster. Anthony Stapley, breaking with Morley, became a member of Cromwell's interim Council of State and was assiduous in attendance during May and June. But he failed to appear at the Council board between 12 July and its last six meetings in October.[52] Stapley's involvement at the national level had been intermittent for some time: he made no recorded appearance in the Rump between April and November 1651.[53] Not surprisingly, in view of his record of inertia in 1653, he was dropped from the new Council of State in November.

Three Sussex men, Anthony Stapley, William Spence and Nathaniel Studley, sat in the shortlived Barebones parliament. The nomination of

Stapley, the most prominent of the county's regicides in national affairs in the summer of 1653, was predictable; it was probably he in turn who nominated the other two. Cromwell must have become better acquainted with Stapley through the work of the Council of State during the weeks following the expulsion of the Rump. He was the obvious man for the Lord General to turn to for sound Sussex nominations. William Spence's family had been one of the most stalwart in parliamentarian Sussex, Nathaniel Studley had proved an energetic committeeman during and after the war. Both had become dependable JPs, pillars of the régime of the Rump in the county.[54] Neither was the kind of 'pitifull creature as were never heard of till these times' with which Cromwell was alleged to have filled the 1653 parliament.[55] Spence's origins were thoroughly respectable: he had undergone the standard gentleman's training at university and an inn of court and had been called to the bar in 1644. Nathaniel Studley came of more modest parish gentry stock, but he also had attended the inns of court.[56] Neither Stapley nor Studley made any discernible impact in the assembly: the latter was named to two committees, the former to one only, on 10 November 'to consider of a new body of the law'.[57] It is unlikely that either of them was on the radical wing of the parliament.[58] But William Spence had probably inherited a strain of radical Puritanism from his father.[59] He was by far the most active of the Sussex members. He was a teller on several occasions, including the crucial division of 17 October on the staying of the proceedings of Chancery for one month. He was an associate of such known radicals as Colonel Blount, Andrew Broughton and John Ireton.[60]

Once the main links between the Sussex magnates and the centre had snapped, there was time, as Cromwell found his feet, for the magnates of Sussex to unite in pursuit of their own interests. While Oliver Cromwell ruled at Whitehall their search for settlement could only be conducted through opposition. This soon took the familiar forms of independence in county government and intransigence at Westminster. In some counties, such as Buckinghamshire and Herefordshire, cliques of obscure men captured control of the Bench in 1653. There was no purge in Sussex. The first renewal of the commission after the expulsion of the Rump, in February 1654, merely brought in five lesser gentry to strengthen administration in the western rapes. In the east a core of established county gentry remained in charge; in the west the careerists of the 1640s were more numerous but a powerful voice among these was that of John Fagge, Morley's brother-in-law. The magnate caucus also continued to dominate the Grand Committee, which after it had lost its power over sequestered estates in 1650 still controlled the collection of assessments. Between 1653 and 1659 the full significance of the Long Parliament's establishment of the Sussex Committee became clear. It had given new authority to an already powerful county oligarchy. The parliamentarian magnate group, led initially by Sir Thomas Pelham, latterly by Herbert Morley, had used the dual institutions of the Bench and the Committee to establish an impregnable grip on the county.[61] Cromwell never dislodged them and when they went into opposition to his Protectorate he found Sussex an intransigent county.

The changing relationship between Herbert Morley and the central government epitomises the difference between the periods from 1642 to 1653 and from 1653 to 1659. Morley's course in the 1640s and early 1650s was that of a man of vision and militancy, one who had broken the bonds of county-mindedness and learnt to judge policies and problems in the light of the national interest. From 1653 his stance became that of an advocate of county supremacy, representing provincialism at its most stubborn and determined. His mood towards Whitehall was similar to that of his father's generation in the 1620s and 1630s. By grasping power and ruling with the support of the army, Cromwell alienated a man who saw parliamentary government as the essence of all that he had fought for. Yet Morley still took the day-to-day security of the county to be his personal concern; he could not lightly relinquish a role that he had occupied with ever-increasing assurance since he first set his whole mind and heart to parliamentary administration in 1642. Recognising the need for a working relationship with the key man at the centre of national affairs, he began to correspond regularly with Secretary Thurloe. But, whereas he had enjoyed an easy relationship with Speaker Lenthall, he had to begin all over again with Thurloe. 'I beseech your pardon for this impertinent troubling you', Morley wrote in 1655 when he sent up some letters taken from a suspected papist.[62] His approach was tentative and uncertain. His intention was merely to open a channel of communication that would enable him to serve his county more effectively.

Under the Instrument of Government Sussex acquired fourteen seats in parliament.[63] At Lewes on 12 July 1654, when the chance came to elect nine county members, the gentry turned to their natural leaders. Radicals like William Spence stood no chance. Sir Thomas Pelham, Henry Shelley and Anthony Stapley, all of whom were in fact either dead or too unwell to sit by September, were obvious choices. The men chosen to represent Sussex who actually assembled on 3 September were all moderates: the Morley clan were in the forefront of the delegation; ex-JPs like Henry Peckham, the recorder of Chichester, and Herbert Springate, a recruiter secluded at Pride's Purge, once more took the public stage; heirs to great estates like Anthony Shirley and John Stapley enjoyed their first taste of Westminster politics; Sir John Pelham, who had inherited Halland in August, rode to London ready to take on his father's role in voicing the country viewpoint. Even the reticent Francis Lord Dacre emerged from his isolation at Herstmonceux.[64] The government had been unable to influence the Sussex elections. Rye ignored the nomination sent by Cromwell's henchman Thomas Kelsey and elected first Herbert Morley, then, in his place, the local gentleman Nathaniel Powell.[65] Whether or not a deliberate intention to further the election of honest, sound country gentry lay behind the parliamentary reapportionment scheme of the Instrument of Government, that was certainly the effect in Sussex.[66]

The first Protectorate parliament is poorly documented, but it is evident from the *Journals* that Morley, Fagge, Peckham, Dacre, Shirley and Stapley were all active members. Five Sussex MPs sat on the committee of privileges.[67] Thus, although the county representation had decreased, its delegates were vocal and energetic.[68] Herbert Morley was the leading figure. His Puritan millenarianism now dimmed, he became the epitome of the sour ex-rumper, a defensive constitutionalist fighting to enlarge the minimal role allotted to parliament. Three times Morley acted as a teller with Sir Richard Onslow, the leading enemy of the Protector in Surrey. He was clearly an important member of the opposition party that filled the vacuum left when the republicans were removed. He was, for instance, teller for the noes when the House divided on the crucial issue of Cromwell's right to nominate members of the council. In December 1654 he brought to the attention of the Commons the refusal of the Clerk of the Commonwealth to accept the due election of his Sussex colleague Sir Thomas Rivers, an intervention which blocked an expedient in the Cromwellian campaign to retain a measure of control over elections.[69] It is hard to say how far the Sussex members went along with Morley. They probably shared his dislike for the authoritarian form of the new constitution, but some of them may have sympathised with the efforts of men like Sir Anthony Ashley Cooper to turn the Protectorate into a form of government acceptable to independently-minded country gentlemen.[70] They all alike desired healing and settling by a régime that turned its back on militarism and the past.

In the first week of November 1655, Major-General William Goffe arrived at Lewes to initiate his supervision of security and local government in Sussex.[71] He chose to begin with Sussex, though his area of responsibility also included Hampshire and Berkshire. The major-generals' experiment evolved from the military response of the Protectorate government to the royalist rising of the spring of 1655. The scheme involved the establishment of new local militias to maintain order county by county.[72] In fact there had been no more sign of willingness to make trouble in Sussex between 1653 and 1655 than in the previous few years. Such disturbances as had occurred had been minor ones. A riotous assembly in the Lurgashall area in the summer of 1653, for instance, was easily suppressed. There was more talk than action. The Rye gentleman, Anthony Norton, for example, declared that 'none but rogues fought against the King and that Cromwell and all that followed him were rogues'.[73] No rising occurred in the county at the time of the western design. The apprehension of Francis Cheynell and the militia commissioners Richard Boughton and Richard Maning about the 'greate deale of danger . . . in respect of home-bred conspiracys' in which Sussex stood seems to have been excessive. Herbert Morley remained watchful for the infiltration of royalist letters and papers at the ports.[74] Furthermore, the corporation of Rye cooperated efficiently with Secretary Thurloe in controlling the entry and departure of strangers by the Dieppe passage. In February 1655, for instance, they detained the French ambassador to the King of Portugal together with several merchants and scholars, until Thurloe gave them all clearance. Security alone could hardly justify Goffe's commission as Major-General of Sussex.[75]

Nor did security become a pressing problem at any stage during the ten months when Goffe was present in Sussex and the neighbouring counties. The Major-General's orders included elaborate provisions for imprisonment, bonds for good behaviour and registration as means of control over dissidents. The scheme was bound to put a brake on royalist activity, even if leniently enforced.[76] But it was easy for a Major-General to be overimpressed by the stories of parliamentarians ready to pay off old scores. Informed by William Freeman that Henry Bishop was 'a most dangerous cavaleere' and that he had been 'a great companion of John Wildman's', Goffe encouraged Freeman to pursue him until, after a game of cat and mouse, the royalist Colonel eventually gave himself up for a spell of imprisonment in London. Goffe soon saw through the bold posturings of the impetuous John Goring. He found him 'a very troublesome fellow in the country', he told Thurloe, 'but I thinke able to doe little hurt, he is such a kind of madd heady fellow'.[77] Other gentry suspected of royalism, such as Adrian May of Rawmere and William Rishton of Earnley, submitted meekly to the registration procedure.[78] Such men posed no real danger to the Cromwellian régime.

Nor did the few gentry who organised a petition on the lines of the radical programme in the Barebones parliament have much chance of reviving their cause. The petition, formulated in the autumn of 1655, was the work of the influential JP Robert Spence of Balcombe and his sons John and William. The latter had already shown his assertively radical bent in the Barebones assembly. The petition called for the abolition of chancery 'and other regulations of the law', of tithes, and of oaths on officeholders, for the disbandment of the army, and for the bringing to trial of the imprisoned Fifth Monarchist leaders Christopher Feake and Thomas Harrison. Goffe reported that it attracted considerable Baptist support, but not enough from gentry to make any headway. Colonel Busbridge told Goffe he 'refused to meddle with it' because of the disbandment clause; other gentry, who may have sympathised with this clause, were doubtless alienated by its radical legal and religious implications. The one group who did need to be taken seriously as a threat to order were the Quakers. In January 1656 Goffe was concerned at their success and spoke of arresting George Fox if an opportunity occurred. But in his campaign against the Quakers Goffe could at least be sure of the united support of the county establishment.[79]

The major-general's constructive achievement outside the sphere of security was unimpressive. In Sussex he made no discernible impact on morality, education, preaching, poor law enforcement, alehouse licensing or the reform of criminal jurisdiction. Indeed he never even attended sessions, although he was appointed as a JP in November 1655 and he appeared at both assizes the following year. A brief for the townsmen of Chichester to make a charitable collection after a disastrous fire is virtually the only administrative decision that bears his imprint.[80] Why did Goffe achieve so little? In the first place the scheme of general supervision of local government was too grandiose. Goffe was a native of Haverfordwest and unacquainted with Sussex. It was impractical to expect an outsider quickly to integrate himself into the complex administrative processes and imbibe the administrative traditions of several counties. Goffe was totally inexperienced in local government. With three counties to look after he was only able to spend an initial fortnight and about four other periods of a few weeks in Sussex over a span of eleven months. Constant travelling and meetings were very exhausting. He confessed himself to be 'soe much tyred, that I can scarse give you an account of my doings' after a visit to Sussex in March 1656; 'moste of the commisoners are tyred and desired to be dismissed for the present', he reported after the first three days of grappling with the business of decimation.[81]

The Protectorate government showed little real understanding of the practical problems involved in the major-generals enforcement of its policies. The business of raising seamen for the navy illustrates its weakness in administrative detail. On 1 February 1656 Goffe received letters about organising impressment in Hampshire and Sussex for a fleet preparing for service on the coast of Spain due to sail in a few weeks. Impressment had by then already run into difficulties in the west country and East Anglia. Goffe discussed the matter with the Hampshire justices and then hurried into Sussex.[82] Acting on his instructions, the JPs in the western rapes undertook the task. But they sent to Portsmouth a landlubber crew, consisting of a tinker, a Quaker, two glass carriers, a hatter, a chairmaker and a tanner with his boy, who was seven years old.[83] Instead of insisting on the impressment of seamen, the justices jumped at the chance of disposing of some of the riffraff of the countryside. When the constables of Gostrow hundred, taking the same unscrupulous line, sent to Rye a wandering sieve-maker with the 'falling sickness' and his wife, plus an aged chimney sweep, lame in one arm, with his family, the mayor declared them 'not fitt for the state's service' and returned them to their places of habitation.[84] The 1656 impressment campaign in Sussex, lacking proper oversight, was a farce, as Herbert Morley warned it would be in a letter to Secretary Thurloe on 20 February.

> Affairs of this nature formerly were wont to be dispatched by commissioners, and not by justices [he pointed out], and there is great reason

> for it in this country, because almost halfe the sea coasts are of an exempt jurisdiction from us, being members of the Cinque Ports.[85]

The press was gravely hampered by an elementary mistake of procedure. The justices lacked the authority to penetrate several of the places such as Rye and Hastings where seamen were most likely to be found. Even if this blunder had been rectified, it was absurd to expect Goffe to provide effective personal supervision of impressment from Christchurch to Rye, when goodwill among his subordinates was almost entirely lacking.

The task set the major-generals was a hard one. Intruders into the provinces, they were bound to depend greatly on support from London. But, from the first, the enormous correspondence filled with queries and requests that reached Secretary Thurloe was more than he could cope with. Goffe, for example, quickly appreciated that copies of the Protector's orders and instructions would be useful for driving commissioners into action and for weeding out the hesitant and fainthearted. He made the point on 13 November and when Thurloe did not respond repeated it on 24 November.[86] More crucial was the whole question of the payment of the major-generals, their militia troops and their officials. It was assumed that the scheme would be self-supporting, that the decimation tax on royalists would raise sufficient money for soldiers, treasurers, clerks, messengers and doorkeepers to be suitably rewarded. This plan was unrealistic. By Christmas Goffe was anxious about the effect on his soldiers' pay of gentry manoeuvring to escape the tax: 'men do now begin to be very industrious to bring their estates to be under £100 per annum', he reported, 'which makes us more earnestly desire an additionall order, that those that have fifty pounds per annum may be taxed'. Others such as Kelsey and Whalley had already made the same or similar requests. They were not heeded.[87]

Cromwell, meanwhile, was proving sympathetic to pressure from well-connected victims of the decimation. Hearing of Sir Edward Ford's efforts to escape, Goffe reminded Thurloe on 28 November of his leading role at Chichester in 1642. A week later he had no choice but to accept the Protector's decision in Ford's favour.[88] At least four others who were initially taxed by the Sussex commissioners were released before the first payment was due on 21 December. Because the central government was so open to pressure, Goffe's hope that Sussex would yield nearer £1,500 than £1,000 was not fulfilled. The initial overall rate was £1,049 a year.[89] During 1656 there were more reductions. Sir Edward Ford persuaded Cromwell to reduce John Caryll's estate from £1,600 to £1,050, whereas the commissioners had originally valued it at £2,500. 'It is earnestly desired he may not gett off', Goffe had written, 'and indeed if he doe, the commissioners will be utterly discouraged'. Henry Bishop obtained freedom from the decimation as well as release from prison after writing an ingratiating letter to Thurloe with information about a suspicious visitor to his home. John Ashburnham's estate was mysteriously reduced in value from £850 to £200.[90] By the end of 1656 the Sussex decimation was yielding a paltry £893 a year. The maintenance of the major-generals and their subordinates had been sabotaged by the gentry, with the apparent compliance of the government.

In February 1656 Goffe at last received directions to pay his men. The form of them confirmed his worst fears. The yield of the decimation was expected to stretch to providing the initial six months pay for all his troops: in fact it would only cover three months. Arrears of pay had become a constant anxiety to Goffe, hindering an effective working relationship with his commissioners and militia troops. The whole scheme rested in the end on the officers of these troops, who were themselves the leading commissioners in each county. They were discouraged and the service was hampered when their pay fell further and further behind. The reduction of troops to eighty men and the dismissal of Colonel Busbridge's troop altogether, expedients adopted by the Council in February and March, did not greatly ease the situation. When Busbridge's troop was disbanded with three months pay for five months service, there were angry words between the Colonel and the Major-General. Goffe faced an ugly scene with the men before they accepted their fate.[91]

The system of decentralised payment of the militias was of course bound to be inequitable. 'I feare those assosiations that rayse least money will have such a pittyfull militia, that the major-general will have little honour or comfort in commanding them', Goffe wrote bitterly to Thurloe in February 1656. He suggested in this letter that a common treasury should be established for receipt and payment of the decimation money. A centralised procedure was subsequently adopted, but it seems never to have been more than a paper plan.[92] By the summer Goffe was distraught about the effect of lack of money on his administration. 'If the worke and ourselves perish for want of our wages', he warned on 24 June, 'it will not, I hope, be laied to our charge.' While he waited hopefully for 'something of the settling of the establishment for the payment of the militia', the new army committee remained inert. 'Oh! how much were it to be wished that things might be done seasonably, that we might not suffer soe much by unnecessary delays', Goffe lamented on 30 June. In August, his administration was still 'ready to starve for want of necessary supplyes of money'.[9] In some counties at least the major-general's scheme was running into the ground for lack of maintenance long before parliament refused to accept the continuance of the decimation. Shortly before the vote of 28 January 1657, which brought the final collapse of the system, Goffe was signing warrants for Thomas Collins, the treasurer at Chichester, to pay the wage due to the Sussex militia troops the previous June. In 1658 Captain Freeman obtained some of the money due to him for expenses from th decimation fund still in Collins's hands. Goffe took the rest, telling Collin he would discharge him in the Exchequer, since 'there was much more du to him than that from the state'. None of the money that came in on the decimation payments of 24 June and 21 December 1656 appears to have reached the abortive general treasury.[94]

Some of the other major-generals undoubtedly attempted and achieved more than William Goffe because they grasped their opportunities more firmly.[95] Goffe was temperamentally unsuited to the administrative task set him. 'I am weake', he wrote with heartfelt feeling as he faced up to 'this difficult affaire'; he referred to himself as a 'poore and inconsiderable creature'; he declared himself 'in many respects unworthy of the employment'. His self-pity betrayed a serious lack of confidence. 'I am very sensible of my great inability to manadge this great trust as I ought', he wrote peevishly on 24 June 1656, 'yett am not convinced of any unfaithfulness'.[96] Lack of support from London encouraged his tendency to self-denigration. Goffe leaned on two emotional props as he struggled with the problems of his major-generalship: his intense Puritan faith and his deep personal attachment to the Protector. Both these aspects of his motivation emerge constantly in his letters to Thurloe. He prayed for Cromwell 'without ceasing', he assured Thurloe, 'I can I hope cheerefully sacrifice my life in the service if need be'. He was shocked to find that ome sought 'to render his Highness unto the people of God as a person voyde of religion or the power of godlines' and he endeavoured to correct such misapprehensions. The millenarianism which he had proclaimed at he Putney debates still gave Goffe strength in the 1650s. 'God can yett aise that designe out of the dust, and make it turne to his prayse, and the omfort of those, that love the Lord Jesus Christ, and wayght for the rise of Antichrist'.[97]

This messianic streak meant much to a man who was timid and querulous by nature. In November 1655 Goffe was worrying about his wife's lack of money and the sale of his coleseed. In the New Year he hoped o settle his family at Winchester but was distracted by Thurloe's failure to btain the Protector's comments on this plan. News of the new parliament in June set him fretting about finding winter lodgings near Westminster. Tact certainly came more easily to Goffe than to some of the major-enerals, since he felt so dependent on and vulnerable to other men's ourtesy and civility. On arrival at Lewes he had the officers of his own oop and those of the local militia dine together, 'and much good cor-espondence appeared, and I trust will continue'. At Chichester he was esitant about taking bonds for security from men who were to be deci-mated: 'to put them upon all the hard termes at ance, it may bee would ot goe down so easily'. Forwarding Chichester's petition for a brief, he oted that some response from London would bring him 'a great reputa-on' in the city, since most of the merchants there had suffered by the ecent fire.[98] Goffe was a man anxious to make friends and afraid of aking enemies.

Yet tact was not enough to attract positive support from the county establishment. The magnates saw Goffe as a man to be lobbied. He might be an upstart military officer but he had the ear of the Protector and Secretary Thurloe. Several magnates met him at Lewes and, in his anxiety to make a favourable impression, Goffe ensured that they got the nominations to the Bench that they wanted.[99] But from the first there was caution beneath the civility of men like John Stapley and Anthony Shirley. They were unlikely to cooperate in a scheme which, by the divisive victimisation of ex-royalists, contradicted the whole spontaneous movement of the gentry community towards closing the unhappy chapter of the 1640s. Goffe's interview with Herbert Morley at Glynde was disheartening. He hoped that the courtesy of a 'kind visit . . . whatever he thinkes of my bussines, will doe noe hurt'. Morley agreed to give Goffe every assistance in so far as his authority as a JP allowed, but he made it clear that beyond that he would have no truck with the Major-General's commission.[100] Morley's developing correspondence with Thurloe during 1656 shows that his eyes were solely on the county's interests. His advice about impressment methods in February was followed by a letter about the effective defence of the coast. With Sir Thomas Pelham and Anthony Stapley both dead, Morley's influence was predominant among the eastern magnates. Goffe abandoned the idea of approaching William Hay or John Fagge, since he knew he could expect a repetition of Morley's haughty behaviour. Hay was still among the most diligent of the eastern justices, but Goffe excused himself from visiting him by reporting that, according to his information he had 'of late not acted in any thing'. It was well known, he explained to Thurloe, that Fagge would not 'stirr a haires bredth without Colonel Morley'. He was 'very free and courteous', but confessed 'he was very glad he was not named to this imployment'.[101] Goffe's arrival to take command of the standing forces in the county, which under the Rump had remained at the Grand Committee's beck and call, was a direct challenge to Morley's clique. The gentry community was bound to close its ranks against him.

'I doe see the stresse of this busines must lie upon the midle sort of men', Goffe concluded after a few days in Lewes. The list of sixteen commissioners that he enclosed in his report reflects his comment. Among those who attended the first meeting at Chichester were lesser gentry recently appointed to the Bench, like Richard Yates and Arthur Bettsworth, and substantial merchants like Richard Maning, mayor of Chichester, and Thomas Ballard, mayor of Arundel. Goffe had nominated John Stapley and Anthony Shirley but neither would act. The business fell quickly into the hands of the commissioned officers of the three militia troops. From the first the leading figure was the assiduous Captain William Freeman, who now broke with the Grand Committee. He advised Goffe about the commission nominations; 'exceeding industrious and helpful' he took charge when Goffe went into Hampshire and Berkshire. The other officers most fully involved were Richard Boughton, Captain Walter

Everenden of Fairlight and Captain Thomas Jenner of Warbleton. Goffe chose the commissioners for their godliness: Everenden, ‘a very honest, sober man’, was one whom ‘the honest men of the country were apt to follow’. Richard Maning was a fierce Puritan ‘much baffled by the corrupt party’ in Chichester, ‘who had kept him from being mayor as long as they could’. Goffe saw his accession to office there as ‘a good providence’. Goffe’s adjutants regarded their troops as a ‘new quickesett hedge, that will for a while need an old hedge about it’, as a potent means of security in the countryside that could one day make Cromwell’s army redundant. They yearned for moral reform, but they were always preoccupied with decimating and with patrolling the county seeking royalists or trouble-makers.[102]

John Busbridge, a survivor of the old-style trained band captains, was the only military commissioner who moved among the county gentry and shared their preconceptions. He was quickly alienated, and predictably was first to defect. Goffe found him thoroughly refractory: he did not attend meetings and was ‘very unapt for business’. A new wife who was ‘very much against his being in publicke employment’, perhaps because she found her husband’s country affairs a distraction from a metropolitan life, the disagreeable major-generals scheme, his quarrel with Rye and a nomination to the shrievalty from which he hastened to get himself discharged, combined in 1656 to turn Busbridge against public service. There was friction between him and the other commissioners over his magnate connections. William Freeman’s faction lobbied Goffe with tales of Busbridge’s wife’s malignancy and of drinking and gaming at his Etchingham home. Yet the confrontation between Busbridge and Goffe, when the latter reduced his troop in March 1656, was civil enough. Busbridge merely affirmed what every county gentleman knew, that Goffe’s agents were a faction of radical Puritans like himself, lacking social prestige and unable to understand the traditions of magnate administration. Like Morley, Fagge and others, Busbridge, an irascible man, decided to keep his hands clean: he ‘suspected some ill dealing from some of his countrymen, and saith, he is now soe much disobliged, that he will never appeare in publicke business more’. In fact he did attend the midsummer sessions the following summer, but that was a social occasion, a very different matter from working with Goffe and his busybody commissioners.[103]

Determining who should pay the decimation tax nine years after the war had ended was no easy task. Goffe and his men relied heavily on the old sequestration books.[104] To the gentry community it was bound to look like the unnecessary reopening of old scores. Some of the victims, like Robert Edsawe, whose clerical father had sent him to join the royalist army, Piers Edgcombe, Lord Lumley, John Covert and Richard Bridger, had certainly born arms against parliament. Two leading recusants whose implication as royalists was well established, John Caryll and Sir Garrett

Kempe, also suffered decimation.[105] But other more ambiguous cases were bound to seem invidious.[106] Several neutrals, including John Lewkenor and Thomas May, found themselves picked upon.[107] Decimation of magnates like John Ashburnham and Sir William Morley was an affront to a community set on reconciliation. Ashburnham's royalist past was well known, but his neighbours' readiness to forgive and forget had enabled him to reintegrate himself into gentry society. In 1650 Anthony Stapley, Herbert Morley and Peter Farnden had agreed to act as his trustees.[108] Goffe was caustic about men who exhibited 'too much innocency as to any of the late designes', yet the western gentry were too sensible to be attracted by the harebrained royalist conspiracies of the mid 1650s. Sir William Morley, for instance, a much respected man, had lived in quiet retirement from public affairs since the outbreak of the civil war. No wonder he took it 'very much to heart, that hee should bee still reckoned a malignant', having told Goffe that he had 'long bin satisfyde of the justness of our cause'.[109]

The Sussex gentry showed their dislike of the vindictive policy of decimation and for those who were identified with it at the county election at Lewes castle in August 1656. Goffe reported the triumph of the county over the military faction: 'Colonel Morley ruled the rost, by the help of a disaffected party, much to the griefe of the honest party . . . it was theire designe to have noe soldier, decemator, or any man that hath salary'. The election return, showing the order in which men were chosen, was a rollcall of the gentry with the most power and prestige. Herbert Morley, Sir John Pelham, John Fagge, John Stapley and Anthony Shirley were the first five on the list. All had sat in 1654. The other four places went to George Courthope, a newcomer to Westminster, Sir Thomas Rivers, who had sat in 1654, and to two experienced parliamentarians of the 1640s, Sir Thomas Parker and Samuel Gott. Henry Peckham again sat for Chichester and Anthony Stapley, the younger son of the regicide, for Lewes. The electioneering efforts of Major-Generals Goffe and Kelsey could not stem the antimilitarist tide. Goffe wrote to the mayor of Arundel, who assured him the town would chose Captain Freeman if Anthony Shirley, their representative in 1654, sat for the county, but in the end Morley swayed the corporation into electing his father-in-law Sir John Trevor instead.[110] Kelsey tried to get the single Rye seat for one of the Commissioners of the Admiralty and Navy. 'Few gentry of your county', he wrote in a bid to sow discord, 'in regard of crossing theire owne interest', would take care to preserve the port's liberties and privileges. The corporation disagreed. Over the years William Hay had worked hard for the town. Recommended fulsomely by his cousin Morley, he won an overwhelming victory at the poll over Kelsey's candidate.[111]

The 1656 elections were thus a demonstration of the failure of the major-generals experiment to impose effective centralised control of th shire. Sussex warns against over-emphasis on the significance of their brief intervention in halting or interrupting the process of reconciliation in the county communities. There at least, Puritan repression never worked, military rule was more a bogey than a reality.[112] Paradoxically the return of the longest established county families to the Bench, begun with Lord Dacre's appointment in 1655, accelerated while Goffe was overlord. One of those who came back into local government was George Courthope, a reputed royalist who helped to defeat the military faction in the 1656 election.[113] William Freeman and his friends in revenge petitioned against Courthope, dramatising his role in organising the 1648 petition, and accusing him of sending money to the King. They even considered alleging that he was dismissed from the Commission of the Peace in 1646 for malignancy and drunkenness. But they failed to make their case.[114]

Decimation still rankled in 1657. When Colonel Culpepper cursed the decimators 'and all the devisers of the decimation' at the Bull Inn in Lewes, he started a celebrated quarrel between John Pellet, who defended the tax, and Henry Woodcock.[115] Nevertheless the county had to be governed. The swordsmen and their moderate opponents were bound to bury their differences when they sat together on the Bench. At Michaelmas sessions in 1656 Richard Boughton, William Freeman and Thomas Jenner sat at Lewes with John Stapley, John Fagge and William Hay. The Chichester Bench that Michaelmas had on its agenda a case which touched on the very issues at stake in the summer election.[116] When a Warnham busybody had procured the lieutenant and corporal of Captain Freeman's troop to search an alehouse in the village, the butcher there had called him an 'informinge rogue'. The butcher had also called Freeman himself and his whole company 'rogues' and sworn several oaths against them. Freeman himself was on the Bench that heard the case. Whatever any of his colleagues may have felt about the militia men, so outright a challenge to a JP's authority could not be treated lightly. The Bench agreed to fine the rash tradesman five pounds.[117] Magisterial cohesion overcame the factional division among the gentry which had emerged under the stress of Cromwellian government.

The county reunited

Herbert Morley and Anthony Stapley had worked in close cooperation as the county's parliamentary bosses in the 1640s. Neither Morley nor Stapley's son John was sympathetic to Cromwell's Protectorate, but they opposed it from opposite viewpoints. Whereas John Stapley fell in with the royalist conspirators and took up the King's cause, Morley stuck to his republican principles and passively resisted the betrayal, as he saw it, of the parliamentary cause. Morley accepted his exclusion from the 1656 parliament with good grace. When a manifesto appeared, with his and

John Fagge's names appended, attacking Cromwell's exclusion of some hundred MPs, he hastened to deny that he 'ever knew of' it. 'I am amazed to hear of it', he wrote to Sir John Trevor on 12 October,

> it beinge my desire, that since I am debarred from exercise of the trust reposed in me by my countrey to serve them in parliament, I am well contented I shall ever live quietly at my owne house, where if any desire to speake with me, they shall assuredly finde me.[118]

During 1657 and 1658 Morley was busy taking recognisances, examining criminals and attending sessions, where he sometimes took the chair. In the summer of 1658 he was fully engaged in the new anti-papist drive in Pevensey rape. In local affairs he was as approachable as ever; his administrative expertise was much in demand.[119]

Herbert Morley's chance to play a part in national politics once again came in 1659 when, with his brother-in-law Fagge, he was elected under the old franchise for the county.[120] In speeches in February and March 1659, Morley showed himself to be a hard-line republican. He castigated those who were willing to overlook the delinquency of Edmund Jones, who had been elected for Brecon. By admitting cavaliers to sit, he claimed, he would be breaking the oath he had just taken to be true and faithful to Richard Cromwell and the liberties of the people. On 18 February, when the House was bogged down in an inconclusive debate about bounding the new Protector's power, Morley tried to bring it back to the essential question of its own rights and liberties, indeed its supremacy. He pointed out forcefully that the Commons might end up putting a double negative upon themselves by giving both Richard Cromwell and the Other House too much power. A fortnight later, Morley gave strong support to Sir Anthony Ashley Cooper over the question of the Commons transacting with the Other House. He warned MPs against being tempted by the government tactic of including in the Other House the old peers who had been faithful. The Cromwellians would hold the majority: the point had already been made by others that imposing bounds on the Other House, once it was recognised, would be wellnigh impossible. Morley described the government's scheme as 'a gilded pill' that 'must be sent down in syrups and sweetmeats'. 'All the gilding and syrups shall not make me pass it', he declared.[121] Throughout the period from 1653 until the Rump was restored, Morley was unwilling to countenance those who saw Protectorates as a better basis for settlement than none. For six years his opposition at Westminster was persistent and forthright.

The news of April 1658 that John Stapley had been arrested as a royalist conspirator amazed the gentry community of Sussex. Edward Chown, who until then had kept the rumours he had heard to himself told his brother Henry and Edward Blaker all he knew when they showed their bewilderment at Stapley's detention. The general disbelief among those who were not involved in the plot is understandable. Stapley had more prestige and influence than anyone, except possibly Sir John Pelham, among the younger generation of county magnates. When the eastern justices pressed Goffe to appoint a *custos rotulorum* in 1655, there was unanimous agreement that he should be given the office in succession to his father.[122] Of course it was the very fact that he was so highly respected which made Stapley such an attractive recruit to the royalist ranks. He was known to be a moderate 'and many would rise with him, who would not follow the cavilliers'. Stapley was not so much headstrong as naïve. He listened to the persuasions of his royalist kin the Gorings and the Campions; he swallowed Dr Hewitt's assurances that Charles was almost ready to invade and that many gentry were engaged in other counties; he was tempted by the glory and the baronetcy that command of the regiment which helped to restore the King might bring; he took fright at Hewitt's insinuations that he was a 'lost man' after his father's treason, if he did not redeem his family's reputation. Stapley was certainly persuaded to accept the leadership of the Sussex wing of the 1658 conspiracy. He was nerved for action by a series of meetings with Hewitt and others. Even so he never distributed the blank commissions that he was persuaded to accept, or showed any energy in sounding out magnate friends and neighbours. He recognised the need to secure Sir John Pelham's support, for example, but excused himself from approaching him, since 'there had been a quarrel between them two'. He sent his brother Anthony, the only man apart from his neighbour Henry Mallory that he himself apparently engaged, to try the mind of Henry Goring of Highden, a senior magnate of considerable standing. When he was arrested in March 1658 Stapley quickly confessed and abjectly begged the Protector's pardon. All his bravado melted into terrified volubility as he sought to satisfy Cromwell and escape the consequences of his rashness.[123]

It would be easy to dismiss the whole Sussex conspiracy, the cloak-and-dagger meetings on the Downs and in manor houses, the inducement of friends at village alehouses, as a foolish escapade. Yet, given the assumptions of the plotters, that Charles would land with a considerable army and that support for him would at once emerge all over south-east England, the talk of a Stuart restoration, which spread from manor to manor in 1657 and early 1658 seemed by no means unrealistic. The county was quite inadequately defended. Rye was the only remaining garrison and Captain Freeman's militia troop could scarcely by itself provide effective surveillance of the western rapes.[124] The capture of Freeman was a first priority in the royalist scheme. The intention to seize Chichester made some sense since it was based on an ingenious plan formulated by the publican of the Dolphin, Henry Binsted, to disarm at daybreak the troop of thirty or so cavalry based in the city. About seventeen county gentry and more than twenty lesser gentry were implicated to a greater or lesser degree in the conspiracy. The planning of the old royalists in the west, men like Henry Bishop, George Gunter and William Smith, was well coordinated with that of eastern agents such as Thomas Geere of Ovingdean and John Mills of Alfriston.[125]

Charles II certainly enjoyed a much wider and more substantial basis of support in Sussex in 1658 than his father had enjoyed in the 1640s. Loyalty to him was by no means confined to the old heartland of Sussex royalism in Chichester rape. Besides active royalists of the 1640s, like John Apsley and Thomas Sackville, and leading Catholics, like Sir Garrett Kempe and John Caryll, there was a whole new generation of gentry who were coming to look to the Stuarts for the healing and settling that was universally desired. Ten men who became JPs at the Restoration expressed some degree of interest in Stapley's conspiracy. On the one hand there was Thomas Woodcock, an enthusiastic plotter who was lucky to be acquitted; on the other there were men like Thomas Nutt, who was keen to discuss the conspiracy with John Stapley but too cautious to do more than imply that he would let his horses be taken if the rising occurred. George Parker, Sir Thomas's eldest son, who had been in the forefront of the 1648 petitioning movement, was equally tightlipped, saying that 'he meant to sleep in a whole skin'.[126] Others were more careless. William Wilson had to distract a party of dragoons who visited Eastbourne Place at Easter 1658 from searching the house by entertaining them with a wheatear pie, while he hastily disposed of some incriminating letters. Distraught at the suspicion that had fallen on her husband, Mary Wilson sought to assure a cousin that he had taken every precaution against it: 'he hath lived retired at home all these times and avoyded all publicke and private meetings, because he would not give cause for the least suspicion'. But Wilson, it seems, had at least been actively soliciting the support of his neighbours Nicholas Gildredge and Thomas Foster. Percy Goring, the younger son of Sir William Goring of Burton, carried dangerous tracts about him as he rode through the Sussex lanes. When he dropped a pamphlet in Sullington street which declared 'that any man or woman that should resist the King should be cut as small herbs to the pot' he almost landed himself in serious trouble.[127]

There were some gentry who made it clear when they were approached that they would have nothing to do with the plot. Richard Lindsey, for example, who was heavily indebted, showed no interest when the busy agent John Pickering, who was one of his clients, tried to engage him over a pint of wine at the Chequer in Maresfield. 'He had suffered much, and was in years, and was resolved to live peaceably', he declared. Pickering's talk of 'troublesome times' did not move this tired and apathetic ex-royalist: 'let come what will come', he would content himself with living under the Protector. John Watson of West Hoathly took much the same line: 'he would do nothing, for he was old and lame'. Any meddling in such affairs, he warned Pickering, was unwise. There seems to have been a widespread but grudging acceptance of the Cromwellian régime in the last months of Oliver's life, particularly among the greatest magnates. John Covert, an ex-royalist colonel who since the war had come to live at Slaugham Place, refused the royalist commission that was offered to him. Henry Goring of Highden was eager enough to discuss the latest rumours about Charles Stuart's invasion places with his dinner guests, but Anthony Stapley found Goring 'wary and shy' when he raised the topic of a rising. In the tense situation when the conspiracy was revealed, the logic of time-serving neutralism led to the course that Walter Burrell was alleged to have followed. He

> was so wise as to procure himself to be nominated as one to be questioned by the state as an actor for Charles Stuart, colourably that he might be the better excused, if the King, meaning Charles Stuart, should come, for not acting for him really.[128]

There was certainly much disbelief in and pessimism about a restoration in 1658. Those who accepted public employment did so not only because they thought they owed it to their county, but because they believed that the Protectorate offered the only possible basis for settlement. 'He wondered that Charles Stuart should be so ill beloved, for he could not hear that anybody loved him', Edward Blaker, the sheriff for 1658, told the royalist William Smith. When Smith later insisted that Charles would land very shortly, Blaker remained totally sceptical, 'for he would not conceive how he should be able to do it'. William Dyke, an active, though aged, Puritan JP, challenged Anthony Stapley's contention that a restoration was the only means to remove the 'many grievances and oppressions' of the people. He was convinced that 'there would be many more if a strange people was brought in amongst us'.[129] The mirage of a vast army over the water, giving heart to the inner circle of conspirators, disturbed many magnates who dreaded the renewal of civil war. The longer the Protectorate lasted, the better chance it seemed to have of becoming permanent. In this sense Cromwell's refusal of the crown, which seemed so great a disaster for those most deeply involved in pressing it in London, may have been quickly accepted by many provincial gentry without further heartsearching. Samuel Gott's reaction was probably not typical. Excluded from the parliament, he had nevertheless followed its debates closely. On 12 May 1657 he wrote dejectedly to his friend John Swynfen:

> That good which we thought we had griped fast in our fists, when we opened them our hands precurd but winde; great were desires and expectations of settlement and because great the disapointments are the more shamefull, hence comes it that persons interested in the late modell gaze on each other as if they beheld something of wonder. I wish we may not loose our hearts for most of us have lost our tongues.[130]

Even without the kingship, the Humble Petition and Advice acquired wider and fuller support from country gentry than the Instrument of Government.[131] Moderate gentry eagerly grasped the county places in

Richard Cromwell's parliament of January 1659. George Courthope, Samuel Gott and Henry Peckham, who had been excluded in 1656, all returned to Westminster; Anthony Shirley and William Hay sat again; the newcomers included John Busbridge, Henry Onslow, George Parker and John Byne, the heir of a family with a tradition of service to the county which had been in eclipse since 1625.[132] Samuel Gott, convinced of the viability of the Humble Petition, once more adopted a Cromwellian stance. When the Commons were floundering over the question of transacting with the Other House, he urged the members to avoid a 'split upon this very rock':

> When we go home what satisfaction will it be to them that sent us, what satisfaction to our consciences? . . . We leave the nation to an arbitrary government. Any government is better than no government, and any civil better than a military government.

Gott's political outlook in 1659, one shared by many of his countrymen if not by Herbert Morley, was based on expediency rather than principle. He based his case on grounds of 'prudence, conveniency, safety and law'. He confessed himself 'little pleased with these Lords', but ridiculed a parliament of one House as a constitutional innovation that the governing class would not tolerate: 'we are but one leg and cannot go but hop up and down without them . . . I have seen a man walk very well with a wooden leg'.[133]

There was a particular reason for the Sussex magnates to pin their faith in the régime which existed and which had survived for four years, a reason which did not apply in some counties. They had maintained a firm hold on the institutions of county government, despite the influx of lesser gentry and merchants as JPs. Furthermore, Oliver Cromwell had succeeded in drawing into active membership of the Commission of the Peace several men of county reputation. Sir John Pelham, William Dyke and Henry Onslow all responded positively to their appointment. In 1656 George Courthope took up once more the administrative tasks he had abandoned ten years before. The assessments, in the east at least, remained in the hands of the traditional rulers.[134] When John Stapley's conspiracy leaked out Goffe's militia commissioners were able to busy themselves for a few weeks with examinations and interrogations, but in normal times the Puritan militants were overshadowed by the prestige and influence of magnates whom the community habitually trusted.[135]

The collapse of Richard Cromwell's Protectorate in April 1659 brought political uncertainty to both the capital and the provinces. 'Times are dead and no money to be payed where owinge', reported John Busbridge from London at the end of the month. He decided to prolong his visit 'to see how thinges goe in this unsettled time'. The return of the Rump in May decided nothing, because it was bound to be at odds with the army leaders and the social basis of its support was too narrow. The summer's outburst of radicalism, the pamphleteering and propaganda about the Good Old Cause, encouraged a growing conviction among moderate gentry that only a Stuart restoration could save the country from anarchy.[136] In early June about 5,000 Fifth Monarchists met for eight hours at Horsham.[137] Later that month the Rump received a petition from 'divers friends to the Good Old Cause' in east Sussex, quickly answered by a JP and gentry sponsored petition.[138] The unpopularity of the Rump was partly due to the authority it gave to 'mean and fanatic spirits' in the provinces. There were widespread purges of militia commissions and Commissions of the Peace. But Sussex went against the general trend, for, with the return of the Rump, the gentry community, deprived for six years of its voices in the Council of State, once more had a patron at the centre.

Herbert Morley was a predictable choice for the new Council of State. The remodelling of the Bench and the militia commission during July reflects his conservative social instincts. The promotion of John Fagge to a place high on the Commission of the Peace, just below Morley himself, is a clear indication of his patronage. Radicals were purged: William Freeman lost his place on both bodies; Thomas Jenner his most energetic colleague in the militia commission was dismissed as a JP; Richard Maning, the Puritan mayor of Chichester whom Goffe had found so agreeable, was dropped from the militia commission.[139] The county gentry, in fact, took a further step in July 1659 towards the restoration of their traditional domination of the shire.

During the summer of 1659 Herbert Morley harnessed the energies of the group of men with whom he had worked most closely from 1649 to 1653 in pursuit of a policy of firm control in the county and active involvement in national affairs at Westminster. He himself had a busy summer, attending the Council regularly and bearing his share of committee work at Westminster with his colleagues John Downes, John Fagge, William Cawley, William Hay and James Temple. He also acted as an Admiralty commissioner.[140] All the active MPs also attended the assizes at East Grinstead on 22 July.[141] A few days later Morley arranged for his brother-in-law Fagge to take overall charge of the county militia, in view of the increasing rumours of a royalist conspiracy in the south-east. Two troops of horse and two of foot were hastily raised to defend the county; Thomas Marshall, a recently appointed justice, was given oversight of Rye with a further troop; Cowdray was garrisoned; Brambletye was searched; Sackville Graves, one of the 1658 conspirators, was among those whom Fagge arrested on suspicion.[142]

Though plans there collapsed in both cases, Surrey and Kent seem to have been much better organised than Sussex to take part in Sir George Booth's rising. There no one this time was prepared to play John Stapley's role.[143] By September Morley was sufficiently confident of the quiescence of his county to agree to a disbandment of the emergency forces. Before leaving London for a brief spell at Glynde, he also responded to the pleas of the Rye corporation for the removal of some soldiers quartered there: 'I have importuned the Councell in your behalfe', he wrote, 'I hope you will take care for the safety of your towne by continuing your watches as formerly, which I undertooke for you'. The essence of Morley's command of the county was his friendly relationship, carefully cultivated, with men who had faithfully worked with him since 1642. 'My brother Fagge and Cousin Hay present their respects to you', he added in a postscript to his letter from Whitehall to the Rye townsmen on 6 September 1659.[144]

Morley's political acumen and zeal for parliamentary government brought him a formidable reputation during the summer and autumn of 1659. His prestige on the vulnerable south coast made him a useful member of the Council, yet his moderation was in striking contrast to the uncompromising republicanism of some others such as Sir Arthur Hesilrige. Already colonel of a foot regiment, he was an obvious choice for appointment when the Rump decreed on 12 October that thenceforth the army should be governed by seven commissioners. Its tense relationship with the army had reached a crisis. But Morley's attempt, with Hesilrige and Colonel Walton, to secure the continuance of the sittings at Westminster by enlisting the help of loyal soldiery was a failure. The unsteadiness of his men forced him to give way and he was subsequently removed from his command. Morley became determined that the nakedly military régime which replaced the Rump should be defeated. During November he met in secret with eight others who saw the restoration of constitutional government as the first priority.[145] Morley seems to have been the first of this council of nine to contact Charles Stuart. John Evelyn's tract *An Apology for the Royal Party: Written in a Letter to a Person of the late Councel of State* was aimed specifically at his old schoolfellow at Southover. Despite diverging political views, Morley and Evelyn had always remained on good terms. It was probably Evelyn who convinced Morley that the time was coming for him to discard his republicanism. The pressure of friends and kin must have weighed on his mind. Morley may well always have regarded the restored Rump as a temporary expedient, tackling the problem of settlement in preparation for a free election. He was becoming disillusioned with Hesilrige's negative policies; like others such as Ashley Cooper, he was coming to see that the country might only find true parliamentary government under the monarchy and the old constitution; at the very least he recognised the need to secure himself against the occurrence of a restoration.

The future was cloudy. During November Morley asked Evelyn to intercede with the King on behalf of himself, Fagge and his Hay relations.[146] On 3 December Morley arrived at Portsmouth with Heselrige and Walton and won over the governor. Their purpose was to reinforce their power in preparation for the march south of General Monck, who had agreed to try to re-establish the parliament. Morley's interest on the south coast made him the crucial figure in the enterprise. Fagge, armed with commissions signed by Thomas Scot as president of the secret council of nine, had begun to raise forces in his support when on 26 December the army régime tottered and the Long Parliament reassembled.[147]

The imposition of the oath abjuring the House of Stuart on members of the new Council of State established on 2 January 1660 caused Morley and Fagge to break with Heselrige and the extreme republicans. Both, like Anthony Ashley Cooper who also declined the oath, were elected but failed to serve. In the restored Rump, on the other hand, Morley was as vocal as ever, teaming up with Cooper in the leadership of a faction which aimed, in open opposition to Heselrige's supporters, to prepare the ground for Monck and to keep open the option of an offer to the King of a 'free return to his own dominions'. 'The parties in the House are diametrically opposite', reported Lord Mordaunt to the King on 16 January.[148] Fagge was a teller against the reading on 3 January of the Bill imposing the oath renunciating the House of Stuart on the whole House. As usual he clung close to Morley. Despite these manoeuvrings, the republicans seem still to have trusted Morley. They made no objection to his appointment as Lieutenant of the Tower on 7 January.[149]

Command of the Tower made Morley's allegiance all the more attractive to the royalists: between 10 and 22 January John Evelyn conducted a vigorous campaign to convert both him and Fagge, who was then engaged in raising a regiment of foot. Morley resisted Evelyn's persuasions, more it seems out of hesitancy and uncertainty about his own fate under the restored King than from any remaining republican scruples. In discussion with Evelyn he was apprehensive about Monck's intentions; a report to Sir Edward Hyde mentioned his awareness of his 'own guilt and breach of faith'. Morley recognised that only Monck could dictate the pace and direction of events. Later Evelyn wrote scornfully in his diary of Morley's 'horrible error and neglect of the counsel I gave him, by which he had certainly don the greate work, with the same ease that Monk did it . . . by which he had then made himselfe the greatest person in England next the King'.[150] But the charge, coloured by Evelyn's pique at the loss of the grandeur that might have come his own way, is unfair. It is true that in late January Morley's position was potentially very strong. Fagge was governor of Portsmouth; his brother William governor of Arundel. Yet he lacked sufficient strength to act independently. In view of this, Morley's course was a wise and realistic one.[151] His control of the Tower and the support of his and Fagge's regiments ensured Monck's smooth entry to London; he was Monck's man on the new army commission of 11 February; he was involved in Monck's negotiations for readmitting the secluded members; he was elected to and regularly attended the Council of State which sat in March, April and May; he remained Lieutenant of the Tower until the King's return.[152] Thus Morley played a principal role in the Restoration of Charles II. He had yearned, as much as any of his

Sussex friends, for a settlement that provided a constitutional voice for independent country gentlemen like himself. In 1659 and 1660 he bent his acute political skills to getting it.

The Sussex gentry, like those of Kent, enthusiastically welcomed the Restoration. At Eastbourne William Wilson personally supervised the celebrations, with bonfires on the Downs and the distribution of claret to the local countrymen. 'He publickly declared', it is recorded, 'that now God be thanked he thought his estate his own and he hoped that every man of them around him would thinke the same'.[153] There were bonfires all over the county. At West Chiltington the churchwardens wasted no time in 'setting up the King's armes'.[154] Sour faces were only to be found among Puritan militants and sectaries. A Twineham labourer, alleged to be a Quaker, excused himself from going to the bonfire with the comment that he did 'not know but that the Kinge maye bee killed within a small tyme'. But Walter Burrell, confident that settlement was at last achieved, decided to give coats to ten men of Cuckfield on 29 May each year of Charles II's reign, 'upon which day the cloathed poor people are to bee ait church to give thanks for the great mercy vouchsafed to these kingdomes by the happy restoration of his Majesty'.[155]

On 30 June the Sussex gentry swarmed into Whitehall to present their address to the King. 'I went with it, and kiss'd his Majesties hand', recorded John Evelyn, who was himself a signatory. The address expressed the county's 'hearty joy' at his 'miraculous and peaceable restauration . . . which wee must ever esteeme the greatest earthly blessing, being now well assured'. In deference to their rank and status, the gentry left one side of the address open for the signatures of the nobility. There the Earls of Northumberland, Dorset and Norwich, the Viscounts Montagu, Lumley and Dacre and Lord Abergavenny boldly spread their names. The rest of the page was tightly packed with the signatures of 104 gentry, a rollcall of the county families, a demonstration of the restored unity of the gentry community: the royalists John Ashburnham, Sir Edward Ford, and George Gunter, the conspirators of 1658, John and Anthony Stapley, Percy Goring and Sir Thomas Woodcock, the parliamentarians Herbert and William Morley, Herbert Springate, Hall Ravenscroft and Thomas Middleton, all joined in welcoming home the exiled King. Young men like Sir John Pelham and John Covert who had inherited grand estates added their names; younger sons of county families who had made their way in the world and established themselves in their native shire, like Bray and Henry Chown who had been bound apprentices in the 1630s, joined the rejoicing. The page was full of names that every Sussex countryman respected: among them were Gorings, Mays, Eversfields, Bynes, Morleys and Lewkenors. Even old Benjamin Pickering, the firebrand Puritan minister of East Hoathly, signed. Only the signatures of the Puritan militants who had acted as Goffe's henchmen and of the surviving regicides were conspicuously absent. James Temple and John Downes were both tried and found guilty. Both of them were still in prison in 1666. William Cawley escaped to live out his life at Vevay in Switzerland.[156]

In the militia commission of March and the Commissions of the Peace of March and July 1660 the county gentry flooded back into power. For the first time peers—Dacre, Dorset and Northumberland—were nominated as militia commissioners. They were accompanied by newcomers to the Bench from the old families such as John Hay, John de la Chambre and Henry Onslow and by old stalwarts like George Courthope and Francis Selwyn. The re-establishment of the lieutenancy under the Earl of Northumberland, the new *custos rotulorum*, in August confirmed the hold of the magnates on the trained bands.[157] The remodelling of the Bench was drastic, though not quite as drastic as in some other counties, such as Warwickshire.[158] The justices who served for the first time all came from well-established families. Many of them sat for Sussex boroughs in the Cavalier Parliament. Several, including William Morley of Halnaker, John Lewkenor, John Covert, and the conspirators of 1658, Thomas Nutt, William Wilson and Thomas Woodcock, shared in the bonanza of baronetcies and knighthoods which Charles II indulged in during his first two years on the throne.[159] Even John Fagge followed his pardon with a baronetcy before the end of 1660. Fagge lived until 1701, serving in parliament from the 1660s until the 1690s. Daniel Defoe visited him at his 'noble ancient seat' of Wiston in 1697, when Fagge showed him some of the prize bullocks he was breeding.

Only Herbert Morley was left out. He was treated harshly and paid £1,000 for his pardon.[160] His wholehearted commitment to the parliamentary cause was remembered and his contribution to the Restoration was ignored. A scapegoat, in August he suffered the humiliation of dismissal from the Commission of the Peace; in the April parliamentary election he was defeated; when the Earl of Northumberland recommended him as a deputy-lieutenant his name was crossed out by Secretary Nicholas.[161] Realising the futility of standing for the county in 1661, Morley hastened to apply to his old friends at Rye. 'Though I am conscious of my own weakness', he wrote a week before the parliament was summoned, 'I shall readily serve with my utmost diligence'. They duly elected him. But Morley never regained his county or national standing before his death in 1667.[162]

Thus the gentry came into their own again. In March 1660 Sir John Pelham visited Henry Goring at Highden. They decided to stand together for the new parliament, sharing the election expenses. Their entertainment of the freeholders when they were elected for the shire was lavish: the bills at the White Horse, the Bull and the other Lewes inns in April came to £505. Pelham and his wife spent extravagantly in London that happy summer season, on clothes and jewellery, at the Cockpit, 'to the drummer and trumpeters', and on cloth and lace, hats and black belts for the servants and footboys. Pelham applied himself to the further enhancement of his prestige and to an energetic role in county government. He became a gentleman in the Privy Chamber and obtained the vice-admiralty of Sussex. Northumberland appointed him a deputy-lieutenant and he at once became the principal figure in the militia of the eastern rapes. At the autumn musters he distributed sack and beer to his men. He bought Poulton's *Statutes*, Dalton's *Justice of the Peace* and *The Compleat Justice* in preparation for his first appearance at Michaelmas on the quarter sessions Bench.[163] The magnates' concern to cement their hold on the county by close liaison with the nobility is indicated by their invitation to Lord Jocelyn Percy, newly appointed a JP at the age of sixteen, to undertake a militia captaincy. His father excused him on the grounds of his youth:

> The experience of a yeare or two more in the world may I hope make him somewhat fitter for imployment, and I shall then be very glad to see him brought into any way of serving his countrie either in a civill or a millitarie capacitie.

The correspondence between Northumberland and his deputies in 1660 breathes an air of confident and amicable cooperation between the greatest men of the shire. County government was once more built on the sure foundation of noble and gentry dominance. 'The carrying things with moderation', concluded Northumberland in a letter of February 1661 with a backward glance at a decade in which he had remained aloof from national and local politics, was the only sure way 'to mentaine the countrie in peace, and that it may long continue in that temper shall be the wishes and endevors of your very affectionate friend and servant'.[164]

Part V

GOVERNMENT AND THE IMPACT OF WAR

15

The County Committee

There is such an antipathy betweene the Committee for sequestracons and us, that there is no way unthought of nor unattempted by them, that might render us and our accons odious and hinder our proceedings.
The Subcommittee of Accounts at Chichester to the Committee for Taking the Accounts of the Kingdom, 30 July 1646.[1]

The service, charge, paynes and trouble [are] soe great . . . so that your petitioner is weekly necessitated to great travell, charge and expence therein, haveing not resided in his usuall place of aboad above two daies in one weeke ever since he tooke appon him the said imployment.
John Stalman, clerk to the county sequestrators, to the Committee for Compounding, December 1650.[2]

Structure and membership

Piecemeal measures during 1643, initiated by John Pym in his drive to create a military and administrative machine for parliament, gave shape and purpose to the embryonic County Committees.[3] Parliamentary organisation began with informal gatherings in manor houses. Then, as the war got under way, the need for formalisation and institutionalisation became apparent. In most counties the development of a County Committee out of the deputy-lieutenancy was gradual and experimental. Nevertheless in Sussex, unlike in Kent and Staffordshire, there was a distinct act of creation.[4] On 18 July 1643 the Commons ordered that forty men 'shall be Committees for the disposing of the affairs of Sussex'. The terms of the order were unusually wide: the Committee was given power to raise money according to the ordinances of parliament, to spend it under the warrant of five committeemen, to raise forces, defend the county and if necessary associate with other counties for mutual defence. A general authorisation to 'execute all orders and ordinances of parliament' covered such important matters as sequestration.[5]

In February 1643 parliament instituted the weekly assessments, in March the sequestration procedure, and in May the compulsory levy of one-fifth on revenue or one-twentieth on goods in place of the Propositions system of loans.[6] Before the Sussex Committee was set up in July, these ordinances had already made essential a fully-fledged structure of Committees in each rape. Basing their practice on the petty sessions, the committeemen met in the inns of market towns. Chichester, Arundel, Horsham and Billingshurst were regular meeting places in the western rapes; the Committee for Hastings rape met at Battle and Robertsbridge; a joint Committee served for Lewes and Pevensey rapes, meeting at Lewes.[7] The membership of these Committees was loosely defined as those nominated in one or other of the parliamentary ordinances who were resident in the rape concerned. But the lists in the ordinances and the *Commons Journals* bear little relation to the active membership. Many of the hundred or so men nominated in 1643 and 1644 were unwilling to serve. Sir William Culpepper, William Michelbourne, Sir William Goring, Sir Thomas Eversfield of Denne, John Alford, Henry Goring of Highden and Thomas Shirley were among the magnates who failed to respond when Herbert Morley tried to attract them into a public role.[8]

In the east there was no problem in staffing the Committees. The brunt of the routine work at Lewes was born by the aged William Newton, Herbert Hay, Thomas Jefferay and Anthony Fowle. In Hastings rape Committee business rested in the capable hands of three well respected JPs Peter Farnden, John Busbridge and Anthony Cruttenden.[9] Lesser gentry like John Everenden regularly attended at Battle and Robertsbridge.[10] In the west it was a different matter. Two substantial gentry, William Gratwick and Henry Bridger, took some part in Arundel rape during 1643, but they soon retired leaving the overworked JPs George Churcher and Ralph Cowper to cope with Committee work on top of their magisterial business.[11] At Chichester Sir John Chapman sat with the merchant Stephen Humphrey and the parish gentlemen Arthur and Peter Bettsworth. The wills of Thomas Milet and Edward Manning indicate the economic status of two typical western committeemen: the former hoped to raise £820 in legacies, the latter £750 from the sale of virtually all their property.[12] Rising men and merchants filled the vacuum in the west.

In some counties a single Committee, sometimes with a permanent headquarters, usually with its own secretariat and a routine of daily or weekly business, engrossed power. Sir Anthony Weldon's General Committee dominated the lathal Committees of Kent.[13] In 1645 and 1646 John Pyne and his henchmen ran the peripatetic Somerset Committee which met in eight towns guarded by a 'Committee troop'.[14] The Staffordshire Committee controlled the civil and military affairs of the whole shire from the county town.[15] Sussex's Grand Committee, sitting at Lewes, delegated more responsibility to the local Committees than some of the other County Committees did. It had to allow the Committee at Chichester considerable discretion in sequestrations business, which was largely concentrated in the western corner of the county. Essentially Sussex's Grand Committee was a magnate caucus body, with a wider effective membership than any of the rape Committees, and dominated by the two most powerful men in the county, Sir Thomas Pelham and Herbert Morley. Activists of lesser gentry status like Simon Everenden and William Freeman seldom appeared at its meetings in the first years of the war. Freeman's gradual acceptance into its inner counsels was a mark of his outstanding service to the parliamentary cause. On the other hand magnates who through neutralism were inactive on the rape Committees sometimes attended. Thus John Alford and Sir William Goring, men much respected throughout the county, were at the meeting to discuss the petition of September 1645.[16] The Grand Committee was a genuine county assembly, a demonstration of gentry unity, a forum for gentry opinion.

Since there was virtually no break in the continuity of quarter sessions administration, the Grand Committee of Sussex never took on such extensive powers as those exercised by the Committees in counties like Kent, Somerset, Dorset and Staffordshire.[17] Nevertheless it was a policy-making body with broad functions, apportioning taxes between the six rapes, maintaining general oversight of impressment and its accounts. It organised musters, informed Speaker Lenthall of county opinion on such matters as the continuance of garrisons and the taking of the National Covenant. It met hastily whenever a crisis loomed.[18] The Grand Committee dealt with ecclesiastical as well as secular affairs, adjudicating on the delinquency of ministers and enforcing ejections.[19] It was responsible for coastal defence as well as the county's inland borders. It acted as the agent of parliament and the Admiralty committee over the salvage of wrecks.[20] After the rising at Horsham in 1648, it determined the fines on those engaged against the parliament.[21] When the discontents of the western rapes reached a climax in 1645, it became a court of appeal hearing grievances against the subordinate local committees.[22]

The strength of parliamentary administration in a particular county depended, amongst other things, on the effectiveness of the communications between London and its Committee. A core of Sussex MPs, dividing their time between London and their homes, was indefatigable in pushing forward parliamentary programmes. In 1648 the House of Commons eventually formalised its system of communication with the provinces, by appointing particular members 'to take care for the signing and sending away of the copies of the letters . . . to the respective commissioners or Committees'. The order, naming Herbert Morley and Edward Apsley as agents, was otiose in Sussex.[23] Since 1642 Morley had consistently ensured the smooth passage of directions to Lewes; when he was away from Westminster Sir Thomas Pelham, Sir Thomas Parker and Henry Shelley acted instead. John Downes and Edward Apsley were agents for Arundel and Bramber rapes, William Cawley for Chichester rape.[24] Only Hastings rape lacked an MP among the core of its Committee during the war, but the committeemen there were well integrated with colleagues at Lewes and Morley's patronage got the governor of Rye, John Fagge, elected as a recruiter.[25]

The reorganisation of the provincial sequestrations machinery in 1650 deprived the County Committees of much of its business, but in Sussex the Grand Committee survived both this upheaval and the removal of certain of its military and ecclesiastical functions during the 1650s. It certainly continued to meet regularly if not as frequently as previously. In 1650 it was busy establishing a new schedule of men liable to find horse and arms for the Rump's militia.[26] In 1652 and again in 1658 it backed its agents' claims for suitable rewards.[27] The enforcement of the assessments continued throughout the 1650s. Some centralisation was certainly attempted in the 1650s but the influence of Sussex gentry over their internal affairs was not significantly reduced.[28]

The defence of the county

Sussex was at the heart of parliament's South-Eastern Association. Its security was dependent on vigorous prosecution of the scheme of mutual defence. The county's contribution to the regional war effort rested largely on two men of outstanding energy and responsibility, Herbert Morley and Anthony Stapley. While Stapley was mainly based on Chichester, where he was governor from 1643 to 1645, Morley roamed the southern counties. Between 1644 and 1646 companies from his regiment fought in Somerset, Dorset, Hampshire and Berkshire and took part in the prolonged siege of Basing House.[29] In June 1645 Morley joined a delegation from Sussex, Surrey and Hampshire to discuss with the Committee of Both Kingdoms a combined strategy towards Basing. Morley was enthusiastic about renewing the siege and promised substantial forces from Sussex.[30] Commissary General Peck, who presided at Chichester over the expenditure of the assessments and sequestrations money which sustained the Sussex regiments, kept methodical accounts which show in detail how the soldiers were paid and equipped, arms and drums were repaired, and the wounded home from the battlefront were tended. The salaries of the officers and men, surgeons, chaplains, master gunner, martial and clerk of the magazine were often in arrears, but seldom more so than six months.[31] Morley and Stapley mounted, organised and led a small but efficiently managed provincial army.

The military role of the Grand Committee at Lewes was complementary to that of Morley's and Stapley's regiments. Sir Thomas Pelham and his colleagues exercised a dual responsibility: to keep the trained bands up to scratch and to enforce with the minimum of delay the impressment levies imposed by parliament.[32] They responded energetically to the New Model ordinance of 17 February 1645. The first press of eighty-seven men from Pevensey and Lewes rapes were delivered at Staines on 9 April.[33] In November 1645 a force bound for Abingdon reached Reading only twelve days after the despatch of the letter of the Committee of Both Kingdoms directing it to be raised.[34] The Grand Committee compensated for the deficiencies in their control of the western rapes by ruthless exploitation of eastern gentry, yeomen and husbandmen. They knew they could rely on the zeal of a town like Rye and afford to ignore its clamours for payment of the £200 they had voted for its defence. Rye had been generous over the Propositions loan; it had agreed to deprive itself of six pieces of ordnance for the defence of Shoreham in the crisis of 1643; its vigour did not appreciably slacken as its protests at the burdens imposed on it mounted.[35] Lesser gentry like John Everenden, diverted from their fields and hop grounds to mustering and training, became the backbone of the defence of Sussex.[36] Many of them might have echoed the protestations of the unfortunate Edward Godman who, incapacitated by gout and lacking 'experience or skill to doe itt', found himself in charge of his neighbourhood foot company. To Pelham in 1644, he stressed his forwardness 'in sending forth men, horses and in other subscriptions beeyound my ability for the advancement of the cause'. 'If itt bee your pleasure that I must goe on the service', he pleaded, surely the Committee did not expect him to bear the extraordinary charge of colours, halberds and other accoutrements that 'afterwards may bee still kept for the countreysuse'.[37]

Sequestrations

Sequestrations revenue was the foundation of the Committee's programme of action to defend the county. There was a strong incentive, therefore, to enforce the sequestration ordinance of 27 March 1643 without delay.[38] In the first full year of the system about £9,500 was raised in Chichester rape, where the bulk of the sequestered estates lay. This was spent on Morley's and Stapley's regiments, on employing an engineer to improve Chichester's fortifications, and on such necessities as gunpowder and shot for the garrison there. The sequestrations revenue was supplemented by the payments in kind of grain, sheep and beer from tenants of sequestered estates to the garrisons at Chichester and Cowdray. In certain cases, such as George Gunter's farm at Racton, the Committee at Chichester employed a bailiff to manage an estate on their behalf.[39]

Four committeemen, Sir John Chapman, George Oglander, William Cawley and Stephen Humphrey, who as treasurer was a key man, meeting regularly at Chichester, shouldered much of the sequestrations work.[40] From the first the business was dogged by administrative difficulties. There were problems in obtaining evidence of men's malignancy, discovering the extent of their estates, finding satisfactory tenants.[41] The Committee quickly became entangled in the intricacies of the gentry's leases, wardships, dowers and annuities. Humphrey explained to William Prynne in November 1644 that the delay in submitting his accounts up to Michaelmas 1643 was due to his troubles in collection, which had been 'soe many by reason of the armies and free quarter taken in most parts of this county that our tenants are much ympoverished and disabled to pay their rents'.[42]

'Responsable men and fitt for this undertaking are very rare in these parts, we have none that begg imployments of us in this kinde', noted the

Chichester Committee in October 1645, when they urged the Committee of Accounts in London not to discourage their agents 'by to much harshness' in demanding speedy accounting.[43] Collectors sometimes failed to keep rentals. The sale of sequestered goods and cattle was often haphazard, carried out privately instead of in the market place as required by the ordinance; goods went at 'a despicable rate'; several accountants kept no registers of what was sold or to whom. When Humphrey, praised by his colleagues for his 'faythfullness and industry', produced his records for the Sub-committee of Accounts, they found them so 'confusedly done' that they knew 'not what to make of it'.[44] Richard Boughton, the county solicitor for sequestrations, was unable to produce a full record of his transactions for the new sequestrations commissioners in 1652. The Grand Committee had by then long since lost track of its proceedings with regard to estates already discharged.[45]

Yet the Grand Committee had some reason for pique in 1650 when it was blamed for the failure to establish systematic record and account keeping:

> We cannot but much wonder to heare that we should be thus payd for our faithfull and troublesome service in that imployment, having dealt therein we dare say with as much faithfulness and advantage to the state as any whatsoever.

The Compounding commissioners had ordered that the Grand Committee should pay a fine of twenty pounds apiece for their neglect.[46] Rough and ready as it was, the sequestrations machinery had been run sufficiently competently to sustain the cause.

The Grand Committee could not eradicate abuses in the sequestration procedure when an insensitive and divisive definition of royalism was applied or the letter of the sequestrations instructions was ignored. Sir Charles Shelley, for instance, was sequestered when he was too young to be lawfully indicted as a recusant.[47] The Committee at Chichester was interminably slow in responding to appeals and in releasing men whom they regarded as particular enemies of the state. They retained the sequestration of the lands of Sir John Morley and John Caryll, for example, for some time after they had been ordered to discharge them by the Committee for Compounding.[48] Arbitrary and spiteful proceedings against delinquents and recusants helped to create the resentment expressed in the 1645 petition to the Grand Committee. The petitioners demanded that

> whoever shall be conceived or accused to be within the compasse of the ordinances for sequestracon may speedily have a faire hearing and soe be discharged or sequestred according to the meritt of his cause knowing their accusers being brought face to face.[49]

The Grand Committee itself could be implacable, as it was in the cases of the Earl of Thanet and Sir Edward Bishop, but by and large it stuck to the rules and was lenient to gentry involved in the royalist campaigns.[50]

The drastic national overhaul of the sequestration and compounding system in 1649 and 1650 involved the replacement of the County Committees by sequestration commissioners who were little more than minions of the Committee for Compounding in London. The new commissioners were given virtually no power to act independently.[51] In most counties three men were appointed, but at first six men served in Sussex, three for the east and three for the west. Stephen Humphrey, by 1650 an expert in sequestration, was the sole survivor of the old Committee. His colleagues were men untried in local government and of markedly lower social status than their predecessors. By 1650 the sequestration revenue for the whole county had dropped, with the progress of compounding, to about £4,500 a year.[52] After the first year of the new system three of the commissioners were dismissed; the other three stumbled on, managing the remaining sequestered estates as best they could, until March 1654, when the administration was again overhauled. Thereafter, Stephen Humphrey and George Stonestreet shared the work, following the dismissal of Henry Stalman, accused of using sequestered lands for his own cony warrens.[53] When the Committee for Compounding wound up its affairs in 1656, Sussex was among the counties with the largest arrears outstanding.[54]

The new commissioners never received adequate support from London. The new men were timid, uncertain about how to give acquittances, about allowances to tenants for repairs, about the whole procedure for letting in which they were hamstrung by the central Committee for Compounding. The questions they sent up to London in 1650 and 1651 were not fully answered.[55] Yet they were bombarded with instructions and queries from the Compounding Committee, the Committee for the Advance of Money and the Barons of the Exchequer.[56] Time and again the commissioners were sent hunting through the muddled 1640s records; time and again they found themselves forced to adapt leasing negotiations in midstream or to submit justifications for the rents they proposed to set.[57] No wonder the Sussex commissioners remained confused and in constant need of reassurance. They were set tasks they were ill-equipped to fulfil.[58]

Neither the commissioners themselves nor their agents received salaries sufficient to cover their expenses. After an exhausting summer and autumn in 1650, Stephen Humphrey and Henry Stalman complained that their charges riding the county to survey and let estates, the expense and hazard of returning money to London and losses from clipped money left them considerably out of pocket. The clerk, John Stalman, who after remonstrations from the commissioners was awarded half a crown a day, found that his daily wage defrayed only about half his expenses between May and December 1650. In response to a virtual ultimatum from the commissioners, the Committee for Compounding gave him a bonus of twenty pounds.[59] Stalman soldiered on, losing his horse on one of his journeys to London to deliver money. His colleague Thomas Buttery, the commissioners' agent, confronted his London masters with greater determination over their failure to pay him enough. When they simply dismissed him in 1654, the whole creaking machinery ground to a halt. Humphrey reported that the accounts for the previous Michaelmas could not 'possibly bee finished without the aid of our former agent'. His request for a 'competent sallery' for Buttery was tersely refused. In 1655 Buttery was still pestering the Committee for Compounding for an allowance for his 'sickness and great charges' in journeying to London in the depths of winter.[60]

The gentry, intent on the restoration of sequestered land to men of status, did everything they could to hinder the commissioners, juggling estates between father and son to avoid penalities, concealing or revealing testamentary or leasing arrangements according to whether or not they made land liable to confiscation.[61] Legal tangles wasted much of the commissioners' time. After a long series of examinations, Humphrey and Stalman failed to establish the state's right to the valuable estates of Newtimber and Michelgrove.[62] Meanwhile the tenants held off paying their rents, while bothering the commissioners about claims for expenses.[63] Despite these pressures, the commissioners made a sincere attempt to combine the maximum returns attainable for the state with a proper concern for the rights and livelihoods of tenants. They constantly reiterated that the rents they contracted for were at customary levels and no one could be found who would pay more. Claims for allowances traditionally accepted were treated sympathetically by the commissioners, but suspiciously by the London authorities. Thus Humphrey and Stalman supported the claim by Sir Thomas Gage's tenants for £100 spent on maintenance and repair of sea walls. Requesting that they should be allowed to cut some of the underwood on Sir Richard Weston's land, in payment of his arrears of rent, the commissioners suggested that the tenants who 'time out of mind had the herbage' of the woodlands should be compensated and that the land should be 'kept for some years from harm by the cattle'.[64]

Once matters had been settled to their satisfaction the commissioners were naturally reluctant to undo them. Thus when, through a procedural misunderstanding, the recusant Ann Henslow's estate had not been surveyed, posted and boxed precisely in the manner directed and she attempted to void the lease, they were uncooperative. 'There was noe greater improvement to bee made', Humphrey and Stonestreet assured the Committee for Compounding, and the tenants had been 'at noe small charge in fenceinge . . . and in trenchinge to bringe the water' into the land. In February 1654 the commissioners protested vigorously at the harsh landlordism of John Wildman, who had bought the sequestered estate of Lord Morley and Mounteagle. They were shocked at his attempt to evict tenants with whom they had contracted at high rents, without six months' notice or any compensation for manuring and repairing their farms, 'whereby themselves and families are likely to be ruined . . . and we ourselves branded with beinge the authors and instruments thereof'. Humphrey and Stalman urged the Committee for Compounding to appeal to Wildman on the tenants' behalf 'that as a gentleman he will have respect to theire great charge and losse in their stock in theis tymes'. The really poor, such as the Hastings tenement squatters on the land of John Rigatt who could not afford to pay their rents, always engaged the commissioners' sympathy.[65]

The sums raised by the Sussex commissioners between 1650 and 1656 were a paltry contribution to the national treasury. But their diligence, despite all odds, was remarkable. They were much on the road and away from home at all times of year.[66] To their London masters they were always polite, always excusing themselves. They invariably ended with protestations of zeal. With the gentry they were patient but firm. There is no doubt that Humphrey, Stalman and Stonestreet gave their hearts to their task. They recognised a responsibility to the state. It was characteristic that, amidst their other preoccupations, they suggested to the Committee for Compounding that the cathedral library at Chichester, which had been left rotting in the Deanery, should be sent up to London by wagon to be 'sold for the use of the state'.[67]

Recent research has illustrated the tenacity and financial resilience of the royalist and catholic gentry who suffered sequestration. Many of them recovered their property through compounding long before the Restoration; ultimately almost all of them did so.[68] Nevertheless, even allowing for some exaggeration in their claims, the Sussex delinquents suffered enormous losses during the civil war. Many of them only emerged from the clutches of the Committee, or the commissioners who succeeded it, after a prolonged struggle. The Earl of Thanet estimated that he lost goods in Sussex worth about £3,000 when his Wiston estate was used to supply both armies in turn during the 1643 campaign. Sir William Ford claimed losses of £4,000 during the sequestration of his Uppark estate, much of which was accounted for by spoil of his mansion, farms, household goods, cattle, sheep and woods. Thomas May alleged that the Chichester Committee confiscated £500 of his personal estate and that Waller's soldiers violently deprived him of a further £2,500. Furnishings, pewter, brass, livestock, crops, his wife's coach, posts and rails, pigeon houses and cony warrens, were ransacked from Sir Edward Bishop's estate at Parham.[69] The direct vengeance of parliamentary soldiers was often fierce. For such men as these the toils of sequestration came as an unhappy aftermath.

The Subcommittee of Accounts

It was not until June 1645 that the Committee for Taking the Accounts of the Kingdom, established in the previous July, was given adequate powers. The central Accounts Committee, sitting in Cornhill, established subcommittees in each county to take the accounts of the treasurers for assessment, loan and sequestration money. No accountants or committeemen were to sit; a new body in each county was envisaged.[70] Sussex welcomed parliament's initiative. It was 'a worke much desired by the country', admitted the committeemen of Bramber rape in November 1645.[71] Suspicion of the Committee's treasurers, particularly when they were also committeemen, was part of a cumulative movement against Committee government. The petitioners of September 1645 wanted five or six independent gentry in each rape, nominated by the knights of the shire, to undertake the treasurerships. They regarded the current treasurers as 'not responsible for so great a trust': in future men should be appointed 'for the space of one yeare and noe more'.[72] If the county distrusted the Committee's agents, the Committee resented the prying into its affairs by the Subcommittee. The county's parliamentary managers would no more tolerate new masters than excessive interference from outside. Thus the new Subcommittee was awkwardly placed between a powerful ruling group jealous of its authority and a disgruntled community clamouring for redress after three years of military administration.

The Subcommittee initially nominated for Sussex was much too small. Separate Subcommittees were clearly needed for each rape, but most of the men named lived in the Chichester area. The proceedings of the Subcommittee for Chichester rape are fully recorded and a mass of accounts that it audited have survived. Elsewhere little seems to have been achieved during the whole four-year period before the central Accounts Committee was discharged in 1649. The Committee at Horsham explained in November 1645 their inertia there by the fact that only one resident of the rape had been appointed. They offered fourteen nominations of minor gentry, men from whom they expected friendly treatment, but several of these were unacceptable since they were accountants. When the Horsham Subcommittee at last met in April 1646, the five members who appeared shunned the business. The 'worke will prove to difficult for us', they told the central Accounts Committee; they laid it aside requesting the assistance of six more gentry 'very fitt for the busines'. In 1646 there was an abortive attempt by the active committeemen in Chichester and Bramber rapes to get things moving in Arundel rape. In the east nothing happened at all until 1647, when a small joint Subcommittee for the three rapes met at Lewes. It at once requested further support, sending to London a list of ten esquires and fourteen gentry who might be prepared to act. Apparently none of them did so. Yet, for all this evidence of hanging back, at least thirty-eight gentry attended meetings of the Sussex Subcommittees at one time or another between 1645 and 1648. In general they were men of distinctly lower social status than the committeemen whose financial dealings they were expected to adjudicate. A few prominent neutrals showed themselves: Sir William Culpepper, Sir William Goring and

William Thomas, for example. But such men, the only men with the prestige to challenge the unrestricted dominance of the Grand Committee's control, were always in a minority.[73]

In some counties such as Hertfordshire, Northamptonshire and Buckinghamshire the Subcommittees accumulated masses of accounts. Elsewhere, as in Essex, the Subcommittee of Accounts was balked throughout by the County Committee.[74] In Sussex only the subcommittee for Chichester rape had a firm identity. It made an energetic start. The accounts of the 1642 subsidy, the assessments for 1643–44 and Commissary Peck's accounts for the county's regiments and garrisons were all obtained, checked and sent to London without delay.[75] Thereafter the Subcommittee was frustrated by the determined obstructionism of the Committee at Chichester in a straightforward struggle for power. The leading committeemen William Cawley and Stephen Humphrey, themselves the principal accountants, enjoyed the support of George Oglander and Sir John Chapman, both influential gentlemen. The leading subcommitteemen were the minor gentlemen Francis Blachford and Thomas Bettsworth and the merchants George Greene, an ex-mayor of the city, and John Farrington. Humphrey treated the Subcommittee with contempt; Cawley joined him in refusing to present his account. A trumped up charge against Francis Blachford, the most militant figure among the Subcommittee activists, enabled them to sequester and imprison him. In retaliation the Subcommittee imprisoned Humphrey. The Grand Committee, in a petition to Speaker Lenthall, testified to Humphrey's diligence. Anthony Stapley accused the Subcommittee of exceeding their powers by imprisoning Humphrey out of mere malice. They complained to the central Committee of Accounts about his 'very high expressions to us'. Stapley maintained that their delegated power was inferior to that of the County Committee, the direct representatives of parliament. Meanwhile the Chichester Committee dealt rigorously with Blachford.[76]

If they had not been so affronted and opposed, declared the Subcommittee in November 1645, 'wee had done more service in a moneth than we have in sixe moneths'. For more than a year the Committee's campaign against them drastically hindered their progress. They refused to submit their order book or the rentals or books of leases of the revenues of the bishopric, but only allowed a clerk to take copies when they were actually sitting, which was two or three times a week at the most. They obtained an order in July 1646 for payment to them of the arrears of the Scottish Loan, which had been laboriously collected by the Subcommittee to pay their clerks and officers. William Cawley and his colleagues intended to discredit the Subcommittee as thoroughly as they could. It was an obvious tactic to deprive it of funds. They succeeded in putting it permanently on the defensive.[77]

The conflict at Chichester was based on rumour and suspicion. The chaotic state of the sequestration administration was well known, and it was generally assumed that men like Cawley and Humphrey had been lining their own pockets. 'The generall complaint of the country being that the state hath much suffered by it', wrote the Subcommittee on 26 December 1645, 'makes them take what course they cann to blurr us'.[78] Any treasurer for sequestrations was likely to be unpopular. Humphrey was certainly an inefficient accountant, but it is not clear that he was corrupt. His obstructions stemmed perhaps from resentment at the Subcommittee's failure to appreciate his difficulties in producing an adequate set of accounts. Allegations of embezzlement against William Cawley, whom the Subcommittee attempted to surcharge with £900 for which he had failed to account, were probably unfair. Witnesses before the Committee deposed that much of the money which Cawley was charged with having received in fines after Waller's reduction of Chichester had in fact been paid direct to Colonel Morley and other officers. Cawley's failure to obtain acquittances in every case was excusable in the confused situation following the fall of the city to parliament. Sir William Waller made this point on his behalf, in a letter to the central Accounts Committee which commended his 'faithful performance' in managing the local parliamentary finances at that time.[79] The proceedings of the Subcommittee have strong undertones of personal vindictiveness.

The success of the Chichester committee in obstructing the Subcommittee of Accounts there seems to have encouraged similar attitudes elsewhere. The Horsham Committee, which had originally been willing it seems to see the accounting done, turned against the Subcommittee there, which found itself 'delayed deluded yea and derided' by the committeemen's daily 'obstruccons and opposicons'. William Freeman brought the business to a standstill by refusing to make the order book available.[80] Samuel Jeake and his friends at Rye condemned the Committee of Accounts and its minions, in their remonstrance of 1648 to Lord General Fairfax, as men 'whose endevours are more to ensnare then to advance the publique good'.[81] Furthermore, lack of funds to pay the officers of the Subcommittees inhibited action. In the eastern rapes the clerk, messengers and doorkeeper were apparently 'ready to desert' in 1647 for lack of pay. The attempt to obtain comprehensive accounts from the localities was a bold venture, but one that easily became submerged in the animosities of county politics and the administrative difficulties it posed.

Assessments 1643–1660

In the period 1541 to 1547 Henry VIII obtained £656,245 from the whole country through parliamentary lay subsidies; between 1643 and 1660 Sussex alone paid towards the weekly and monthly assessments, together with the assessments for the armies in Scotland and Ireland, a total of around £525,000.[82] This is the measure of the astonishing success of the assessments. For seventeen years Sussex paid an average of about £36,000

For the first time in the seventeenth century the wealth of provincial England was effectively harnessed to the needs of the state. Once the new system of national taxation was established, the arrears left uncollected were remarkably small. The final accumulated arrears on the accounts of Edward West and William Alcock for the period 1645 to 1650 were only about £4,519, less than 3 per cent of the total charge. £253,167 charged on the county between December 1650 and September 1660 was collected in full.[83]

The success of the assessment owed nothing to radically new procedures.[84] High collectors for each rape still bore responsibility for bringing in the money. Gentlemen who had acted as commissioners in the 1620s and in 1642 organised the assessments as county committeemen in the 1640s and 50s. When Laurence Ashburnham and John Busbridge called a meeting at Battle in 1643 to initiate the next tax by nominating assessors and collectors they were on familiar ground.[85] Nor was the method of assessment new. The system of the poundage rate used in 1642 was generally applied. The assessors became used to juggling with the figures in order to reach a rate that would bring in the required sum from a particular village on each occasion. For instance, when the national assessment was reduced from £120,000 a month to £90,000 a month in 1654, the Cuckfield taxpayers paid at sixpence instead of eightpence poundage.[86] Men found themselves paying different poundages for their lands in different villages, since the distribution of the tax was always rough and ready.[87]

The assessment involved unprecedentedly large sums of money and it was initiated at a time when administration was already much disrupted by the civil war. Not surprisingly it took some time to establish. The Commons gave two MPs special responsibility for oversight of the assessments in each county. Sussex committeemen were to ensure that money was paid direct to John Baker at his home in Mayfield. Throughout the spring and summer of 1643 the Commons used the Sussex MPs as agents to speed collection of the first assessments. Again in 1645 they urged Sussex members returning home to accelerate the collection of the tax.[88] It was a full ten years before the problem of extracting money on time from dilatory towns and villages was solved. But in the long run vigorous enforcement brought home the lesson that the badgering would go on till the money was paid. The Grand Committee's use of the threat of free quarter 'without allowance for the same as a deserved punishment' probably assisted the swift payment of a new assessment of December 1647. In Lewes and Pevensey rapes money was coming in very slowly at that time. Much of it for these years was not in fact paid until the early 1650s, but collection never ground to a halt.[89] Whereas in the 1640s the mayor of Rye was constantly under pressure from committeemen, in the next decade the town paid up regularly.[90] The streamlining of collection by placing full responsibility on a receiver-general, and the appointment of Edward West in 1646 as agent with special responsibility for arrears, helped the system to run more smoothly. In the 1650s William Alcock, who combined the receivership with the clerkship of the peace, achieved a high standard of efficiency.[91]

The impact of the assessments was bound to reach deep into the pockets of every level of society above the very poor. A Grand Committee ruling that landlords should pay three-quarters and tenants one-quarter of sums charged on leasehold and copyhold land was an attempt to give gentlemen some relief. Deductions by tenants for assessments they had paid nevertheless cut sharply into magnate rent rolls.[92] The direct charges on their lands held in demesne were harsh enough: Francis, Lord Dacre paid just over seventy pounds between September 1643 and the following September, Sir Thomas Pelham contributed more than £161 in the accounting year 1643–44.[93] The escalation of the charge on lesser gentry was equally striking. John Everenden, who had paid only three pounds in all for the five subsidies voted by parliament in 1628, paid more than £163 over the period 1643 to 1652.[94] Yet men of this kind could afford the new level of taxation much more easily than the townsmen of a community such as Rye, which was struggling against a multitude of economic pressures. In Rye in the 1640s only the very poor seem to have been excused; 308 individuals were included in a tax made by the mayor and jurats in October 1644: some men paid on their lands, many on their goods, some on both; some men paid a pound or more, many were charged a single shilling. Numerous fishermen as well as fellmongers, cordwainers, bricklayers, basketworkers, glovers, tanners and gardeners contributed to another tax levied at Rye in 1660.[95]

Rye did its utmost to obtain some release from the grinding weight of the assessments. In 1645 the mayor regarded Peter Farnden as a promising advocate with the Committee at Battle. Reminding him of his promise that the town should be allowed to argue its case for an abatement, he pointed out 'how easely' Hastings and Winchelsea were treated. On another occasion, in 1653, the mayor informed the Committee that he could not conceive that an increase in the town's charge of forty shillings was intended with Rye 'very high already'. He disingenuously attributed the new rate 'to some fault of the scribe' and deducted the excess. In 1656 the Committee tried to impose an extra ten pounds on Rye: this time the town petitioned the Committee of the Army and sought to pit Herbert Morley against the committeemen of Hastings rape. They crowed with delight at paying off an old score against John Busbridge, with whom they had been at loggerheads over his lenience to a gentleman living on the edge of the town's liberty. Busbridge was 'very angry and high and said he had done it and he would owne it and would shew his reasons above' when he was summoned to London for increasing the tax on Rye.[96]

Committeemen enjoyed much discretion and they did not hesitate to give favour where they wished. The familiar pattern of pressure, patronage and partiality, so characteristic of taxation in the seventeenth century, recurred with the assessments. There was much argument over apportionment between the rapes. This was not resolved until 1649, when it was agreed that Pevensey and Hastings rapes should bear the greatest load and Lewes and Bramber rapes the lightest.[97] It can hardly have been merely coincidence that the hundred of Willingdon suddenly escaped at an extraordinarily low sum in 1645 when a rate was set by three committeemen, one of whom was Francis Selwyn of Friston; or that the demands made on Lewes and Southover were drastically reduced in 1648 when the Lewes gentleman Ambrose Traiton settled the matter with the help of Thomas Springate.[98] When Anthony Fowle and Herbert Morley wanted to reduce a tax on Lewes rape by £456 in 1645, they simply left eight hundreds at the previous level and handed out large abatements to the other hundreds and to the borough of Lewes.[99] No wonder men complained about the unbridled power of committeemen.

Open resistance to the assessments was an important element in the movement of protest against the hardships imposed during the war on the western rapes.[100] There were the usual rating disputes. Moreover there were, as usual, a few rebellious spirits ready to challenge the masters of the county: a Herstmonceux yeoman refused to pay his rate of eleven shillings in 1645; a Shoreham gentleman, armed with a pistol, swore 'by the Lord's wounds he would pistoll whomsoever should come to gather any tax of him or distrayne' in 1654; the same year a Shipley gentleman threatened to make a collector who distrained his cows 'fly the country'.[101] Overall though it is the lack of opposition to the assessments that remains striking. The parliamentary and Cromwellian authorities taught the Stuarts just how much money could be squeezed year by year from the mass of their subjects.

16

Administration and the civil war

Local administration was severely disrupted by the civil war in most of the southern and midland counties. The regular assize circuits were not held between 1642 and 1645.[1] Quarter sessions were suspended from 1642, until 1645 in Warwickshire and until 1646 in Hampshire and Somerset.[2] In Wiltshire the war 'gave the nascent system a fundamental shock'.[3] There was less military activity in Sussex than in these counties and consequently the traditional processes of government never came to a complete standstill. Nevertheless administration was greatly hampered by the unsettled conditions. No assizes were held in 1643; a full file of papers testifies to the heavy load of business before the summer assizes at Lewes in September 1644, but the files for 1645 and 1646 are scanty and apparently incomplete. It was not until 1646 that the twice-yearly visits of the judges to Sussex were put on their normal footing.[4] Twice in the western division, at Easter 1643 and Epiphany 1644 which fell in the midst of the siege of Arundel, sessions were omitted. The temporary breakdown of the shrievalty in 1643 is indicated by an order of the Bench at Michaelmas sessions that, since the sheriff John Baker was not able to enforce a writ of restitution through the under-sheriff and bailiffs, the constables of the hundred of Box and Stockbridge should restore an Aldingbourne widow to her lands.[5]

Besides political disruption, many provincial Benches suffered from short staffing in the 1640s. Attendances at sessions dropped sharply in Warwickshire, Somerset and Denbighshire.[6] Five times between 1643 and 1649 only two or three justices appeared on the western Bench in Sussex and on six other occasions four justices sat. During 1643 the deficiency of manpower in the west was acute: six JPs in all were active but only four of them attended sessions. This, rather than general disorder, most probably accounts for the abandonment of the Easter sessions in that year. Until 1646 a skeleton commission kept the administration going in west Sussex. The partnership between Ralph Cowper and George Churcher was the mainstay. The parliamentary caucus also relied on neutrals ready to carry out the customary duties of their office. They even allowed Thomas May, despite his reputation for royalism, to remain active as a JP until 1644. Assistance from eastern gentry like Herbert Morley and Anthony

Stapley brought some relief to the few overworked western justices. At Michaelmas 1644 for instance, four JPs attended at both Lewes and Petworth. Attempts in 1644 to persuade more of the prominent western neutrals, men like Sir Thomas Eversfield of Denne, into an active role were unsuccessful. Early in 1646, though, Sir William Goring of Burton and Henry Goring of Washington came back into harness. Royalist and neutralist defections also weakened the eastern Bench between 1642 and 1646, but at no time was a large part of the division entirely devoid of oversight. There also, dependence on the labours of neutrals like William White, William Thomas and Laurence Ashburnham became necessary.[7]

War brought a hiatus in the recently established petty sessions system.[8] Monthly meetings were the first kind of business to be dropped when a critical shortage of manpower faced the Commission. They were restored in Hastings rape by 1647 and in Pevensey rape by 1649, but specific references to their being held again in the west do not occur until 1651.[9] In the interim the JPs relapsed into a much fuller use than during the 1630s of the informal and haphazardly arranged meetings, in each other's homes and local inns, which had characterised magisterial business in the Elizabethan period. The clear distinction between petty sessions courts and private hearings was temporarily abandoned. In Bramber and Arundel rapes some meetings attended by several justices were apparently held. Immediately Peter Farnden and John Busbridge joined the Bench in 1644 they held a 'public meeting' with the purpose of confirming new overseers of the poor in Hastings rape, a matter that would normally have been routine petty sessions business. Likewise, in the north part of Buttinghill hundred in 1647, three JPs summoned overseers to a private house in Cuckfield to deliver their accounts.[10]

The civil war created new tasks for the JPs and exacerbated certain problems. An urgent priority in 1647, for instance, was the repair of Moultbridge, which had been dismantled to prevent the royalists moving eastwards in 1643. The poverty of the parishioners of St Pancras became chronic following the siege of Chichester in 1642. Vagrancy reached alarming dimensions in the mid-1640s.[11] But only a very few soldiers appeared before the Sussex magistrates. Herbert Hay interrogated an Arlington man in 1645 who had stolen away from his colours when the opportunity arose and had 'come home to his mother', leaving his coat and sword at the house of an acquaintance in Ringmer. The same autumn a discharged soldier, on the way home to Kent, was indicted for stealing linen from Lady Courthope's hedge at Whiligh. Another soldier, apprehended in 1648, was one of a gang that had broken through a watch at Chiddingstone and 'committed misdemeanours by drawing of swords, cokking of pistolls and thretninge words' at a Withyham alehouse. During the summer campaign he had served on both sides in turn: in Monmouthshire, marching under Lieutenant-General Cromwell, 'being behind his cullers and asking which way his cullers were gon, he was set upon by the countrey people'.[12]

There was a partial breakdown in many spheres of government during the 1640s. Between 1645 and 1650 persistent efforts were needed to bring in arrears to the county funds.[13] The repair of highways and bridges was much neglected until 1645, when presentments of defaults began to occur again.[14] Bridge repair was not properly taken in hand until 1651. Some of the Arun bridges were by then 'totally fallen downe' and the Rother bridges were hardly in a better condition. Considerable expenditure was required in the 1650s to bring the county's communications up to the pre-civil war standard.[15] The state of the county gaol at Horsham was a matter of constant anxiety, dispute and expense from 1636 onwards, when the assize judges declined to support a proposal from the western Bench that it should be replaced with a new gaol at Lewes. The gaol was 'rebuilt' at the direction of the assize judges, in 1641, but most inefficiently.[16] By 1649 it was 'not of sufficient strength to hold the prisoners by reason whereof diverse have made escapes'.[17] Between 1651 and 1656 the county paid out £460 for work on the gaol that should have been done in the 1640s had it been possible to raise the money.[18] During the 1640s, the Bench was struggling to pay off the accumulated arrears of a previous gaoler.[19]

The deficiencies in the government of Sussex during and immediately after the civil war are obvious, yet the competence and vigour with which a small group of active justices maintained order under difficult conditions was remarkable. The parliamentary Bench proved itself flexible and ready to experiment. The decision to hold all the sessions of the years 1643 to 1648 at Arundel, Petworth or Horsham rather than Chichester, for example, was a commonsense move when the effective Commission was concentrated in Arundel and Bramber rapes.[20] The expedient of ordering constables in Hastings rape to pay charitable uses money direct to the master of the Battle house of correction, or to a receiver there who acted as paymaster of the bridewell, was a sensible attempt to ease the flow of money to its destination.[21] The Bench's policy of granting charitable collections for the unfortunate and needy by their own authority, when the machinery of letters patent broke down, illustrates their concern that the community should not suffer from disruption of the agencies of the state.[22]

A fruitful and easy relationship between the Bench and the County Committee, institutions enjoying a substantial overlap of membership, strengthened the hands of the justices. A dispute between Fernhurst and Midhurst over the taxation of some lands in 1647 was referred to the Committee at Chichester. Seeking to strengthen the gaol in 1649, the JPs requested the Committee at Horsham to take care of the work.[23] The provost marshal appointed by the Horsham Committee to rid the iron-working district around Warnham of vagrants performed a task customarily the responsibility of the Bench.[24] In turn the justices occasionally brought their authority to bear against someone reluctant to pay taxes for the defence of the state, and they regularly granted pensions to maimed soldiers on the recommendation of the committeemen.[25] Thus the relationship was reciprocal and the intimate personal ties of the parliamentary caucus brought cohesion to county government at a time when it was threatened with collapse.

APPENDICES

I PRESENTMENTS AT VISITATIONS

[i] Archdeaconry of Chichester 1623–26

Date	Total presentments	Positive presentments	Percentage positive
Easter 1623	124	85	69
Easter 1624	124	74	60
Easter 1625	124	55	45
Summer 1625	132	77	58
Michaelmas 1625	124	28	23
Easter 1626	124	45	36
Summer 1626	124	42	34
Michaelmas 1626	124	29	23
Average	125	54	43

Source: Johnstone, pp. 59–126.
Note. The summer 1625 visitation included the Dean of Chichester's peculiar.

[ii] Archdeaconry of Lewes 1637–39

Date	Total presentments	Positive presentments	Percentage positive
Easter 1637	150	79	53
September 1637	150	66	44
Michaelmas 1637	150	38	25
Easter 1638	150	76	50
September 1638	150	78	52
Michaelmas 1638	150	24	16
Easter 1639	150	54	36
Average	150	59	39

Source: WSRO Ep II/15/1.

II THE COMMISSION OF THE PEACE 1625–60

This appendix provides information about the membership of the Commission of the Peace in the period 1625–60. It is based on the following sources: BM, Harleian MS 1622, Sloane MS 577; E 1238 (4): *Liber Pacis*, Michaelmas 1650; ESRO, Sessions Rolls 20–55, QSOB 1650–55, 1655–60; PRO, Assizes 35/67–101, C 193/12/1, 2, 13/1, 3–6, C 220/9/4, SP 16/212, Index 4211–14; WSRO, Sessions Rolls 14–45; Redwood. For discussion of these sources, which are also used for Appendix III, see *BIHR*, XXXII (1959), 221–42.

Sections (ii)–(viii) show the changing composition of the Commission of the Peace rape by rape; 163 resident gentry who sat on the Bench between 22 December 1625 and 30 July 1660 are included. Exclusion from and death in office are indicated by the signs noted on page 349.

[i] Resident gentry on the Commission of the Peace 1625–60

Rape	*Commission of the Peace*										
	30 March 1625	*22 Dec. 1625*	*12 March 1630*	*20 Feb. 1635*	*13 July 1639*	*20 July 1642*	*6 Feb. 1644*	*1 March 1649*	*20 Feb. 1654*	*2 July 1657*	*15 Oct. 1660*
Chichester	6	6	7	6	8	10	5	9	10	12	8
Arundel	6	2	4	3	3	5	3	3	6	6	8
Bramber	8	4	5	6	3	4	5	6	7	7	10
Lewes	6	4	4	3	2	4	8	5	6	4	7
Pevensey	12	6	10	9	9	7	11	10	10	10	7
Hastings	7	5	4	5	3	7	2	3	3	9	9
Residence uncertain	3	–	–	–	–	–	–	–	1	1	3
Total	48	27	34	32	28	37	34	36	43	49	52

[II] West Sussex Justices of the Peace: Rape of Chichester

1625 6 7 8 9 30 1 2 3 4 5 6 7 8 9 40 1 2 3 4 5 6 7 8 9 50 1 2 3 4 5 6 7 8 9 60 1

Name	*Home*
Bowyer, Sir Thomas	North Mundham
Ford, Sir William	Harting
Gray, Thomas	Woolbeding
Jordan, Nicholas	Chichester
Lewkenor, Richard	West Dean
Thorne, William	Chichester
Whatman, Thomas	Chichester
Nevill, William	Chichester
Lewkenor, Christopher	West Dean
Morley, Sir William	Boxgrove
Steward, Richard	Chichester
May, Thomas	Mid Lavant
Pay, Laurence	Upmarden
Jermyn, Philip	Racton
Norton, Sir Gregory	West Thorney
Ford, Sir Edward	Harting
Cowper, John	Harting
Morley, Sir John	West Dean
Wolfe, Nicholas	Chichester
Cawley, William	Chichester
Downes, John	Chichester
Oglander, George	Chichester
Chapman, Sir John	Westhampnett
Steward, Humphrey	Trotton
Bettsworth, Peter	Rogate
Peckham, Sir Henry	Boxgrove
Humphrey, Stephen	Chichester
Boughton, Richard	Chichester
Yalden, William	Lodsworth
Bettsworth, Arthur	Chithurst
Cawley, William	Chichester
Knowles, Richard	Upwaltham
Maning, Richard	Chichester
Bettsworth, Thomas	Rogate
Carr, Alan	Chichester
Downes, Richard	Chichester

Exclusion from office

Died in office where date known

Died in office where date unknown

[iii] West Sussex Justices of the Peace: Rape of Arundel

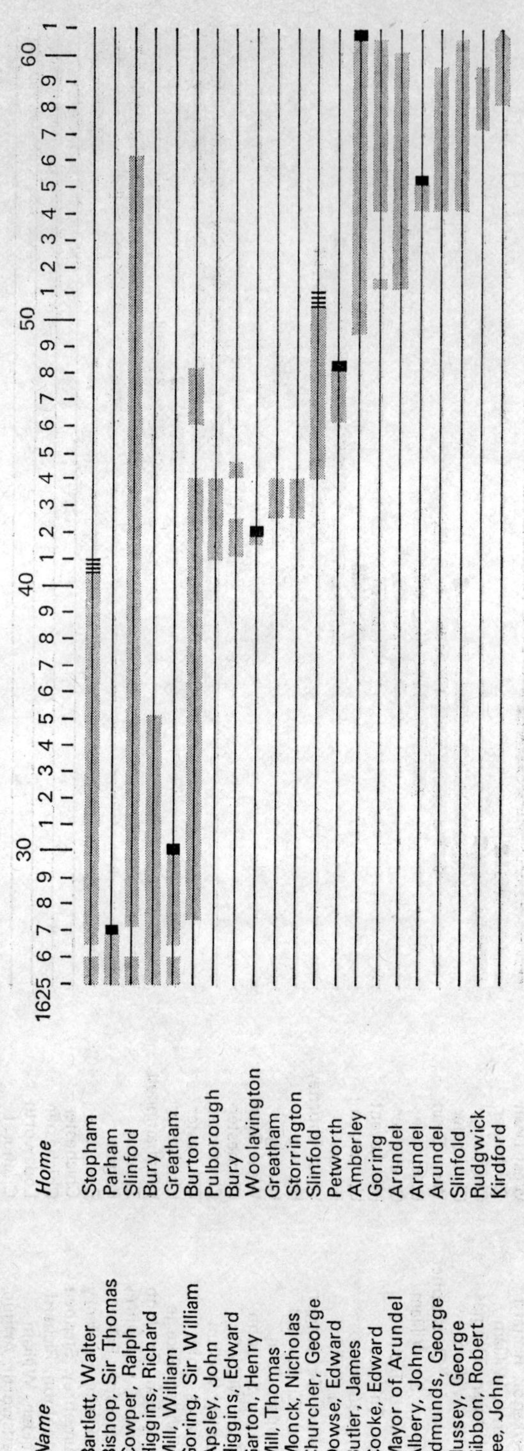

[iv] West Sussex Justices of the Peace: Rape of Bramber

Name	Home
Alford, Edward	Durrington
Comber, William	Shermanbury
Michell, Edward	Horsham
Middleton, John	Horsham
Goring, Sir Henry	Washington
Leedes, Sir John	Steyning
Alford, Sir John	Durrington
Farnfould, Sir Thomas	Steyning
Middleton, Thomas	Horsham
Apsley, Edward	Thakeham
Eversfield, Sir Thomas	Horsham
Marlott, William	Shoreham
Ravenscroft, Hall	Horsham
Temple, James	Clapham
Fagg, Sir John	Wiston
Freeman, William	Cowfold
Michell, Edward	Horsham
Yeates, Richard	Warnham
Fenwick, John	Warminghurst
Onslow, Henry	Warnham
Byne, John	Washington

1625 6 7 8 9 30 1 2 3 4 5 6 7 8 9 40 1 2 3 4 5 6 7 8 9 50 1 2 3 4 5 6 7 8 9 60 1

[v] East Sussex Justices of the Peace: Rape of Lewes

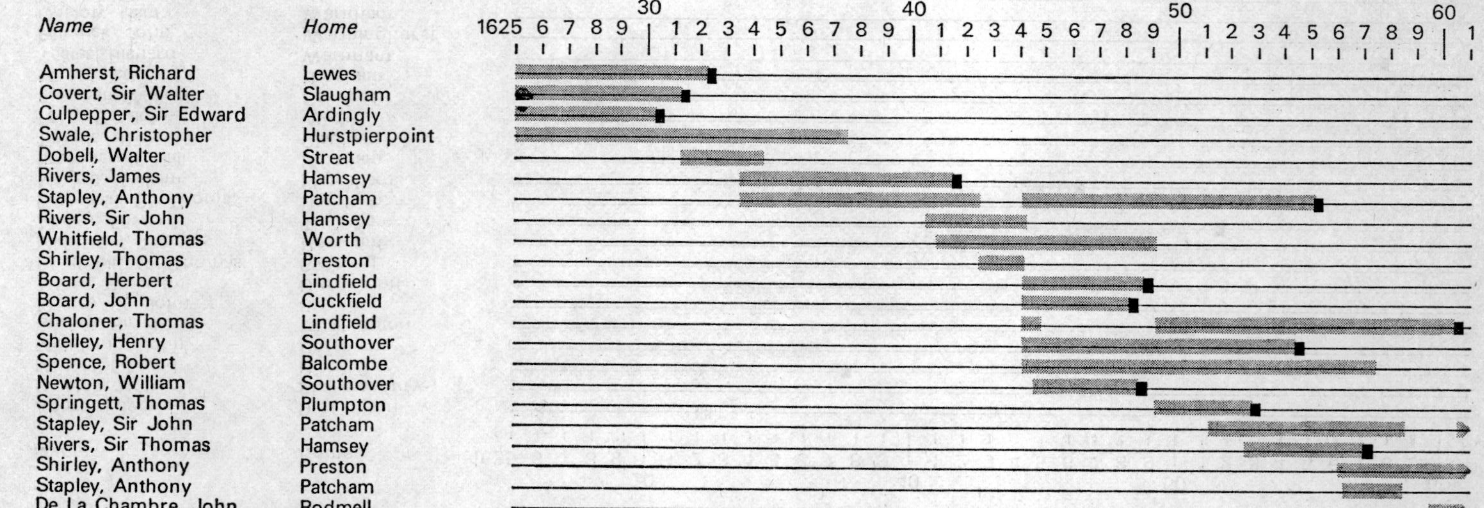

[vi] East Sussex Justices of the Peace: Rape of Pevensey

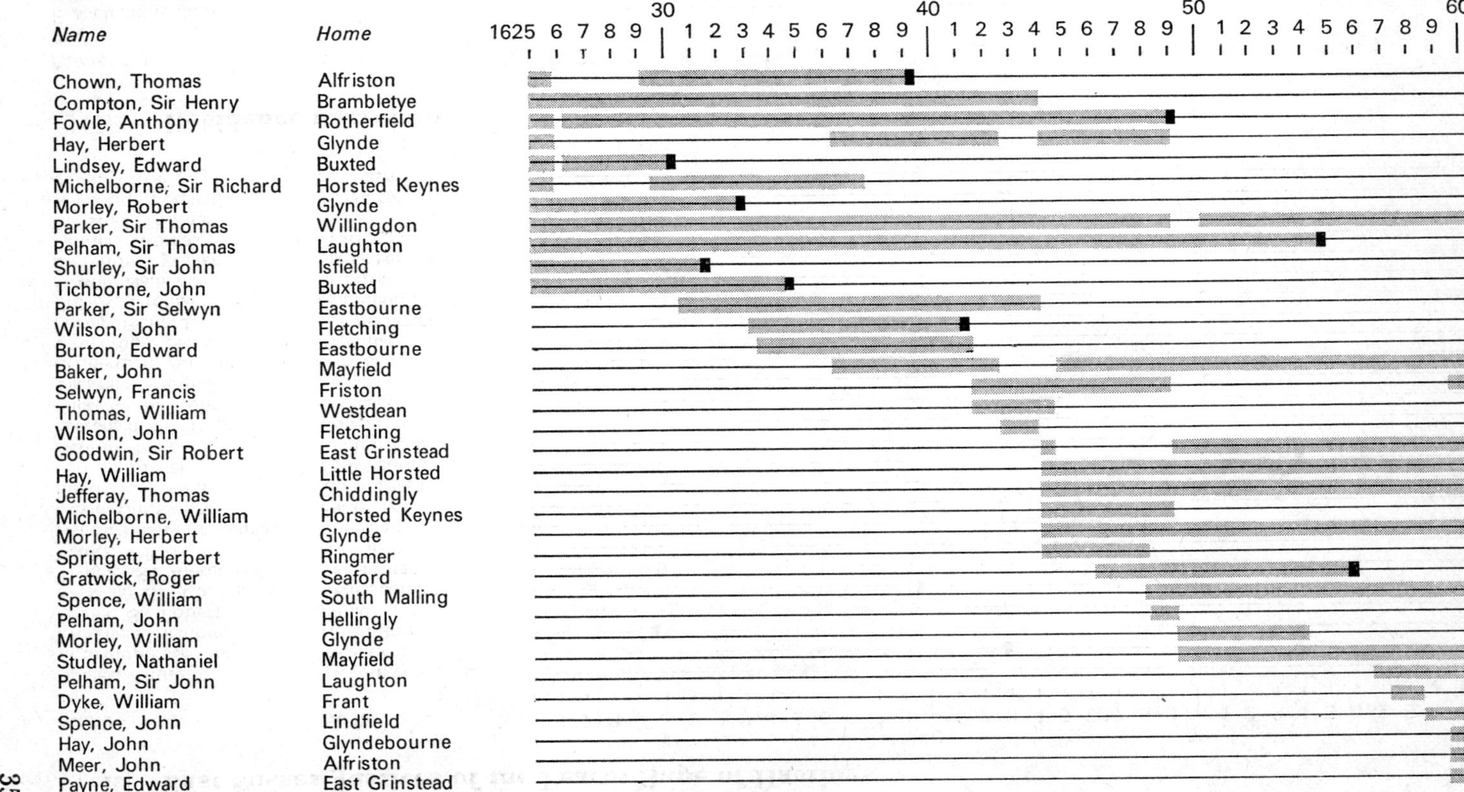

[vii] East Sussex Justices of the Peace: Rape of Hastings

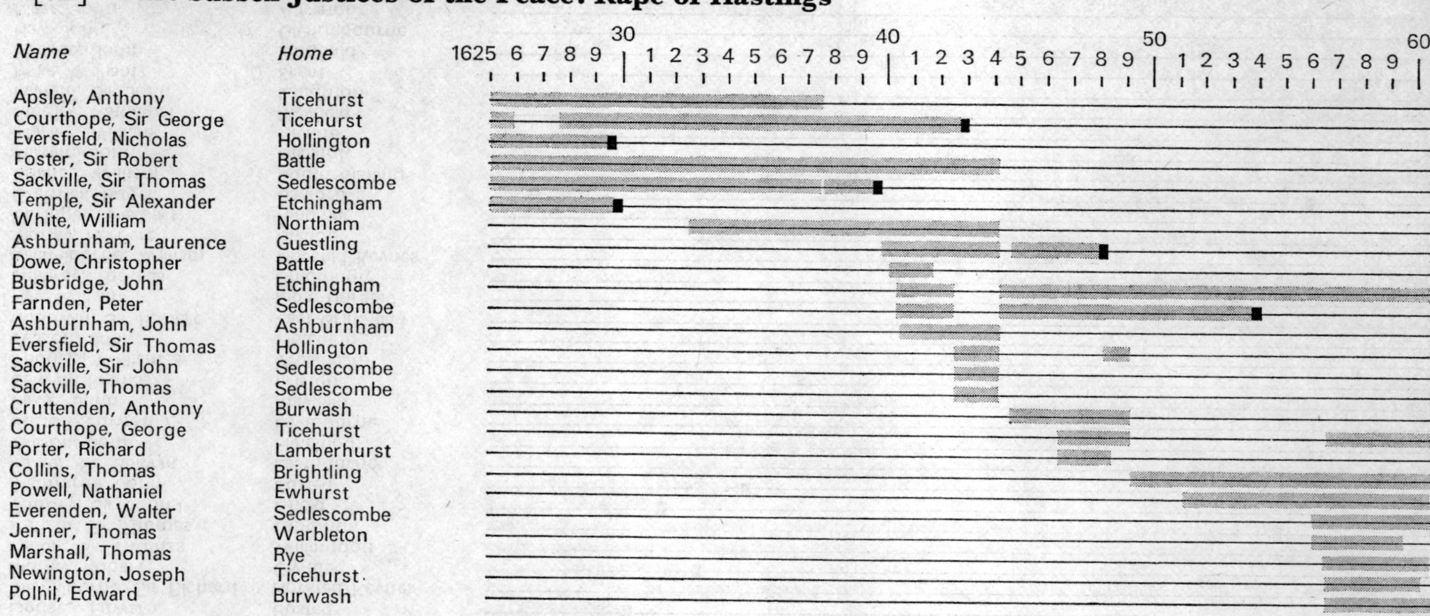

Name	*Home*
Apsley, Anthony	Ticehurst
Courthope, Sir George	Ticehurst
Eversfield, Nicholas	Hollington
Foster, Sir Robert	Battle
Sackville, Sir Thomas	Sedlescombe
Temple, Sir Alexander	Etchingham
White, William	Northiam
Ashburnham, Laurence	Guestling
Dowe, Christopher	Battle
Busbridge, John	Etchingham
Farnden, Peter	Sedlescombe
Ashburnham, John	Ashburnham
Eversfield, Sir Thomas	Hollington
Sackville, Sir John	Sedlescombe
Sackville, Thomas	Sedlescombe
Cruttenden, Anthony	Burwash
Courthope, George	Ticehurst
Porter, Richard	Lamberhurst
Collins, Thomas	Brightling
Powell, Nathaniel	Ewhurst
Everenden, Walter	Sedlescombe
Jenner, Thomas	Warbleton
Marshall, Thomas	Rye
Newington, Joseph	Ticehurst
Polhil, Edward	Burwash

[viii] Residence uncertain.

Name

1625 6 7 8 9 30 1 2 3 4 5 6 7 8 9 40 1 2 3 4 5 6 7 8 9 50 1 2 3 4 5 6 7 8 9 60 1

Beauchampe, John
Wilson, Alexander
Smith, Richard

[ix] The social status of Justices of the Peace 1625–60

Status	Commission of the Peace								
	30 March 1625	*12 March 1630*	*20 Feb. 1635*	*20 July 1642*	*6 Feb. 1644*	*1 March 1649*	*20 Feb. 1654*	*2 July 1657*	*15 Oct. 1660*
Baronets	3	5	4	7	1	1	1	0	5
Knights	14	7	7	11	2	3	1	1	4
Gentry in 1634 Visitation	24	18	16	17	25	19	19	21	26
Other county gentry	3	1	1	1	1	1	1	1	3
Clergy	3	3	4	–	–	–	–	1	1
Lesser gentry/ Merchants	1	–	–	1	5	12	21	25	13
Total	48	34	32	37	34	36	43	49	52

[x] The Justices of the Peace and higher education 1625–60

	Commission of the Peace								
	30 March 1625	12 March 1630	20 Feb. 1635	20 July 1642	6 Feb. 1644	1 March 1649	20 Feb. 1654	2 July 1657	15 Oct. 1660
University only	8	5	6	6	3	4	4	9	11
Inns of Court only	9	7	7	9	9	7	8	7	4
University and Inns	15	13	11	15	11	10	8	9	14
Total	32	25	24	30	23	21	20	25	29
Size of Commission	48	34	32	37	34	36	43	49	52
Total as percentage of whole Commission	67	74	75	80	68	58	47	51	56

[xi] Family continuity on the Commission of the Peace 1625–60

Relative on Commission	*Commission of the Peace*								
	30 March 1625	*12 March 1630*	*20 Feb. 1635*	*20 July 1642*	*6 Feb. 1644*	*1 March 1649*	*20 Feb. 1654*	*2 July 1657*	*15 Oct. 1660*
Father/Uncle	12	8	8	14	11	7	10	11	19
Grandfather/ Great-uncle	2	4	5	6	2	1	1	–	2
Total	14	12	13	20	13	8	11	11	21
Size of Commission	48	34	32	37	34	36	43	49	52
Total as percentage of whole Commission	29	35	41	54	38	22	26	22	40

III QUARTER SESSIONS 1625–60

[i] The performance of Justices of the Peace in attending Quarter Sessions 1625–60 (Data before 1642 is incomplete)

%	*0*	*0–25*	*25–50*	*50–75*	*75–100*	*Total*
JPs appointed before April 1641	7	12	24	17	10	70
JPs appointed after April 1641	28	19	20	17	9	93
All Justices	35	31	44	34	19	163
Percentages of all JPs	22	19	26	21	12	100

[ii] The attendance of Justices of the Peace at Quarter Sessions 1625–60 (Data before 1642 is incomplete)

Divisions and dates	*2–3*	*4–5*	*7–9*	*10–13*	*14–17*	*Sessions held*
Midsummer sessions 1625–1660	–	5	8	11	2	26
Eastern sessions 1625–1642	–	3	11	12	4	30
Eastern sessions 1643–60	1	13	14	19	7	54
Western sessions 1625–42	–	8	11	8	–	27
Western sessions 1643–60	5	17	18	12	–	52
All sessions	6	46	62	62	13	189
Percentages	3.1	24.9	33.0	33.0	7.0	100

IV POOR RELIEF CASES AND THE HARVEST 1625–59

Harvest year	Quality of harvest	Quarter sessions	Funds from parish	Funds from individual	Housing	Housing and parish funds	Settlement	Enforcement	Total	Total new cases
1625	Average	5	–	1	–	–	2	1	4	3
1626	Good	7	3	1	2	–	–	–	6	6
1627	Good	5	2	–	–	–	–	–	2	2
1631	Average	2	–	–	–	–	2	–	2	2
1632	Deficient	4	1	3	–	–	3	–	7	7
1635	Average	3	1	–	1	–	8	2	12	10
1636	Average	7	4	1	–	1	19	2	27	25
1637	Deficient	7	1	1	3	–	11	1	17	16
1638	Average	7	1	1	–	–	5	1	8	7
1639	Good	7	2	–	–	–	12	2	16	14
1640	Average	6	3	1	–	–	2	–	6	6
1641	Good	7	3	4	1	1	6	5	20	15
1642	Average	6	1	–	1	–	7	2	11	9
1643	Good	6	3	1	–	1	11	2	18	16
1644	Good	7	5	–	–	–	9	1	15	14
1645	Good	7	7	–	–	1	6	–	14	14
1646	Deficient	7	4	–	1	–	8	2	15	13
1647	Bad	7	4	1	1	1	10	3	20	17
1648	Bad	7	13	2	1	2	6	6	30	24
1649	Bad	7	9	3	–	–	14	2	28	26
1650	Deficient	6	7	1	–	–	11	3	22	19
1651	Average	7	5	1	2	–	14	4	26	22
1652	Good	7	6	–	–	1	9	1	17	16
1653	Abundant	7	6	–	–	–	6	1	13	12
1654	Abundant	7	6	–	–	1	12	2	21	19
1655	Good	7	7	–	–	–	6	1	14	13
1656	Average	7	11	1	2	–	15	1	30	29
1657	Deficient	7	6	1	–	1	14	3	25	22
1658	Bad	7	4	4	–	1	18	1	28	27
1659	Deficient	6	8	5	4	1	8	3	29	26
Total		189	133	33	19	12	254	52	503	451

Sources: WSRO, Sessions Rolls 14–45; ESRO, Sessions Rolls 20–55, QSOB 1650–55, 1655–60; Redwood. Harvest categories are from Hoskins, *Agricultural History Review*, xvi (1968), 15–31. See above, pp. 156–7

V TAXATION

Figures throughout this appendix are to the nearest pound or shilling. Tarring, Patching and Marlpost tithing have been included in Brightford hundred. The data for 1610, 1626, 1628 and 1642 is incomplete.

1610: the sum of the two payments which made up the single subsidy granted by the statute 7 James I, c.23: PRO, E 179/191/350, 357, 359.

1626: the second subsidy paid under the statute 1 Charles I, c.6: PRO, E 179/191/377a.

1628: for Arundel, Bramber and Lewes rapes and the city of Chichester the third, for Hastings rape the fourth, subsidy paid under the statute 3 Charles I, c.8: PRO, E 179/191/380, 381, 383, 385.

1635: £250 of the assessment of £5,000 on Sussex in the ship money writ of 1635 was paid by the Cinque Ports. The clergy, who did not contribute to the subsidies in these tables, paid £400 of the £4,750 raised by the county: PRO, SP 16/317/97.

1636: the assessment for ship money in 1636 was on the same basis as the previous year. The clergy contributed about £460 on this occasion: PRO, SP 16/351/89.

1642: the first payment under the statute granting a tax of £400,000 'for the necessary defence and great affaires of the Kingdoms of England and Ireland', 16 Charles I, c.32: £10,915 was demanded from Sussex in two payments: PRO, E 179/191/360, 387–89, 258/12.

[i] The yield of the subsidy, ship money and the Act for £400,000 1610–42

Rape	*1610*	*1626*	*1628*	*1635*	*1636*	*1642*
Chichester	–	324	–	784	888	680
Arundel	–	232	194	812	708	969
Bramber	195	165	131	588	582	863
Lewes	–	199	145	608	648	–
Pevensey	–	266	–	975	970	910
Hastings	–	136	117	862	877	910
City of Chichester	88	64	54	121	77	230
Total	–	1386	–	4750	4750	–

[ii] The yield of the subsidy, ship money and the Act for £400,000 in Bramber rape 1610–42

Hundred–Borough	*1610*	*1626*	*1628*	*1636*	*1642*
Brightford	45– 4	41–12	31–12	92– 7	130–18
Fishergate	4–14	1–12	1– 0	23– 0	36–16
Burbeach	9–14	7– 7	5–17	62– 0	104– 6
Steyning	–	28– 3	15– 6	50– 0	44– 3
Tipnoak	10– 4	–	8– 0	56– 0	68–12
Windham	–	–	7–12	28– 0	41– 7
West Grinstead	35– 7	–	19– 3	66– 0	123–14
Shinglecross	24–18	–	16– 0	54– 0	81–17
East Easewithe	–	–	15–16	59–10	42–16
Shoreham	4– 1	3–11	2–13	10– 0	16–19
Steyning	–	2–16	1– 7	18– 0	57–16
Horsham	–	7–17	7– 0	60– 0	58– 6
Bramber	–	–12	–	3– 0	5– 9
Total	194–13	165– 0	131– 6	581–17	862–19

[iii] The yield of the subsidy in the city of Chichester 1625–28

	1626			*1628*		
	Lands	*Goods*	*Total*	*Lands*	*Goods*	*Total*
Commissioners	1– 4	3– 6	4–10	2– 8	1–17	3– 5
Assessors	– 4	6–11	6–15	– 8	5– 4	5–12
East Street	4–16	8– 0	12–19	1– 8	3– 6	4–15
The Close	–16	2–13	3– 9	–12	3– 4	3–16
South Street	1–12	4–10	6– 4	–16	6– 0	6–16
West Street	7– 0	7–12	15– 0	6– 0	7–19	13–19
North Street	4–12	6– 6	10–18	3–16	7– 9	11– 6
Pallant	– 4	3–17	4– 1	– 4	2–19	3– 3
Total	20– 8	42–15	63–16	15–12	37–18	52–12

[iv] Taxpayers in Bramber rape 1610–42

Hundred–Borough	*1610*	*1626*	*1628*	*1642*
Brightford	109	87	72	272
Fishergate	13	6	3	45
Burbeach	24	24	17	145
Steyning	39	28	25	91
Tipnoak	32	32	30	151
Windham	26	29	24	81
West Grinstead	69	62	47	319
Shinglecross	55	53	48	186
East Easewithe	49	56	49	126
Shoreham	12	9	7	40
Steyning	13	9	5	153
Horsham	28	31	26	328
Bramber	1	3	–	22
Total	470	429	353	1959

[v] Subsidymen in the city of Chichester 1610–28

	1610			*1626*			*1628*		
	Lands	*Goods*	*Total*	*Lands*	*Goods*	*Total*	*Lands*	*Goods*	*Total*
Commissioners	–	5	5	1	5	6	2	3	5
Assessors	–	9	9	1	9	10	2	8	10
East Street	3	22	25	9	14	23	7	7	14
The Close	2	6	8	3	5	8	3	5	8
South Street	6	10	16	7	8	15	4	9	13
West Street	3	14	17	13	14	27	11	15	26
North Street	7	17	24	11	14	25	16	11	27
Pallant	3	10	13	1	7	8	1	5	6
Total	24	93	117	46	76	122	46	63	109

[vi] **Subsidymen paying on lands and goods in Bramber rape 1610–28**

	Lands			Goods		
Hundred–Borough	*1610*	*1626*	*1628*	*1610*	*1626*	*1628*
Brightford	72	72	69	37	15	3
Fishergate	8	4	1	5	2	2
Burbeach	13	21	16	11	3	1
Steyning	26	19	22	13	9	3
Tipnoak	30	31	29	2	1	1
Windham	26	28	24	–	1	–
West Grinstead	55	58	45	14	5	2
Shinglecross	51	53	48	4	–	–
East Easewithe	37	51	48	12	5	2
Shoreham	6	4	4	6	5	3
Steyning	8	8	4	5	1	1
Horsham	28	30	26	–	1	–
Bramber	1	3	–	–	–	–
Total	361	381	336	109	48	18

[vii] **Subsidy payments on lands and goods in Bramber rape 1626–28**

	Lands		Goods	
Hundred–Borough	*1626*	*1628*	*1626*	*1628*
Brightford	32– 8	39–18	7– 4	1–12
Fishergate	–16	– 4	–16	–16
Burbeach	5– 4	5– 2	1– 7	–13
Steyning	22–12	13–11	5–11	1–14
Shoreham	1– 0	–16	2–11	1–17
Steyning	2– 8	–16	– 8	–11
Horsham	7– 4	7– 0	–13	–
Bramber	–12	–	–	–

[viii] Ship money collections

Writ	Sheriff	Charge	Arrears	Percentage
October 1634	Sir William Culpepper	6,735*	70–13–2	1.1
August 1635	Sir William Culpepper†	5,000	–	–
August 1636	Sir Edward Bishop	5,000	31–15–0	0.6
October 1637	Anthony Fowle	5,000	–	–
November 1638	Anthony Foster	1,800	–	–
November 1639	Edward Apsley	5,000	2,804–12–0	56.1

Source: Figures for 1635 to 1639 from M. D. Gordon, 'The collection of ship money in the reign of Charles I', *TRHS*, iv (1910), 160; for 1634 from PRO, SP 16/296/58.

* This sum was charged on Sussex and Kent together.

† Twenty-two per cent of this collection was made by Sir William Morley who succeeded Sir William Culpepper as sheriff in January 1636.

REFERENCES

Abbreviations

Add	Additional (MS).
AO	C. H. Firth and R. S. Rait, eds. *Acts and Ordinances of the Interregnum 1642-1660*, 2 vols. (London, 1911).
APC	*Acts of the Privy Council.*
Barnes	T. G. Barnes, *Somerset 1625-1640* (Oxford, 1961).
BIHR	*Bulletin of the Institute of Historical Research.*
Blackwood	B. G. Blackwood, *The Lancashire Gentry 1625-60: A Social and Economic Study* (Oxford, D.Phil. Thesis, 1973).
BM	British Museum.
Boynton	L. Boynton, *The Elizabethan Militia* (London, 1967).
Brent	C. E. Brent, *Employment, Land Tenure and Population in Eastern Sussex, 1540-1640* (Sussex D.Phil. Thesis, 1973).
CCAM	*Calendar of the Committee for Advance of Money.*
CCC	*Calendar of the Committee for Compounding.*
CJ	*Journal of the House of Commons.*
Cliffe	J. T. Cliffe, *The Yorkshire Gentry* (London, 1969).
CSPD	*Calendar of State Papers Domestic.*
DL Book	'Booke concerning the Deputy Leiuetennantshipp', manuscript in East Sussex Record Office.
DNB	*Dictionary of National Biography.*
EHR	*English Historical Review.*
Everitt	A. Everitt, *The Community of Kent and the Great Rebellion* (Leicester, 1966).
ESRO	East Sussex Record Office.
GMR	Guildford Muniment Room.
Hassell Smith	A. Hassell Smith, *County and Court* (Oxford University Press, 1974).
HLRO	House of Lords Record Office.
HMC	*Historical Manuscripts Commission.*
HMCP	*HMC Portland MSS.*
HMCR	*HMC Rye MSS.*
Johnstone	H. Johnstone, ed. *Churchwardens Presentments: Archdeaconry of Chichester* (Sussex Record Society, XLIX, 1947-8).
Keeler	M. F. Keeler, *The Long Parliament* (Philadelphia, 1954).
LJ	*Journal of the House of Lords.*
Manning	R. B. Manning, *Religion and Society in Elizabethan Sussex* (Leicester, 1969).
Morrill	J. S. Morrill, *Cheshire 1630-1660* (Oxford, 1974).
Mousley	J. E. Mousley, 'Sussex Country Gentry in the Reign of Elizabeth' (Ph.D. thesis, London, 1956).
PCR	*Privy Council Registers in Facsimile.*
PRO	Public Record Office.
QSOB	Quarter Sessions Order Book.

Quintrell	B. W. Quintrell, 'The Government of the County of Essex 1603-1642' (PhD thesis London, 1965).
Redwood	B. C. Redwood, *Quarter Sessions Order Book 1642-1649* (Sussex Record Society, LIV, 1954).
Richmond	B. J. Richmond, 'The Work of the Justices of the Peace in Hampshire 1603-1640' (MPhil thesis, Southampton, 1969).
RO	Record Office.
SAC	*Sussex Archaeological Collections.*
SNQ	*Sussex Notes and Queries.*
SR	*Statutes of the Realm.*
SRS	Sussex Record Society.
Stone	L. Stone, *The Crisis of the Aristocracy* (Oxford, 1965).
Thomas-Stanford	C. Thomas-Stanford, *Sussex in the Great Civil War and the Interregnum* (London, 1910).
TRHS	*Transactions of the Royal Historical Society.*
TSP	T. Birch, ed. *A Collection of the State Papers of John Thurloe*, 7 vols (1742).
Univ. Birmingham Hist. J.	*University of Birmingham Historical Journal.*
VCH	*Victoria County History.*
VCHS	*Victoria County History of Sussex*, 6 vols (1905-53).
Visitation 1634	W. Bruce Bannerman, ed. *The Visitations of Sussex 1530 and 1633-4* (Harleian Society, LIII, 1905).
Visitation 1662	A. W. Hughes Clarke, ed. *The Visitation of Sussex 1662* (Harleian Society, LXXXIX, 1937).
WSRO	West Sussex Record Office.

References

1. Communications, towns, agriculture and industry

1. *Camden's Britannia 1695* (David & Charles, 1971), p. 166.
2. BM, Add MS 33147, fol. 247r.
3. Brent, pp. 122–63, 239–58. C. Brent, 'Beyond beginnings', in W. Lamont, ed. *The Realities of Teaching History: Beginnings* (University of Sussex, 1972), pp. 107–8; R. Garraway Rice, ed. *West Sussex Protestation Returns 1641–2* (SRS, v, 1906).
4. PRO, SP 14/116/36. I am grateful to Mr Colin Brent for information about the distribution of population in East Sussex.
5. ESRO, Dunn MS 51/60.
6. Thomas-Stanford, pp. 6–7; J. Parkes, *Travel in England in the Seventeenth Century* (Oxford University Press, 1925), pp. 14–15.
7. ESRO, Sessions Rolls 49, outer membrane; *SAC*, iv (1851), 256; PRO, Assizes 35/76/9.
8. ESRO, Sessions Rolls 30–36; WSRO, Sessions Rolls 25–28; Barnes, pp. 63–4, 183.
9. WSRO, Sessions Rolls 71/16.
10. *SR*, iv, part 1, 726–7, part 2, 919–20; *APC 1628–9*, no. 235.
11. PRO, SP 16/216/76. See also J. Crofts, *Packhorse, Wagon and Post* (Routledge, 1967), pp. 14–19.
12. E. Straker, *Wealden Iron* (Bell, 1931), pp. 185–6; PRO, Assizes 35/71/9/13.
13. ESRO, Sessions Rolls 50/10.
14. D. Defoe, *A Tour through Great Britain* (1707), p. 125; L. G. Wickham Legg, ed., 'A relation of a short survey of the western counties', *Camden Society*, third series, lii (1936), 29.
15. *Ibid*, 27–8; J. B. Caldecott, 'John Taylor's tour of Sussex in 1653', *SAC*, lxxxi (1940), 29.
16. R. F. Dell, ed. *The Records of Rye Corporation* (Lewes, E. Sussex County Council, 1962), map facing p. 161; H. L. Turner, *Town Defences in England and Wales* (London, J. Baker, 1970), pp. 159–63; L. A. Vidler, *A New History of Rye* (Hove, 1934), p. 62.
17. ESRO, Rye MS 47/107; A. J. F. Dulley, 'The early history of the Rye fishing industry', *SAC*, cvii (1969), 53–4.
18. ESRO, Sessions Rolls 38/1; *HMCR*, p. 196.
19. ESRO, Sessions Rolls 50, outer membrane, QSOB 1655–60, fol. 61r.
20. W. G. Hoskins, *Local History in England* (Longman, 1959), p. 177.
21. *VCHS*, iii, 78–9; *Camden Society*, third series, lii (1936), 34; G. S. Burrows, *Chichester: A Study in Conservation* (HMSO, 1968), pp. 9, 23–7, 83.
22. *VCHS*, iii, 23 and map facing, 82; Burrows, *Chichester*, p. 5.
23. Garraway Rice, *West Sussex Protestation Returns*, pp. 43–57.
24. PRO, E179/191/377a.
25. Brent, pp. 336-45; *VCHS*, vii, 7–8; *Camden Society*, third series, lii (1936) 30; Lamont, ed. *Realities of Teaching History*, pp. 108–9.
26. W. H. Godfrey, 'The High Street, Lewes', *SAC*, xciii (1955), 1–33.

27. PRO, Prob 11/181/183; W. H. Godfrey, ed., *The Book of John Rowe* (SRS, xxxiv, 1928), 8–16.
28. A. Everitt, 'The Marketing of Agricultural Produce', in J. Thirsk, ed. *Agrarian History of England* (Cambridge, 1967), iv, 467–75; Brent, pp. 293–6.
29. ESRO, Frewen MS 520, fols. 36r, 41r, 47v, 53v, 54v, 57r.
30. G. H. Kenyon, 'Petworth Town and Trades 1610–1760', *SAC*, xcvi (1958), 35–107; xcviii (1960), 71–117.
31. Thirsk, ed. *Agrarian History*, iv, 56–7; E. Kerridge, *The Agricultural Revolution* (Allen & Unwin, 1967), pp. 51–3; J. Cornwall, 'Farming in Sussex 1560–1640', *SAC*, xcii (1954), 60–3.
32. Thirsk, ed. *Agrarian History*, iv, 59–61; Kerridge, *Agricultural Revolution*, pp. 132–6, 170–1; G. Fussell, 'Four centuries of farming systems in Sussex', *SAC*, xc (1951–2) 68–9; J. Cornwall, 'Agricultural Improvement 1560–1640', *SAC*, xcviii (1960), 122–3.
33. *SAC*, xcii (1954), 64–5, 79–81.
34. G. H. Kenyon, 'Kirdford Inventories 1611–1776', *SAC*, xciii (1955), 78–156.
35. ESRO, DL Book, fol. 29r; PRO E 401/2586.
36. Stone, pp. 277–9.
37. BM, Add MS 33144–9, 33154, 33155.
38. *HMC De L'Isle and Dudley MSS*, vi, 441–2; BM, Add MS 33084, fol. 64r.
39. BM, Add MS 33144, fols. 107–117, 33145, fol. 78v, 33146, fol. 129r.
40. *Ibid*, Add MS 33145, fols. 7v, 12r, 16v, 18v, 27v, 58v, 120r.
41. *Ibid*, fols. 64v, 69v, 33147, fols. 8r, 12r.
42. *SAC*, xciii (1955), 85–6.
43. BM, Add MS 33145, fols. 104v, 132,r 142r, 33147, fols. 19r, 29v, 40r.
44. Stone, pp. 303, 347.
45. BM, Add MS 33145, fols. 33v, 39r, 43r, 45v, 46v, 61r, 62r, 75r.
46. *Ibid*, fols. 2–59, 33147, fols. 3–22.
47. *Ibid*, Add MS 33144, fols. 49v, 52v, 59v, 64v, 70r, 72v; Stone, p. 301.
48. BM, Add MS 33144, 33147; *SAC* xcii (1954), 92; Thirsk, *Agrarian History*, iv, 538–42; Everitt, pp. 28, 32.
49. BM, Add MS 33145, fols. 4v, 9r, 25r, 26r, 27v, 30r, 67r, 114v, 33147, fols. 18v, 19v, 24r, 25v.
50. *Ibid*, Add MS 33145, fols. 5r, 12r, 15r, 47r, 120v, 33147, fols. 9v, 15r, 21v, 31v, 32r; *SAC*, xcii (1954), 77.
51. ESRO, Frewen MS 520, fols. 10r, 14r, 20r, 47v, 52v, 55v.
52. *Ibid*, fols. 50v, 56r, 57r.
53. *Ibid*, fols. 47v, 48r, 50, 52v, 55v, 67r, 68v, 74v.
54. *Ibid*, fols. 47v, 52v, 55v, 62v, 77–83.
55. *Ibid*, fols. 47–62, 68v, 74r, 79v.
56. *Ibid*, fols. 47r, 55v, 68v, 74r, 77v.
57. *Ibid*, fols. 47v, 52v, 55v, 62v, 74r, 77v.
58. *Ibid*, fols. 43v, 50v, 53, 56, 67v, 74v.
59. *Ibid*, fols. 32v, 38v, 39r, 50v, 56v, 69v, 78v, 79r.
60. *Ibid*, Hickstead Place MS 467. Extracts appeared in E. Turner, 'On the Domestic Habits and Mode of Life of a Sussex Gentleman', *SAC*, xxiii (1871). 36–72.
61. Straker, *Wealden Iron*, pp. 52–9; J. L. Parsons, 'The Sussex Iron works', *SAC*, xxxii (1882), 21–3; BM, Add MS 33084, fol. 83; H. R. Schubert, *History of the British Iron and Steel Industry from c. 450 BC to AD 1775* (Routledge, 1957), pp. 368–9.
62. Straker, *Wealden Iron*, pp. 251, 275–6, 299.
63. PRO, E 401/2586, SP 14/127/79, 81.
64. *SAC*, xxxii (1882), 30–2; ESRO, Dunn MS 46/1.
65. *CSPD 1619–23*, p. 12; *CSPD 1653–4*, p. 80.
66. Straker, *Wealden Iron*, pp. 141–77.

67. *CSPD 1653–4*, p. 80.
68. ESRO, Dunn MS 47/1.
69. PRO, Prob 11/281/189; Straker, *Wealden Iron*, p. 379.
70. *Camden Society*, third series, lii (1936), 38; Straker, *Wealden Iron*, pp. 425, 430.
71. BM, Add MS 33144, fol. 18v, 33146, fols. 2r, 132v, 133r, 33148, fols. 74r, 93v, 33154, *passim*, 33155, fols. 1–98.
72. J. H. Andrews, 'Chichester and the Grain Trade 1650–1750', *SAC*, xcii (1954), 93–105; T. Willan, *The English Coasting Trade 1600–1750* (Manchester University Press, 1938), p. 147.
73. *Camden Society*, third series, lii (1936), 30.
74. J. H. Farrant, 'The Evolution of Newhaven Harbour and the Lower Ouse before 1800', *SAC*, cx (1972), 47–51.
75. Brent, pp. 306–25.
76. PRO, SP 16/136/13; SP 18/126/118, 128; ESRO, Rye MS 47/158.
77. Willan, *English Coasting Trade*, p. 149; Brent, pp. 319–36.
78. ESRO, Rye MS 47/145, 99/14, 15, 21, 23, 25; Dell, ed. *The Records of Rye Corporation*, pp. 92–7; J. K. Gruenfelder 'Rye and the Parliament of 1621', *SAC*, cvii (1969), 25–6; J. H. Andrews, 'Rye Harbour in the Reign of Charles II', *SAC*, xciv (1956), 35–42.
79. Rye MS 47/144–6, 152; below p. 238.
80. *HMCR*, pp. 133–56; *CSPD 1619–23*, pp. 339, 345, 409; *CSPD 1623–5*, p. 228; *CSPD 1629–31*, pp. 534, 559–60; *CSPD 1631–3*, pp. 51–2, 78, 303, 316; *SAC*, cvii (1969), 27–8; Thomas-Stanford, p. 279; A. J. F. Dulley, 'The Early History of the Rye Fishing Industry', *SAC*, cvii (1969), 54–64.
81. ESRO, Rye MS 47/147.
82. *Ibid*, 47/146; *HMCR*, pp. 217–8.

2. The gentry community

1. *SAC*, ii (1849), 99–100.
2. BM, Add MS 33084, fol. 73r.
3. ESRO, Dunn MS 51/61.
4. L. Stone, *Social Change and Revolution in England* (Longman, 1965); J. H. Hexter, 'Storm over the gentry', in *Reappraisals in History* (Longmans, 1967); Cliffe; Everitt; H. A. Lloyd, *The Gentry of South West Wales 1540–1640* (University of Wales Press, 1968).
5. A. Everitt, *Change in the Provinces: the Seventeenth Century* (Leicester University Department of English Local History, Occasional Papers, second series, i, 1969), p. 56; PRO, Prob 11/168/65; *Visitation 1662*, p. 78.
6. Manning, pp. 221–37.
7. Below, pp. 231–2.
8. Below, pp. 175–201.
9. Below, p. 99.
10. Mousley, pp. 593–8; W. P. D. Murphy, ed. '*The Earl of Hertford's Lieutenancy Papers 1603–12*' (Wiltshire Record Society, xxiii, 1969), 1–5; *VCH Wiltshire*, v, 80–6, 135.
11. Stone, pp. 106, 374, 428, 436–7, 475, 555, 761; F. Hull, ed., 'The Tufton Sequestration Papers 1644–7', in *A Seventeenth Century Miscellany* (Kent Records, xvii, 1960), 35–7.
12. R. J. N. Swales, 'Local Politics and the Parliamentary Representation of Sussex' (PhD thesis, Bristol, 1964), p. 32.
13. Mousley, p. 250.
14. Manning, p. 234; J. E. Neale, *The Elizabethan House of Commons* (Cape, 1963), pp. 63–4; R. B. Manning, 'Anthony Browne, 1st Viscount Montagu: the influence in county politics of an Elizabethan Catholic nobleman', *SAC*, cxvi (1968), 103–12.

15. T. G. Barnes and A. Hassall Smith, 'Justices of the Peace from 1588 to 1688 – a revised list of sources', *BIHR*, xxxii (1959), 227.
16. ESRO, Rye MS 47/113.
17. V. Sackville-West, ed. *The Diary of Lady Anne Clifford* (London, 1923), pp. 82, 107.
18. ESRO, Frewen MS 520, fol. 34r; BM, Add MS 33145, fol. 142v.
19. *CSPD 1628–9*, p. 595; *APC 1630–1*, no. 92.
20. PRO, Prob 11/157/33, 52, 161/61.
21. Sackville-West, ed. *Lady Anne Clifford*, pp. 31–2; ESRO, Sessions Rolls 12–29.
22. Lord Leconfield, *Petworth Manor in the Seventeenth Century* (Oxford University Press, 1954), p. 6; Stone, pp. 290–1.
23. PRO, Prob 11/204/60; Keeler, pp. 158–9.
24. Manning, pp. 268–70; Mousley, *passim.*
25. Everitt, pp. 45–6; A. Everitt, *Change in the Provinces* (Leicester University Press, 1969), p. 27.
26. BM, Add MS 33145, fols. 124v, 126r.
27. Stone, pp. 579–81.
28. PRO Prob 11/168/75, 171/81; I. Nairn and N. Pevsner, *Sussex* (Penguin, 1965), p. 508.
29. PRO, Prob 11/159/62, 311/100; Nairn and Pevsner, *Sussex*, pp. 369, 545, 629.
30. *Visitation 1662*, pp. 60, 174; *CCC*, 2458.
31. Everitt, *Change in the Provinces*, pp. 13–14.
32. *Visitation 1662*, pp. 2, 64.
33. PRO, Prob 11/159/5, 162/75.
34. *Ibid*, Prob 11/157/62, 179/64.
35. ESRO, Dyke Hutton MS 825, 844; PRO E 401/2586.
36. *Visitation 1662*, p. 38.
37. Essex RO, D/DL E 22, 7 Dec. 1644, 19 July 1645, 29 Aug. 1646, 28 June 1649.
38. BM, Add MS 33145, fol. 217r, 33148, fol. 66r.
39. *Camden Society*, third series, lii (1936), 29–38.
40. Mousley, pp. 312–14.
41. Nairn and Pevsner, *Sussex*, pp. 31–2, 54–5, 398, 471, 549, 607.
42. J. H. Cooper, 'The Coverts', *SAC*, xlvii (1904), 138–9 and plates.
43. W. H. Godfrey, 'Brambletye', *SAC*, lxxxii (1931), 1–19.
44. W. G. Hoskins, 'The rebuilding of rural England', *Past and Present*, iv (1953), 44–59; Everitt, pp. 28–33; J. P. Ferris, 'The gentry of Dorset on the eve of the Civil War', *Genealogists Magazine*, xv, (1965), 114; articles by R. T. Mason in *SAC*, lxxx–ci (1939–63).
45. Nairn and Pevsner, *Sussex*, p. 32.
46. *SAC*, xx (1863), 232; *VCHS*, ii, 297–8.
47. BM, Add MS 33145, fols. 4r, 9, 16r, 100r.
48. *Ibid*, Add MS 33084, fol. 60r.
49. *SR*, iv, part ii, 1088–9.
50. ESRO, Sessions Rolls 49/77.
51. *Ibid*, 53/57.
52. Redwood, pp. 20, 108, 122, 198.
53. PRO, St. Ch 8/32/6, 40/14, 84/21–4, 111/4, 7, 197/1, 227/13, 303/27, 304/11.
54. Redwood, p. xxiii; Bodleian, Rawlinson MS B 431; ESRO, QSOB 1650–5, fols 36r, 59v; J. Lister, ed., *West Riding Sessions Records*, ii (Yorkshire Archaeological Society Record Series, liii, 1915), x–xiv.
55. WSRO, Sessions Rolls 86/50.
56. BM, Add MS 33145, fol. 12r, 33147, fols 6v, 16v, 235r; *Camden Society*, third series, lii (1936), 37; G. Batho, 'The Percies at Petworth 1574–1632', *SAC*, xcv (1957), 16–18.
57. BM, Add MS 33145, fols 2v, 9r, 11v, 19r, 35v, 47v, 54v, 75v.

58. BM, Add MS 33084, fol. 78r, 33145, fol. 186v; *SAC*, ii (1849), 100, xlviii (1905), 126–7.
59. A. Macfarlane, *The Family Life of Ralph Josselin* (Cambridge University Press, 1970); B. Schofield, ed., *The Knyvett Letters* (Constable for Norfolk Record Society 1949); D. Gardiner, ed., *The Oxinden Letters 1607–1642* (Sheldon, 1933); J. Thirsk, 'The family', *Past and Present*, xxvii (1964), 116–22.
60. PRO, Prob 11/168/75, 234/85, 308/59, SP 23/104, 144; *SAC*, xlvii (1904), 75; Stone, pp. 594–600, 609–17.
61. ESRO, Frewen MS 4233, nos 5–23, 42–4, 76–88; T. W. W. Smart, 'A biographical sketch of Samuel Jeake senior of Rye', *SAC*, xiii (1861), 60–2.
62. *SAC*, xi (1859), 17.
63. *HMC Rutland MSS*, p. 520.
64. BM, Add MS 33145, fols 129r, 136r, 147v, 176r, 187v, 207v, 33148, fols 12v, 25r.
65. *Ibid*, Add MS 33148, fols 56r, 63r, 33149, fol. 274r; PRO, Prob 11/241/456.
66. Sussex Archaeological Society, Accession 1295; Stone, p. 644; BM, Add MS 33137, fols 65–6.
67. *HMC De L'Isle and Dudley MSS*, vi, 441–2, 614.
68. BM, Add MS 33145, fols 9, 15v, 30v, 31r, 37v, 44r.
69. ESRO, Frewen MS 4223, no. 84.
70. *Ibid*, Dunn MS 51/50; W. Notestein, 'The English Woman 1580–1650' in J. H. Plumb, ed., *Studies in Social History* (Longmans, 1955), pp. 77–8.
71. *SAC*, xiii (1861), 62; ESRO, Frewen MS 520, fol. 17r.
72. Stone, p. 590.
73. PRO, Prob 11/151/14, 161/12, 164/86, 181/183, 241/456, 311/100.
74. *Ibid*, Prob 11/159/5, 180/102, 185/13, 252/4; W. Budgen, ed., *Sussex Deeds and Documents* (SRS, xxix, 1942), 179; Macfarlane, *Ralph Josselin*, p. 123.
75. PRO, Prob 11/171/81, 311/100.
76. *Ibid*, Prob 11/164/86, 180/102, 227/111, 161/12.
77. *Ibid*, Prob 11/151/5, 161/12, 252/4, 314/57.
78. *SAC*, xi (1859), 31.
79. Sackville-West, ed., *Lady Anne Clifford*, pp. 85, 105; G. C. Williamson, *Lady Anne Clifford* (SR Publishers, 1967), pp. 128–9.
80. T. Barrett-Lennard, *An Account of the Families of Barrett and Lennard* (London, 1908), p. 291; *SAC*, xlviii (1905), 128–34.
81. PRO, Prob 11/308/59; *TSP*, iv, 190.
82. BM, Add MS 33145, fols 83v, 123v, 159v, 33148; WSRO, Ep 11/16/103A.
83. BM, Add MS 33148, fols 19v, 25r, 30v, 93r; 33149, fols 209, 248r, 255r; ESRO, Dunn MS 51/48, 53, 54; Stone, pp. 592–3; Macfarlane, *Ralph Josselin*, pp. 105–25.
84. Essex RO, D/DL E22. 15 Jan. 1648; *SAC*, xlviii (1905), 135; WSRO, Ep 11/15/1, fols 7r, 18v; Macfarlane, *Ralph Josselin*, pp. 205–10; S. C. Lomas, 'The Memoirs of Sir George Courthope', *Camden Society*, third series, xiii (1907), 103.
85. BM, Add MS 33145, fols 81r, 83v, 98r, 104v, 118v, 123v, 33147, fols 227v, 231v; 33148, fol. 35v.
86. ESRO, Frewen MS 520, fol. 29r; R. W. Blencowe, 'Paxhill and its neighbourhood' *SAC*, xi (1859), 30.
87. J. Simon, *Education and Society in Tudor England* (Cambridge University Press, 1966), pp. 369–403; K. Charlton, *Education in Renaissance England* (Routledge, 1965), pp. 89–130; A. J. Fletcher, 'The expansion of education in Berkshire and Oxfordshire 1500–1670', *British Journal of Educational Studies*, xv (1967), 57–9.
88. B. Simon, ed., *Education in Leicestershire 1540–1940* (Leicester University Press, 1968), p. 41; M. Spufford, 'The schooling of the peasantry in Cambridgeshire 1575–1700', in J. Thirsk, ed., *Land, Church and People* (*Agricultural History Review*, special number, 1970), pp. 112–47.
89. WSRO, Ep I/22/1; *SNQ*, xlv, 271; *VCHS*, ii, 407–24; below, pp. 69–70.

90. ESRO, Frewen MS 520, fols 41r, 42, 53v, 56r, 59v; E. S. De Beer, ed., *The Diary of John Evelyn* (Oxford University Press, 1955), i, 9, 11, 15–16; *VCHS*, ii, 414–5.
91. ESRO, Hickstead Place MS 467, pp. 21, 23; BM, Add MS 33145, fol. 11r; De Beer, ed., *Evelyn's Diary*, iii, 65.
92. PRO, Prob 11/159/5, 204/130.
93. H. F. Kearney, *Scholars and Gentlemen* (Faber, 1970), pp. 15–33; L. Stone, 'The educational revolution in England 1560–1640', *Past and Present*, xxviii (1964), 41–80.
94. ESRO, Frewen MS 520, fol. 43v; J. Foster, *Alumni Oxonienses* (Oxford, 1891), p. 474.
95. BM, Add MS 33145, fols 16v, 41v, 58v, 67r, 80r, 101v; Foster, *Alumni Oxonienses*, p. 1138.
96. BM, Add MS 33145, fols 53v, 60v, 73r, 80r, 83v, 33148, fol. 99r.
97. *Ibid*, fols 104v, 123v, 129v, 152v, 157v, 166v, 33084, fol. 57r; J. and J. A. Venn, *Alumni Cantabrigienses* (Cambridge, 1922), iii, 336.
98. Stone, p. 701; J. W. Stoye, *English Travellers Abroad* (Cape, 1952), pp. 98, 177, 402; Cliffe, pp. 77–80.
99. BM, Add MS 33084, fol. 48r.
100. *Camden Society*, third series, xiii (1907), 96, 104–36.
101. BM, Add MS 33084, fol. 53r.
102. PRO, Prob 11/157/52.
103. *Ibid*, Prob 11/221/69.
104. *CSPD 1637*, pp. 238–9; *CSPD 1638–9*, pp. 46–7; *SAC*, xlv (1902), 209.
105. F. J. Fisher, ed., 'The state of England Anno Dom. 1600', *Camden Society*, third series, lii (1936), 24; J. Thirsk, 'Younger sons in the seventeenth century', *History*, liv (1969), 358–77.
106. PRO, Prob 11/171/81, 181/183, 266/278. See also Lloyd, *Gentry of South West Wales*, pp. 50–1; Ferris, *Genealogists' Magazine*, xv (1965), 107.
107. PRO, Prob 11/156/83, 159/5, 179/64, 180/102, 204/83, 336/55.
108. *Ibid*, Prob 11/328/166; *Camden Society*, third series, xiii (1907), 116–17; *Visitation 1662*, pp. 24–6.
109. *SAC*, xi (1859), 17–26; Cliffe, pp. 83–5.
110. ESRO, Dunn MS 51/67.
111. BM, Add MS 33145, fols 83v, 89r, 98r, 104v, 113v, 118v; Charlton, *Education in Renaissance England*, pp. 205–13.
112. ESRO, Dunn MS 51/53, 62, 64.
113. Sackville-West, ed., *Lady Anne Clifford*, pp. 106–7.
114. ESRO, Dunn MS 51/51, 60–6.
115. PRO, Prob 11/162/75, 181/183, 204/61, 227/148, 252/4; 243/83, 96; Budgen, ed., *Sussex Deeds and Documents*, p. 126; Stone, pp. 637–42; Keeler, p. 271.
116. BM, Add MS 33143, fols 47v, 98v; Essex RO, D/DL E22; *Camden Society*, third series, lii (1936), 38.
117. BM, Add MS 33147, fols 141r, 168r, 33148, fols 101r, 33149, fols 242v, 257r; Essex RO, D/DL E22, 17 May 1645, 4 Sept 1648; T. Barrett Lennard, 'Extracts from the Household Account Book of Herstmonceux Castle', *SAC*, xlviii (1905), 121.
118. BM, Add MS 33147, fols 218r–222v.
119. PRO, Prob 11/164/86, 113.
120. BM, Add MS 33148, fols 50v, 62r.
121. PRO, Prob 11/151/14, 159/5, 308/59.
122. *Ibid*, Prob 11/252/4, 311/95.
123. *SAC*, xcv (1957), 15.
124. ESRO, Frewen MS 520, fols 22r, 79.
125. BM, Add MS 33145, 33147, 33148–9; Essex RO, D/DL E22; R. Bird, ed., *The Journal of Giles Moore* (SRS, lxiii, 1971), p. 19; Brent, pp. 306–7.
126. R. S. Roberts, 'The personnel and practice of medicine in Tudor and Stuart England', *Medical History*, vi (1962), 363–82.

127. F. W. Steer, 'The possessions of a Sussex Surgeon', *Medical History*, ii (1958), 134–6.
128. WSRO, Ep I/22/1; J. F. Williams, ed., *Bishop Redman's Visitation* (Norfolk Record Society, xviii, 1946), p. 26.
129. J. H. Raach, *A Directory of English Country Physicians 1603–43* (Dawsons Pall Mall, 1962), p. 116; *Visitation 1662*, p. 83; Essex RO, D/DL E22, 8 Nov. 1645, 6 Nov. 1647, 12 Feb. 1648; *SAC*, xlviii (1905), 121.
130. BM, Add MS 33145, fols 77r, 116r, 159r, 201v, 210r.
131. PRO, Prob 11/241/456.
132. BM, Add MS 33145, fols 23r, 67r, 109r, 119, 163v, 213r, 33148, fols 29–38, 44r, 49r, 56–7, 101r, 33149, fol. 257r; C. H. Firth, *Cromwell's Army* (Methuen, 1962), p. 253.
133. BM, Add MS 33147, fols 89r, 90r, 100v, 101v, 115v, 125v, 157r, 186r.
134. ESRO, Frewen MS 520, fol. 55r, 4223, no. 31.
135. *Ibid*, Dunn MS 37/5, Frewen MS 606.
136. Johnstone, pp. 82, 92; K. Thomas, *Religion and the Decline of Magic* (Weidenfeld & Nicolson, 1971), pp. 177–211, 633–4; below, pp. 162–3.
137. F. J. Fisher, 'London as an "engine of economic growth' ", in J. S. Bromley and E. H. Kossman, eds, *Britain and the Netherlands*, iv (The Hague, 1971), 1–16; C. Russell, *The Crisis of Parliaments* (Oxford University Press, 1971), pp. 172–4.
138. PRO, Prob 11/168/75, 186/86, 227/111; Crofts, *Packhorse, Waggon and Post*, pp. 109–24; Cliffe, pp. 109–10.
139. PRO, Prob 11/161/61.
140. ESRO, Frewen MS 520, fols 17r, 34v, 36v; Dunn MS 49/22, 51/3.
141. Bird, ed., *Journal of Giles Moore*, pp. 16, 22, 27, 156, 180–2, 279–80.
142. BM, Add MS 33145, 33148.
143. Everitt, *Change in the Provinces*, pp. 10–11; Everitt, pp. 42–3, 328; B. G. Blackwood, 'The marriages of the Lancashire gentry on the eve of the Civil War', *Genealogists' Magazine*, xvi (1970), 321–8; *Genealogists' Magazine*, xv (1965), 108; Morrill, p. 4.
144. L. Hutchinson, *Memoirs of Colonel Hutchinson* (Dent, Everyman, 1965), p. 7; Mousley, pp. 115–28.
145. PRO, Prob 11/159/62, 208/70.
146. *Ibid*, Prob 11/161/12, 212/65.
147. BM, Add MS 33144–5, 33147–9; Keeler, p. 302.
148. BM, Add MS 33058, fol. 71v, 33145, fols 107v, 117v, 142v, 164v.
149. *SAC*, ii (1849), 99; Essex RO, D/DL E22.
150. Macfarlane, *Ralph Josselin*, pp. 144–5.
151. BM, Add MS 33145, fols 20v, 58r, 59r, 66r, 68r, 80r, 146v; PRO, Prob 11/161/12.
152. Essex RO, D/DL E22, 27 Jan. 1644, 15 March 1645.
153. BM, Add MS 33145, fols 77r, 111v, 33148, fols 56v, 57r; PRO, Prob 11/241/456; M. A. Lower, *Historical and Genealogical Notices of the Pelham Family* (1873), p. 44.
154. BM, Add MS 33145, fols 73v, 109r; Bird, ed., *Journal of Giles Moore*, p. 324; Essex RO, D/DL E22; see also Macfarlane, *Ralph Josselin*, p. 150.
155. BM, Add MS 33147, fol. 135r; ESRO, Frewen MS 520, fol. 51r.
156. Essex RO, D/DL E22, 6 Nov. 1647.
157. BM, Add MS 33145, 33147, 33149.
158. BM, Add MS 33145, fols 14r, 33r, 80r, 88r, 95r, 98r, 165r, 184v.
159. *Ibid*, fols 38v, 46r, 53r, 97r, 134r, 140r, 167r, 217r; Sir G. Isham, ed., *The Correspondence of Bishop Brian Duppa and Sir Justinian Isham* (Northamptonshire Record Society, xvii, 1955), p. 57.
160. BM, Add MS 33084, fol. 78r; 33148, fols 61v, 62r.
161. Stone, pp. 234–42. J. S. Cockburn, *A History of English Assizes* (Cambridge University Press, 1972), pp. 103–6, 144–6.
162. BM, Add MS 33145, fols 1–125, 33188, fols 132–79.
163. Everitt, *Change in the Provinces*, p. 43.
164. ESRO, Dunn MS 51/55.

165. *CSPD 1638–9*, p. 169.
166. PRO, SP 16/166/66.
167. *SAC*, iii (1850), 223–4.
168. PRO, SP 16/223/1.
169. *Ibid*, SP 16/369/58, 169; Keeler, p. 302; Thomas-Stanford, pp. 19–21.
170. *CSPD 1633–4*, p. 423; *CSPD 1634–5*, pp. 308, 471; PRO, SP 16/289/98; *CSPD 1635–6*, p. 74; *CSPD 1640*, p. 542; *HMC De l'Isle and Dudley*, vi 192.
171. J. Rushworth, *Historical Collections* (1691), iv, 459–60; W. H. Coates, ed., *The Journal of Sir Simonds D'Ewes* (New Haven, 1942), pp. 339–40.
172. M. A. Lower, 'The trial and execution of Thomas Lord Dacre', *SAC*, xix (1867), 170–91.
173. PRO, St. Ch 8/71/12, 86/12, 99/12, 111/4, 265/25, 283/7.
174. *Ibid*, St. Ch 8, 9, *passim.*
175. PRO, St. Ch 8/273/30.
176. *Ibid*, St. Ch 8/195/28.
177. *Ibid*, St. Ch 8/67/4, 153/22, 160/5; *SAC*, xlviii (1905), 128–32.
178. *SAC*, xi (1859), 11–13.
179. WSRO, Sessions Rolls 2/123–4.
180. Stone, pp. 229–31; W. T. MacCaffrey, 'Talbot and Stanhope: an episode in Elizabethan politics', *BIHR*, xxxiii (1960), 73–85.
181. PRO, St. Ch 8/294/23.
182. *Ibid*, SP 16/223/1, St. Ch 8/195/28.

3. The Puritan mind

1. ESRO, Frewen MS 4223, no. 31.
2. *Ibid*, no. 71.
3. *Ibid*, Frewen MS 520, fol. 8v.
4. C. Hill, *Society and Puritanism in Pre-Revolutionary England* (Secker & Warburg, 1964), pp. 13–29; P. McGrath, *Papists and Puritans under Elizabeth I* (Blandford Press, 1967), pp. 32–46; N. R. N. Tyacke, 'Puritanism, Arminianism and Counter-Revolution', in C. Russell, ed., *The Origins of the English Civil War* (Oxford University Press, 1973), pp. 119–43.
5. P. Collinson, *The Elizabethan Puritan Movement* (Cape, 1967), pp. 26–7.
6. B. Hall, 'Puritanism: the problem of definition', in Ecclesiastical History Society, *Studies in Church History* (Nelson, 1965), ed. G. J. Cuming, ii, 283–96.
7. Collinson, *Elizabethan Puritan Movement*, p. 27.
8. Thirsk, ed., *Agrarian History*, iv, 109–12; Everitt, *Change in the Provinces*, p. 36; R. C. Richardson, *Puritanism in North-west England* (Manchester University Press, 1972), p. 94; Thirsk, *Past and Present*, xxvii (1964), 118; D. G. Hey, 'The pattern of nonconformity in South Yorkshire', *Northern History*, viii (1973), 86–118.
9. J. A. F. Thomson, *The Later Lollards* (Oxford University Press, 1965), pp. 172–91.
10. Manning, pp. 37–8; *VCHS*, ii, 22, 32; Thomas-Stanford, p. 24.
11. G. R. Elton, *Policy and Police* (Cambridge University Press, 1972), pp. 85–9; *VCHS*, ii, 18.
12. W. Holloway, *History of Rye* (London, 1847), pp. 600–1; *VCHS*, ii, 27.
13. *VCHS*, ii, 22; Manning, pp. 37, 192–9; Collinson, *Elizabethan Puritan Movement*, pp. 171–4, 209–13, 249–62, 280, 283.
14. *CSPD 1635*, p. xliii.
15. P. M. Johnston, 'Ancient paintings at "Pekes" Chiddingly', *SAC*, liii (1910), 141; M. Spufford, 'The scribes of villagers' wills in the sixteenth and seventeenth centuries and their influence', *Local Population Studies*, vii (1971), 28–43; A. G. Dickens, *Lollards and Protestants in the Diocese of York* (Oxford University Press, 1959), pp. 171–2, 215–17.

16. PRO, Prob 11/178/168, 181/183.
17. *Ibid*, Prob 11/159/62, 161/61.
18. J. F. H. New, *Anglican and Puritan* (A. and C. Black, 1964), pp. 15–16; W. Haller, *The Rise of Puritanism* (Columbia University Press, 1957), pp. 193–4.
19. PRO, Prob 11/180/102, 185/13, 201/189, 214/183.
20. *Ibid*, Prob 11/156/101, 157/33, 162/11, 181/192, 264/61.
21. Tyacke, 'Puritanism, Arminianism and Counter-Revolution', in Russell, ed., *Origins of the Civil War*, pp. 120–3.
22. C. Hill, *Puritanism and Revolution* (Heinemann, 1962), pp. 216–17; New, *Anglican and Puritan*, pp. 5–29; C. H. and K. George, *The Protestant Mind of the English Reformation* (Princeton University Press, 1961), pp. 23–72.
23. PRO, Prob 11/178/168, 181/183, 241/456, 264/183, 316/16.
24. Thomas, *Religion and the Decline of Magic*, pp. 469–77.
25. PRO, Prob 11/161/61, 204/99, 274/83.
26. New, *Anglican and Puritan*, pp. 76–81.
27. PRO, Prob 11/156/101, 178/168, 181/183, 234/83, 264/183, 316/16; Cliffe, p. 257.
28. ESRO, Dunn MS 51/64.
29. *Ibid*, Frewen MS 4223, nos 30–9, 58, 71; O. C. Watkins, *The Puritan Experience* (Routledge, 1972), pp. 9–12.
30. J. Maynard, *A Shadow of the Victory of Christ* (1646), pp. 21–2.
31. ESRO, Frewen MS 520, fol. 8r, 4223, no. 36.
32. Haller, *Rise of Puritanism*, pp. 89–91, 128–72.
33. ESRO, Frewen MS 4223, nos. 31, 38, 87.
34. *Ibid*, nos. 37, 38, 71, 85.
35. Thomas, *Religion and the Decline of Magic*, pp. 78–112; George, *Protestant Mind of the English Reformation*, pp. 105–14.
36. ESRO, Frewen MS 4223, no. 82; *HMCR*, p. 223; T. W. W. Smart, 'Extracts from the manuscripts of Samuel Jeake', *SAC*, ix (1857), 57.
37. ESRO, Frewen MS 4223, nos. 33, 77.
38. *Ibid*, nos. 84, 91.
39. ESRO, Dunn MS 51/48, 53, Frewen MS 4223, no. 95.
40. E. M. Bell-Irving, *Mayfield* (London, 1903), pp. 97–8.
41. William Salt Library, 454 (Swynfen MSS), no. 11; ESRO, Dunn MS 51/60, 66.
42. *VCHS*, ii, 32; Thomas, *Religion and the Decline of Magic*, p. 104.
43. ESRO, Frewen, MS 4223, no. 90; Thomas, *Religion and the Decline of Magic*, pp. 82–3.
44. ESRO, Frewen MS 4223, nos 16, 31, 59, 66.
45. BM, E 1407: S. Gott, *An Essay of the True Happiness of Man* (1650).
46. ESRO, Frewen MS 4223, no. 96.
47. *Ibid*, nos 11, 30, 31.
48. W. H. Blaauw, 'Passages of the Civil War in Sussex', *SAC*, v (1853), 69–71; Thomas-Stanford, pp. 114–18.
49. J. H. Cooper, 'Cuckfield families', *SAC*, xliii (1900), 13–14.
50. ESRO, Frewen MS 4223, nos 31, 45; *SAC*, xiii (1861), 58–9.
51. Thomas, *Religion and the Decline of Magic*, pp. 88–9; C. Hill, *God's Englishman* (Weidenfeld & Nicolson, 1970), pp. 217–50.
52. ESRO, Frewen MS 4223, nos 31, 90.
53. *Ibid*, Frewen MS 520, fol. 1v; PRO, Prob 11/227/148.
54. R. H. Tawney, *Religion and the Rise of Capitalism* (London, 1926); C. Hill, 'Protestantism and the Rise of Capitalism', in F. J. Fisher, ed., *Essays in the Economic and Social History of Tudor and Stuart England* (Cambridge University Press, 1961), pp. 15–39; George, *Protestant Mind of the English Reformation*, pp. 117–73; M. J. Kitch, *Capitalism and the Reformation* (Longmans, 1967).
55. ESRO, Dunn MS 51/61, Frewen MS 4223, no. 37; Hill, *Society and Puritanism*, pp. 443–81; Collinson, *Elizabethan Puritan Movement*, pp. 374–80; Richardson, *Puritanism*

in North-west England, pp. 90–7; George, *Protestant Mind of the English Reformation*, pp. 257–305.
56. PRO, Prob 11/180/102.
57. *SAC*, xi (1859), 17–18; ESRO, Dunn MS 51/62.
58. W. P. Breach, 'William Holland, alderman of Chichester, and the Steyning grammar school', *SAC*, xliii (1900), 79; ESRO, Rye MS 112/2, 3, 113/1a; Vidler, *History of Rye*, pp. 73–4; W. V. Cooper, *History of Cuckfield* (Haywards Heath, 1912), pp. 141–2.
59. ESRO, Frewen MS 4223, nos 35, 38, Dunn MS 49/22; G. H. Kenyon, 'Petworth town and trades 1610–1760, Part I', *SAC*, xcvi (1958), 70.
60. *Ibid*, Dunn MS, 51/62, Frewen MS 4223, nos 31, 32.
61. PRO, Prob 11/264/183, 300/209; Haller, *Rise of Puritanism*, pp. 91–2; Hill, *Puritanism and Revolution*, pp. 215–18.
62. ESRO, Frewen MS 4223, no. 35; *SAC*, xiii (1861), 57–8; Haller, *Rise of Puritanism*, p. 79.
63. WSRO, Sessions Rolls 49/38; Hill, *Society and Puritanism*, p. 447; *DNB*.
64. *DNB*; BM, E1407: Gott, *An Essay of the True Happiness of Man*.
65. Hill, *Society and Puritanism*, pp. 30–78; P. S. Seaver, *The Puritan Lectureships: politics of religious dissent, 1560–1662* (Stanford University Press, 1970), pp. 15–54.
66. *VCHS*, ii, 26.
67. ESRO, Frewen MS 4223, nos 25–8; *SAC*, ix (1857), 45–9; Manning, pp. 166–217; Collinson, *Elizabethan Puritan Movement*, pp. 453–4; *HMC Salisbury MSS*, xv, 262–3, 390.
68. Johnstone, p. xxviii; WSRO, Ep II/15/1; W. C. Renshaw, 'Notes from the Act Books of the Archdeaconry Court of Lewes', *SAC*, xlix (1906), 61.
69. *HMCR*, p. 67.
70. ESRO, Frewen MS 4223, no. 40; *SAC*, xiii (1861), 60.
71. PRO SP 14/153/91, 158/24, 160/60, 173/67, St. Ch 8/707/7; *HMCR*, pp. 162, 170; *CSPD 1623–5*, p. 118; Seaver, *Puritan Lectureships*, p. 98; *SAC*, xlix (1906), 60; Thomas-Stanford, pp. 30–1.
72. Hill, *Society and Puritanism*, pp. 79–123.
73. BM, Add MS 33145, fol. 27v.
74. PRO, SP 16/261, fol. 83; Seaver, *Puritan Lectureships*, pp. 18, 109; R. Howell, *Newcastle-upon-Tyne and the Puritan Revolution* (Oxford University Press, 1967), pp. 105, 111.
75. *HMC House of Lords MSS*, p. 61; *VCHS*, ii, 36; *CJ*, ii, 754; Thomas-Stanford, pp. 136–7.
76. Bodleian, Tanner MS 148, fols 32–7; W. C. Renshaw, ed., *Ecclesiastical Returns for 86 Parishes in East Sussex 1603* (SRS, iv, 1905), 5–17; Collinson, *Elizabethan Puritan Movement*, p. 188; Richardson, *Puritanism in North-west England*, pp. 126–8; Cliffe, p. 268; B. Magee, *The English Recusants* (Burns & Oates, 1938), p. 38.
77. PRO, Prob 11/227/117, 152; W. D. Peckham, 'The acts of Bishop Montagu', *SAC*, lxxxvi (1947), 151; *DNB*.
78. S. Arnott, 'Contributions towards a parochial history of Hollington', *SAC*, xxi (1869), 139–40.
79. Bell Irving, *Mayfield*, pp. 100–1; *DNB*.
80. PRO, Prob 11/159/5, 161/12, 185/13, 234/86, 311/95.
81. C. Hill, *Economic Problems of the Church* (Oxford University Press, 1956), pp. 182–3; Thomas, *Religion and the Decline of Magic*, p. 603; Collinson, *Elizabethan Puritan Movement*, p. 370.
82. PRO, Prob 11/201/189, 256/249, 311/95; Cliffe, pp. 259–60.
83. BM, Add MS 33148, fol. 57r.
84. Manning, pp. 188–217.

85. *SAC*, xlix (1906), 54, 55; W. C. Renshaw, 'Notes from the Act books of the court for the deanery of South Malling', *SAC*, l (1907), 41; Thomas-Stanford, pp. 26–7.
86. WSRO, Ep ii/15/1, p. 13; Richardson, *Puritanism in North-west England*, pp. 45–7.
87. *SAC*, xlix (1906), 59–60; WSRO, Ep ii/9/23, fol. 4r.
88. W. Laud, *Works* (Oxford, 1853), v, part ii, 330, 334, 343, 369–70.
89. Richardson, *Puritanism in North-west England*, pp. 21–36.
90. *SAC*, xlix (1906), 58; Richardson, *Puritanism in North-west England*, pp. 74–6; Collinson, *Elizabethan Puritan Movement*, pp. 94–6.
91. WSRO, Ep ii/15/1, pp. 33, 50; Richardson, *Puritanism in North-west England*, pp. 113–14.
92. Stone, pp. 572–9; Thomas, *Religion and the Decline of Magic*, pp. 66, 604–5; Collinson, *Elizabethan Puritan Movement*, pp. 370–1; Richardson, *Puritanism in North-west England*, p. 30.
93. PRO, Prob 11/164/86, 113, 182/32.
94. *Ibid.* Prob 11/157/33, 204/99, 264/61, 246/205, 264/183, 300/209.
95. Stone, pp. 579–81; Cliffe, p. 280.
96. PRO, Prob 11/311/100; Nairn and Pevsner, *Sussex*, pp. 622, 629; above, p. 25.
97. Nairn and Pevsner, *Sussex*, pp. 58, 414–15, 588.
98. PRO, Prob 11/299/110; *Visitation 1662*, p. 33.
99. Redwood, p. 156.

4. The enforcement of Arminianism

1. PRO, SP 16/442/137.
2. ESRO, Sessions Rolls 51/21.
3. Tyacke, 'Puritanism, Arminianism and counter-revolution', in Russell, ed., *Origins of the English Civil War*, pp. 119–43; H. Swartz, 'Arminianism and the English Parliament', *Journal of British Studies*, xii (1973), 41–68; Russell, *Crisis of Parliaments*, pp. 210–17.
4. F. W. Steer and I. M. Kirby, *The Records of the Bishops . . . of the Diocese of Chichester* (Chichester, Sussex Record Office, 1966), pp. xxii–xxiii.
5. H. R. Trevor-Roper, *Archbishop Laud* (2nd edn, Macmillan, 1962), pp. 73–7; Gardiner, *History of England*, v, 352, 362, 372–3; Laud, *Works*, v, 75, 100; Isham, ed., *Duppa-Isham Correspondence*, pp. xvi–xxxi.
6. G. Ormsby, ed., *The Correspondence of John Cosin* (Surtees Society, i, 1868), 42, 68, 73, 97.
7. Manning, p. 16; P. Hembry, *The Bishops of Bath and Wells 1540–1640* (Athlone Press, 1967), pp. 228–31.
8. PRO, SP 16/210/36, 474/59; Ormsby, ed., *Cosin Correspondence*, pp. 22, 37, 45; J. Le Neve, *Fasti Ecclesiae Anglicanne 1541–1857* (Athlone Press, 1971), ii, *Chichester Diocese*, 75.
9. PRO SP 16/385/68; Le Neve, *Fasti 1541–1857*, ii, 7, 13, 16, 21, 58, 75; F. W. Steer, 'Bishop Montagu's personal accounts', *SAC*, xcv (1957), 37–9.
10. PRO, SP 16/474/59; Le Neve, *Fasti 1541–1857*, ii, 13, 16, 60; Ormsby, ed., *Cosin Correspondence*, pp. 71–3, 86; Isham, ed., *Duppa-Isham Correspondence*, pp. 196–203; A. G. Matthews, *Walker Revised* (Oxford University Press, 1948), p. 355.
11. BM, 700 g 3: C. Dowe, *Innovations unjustly charged upon the present Church and State* (1637); W. Prynne, *Canterburies Doome* (1646), pp. 190, 207, 357; C. Hill, *Antichrist in Seventeenth-Century England* (University of Newcastle, 1971), pp. 33–40.
12. PRO SP 16/442/137; Matthews, *Walker Revised*, p. 361; F. E. Sawyer, 'Proceedings of the Committee of Plundered Ministers relating to Sussex', *SAC*, xxx (1880), 122–3.

13. Matthews, *Walker Revised*, pp. 353–62.
14. Venn, *Alumni Cantabrigienses*, iii, 322; Foster, *Alumni Oxonienses*, 1128; Tyacke, 'Puritanism, Arminianism and Counter-Revolution' in Russell, ed., *Origins of the English Civil War*, pp. 139–40.
15. G. M. Cooper, 'Berwick Parochial Records', *SAC*, vi (1856), 223–38.
16. *SAC*, xcv (1957), 28–41; Hembry, *Bishops of Bath and Wells*, pp. 231–2.
17. *CSPD 1629–31*, pp. 122, 124; Hill, *Economic Problems of the Church*, pp. 310–16; *DNB*; B. P. Levack, *The Civil Lawyers in England 1603–41* (Oxford University Press, 1973) p. 258.
18. Xerox copies of printed versions of these articles are available in a bound volume in WSRO. See also PRO, SP 16/499/71; Kenyon, *Stuart Constitution*, pp. 137–46; E. Cardwell, *Synodalia*, i, 245–329.
19. Collinson, *Elizabethan Puritan Movement*, pp. 356–74; Richardson, *Puritanism in North-west England*, pp. 29, 74–85.
20. PRO SP 16/499/71; Laud, *Works*, v, part ii, 419–35.
21. Trevor-Roper, *Laud*, pp. 189–94; New, *Anglican and Puritan*, p. 74; R. W. Ketton-Cremer, *Norfolk in the Civil War* (Faber, 1969), pp. 62–6.
22. Thomas, *Religion and the Decline of Magic*, pp. 177–212, 477–86.
23. Worcester College, Oxford, AA 8/16 (48): *Articles to be enquired of in the ordinary visitation of . . . Dr Hutchinson.* Bishop Duppa's and Dr Marsh's articles are in the WSRO volume of xeroxes.
24. Cooper, *History of Cuckfield*, pp. 48–9.
25. WSRO, Ep i/22/1; Ep ii/15/1, pp. 3, 33, 43, 55, 58, 83; *CSPD 1641–3*, p. 547.
26. R. A. Marchant, *The Church under the Law* (Cambridge University Press, 1969), pp. 114–235; E. R. C. Brinkworth, 'The Laudian Church in Buckinghamshire', *Univ. Birmingham Hist. J.*, v (1955–56), 40.
27. WSRO, Ep i/22/1. For the purchase of books of articles see PAR 59/9/2/6, 197/9/1.
28. *Ibid*, Ep ii/15/1, pp. 46, 48, 53, 83.
29. *Ibid*, Ep i/22/1.
30. Marchant, *Church under the Law*, p. 134.
31. WSRO, Ep i/22/1.
32. *Records of Bucks*, vii, 97–114.
33. WSRO, Ep i/23/5; Williams, ed., *Bishop Redman's Visitation 1597*, 8–9.
34. Johnstone; WSRO, Ep ii/15/1; Appendix I.
35. Marchant, *Church under the Law*, pp. 196–203.
36. WSRO, Ep i/22/1, 26/2.
37. *Ibid*, Ep i/26/2, fols 2v, 8, 12r, 30r, 33r, 34r, 35r, 37r.
38. *Ibid*, fols 2r, 4r, 17r.
39. *Ibid*, fols 6r, 9r, 22r, 25r, 34v.
40. WSRO, PAR 21/9/1, fols 137–47; Ep i/26/2, fol. 31r.
41. *Ibid*, Ep i/17/27, Ep i/26/2, fol. 37r, PAR 48/9/1, fols 10v–11r.
42. *Ibid*, PAR 59/9/2/1–11.
43. Marchant, *Church under the Law*, pp. 200–1; R. A. Marchant, 'The restoration of Nottinghamshire churches', *Thoroton Society Transactions*, lxv (1961), 57–93; R. F. B. Hodgkinson, 'Extracts from the Act Books of the Archdeacons of Nottingham', *Thoroton Society Transactions*, xxxi (1927), 128–37; *Univ. Birmingham Hist. J.*, v, (1955–56), 31, 41–7.
44. ESRO, Sessions Rolls 51/21.
45. Johnstone, pp. xxxvii, 101, 104, 119; Hill, *Society and Puritanism*, p. 157; *Univ. Birmingham Hist. J.*, v (1955–56), 50–1.
46. Johnstone, pp. 66, 114; WSRO, Ep ii/9/23, fol. 13r; *Records of Bucks*, vii, 108.
47. Thomas, *Religion and the Decline of Magic*, pp. 159–66; Hill, *Society and Puritanism*, pp. 472–3; *Univ. Birmingham Hist. J.*, v (1955–56), 51–3.

48. WSRO, Ep ii/9/23, fols 4v, 12v, Ep ii/15/1, pp. 13, 16, 17, 21, 22, 33, 45, 59, 83; *SAC*, xlix (1906), 61, l (1907), 42; Johnstone, pp. 101, 126.
49. WSRO, Ep ii/15/1, p. 24.
50. *SAC*, l (1907), 42.
51. Manning, p. 174; Hill, *Economic Problems of the Church*, pp. 224–41.
52. WSRO, Ep i/22/1, Ep ii/15/1, pp. 46, 71; *SAC*, l (1907), 44. For this offence and others touched on in this chapter see J. Addy, *The Archdeacons and Ecclesiastical Discipline in Yorkshire 1598–1714*, St Anthony's Hall Publications, York, no. 24 (1963).
53. Johnstone, p. xxviii; Williams, ed., *Bishop Redman's Visitation*, pp. 14, 17; T. F. Palmer, ed., *Act Book of the Archdeacon of Taunton* (Somerset Record Society, xliii, 1928), 10.
54. WSRO, Ep i/22/1; R. A. Marchant, *Puritans and the Church Courts in the Diocese of York* (Longmans, 1960), p. 65; Williams, ed., *Bishop Redman's Visitation*, pp. 17–18; *Records of Bucks*, vii, 105; Rushworth, *Historical Collections*, iv, 22.
55. WSRO, Ep i/17/22, fol. 21r, Ep ii/15/1, pp. 5, 27, 37, 38; Johnstone, p. xxviii.
56. *CSPD 1635*, pp. xlii–xliv; Trevor-Roper, *Laud*, pp. 192–5.; *SAC*, xxxi (1881), 174.
57. *Records of Bucks*, vii, 105; *CSPD 1635*, pp. 26–7.
58. WSRO, Ep i/17/27, fol. 11v, Ep i/26/2, fols 29r, 31r, 33r; *Thoroton Society Transactions*, lxv (1961), 62.
59. WSRO, Ep ii/15/1, p. 19; R. C. Hussey, 'Some Entries in Salehurst Parish Books', *SAC*, xxv (1873), 153.
60. WSRO, Ep i/261, 2, fol. 35r; ESRO, Sessions Rolls 51/21; see p. 76.
61. *Records of Bucks*, vii, 101–2; *Univ. Birmingham Hist. J.*, v (1955–56), 45–6.
62. ESRO, Rye MS 47/123/3; Thomas-Stanford, pp. 29–30.
63. Trevor-Roper, *Laud*, pp. 151–5; Russell, ed., *Origins of the Civil War*, p. 138; T. F. Palmer, ed., *Colectanea* ii (Somerset Record Society, xliii, 1928), 177–203.
64. *SAC*, xlix (1906), 64.
65. WSRO, Ep ii/15/1, p. 60; J. H. Cooper, 'The Vicars and Parish of Cuckfield in the Seventeenth Century', *SAC*, xlv (1902), 27.
66. WSRO, Ep i/26/2.
67. *Ibid*, PAR 21/9/1, fol. 145, PAR 48/9/1, fol. 10v, PAR 59/9/2/3; *SAC*, xlv (1902), 27.
68. WSRO, Ep ii/9/23, fol. 127v, Ep ii/15/1; *Univ. Birmingham Hist. J.*, p. 46.
69. *Ibid*, Ep ii/9/23, fols 125–7, Ep ii/15/1, pp. 47, 68.
70. *Ibid*, Ep ii/9/23, fols 126, 128v, Ep ii/15/1, pp. 56–8.
71. *Ibid*, Ep ii/9/23, fol. 2r, Ep ii/15/1, pp. 25, 51.
72. *Ibid*, Ep ii/9/23, fols 56r, 57r; *SAC*, xlix (1906), 63; Trevor-Roper, *Laud*, p. 155; Hembry, *Bishops of Bath and Wells*, pp. 230–1.
73. *Records of Bucks*, vii, 110.
74. J. S. Morrill, 'Puritanism and the Church in the diocese of Chester', *Northern History* viii (1973), 150–4; Morrill, pp. 19–21; Levack, *Civil Lawyers in England*, pp. 177–8; Marchant, *Church under the Law*, pp. 48–9, 232–4; Ketton-Cremer, *Norfolk in the Civil War*, pp. 62–88; Quintrell, pp. 299–306.
75. PRO, SP 16/442/137; above, p. 76.
76. W. Notestein, ed., *The Journal of Sir Simonds D'Ewes* (Yale University Press, 1923), pp. 282–3.
77. A. C. Wood, *Nottinghamshire in the Civil War* (Oxford University Press, 1937), pp. 11–12; Morrill, pp. 44–53; D. Underdown, *Somerset in the Civil War and Interregnum* (David & Charles, 1973), pp. 26–7.
78. PRO, Index 4212, 16 August 1641; WSRO, Ep i/17/27, Ep ii/9/24; Hembry, *Bishops of Bath and Wells*, pp. 246–7; Steer and Kirby, *Records of Diocese of Chichester*, pp. 6, 18, 19, 25, 100.
79. ESRO, Rye MS 47/133.
80. BM, E 134 (35): *Two Petitions of Sussex*.

5. Catholicism and fear of popery

1. PRO SP 14/160/60.
2. BM, E 134 (85): *Two Petitions of Sussex* (1642).
3. J. Bossy, 'The character of Elizabethan Catholicism', *Past and Present*, xxi (1962), 39–57; Manning, pp. 151–65; J. Miller, *Popery and Politics in England 1660–1688*, (Cambridge University Press, 1973), pp. 3–27.
4. J. Bossy, 'The English Catholic Community 1603–1625', in A. G. R. Smith, ed., *The Reign of James VI and I* (Macmillan, 1973), pp. 101–5.
5. McGrath, *Papists and Puritans under Elizabeth I*, p. 29; C. Cross, *The Royal Supremacy in the Elizabethan Church* (Allen & Unwin, 1969), pp. 110–11.
6. BM, Harleian MS 703, fol. 52r.
7. Manning, pp. 268–70; Cliffe, pp. 174–88.
8. *SR*, iv, part ii, 1071–7; Russell, *Crisis of Parliaments*, pp. 265–6; H. Bowler, ed., *Recusant Roll No. 2* (Catholic Record Society, lvii, 1965), xii–xlvii; Miller, *Popery and Politics*, pp. 51–66.
9. *Records of Bucks*, vii, 105; *CSPD 1635*, p. 26; Cockburn, *History of English Assizes*, pp. 211–12.
10. WSRO, Ep i/15. I am grateful to Mr Timothy McCann for making available to me his analysis of these returns.
11. WSRO, Ep i/22/1, Ep ii/14/1; Sessions Rolls 14.
12. PRO, E 179/191/377a; ESRO, Sessions Rolls 51/2–20, 119/54, 120/46; WSRO, Sessions Rolls 14, 42/40/5, 90/62, Ep. i/15.
13. Rushworth, *Historical Collections*, v, 166.
14. *AO*, ii, 1170–80; *SR*, iv, part 2, 1074; Miller, *Popery and Politics*, p. 54; J. T. Rutt, ed., *Burtons Diary* (1828), ii, pp. 148–55, 169, 310.
15. Garraway Rice, *West Sussex Protestation Returns*, pp. 64–5.
16. WSRO, Ep i/22/1, Ep ii/15/1, p. 54; ESRO, Sessions Rolls 51/20; PRO, E 179/191/377a, 385.
17. *HMCP*, i, 1; Redwood, *passim*.
18. WSRO, Ep i/14/1; ESRO, Sessions Rolls 51/19; PRO, Assizes 35/84/8.
19. WSRO, Sessions Rolls 14/15/21; PRO, SP 23/212/287, 293, 319.
20. PRO, SP 23/212/295–6.
21. Smith, ed., *Reign of James VI and I*, p. 101.
22. PRO, SP 23/212/294–5, 316; *CCC*, 1960–61; W. D. Cooper, 'Royalist compositions in Sussex during the Commonwealth', *SAC*, xix (1867), 116–20.
23. WSRO, Ep ii/15/1, pp. 54, 76; Magee, *English Recusants*, pp. 141, 146; Manning, pp. 151–65, 268–70.
24. PRO, E 179/191/377a; Manning, pp. 159–64; A. C. Southern, ed., *An Elizabethan Recusant House* (London/Glasgow, 1954); Cross, *Royal Supremacy in the Elizabethan Church*, p. 113; Smith, ed., *Reign of James VI and I*, p. 103.
25. ESRO, Sessions Rolls 51/6, 120/45; WSRO, Ep ii/15/1, p. 78.
26. WSRO, Sessions Rolls 51/2–20.
27. *Ibid*, Sessions Rolls 14/15/21, 42/1, 90/62; Garraway Rice, ed., *West Sussex Protestation Returns*, p. 158.
28. PRO, E 179/191/377a.
29. WSRO, Ep i/15; T. J. McCann, 'The Catholic recusancy of Dr John Bullaker of Chichester, 1574–1627', *Recusant History*, xi (1971), 75–85.
30. Manning, pp. 153–160; *SAC*, cvi (1968), 103–112.
31. WSRO, Sessions Rolls 14/15/22, 90/62, Ep i/15, Ep i/17/28, fols 30–1; C. E. Welch, 'Roman Catholic recusants at Midhurst in 1641', *SNQ*, xiv (1954–57), 166–9.
32. PRO, E 179/191/390.
33. WSRO, Ep ii/2/1, fol. 91v. I owe this suggestion to Mr Timothy McCann.
34. Garraway Rice, ed., *West Sussex Protestation Returns*, pp. 127–8.

35. Westminster Cathedral Archives, AAW, vol. xxiv, fol. 639. I am grateful to Mr Timothy McCann for this reference.
36. Smith, ed., *The Reign of James VI and I*, pp. 98–102; Miller, *Popery and Politics*, pp. 28–50.
37. Manning, p. 252; WSRO, Sessions Rolls 14/15/22, Ep i/15.
38. Johnstone, p. 102.
39. *HMC 3rd Report*, appendix, p. 277.
40. *The Dublin Review*, dxii (1967), 169. I am grateful to Mr Timothy McCann for this reference.
41. R. E. Scantilebury, *The Registers and Records of Brockhampton* (Catholic Record Society xliv, 1949), 2.
42. PRO, SP 23/212/293.
43. Stone, p. 614; *Visitation 1662*, pp. 66–7.
44. *Visitation 1634*, pp. 8–9, 53–4; *Visitation 1662*, p. 51; *CCC*, 1811; PRO, Prob. 11/234/98; M. E. Finch, *The Wealth of Five Northamptonshire Families* (Northamptonshire Record Society, xix, 1956), pp. 66–99.
45. PRO, Prob 11/164/86, 113.
46. BM, Add MS 33145, fols 38v, 61v.
47. PRO, E 179/191/377a; *CSPD 1627–8*, p. 461.
48. *HMCP*, i, 1.
49. PRO, SP 23/116/873; Manning, pp. 135, 268.
50. PRO, SP 16/467/104; Miller, *Popery and Politics*, pp. 16–17, 58–68.
51. *CCC*, 1960, 2211; PRO, SP 23/212/293.
52. PRO, Prob 11/234/98; *CCC*, 3011–12.
53. R. Clifton, 'Fear of Popery', in Russell, ed., *Origins of the English Civil War*, pp. 144–67; R. Clifton, 'The popular fear of Catholics during the English Revolution', *Past and Present*, lii (1971), 23–55; C. Z. Wiener, 'The beleaguered isle', *Past and Present*, li (1971), 27–62; Hill, *Antichrist in Seventeenth-Century England*, pp. 1–40; Miller, *Popery and Politics*, pp. 67–90.
54. WSRO, PAR 197/9/1.
55. PRO, SP 16/478/69; Magee, *English Recusants*, pp. 94–7.
56. Coates, ed., *Journal of Sir Simonds D'Ewes*, p. 172.
57. BM, Lansdowne MS 82, fol. 103; *APC 1618–19*, p. 199; PRO SP 14/107/50.
58. *APC 1615–16*, p. 33.
59. PRO, SP 14/107/50; *APC 1618–19*, p. 199.
60. PRO, SP 16/467/104; *Past and Present*, lii (1971), 26.
61. BM, Harleian MS 703, fol. 154r; *APC 1615–16*, pp. 33–4.
62. PRO, SP 14/160/60; *HMCR*, p. 170; ESRO, Frewen MS 4223, no. 47; *SAC*, xiii (1861), 59.
63. Below p. 284–5.
64. PRO, SP 16/11/39.
65. *Past and Present*, lii (1971), 26–8; Russell, ed., *Origins of the English Civil War*, pp. 158–9.
66. *CJ*, ii, 46, 58; WSRO, Sessions Rolls 42/40/5; ESRO, Sessions Rolls 51/6, 7, 20.
67. *CJ*, ii, 267; *CSPD 1641–3*, p. 100; Coates, *Journal of Sir Simonds D'Ewes*, p. 172.
68. BM, E 134 (35): *Two Petitions of Sussex* (1642).
69. ESRO, Rye MS 47/137.
70. Russell, ed., *Origins of the English Civil War*, pp. 163–7.

6. Achieving the millennium

1. Bodleian, Dep C MS 163, no. 263.
2. ESRO, Frewen MS 4223, no. 90.
3. *Ibid*, no. 96.

4. B. Capp, *The Fifth Monarchy Men* (Faber, 1972), pp. 23–75; B. Capp, 'Godly rule and English millenarianism', *Past and Present*, lii (1971), 106–17; Hill, *Antichrist in Seventeenth-Century England*, pp. 78–145.
5. ESRO, Frewen MS 4223, nos 54, 56; *SAC*, ix (1857), 49–54.
6. ESRO, Dunn MS 51/55, 56.
7. B. Pickering, *A Firebrand Pluckt out of the Burning* (1645), pp. 16–19; J. F. Wilson, *Pulpit in Parliament* (Princeton University Press, 1969), pp. 189–235.
8. Capp, *Fifth Monarchy Men*, p. 50.
9. ESRO, Frewen, MS 4223, no. 53.
10. *TSP*, V, 779.
11. C. Cross, 'The Church in England 1646–1660', in Aylmer, ed., *The Interregnum*, pp. 99–120; J. P. Kenyon, *The Stuart Constitution* (Cambridge University Press, 1966), pp. 251–69.
12. *SAC*, xxxi (1881), 171, 188; *AO*, ii, 968–75.
13. *SAC*, xxxi (1881), 169–70; *CJ*, iv, 707, vii, 366; Wilson, *Pulpit in Parliament*, pp. 127, 168, 183, 212–13, 264, 269; Morrill, pp. 163–6, 241.
14. *AO*, ii, 983; PRO SP 18/42/70i, 78/241; A. G. Matthews, *Calamy Revised* (Oxford University Press, 1934), p. 491.
15. *CSPD 1635*, p. xlii–xliii.
16. *DNB*; Wilson, *Pulpit in Parliament*, pp. 82, 124, 187, 190, 241, 244, 247; Capp, *Fifth Monarchy Men*, p. 47.
17. *SAC*, xxxi (1881), 178.
18. WSRO, PAR 149/1/1/1, fols 42v–43r.
19. PRO, SP 28/135, fol. 78r.
20. *SAC*, xxxi (1881), 178, 181, 197; Matthews, *Walker Revised*, pp. 355, 358.
21. WSRO, Sessions Rolls 51/52/1; PRO SP 18/42/70i, 66/60ii; *AO*, ii, 983.
22. ESRO, PAR 516/29/1, 2.
23. Bodleian, Tanner MS 62, fol. 493r; S. R. Gardiner, *History of the Great Civil War*, (London, 1886), i, 173–4.
24. *SAC*, xxxi (1881), 175; WSRO, PAR 183/9/1, fols 35v–37r.
25. Bodleian, Dep C MS 160, no. 36.
26. *SAC*, xxx (1880), 112–36, below, p. 288.
27. House of Lords Record Office, 23 June 1660: Petition of Benjamin Blaxton.
28. *SAC*, v (1852), 72–9.
29. WSRO, PAR 27/1/1/1, fol. 109; Matthews, *Walker Revised*, pp. 354–61.
30. *SAC*, xxvi (1875), 94; xxx (1880), 128, 133–6; xxxi (1881), 173–85; Matthews, *Walker Revised*, 355, 358–9, 361; Thomas-Stanford, pp. 138–50.
31. Matthews, *Walker Revised*, p. xiv; Manning, p. 15; Morrill, p. 167.
32. BM, Add MS 33084, fol. 71r.
33. *SAC*, iv (1851), 259–61; xxxvi (1888), 139.
34. *Ibid*, v (1852), 78, xxxi (1881), 188–91.
35. *Ibid*, xxxi (1881), 172; Bodleian, Dep C MS 163, no. 263; above, p. 105.
36. Bodleian, Tanner MS 60, fols 252r, 254r.
37. *AO*, ii, 968–75, 983; PRO, SP 25/78/238, 241; *CCC*, pp. 1215, 1863; Thomas-Stanford, pp. 293–6.
38. F. E. Sawyer, 'Proceedings of the Committee of Plundered Ministers Relating to Sussex', *SAC*, xxxvi (1888), 136–59; Aylmer ed., *The Interregnum*, p. 104.
39. PRO. SP 16/66/60, 61.
40. *Ibid*, SP 18/42/70.
41. *CJ*, iv, 719; *SAC*, xxxvi (1888), 144–5; *VCHS*, ii, 36.
42. *CSPD 1631–3*, p. 491; Seaver, *Puritan Lectureships*, pp. 163, 252. I am grateful to Professor Paul Seaver for additional information about William Martin.
43. C. E. Welch, 'Commonwealth Unions of Benefices in Sussex', *SNQ*, xv (1958–62), 119; Matthews, *Calamy Revised*, pp. 342–3.

44. *SAC*, xxxvi (1888), 140–1; *SNQ*, xv (1958–62), 116–20; *CSPD 1657–8*, pp. 82, 168, 293, 375–6; W. A. Shaw, *A History of the English Church 1640–1660* (London, 1900), ii, 248–53.
45. Bodleian, Dep C MS 169, no. 36.
46. Aylmer, ed., *The Interregnum*, pp. 99–120; R. S. Bosher, *The Making of the Restoration Settlement* (London, 1951), pp. 1–48; G. F. Nuttall, 'Congregational Commonwealth incumbents', *Transactions of the Congregational Historical Society*, xiv (1940–44), 155–67.
47. Matthews, *Calamy Revised*, pp. 381, 465, 535.
48. PRO, SP 18/42/70.
49. Capp, *Fifth Monarchy Men*, pp. 176, 254; Matthews, *Calamy Revised*, p. 396.
50. Thomas-Stanford, pp. 101–10.
51. BM, E 688 (11): N. Smith, *A Warning to the World* (1653).
52. Matthews, *Calamy Revised*, p. 466.
53. BM, E 804 (4): *The Declaration and Agreement of the Ministers of the County of Sussex* (1653); Aylmer, ed., *The Interregnum*, pp. 108–10; Worden, *The Rump Parliament*, pp. 322–4.
54. WSRO, PAR 51/9/2/17; *SAC*, v (1852), 72–9.
55. Capp, *Fifth Monarchy Men*, pp. 50–1; *CCC*, p. 1215.
56. BM, Add MS 33145, fol. 184v; ESRO, Frewen MS 520, fols 49v, 50v.
57. ESRO, Frewen MS 4223, no. 90.
58. PRO, SP 18/66/61.
59. Matthews, *Calamy Revised*, pp. 5–6; T. W. W. Smart, 'A notice of Rev. John Allin, Vicar of Rye, 1653–1662, an ejected minister', *SAC*, xxxi (1881), 123–56. I am grateful for information about John Allin to Professor Paul Seaver.
60. *HMCR*, p. 220; ESRO, Rye MS 47/145, 148.
61. ESRO, Rye MS 47/162.
62. ESRO, Rye MS 47/137, 143, 144, 148, 154.
63. ESRO, Frewen MS 4223, nos 53–5.
64. De Beer, ed., *Diary of John Evelyn*, iii, 67.
65. *HMCR*, pp. 220, 229.
66. ESRO, Rye MS 47/146.
67. *HMCR*, p. 144; Dell, ed., *The Records of Rye Corporation*, p. xiv; Thomas-Stanford, p. 231.
68. WSRO, Sessions Rolls 51/52/1; Hill, *Society and Puritanism*, pp. 145–218.
69. *SR*, v, 1, 25; *AO*, i, 420–2, ii, 383–7; G. E. Aylmer, *The State's Servants* (Routledge, 1973), p. 307.
70. Above, pp. 83–9.
71. WSRO, Sessions Rolls 72/11; ESRO, QSOB 1655–60, fols 56v, 67v.
72. WSRO, PAR 197/29/3.
73. ESRO, QSOB 1655–60, fol. 60r.
74. WSRO, Sessions Rolls 55/53/5.
75. Below, pp. 152–5.
76. ESRO, Sessions Rolls 102/8.
77. Hill, *Society and Puritanism*, pp. 190–1; T. G. Barnes, 'County politics and a Puritan cause celèbre: Somerset Churchales, 1633', *TRHS*, ix (1959), 103–22.
78. B. W. Blencowe, 'Extracts from the parish registers and other parochial documents of East Sussex', *SAC*, iv (1851), 255; Redwood, p. xxiii.
79. *SR*, v, 1; ESRO, Sessions Rolls 53/132.
80. *AO*, i, 420–2; Redwood, pp. xxii–xxiii, 76–7; ESRO, QSOB 1650–5, fol. 33v.
81. J. Furley, *Quarter Sessions Government in Hampshire in the Seventeenth Century* (Winchester, 1937), pp. 71, 83; below, pp. 159–60.
82. Thomas, *Religion and the Decline of Magic*, pp. 502–12.
83. WSRO, Sessions Rolls 86/2.

84. *Ibid*, Sessions Rolls 91/50; *AO*, ii, 393–6; Redwood, pp. 107, 207; ESRO, QSOB 1650–5, fol. 64v; *TSP*, iv, 229.
85. WSRO, Sessions Rolls 53/54/39; Redwood, *passim*; ESRO, QSOB 1650–5, 1655–60.
86. Below, p. 304.
87. Hill, *Society and Puritanism*, p. 377.
88. WSRO, PAR 293/12/1; Redwood, p. 97.
89. Below, pp. 156–9.
90. Redwood, pp. xxii, 77, 97; WSRO, Sessions Rolls 53/54/1.
91. *AO*, i, 1065–70.
92. WSRO, PAR 59/9/2/19–23, 197/9/1.
93. ESRO, QSOB 1655–60, fols 3v, 19v, 24v, 42v.
94. S. C. Ratcliff and H. C. Johnson, eds, *Warwick County Records* (Warwick, 1935–39), III, xxiv; Hill, *Society and Puritanism*, p. 437.
95. ESRO, QSOB 1650–5, fols 2r, 22r.
96. WSRO, PAR 59/9/2/14–23, 197/9/1.
97. *Ibid*, Sessions Rolls 77/8, 86/54, 97/50.
98. *Ibid*, PAR 293/12/1; *SAC*, xxiii (1871), 46.
99. ESRO, QSOB 1655–60, fols 44r, 58r, 69v, 70r, 72v, 76r, 77r.
100. *Ibid*, fols 19r, 38r, 42v, 51r, 53r, 65v, 78r.
101. *Ibid*, fol. 72v.
102. *AO*, ii, 715–18.
103. L. F. Salzman, ed., *The Parish Register of Glynde* (SRS, xxx, 1924), 24, 36, 38–40; W. C. Renshaw, ed., *The Parish Registers of Cuckfield* (SRS, xiii, 1911), 117–19; J. Dale, 'Churchwardens accounts, Bolney parish', *SAC*, vi (1853), 251.
104. Holloway, *History of Rye*, p. 508; Salzman, ed., *Parish Register of Glynde*, pp. 40–1.
105. G. Davies, *The Early Stuarts* (Oxford University Press, 1937), pp. 200–1.
106. WSRO, PAR 16/1/1/1; ESRO, QSOB 1650–5, fol. 57r; *SAC*, vi (1853), 251; J. Cooper, 'The hundred of Swanborough', *SAC*, xxix (1879), 160; R. G. Rice, 'Warnham: the registers and vicars', *SAC*, xxxiii (1883), 156; F. W. T. Atree, 'Wivelsfield', *SAC*, xxxvi (1888), 20; W. P. Breach, 'Steyning marriages during the Commonwealth', *SAC*, xlii (1899), 111–16.
107. M. A. Lower, 'Parochial history of Chiddingly', *SAC*, xiv (1862), 246.
108. ESRO, QSOB 1655–60, fol. 5v; Renshaw, ed., *Parish Registers of Cuckfield*, p. 117; E. H. Bates-Harbin, and M. C. B. Dawes, eds, *Somerset Quarter Sessions Records*, (Somerset Record Society, xxiii, xxiv, xxviii, xxxiv, (1907–19), III, xlviii.
109. J. T. Rutt, ed., *Diary of Thomas Burton* (London, 1828), ii, 67–74.
110. Renshaw, ed., *Parish Registers of Cuckfield*, p. 119; Salzman, ed., *Parish Register of Glynde*, pp. 40–1.
111. P. Collinson, *The Godly: aspects of popular Protestantism in Elizabethan England* (papers presented to the Past and Present Conference on Popular Religion, 1966), p. 22; Collinson, *Elizabethan Puritan Movement*, p. 381.
112. ESRO, Frewen MS 4223, no. 30.
113. *Ibid*, nos 40, 46–7.
114. *Ibid*, nos 46–7; *SAC*, xiii (1861), 59, above, p. 103.
115. ESRO, Frewen MS 4223, no. 49.
116. *Ibid*, nos 48, 64, 67, 68, 74, 75; *SAC*, xiii (1861), 60; Holloway, *History of Rye*, pp. 550–1.
117. ESRO, Frewen MS 4223, nos 90, 91.
118. *Ibid*, no. 70; *SAC*, xiii (1861), 60.
119. Aylmer, ed., *The Interregnum*, pp. 116–20.
120. WSRO, Ep i/22/1.
121. Walker, *Calamy Revised*, p. 396; *TSP*, iv, 151; Capp, *Fifth Monarchy Men*, pp. 176, 178, 259.
122. Capp, *Fifth Monarchy Men*, pp. 111, 133.

123. *TSP*, iv, 151, 161, 593.
124. W. Figg, 'Extracts from documents illustrative of the sufferings of the Quakers in Lewes', *SAC*, xvi (1864), 65–74; N. Penney, ed., *The First Publishers of Truth* (London, 1907), pp. 233–7; *VCHS*, ii, 37–9; W. C. Braithwaite, *The Beginnings of Quakerism* (Cambridge University Press, 1955), p. 399; W. Armistead, ed., *The Journal of George Fox* (London, 1852), pp. 221–2.
125. PRO, SP 18/153/11, 15; WSRO, Sessions Rolls 83/69.
126. *TSP*, iv, 642; PRO, SP 18/153/13; Braithwaite, *Beginnings of Quakerism*, pp. 398–9.
127. PRO, SP 18/183/53.
128. WSRO, Sessions Rolls 932/64, 65.
129. ESRO, QSOB 1655–60, fol. 6r; WSRO, Sessions Rolls 84/38, 39; *SAC*, xvi (1864), 75–7.
130. Russell, *Crisis of Parliaments*, p. 367.
131. ESRO, QSOB 1655–60, fol. 6r; PRO, SP 18/153/11, 183/53; W. Albery, *A Millennium of Facts in the History of Horsham* (Horsham, 1947), pp. 407–54.
132. *SAC*, xvi (1864), 75–8.
133. ESRO, QSOB 1655–60, fols 6r, 23v, 28v, 31r, 46r, 50v, 55r, 56v, 62v, 64v.
134. *Ibid*, fols 16v, 37r; *SAC*, xvi (1864), 75; Braithwaite, *Beginnings of Quakerism, passim*; Gardiner, *History of England during the Commonwealth and Protectorate* (London, 1901), iii, 288–9.
135. PRO, SP 18/153/11, 183/53.
136. WSRO, Sessions Rolls 84/38, 39; ESRO, QSOB 1655–60, fols 12r, 27v; *SAC*, xvi (1864), 72.
137. ESRO, QSOB 1655–60, fol. 367r.
138. PRO, SP 18/153/11–16; Thomas-Stanford, pp. 290–3; W. K. Jordan, *The Development of Religious Toleration in England* (Allen & Unwin, 1938), iii, 176–9.
139. Bosher, *Making of the Restoration Settlement*, pp. 219–77.
140. House of Lords Record Office, 23 June 1660: Petition of Robert Tomlinson; *HMC 7th Report*, appendix, pp. 104–8; WSRO, PAR 27/1/1/1, fol. 109.
141. *SAC*, xxxi (1881), 185.
142. ESRO, Sessions Rolls 128/11; Matthews, *Calamy Revised*, pp. 42, 302.
143. Matthews, *Calamy Revised*, pp. 42–3, 450, 538; D. R. Lacey, *Dissent and Parliamentary Politics in England 1661–1689* (New Brunswick, 1969), pp. 391–2, 426–7, 442.
144. J. H. Cooper, 'A religious census of Sussex in 1676', *SAC*, xlv (1902), 142–8; and, 'Return of conventicles in Sussex 1669', *SAC*, li (1908), 1–5.
145. *SAC*, xiii (1861), 62–79.

7. The framework of government

1. BM, Harleian MS 703, fol. 16.
2. *Ibid*, Add MS 33084, fol. 40r.
3. WSRO, Sessions Rolls 66/10.
4. Redwood, pp. xiii–xvii, 210–14; Barnes, pp. 71–80, 91–5; Quintrell, pp. 37–113; T. G. Barnes, ed., *Somerset Assize Orders* (Somerset Record Society, lxv, 1959), xii–xxxvi; A. Hassell-Smith, 'Justices at work in Elizabethan Norfolk', *Norfolk Archaelogy*, xxxiv, part 2 (1967), 93–110; S. A. Peyton, *Minutes of Proceedings in Quarter Sessions* (Lincoln Record Society, xxv, 1931 for 1928), I, xii–cxxx, 4.
5. PRO, Indices 4211–14, Assizes 35/67–101; *BIHR*, xxxii (1959), 221–42; Appendix II.
6. F. Bamford, ed., *A Royalist's Notebook* (Constable, 1936), p. 246.
7. Cockburn, *A History of English Assizes*, pp. 156–63; J. H. Gleason, *The Justices of the Peace in England* (Oxford University Press, 1969), pp. 49, 61–2; A. Hassell-Smith,

'The Elizabethan Gentry of Norfolk: Office Holding and Faction' (DPhil thesis, London, 1959), chapter 3.

8. Mousley, pp. 308–11; BM, Add MS 38139; PRO, C 193/13/1; Stone, pp. 65–128.
9. Hassell-Smith, pp. 76–86.
10. Cited in Cockburn, *History of English Assizes*, p. 162.
11. Cited in *ibid*, p. 157; Gleason, *Justices of the Peace*, pp. 60, 63.
12. Sir H. Ellis, 'Certificate concerning the JPs in Sussex in 1587', *SAC*, ii (1849), 60.
13. Cockburn, *History of English Assizes*, pp. 157–63.
14. BM, Harleian, MS 703, fol. 165v.
15. PRO, SP 16/442/137; Gleason, *Justices of the Peace*, pp. 63–4; *CSPD 1619–23*, p. 332; Barnes, pp. 313–16.
16. Appendix, II(i).
17. PRO, Index 4212, 7 July 1637; Barnes, pp. 305–6.
18. PRO, Index 4212, 20 Feb. 1635; SP 16/177/61, 191/45, 210/57, 250/42; Teirney, *History of Arundel*, p. 433.
19. PRO, Index 4212, 20 Feb. 1635; SP 16/202/41, 210/92, 243/18, 262/15; WSRO, Sessions Rolls 14–26.
20. Barnes, pp. 299–310.
21. Below, pp. 143.
22. ESRO, DL Book, fol. 15r, Sessions Rolls 20, 22; PRO, Assizes 35/67/8/85.
23. PRO, Index 4212, 7 July 1637.
24. Barnes, p. 45; Richmond, p. 86.
25. PRO, C 193 /13/1.
26. PRO, SP 16/442/137; Index 4212, 24 February 1640.
27. BM, Add MS 33084, fol. 40r.
28. Appendix II (ix).
29. *TSP*, iv, 151, 161, 190, v, 172; PRO, Index 4213, 26 Jan., 14 April, 18 July, 1656.
30. PRO, C 193/13/1; Appendices II (ii)–(viii); Underdown, *Pride's Purge*, p. 344; Underdown, *Somerset in the Civil War and Interregnum*, p. 185.
31. BM, Add MS 33084, fol. 83v; Cockburn, *History of English Assizes*, p. 160; Appendix II(i).
32. BM, Add MS 33084, fol. 40r; PRO, Prob 11/204/83.
33. *Visitation 1662*, p. 33.
34. *CSPD 1645–7*, p. 210; *CSPD 1655*, p. 4; *HMCR*, pp. 225, 230, 236; *Visitation 1662*, p. 38, 43, 103; PRO, Prob 11/300/209; for Polhill see *DNB*; see pp. 281–2.
35. ESRO, Glynde MS 1229; Frewen MS 520.
36. Below p. 219.
37. Redwood, p. 146; ESRO, QSOB 1650–5, fol. 13r.
38. *HMCP*, i, 465.
39. PRO, E 179/191/398, SP 28/181; ESRO, Sessions Rolls 47/4.
40. BM, Harleian MS 703, fol. 165v.
41. *Visitation 1634*.
42. *CSPD 1639–40*, p. 65; *Visitation 1662*, p.p 10, 43, 119; PRO, Prob 11/299/177.
43. D. E. Howell James, ed., *Norfolk Sessions Order Book 1650–1657* (Norfolk Record Society, xxvi, 1955), pp. 4–5.
44. PRO, Prob 11/247/247.
45. Underdown, *Pride's Purge*, pp. 311–12; Underdown, *Somerset in the Civil War and Interregnum*, pp. 140–1, 149, 169–70; A. L. Beier, 'Poor relief in Warwickshire 1630–1660', *Past and Present*, xxxv (1966), 93–4; Pennington and Roots, eds, *The Committee at Stafford*, pp. xxii–xxiii.
46. Appendix II(ix). Cf. Morrill, pp. 224–5, and Blackwood, pp. 208–10.
47. Gleason, *Justices of the Peace*, pp. 87–8; Richmond, p. 97; Appendix II(x).

48. Appendix II(xi).
49. BM, Add MS 38139; Gleason, *Justices of the Peace*, p. 259; Mousley, pp. 427–8, 474–5, 485–6, 754–5.
50. Underdown, *Pride's Purge*, 309–11; Underdown, *Somerset in the Civil War and Interregnum*, pp. 157–8.
51. Appendix II.
52. BM, Harleian MS 703, fol. 16; Redwood, p. xx.
53. ESRO, QSOB 1650–5, fol. 55v, Sessions Rolls 104/97.
54. *A Descriptive Report on the Quarter Sessions Records* (Lewes, 1954), p. 2.
55. BM, Add MS 33145, fols 9v, 12v, 45v, 58v, 59v; ESRO, Frewen MS 520, fols 32r, 34r, 39r, 42r; Cockburn, *History of English Assizes*, pp. 1–11, 153–261.
56. F. G. Emmison, 'The Elizabethan assize files with particular reference to the county of Essex', *Bulletin of Local Archivists*, xiii (1954), 2–12; Barnes, ed., *Somerset Assize Orders*, pp. xx–xxx.
57. PRO, Assizes 35/67–101; Redwood, *passim*; Barnes, pp. 51–3.
58. PRO, Assizes 35/77/6, 82/5, 94/9.
59. WSRO, Sessions Rolls 32, outer membrane; ESRO, QSOB 1650–5, fol. 64r.
60. Redwood, pp. 40–1.
61. Cited in Barnes, ed., *Somerset Assize Orders*, p. xxvi.
62. *Ibid*, p. xxii; *CSPD 1631–3*, pp. 535–6; *CSPD 1635*, pp. 128–9; *CSPD 1635–6*, p. 247.
63. Hassell-Smith, *Norfolk Archaeology*, xxxiv (1967), 93–110.
64. J. Hurstfield, 'County Government 1530–1660', *VCH Wiltshire*, v, 93.
65. S. C. Ratcliffe and H. C. Johnson, ed., *Warwick County Records* (Warwick, 1935), i, 5; J. Willis Bund, ed., *Worcestershire Quarter Sessions Rolls* (Worcester, 1900), ii, 395.
66. Quintrell, pp. 55–8.
67. Barnes, pp. 82, 179–9.
68. *SAC*, ii (1849), 58.
69. Below, pp. 177–8, 202–5.
70. PRO, SP 16/192/99, 247/46.
71. Bodleian, Tanner MS 148 fol. 12.
72. PRO, SP 16/328/74, 426/37; ESRO, Sessions Rolls 46/1.
73. PRO, SP 16/191/45, 203/34, 314/103.
74. Barnes, pp. 41, 82; Quintrell, pp. 48–9.
75. PRO, SP 16/239/4, 250/43.
76. *Ibid*, SP 16/426/19, 37.
77. ESRO, QSOB 1950–5, 1655–60, *passim*; Morrill, pp. 233–41; below, pp. 218–9.
78. See the minutes of meetings in Ratcliff and Johnson, eds. *Warwick County Records*, I, xxx–xxxii.
79. ESRO, Sessions Rolls 36/5, QSOB 1655–60, fol. 29v.
80. Barnes, pp. 56–7.
81. For a selection of printed examinations see Willis Bund, ed., *Worcestershire Quarter Sessions Rolls.*
82. ESRO, Sessions Rolls 22/116, 122, 126, 128.
83. F. G. Emmison, *Elizabethan Life: disorder* (Essex Record Office, 1970), p. 285.
84. G. Leveson-Gower, 'Notebook of a Surrey Justice', *Surrey Archaeological Collections*, ix (1888), 161–232.
85. ESRO, Sessions Rolls 104/74–7.
86. Redwood, pp. 31, 34–5, 44.
87. ESRO, Sessions Rolls 85/1–2.
88. Below, p. 169.
89. M. Weinbaum, ed., *British Borough Charters 1307–1660* (Cambridge University Press, 1943), pp. 114–15; M. Reed, 'The Keeping of Sessions of the Peace in the Borough of Hastings', *SAC*, c (1962), 46–59.

90. ESRO, Rye MS 47/109.
91. *Ibid*, 47/117; F. Hull, ed., *A Calendar of the White and Black Books of the Cinque Ports* (HMC Joint Publication series, 5, London, 1966), pp. 454, 461, 465; ESRO, Rye MS 47/152, 154, 156, 159.
92. Steer, *Chichester City Charters*, p. 19.
93. Bodleian, Tanner MS 148, fols 12–15. There is no evidence to support the view that this charter transferred the Close to the jurisdiction of the city. *VCH Sussex*, iii, 96; A. Ballard, *A History of Chichester* (Chichester, 1929), p. 63; below, p. 234–5.
94. Bodleian, Rawlinson MS B 431, fol. 9r; W. C. Renshaw, 'The Hundred of Buttinghill', *SAC*, lviii (1916), 6–20; J. R. Daniel-Tyssen, 'The parliamentary surveys of the county of Sussex', *SAC*, xxiii (1871), 217–313; *SAC*, xlviii (1905), 29–30.
95. PRO, SP 16/247/46.
96. Redwood, p. 184; Barnes, p. 128.
97. Godfrey, ed., *The Book of John Rowe*; T. W. Horsfield, *History of Lewes* (Lewes, 1824), pp. 321–3.
98. BM, Add MS 33144, 33171–83.
99. ESRO and WSRO, Sessions Rolls, QSOB 1650–5, 1655–60, Redwood.
100. Redwood, pp. 1, 60, 82, 143; ESRO, QSOB 1650–5, fol. 9r.
101. ESRO, Sessions Rolls 124/7.
102. De Beer, ed., *The Diary of John Evelyn*, ii, 11–12.
103. J. S. Cockburn, ed., *Somerset Assize Orders 1640–59* (Somerset Record Society, lxxi, 1971), xiii, xxii; Mousley, pp. 283–4, 303–6; Hassell-Smith, pp. 139–54.
104. Cliffe, p. 254.
105. PRO, C 227/30, 31.
106. Above, p. 130.
107. PRO, Prob 11/314/57.
108. Barnes, pp. 124–42; Cliffe, pp. 250–5.
109. ESRO, Sessions Rolls 109/50.
110. BM, Harleian MS 703, fol. 143r.
111. Redwood, pp. 81–2; WSRO, Sessions Rolls 90/45.
112. GMR, Losely MS 769/1 (i).
113. Redwood, p. 123.
114. *Ibid*, p. xiii and Appendix B. For a full account of the clerk's duties see T. G. Barnes, *The Clerk of the Peace in Caroline Somerset* (Leicester, 1961), pp. 22–9.
115. PRO, Prob 11/182/32.
116. See Sir E. Stephens, ed., *The Clerks of the Counties* (London, 1961), pp. 37–8; Lister, ed., *West Riding Sessions Records*, ii, 403–4.
117. Budgen, ed., *Abstracts of Sussex Deeds*, pp. 9, 37; PRO, Prob 11/234/85.
118. WSRO, Sessions Rolls 44/2, 3, 66/10.
119. *Ibid*, 49/10.
120. WSRO, PAR 59/57/1/13; Hassell Smith, p. 87; Barnes, p. 75.
121. See for instance BM, Add MS 33144, fol. 1v.
122. WSRO, Sessions Rolls 22/21/1; ESRO, Sessions Rolls 33/2.
123. S. C. Newton, 'Staffordshire Quarter Sessions: archives and procedure', in M. W. Greenslade, ed., *Essays in Staffordshire History* (Staffordshire Record Society, fourth series, vi, 1970), 66–85.
124. Redwood, pp. vii–xii; H. C. Johnson, ed., *Minutes of Proceedings in Sessions 1563 and 1574 to 1592* (Wiltshire Arch. and Natural History Soc. Records Branch, iv, 1949); Barnes, *Clerk of the Peace*, p. 6; F. G. Emmison and I. Gray, *County Records* (London, 1948).
125. Below, p. 218.
126. For the duties of constables and headboroughs see Peyton, *Proceedings in Quarter Sessions*, I, xliii–xlv, l–liii.

127. Godfrey, ed., *Book of John Rowe*, p 141.
128. Redwood, pp. 38, 72; WSRO, Sessions Rolls 40, outer membrane; ESRO, QSOB 1650–5, fols 40, 64r, 1655–60, fols 7r, 34v, 40r, 55v, 73r.
129. Redwood, p. 163.
130. Godfrey, ed., *Book of John Rowe*, p. 139; Peyton, *Proceedings in Quarter Sessions*, I, lxiii–lix.

8. The enforcement of order

1. BM, Lansdowne MS 53, fol. 165.
2. PRO, SP 16/383/20.
3. WSRO, Sessions Rolls 60/63.
4. Willan, *English Coasting Trade*, p. 147; J. H. Andrews, 'The Port of Chichester and the grain trade 1650–1750', *SAC*, xlii (1954), 93–105; A. Woodworth, *Purveyance for the Royal Household in the Reign of Queen Elizabeth* (American Philosophical Society, Transactions, new series, vol. 35, part 1, 1946).
5. PRO, SP 16/118/19.
6. *APC 1629–30*, nos 197, 205, 278.
7. *Ibid*, no. 1031.
8. PRO, SP 16/98/104, 153/12, 162/14; *APC 1629–30*, nos 596, 935, 947, 952; M. Hawkins, 'The Government: its role and its aims', in Russell, ed., *Origins of the English Civil War*, pp. 51–7.
9. PRO, SP 16/383/20.
10. Richmond, p. 295; F. G. Emmison, *Elizabethan Life: disorder* (Essex Record Office, 1970), pp. 64–5; A. J. Fletcher, *Tudor Rebellions* (Longmans, 1968), pp. 112–13.
11. Bamford, *A Royalist's Notebook*, p. 53; W. G. Hoskins, 'Harvest fluctuations and English economic history 1620–1759', *Agricultural History Review*, xvi (1968), 15–31.
12. *APC 1630–1*, no. 328; PRO SP 16/177/61, 185/80, 192/98.
13. *APC 1630–1*, nos 453, 890.
14. PRO, SP 16/192/98, 204/99, 210/57.
15. E. P. Thompson, 'The moral economy of the English crowd in the eighteenth century', *Past and Present*, l (1971), 76–136.
16. ESRO, Sessions Rolls 41/21.
17. BM, Add MS 33145, fol. 222r.
18. PRO, SP 16/192/99.
19. E. M. Leonard, *The Early History of English Poor Relief* (Cambridge, 1900), pp. 188–92; Quintrell, p. 221; Richmond, pp. 362–71.
20. PRO, SP 16/189/15.
21. J. Thirsk and J. P. Cooper, eds., *Seventeenth-Century Economic Documents* (Oxford University Press, 1972), pp. 36, 343–7.
22. PRO, SP 16/185/80, 203/102, 210/57.
23. *Ibid*, SP 16/204/99.
24. *Ibid*, E 190/763–7.
25. ESRO, Rye MS 47/127.
26. *Ibid*, 47/115; PRO, SP 16/185/80.
27. *APC 1630–1*, nos 692, 903, 1001.
28. PRO, SP 16/190/51; ESRO, Rye MS 47/115.
29. WSRO, Sessions Rolls 3/99, 16/2.
30. ESRO, Sessions Rolls 98/1, 102/8.
31. *Ibid*, 21/114, 22/127, 134, 39/95; Quintrell, p. 227.
32. Johnstone, pp. xxxvii, 1–127; above, p. 87.
33. BM, Harleian MS 703, fol. 173r; ESRO, DL Book, fol. 19r, QSOB 1650–5, fol. 470; Barnes, p. 78.

34. ESRO, Rye MS 47/145, Sessions Rolls 102/8; P. Clark, 'The migrant in Kentish towns 1580–1640', in Clark and Slack, eds., *Crisis and Order in English Towns 1500–1700*, pp. 139–41; Richmond, pp. 233–6.
35. ESRO, Sessions Rolls 98/1; QSOB 1655–60, fol. 58v; Morrill, pp. 244–5.
36. WSRO, Sessions Rolls 12/12/5; ESRO, Sessions Rolls 30/61; Richmond, p. 251.
37. ESRO, Sessions Rolls 15/1, 27/1, 30/2, 34/1, 49/1, 60/1.
38. WSRO, Sessions Rolls 2, outer membrane; Redwood, p. 129.
39. PRO, SP 16/191/63, 192/99.
40. Redwood, pp. 51–2, 56, 177, 191.
41. ESRO, Sessions Rolls 28/89, 102/8; QSOB 1650–5, fol. 20r.
42. Barnes, pp. 65–6, 193.
43. ESRO, Sessions Rolls 1–62; WSRO, Sessions Rolls, 1–49; BM, Harleian MS 703, fol. 19; Quintrell, p. 228; below, p. 224.
44. Redwood, pp. 51, 70–1; WSRO, Sessions Rolls, 51/52/50.
45. W. K. Jordan, *Philanthropy in England* (Allen & Unwin, 1959), pp. 143–239; Hill, *Puritanism and Revolution*, pp. 215–38; C. Hill, *Society and Puritanism in Pre-Revolutionary England* (Secker & Warburg, 1964), pp. 259–97.
46. WSRO, Visitation Articles 1586.
47. ESRO, Frewen MS 520, fols 31v, 57r; Essex RO, D/DL E 22, 16–23 Dec. 1643, 14–21 Dec. 1644, 20–27 Dec. 1645, 19–26 Dec. 1646; BM, Add MS 33145, fols 8v, 17r, 40v, 66v, 93r.
48. ESRO, PAR 516/31/1; BM, Add MS 33145, fols 26r, 32v, 59v, 68v.
49. PRO, Prob 11/161/12; *SAC*, xlviii (1905), 146; above, p. 150.
50. PRO, Prob 11/311/95; *SAC*, xliii (1900), 69–70.
51. *VCH Sussex*, ii, 101; Bodleian, Tanner MS 149, fol. 114, Rawlinson MS B 431, fol. 34r; PRO, SP 16/190/50, 191/45.
52. WSRO, Ep i/16/1, fol. 5r.
53. Appendix IV; A. L. Beier, 'Poor relief in Warwickshire 1630–60', *Past and Present*, xxxv (1966), pp. 77–100.
54. PRO, SP 16/189/6.
55. WSRO, PAR 465/6/1, 516/31/1.
56. *Ibid*, PAR 59/57/1, 86/37/1; Ep i/16/1.
57. P. Slack, 'Poverty and politics in Salisbury 1587–1666', in Clark and Slack, eds *Crisis and Order in English Towns*, pp. 164–203.
58. ESRO, QSOB 1655–60, fols. 11v, 19v; Beier, *Past and Present*, xxxv (1966), 82.
59. ESRO, Sessions Rolls 20/1, 33/33, 51/22.
60. *Ibid*, PAR 516/31/1; see also E. M. Hampson, *The Treatment of Poverty in Cambridgeshire* (Cambridge University Press, 1934), pp. 42–8.
61. PRO, SP 16/188/34, 189/6, 191/45, 63, 328/74, 426/37; ESRO, Frewen MS 520, fol. 41r; BM, Add MS 33145, fol. 93v.
62. PRO, SP 16/192/99; *CSPD 1637*, p. 290; ESRO, QSOB 1650–5, fol. 2v; Morrill, pp. 247–8.
63. ESRO, PAR/516/33; Sessions Rolls 26, outer membrane; *SAC*, xlviii (1905), 28.
64. PRO, SP 16/191/45, 210/92, 220/41, 247/46, 263/82; see also Hampson, *Treatment of Poverty in Cambridgeshire*, pp. 48–50.
65. PRO, SP 16/328–425.
66. Barnes, *Somerset Assize Orders*, p. 63; ESRO, QSOB 1650–5, fol. 68v; WSRO, Sessions Rolls 16/18/1.
67. WSRO, Sessions Rolls 16/14/84.
68. Redwood, pp. 96, 106, 146, 152–3,; ESRO QSOB 1650–5, fol. 18r; see also Barnes, p. 186; W. B. Willcox, *Gloucestershire 1590–1640* (Yale University Press, 1940), p. 71.
69. WSRO, Sessions Rolls 71/8; Thomas-Stanford, p. 61.

70. Redwood, p. 196; ESRO, QSOB 1650–5, fols 14r, 18r, 21v.
71. Redwood, p. 171; ESRO, QSOB 1650–5, fols 2v, 27r, 30r, 41v, 1655–60, fols 7r, 11r, 15r, 49r, 70v, 74r, 79v.
72. Redwood, p. 145; Thomas, *Religion and the Decline of Magic*, pp. 526–30; MacFarlane *Ralph Josselin*, p. 194.
73. WSRO, Sessions Rolls 5/64, 85/49.
74. N. Z. Davis, 'The reasons of misrule: youth groups and charivaris in sixteenth-century France', *Past and Present*, l (1971), 45.
75. Johnstone, p. 116; ESRO, Sessions Rolls 15/3; Barnes, p. 57; Emmison, *Elizabethan Life: disorder*, pp. 139–47; Willis Bund, ed., *Worcestershire Quarter Sessions Rolls*, II, cxxxvi.
76. Johnstone, p. 116; WSRO, Ep i/15/1, p. 81.
77. Johnstone, *passim*; WSRO, Ep i/15/1, *passim*; Marchant, *Church under the Law*, p. 219; Quintrell, p. 170.
78. PRO, Assizes 35/91–100; Aylmer, *The State's Servants*, p. 307.
79. ESRO, Sessions Rolls 53/23, 56/114; Redwood, p. 206.
80. WSRO, EP i/15/1, pp. 3, 14, 17; ESRO, QSOB 1655–60, fol. 47r.
81. *AO*, ii, 387–9; Gardiner, *Commonwealth and Protectorate*, ii, 83; ESRO, QSOB 1655–60, fols 60r, 65v.
82. WSRO, Ep i/15/1, p. 3; ESRO, Sessions Rolls 28/93; Johnstone.
83. ESRO, Sessions Rolls 21/146, 36/66.
84. PRO, SP 16/89/59, 91/13, 164/45.
85. ESRO, Sessions Rolls 55/82; WSRO, Ep i/15/1, pp. 79–81, Sessions Rolls 31/7; Thomas, *Religion and the Decline of Magic*, p. 529.
86. WSRO, Sessions Rolls 29/8, 42/50, 43/63, 46/5.
87. ESRO, Sessions Rolls 24/1, 55/82.
88. *Ibid*, 65/26; WSRO, Sessions Rolls 14/15/2.
89. ESRO, Sessions Rolls 12/20, 24, 38/138; WSRO, Sessions Rolls 31/7; Thomas, *Religion and the Decline of Magic*, p. 9.
90. C. L. Ewen, *Witch Hunting and Witch Trials* (London, 1929), pp. 99, 246–7; Thomas, *Religion and the Decline of Magic*, pp. 435–583; A. Macfarlane, *Witchcraft in Tudor and Stuart England* (London, 1970).
91. *CSPD 1656–7*, p. 424; M. A. Lower, 'Story of Witchcraft at Brightling', *SAC*, xviii (1866), 111–13.
92. *HMCR*, 139–40; Thomas, *Religion and the Decline of Magic*, pp. 609, 634; G. S. Butler, 'Appearance of Spirits in Sussex', *SAC*, xiv (1862), 25–32.
93. ESRO, Rye MS 47/138; *HMCR*, pp. 215–16; Thomas, *Religion and the Decline of Magic*, pp. 124, 445, 551.
94. ESRO, Sessions Rolls 18/59, 60.
95. WSRO, Sessions Rolls 78/51, 52; F. G. Emmison, *Elizabethan Life: Morals and the Church Courts* (Essex County Council, 1973), pp. 2–5.
96. WSRO, Visitation Articles 1586, 1600.
97. Thomas, *Religion and the Decline of Magic*, pp. 177–252; Macfarlane, *Witchcraft in Tudor and Stuart England*, pp. 115–34; above, p. 42.
98. WSRO, Sessions Rolls 2/99; Johnstone, pp. 82, 92.
99. WSRO, Sessions Rolls 7/8/50. I am grateful to Mr Keith Thomas for his comments on this case.
100. WSRO, Ep i/22/1; Ep ii/15/1; Johnstone, *passim*.
101. Barnes, p. 61; Quintrell, pp. 211–12.
102. P. Laslett, *The World We Have Lost* (Methuen, 1965), pp. 128–49.
103. WSRO, Sessions Rolls 18/40, 65/10/29, 83/72; ESRO, Sessions Rolls 22/133, 66/91, 93/94a, 125/71.
104. Redwood, pp. 42, 112, 190–1; Barnes, *Somerset Assize Orders*, p. 65; below, p. 223.

105. ESRO, Sessions Rolls 3, 8, outer membranes; Redwood, pp. 117, 174; Barnes, p. 61; Quintrell, pp. 208–11; Willcox, *Gloucestershire*, pp. 67–9; Marchant, *Church under the Law*, pp. 224–5.
106. ESRO, Sessions Rolls 17/11.
107. *Ibid*, QSOB 1650–5, fol. 11r; Redwood, p. 85.
108. ESRO, Sessions Rolls 94/62, 63; WSRO, Sessions Rolls 83/72.
109. ESRO, Sessions Rolls 66/92; Redwood, pp. 53–80.
110. WSRO, Ep ii/15/1, p. 73; Thirsk, ed., *Agrarian History of England*, iv, 409–12, 462–4; above, p. 88.
111. PRO, SP 16/383/12.
112. P. Clark, 'The migrant in Kentish towns 1580–1640', in Clark and Slack, eds, *Crisis and Order in English Towns*, pp. 117–63; see also, J. Cornwall, 'Evidence of population mobility in the seventeenth century', *BIHR*, xl (1967), pp. 143–52.
113. PRO, SP 16/393/85, 425/85; P. Spufford, 'Population movement in seventeenth-century England', *Local Population Studies*, iv (1970), pp. 41–50.
114. BM, Add MS 33147, fols 17r, 130v, 223v; ESRO, Sessions Rolls 22/114, 65/53, Rye MS 47/145, 146.
115. ESRO, Sessions Rolls 32, 33; Quintrell, p. 200; Willis Bund, ed., *Worcestershire Sessions Rolls*, II, lxiii.
116. Above, p. 139.
117. ESRO, Sessions Rolls 9/94, 95, 20/65, 74/76, 22/109, 66/79, 70/77.
118. *Ibid*, 66/79.
119. WSRO, Sessions Rolls 60/63; above, p. 147.
120. ESRO, Sessions Rolls 10/72, 33/2.
121. *Ibid*, 65/92, 93; PRO, Assizes 35/85/1.
122. ESRO, Sessions Rolls 44/3, 66/79; above, p. 144.
123. ESRO, QSOB 1655–60, fol. 36r; Sessions Rolls 11/7a/53, 54.
124. Willis Bund, ed., *Worcestershire Sessions Rolls*, ii, 485; WSRO, Sessions Rolls 29, 40, outer membranes, 56/42/57; below, p. 200.
125. PRO, SP 16/426/19.
126. Quintrell, pp. 204–5; Richmond, pp. 281–2.
127. ESRO, Sessions Rolls 9/118; WSRO, Sessions Rolls 43/81; Redwood, p. xix; Godfrey, ed., *Book of John Rowe*, pp. 152–5; Horsfield, *History of Lewes*, p. 217.
128. ESRO, QSOB 1650–5, fols 9r, 14v, 30r, 40v, 1655–60, fols 15v, 27r, 32v.
129. *Ibid*, QSOB 1650–5, fols 16v, 31, 46v; 1655–60, fols 8r, 44v, 75r.
130. ESRO, Sessions Rolls 10/72, 11/7a/54, 33/2.
131. ESRO, PAR 416/32/2/2, 3, QSOB 1655–60, fol. 75v; Richmond, pp. 323–6.
132. ESRO, Sessions Rolls 107/59; WSRO, Sessions Rolls 75/37.
133. WSRO, Sessions Rolls 39, outer membrane, 44/45; Ratcliff and Johnson, *Warwick County Records*, IV, xxxiii.
134. *SR*, iv, part 2, 899–900, v, 401–5; Barnes, *Somerset Assize Orders*, pp. 65–9.
135. ESRO, QSOB 1655–60, fol. 15v; Richmond, pp. 326–30; Cockburn, *History of English Assizes*, pp. 169–70.
136. WSRO, Sessions Rolls 57/58/3, 78; Redwood, pp. 106; ESRO, QSOB 1655–60, fols 41r, 45v.
137. WSRO, Sessions Rolls 27, outer membrane; ESRO, QSOB 1650–5, fol. 68r, 1655–60, fol. 1v.
138. WSRO, Sessions Rolls 53/54/44; Redwood, p. 70; ESRO, QSOB 1655–60, fol. 35v.
139. ESRO, QSOB 1650–5, fol. 18r; WSRO, Sessions Rolls 77/2, 78/12; Redwood, pp. 18, 47, 76, 112, 204.
140. P. Styles, 'The evolution of the law of settlement', *Birmingham Hist. J.*, ix (1963), 33–63; G. Taylor, *The Problems of Poverty 1660–1834* (Longmans, Seminar Studies, 1969), pp. 26–9; Ratcliff and Johnson, eds, *Warwick County Records*, IV, xxiv.
141. PRO, SP 16/151/32, 239/25.

142. *Ibid*, SP 16/138/68 iii, 161/47.
143. R. G. Marsden, 'The Vice-Admirals of the coast', *EHR*, xxii (1907), 468–77; E. Welch, *The Admiralty Court Book of Southampton* (Southampton Record Series, xiii, 1968).
144. PRO, SP 16/109/81, 82, 111/13, 133/18, 37.
145. WSRO, Ep i/55/1–51; 88/1.
146. *Ibid*, Ep i/55/1–9; *EHR*, xxii (1907), 751.
147. PRO, SP 16/365/9, 94–6, 368/56, 60, 369/81; *CSPD 1637*, pp. 321–2.
148. PRO, SP 16/364/3i, 7.
150. *Ibid*, SP 16/139/85.
151. *SAC*, xi (1859), 27.
152. BM, Add MS 33145, fol. 95v, 33144, fols 47v, 50v, 54v, 112v, 33145, fols 59r, 61r.
153. PRO. SP 16/139/85, 168/29, 170/21, 31, 34.
154. PRO, SP 16/170/31.
155. PRO, SP 16/239/25.
156. PRO, SP 16/291/52, 63, 73, 121, 293/41, 98, 99.
157. D. O. Shilton and R. Holworthy, eds, *High Court of Admiralty Examinations* 1637–38 (Anglo-American Records Foundation, 1932), pp. 101–2.
158. PRO, SP 16/151/32.

9. The exact militia

1. BM, Harleian MS 703, fol. 173v.
2. ESRO, DL Book, fol. 43v.
3. Boynton, pp. 239, 240–2.
4. For the obligations of lieutenants see G. Scott Thomson, *Lords Lieutenants in the Sixteenth Century* (London, 1923); Barnes, pp. 98–102; Boynton.
5. *CSPD 1623–5*, p. 300; J. C. Sainty, *Lieutenants of Counties 1585–1642* (*BIHR* Special Supplements 8, 1970), pp. 34–5.
6. Clarendon, *History of the Rebellion*, i, 76.
7. R. W. Kenny, *Elizabeth's Admiral: the political career of Charles Howard, Earl of Nottingham* (Johns Hopkins Press, 1970).
8. W. Rye, ed., *State Papers relating to Musters, Beacons, Shipmoney in Norfolk* (Norwich, 1907), pp. 166, 172; Boynton, pp. 271–2.
9. Sainty, *Lieutenants of Counties*, pp. 10–11.
10. For nomination see G. Scott Thomson, 'The origin and growth of the office of deputy lieutenant', *TRHS*, 4th series, v, 1922, 154.
11. Sainty, *Lieutenants of Counties*, p. 3.
12. BM, Harleian MS 703; for lieutenancy record keeping in Elizabeth's reign see Boynton, p. 49.
13. *CSPD 1581–90*, p. 518, quoted in Boynton, p. 177, where Covert and Sir Thomas Palmer are mistakenly referred to as deputy-lieutenants of Kent.
14. *CSPD 1623–5*, p. 300.
15. W. K. Jordan, *Men of Substance*, pp. 12–24.
16. PRO, Index 4211 (Crown Office Doquet Book 1615–29), fol. 186r; Barnes p. 102
17. BM, Harleian MS 703, fol. 44r.
18. *APC 1626*, pp. 221, 224; *CSPD 1627–8*, p. 461.
19. PRO, Index 4211, fol. 210r; below, p. 351.
20. *APC 1630–1*, no. 983; PRO, SP 16/407/66.
21. ESRO, DL Book, fol. 24v, C. Thomas-Stanford, 'The Sussex musters of 1618', *SAC*, lix (1918), 122–4.
22. BM, Harleian MS 703, fol. 157r.
23. *Ibid*, fol. 136r, Add MS 38139; *SAC*, lix (1918), 118–19; PRO, c 193/13/1.
24. For Somerset, see Barnes, p. 116.

25. Above, p. 17.
26. For evidence of 'a widespread disinclination to serve' see Boynton, pp. 283–7; Murphy, ed., *Hertford's Lieutenancy Papers*, 11.
27. BM, Harleian MS 703, fols 159, 164r.
28. *Ibid*, fol. 153r.
29. BM, Harleian MS 703, fol. 157v.
30. *Ibid*, fol. 164r.
31. ESRO, DL Book, fol. 15r.
32. ESRO, DL Book, fol. 73v.
33. *Ibid*, fols 26v–27, 29r; see also Barnes, p. 114.
34. *Visitation 1622*, pp. 12–13, 16–17.
35. *APC 1625–6*, pp. 29, 181; *APC 1626*, p. 13.
36. *APC 1626*, pp. 221, 224; *CSPD 1627–8*, p. 461.
37. ESRO, DL Book, fols 20, 29r, 36v.
38. *Ibid*, fol. 15r.
39. BM, Harleian MS 703, fols 163v, 164v.
40. *Ibid*, fol. 163r; Boynton, p. 240.
41. For slackness during 1603–12, see Murphy, ed., *Hertford's Lieutenancy Papers*, particularly pp. 13–14.
42. BM, Harleian MS 703, fol. 153r.
43. Boynton, pp. 212–15; *APC 1613–14*, pp. 552–5.
44. BM, Harleian MS 703, fol. 156v.
45. *APC 1615–16*, pp. 228–31.
46. *APC 1615–16*, pp. 516–19; *APC 1616—17*, pp. 305–7; *APC 1618–19*, pp. 118–20, 363–6.
47. BM, Harleian MS 703, fol. 158v.
48. *Ibid*, fol. 163.
49. *APC 1619–21*, p. 10; Sackville-West, ed., *Diary of Lady Anne Clifford*, p. 92.
50. BM, Harleian MS 703, fol. 172r.
51. *Ibid*, fol. 173v.
52. *SAC*, lix (1918), 121.
53. ESRO, DL Book, fol. 1v.
54. *Ibid*, fol. 5.
55. *SAC*, lix (1918), 124; WSRO, Add MS 2741.
56. ESRO, DL Book, fols 24v, 38r.
57. *Ibid*, fols 24v, 25v, 26r, 28r; *APC 1625–6*, pp. 484–5, 496–9; *APC 1626*, pp. 72–4; Barnes, p. 246; Gardiner, *History of England*, vi, 124.
58. *SAC*, lix (1918), 120–4.
59. *Ibid*, 118–19; ESRO, DL Book, fols 11, 24v, 28v.
60. ESRO, DL Book, fols 11, 48r.
61. *Ibid*, fol. 69r.
62. *Ibid*, fol. 38r.
63. *Ibid*, Dunn MS 52/5/1.
64. *SAC*, lix (1918), 118.
65. ESRO, DL Book, fol. 18r.
66. *Ibid*, Dunn MS 51/1.
67. *Ibid*, Dunn MS 52/5/3.
68. *Ibid*, Dunn MS 52/5/4.
69. PRO, SP 16/381/66.
70. BM, Harleian MS 703, fol. 162r; *APC 1623–5*, pp. 8–9; Boynton, pp. 238–40, 249.
71. ESRO, DL Book, fols 5r, 6r, 18r.
72. *Ibid*, Dunn MS 52/5/1, 3, 4; WSRO, Add MS 2741; *SAC*, lix (1918), 123.
73. PRO, SP 16/381/66.
74. BM, Add MS 33143, fol. 59v; 33145, fols 3r, 8r, 14v, 17v, 19r.

75. PRO, Prob 11/159/62.
76. *SAC*, lix (1918), 120–4.
77. ESRO, DL Book, fols 5r, 6r.
78. *Ibid*, Frewen MS 520, fol. 33r.
79. *Ibid*, DL Book, fols 12v, 13; *APC 1626*, p. 27; Boynton, pp. 246–8; Barnes, pp. 249–50.
80. ESRO, Dunn MS 51/1.
81. PRO, SP 16/233/11.
82. ESRO, DL Book, fols 64r, 69r.
83. *Ibid*, fol. 60v; Boynton, pp. 252–3; Barnes, pp. 252–3.
84. BM, Add MS 33145, fol. 18v.
85. ESRO, DL Book ,fol. 75r.
86. Bodleian Library, Rawlinson MS B431, fol. 16r.
87. Boynton, pp. 268–9. For a different view of the 1630s see Barnes, pp. 258–71.
88. ESRO, DL Book, fol. 18r.
89. *Ibid*, fol. 5v.
90. *PCR*, iv, 608–9.
91. *SAC*, lix (1918), 118.
92. BM, Add MS 33145, fol. 4v.
93. BM, Harleian MS 703, fol. 157.
94. *APC 1621–3*, p. 18; BM, Harleian MS 703, fols 170v, 172r.
95. ESRO, DL Book, fol. 18r; PRO, SP 16/381/66.
96. *APC 1617–18*, p. 58; *SAC*, lix (1918), 124.
97. ESRO, DL Book, fols 10, 11v; Barnes, p. 246.
98. Boynton, pp. 106, 180, 225; Murphy, *Hertford's Lieutenancy Papers*, pp. 11–13; for Hampshire, see Richmond, pp. 464–7 and Norfolk, Hassell Smith, pp. 279, 286–7.
99. *APC 1613–14*, pp. 144–5.
100. BM, Harleian MS 703, fol. 154r.
101. *Ibid*, fols 156v, 157.
102. *SAC*, lix (1918), 118–21.
103. PRO, SP 14/181/36.
104. ESRO, DL Book, fols 24v, 26r, 28.
105. *Ibid*, fol. 48r.
106. *APC 1627–8*, p. 140.
107. BM, Harleian MS 703, fol. 172r.
108. *SAC*, lix (1918), 124.
109. PRO, SP 14/112/37.
110. Boynton, pp. 209–10; Hassell Smith, pp. 290–3.
111. BM, Harleian MS 703, fol. 172r.
112. Boynton, pp. 276–80.
113. PRO, SP 16/112/37.
114. Rye, ed., *State Papers relating to Norfolk*, pp. 17–18.
115. Boynton, pp. 292–7; Barnes, pp. 261–71, 281–98; T. H. Breen, 'English origins and New World development', *Past and Present*, lvii (1972), 81.
116. Rye, ed., *State Papers relating to Norfolk*, pp. 141–3.
117. G. Scott Thomson, ed., *The Twysden Lieutenancy Papers* (Kent Archaeological Society Records, x, 1926), 17–20, 42–7.
118. ESRO, DL Book, fol. 11v; M. A. Lower *Survey of the Coast of Sussex* (1870).
119. PRO, SP 16/87/81.
120. *Ibid*, SP 16/112/49.
121. *Ibid*, SP 16/289/18.
122. *Ibid*, SP 16/136/13, 151/32, 161/46; *APC 1628–9*, no. 1118.
123. ESRO, Rye MS 47/107.
124. PRO, SP 16/87/81, 289/18.

125. *VCH Sussex*, ii, 156; *APC 1627*, p. 129; *Camden Society*, lii (1936), 28; ESRO, Rye MS 47/127.
126. BM, Harleian MS 703, fols 164, 165v; PRO, SP 16/289/18.
127. ESRO, DL Book, fol. 38r.
128. *APC 1627*, p. 437; *CSPD 1627–8*, pp. 68, 87; *VCH Sussex*, ii, 155; *HMCR*, p. 213.
129. M. A. Lower, 'Memorials of Seaford', *SAC*, vii (1854), 104.
130. PRO, SP 16/161/46.
131. BM, Harleian MS 703, fol. 164v.
132. *Ibid*, fols 142v, 164.
133. ESRO, DL Book, fol. 11v.
134. *Ibid*, fol. 38r.
135. *Ibid*, fol. 38; PRO, SP 16/89/9; Boynton, p. 260.
136. ESRO, DL Book, fol. 49r; PRO, SP 16/70/89.
137. *CSPD 1638–9*, p. 484; BM, Add MS 33508, fol. 67r; Salzman, ed., *Town Book of Lewes*, pp. 64–5.
138. BM, Add MS 33145, fol. 114v.
139. PRO, SP 16/407/66; *PCR*, v, 181–2.
140. ESRO, DL Book, fol. 9r; E. Thomson, ed., *The Chamberlain Letters* (Murray, 1965), p. 151; for beacons in the Elizabethan period, see Boynton, pp. 132–9, plate 10.
141. ESRO, DL Book, fol. 24v, 38.
142. *Ibid*, fol. 49r; Sessions Rolls 27/95.
143. *Ibid*. DL Book, fol. 51r.
144. WSRO, Session Rolls 22, outer membrane.
145. PRO, SP 16/89/32.
146. BM, Add MS 33145, fol. 21r.
147. For a brief account see J. R. Jones, *Britain and Europe in the Seventeenth Century* (E. Arnold, 1966), pp. 19–22.
148. *APC 1627*, p. 48v; *APC 1627–8*, pp. 60–1; ESRO, DL Book, fol. 50v.
149. PRO, SP 16/62/6.
150. ESRO, DL Book; BM, Harleian MS 703, fol. 175v.
151. *Ibid*. fol. 50v.
152. Bodleian Library, Rawlinson MS B 431, fol. 8r.
153. WSRO, Session Rolls 23/60.
154. ESRO, DL Book, fols 3r, 8r, 47r.
155. *Ibid*, fols 8r, 46r; *APC 1625–6*, pp. 42–5; *APC 1627*, pp. 216–17.
156. *APC 1623–5*, pp. 351–2; BM, Harleian MS 703, fol. 175v.
157. *APC 1623–5*, pp. 376–7; ESRO, DL Book, fol. 3r.
158. *PCR*, ix, 393–6, x, 472–3.
159. *CSPD 1640*, pp. 202, 539–40; *HMC Rutland MSS*, i, 520.
160. BM, Harleian MS 703, fol. 175v.
161. ESRO, DL Book, fol. 18.
162. *APC 1625–6*, p. 210.
163. *APC 1627*, p. 43.
164. ESRO, DL Book, fol. 49r; *APC 1629–30*, no. 178.
165. ESRO, DL Book, fol. 8r; PRO, SP 16/62/20, 21, 23.
166. ESRO, DL Book, fols 35, 37r; *APC 1626*, pp. 223–4.
167. ESRO, DL Book, fols 14, 20, 21r; *APC 1625–6*, pp. 326–7; PRO, SP 16/34/91.
168. ESRO, DL Book, fol. 36r.
169. *Ibid*, fols 39, 40r; PRO, SP 16/47/43.
170. Below, pp. 211–2.
171. ESRO, DL Book, fol. 40v, 41r.
172. *Ibid*, fols 43, 46v; *APC 1627*, rp. 130–1, 143, 183–6.
173. PRO, SP 16/60/35; 61/20, 68; 62/6, 27.
174. *Ibid*, SP 16/62/3, 6.

175. Appendix V(i).
176. PRO, SP 16/16/68, 562/56.
177. Barnes, p. 255.
178. ESRO, DL Book, fols 53, 57r, 59r; *APC 1627–8*, pp. 142–3, 176–7, 183; *CSPD 1627–8*, p. 444.
179. ESRO, DL Book, fol. 59v; PRO, SP 16/93/57.
180. ESRO, DL Book, fol. 61r; PRO, SP 16/108/81.
181. PRO, SP 16/86/62.
182. ESRO, DL Book fol. 54r.
183. *Ibid*, fol. 55r; *APC 1627–8*, pp. 173, 180.
184. ESRO, DL Book, fol. 54v.
185. *Ibid*, fols 66, 67r; *APC 1628–9*, no. 127; PRO, SP 16/111/19.
186. *APC 1628–9*, nos 488, 491, 549.
187. L. Boynton, 'Billeting: the example of the Isle of Wight', *EHR*, lxxiv (1959), 26–7, 36–7.
188. *APC 1628–9*, nos 488, 491, 549.
189. *Ibid*, no. 317; *APC 1627–8*, pp. 373, 490; ESRO, DL Book, fol. 63r; PRO, SP 16/111/19.
190. G. E. Aylmer, 'St Patrick's Day 1628 in Witham, Essex', *Past and Present*, lxi (1973), 139–48; Barnes, p. 258; Boynton, *EHR*, lxxiv, 37–40; *CSPD 1631–3*, p. 381; A. R. Bayley, *The Great Civil War in Dorset* (Taunton, 1910), p. 12.
191. *CSPD 1628–9*, p. 63; PRO, SP 16/233/11; *CJ*, i, 902.
192. *APC 1626*, pp. 221, 224; *CSPD 1627–8*, p. 461; ESRO, DL Book, fol. 456.
193. L. Boynton, 'Martial law and the Petition of Right', *EHR*, lxxix (1964), 255–84.
194. ESRO, Sessions Rolls 25/70; WSRO, Sessions Rolls 23/120.
195. L. Boynton, 'The Tudor Provost-Marshal', *EHR*, lxxvii (1962), 437–55; Hassell Smith, pp. 130–3.
196. *SAC*, xlviii (1905), 26; *CSPD 1611–18*, p. 460.
197. ESRO, DL Book, fol. 4; *APC 1623–5*, p. 396.
198. ESRO, DL Book, fol. 27v, 29r.
199. WSRO, Sessions Rolls, 29, 40, outer membranes; see above, p. 167.
200. BM, Add MS 33145, fols 3r, 18v.
201. Barnes, pp. 257–80, Boynton, pp. 269–97.
202. ESRO, DL Book, fol. 1v.

10. The taxation of the country

1. ESRO, Sessions Rolls 27/95.
2. *Ibid*, DL Book, fol. 40v.
3. R. S. Schofield, 'Parliamentary Lay Taxation 1485–1547' (PhD thesis, Cambridge University, 1963); F. C. Dietz, *English Public Finance 1558–1641* (London, 1932), pp. 380–97; H. Miller, 'Subsidy Assessment of the Peerage in the Sixteenth Century'. *BIHR*, xxviii (1955), pp. 15–34.
4. Quintrell, pp. 310–18.
5. Below, pp. 215–7.
6. PRO, E 179/191/383, 384; *SAC*, ix (1857), 105.
7. PRO, E 179/191/380.
8. Bodleian, Rawlinson MS B 431, fol. 7r; *CSPD Addenda 1625–49*, p. 345.
9. PRO, E 179/191/377a, 384, 385.
10. W. H. Blaauw, 'The defence of Sussex and the south coast from invasion', *SAC*, xi (1859), 170.
11. Mousley, pp. 370–81.
12. Thirsk and Cooper, eds, *Seventeenth-Century Economic Documents*, pp. 608–9.
13. PRO, SP 14/122/89; BM, Add MS 33145, fols 2r, 22r, 23r.

14. PRO, E 179/191/377a.
15. *Ibid*, E 179/191/377a, 382, 385, 406; SP 14/122/89.
16. *Ibid*, E 179/191/378, 381, 383–5, 406.
17. *Ibid*, E 179/191/377a, 384; Quintrell, pp. 319–23.
18. Appendices, V(i), (ii) and (viii).
19. M. D. Gordon, 'The collection of ship money in the reign of Charles I', *TRHS*, iv (1910), 149.
20. PRO, E 179/191/377a; SP 16/344/77.
21. Bodleian, Rawlinson MS 431 B, fol. 18v; PRO, SP 16/306/51; Barnes, pp. 211–12; Thirsk and Cooper, eds, *Seventeenth-Century Economic Documents*, pp. 618–21; BM, Add MS 33145, fols 84–114.
22. PRO, E 179/191/380; WSRO, CAP 1/4/10/13.
23. Barnes, pp. 203–37; Dietz, *English Public Finance*, pp. 396–7; *CSPD 1635*, p. 558.
24. *CSPD 1634–5*, p. 569.
25. *Ibid*, p. 602; *CSPD 1635*, p. 361; *CSPD 1635–6*, p. 178.
26. *CSPD 1635–6*, pp. 196, 267, 458; *CSPD 1636–7*, p. 78.
27. PRO, SP 16/329/37; *TRHS*, iv (1910), 160.
28. ESRO, Rye MS 47/126; *CSPD 1637*, p. 544.
29. TRHS iv (1910), 156–61; Appendix V(viii).
30. PRO, SP 16/344/10, 376/134; Manning, pp. 153–7, 243–4, 270.
31. PRO, SP 16/356/60; *CSPD 1637*, p. 123.
32. *CSPD 1637*, pp. 123, 254, 363, 375; Appendix V(viii).
33. Thirsk and Cooper, *Seventeenth-Century Economic Documents*, pp. 618–20.
34. PRO, E 179/191/380–5, SP 16/306/51, 351/89, 376/108.
35. Barnes, pp. 203–43; Zagorin, *The Court and the Country*, pp. 115–16; Ketton-Cremer, *Norfolk in the Civil War*, pp. 89–103; E. A. Andriette, *Devon and Exeter in the Civil War* (David & Charles, 1971), pp. 33–5; above, pp. 188–9.
36. *CSPD 1639–40*, p. 377; *PCR*, viii, 257–8.
37. PRO, SP 16/446/56, 469/70.
38. ESRO, Rye MS 47/126; PRO, SP 16/317/97, 351/89.
39. WSRO, Cap 1/4/10/13; PRO, SP 16/311/63, 317/97, 335/66, 351/89; *CSPD 1637*, p. 197; above, p. 235–6.
40. BM, Add MS 33145, fols 94r, 95r, 100v, 104r.
41. Thirsk and Cooper, *Seventeenth-Century Economic Documents*, pp. 620–3.
42. PRO, SP 16/306/51, 344/77, 376/108.
43. Notestein, ed., *Journal of Sir Simonds D'Ewes*, pp. 43–4; Coates, ed., *Journal of Sir Simonds d'Ewes*, pp. 120–1, 284–5, 288, 323; *SR*, v, 145–67; C. Russell, 'Parliament and the King's finances', in Russell, ed., *Origins of the English Civil War*, pp. 106–16.
44. PRO, E 179/191/360, 387–9, 258/12, SP 28/181; ESRO, Rye MS 82/3.
45. PRO, E 179/191/384, 388, 389, 258/12; BM, Add MS 33145, fol. 148r; Quintrell, pp. 324–6.
46. Russell, ed., *The Origins of the English Civil War*, pp. 98–106.
47. Dietz, *English Public Finance*, pp. 115, 149, 158, 186, 194, 227–8, 235–8; Gardiner, *History of England*, ii, 261–8, iii, 380, iv, 294–5, vi, 125, 143., vii, 166–7; Quintrell, pp. 326–37.
48. Gardiner, *History of England*, ii, 262.
49. ESRO, DL Book, fols 15v, 16r, 17r; Barnes, p. 162.
50. ESRO, DL Book, fols 31, 33; WSRO, Sessions Roll 16; PRO, Assizes 35/68/8.
51. ESRO, DL Book, fols 32, 34.
52. PRO, SP 16/33/109.
53. ESRO, DL Book, fol. 17r.
54. Gardiner, *History of England*, ii, 268.
55. PRO, E 178/5678, E 198/4/32, E 407/35.

56. *Ibid*, E 401/2586.
57. Above, pp. 195–6.
58. PRO, E 401/2586, E 407/35.
59. PRO, E 178/5678, E 407/35; Sir H. Ellis, 'Compositions for knighthood, temp. Charles I', *SAC*, xvi (1864), 45–51; Barnes, pp. 168–9; Cliffe, pp. 296–301.
60. PRO, E 401/2586; *APC 1625–6*, p. 371; BM, Add MS 33145, fol. 2v.
61. PRO, E 179/191/377a, E 407/35.
62. PRO, SP 14/127/79, 81, SP 16/89/5.
63. Rushworth, *Historical Collections*, iii, 911–14.
64. ESRO, DL Book, fol. 34v; above, p. 196.
65. PRO, E 178/5678.
66. A. Woodworth, *Purveyance for the Royal Household in the Reign of Queen Elizabeth* (Transactions of the American Philosophical Society, new series, xxv, Philadelphia, 1945); G. E. Aylmer, 'The last years of purveyance', *Economic History Review*, x (1957), 81–93.
67. BM, Harleian MS 703, fols 143v, 144v, 171r, 173r; ESRO, Sessions Rolls 16, 27, 28; W. Hudson, 'Extracts from the First Book of the Parish of Southover', *SAC*, xlviii (1905), 25; Thirsk and Cooper, eds, *Seventeenth-Century Economic Documents*, pp. 628–9; Hassell Smith, pp. 293–302.
68. BM, Add MS 33145, fols 4v, 7r, 11r, 15v, 21, 23r; ESRO, Frewen MS 520, fols 11v, 19r, 31v, 39v.
69. ESRO, PAR 516/37/3/1a, Frewen MS 520, fol. 4r.
70. *Ibid*, Sessions Rolls 26/73, 29/89.
71. BM, Harleian MS 703, fol. 135r.
72. WSRO, Sessions Rolls 14/15/2, 3; I am grateful to Mr Graham Bungard for information about Isack Bungar.
73. *SAC*, cvii (1969), 51–2.
74. BM, Harleian MS 703, fols 135, 145r, 155r, 159r.
75. ESRO, DL Book, fol. 65r.
76. *APC 1629–30*, no. 1088; *CSPD 1636–7*, pp. 27, 32; *CSPD 1637–8*, pp. 441, 480; *CSPD 1639*, pp. 305–6; BM, Add MS 33145, fols. 73r, 96v.
77. *CSPD 1638–9*, p. 353.
78. ESRO, QSOB 1650–5, fol. 6v.
79. WSRO, Sessions Rolls 43/3; ESRO, Frewen MS 520; BM, Add MS 33145; Add MS 33149, fols 243r, 253v, 259r; Redwood; *SAC*, xlviii (1905), 25.
80. Redwood, pp. 41, 63, 74, 80, 85.
81. ESRO, QSOB 1650–5, fol. 13r.
82. ESRO, Glynde, MS 97.
83. WSRO, Sessions Rolls 12; Redwood; ESRO, QSOB 1650–55, 1655–60.
84. WSRO, Sessions Rolls 25/2.
85. ESRO, Sessions Rolls 39, QSOB 1955–60, fols 21v, 45v; WSRO, Sessions Rolls 40; BM, Add MS 33145, fol. 133v; GMR, Losely MS 1084/31; Ratcliff and Johnson, eds, *Warwickshire County Records*, ii (1936), xxix; Richmond, p. 425; E. Melling, ed., *Kentish Sources*, iv: *The Poor* (Maidstone, 1964), p. 50; Aylmer, *The State's Servants*, p. 311.
86. ESRO, Sessions Rolls 42; Redwood, p. 87.
87. Redwood, p. 129.
88. ESRO, Sessions Rolls 41, 45, QSOB 1655–60, fols 40r, 43r, 61v; Redwood, pp. 8, 28, 91.
89. WSRO Sessions Rolls 82/2.
90. ESRO, Frewen MS 520; BM, Add MS 33145; above, p. 156.
91. Below, p. 226–7.
92. ESRO, Sessions Rolls 21/5, 7, 27/95.
93. *Ibid*, 38/2; QSOB 1650–55, fol. 32r; Redwood, p. 200.

94. ESRO, Sessions Rolls 28/3/7; Godfrey, ed., *Book of John Rowe*, pp. 126–31; *SAC*, lviii (1916), 6–20; G. D. Johnson, 'The Repair of Sussex Bridges', *SAC*, xci (1953), 164–72; Barnes, pp. 63–4.
95. ESRO, QSOB 1650–55, fol. 13r.
96. Redwood, p. 104.
97. *Ibid*, pp. 4, 83; *SAC*, xci (1953), 174.
98. ESRO, QSOB 1650–55, fols 44v, 58v, 1655–60, fols 10v, 40r, 45r; *SAC*, xci (1953), 165–8.
99. ESRO, Sessions Rolls 12/33; *VCH Wiltshire*, v, 97–8.
100. ESRO, QAF/1/E1, Sessions Rolls 36/1, 45/16.
101. WSRO, Sessions Rolls 79/6; ESRO, QSOB 1650–55, fol. 43r, 1655–60, fol. 31v.
102. ESRO, QAF/1/E1, Glynde MS 97.
103. *Ibid*, QSOB 1650–55, fols 21r, 25v, 56v, 60r, 63v, 67v, 1655–60, fols 4v, 10r, 17r, 19v.
104. *Ibid*, Sessions Rolls 22; Redwood, pp. 70, 114, 142.
105. ESRO, Sessions Rolls 41/1.
106. *Ibid*, QSOB 1650–55, fols 6v, 31, 38v.
107. ESRO, QSOB 1655–60, fol. 3v.

11. The administrative achievement

1. WSRO, Sessions Rolls 16/18/5.
2. PRO, SP 16/192/98.
3. ESRO, Sessions Rolls 1–128; QSOB 1650–55, 1655–60; WSRO, Sessions Rolls 1–98
4. Richmond, p. 65.
5. ESRO, Sessions Rolls 30; WSRO, Sessions Rolls 27–44; PRO, SP 16/239/4, 265/33, 328/74; Steele, *Tudor and Stuart Proclamations*, nos 1594, 1630, 1642; N. J. Williams, ed., *Tradesmen in Early Stuart Wiltshire* (Wiltshire Archaeological and Natural History Records Branch, xv, 1960 for 1959), xi–xv.
6. PRO, E 180/141.
7. Bodleian, Rawlinson MS B 431, fols 11v, 12r, 14v, 16r; WSRO, Sessions Rolls 29–31; PRO, SP 16/351/106.
8. ESRO, QSOB 1655–60, fol. 68r.
9. *Ibid*, QSOB 1650–55, fols 6v, 31, 36v, 38v.
10. WSRO, Sessions Rolls 22; ESRO, QSOB 1650–55, fol. 13r.
11. WSRO, Sessions Rolls 40; Redwood, p. 30.
12. Redwood, p. 129; ESRO, QSOB 1650–55, fols 32v, 48r; 1655–60, fols 5r, 27r.
13. Appendix III(i).
14. For this and the following paragraphs see Appendix II and the sources there cited.
15. Above, p. 135.
16. Quintrell, pp. 66–7; Richmond, pp. 106–7; Gleason, *Justices of the Peace*, p. 105.
17. Appendix III(ii).
18. Gleason, *Justices of the Peace*, pp. 106–12.
19. ESRO, Sessions Rolls 102/3, 121/1; WSRO, Sessions Rolls 71/5, 10, 11; 72/6, 7.
20. ESRO, Sessions Rolls 47; above, p. 93.
21. Barnes, pp. 70–1.
22. Above, pp. 145.
23. *TSP*, iv, 394; ESRO, Rye MS 47/154, 156; Redwood, pp. 62, 67, 73, 177, 202; above, p. 141.
24. PRO, Prob 11/268/407.
25. *Ibid*, C 193/13/1, SP 16/192/98, 266/1, 276/66, 328/77, 351/106, 364/120.
26. ESRO, Sessions Rolls 21, 23–29.
27. PRO, SP 16/364/121; ESRO, Sessions Rolls 56.
28. WSRO, Sessions Rolls 51, 52; ESRO, QSOB 1650–55.

29. PRO, C 193/13/1.
30. ESRO, Sessions Rolls 20–9.
31. *Ibid*, Sessions Rolls 82–127.
32. PRO, Prob 11/311/95; Manning, p. 242.
33. ESRO, Sessions Rolls 20–1, 25–7; PRO, SP 16/189/15.
34. PRO, SP 16/164/45.
35. *Ibid*, Prob 11/161/12.
36. ESRO, QSOB 1655–60, fol. 80r.
37. *TSP*, v, 287.
38. Redwood, pp. 93, 95, 151, 162, 176, 182, 193; WSRO, Sessions Rolls 26; ESRO, QSOB 1650–55, fol. 20r, 1655–60, fol. 34r.
39. Redwood, p. 31.
40. But see Barnes, pp. 76–7.
41. Redwood, pp. 22, 76, 131, 139, 152, 176–7; ESRO, QSOB 1650–55, fol. 59v, 1655–60, fols 56v, 64v.
42. WSRO, Sessions Rolls 85/48; ESRO, Sessions Rolls 106/27, 28.
43. Redwood, p. 80; Peyton, *Minutes of Proceedings in Quarter Sessions*, pp. xx–xxi; Barnes, pp. 140–1.
44. ESRO, QSOB 1650–55, fol. 55r.
45. *TSP*, iv, 240; *CSPD 1645–7*, p. 210; *CCC*, p. 673; CAM, p, 1203.
46. PRO, SP 28/181.
47. Cockburn, *History of English Assizes*, pp. 178–87.
48. Roots, 'Swordsmen and decimators—Cromwell's major-generals', in Parry, ed., *The English Civil War and After*, pp. 78–92.
49. PRO, Index 3421: 22 Nov. 1655.
50. Barnes, pp. 172–202.
51. Quintrell, pp. 61–3, 228–30; above, pp. 137–8, 153–4, 157–8.
52. Barnes, p. 181.
53. PRO, SP 16/189/6, 192/99.
54. PRO, SP 16/250/43, 265/33, 314/103, 328/82, 348/43, 364/8, 121, 383/25, 393/85.
55. *Ibid*, SP 16/189–426; Cockburn, *History of English Assizes*, p. 186.
56. PRO, SP 16/191/45, 63, 201/34, 202/41, 203/34.
57. *Ibid*, SP 16/202/41, 203/34, 220/41, 250/42, 262/15.
58. *Ibid*, SP 16/220/51.
59. *Ibid*, SP 16/243/19, 329/65.
60. Aylmer, *The State's Servants*, pp. 308–11; above, pr. 166–70.
61. Redwood, p. 22.
62. ESRO, Sessions Rolls 9/102; Morrill, pp. 227–8.
63. *Ibid*, Sessions Rolls 86/52.
64. *Ibid*, Sessions Rolls 16/18/5; ERSO, QSOB 1650–55, fol. 34r.
65. ESRO, Sessions Rolls 21/109, 56/16, 18.
66. WSRO, Sessions Rolls 82/5, 98/61.
67. *Ibid*, Sessions Rolls 81/86; ESRO, Sessions Rolls 29/71.
68. Redwood, p. 43.
69. ESRO, Sessions Rolls 39/2.

12. Opposition and conflict 1603–1642

1. M. A. Tierney, *The History of Arundel* (London, 1834), ii, 433.
2. PRO, SP 16/442/137.
3. *Ibid*, SP 16/450/39.
4. J. E. Neale, *The Elizabethan House of Commons* (Cape, 1963), pp. 185–8; Swales, *Parliamentary Representation of Sussex*, pp. 46–93, 113–19.

5. Swales, *Parliamentary Representation of Sussex*, pp. 93–118; R. E. Ruigh, *The Parliament of 1624: politics and foreign policy* (Harvard University Press, 1971), p. 101.
6. Neale, *The Elizabethan House of Commons*, pp. 64, 204–12, 250–60.
7. Ruigh, *Parliament of 1624*, pp. 133–4.
8. A. H. Stenning, 'Members of Parliament for Sussex', *SAC*, xxxiii (1883), 69–89.
9. D. H. Willson, ed., *The Parliamentary Diary of Robert Bowyer* (Minneapolis University Press, 1931), pp. 314, 366; E. R. Foster, ed., *Proceedings in Parliament 1610* (Yale University Press, 1966).
10. R. Zaller, *The Parliament of 1621: a study in constitutional conflict* (University of California Press, 1971), pp. 150–6; W. Notestein, F. H. Relf, H. Simpson, eds, *Commons Debates 1621* (New Haven, 1935), ii, 208–9, 474, iii, 341, iv, 32, vi, 50, 229, vii, 620–1; above, pp. 147–52.
11. PRO, Index 4211, 27 October 1626; Willson, ed., *The Diary of Robert Bowyer*, pp. 195–6, 207, 340, 342–4.
12. T. L. Moir, *The Addled Parliament* (Oxford University Press, 1958), pp. 84, 124, 129, 130; D. H. Willson, *The Privy Councillors in the House of Commons* (Minneapolis University Press, 1940), pp. 118, 155, 213; S. R. Gardiner, *History of England from the Accession of James I to the Outbreak of the Civil War* (London, 1883–84), iv, 41, 69, 233, 341, 400; H. Hulme, *Sir John Eliot* (Allen & Unwin, 1957), pp. 227, 229, 252; S. R. Gardiner, ed., *Debates in the House of Commons 1625* (Camden Society, vi, 1873), pp. 121, 146.
13. Notestein, ed., *Commons Debates*, ii, 120–1, iii, 434–5, vii, 321, 329; P. Zagorin, *The Court and the Country* (Routledge, 1969), pp. 86–7.
14. *CSPD 1625–6*, pp. 354–5; Gardiner, *History of England*, vi, 118–21.
15. Notestein, ed., *Common Debates 1621*, ii, 120, iii, 433, iv, 43; *CJ*, i, 523.
16. BM, Harleian MS 7614.
17. P. Clark and P. Slack, eds, *Crisis and Order in English Towns* (Routledge, 1972), pp. pp. 19–23; Everitt, *Change in the Provinces*, pp. 45–6.
18. Manning, p. 11; Godfrey, ed., *The Book of John Rowe*, p. 170; L. F. Salzman, ed., *The Town Book of Lewes* (SRS, xlviii, 1946), 131; ESRO, Seaford MS 6, p. 290; *HMC 13th Report*, Appendix ii(ii), 358–9.
19. PRO, E 179/191/377a; Neale, *The Elizabethan House of Commons*, pp. 250–1; Vidler, *History of Rye*, p. 73.
20. *HMCR*, pp. 44–5.
21. Tierney, *The History of Arundel*, ii, 432–4.
22. Bodleian, Tanner MS 148, fols 12–15; F. Steer, *Chichester City Charters* (Chichester Papers, iii, 1956), p. 19; above, p. 141.
23 *CSPD 1635–6*, p. 539; P. Slack, 'Poverty and politics in Salisbury 1597–1666', in Clark and Slack, eds, *Crisis and Order in English Towns*, pp. 187–8; A. Dyer, *The City of Worcester in the Sixteenth Century* (Leicester University Press, 1973), 195, 233–5; J. K. G. Taylor, 'The civil government of Gloucester 1640–46', *Transactions of the Bristol and Gloucestershire Archaeological Society*, lxvii (1946–48), pp. 60–1.
24. WSRO, Sessions Rolls 14–21.
25. Bodleian, Tanner MS 148, fols 12–15.
26. *CSPD 1635*, p. xliii; Laud, *Works*, v, part 2, 486.
27. PRO, SP 16/311/73; WSRO, CAP 1/4/10/13.
28. PRO, SP 16/311/73, 325/60–2, 74; Bodleian, Tanner MS 148, fols 12–15; *CSPD 1636–7*, pp. 215–16.
29. PRO, SP 16/325/74; Bodleian, Tanner MS 148, fols 14–15.
30. ESRO, Rye MS 47/116; above, p. 141.
31. *Ibid*, Rye MS 47/108; *HMCR*, p. 173; *SAC*, xxxiii (1883), 85; *SAC*, cvii (1969), 23–35.
32. ESRO, Rye MS 47/117, 118.
33. *Ibid*, Rye MS 47/113; *HMCR*, pp. 179–80.

34. Above, pp. 71, 117–9.
35. PRO, SP 16/35/74.
36. *Ibid*, SP 16/233/11.
37. PRO, SP 16/35/72, 73, 76, 228/26, 28, 231/69, 232/10, 233/34; *CSPD 1633–4*, pp. 69, 110; *APC 1626*, pp. 254, 264.
38. PRO, SP 16/34/74, 75.
39. PRO, St. Ch 9/1/20, 220/30.
40. ESRO, Rye MS 47/111, 113; WSRO, Ep ii/9/23, fol. 27r.
41. ESRO, Rye MS 47/133.
42. Above, pp. 43–4.
43. *CSPD 1631–3*, p. 68; *CSPD 1635–6*, p. 57; Keeler, p. 280.
44. G. E. Aylmer, *The King's Servants* (Routledge, 1961), p. 418; *Camden Society*, third series, xiii (1907), p. 137.
45. Zagorin, *Thd Court and the Country*; above, p. 36.
46. Aylmer, *The King's Servants*, p. 127; *CSPD 1627–8*, p. 517; R. Ashton, *The Crown and the Money Market* (Oxford University Press, 1960), pp. 167–8, 174–5; Stone, pp. 428, 475.
47. Keeler, p. 89; Aylmer, *The King's Servants*, p. 284; *CSPD 1631–3*, p. 378; *CSPD 1633*, pp. 17, 140; *CSPD 1639–40*, pp. 331, 537.
48. *CSPD 1639–40*, p. 607.
49. *CSPD 1635–6*, p. 4; Keeler, pp. 173–4; *CCC*, 93; PRO, Prob 11/192/11.
50. Zagorin, *The Court and the Country*, pp. 33–9, 74–118.
51. For a full discussion see chapters 9 and 10.
52. See the maps on pp. 46, 50.
53. PRO, Index 4211; above, pp. 130–1.
54. PRO, SP 14/127/79, 81, SP 16/89/5; Rushworth, *Historical Collections*, iii, 914; Keeler, pp. 301–2, 323, 349; below, pp. 211–5.
55. PRO, SP 16/442/137.
56. *CSPD 1640*, p. 520.
57. Laud, *Works*, v, part ii, 330, 369–70; above, p. 73.
58. ESRO, Sessions Rolls 44.
59. PRO, SP 16/442/137.
60. WSRO, Sessions Rolls 16, 31; ESRO, Sessions Rolls 35, 42, 46.
61. Above, pp. 45, 130.
62. ESRO, Rye MS 47/131/39/2; J. K. Gruenfelder, 'The election to the Short Parliament, 1640', in H. S. Reinmuth, ed., *Early Stuart Studies* (Minneapolis University Press, 1970), pp. 180–230.
63. BM, Add MS 33145, fol. 126r; PRO, SP 16/442/137.
64. PRO, SP 16/447/43.
65. *SAC*, xxxiii (1883), 85–6; *CJ*, ii, 3, 10; *HMC 4th Report*, appendix, House of Lords MSS, 25.
66. PRO, SP 16/442/137; Keeler, p. 67.
67. J. Wentworth-Fitzwilliam, *Parham in Sussex* (London, 1948), pp. 50–6; *APC 1629–30*, no. 1198.
68. *MHC 4th Report*, appendix, House of Lords MSS, 25; *CJ*, ii, 18; Reinmuth, ed., *Early Stuart Studies*, p. 206.
69. J. H. Plumb, 'The growth of the electorate in England from 1600 to 1715', *Past and Present*, lv (1969), 94–107.
70. *CJ*, ii, 10; Keeler, pp. 191–2; *SAC*, xx (1868), 155; Reinmuth, ed., *Early Stuart Studies*, pp. 202, 214.
71. J. K. Gruenfelder, 'The spring parliamentary election at Hastings, 1640', *SAC*, cv (1967), 49–55; Reinmuth, ed., *Early Stuart Studies*, pp. 206, 222, 230.
72. *CSPD 1639–40*, pp. 565, 607.
73. PRO, SP 16/450/8, 39, 52.

74. *Ibid*, SP 16/450/6.
75. *Past and Present*, lv (1969), 101–3.
76. PRO, SP 16/450/52; *CSPD 1639–40*, p. 607.
77. PRO, SP 16/450/39i.
78. ESRO, Rye MS 47/131/39/2, 5.
79. *Ibid*, Rye MS 47/131/39/3, 4, 6, 7, 8, 10, 13; Reinmuth, ed., *Early Stuart Studies*, pp. 199–200.
80. ESRO, Rye MS 47/13/39/1.
81. *CJ*, ii, 7, 10.
82. Rushworth, *Historical Collections*, iii, 1182–3; above, p. 207.
83. *CSPD 1640*, p. 520.
84. *CSPD 1637–8*, p. 595; *CSPD 1640*, pp. 575, 583.
85. Keeler, pp. 6–11; BM, Add MS 33145, fol. 132v.
86. PRO, C 219/43, part ii/213.
87. *SAC*, xxxiii (1883), 87–9; Keeler, pp. 66–8, 76–8; W. K. Jordan, *Men of Substance* (University of Chicago Press, 1942), pp. 9–37, 140–78.
88. PRO, C 219/47, part ii/208; *CJ*, ii, 30, 58; Keeler, p. 67.
89. PRO, SP 16/469/82, 86, 107; R. N. Kershaw, 'The elections for the Long Parliament 1640', *EHR*, xxxviii (1923), 498–9; Keeler, pp. 76–7.
90. ESRO, Rye MS 47/133; Keeler, p. 77.
91. *CJ*, ii, 51, 63, 86, 89; Keeler, pp. 10, 67.
92. *CJ*, ii, 302, 313, 333, 337; Coates, ed., *The Journal of Sir Simonds D'Ewes*, pp. 126, 236, 260.
93. ESRO, Rye 47/133; Zagorin, *The Court and the Country*, pp. 203–6.
94. ESRO, Dunn MS 51/54.
95. *Ibid*, Rye MS 47/133.
96. BM, Add MS 33145, fols 134r–140r; above, p. 43.
97. *CJ*, ii, 24, 54, 73, 105, 107, 113, 115, 130, 205; Keeler, pp. 113, 191–2, 209, 280, 296, 302, 323–4, 349.
98. *CJ*, ii, 21; Keeler, pp. 83, 170, 252, 271, 273, 280, 322.
99. *CJ*, ii, 288; Coates, ed., *The Journal of Sir Simonds D'Ewes*, pp. 1–19, 44.
100. PRO, Index 4211, 16 August 1641; ESRO, Sessions Rolls 54.
101. Gardiner, *History of England*, ix, 122, 137, 313, x, 2; *CSPD 1641–3*, pp. 42, 46.
102. BM, Add MS 33145, fol. 142v; PRO, SP 16/483/88.
103. BM, Add MS 33058, fol. 69r; *AO*, i, 2.
104. *CJ*, ii, 438; *LJ*, iv, 591.
105. Above, pp. 93, 104.
106. BM, E 134 (35): *Two Petitions of Sussex* (1642); A. J. Fletcher, 'The Derbyshire petitions and the outbreak of the civil war', *Derbyshire Archaeological Journal*, forthcoming.

13. The county at war 1642–1648

1. Bodleian, Dep C MS 153/102.
2. *Ibid*, Dep C MS 154/31.
3. ESRO, Frewen MS 4223, no. 56.
4. C. V. Wedgwood, *The King's War* (Collins, 1958), pp. 93–101; Zagorin, *The Court and the Country*, pp. 295–351; I. A. Roots, *The Great Rebellion* (Batsford, 1966), pp. 56–74.
5. BM, Add MS 33058, fol. 69r; *CJ*, ii, 593, 606, 616.
6. Above, pp. 209–10.
7. *CJ*, ii, 651, 742, 746.
8. Salzman, ed., *The Town Book of Lewes*, 66.
9. Redwood, p. 9.

10. PRO, E 179/191/390.
11. *CJ*, ii, 631.
12. *SAC*, v (1852), 73–7.
13. ESRO, Sessions Rolls 57/60, 62, 63, 65; Redwood, pp. xxii, 16.
14. Garraway Rice, ed., *West Sussex Protestation Returns.*
15. PRO, E 179/191/390; *CJ*, ii, 754.
16. Bodleian, Dep C MS 153/102; see the epigraph to this chapter.
17. PRO, Index 4212, 20 July 1642.
18. R. Steele, *Tudor and Stuart Proclamations* (Clarendon Press, 1960), nos 2186, 2194.
19. *CJ*, ii, 681, 772; Losely House, Losely MS, bound letters, v, 131.
20. Gardiner, *History of England*, x, 216; G. N. Godwin, *The Civil War in Hampshire* (Southampton and London, 1904), pp. 9–23.
21. *CJ*, ii, 754; WSRO, CAP 1/4/10/13.
22. Above, p. 54.
23. Keeler, pp. 83, 113, 271, 280–1.
24. *CJ*, ii, 715; BM, E 112 (15): *Some Special and Considerable Passages.*
25. *CJ*, ii, 717; BM E 114 (3): *Exceeding Good Newes from Oxfordshire*; Thomas-Stanford, pp. 39–40.
26. *CJ*, ii, 744, 745, 759, 806.
27. *Ibid*, 754, 810, 834, 835; PRO, SP 23/177/9, 179/693, 223/871.
28. BM, 669 f5 (97): *A Proclamation ... to the Inhabitants ... of Sussex*; Clarendon, *History of the Rebellion* (Oxford, 1888), ii, 446.
29. BM, E 128 (28): *Special Passages*, 22–29 Nov. 1642, p. 132; Wedgwood, *The King's War*, pp. 133–5.
30. PRO, SP 19, SP 23; *TSP*, iv, 258.
31. BM, E 84(4): *The Kingdomes Weekly Intelligencer*, 27 Dec 1642–3 Jan 1643, p. 7.
32. Bodleian, Dep C MS 153/102.
33. HLRO, Main Paper Series, Draft order for opposing Mr Ford, 18 Nov. 1642.
34. Bodleian, Dep C MS 153/102; *HMCP*, i, 72–3.
35. BM, E 242 (26): *A Perfect Diurnal*, 24 Nov. 1642; Thomas-Stanford, pp. 42–7.
36. PRO, SP 19/117/12, 13, 14, 139/7, SP 23/176/205; *CJ*, ii, 834.
37. PRO, SP 23/229/17.
38. Bodleian, Dep C MS 153/102; PRO, SP 19/139/7, SP 23/212/287.
39. *CJ*, ii, 858; BM, E 242 (28), (37), E 244 (9): *England's Memorable Accidents*, 26 Nov. 1642, 2 Dec. 1642, 5 Dec. 1642.
40. *CJ*, ii, 874.
41. BM, E 242 (28), E 244 (16): *England's Memorable Accidents*, 26 Nov. 1642, 15 Dec. 1642; E 242 (35): *A Perfect Diurnal*, 3 Dec. 1642; Thomas-Stanford, pp. 48–9; Godwin, *Civil War in Hampshire*, p. 55.
42. HLRO, Main Paper Series, Petition of Thomas Alse and John Palmer, 16 May 1643.
43. BM, E 244 (28): *A Continuation of Certain Special and Remarkable Passages*, 26–30 Dec. 1642, p. 6.
44. *Ibid*, E 84 (22): *A True Relation ... of the taking of Chichester*; E 83 (36): *Brave Newes of the taking ... of Chichester*; *SAC*, v (1852), 41–5; Thomas-Stanford, pp. 50–63; Godwin, *Civil War in Hampshire*, pp. 55–9; Hilary Turner, *Town Defences in England and Wales* (J. Baker, 1971), pp. 154–5.
45. Clarendon, *History of the Rebellion*, ii, 446.
46. W. D. Peckham, 'Chichester in the Civil War', *SNQ*, xiii (1950), 11–14.
47. BM, 169 f5 (97): *A Proclamation ... to the Inhabitants ... of Sussex.*
48. *DNB*; Keeler, p. 280; *Visitation 1634*, p. 48; R. F. Dell, ed., *The Glynde Place Archives* (East Sussex County Council, 1964), pp. xv–xviii.
49. PRO, Prob 11/162/111; above, p. 63.
50. Thomas-Stanford, p. 73.

51. *HMCP*, i, 178; BM, E 54 (4): *The Sea Gull or the New Apparition* (1644), E 3 (21): *The Sussex Picture* (1644); Thomas-Stanford, pp. 153–6.
52. Fletcher, 'Petitioning and the outbreak of the Civil War in Derbyshire', *Derbyshire Archaeological Journal*, forthcoming; Morrill, pp. 23–5, 139–79; Underdown, *Somerset in the Civil War*, pp. 121–74.
53. ESRO, Frewen MS 520, fol. 48v.
54. ESRO, Rye MS 47; above, pp. 105–6.
55. *CJ*, iii, 43.
56. *Ibid*, ii, 940–1, 978, 990, 992; Everitt, p. 188.
57. *CJ*, iii, 171; Bodleian, Dep C MS 154/21.
58. Everitt, p. 148.
59. ESRO, Frewen MS 4223, no. 54; *SAC*, ix (1856), 49; Wedgwood, *The King's War*, pp. 207–9; Gardiner, *History of the Great Civil War*, i, 182–3.
60. *SAC*, v (1852), 73–7.
61. Thomas-Stanford, p. 73; *SAC*, v (1852), 78–9; Matthews, *Walker Revised*, pp. 354, 358.
62. Bodleian, Dep C MS 154/9, 163/263; *DNB*.
63. Below, pp. 329–31, 337–8.
64. Bodleian, Dep C MS 154/83.
65. BM, Add MS 33084, fol. 38r.
66. ESRO, Frewen MS, fols 48v–49r.
67. Bodleian, Dep C MS 163/263; ESRO, Sessions Rolls 62/3.
68. BM, 669 f5 (139): *His Majesty's Proclamation forbidding all his Loving Subjects . . . to Raise Forces . . .*; Bodleian, Dep C MS 154/21, 164/60; Everitt, pp. 186–200.
69. Bodleian, Dep C MS 154/31; PRO, SP 16/498/41; Thomas-Stanford, p. 69; see also the epigraph to this chapter.
70. Clarendon, *History of the Rebellion*, iii, 329–32; BM, E 79 (18): *Mercurius Aulicus*, 10–16 Dec. 1643, pp. 707–8; Thomas-Stanford, pp. 69–73.
71. Gardiner, *History of the Great Civil War*, i, 297–8.
72. Bodleian, Dep C MS 169/36.
73. Thomas-Stanford, p. 74; F. T. R. Edgar, *Sir Ralph Hopton: King's man in the West 1642–52* (Oxford University Press, 1968), pp. 150–1.
74. ESRO, Frewen MS 520, fol. 49r.
75. Redwood, p. 133.
76. ESRO, Frewen MS 4223, no. 56; D. G. C. Elwes, *Castles, Mansions and Manors of Western Sussex* (London, 1876), p. 48; Thomas-Stanford, pp. 73–81; *SAC*, v (1852), 57–60; Bodleian, Dep C MS 169/36; BM, E 252 (11): *A Perfect Diurnal*, 21, 11–18 Dec. 1643.
77. *CJ*, iii, 292; *AO*, i, 333–9; BM, E 75 (2): *Declaration . . . that the towne and county of Southampton, Sussex, Surrey and Kent shall associate themselves . . .*; Everitt, p. 201.
78. BM, E 79 (29): *The True Informer*, 15, 23–30 Dec. 1643, p. 115.
79. ESRO, Frewen MS 4223, no. 56.
80. Clarendon, *History of the Rebellion*, iii, 334.
81. BM, E 79 (9): *The True Informer*, 14, 16–23 Dec. 1643, pp. 106–8; E 81 (10): *A Full Relation of the Taking of Arundel* (1644); E 81 (12): *An Exact and True Relation of the Taking of Arundel* (1644); E 81 (14): *The Weekly Account*, 19, 10 Jan. 1644; E 252 (12): *A Perfect Diurnal*, 22, 18–25 Dec. 1643; Thomas-Stanford, pp. 82–98; Godwin, *Civil War in Hampshire*, pp. 140–52; Edgar, *Sir Ralph Hopton*, pp. 153–4, *SAC*, xxviii (1878), 97–113.
82. *CJ*, iii, 681; *CSPD 1644–5*, pp. 85, 100; B. Whitelocke, *Memorials* (1682), p. 109.
83. *CSPD 1644–5*, pp. 237–42; Clarendon, *History of the Rebellion*, iv, 8–10; Wedgwood, *The King's War*, p. 381.
84. *CSPD 1645–7*, p. 355.

85. BM, E 81 (12): *An Exact and True Relation of the Taking of Arundel*, p. 2; ESRO, Frewen MS 4223, no. 56.
86. PRO, SP 28/135, fols 135–8.
87. ESRO, Frewen MS 4223, no. 56.
88. PRO, SP 28/135, fols 78r, 80r, 82r, 109r, 110r, 113r, 267r; Redwood; ESRO, Sessions Rolls 85/1, 2.
89. Essex Ro, D/DL E 22; BM, Add MS 33145; ESRO, Frewen MS 520.
90. ESRO, Rye MS 47/135, 137.
91. Tierney, *History of Arundel*, pp. 714–15.
92. PRO, SP 23/223/871; above, pp. 158–9.
93. T. W. Webb, ed., *Military Memoir of Colonel John Birch* (Camden Society, new series, vii, 1873), 217.
94. BM, Add MS 33058, fol. 71; Bodleian, Dep C MS 169/36. For the structure of the County Committee, see below, pp. 325–7.
95. D. Underdown, *Pride's Purge* (Oxford University Press, 1971), pp. 24–44; C. Holmes, 'Colonel King and Lincolnshire politics', *Historical Journal*, xvi (1973), 471–84; Wedgwood, *The King's War*, pp. 403–4, 436–7; Gardiner, *History of the Great Civil War*, ii, 264–5, 273, 305–6.
96. BM, E 302 (18): *A True Relation of the Rising of the Clubmen in Sussex*, E 303 (15): *The True Informer*, 21–27 Sept. 1643, p. 178; *CCC*, pp. 921, 983.
97. BM, E 302 (33): *The Kingdome's Weekly Intelligencer*, 16–23 Sept. 1645; Bodleian, Tanner, MS 60, fols 251r, 254r.
98. Underdown, *Pride's Purge*, pp. 76–105, 281, 355–6; W. G. Hoskins, 'Harvest fluctuations and English economic history', *Agricultural History Review*, xvi (1968), 29.
99. Bodleian, Dep C MS 158/31.
100. BM, E 452 (28): *The Moderate Intelligencer*, 173, 6–13 July 1648; *CSPD 1648–9*, pp. 145–6, 153, 169.
101. BM, 669, f12 (60): *A Letter from Horsham.*
102. Bodleian, Dep C MS 163/290; BM, E 451 (13): *The Resolution of the Prince of Wales concerning his coming into England* (1648).
103. Bodleian, Dep C MS 158/31; below, pp. 291–2.
104. BM, E 451 (18): *The Moderate*, 29 June–6 July 1848, p. 1422.
105. D. H. Pennington and I. A. Roots, *The Committee at Stafford* (Manchester University Press, 1957), pp. xxvi–lxxiv; Morrill, pp. 190–203; Underdown, *Somerset in the Civil War*, pp. 133–7.
106. Bodleian, Tanner MS 60, fol. 254v; *CSPD 1644–45*, p. 323.
107. BM, E 93 (4): *Certain Informations*, 6–13 March 1644, p. 63, E 99 (15): *Certain Informations*, 17–24 April 1644, p. 110.
108. Bodleian, Dep C MS 155/120, 158/31.
109. *Ibid*, Tanner MS 60 fols 252–4; BM, E 44 (7): *New Propositions Agreed upon by the Lords and Commons*, p. 3.
110. Firth, *Cromwell's Army*, pp. 216–19; Pennington and Roots, eds, *The Committee at Stafford*, p. xliii.
111. Bodleian, Tanner MS 60, fol. 254r.
112. *CJ*, iii, 362, 368, 393, 400, 401, 403; BM, E 81 (23): *The Parliament Scout*, 29, 5–12 Jan. 1644.
113. J. S. Morrill, 'Mutiny and discontent in English provincial armies', *Past and Present*, lxi (1972), 64.
114. Bodleian, Tanner MS 60, fol. 254r; *CJ*, iii, 403, 407, iv, 28; Whitelocke, *Memorials*, p. 120; Thomas-Stanford, p. 166.
115. Bodleian, Tanner MS 60, fols 252r, 253r.
116. BM, E 302 (9): *The True Informer*, 14–20 Sept. 1645, p. 175; Bodleian, Dep C MS 155/120.
117. Underdown, *Pride's Purge*, pp. 35–44; *Past and Present*, lvi (1972), 49–74.

118. Bodleian, Dep C MS 156/255.
119. *CJ*, v, 103; *CSPD 1645–7*, p. 355; *Past and Present*, lvi (1972), 72.
120. BM, E 447 (7): *New Propositions Agreed upon by the Lords and Commons*, p. 3.
121. Stone, *Social Change and Revolution*, pp. xi–xxvi; Hexter, *Reappraisals in History*, pp. 117–62.
122. B. Manning, 'Neutrals and Neutralism in the English Civil War 1642–46 (DPhil thesis, Oxford, 1957); A. M. Everitt, *The Local Community and the Great Rebellion* (Historical Association, 1969); Cliffe, pp. 336–62; Morrill, pp. 69–74.
123. *CJ*, ii, 537, 564, 618; Coates, ed., *Journal of Sir Simonds D'Ewes*, p. 295.
124. PRO, SP 16/220/45, 236/69, 242/67, 314/24, 441/114; Keeler, pp. 89, 252.
125. *CJ*, ii, 750, 834, 860; *CCC*, pp. 1237, 1493; Thomas-Stanford, pp. 39–40, 254–7.
126. Sackville West, ed., *Diary of Lady Anne Clifford*, p. 106; Coates, ed., *Journal of Sir Simonds D'Ewes*, p. 52; *CJ*, iii, 142.
127. PRO, SP 23/113/964; *CCC*, pp. 838, 921, 1084, 1299.
128. *CCC*, pp. 849–50; *CCAM*, p. 508; Wentworth-Fitzwilliam, *Parham in Sussex*, pp. 59–61; *HMCP*, i, 72; Thomas-Stanford, pp. 124–5.
129. Bodleian, Dep C MS 154/83; PRO, SP 28/246.
130. *CCC*, p. 1215.
131. Keeler, p. 248; *HMCP*, i, 72.
132. *CCC*, pp. 907, 940, 1637, 1981, 2051; PRO, SP 23/113/958, 228/131.
133. *CCC*, pp. 839, 982, 2099; PRO, SP 23/210/593; above, pp. 54–5.
134. *CJ*, ii, 831, 834.
135. Matthews, *Walker Revised*, pp. 353–62; *SAC*, xi (1858), 24–29, xxx (1880), 122–3, xxxi (1881), 200, xxxvi (1888), 156.
136. Bodleian, Dep C MS 169/36.
137. *CCC*, pp. 1242, 2211; above, p. 262.
138. Appendix II(ii)–(viii).
139. PRO, SP 16/89/5, Prob 11/204/99, 299/110; Manning, p. 209; *Visitation 1662*, pp. 28–9, 79–80; below, p. 326.
140. PRO, Prob 11/162/111, 227/111, 150, 316/16; *Visitation 1662*, pp. 15, 58–9; Dell, *The Glynde Place Archives*, p. xvii.
141. PRO, Prob 11/162/111.
142. BM, Add MS 33084, fols 46–47r; V. A. Rowe, *Sir Henry Vane the Younger* (Athlone Press, 1970), pp. 15–115.
143. BM, Add MS 33084, fols 64r, 67r.
144. BM, Add MS 33145; Redwood, pp. 66–162; *CJ*, iv, 14, 75; ESRO, Rye MS 82.
145. BM, Add MS 33084, fols 65r, 69r.
146. Kent RO, Sackville MS U 269 C7/2.
147. ESRO, Frewen MS 520; Essex RO, D/DL E 22.
148. PRO, SP 28/135, fols 53–118, 247–93.
149. *CJ*, ii, 996, iii, 171, 177, 666; BM, Add MS 31116, fol. 107r; Underdown, *Pride's Purge*, pp. 34–5.
150. ESRO, Frewen, MS 4223 no. 55; *CSPD 1644*, pp. 24–5; *CSPD 1644–5*, pp. 227, 323; *AO*, i, 413–18; *CJ*, iii, 324, iv, 36; Thomas-Stanford, pp. 95–6, 156–7.
151. *Visitation 1662*, p. 18; *CSPD 1641–3*, p. 361; *SAC*, xi (1858), 24; *Camden Society*, third series, xiii (1907), 137–9.
152. *HMCP*, i, 111; *CJ*, ii, 761; *HMC 5th Report*, appendix, p. 53; Thomas-Stanford, p. 70; K. Lindley, 'The part played by the Catholics', in B. Manning, ed., *Politics, Religion and the English Civil War* (E. Arnold, 1973), pp. 127–76.
153. *CCC*, pp. 2947, 3011, 3175.
154. ESRO, Hickstead Place MS 467.
155. Barrett-Lennard, *Families of Lennard and Barrett*, p. 280; E. Venables, 'The Castle of Herstmonceux and its Lords', *SAC*, iv (1851), 160; Thomas-Stanford, pp. 207–9.

156. Essex RO, D/DL E 22; Keeler, pp. 348–9; Everitt, pp. 194, 197; P. Laslett, ed., *Patriarcha and other Political Works of Sir Robert Filmer* (Oxford University Press, 1949), pp. 1–10.
157. PRO, SP 23/176/205–6, 211, 229, 231; Keeler, p. 271.
158. PRO, SP 23/179/693–6.
159. ESRO, Danny MS 64.
160. *CJ*, ii, 873, ii, 227, 681; *CCAM*, p. 420; Bodleian, Tanner MS 60, fol. 255; Keeler, p. 83.
161. PRO, Prob 11/208/70; *CCC*, p. 1071; see map on p. 46.
162. BM, Add MS 33084, fol. 65r.
163. *CJ*, ii, 124, iii, 77, 171, 227, 256; PRO, Prob 11/212/65; Keeler, p. 170; G. Isham and M. Toynbee, 'Sir Thomas Eversfield and his Two Wives', *SNQ*, xiv, 15 (1957), 253–9.
164. Redwood; ESRO, Sessions Rolls 55–63, Rye MS 82.
165. BM, Add MS 33084, fol. 40r; *CJ*, iii, 156, 354, 516.
166. Redwood; ESRO, Sessions Rolls 55–81; PRO, Index 4213, 21 Feb. 1646.
167. *CJ*, ii, 874, iii, 607, 646; Whitelock, *Memorials*, p. 96; Thomas-Stanford, pp. 156–7.
168. *CJ*, iii, 607, iv, 14, v, 615, 640, 664; BM, E 454 (5): *Kingdome's Weekly Intelligencer*, 18–25 July 1648; Keeler, pp. 273–4.
169. Bodleian, Dep C MS 169/36.
170. BM, E 81 (10): *A Full Relation of the taking of the Castle of Arundel* (1644); *CCC*, p. 2051.

14. The search for settlement 1648–1660

1. ESRO, PAR 516/29/4.
2. *TSP*, v, 190.
3. BM, Add MS 33084, fol. 83v.
4. PRO, SP 23/176/637, 639, 177/8, 13, 15.
5. ESRO, Danny MS 63.
6. Underdown, *Pride's Purge*, pp. 45–105; ESRO, Frewen MS 4223, no. 73.
7. *CJ*, v, 591; BM, E 447 (7): *New Propositions Agreed upon by the Lords and Commons*, p. 5; ESRO, PAR 576/29/4.
8. BM, E 522 (40): *Perfect Occurences*, 76, 9–16 June 1648.
9. HLRO, 9 June 1648; The Petition of Sussex.
10. *TSP*, v, 382–3; *AO*, i, 1242.
11. ESRO, Frewen MS 4223, no. 76; Thomas-Stanford, pp. 214–16; Underdown, *Pride's Purge*, pp. 106–42; C. Hill, *Puritanism and Revolution* (Heinemann, 1962), pp. 50–122.
12. B. Worden, *The Rump Parliament* (Cambridge University Press, 1974), p. 40.
13. C. V. Wedgwood, *The Trial of Charles I* (Collins, 1964), pp. 101, 157–8; Thomas-Stanford, pp. 317–19.
14. Worden, *Rump Parliament*, p. 62.
15. Underdown, *Pride's Purge*, pp. 184–5, 208–56, 367–87; Thomas-Stanford, p. 219.
16. *CJ*, v, 572, 649, vi, 574, vii, 249–61; *DNB*; Underdown, *Pride's Purge*, pp. 52, 188, 251.
17. Worden, *Rump Parliament*, pp. 29–30, 71, 174, 222, 256, 259, 281, 284, 301, 313; Dell, ed., *Glynde Places Archives*, p. xix.
18. Underdown, *Pride's Purge*, pp. 258–306; Worden, *Rump Parliament*, pp. 23–102; Morrill, p. 187.
19. *CJ*, vi, 134.
20. PRO, Index 4213, 26 Feb. 1649, 1 March 1649, 11 March 1650; Redwood, p. xxv.

21. PRO, Index 4213, 6 July 1649, 3 March 1651, 3 July 1651, 4 March 1652, 7 July 1652, 11 October 1652.
22. ESRO, Rye MS 82/9–40, Sessions Rolls 83–98, QSOB 1650–55, fols 1–44; WSRO, Sessions Rolls 65–75; Redwood, pp. 170–204.
23. Appendix II.
24. *AO*, ii, 397–402; Underdown, *Somerset in the Civil War*, pp. 167–8; Worden, *Rump Parliament*, p. 224.
25. ESRO, Rye MS 47/143; *CSPD 1650*, pp. 348, 511.
26. PRO, SP 23/170/87; *CSPD 1651*, pp. 358, 374, 381, 444.
27. WSRO, CAP 1/30/6, Ep i/11/21, fol. 34; below, pp. 331–3.
28. ESRO, Dunn MS 47/1.
29. William Salt Library, MS 454 (Swynfen); Underdown, *Pride's Purge*, pp. 262–8; Q. Skinner, 'Conquest and Consent: Thomas Hobbes and the Engagement Controversy', in Aylmer, ed., *The Interregnum*, pp. 79–98; J. M. Wallace, *Destiny his Choice: The Loyalism of Andrew Marvell* (Cambridge, University Press 1968), pp. 43–68.
30. BM, E 1407: *An Essay of the True Happiness of Man* (1650); Underdown, *Pride's Purge*, p. 56.
31. *CSPD 1649–50*, p. 440; Underdown, *Pride's Purge*, p. 300.
32. PRO, SP 28/291.
33. F. A. Inderwick, 'The Rye engagement', *SAC*, xxxix (1894), 16–27.
34. WSRO, PAR 21/9/2/21, 59/9/2/21, 197/9/1.
35. ESRO, Danny MS 284; Redwood, pp. 175, 180.
36. *CSPD 1649–50*, pp. 63, 68.
37. *CSPD 1650*, pp. 462–3; *CSPD 1651*, pp. 374, 381.
38. *CSPD 1651*, p. 458; *CJ*, vii, 24–5.
39. *CSPD 1651*, pp. 275, 341, 503.
40. *CSPD 1649–50*, p. 574; WSRO, Sessions Rolls 75/5; Morrill, pp. 255–6.
41. PRO, SP 23/169/555–7.
42. ESRO, Sessions Rolls 99/63, 64.
43. Thomas-Stanford, pp. 251–63; F. E. Sawyer, 'Captain Nicholas Tettersell and the Escape of Charles II', *SAC*, xxxii (1882), 81–104.
44. *HMCP*, i, 582; D. Underdown, *Royalist Conspiracy in England* (Yale University Press, 1960), pp. 36–8.
45. *CSPD 1649–50*, pp. 161, 179, 200, 260; *CSPD 1650*, pp. 341, 558; *CSPD 1651*, pp. 169, 172, 242; *CSPD 1655*, p. 110; J. R. Jones, *Britain and Europe in the Seventeenth Century* (E. Arnold, 1966), pp. 47–55.
46. BM, E 674 (6): *Mercurius Politicus*, 115, 12–19 Aug. 1652; *CSPD 1651–2*, pp. 360, 405; *CSPD 1652–3*, pp. 8, 36, 352; *CSPD 1653–4*, p. 572; Whitelocke, *Memorials*, p. 533.
47. *CSPD 1651–2*, p. 237; BM, E 683 (19): *The Moderate Intelligencer*, 166, 1–8 Dec. 1652, E 683 (21): *A Perfect Account*, 101, 1–8 Dec. 1652; Thomas-Stanford, pp. 264–74.
48. Above, pp. 188–92.
49. Redwood, p. 172.
50. Worden, *Rump Parliament*, p. 256; *CSPD 1649–50*, pp. 122, 161, 179, 201, 211, 260, 268–9; *CSPD 1650*, pp. 145, 341; *CSPD 1651*, pp. 169, 172; *CSPD 1651–2*, pp. 201, 339; *CSPD 1653–4*, pp. 62, 541, 572.
51. *CSPD 1652–3*, pp. xxiii, 49, 128, 231, 250, 266, 273, 510; Worden, *Rump Parliament*, pp. 281, 339.
52. *CSPD 1652–3*, pp. xxxiv–xli, 333, 347, 402, 415, 425.
53. Worden, *Rump Parliament*, pp. 281, 339.
54. Redwood; ESRO QSOB 1650–55, fols 1–47, Sessions Rolls 83–99.
55. A. Woolrych, 'The Calling of Barebone's Parliament', *EHR*, lxxx (1965), pp. 500–1.

56. *Visitation 1634*, pp. 99–101, 150; *Visitation 1662*, p. 103; Venn, *Alumni Cantabrigienses*, iv, 131; Horsfield, *History of Lewes*, ii, 172.
57. *CJ*, vii, 348.
58. *AO*, ii, 975; *CSPD 1655*, p. 68.
59. PRO, Prob 11/264/183, 354/87.
60. *CJ*, vii, 288, 300–1, 315; K. H. D. Haley, *The First Earl of Shaftesbury* (Oxford University Press, 1968), p. 73. I am grateful to Professor Austin Woolrych for information about the Sussex members of Barebones.
61. PRO, Index 4213, 20 Feb. 1654; ESRO, QSOB 1650–55, 1655–60, Sessions Rolls 83–120; Underdown, *Pride's Purge*, pp. 340–1; Cockburn, *History of English Assizes*, pp. 186–7; below, p. 327.
62. *TSP*, iii, 369.
63. V. F. Snow, 'Parliamentary reapportionment proposals in the Puritan Revolution', *EHR*, lxxiv (1959), 440–2.
64. *HMCR*, p. 223; *SAC*, xxxiii (1883), 90; PRO, Prob 11/241/455, 246/189; BM, Add MS 33148 fol. 56.
65. ESRO, Rye MS 47/148, 151, 152.
66. H. R. Trevor-Roper, *Religion, the Reformation and Social Change* (Macmillan, 1967), pp. 371–4; Roots, *The Great Rebellion*, p. 182.
67. *CJ*, vii, 366, 368, 370, 380–1.
68. *EHR*, lxxiv (1959), 429.
69. *CJ*, vii, 384, 394–5, 409, 412, 414, 418.
70. Gardiner, *History of the Commonwealth and Protectorate*, iii, 34–68; Trevor-Roper, *Religion, the Reformation and Social Change*, pp. 376–8; Haley, *First Earl of Shaftesbury*, pp. 85–8.
71. *TSP*, iv, 151.
72. D. W. Rannie, 'Cromwell's Major Generals', *EHR*, x (1895), 471–506; Roots, 'Swordsmen and decimators', in R. H. Parry, ed., *The English Civil War and After 1642–1658* (Macmillan, 1970), pp. 78–92; Aylmer, *The State's Servants*, pp. 312–14; Thomas-Stanford, pp. 282–90.
73. ESRO, QSOB 1650–55, fol. 49v; *HMCR*, p. 223.
74. *TSP*, iii, 324, 369.
75. ESRO, Rye MS 47/152; *HMCR*, pp. 224–5.
76. Underdown, *Royalist Conspiracy*, pp. 159–77.
77. *TSP*, iv, 161, 190, 229, 344–5; Redwood, pp. 107, 207; M. Ashley, *John Wildman* (Cape, 1947), pp. 86, 119–20.
78. BM, Add MS 19516, fols 5v, 7r.
79. *TSP*, iv, 151, 161, 408, 642; above, pp. 120–2.
80. PRO, Index 4213, 22 Nov. 1655; *TSP*, iv, 414, 582, v, 287; *CSPD 1655–6*, p. 127.
81. *EHR*, vii (1892), 717–20; *TSP*, iv, 208, 642; Kenyon, *Stuart Constitution*, pp. 348–50; *CSPD 1655*, pp. 296, 344, 390.
82. *TSP*, iv, 497; *CSPD 1655–6*, pp. 157–60; *HMCR*, p. 227; Gardiner, *Commonwealth and Protectorate*, iii, 464–6.
83. *CSPD 1655–6*, p. 489.
84. ESRO, Rye MS 47/154.
85. *TSP*, iv, 549.
86. *Ibid*, iv, 190, 239.
87. *Ibid*, iv, 344–5; *EHR*, x (1895), 484–7.
88. *TSP*, iv, 258, 285.
89. *Ibid*, iv, 218, 497; PRO, SP 28/181.
90. *TSP*, iv, 643, v, 442; PRO, SP 28/181; Underdown, *Royalist Conspiracy*, p. 176; Morrill, p. 260.
91. *TSP*, iv, 497, 525, 582, 593, 642; *CSPD 1655–6*, pp. 140, 200.

92. *TSP*, iv, 497; *EHR* x, (1895), 488–9; *CSPD 1655–6*, pp. 262–3, 367–8.
93. *TSP*, v, 151, 171, 341, 365.
94. PRO, SP 28/181, 246; *CJ*, vii, 483; C. H. Firth, *The Last Years of the Protectorate* (London, 1909), pp. 105–25.
95. Parry, ed., *English Civil War and After*, pp. 80–7; Morrill, pp. 245, 273–87.
96. *TSP*, iv, 151, 190, 752, v, 151.
97. *Ibid*, iv, 190, 498; Lamont, *Godly Rule*, p. 22; *DNB*.
98. *TSP*, iv, 151, 208, 217, 285, 408, 414, 526.
99. Above, p. 131.
100. *TSP*, iv, 161.
101. *Ibid*, iii, 369, iv, 151, 161, 190, 549, 574.
102. *Ibid*, iv, 151, 160–1, 190, 208, 229, 285, 394, 642; PRO, SP 28/246.
103. *TSP*, iv, 151, 394, 408–9, 642; ESRO, Rye MS 47/137, 154, 156, QSOB 1655–60, fol. 37v.
104. *TSP*, iv, 208.
105. *CCC*, pp. 916, 1960.
106. *CCC*, pp. 858, 920, 1069, 1082, 1568,; PRO SP 28/181; Keeler, pp. 163–4; Matthews, *Walker Revised*, p. 355.
107. *CCC*, pp. 834, 952, 1215; Keeler, p. 271.
108. PRO, Prob 11/338/47.
109. *TSP*, iv, 208.
110. *Ibid*, iv, 341; *SAC*, xxxiii (1883), 91.
111. ESRO, Rye MS 47/137–48, 153, 154.
112. D. Underdown, 'Settlement in the counties 1653–1658', in G. E. Aylmer, ed., *The Interregnum* (Macmillan, 1972), pp. 165–82; Aylmer, *The State's Servants*, p. 314.
113. PRO, Index 4213, 10 March 1655, 18 July 1656; below, p. 131.
114. *TSP*, iv, 341, 382–3; *Camden Society*, third series, xiii (1907), 141–5.
115. *TSP*, v, 779; Thomas-Stanford, pp. 326–7.
116. ESRO, QSOB 1655–60, fols 21v, 24r.
117. *Ibid*, Sessions Rolls 86/53, QSOB 1655–60, fol. 23v.
118. *TSP*, v, 456, 491; Thomas-Stanford, p. 290; Firth, *Last Years of the Protectorate*, pp. 11–23.
119. ESRO, QSOB 1655–60, fols 29–58, Sessions Rolls 119/54, 120–46.
120. *SAC*, xxxiii (1883), 91–2.
121. J. T. Rutt, ed., *Diary of Thomas Burton* (London, 1828), iii, 237, 337, iv, 58–9; G. Davies, *The Restoration of Charles II* (University of California Press, 1955), pp. 59–61; Haley, *Shaftesbury*, pp. 97–103.
122. *TSP*, iv, 394, vii, 103, 111; PRO, Index 4213, 26 Jan. 1656.
123. *TSP*, vii, 25, 65–9, 74–5, 77–83, 85–7, 88–90; Thomas-Stanford, pp. 296–300; Firth, *Last Years of the Protectorate*, pp. 58–70; Underdown, *Royalist Conspiracy*, pp. 209–27.
124. ESRO, Rye MS 47/158, 82/81; *CSPD 1658–9*, p. 71; *HMCR*, p. 223.
125. *TSP*, i, 710, vii, 67–8, 77, 80, 82–3, 89, 93, 99; *Calendar of the Clarendon State Papers* (Oxford, 1869–1870), iv, 20; Ashley, *John Wildman*, pp. 118–20.
126. *TSP*, i, 710, vii, 61, 67, 79, 89, 94, 99, 162–3.
127. *SAC*, xi (1859), 28–9; Thomas-Stanford, pp. 300–1; *TSP*, vii, 67, 104.
128. *TSP*, vii, 78–9, 86, 116–17; PRO, SP 23/185/429.
129. *TSP*, vii, 83, 87, 92–3, 103.
130. William Salt Library, MS 454 (Swynfen), no. 11; Firth, *Last Years of the Protectorate*, i, 167–94.
131. A. Woolrych, 'Last Quests for Settlement 1657–60', in Aylmer, ed., *The Interregnum*, pp. 181–8, see also pp. 18–19, 26–7.
132. *SAC*, xxxiii (1883), 91–3; PRO, SP 18/130/29; ESRO, Rye MS 47/153; *HMCR*, pp. 232–3.

133. Rutt, ed., *Burton's Diary*, iii, 144, iv, 56–8; Davies, *Restoration of Charles II*, p. 48.
134. ESRO, QSOB 1650–55, 1655–60, Sessions Rolls 83–123; WSRO, Sessions Rolls 65–94; below, pp. 336–9.
135. *TSP*, vii, 95, 104–5, 111.
136. ESRO, Dunn MS 51/63; Davies, *Restoration of Charles II*, pp. 86–122; Aylmer, ed., *The Interregnum*, pp. 181–200; A. H. Woolrych, 'The good old cause and the fall of the Protectorate', *Historical Journal*, xiii (1957), 133–61.
137. *Clarendon Calendar*, iv, 220.
138. *CJ*, vii, 687, 698.
139. PRO, Index 4213, 6 July 1659; Assizes 35/99/10, 100/6; *AO*, ii, 1333–4; *CJ*, vii, 654, 727; above, p. 131.
140. *CSPD 1658–9*, pp. xxiv, 375, 382, 390; *CSPD 1659–69*, pp. xxiii–xxiv; *CJ*, vii, 644–797; Thomas-Stanford, pp. 306–7.
141. PRO. Assizes 35/100/6.
142. *CSPD 1659–60*, pp. 52, 61, 71, 99, 107, 111–12, 140, 173; *TSP*, vii, 99; Thomas-Stanford, pp. 307–10.
143. Underdown, *Royalist Conspiracy*, pp. 267–8; Everitt, pp. 302–5; Clarendon Calendar, iv, 283, 329, 343, 371.
144. ESRO, Rye MS 47/161; *CJ* vii, 773.
145. *CJ*, vii, 731, 796; BM, E 1000 (7): *Weekly Intelligencer*, 11–18 Oct. 1659, p. 188; Davies, *Restoration of Charles II*, pp. 144–80; Haley, *Shaftesbury*, pp. 115–18; E. Ludlow, *Memoirs* (Oxford, 1894), ii, 69, 134, 137–40; C. H. Firth, ed., *The Clarke Papers*, iv (Camden Society, new series, lxii, 1901), 60–2, 71, 298.
146. *CJ*, vii, 648; Davies, *Restoration of Charles II*, p. 118; Haley, *Shaftesbury*, pp. 115–18; E. S. De Beer, 'Evelyn and Colonel Herbert Morley in 1659 and 1660', *SAC*, lxxviii (1937), 178–9.
147. BM, E 773 (26): *Mercurius Politicus*, 8–15 Dec. 1659, p. 946; Davies, *Restoration of Charles II*, pp. 180–9; Whitelock, *Memorials*, p. 691; Aylmer, ed., *Interregnum*, pp. 200–2; Firth, ed., *The Clarke Papers*, iv, 165–6; *Clarendon Calendar*, iv, 481.
148. *CJ*, vii, 800; R. Baker, *A Chronicle of the Kings of England* (1684), p. 678; *Clarendon State Papers* (1786), iii, 650, 655; Haley, *Shaftesbury*, pp. 124–5.
149. *CJ*, vii, 803, 805, 807.
150. De Beer, ed., *Evelyn's Diary*, iii, 237–40; *SAC*, lxxviii (1937), 180–3; *Clarendon State Papers*, iii, 655; Thomas-Stanford, pp. 312–15.
151. A. H. Nethercot, 'John Evelyn and Colonel Herbert Morley in 1659–60', *Huntingdon Library Quarterly*, i (1937), 439–46.
152. Baker, *Chronicle*, p. 679; *CJ*, vii, 849; *CSPD 1659–60*, pp. xxvi–xxvii.
153. *SAC*, xi (1859), 31; Everitt, pp. 312–18.
154. WSRO, PAR 48/9/1, fol. 18r.
155. *Ibid*, Sessions Rolls 98/60; *SAC*, xliii (1900), 15.
156. PRO, SP 29/1/46; De Beer, ed., *Evelyn's Diary*, iii, 249.
157. *AO*, ii, 1444; PRO, SP 29/11/195–6, Index 4213, 27 April 1660, Index 4214, 11 August 1660; *LJ*, vii, 266, 274.
158. PRO, Index 4213, 1 March 1660, 4214, 30 July 1660; Ratcliff and Johnson, eds, *Warwick Country Records*, IV, xiv–xxiii; above, p. 131.
159. *SAC*, xxxiii (1883), 93; Thomas-Stanford, pp. 315–16.
160. De Beer, ed., *Evelyn's Diary*, iii, 245; *SAC*, lxxxvii (1837), 182–3; Defoe, *Tour through Great Britain* (London, 1927), p. 131.
161. PRO, Index 4214, 31 August 1660; SP 29/11/196.
162. *HMCR*, pp. 238–40.
163. BM, Add MS 33137, fols 74r, 33148, fols 104–10; ESRO, QSOB 1655–60, fol. 80r.
164. BM, Add MS 33084, fol. 83.

15. The county committee

1. PRO, SP 28/256.
2. *Ibid*, SP 23/120/371.
3. J. Hexter, *The Reign of King Pym* (Harvard University Press, 1961), pp. 13–30.
4. Pennington and Roots, *The Committee at Stafford*, pp. xv–xvii; Everitt, pp. 128–9; Morrill, pp. 82–9; B. W. Quintrell, 'The Divisional Committee for Southern Essex during the Civil War and its part in Local Administration' (MA thesis, Manchester University, 1962), pp. 1–24; A. M. Johnson, 'Buckinghamshire 1640 to 1660: a study in county politics' (MA thesis, University of Wales, 1963), pp. 91–100.
5. *CJ*, iii, 171, 177, 200.
6. *AO*, i, 85–100, 106–17, 145–55.
7. ESRO, Rye MS 47, 82; PRO, SP 28/246; *CCC*, p. 2769.
8. *CJ*, iii, 45, 173; Bodleian, Dep C MS 163/263; HLRO, 18 May 1643: Draft orders for Committees for sequestration and weekly assessments in Sussex.
9. PRO, SP 28/246, 179/191; ESRO, Rye MS 82.
10. ESRO, Frewen MS 520, fols. 48–9.
11. PRO, SP 19/90/23.
12. *Ibid*, Prob 11/255/178, 259/407.
13. Everitt, pp. 126–85; A. Everitt, ed., 'An account book of the Committee of Kent for 1647 and 1648', in *A Seventeenth Century Miscellany*, pp. 115–52.
14. Underdown, *Somerset in the Civil War*, pp. 121–37.
15. Pennington and Roots, *Committee at Stafford*, pp. xv–xvii.
16. Bodleian, Tanner MS 60, fol. 255r, Dep C MS 163/290.
17. Everitt, pp. 126–85; Underdown, *Somerset in the Civil War*, pp. 121–37; C. H. Mayo, *Minite Books of the Dorset Standing Committee* (Exeter, 1902), pp. xxiv–xxvii; Pennington and Roots, *Committee at Stafford*, pp. xi–lxxiv.
18. ESRO, Rye MS 47/143; PRO, SP 28/246; BM, Add MS 33084, fol. 69r; Bodleian, Dep C MS 169/113, Tanner MS 62, fol. 493r.
19. Above, pp. 108–9.
20. ESRO, Rye MS 47/135, 137; *CJ*, iv, 33; *CSPD 1650*, p. 9.
21. PRO, SP 23/105/575.
22. Above, p. 271–2.
23. *CJ*, vi, 30.
24. *CJ*, iii, 4, 15, 324, iv, 14, 41, 75, 84, 168, 192, 318, v, 400, 614; *AO*, i, 139.
25. D. Underdown, 'Party management in the recruiter elections', *EHR*, lxxxiii (1968), 240.
26. *CSPD 1650*, pp. 187, 330, 341, 348, 351; ESRO, Rye MS 47/143; PRO, SP 23/169/571; Underdown, *Somerset in the Civil War*, pp. 163–70; Johnson, 'Buckinghamshire 1640–60', pp. 286–90.
27. PRO, SP 28/181.
28. Everitt, pp. 286–97; Underdown, *Pride's Purge*, pp. 301–2; above p. 244.
29. *CSPD 1644–5*, pp. 2, 134, 348, 541, 584; *CSPD 1645–7*, pp, 30, 196, 206, 347; *CJ*, iii, 43, 487, 520, iv, 168, 319; Thomas-Stanford, p. 160.
30. *CSPD 1644–5*, pp. 460, 488, 510, 560.
31. PRO, SP 28/135, fols 53–118, 247–93; Thomas-Stanford, pp. 158–9.
32. Above, p. 266.
33. PRO, SP 28/246, SP 16/514/8; ESRO, Rye MS 47/136, PAR 516/29/1; *CJ*, iv, 85, 318.
34. *CSPD 1645–7*, pp. 222–3, 231, 252, 260; *CJ*, iv, 334, 409, 618; *AO*, i, 614–26, 653–5.
35. ESRO, Rye MS 47/135, 136; *HMCR*, pp. 213–14.
36. ESRO, Frewen MS 520, fols 49–51.
37. BM, Add MS 33084, fols 38r, 69r.

38. *AO*, i, 106–17; Pennington and Roots, *Committee at Stafford*, pp. xxxv–xl; Everitt, pp. 131–2, 160–2; Johnson, 'Buckinghamshire 1640–60', pp. 132–9; P. G. Holiday, 'Royalist Composition Fines and Land Sales in Yorkshire 1645–1665' (PhD thesis, Leeds University, 1966), pp. 33–40.
39. PRO, SP 28/214.
40. *CJ*, iii, 148, 227; PRO, SP 23/105/560, 583, 223/861, 260/51.
41. Quintrell, 'Committee for Southern Essex', pp. 83–92; Holiday, 'Royalist Composition Fines', pp. 38–40, 61–3.
42. PRO, SP 16/503/67.
43. *Ibid*, SP 16/511/53.
44. *Ibid*, SP 16/511/34, 58.
45. *Ibid*, SP 23/170/87, 253/133.
46. *Ibid*, SP 23/253/38.
47. *Ibid*, SP 23/116/883–935, 212/287–333; *CCC*, pp. 1960–1, 2370–1; Morrill, pp. 71–3, 212–15.
48. PRO, SP 23/103/113, 117, 121, 125, 113/961, 228/273; Holiday, 'Royalist Composition Fines', p. 59.
49. Bodleian, Tanner MS 60, fols 252v, 254v.
50. PRO, SP 23/223/881; Hull, ed., 'Tufton sequestration papers', in *A Seventeenth Century Miscellany*, pp. 45–53; Everitt, p. 142; Wentworth-Fitzwilliam, *Parham in Sussex*, p. 59; above p. 278.
51. *AO*, ii, 329–35; *CCC*, pp. xiii–xv, 160, 162, 167, 170–1, 188; Everitt, pp. 288–91; Underdown, *Somerset in the Civil War*, pp. 163–7; Johnson, 'Buckinghamshire 1640–60', pp. 282–6.
52. *CCC*, pp. 172, 374–5.
53. *Ibid*, pp. xx, 673, 726, 2280, 2473; Everitt, p. 290.
54. PRO, SP 23/260/67.
55. *Ibid*, SP 23/249/42, 251/27–9, 255/71, 74.
56. *Ibid*, SP 19/86/18, SP 23/251/29; *CCC*, pp. 170–1.
57. PRO, SP 23/169/465, 473, 475, 493–4, 593, 170/71.
58. *Ibid*, SP 23/152/27, 255/74; *CCC*, pp. 171, 231.
59. *CCC*, pp. 170–2, 198, 374–5.
60. PRO, SP 23/120/373, 170/85, 260/267; *CCC*, pp. 475, 683, 727.
61. PRO, SP 23/105/566–7, 587–9, 169/449, 487, 497, 547, 187/981, 228/281, 255/75.
62. *Ibid*, SP 23/132/619; *CCC*, pp. 2370–1, 2458.
63. PRO, SP 23/169/441, 170/87, 89, 253/133.
64. *Ibid*, SP 23/169/471, 473, 567, 254/52, 255/60.
65. *Ibid*, SP 23/169/447, 505, 239/72; Ashley, *John Wildman*, pp. 71–2.
66. *Ibid*, SP 23/169, 170, 253/133.
67. *Ibid*, SP 23/169/471, 255/76.
68. J. Thirsk, 'The Sale of Delinquents' Estates during the Interregnum and the Land Settlement at the Restoration' (PhD thesis, London University, 1950); J. Thirsk, 'The sales of royalist lands during the Interregnum', *Economic History Review*, 2nd series, v (1953), 188–207; J. Thirsk, 'The Restoration land settlement', *Journal of Modern History*, xxvi (1954), 315–28; P. G. Holiday, 'Land sales and repurchases in Yorkshire after the Civil Wars, 1650–1670', *Northern History*, v (1970), 67–92.
69. PRO, SP 19/104/89, SP 23/176/223, 223/871; Hull, ed., 'Tufton Sequestration Papers', pp. 43, 60–2; Wentworth-Fitzwilliam, *Parham in Sussex*, p. 60.
70. *AO*, i, 468–70, 717–22; D. H. Pennington, 'The Accounts of the Kingdom 1642–49', in F. J. Fisher, ed., *Essays in the Economic and Social History of Tudor and Stuart England* (Cambridge University Press, 1961), pp. 182–203.
71. PRO, SP/255.
72. Bodleian, Tanner MS 60, fols 252v, 254r.
73. PRO, SP 28/135, 181, 214, 246, 255–7.

74. Fisher, ed., *Essays in Economic and Social History*, pp. 194–9; Quintrell, 'Committee for Southern Essex', pp. 78–81; Johnson, 'Buckinghamshire 1640–60', pp. 151–61.
75. PRO, SP 28/135, 246.
76. *Ibid*, SP 16/511/34, 58, SP 28/246, 255, 256; Bodleian, Dep C MS 156/32.
77. PRO, SP 16/514/66, SP 28/256.
78. *Ibid*, SP 16/511/58.
79. *Ibid*, SP 16/514/64, SP 28/246; *CSPD 1645–7*, p. 447.
80. PRO, SP 28/257.
81. ESRO, Frewen MS 4223, no. 76.
82. Schofield, *Parliamentary Lay Taxation 1485–1547*; *AO*, i, 86, 224, 531, 615, 631, 958, 1073, ii, 29, 53, 292, 456, 655, 903, 1030.
83. Kent RO, Sackville MS 08/2; PRO, SP 28/181.
84. M. Ashley, *Financial and Commercial Policy under the Cromwellian Protectorate* (Cass, 2nd edn, 1962), pp. 72–4.
85. *AO*, i, 139; ESRO, Rye MS 82/1–5; PRO, E 179/191/393–407.
86. GMR, Losely MS 1084/29, 1530/1.
87. PRO, SP 28/246.
88. *CJ*, iii, 43, 182, iv, 41, 75, 84.
89. PRO, SP 28/181, 246; BM, Add MS 33058, fol. 77r.
90. ESRO, Rye MS 47/148, 82/5–8, 19–23.
91. *Ibid*, Rye MS 47/140; PRO, SP 16/513/62; *CSPD 1651*, pp. 195, 282–3; *CSPD 1651–2*, p. 57.
92. *AO*, i, 96; ESRO, Rye MS 82/17; BM, Add MS 33084, fol. 40r; Aylmer, *The State's Servants*, pp. 318–25; Morrill, p. 97.
93. Essex RO, D/DL E 22, 16 Sept. 1643–16 Sept. 1644; BM, Add MS 33145, fols 155–64; PRO, SP 18/1/96.
94. ESRO, Frewen MS 520, fols 47–77.
95. *Ibid*, Rye MS 82/11, 63, 69, 82.
96. *Ibid*, Rye MS 47/137, 156.
97. Kent RO, Sackville MS 08/2; PRO, SP 28/181.
98. PRO, E 179/191/392, 395, 397, 401, 407, SP 28/246.
99. *Ibid*, SP 16/513/62, E 179/191/393.
100. Bodleian, Dep C MS 155/20; above, p. 274.
101. Redwood, pp. 75, 116; WSRO, Sessions Rolls 80/66, 81/83.

16. Administration and the civil war

1. Cockburn, *History of English Assizes*, p. 241.
2. Ratcliff and Johnson, eds, *Warwick County Records*, ii (1936), xxiv–xxvi; Richmond, p. 568; Furley, *Quarter Sessions Government in Hampshire*, p. 81; Bates-Harbin, *Somerset Quarter Sessions Records*, iii (1912), xxv–xxxi.
3. *VCH Wiltshire*, v, 106.
4. PRO. Assizes 35/84–7; Redwood, p. xxiv.
5. Redwood, pp. xxi, 38.
6. Ratcliff and Johnson, eds, *Warwick County Records*, II (1936), xxi, III (1937), xxi, IV (1938), xxv; Bates-Harbin, *Somerset Quarter Sessions Records*, I (1907), xxiv, II (1908), xiv, III (1912), xxiv; *Trans. Soc. Cymmrodorion* (1942), 114.
7. Redwood; WSRO, Sessions Rolls 47–56; ESRO, Sessions Rolls 58–71; Appendix xxiv.
8. Redwood, pp. 28, 30, 38, 39.
9. *Ibid*, pp. 137, 188; ESRO, QSOB 1650–55, fols 14r, 36v.
10. Redwood, pp. 52, 59, 93; ESRO, PAR 576/29/3; above, p. 138.
11. Redwood, pp. xx, 133; above, pp. 166–7.
12. ESRO, Sessions Rolls 70/76, 77, 80/64, 65.

13. Redwood, p. xxi, above, p. 217.
14. ESRO, Sessions Rolls 68; Redwood.
15. Redwood, pp. 65, 71, 82, 84; ESRO, QSOB 1950–55, fols 13r, 35v; *SAC*, xci (1953), 165–72.
16. ESRO, Sessions Rolls 34/1; WSRO, Sessions Rolls 43/81.
17. Redwood, pp. 89, 174.
18. ESRO, QSOB 1650–55, fols 17v, 26r, 33v, 45r, 50r, 1655–60, fols 21v, 55v.
19. GMR, Losely MS 769/1, 2; Albery, *History of Horsham*, pp. 370–3; Redwood, pp. 26, 37, 58, 89, 107, 117, 123, 140.
20. Redwood, pp. 25–162.
21. *Ibid*, pp. 119, 125.
22. *Ibid*, pp. 85, 105, 129; ESRO, Frewen MS 520, fol. 54r; Ratcliff and Johnson, eds, *Warwick County Records*, iii (1937), xxix–xxx.
23. Redwood, pp. xxi, 116, 174.
24. WSRO, Sessions Rolls 56/42/57.
25. ESRO, QSOB 1650–55, fol. 18r; WSRO, Sessions Rolls 56.

Bibliography

This bibliography contains a complete list of the manuscript sources cited in the text, together with their locations, and a select list of the more important printed sources. Pamphlets and newsbooks cited in the text are not listed below but will be found in G. Fortescue, ed., *Catalogue of the Pamphlets, Newspapers, and Manuscripts relating to the Civil War, the Commonwealth, and Restoration, collected by George Thomason*, 2 vols (London, 1908).

I Manuscripts

Bodleian Library

Dep C 153–6, 158, 163, 164, 169 (Nalson Papers) Letters to Speaker Lenthall.
Rawlinson B 431 Precedent Book of a Sussex JP.
Tanner 59, 60, 62 Letters to Speaker Lenthall and the Earl of Northumberland.
Tanner 148 Notes on the dispute at Chichester between the Chapter and the corporation (fols 12–15). Notes on the patronage of Sussex benefices (fols 32–7).
Tanner 149 Return of Hospitals in the Diocese of Chichester (fol. 114).

British Museum

Additional 5697 Pelham burials at Laughton (fol. 265).
19516 Letters to the Major-generals 1656.
31116 Whitaker's Diary.
33058 Pelham correspondence 1642–1645.
33084 Pelham correspondence 1644.
33137 Miscellaneous Pelham papers.
33143–9 Farming, household and personal accounts of the Pelham family 1620–1660.
33154–5 Ironworks accounts of the Pelham family.
33171–85 Pelham court books.
33188 Legal papers of the Pelham family.
38139 *Liber pacis*, July–October 1604.
34013 Major-generals' lists of suspected persons.
Harleian 703 Sir Walter Covert's letter book.
1622 *Liber pacis*, January 1626.
7614 Edward Alford's notes on proclamations.
Lansdowne 82 Report of the Sussex deputy-lieutenants on catholicism in the county (fol. 103).
Sloane 577 *Liber pacis*, March 1652.

East Sussex Record Office, Lewes

Corporations: Rye 1 Hundred, sessions, and assembly books.
47 General files.
82 Assessments 1642–1660.
Seaford 6 Corporation proceedings.

Families	Danny 63	Correspondence between Herbert Morley and Sir William Campion 1645.
	284	Letter from William Hippisley to the Earl of Norwich, 1649.
	Dunn 37	Walter Roberts's accounts and recipe books.
	46–9	Roberts's family iron accounts and inventories.
	51	Correspondence of John and Anna Busbridge, Anne Farnden and John Roberts.
	52	Muster rolls.
	Dyke Hutton 825, 844	Papers of Stephen Pankhurst.
	Frewen 520	Account book of John Everenden.
	606, 611	Recipes, remedies, cures.
	4223	Letter book of Samuel Jeake.
	Glynde 87–95	Shrievalty documents of the Morley family.
	97	County rate for the charitable uses, maimed soldiers and gaol funds, 1653.
	Hickstead Place 467	Account book of Anthony Stapley of Hickstead.
Lieutenancy		'Booke concerning the Deputy Leiuetennantshipp' 1624–31
Parishes	293/12/1	East Chiltington church book.
	416/32	Lindfield settlement papers.
	426/1/1/1	Newhaven parish register.
	465/6/1	Rotherfield overseers accounts.
	465/10/1	Rotherfield churchwardens book.
	576/29	Worth parish documents: Committee warrants, 1648 petition of Sussex.
	516/31	Worth overseers accounts.
	516/33	Worth apprenticeship indentures.
	516/37	Worth purveyance and assessment records.
Local government	QAF/1/E1	Tax for maimed soldiers, 1624.
	QR/E	Sessions rolls, 1594–1660.
	Q1/EW1,2	Indictment books, 1623–32, 1652–1789.
	QE/EW1	Certioraries, fines and estreats, 1642–59.
	QO/EW2,3	Order books 1650–55, 1655–60.
	Accession 1461	Proceedings of the Commissioners of Sewers in th Ouse valley.
Wills	CCC	Archdeaconry of Lewes.

Essex Record Office, Chelmsford

D/DL	E 22	The account book of Francis, Lord Dacre, 1643–49.

Guildford Muniment Room

Losely	769/2	Articles exhibited against Richard Luckins, gaoler.
	1084/29	Cuckfield assessment certificate, 1654.
	1084/13	Cuckfield poor rate, 1651.
	1530/1	Cuckfield assessment certificates, 1651, 1654.

House of Lords Record Office

Main paper series, 1642–60.

Kent Record Office, Maidstone

Sackville	C7/2	Letter from the Sussex Committee to the Earl of Dorset, 1644.
	08/2	Note of the treasures for the assessments, 1644–46. Certificate of assessments, 1644–49.

Losely Manor, Surrey

Losely Bound Letters, v, James Gresham to Sir Poynings More, 1642 (no. 131).

Public Record Office

Assizes	35/67–101	Home Circuit, indictments and other documents, 1625–60.
Chancery	193/12–13	Crown office, JP lists, 1621–58.
	219/43, 47	Petty Bag office, parliamentary election indentures, 1642.
	220/9/4	Petty Bag office, *liber pacis*, Oct. 1660–Dec. 1662.
	227	Petty Bag office, sheriff rolls, 1625–40.
	Index 4211–4	Crown Office docket books, 1625–60.
Exchequer	E 163/18/12	King's Remembrancer, miscellanea, *liber pacis*, October 1628.
	E 178/5678	KR, special commissions of enquiry: compositions for knighthood, 1630–32.
	E 179/191, 258, 291	KR, subsidies, assessments, collection for the protestants in Ireland 1642.
	E 180/141	KR, lenten recognisances, 1619.
	E 198/4/32	KR, accounts of collectors of compositions for knighthood, 1630–32.
	E 401/2586	Exchequer of Receipt, register of privy seal loans, 1625–26.
	E 407/35	Exchequer of Receipt, compositions for knighthood, 1630–32.
Probate	Prob 11	Prerogative Court of Canterbury Wills.
Star Chamber	St. Ch. 8	Star Chamber proceedings, James I.
	St. Ch. 9	Star Chamber proceedings, Charles I.
State Papers	SP 14	State Papers Domestic, James I.
	SP 16	State Papers Domestic, Charles I.
	SP 18	State Papers Domestic, Interregnum.
	SP 19	Committee for Advance of Money.
	SP 23	Committee for Compounding.
	SP 25	Council of State order books.
	SP 28/135	Accounts of treasurers for Sussex regiments.
	SP 28/181, 246	Assessments, decimation: certificates, warrants.
	SP 28/255–7	Sub-committee of Accounts: correspondence.
	SP 28/291	Recusant estates.
	SP 29	State Papers Domestic, Charles II.

Sussex Archaeological Society, Barbican House, Lewes

Accession	1295	Settlement for the marriage of John Pelham and Lucy Sidney, 1647.
Gage	Box 19	Recusancy papers of Sir John Gage.

Westminster Cathedral Archives

AAW,	Vol. xxiv	Letter of the catholic clergy in Sussex, 1631.

West Sussex Record Office

Chapter	CAP 1/4/10/13	Ship money accounts for the Close at Chichester, 1635.
	CAP 1/30/6	Indenture for the purchase by John Downes of the Deanery at Chichester, 1649.
Chichester Archdeaconry	Ep i/15	Presentments of recusants to assizes 1624–28.
	Ep i/16/1	Overseers accounts, St. Andrew's, Chichester.
	Ep i/17/22	Detection book, 1626–29.
	Ep i/17/27	Detection book, 1637–41.
	Ep i/29/14	Metropolitical visitation papers, 1635.

	Ep i/22/1	Churchwardens presentments, 1606–41.
	Ep i/23/1, 5	Registers of presentments, 1571, 1579.
	Ep i/26/2	Church inspection book, 1636.
	Ep i/55	Vice-admiralty court papers, 1638–88.
	Ep i/88/1	Notes on vice-admiralty court procedure.
Lewes	Ep ii/2/1	Marriage Licence Register 1586–1613.
Archdeaconry	Ep ii/9/23	Detection book, 1636–39.
	Ep ii/9/24	Detection book 1639–41.
	Ep ii/10/103A	East Hoathly parish register transcripts.
	Ep ii/14/1	Churchwardens presentments, 1640–41.
	Ep ii/15/1	Register of presentments, 1637–39.
Lieutenancy	Add 2741	Militia papers 1621.
Parishes	16/1/1/1	Upper Beeding parish register.
	21/9/1–2	Billingshurst churchwardens accounts.
	27/1/1/1	Boxgrove parish register.
	48/9/1	West Chiltington churchwardens accounts.
	59/9/2	Cowfold churchwardens accounts.
	59/57/1	Cowfold overseers accounts.
	86/37/1	Fittleworth overseers accounts.
	149/1/1/1	Petworth parish register.
	183/9/1	Steyning churchwardens accounts.
	183/31	Steyning overseers accounts.
	183/33	Steyning apprenticeship indentures.
	197/9/1	Tillington churchwardens accounts.
	197/29/3	Tillington parish documents: warrant from JPs.
Local government	QR/W	Quarter sessions rolls, 1594–1660.

William Salt Library, Stafford

454	Swynfen	Letters from Samuel Gott to John Swynfen, 1650, 1657.

II Printed sources

A. Primary works

Barnes, T. G. ed. *Somerset Assize Orders* (Somerset Record Society, lxv, 1959).

Bates Harbin, E. H. and Dawes, M. C. B. eds, *Somerset Quarter Sessions Records* (Somerset Record Society, xxiii, xxiv, xxviii, xxxiv, 1907–19).

Bird, R. ed. *The Journal of Giles Moore* (SRS, lxiii, 1971).

Budgen, W. ed. *Sussex Deeds and Documents* (SRS, xxix, 1942).

Calendar of the Clarendon State Papers (Oxford, 1869–70).

Earl of Clarendon, *History of the Rebellion* (Oxford, 1888).

Coates, W. H. ed. *The Journal of Sir Simonds D'Ewes* (Yale University Presss, 1942).

Cockburn, J. S. ed. *Somerset Assize Orders 1640–59* (Somerset Record Society, lxxi, 1971).

De Beer, E. S. ed. *The Diary of John Evelyn* (Oxford University Press, 1955).

Garraway Rice, R. ed. *West Sussex Protestation Returns 1641–42* (SRS, v, 1906).

Godfrey, W. H. ed. *The Book of John Rowe* (SRS, xxxiv, 1928).

Historical Manuscripts Commission, *De L'Isle and Dudley MSS.*

Historical Manuscripts Commission, *House of Lords MSS.*

Historical Manuscripts Commission, *Rutland MSS.*

Historical Manuscripts Commission, *Salisbury MSS.*

Howell James, D. E. ed. *Norfolk Sessions Order 1650–57* (Norfolk Record Society, xxvi, 1955).

Laud, W. *Works* (Oxford University Press, 1853).
Lister, J. ed. *West Riding Sessions Records*, ii (Yorkshire Archaeological Society Record Series, liii, 1915).
Lomas, S. C. 'The Memoirs of Sir George Courthope', *Camden Society*, third series, xiii (1907).
Murphy, W. P. D. ed. *The Earl of Hertford's Lieutenancy Papers 1603–12* (Wiltshire Record Society, xxiii, 1969).
Notestein, W. ed. *The Journal of Sir Simonds D'Ewes* (Yale University Press, 1923).
Palmer, T. F. ed. *Act Book of the Archdeacon of Taunton* (Somerset Record Society, xliii, 1928).
Pennington, D. H. and Roots, I. A. *The Committee at Stafford 1643–45* (Manchester University Press, 1957).
Peyton, S. A. ed. *Minutes of Proceedings in Quarter Sessions* (Lincoln Record Society, xxv, 1931 for 1928).
Ratcliff, S. C. and Johnson, H. C. eds, *Warwick County Records* (Warwick, 1935–39).
Rushworth, J. *Historical Collections* (1692).
Sackville-West, V. ed. *The Diary of Lady Anne Clifford* (London, 1923).
Salzman, L. F. ed. *The Town Book of Lewes* (SRS, xlviii, 1946).
Thirsk J. and Cooper, J. P. eds, *Seventeenth-Century Economic Documents* (Oxford University Press, 1972).
Whitelocke, B. *Memorials* (1682).
Wickham Legg, L. G. ed. 'A relation of a short survey of the western counties', *Camden Society*, third series, lii (1936).
Williams, J. F. ed. *Bishop Redman's Visitation* (Norfolk Record Society, xviii, 1946).
Willis Bund, J. ed. *Worcestershire Quarter Sessons Rolls* (Worcester, 1900).

B. Secondary works

Albery, W. *A Millennium of Facts in the History of Horsham* (Horsham, 1947).
Aylmer, G. E. ed. *The Interregnum* (Macmillan, 1972).
Aylmer, G. E. *The King's Servants* (Routledge, 1961).
Aylmer, G. E. *The State's Servants: the Civil Service of the English Republic 1649–60* (Routledge, 1973).
Bamford, F. ed. *A Royalist's Notebook* (Sir John Oglander) (Constable, 1936).
Barnes, T. G. and Hassell Smith, A., 'Justices of the Peace from 1588 to 1688—a revised list of sources', *BIHR*, xxxii (1959).
Barrett-Lennard, T. *An Account of the Families of Barrett and Lennard* (London, 1908).
Barrett-Lennard, T., 'Extracts from the Household Account Book of Herstmonceux Castle', *SAC*, xlviii (1905).
Beier, A. L., 'Poor relief in Warwickshire 1630–1660', *Past and Present*, xxxv (1966).
Bell-Irving, E. M. *Mayfield* (London, 1903).
Blencowe, R. W., 'Paxhill and its neighbourhood', *SAC*, xi (1859).
Brinkworth, E. R. C., 'The Laudian Church in Buckinghamshire', *University of Birmingham Historical Journal*, v (1955–56).
Capp, B. S. *The Fifth Monarchy Men* (Faber, 1972).
Clark, P. and Slack, P. eds, *Crisis and Order in English Towns 1500–1700* (Routledge, 1972).
Cockburn, J. S. *A History of English Assizes 1558–1714* (Cambridge University Press, 1972).
Collinson, P. *The Elizabethan Puritan Movement* (Cape, 1967).
Cooper, W. D., 'Royalist compositions in Sussex during the Commonwealth', *SAC*, xix (1867).
Cooper, W. V. *History of Cuckfield* (Haywards Heath, 1912).
De Beer, E. S., 'Evelyn and Colonel Herbert Morley in 1659 and 1660', *SAC*, lxxviii (1937).
Dell, R. F. ed. *The Glynde Place Archives* (Lewes, E. Sussex County Council, 1964).

Dell, R. F. ed. *The Records of Rye Corporation* (Lewes, E. Sussex County Council, 1962).
Dietz, F. C. *English Public Finance 1558–1641* (London, 1932).
Everitt, A. *Change in the Provinces: the Seventeenth Century* (Leicester University Department of English Local History, Occasional Papers, second series, i, 1969).
Ferris, J. P., 'The gentry of Dorset on the eve of the Civil War, *Genealogists' Magazine*, xv (1965).
Foster, J. *Alumni Oxonienses* (Oxford, 1891).
Furley, J. *Quarter Sessions Government in Hampshire in the Seventeenth Century* (Winchester, 1937).
Gardiner, S. R. *History of England during the Commonwealth and Protectorate* (London, 1901).
Gardiner, S. R. *History of England from the Accession of James I to the Outbreak of the Civil War* (London, 1883–84).
Gardiner, S. R. *History of the Great Civil War* (London, 1886).
Gleason, J. H. *The Justices of the Peace in England* (Oxford University Press, 1969).
Godwin, G. N. *The Civil War in Hampshire* (Southampton and London, 1904).
Haller, W. *The Rise in Puritanism* (Columbia University Press, 1938).
Hill, C. *Antichrist in Seventeenth-Century England* (University of Newcastle, Riddell Memorial Lectures, 1971).
Hill, C. *Economic Problems of the Church* (Oxford University Press, 1956).
Hill, C. *Puritanism and Revolution* (Heinemann, 1962).
Hill, C. *Society and Puritanism in Pre-Revolutionary England* (Secker & Warburg, 1964).
Holloway, W. *History of Rye* (London, 1847).
Hurstfield, J., 'County Government 1530–1660', *VCH Wiltshire*, v (1957).
Horsfield, T. W. *History of Lewes* (Lewes, 1824).
Johnson, A. M. 'Buckinghamshire 1640–1660: a study in county politics' (University of Wales, MA thesis, 1963).
Ketton-Cremer, R. W. *Norfolk in the Civil War* (Faber, 1969).
Leonard, E. M. *The Early History of English Poor Relief* (Cambridge, 1900).
Lloyd, H. A. *The Gentry of South-West Wales 1540–1640* (University of Wales Press, 1968).
Macfarlane, A. *The Family Life of Ralph Josselin* (Cambridge University Press, 1970).
Marchant, R. A. *The Church under the Law* (Cambridge University Press, 1969).
Marchant, R. A., 'The restoration of Nottinghamshire churches', *Thoroton Society Transactions*, lxv (1961).
Matthews, A. G. *Calamy Revised: being a revision of Edmund Calamy's Account of the Ministers and Others Ejected and Silenced 1660–62*, (Oxford University Press, 1934).
Matthews, A. G. *Walker Revised: being a revision of John Walker's 'Suffering of the Clergy during the Grand Rebellion, 1642–1660'*, (Oxford University Press, 1948).
Mawer, A. and Stenton, F. M. *The Place Names of Sussex* (Cambridge University Press, 1929–30).
Mayo, C. H. ed. *Minute Books of the Dorset Standing Committee* (Exeter, 1902).
Miller, J. *Popery and Politics in England 1660–1688* (Cambridge University Press, 1973).
Nairn, I. and Pevsner, N. *Sussex* (Penguin (Buildings of England), 1965).
Quintrell, B. W., 'The Divisional Committee for Southern Essex during the Civil War and its part in Local Administration' (MA thesis, Manchester University, 1962).
Renshaw, W. C., 'Notes from the Act Books of the Archdeaconry Court of Lewes', *SAC*, xlix (1906).
Renshaw, W. C., 'Notes from the Act Books of the Court for the Deanery of South Malling', *SAC*, l (1907).
Renshaw, W. C., 'The hundred of Buttinghill', *SAC*, lviii (1916).
Roots, I. A. *The Great Rebellion 1642–60* (London, Batsford, 1966).
Russell, C. *The Crisis of Parliaments* (Oxford University Press, 1971).
Russell, C. ed. *The Origins of the English Civil War* (Macmillan, 1973).
Sawyer, F. E., 'Proceedings of the Committee of Plundered Ministers Relating to Sussex', *SAC*, xxx (1880), xxxi (1881), xxxvi (1888).

Smart, T. W. W., 'A biographical sketch of Samuel Jeake, senior of Rye', *SAC*, xiii (1861).
Smart, T. W. W., 'Extracts from the manuscripts of Samuel Jeake', *SAC*, ix (1857).
Steer, F. W. and Kirby, I. *The records of the bishops . . . of the diocese of Chichester* (Chichester, W. Sussex Record Office, 1966).
Straker, E. *Wealden Iron* (London, 1931).
Swales, R. J. N., 'Local politics and the parliamentary representation of Sussex' (PhD thesis, Bristol, 1964).
Thirsk, J. ed. *The Agrarian History of England 1500–1640*, iv (Cambridge University Press, 1967).
Thomas, K. V. *Religion and the Decline of Magic* (Weidenfeld & Nicolson, 1971).
Thomas-Stanford, C., 'The Sussex musters of 1618', *SAC*, lix (1918).
Tierney, M. A. *The History of Arundel* (London, 1834).
Trevor-Roper, H. R. *Archbishop Laud* (Macmillan, 2nd edn, 1962).
Underdown, D. *Pride's Purge: Politics in the Puritan Revolution* (Oxford University Press, 1971).
Underdown, D. *Royalist Conspiracy in England* (Yale University Press, 1960).
Underdown, D. *Somerset in the Civil War and Interregnum* (Newton Abbot, David & Charles, 1973).
Venn, J. and J. A. *Alumni Cantabrigienses* (Cambridge, 1922).
Watkins, O. C. *The Puritan Experience* (Routledge, 1972).
Wedgwood, C. V. *The King's Peace* (Collins, 1955).
Wedgwood, C. V. *The King's War* (Collins, 1958).
Wentworth-Fitzwilliam, J. *Parham in Sussex* (London, 1948).
Willcox, W. B. *Gloucestershire 1590–1640* (Yale University Press, 1940).
Worden, B. *The Rump Parliament* (Cambridge University Press, 1974).
Zagorin, P. *The Court and the Country: The beginning of the English Revolution* (Routledge, 1969).

INDEX

Heads of gentry families of county status between 1600 and 1660 are distinguished by full reference to their home and parish. When the parish where a man lived is given merely for purposes of identification it appears in brackets. Except in a few obvious cases, the county is given for all places outside Sussex. Grid references in brackets for places within the county refer to the map following page 445. Where entries include sub-headings the listing of topics is alphabetical; in town entries places and buildings are listed alphabetically before topics.

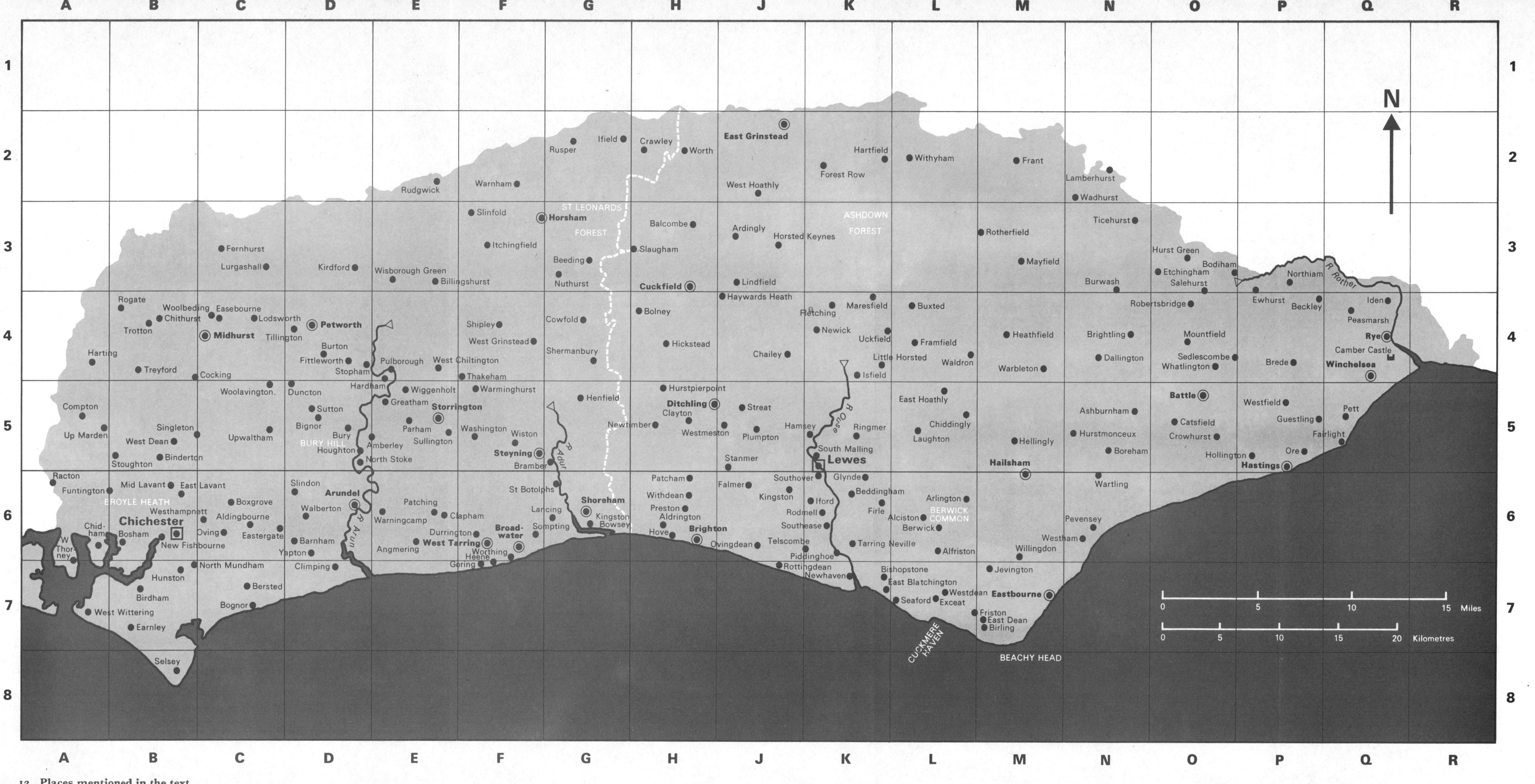

A B C D E F G H J K L M N O P Q R
1 2 3 4 5 6 7 8
N
East Grinstead
Ifield
Crawley
Worth
Rusper
Hartfield
Withyham
Frant
Forest Row
Lamberhurst
Rudgwick
Warnham
West Hoathly
Wadhurst
Slinfold
Horsham
ST LEONARDS
FOREST
Balcombe
Ardingly
Horsted Keynes
ASHDOWN
FOREST
Ticehurst
Rotherfield
Itchingfield
Slaugham
Fernhurst
Lurgashall
Kirdford
Wisborough Green
Billingshurst
Beeding
Nuthurst
Cuckfield
Lindfield
Mayfield
Hurst Green
Bodiham
Etchingham
Salehurst
Burwash
Northiam
R. Rother
Rogate
Woolbeding
Easebourne
Chithurst
Lodsworth
Trotton
Midhurst
Tillington
Petworth
Haywards Heath
Bolney
Fletching
Maresfield
Buxted
Robertsbridge
Ewhurst
Beckley
Iden
Peasmarsh
Shipley
Cowfold
West Grinstead
Newick
Uckfield
Framfield
Heathfield
Brightling
Mountfield
Rye
Hickstead
Burton
Fittleworth
Harting
Treyford
Cocking
Stopham
Pulborough
West Chiltington
Shermanbury
Chailey
Little Horsted
Waldron
Dallington
Sedlescombe
Whatlington
Brede
Camber Castle
Winchelsea
Warbleton
Isfield
Woolavington.
Duncton
Hardham
Thakeham
Wiggenholt
Warminghurst
Hurstpierpoint
Henfield
Greatham
Storrington
Ditchling
Streat
East Hoathly
Battle
Westfield
Compton
Sutton
Clayton
Ashburnham
Catsfield
Pett
Bignor
Parham
Chiddingly
Guestling
Singleton
Upwaltham
Bury
Washington
Wiston
Newtimber
Westmeston
Plumpton
Hamsey
Ringmer
Laughton
Hellingly
Hurstmonceux
Crowhurst
Fairlight
Up Marden
West Dean
BURY HILL
Houghton
Amberley
Sullington
Steyning
R. Adur
South Malling
Boreham
Hollington
Ore
Stoughton
Binderton
North Stoke
Bramber
Stanmer
Lewes
Hailsham
Hastings
Racton
Mid Lavant
East Lavant
Slindon
Patcham
Falmer
Southover
Glynde
Funtington
St Botolphs
Withdean
Kingston
Beddingham
Arlington
Wartling
BROYLE HEATH
Boxgrove
Arundel
Patching
Lancing
Shoreham
Preston
Iford
Firle
BERWICK
COMMON
Westhampnett
Aldingbourne
Walberton
Warningcamp
Clapham
Kingston
Bowsey
Aldrington
Rodmell
Alciston
Chichester
Chid-
ham
Bosham
Oving
Eastergate
R. Arun
Sompting
Broad-
water
Hove
Brighton
Southease
Berwick
Pevensey
W
Thorney
New Fishbourne
Barnham
Durrington
West Tarring
Ovingdean
Telscombe
Tarring Neville
Westham
Angmering
Heene
Worthing
Piddinghoe
Alfriston
Willingdon
Yapton
Goring
Rottingdean
Newhaven
R. Ouse
Hunston
North Mundham
Climping
Bishopstone
Jevington
Bersted
East Blatchington
Westdean
Birdham
Seaford
Exceat
Eastbourne
Bognor
West Wittering
Friston
East Dean
Birling
Earnley
CUCKMERE
HAVEN
BEACHY HEAD
Selsey
0 5 10 15 Miles
0 5 10 15 20 Kilometres